THE YEARBOOK OF EDUCATION LAW 2023

Charles J. Russo, J.D., Ed.D. and Jeffrey C. Sun, J.D., Ph.D., editors

Published by Education Law Association
Philadelphia, Pennsylvania, USA

The Education Law Association improves education by promoting interest in and understanding of education law.

Join the social learning community at EducationLaw.org.

The opinions expressed in this publication are those of the authors and do not represent the official views of the Education Law Association.

© 2024 Education Law Association

All rights reserved. No part of this publication may be reproduced, distributed, or transmitted in any form or by any means, including photocopying, recording, or other electronic or mechanical methods, without the publisher's prior written permission, which may be sought by visiting EducationLaw.org.

ISBN-13: 978-1-56534-195-1
ISBN-10: 1-56534-195-3

EDITORS

Charles J. Russo, M.Div., J.D., Ed.D., is the Joseph Panzer Chair in Education in the School of Education and Health Sciences, Director of its Ph.D. Program, and Research Professor of Law in the School of Law at the University of Dayton. Dr. Russo served as 1998-99 President of the Education Law Association, and was the 2002 recipient of its McGhehey (Achievement) Award, the 2021 Distinguished Scholar Award from the American Educational Research Association's Special Interest Group on Religion & Education, and the 2021 Lifetime Achievement Award from the South African Education Law Association. Dr. Russo authored or co-authored more than 300 articles in peer-reviewed journals; authored, co-authored, edited, or co-edited 75 books, totaling nearly 1,200 publications. Dr. Russo also has spoken extensively on issues in education law in thirty-four of the United States and thirty-one other nations. In addition, he edits two journals and serves on over a dozen editorial boards.

Having spoken in thirty-four states and thirty-one nations outside the United States on all six inhabited continents, Russo taught summer courses in England, Spain, and Thailand. Internationally, he serves or has served as a Visiting Professor at the University of Notre Dame of Australia Faculty of Law in Sydney, Queensland University of Technology in Brisbane, and the University of Newcastle, Australia; the University of Sarajevo, Bosnia and Herzegovina; South East European University, Macedonia; the Potchefstroom and Mafeking Campuses of Northwest University, Potchefstroom, South Africa; the University of Malaya in Kuala Lumpur, Malaysia; the University of Sao Paulo, Brazil; Yeditepe University, Istanbul Turkey; Inner Mongolia University for the Nationalities, Tongliao, Inner Mongolia; and Peking University in Beijing, China. He is currently a Visiting Professor at Capital Normal University in Beijing.

Before joining the Faculty at the University of Dayton as Professor and Chair of the Department of Educational Administration in July 1996, Dr. Russo taught at the University of Kentucky in Lexington, Kentucky, from August 1992 to July 1996 and at Fordham University in his native New York City from September 1989 to July 1992. He taught high school for eight and one half-years, both prior to and after graduation from law school.

He received a Bachelor of Arts degree in Classical Civilization (1972), Juris Doctor Degree (1983), and Doctor of Education degrees in Educational Administration and Supervision (1989) from St, John's University in New York City. He received a Master of Divinity degree from the Seminary of the Immaculate Conception in Huntington, New York (1978). He received a Ph.D. Honoris Causa from Potchefstroom University, now the Potchefstroom Campus of Northwest University, in Potchefstroom, South Africa, in May 2004, for his contributions to the field of Education Law.

Jeffrey C. Sun, J.D., Ph.D., is Professor of Higher Education and Law, Distinguished University Scholar, Associate Dean for Innovation and Strategic Partnerships, and Director of the SKILLS Collaborative (a research and policy center examining workforce development and legal issues to career/ professional postsecondary education) at the University of Louisville. He is also Counsel at Manley Burke.

His research and practice areas focus on higher education law and professional/career education policies and practice. Dr. Sun has served as Project Director and Principal Investigator for over $25 million in grants and contracts.

He has published approximately 100 scholarly works and is co-author of ten books, including *Law, Policy, and Higher Education* (Carolina Academic Press, 2012); Law & Education Inequality: Removing Barriers to Educational Opportunities (Information Age Publishing, 2015); *Student Clashes on Campus: A Leadership Guide to Free Speech* (Routledge); and Academic Leadership and Governance of Higher Education: A Guide for Trustees, Leaders, and Aspiring Leaders of Two- and Four-Year Institutions (Stylus Publishing, 2nd Edition, 2022).

Dr. Sun received a BBA and an MBA from Loyola Marymount University, a law degree (J.D.) from the Moritz College of Law at The Ohio State University, and an M.Phil. and a Ph.D. from Columbia University.

CONTRIBUTORS

Sarah Barber, J.D., Attorney Advisor at U.S. Department of Justice Executive Office for Immigration Review, Slidell, La.

Erin Biolchino, J.D., Ed.D., Assistant Professor of Educational Leadership, California State University, Long Beach, Long Beach, Ca.

Joy Blanchard, Ph.D., Associate Professor, Lutrill and Pearl Payne School of Education, Louisiana State University, Baton Rouge, La.

Susan C. Bon, J.D., Ph.D., Professor of Education and Law; Affiliate Professor, Joseph F. Rice School of Law; University of South Carolina, Columbia, S.C.

Jyllian R. Bradshaw, J.D., Senior Associate, Porter Wright Morris & Arthur LLP, Dayton, Ohio, Adjunct Professor, University of Dayton, Dayton, Ohio

Clarissa Bruton, J.D., Research Manager of Law and Policy, University of Louisville, Louisville, Ky.

Christine Collins-Otto, M.S., Senior Educational Services and Bridges Director, Multnomah Educational Service District, Portland, Ore.

Amy L. Dagley, Ph.D., Associate Professor, Educational Leadership, University of Alabama at Birmingham, Birmingham, Ala.

David L. Dagley, Ph.D., J.D., Professor Emeritus, Educational Leadership, University of Alabama, Tuscaloosa, Ala.

Gillian Foss, Ph.D., School of Education, Louisiana State University, Baton Rouge, La.

Beth Godett, Ed.D., J.D., Adjunct Professor of Education Law and Policy at Boston College, Rider University, Farleigh Dickinson University.

Jeffrey S. Greenley, J.D., M.B.A., Superintendent, Belpre City Schools, Belpre, Ohio

Jesse Hagan, J.D., Assistant County Attorney, Louisville, Ky.

Diane M. Holben, Ed.D., Associate Professor of Professional & Secondary Education, East Stroudsburg University, East Stroudsburg, Pa.

Elizabeth T. Lugg, J.D., Ph.D., Associate Professor, Educational Law, Illinois State University, Normal, Ill.

Raquel Muñiz, J.D., Ph.D., Assistant Professor, Lynch School of Education & Human Development; Assistant Professor, School of Law, Boston College, Boston, Mass.

Allan G. Osborne, Jr., Ed.D., Retired Principal, Snug Harbor Community School, Quincy, Mass.; Editor, West's *Education Law Reporter*.

Barbara Qualls, Ph.D., Associate Professor and Director, M.Ed.-Leadership/Advanced Certification Programs, Stephen F. Austin State University, Nacogdoches, Tex.

Jeffrey C. Sun, J.D., Ph.D., Professor of Higher Education and Law, Distinguished University Scholar, Associate Dean for Innovation and Strategic Partnerships, and Director of the SKILLS Collaborative at the University of Louisville, Louisville, Ky. He is also Counsel at Manley Burke.

CONTENTS

1 – School Governance 1

2 – School Employment 37

3 – Students in K-12 Schools 87

4 – Bargaining 120

5 – Students with Disabilities 129

6 – Torts 177

7 – Sports 210

8 – Higher Education Administration & Faculty 227

9 – Students in Higher Education 267

10 – Federal and State Legislation 309

Chapter 1

SCHOOL GOVERNANCE

Barbara Qualls, Ph.D.[1] and Diane M. Holben, Ed.D.[2]

Introduction	3
Systemic Governance Issues	3
Constitutional Issues	3
Religion	3
First Amendment	4
Fourth Amendment	7
Due Process	8
Adequate Education	8
Equal Protection	9
Elections	10
Board Operations and Authority Issues	11
Taxation	12
Finance	15
Charter Schools	17
Administration	17
Funding	17
Other Charter School Cases	18
Localized Governance Issues	19
Bidding & Awarding of Contracts	19
Breach of Contract	20
Copyright Infringement	22
Insurance	22
Property Rights	23
Public Records and Freedom of Information Act (FOIA)	25
School Boundaries	26
Transportation	27

---

[1] Associate Professor and Director, M.Ed.-Leadership/Advanced Certification Programs, Stephen F. Austin State University, Nacogdoches, Tex.
[2] Associate Professor of Professional & Secondary Education, East Stroudsburg University, East Stroudsburg, PA.

Procedural Issues	27
COVID-19	28
Conclusion	29
Alphabetical List of Cases	31
Cases by Jurisdiction	33

Introduction

This chapter summarizes litigation on K-12 governance issues in 2022. Compared to 2021, the total number of cases decreased. The chapter is organized into two main sections: systemic governance issues and local governance issues. The school governance section includes forty-nine cases involving questions of constitutionality, jurisdiction, board operation, taxation and finance, and charter schools.

The local governance section includes nineteen cases with legal bases predominantly involving state and local statutes related to bidding and awarding of contracts; breach of contract; denial of insurance coverage; property rights; public records and the Freedom of Information Act (FOIA); school boundaries; and transportation of students. The two cases litigated in the federal court system concerned bankruptcy proceedings and copyright infringement law. Considering jurisdiction, five of these cases are from New York, three from Texas, and two from Illinois with the remaining cases distributed among nine additional states. The cases were clustered mainly among the subtopics of breach of contract, property rights, school boundaries, and public records/FOIA. Finally, one case from Florida involved jurisdictional issues while two cases from Florida and one from Pennsylvania concerned litigation related to the COVID-19 pandemic.

Systemic Governance Issues

Constitutional Issues

Religion

In *Carson ex rel. O.C. v. Makin*, the Supreme Court reversed and remanded orders of the First Circuit and the federal trial court in Maine in favor of the state commissioner of education who denied parents the opportunity to participate in its tuition assistance program's.[3] The program allowed parents to select a secondary school for their children if they lived in a school district lacking a secondary school or a contract with a specific school in another system. The state refused to let the parents participate because of language preventing the use of government funding sources from

---

[3] 142 S. Ct. 1987, 403 Educ. L. Rep. 377 (2022).

flowing to sectarian schools. The Supreme Court reversed earlier orders to the contrary, reasoning that the "nonsectarian" requirement violated the parents' rights under the Free Exercise Clause because it was neither neutral toward religion nor did it allow them the opportunity to send their children to the schools of their choice. Two dissents distinguished this case by pointing to the specific language of "may" and "must" concerning the conditions under which funds may/must be directed to private schools.

The Sixth Circuit, in a case from Michigan, considered whether a mask mandate violated the Free Exercise Clause of the First Amendment.[4] Because the state rescinded the mask mandate, the court dismissed the claim as moot.[5]

In Vermont, the federal trial court rejected the secretary of the state's Agency of Education's requests for immunity after he denied parents the opportunity to participate in a Town Tuition Program designed to provide publicly funded education for students who live in towns without public schools.[6] The court wrote that because the secretary's rendering of religious schools ineligible for the program had a causal relationship to the parents' complaint, he was not protected by sovereign immunity. However, the court rejected the co-plaintiff diocese's request for third-party standing.

First Amendment

The Fourth Circuit affirmed a federal trial court in Virginia's rejection of a father's claims following the issuance of no-trespass letters prohibiting him from being on school property or at school events.[7] The no-trespass letters were in response to the father's behavior and conduct at back-to-school nights, PTA meetings, and the use of his children to spread his views on school administration. As a result, the father argued that the board violated his First and Fourteenth Amendment rights. The court held that res judicata barred the father's claims against the board due to his previous lawsuit in state court that was fully adjudicated. Further, the court found that the father failed to demonstrate any of the three elements of First Amendment retaliation: that he engaged in a protected activity, that the defendants acted in a way that violated his rights, or that a causal relationship existed between his protected activity and their conduct.

---

[4] Resurrection Sch. v. Hertel (a), 35 F.4th 524, 403 Educ. L. Rep. 109 (6th Cir. 2022).
[5] Resurrection Sch. v. Hertel (b), 569 F. Supp. 3d 658, 403 Educ. L. Rep. 737 (W.D. Mich. 2021).
[6] A.H. ex rel. Hester v. French, 555 F. Supp. 3d 21, 401 Educ. L. Rep. 203 (D. Vt. 2021).
[7] Davison v. Rose, 19 F.4th 626, 397 Educ. L. Rep. 459 (4th Cir. 2021).

The Seventh Circuit affirmed a federal trial court in Wisconsin's grant of summary judgment in favor of a district attorney when a transgender individual convicted of sex offenses challenged the state law prohibiting convicted sex offenders from legally changing their names.[8] The plaintiff was convicted before the name change statute was enacted, so both her birth name and her chosen name are included on the registry; her challenge is to the inability to legally change her name to her chosen name. She argued that this statute violated the First Amendment by forcing her to display and disclose a name she objected to, regulating expressive conduct by forbidding her from changing her name, and impermissibly excluding her from a limited public forum. The court agreed that the plaintiff failed to establish a legal basis for her argument that the state name change statute violated her constitutional rights to free speech.

Litigation from the Ninth Circuit addressed issues about expression rights protected by the First Amendment. In one case, two trustees in California established social media platforms during their campaigns for office, then maintained them after the election.[9] Designed as a way to communicate with constituents, the sites were also used by one set of parents to post repetitive criticisms of the two trustees and the board. The trustees installed a word filter and eventually blocked the critics. In response to the parental claim that the block violated their First Amendment expression rights, the court affirmed that the trustees violated their free speech rights by blocking their comments from the designated public forum.

One case generated two opinions from the Ninth Circuit concerning the right of a vendor to post political commentary on his personal social media accounts. The principal, named shareholder in an event venue where historical reenactments took place and where school board officials had scheduled field trips for many years, posted a series of comments critical of some national political figures.[10] The business event venue and the shareholder-poster maintained separate social media accounts. After multiple complaints, the board stopped scheduled field trips to the venue. The shareholder and vendor claimed that the board retaliated against them for the social media posts. On further review of an order in favor of the board and its officials, the panel reversed in part and remanded. Specifically, the court thought the relationship between the vendor-shareholder and board was such that the *Pickering*

---

[8] Krebs v. Graveley, 861 F. App'x 671, 395 Educ. L. Rep. 671 (7th Cir. 2021).
[9] Garnier v. O'Connor-Ratliff, 41 F.4th 1158, 405 Educ. L. Rep. 715 (9th Cir. 2022).
[10] Riley's Am. Heritage Farms v. Elsasser (a), 29 F.4th 484, 401 Educ. L. Rep. 64 (9th Cir. 2022).

framework, balancing the degree to which an employer can regulate speech, was justified. The court thought that the vendor-shareholder established a prima facie case for retaliation. In addition, the court raised questions as to whether the severance of the relationship between the board and vendor was district-wide or whether individual schools could decide to continue the field trips. The court later issued a second opinion clarifying the denial of a petition for rehearing.[11]

Three federal trial courts heard First Amendment free expression cases. A candidate for a county school board seat sued state government officials, contending that the provision of the Florida Election Code that prohibited candidates for nonpartisan offices, such as school boards, from campaigning on party affiliation violated the Free Expression Clause of the First Amendment.[12] The court granted the candidate's motion for a preliminary injunction against enforcement of the provision because the portion about candidates for nonpartisan office could be removed without damage to the remainder of the provision and was presumptively unconstitutional in that it was not narrowly tailored to serve a compelling government interest.

A political party committee and canvassers challenged Idaho's campaign-free-election-zone law because they were asked to leave the property of an elementary school where an election occurred while they were electioneering.[13] The plaintiffs filed for a temporary and permanent injunction, concurrently with their complaint, to keep the board from preventing their electioneering more than 100 feet from the polling place buildings. The federal trial court held for the school board, denying all parts of the complaint and requests for injunctive relief, stating that, for First Amendment purposes, the elementary school used as a polling place was either a nonpublic or limited public forum on election day.

At issue in a federal trial court in Pennsylvania, a group of citizens objected to a board policy that gave the presiding officer the authority to interrupt or terminate public comments for being too long, personally directed, abusive, obscene, or irrelevant.[14] The objections included viewpoint discrimination in applying the policies and that the policies restricting speech were subjective and vague. The court granted the plaintiff's request for an injunction because the policy improperly restricted their speech.

---

[11] Riley's Am. Heritage Farms v. Elsasser (b), 32 F.4th 707, 402 Educ. L. Rep. 67 (9th Cir. 2022).
[12] Hetherington v. Madden, 558 F. Supp.3d 1187, 401 Educ. L. Rep. 814 (N.D. Fla. 2021).
[13] Tyler v. Coeur d'Alene Sch. Dist. 271, 568 F. Supp. 3d 1071, 403 Educ. L. Rep. 631 (D. Idaho 2021).
[14] Marshall v. Amuso, 571 F. Supp. 3d 412, 404 Educ. L. Rep. 571 (E.D. Pa. 2021).

In the only non-federal case involving the First Amendment, the Supreme Court of Illinois affirmed the defendant's conviction for disorderly conduct. The conviction arose from the defendant's telephone call with a private school administrator in which the former, while allegedly gathering information to transfer his child to the school, asked about its security measures and talked extensively about gun violence, causing a lockdown and police presence at the school. The defendant argued that his speech was protected by the First Amendment, therefore, his conviction was improper. The disorderly conduct statute at issue here prohibits unreasonable conduct that knowingly alarms or disturbs another or provokes a breach of peace. The court conceded that the defendant engaged in speech under the First Amendment, but it applied the true threats exception that bars "statements where the speaker means to communicate a serious expression of an intent to commit an act of unlawful violence to a particular individual or group of individuals"[15] from protection. The court affirmed that, because the defendant's speech fell under the true threats exception, it was not protected by the First Amendment and so upheld his conviction.

Fourth Amendment

The Fourth Circuit affirmed a federal trial court in Virginia's denial of the defendant's motion to suppress after he was indicted for conspiring to distribute and possession with intent to distribute methamphetamine and using/carrying a firearm during a drug trafficking crime.[16] The defendant argued that the firearm and drug evidence should be suppressed because the deputy lacked reasonable suspicion for the stop, violating the Fourth Amendment's prohibition on "unreasonable searches and seizures." The defendant was parked erratically on a high school campus at the time the school resource officer initiated the stop, and an administrator had seen a crossbow in the vehicle. The court rejected the defendant's argument that, because possession of a crossbow on school grounds is not illegal under state law, there was no reasonable suspicion to stop him. According to the court, even ignoring the defendant's possession of a crossbow on school grounds, the deputy had reasonable suspicion for the stop considering the defendant trespassed on school property, committed a parking violation, and operated a vehicle under the influence at the time of the stop.

---

[15] People v. Swenson, 181 N.E.3d 116, 125, 400 Educ. L. Rep. 307 (Ill. 2020).
[16] U.S. v. Coleman, 18 F.4th 131, 396 Educ. L. Rep. 392 (4th Cir. 2021).

Police officers employed by a municipality and the school board arrested a man who resisted their attempts to subdue him, and he died of injuries he sustained while in custody.[17] The man's family sued the municipality and the board alleging Fourth Amendment violations, including false arrest, excessive force, civil conspiracy, and deliberate indifference. The complex facts of the case resulted in an equally complex decision where a federal trial court in Texas found in favor of the family on their claims of excessive force and unreasonable seizure but not for civil conspiracy or deliberate indifference. The court dismissed the charges against the employee and board.

Due Process

In South Carolina, plaintiffs challenged a state law about disturbing school operations and disorderly conduct that was amended to exclude enforcement on students enrolled in schools.[18] Students and the nonprofit organization representing those who had been impacted by the law prior to its having been amended sought a declaratory judgment against the state attorney general and to remove records of its enforcement before the amendment. The federal trial court granted the plaintiffs' motion on the basis that the earlier version of the state law was unconstitutionally vague as applied to elementary and secondary students, violating the Due Process Clause.

An appellate court in North Carolina heard a case involving motorists who received traffic citations from red light cameras and sued the city and county board of education, claiming that the program authorizing the cameras violated the state constitution provision for using county school funds and due process.[19] The court remanded the case with instructions, stating that the agreement between the city and the board concerning the proceeds from the red light camera program did not meet constitutional requirements.

Adequate Education

The First Circuit affirmed the Rhode Island federal trial court's dismissal of the plaintiff students' claims for violations of the Constitution's Equal Protection, Due Process, and Privileges and Immunities Clauses.[20] A group of public-school students sued the

---

[17] Rivera v. City of Pasadena, 555 F. Supp. 3d 443, 401 Educ. L. Rep. 259 (S.D. Tex. 2021).
[18] Kenny v. Wilson, 566 F. Supp. 3d 447, 402 Educ. L. Rep. 778 (D.S.C. 2021).
[19] Fearrington v. City of Greenville, 871 S.E.2d 366, 402 Educ. L. Rep. 442 (N.C. App. 2022).
[20] A.C. by Waithe v. McKee, 23 F.4th 37, 396 Educ. L. Rep. 603 (1st Cir. 2022).

state and various officials, alleging the state failed to provide an adequate civics education in its public schools. The court first held that students do not have a fundamental constitutional right to an adequate civics education, only to a "minimally adequate education." The court pointed out that this right is only violated when a state action radically or absolutely denies the student of any "educational opportunity." The court was convinced that the state's approach to civics education was sufficient to satisfy rational basis review on the students' equal protection and due process claims while rejecting their claim that inadequate civics education violated the Privileges and Immunities Clause.

The Supreme Court of New Hampshire affirmed the denial of the state's motions to dismiss and for summary judgment on the school boards' claims for inadequate funding under the state constitution.[21] Specifically, the boards alleged that "the amount of per-pupil base adequacy aid set forth…to fund an adequate education is unconstitutional as applied." The court agreed that the state did fail to adequately fund education because the districts alleged that they only received $3,636.06 per pupil from the state and had to supplement that by raising additional funds the local taxes to provide a constitutionally adequate education. The court agreed that $3,636 per student was inadequate.

Equal Protection

The federal trial court in Massachusetts remanded and vacated a rule provision from the final Title IX rule published by the Department of Education setting new standards for sexual harassment, new investigation procedures, and changing the procedural safeguards for the accused under Title IX.[22] Organizations that advocated for sexual violence victims and individuals brought this action against various officials and departments alleging the final rule violated the Administrative Procedures Act and the Equal Protection Clause. The court found that only one individual plaintiff and one organization had standing to bring the current suit. The remaining two plaintiffs argued that thirteen provisions of the Final Rule were unlawful because they "effectively undermine the purpose of Title IX." Because the court accepted the new rule's interpretation of Title IX as rational and consistent with its original language, it posited that the plaintiffs failed to establish that it treated sexual harassment differently and

---

[21] Contoocook Vall. Sch. Dist. v. State, 261 A.3d 270, 396 Educ. L. Rep. 725 (N.H. 2021).
[22] Victim Rts. Law Ctr. v. Cardona, 552 F.Supp.3d 104, 400 Educ. L. Rep. 478 (D. Mass. 2021).

less favorably than harassment allegations based on race, color, national origin, or disability.

Elections

In 2022, five cases addressed issues involving K-12 schools and elections. The Supreme Court of Vermont affirmed the state's motion to dismiss an elementary student's claim alleging the school board's method for electing school board members violated the state constitution and denial of his motion to amend his complaint.[23] The student argued that the act allowed eighteen school boards to vote for school board members in a way that deprived children in rural areas of equal educational opportunities under the state constitution. On further review of the dismissal of the plaintiff's claims due to a lack of standing, the court affirmed, holding that the student failed to state an injury as required to establish such status.

An elector challenged the results of a board of canvassers' recount of a local school board referendum on whether the board would be permitted to exceed the revenue limits enumerated in state law.[24] The first tally resulted in a five-vote margin of victory for the "Yes" votes, with over 33,000 votes cast. Over seven days, a recount was conducted where the result was again a five-vote margin of victory for the "Yes" votes, even though the total had changed with contested ballots removed. The Supreme Court of Wisconsin affirmed that the statute on opening ballots and correcting errors in contested elections did not provide an individual elector an independent right to have the ballots opened and re-counted.

In Massachusetts, a candidate was declared ineligible to serve on a school committee because the city and its election commission determined he did not live there.[25] On further review granting the candidate's request for a permanent injunction, an appellate panel decided that, because the statute concerning residential tax exemption did not prove that he lived elsewhere and the fact that his civic life took place in the city must be considered in determining his place of residence, he was eligible to serve on the committee.

An appellate court in New York affirmed the denial of a county board of elections' motion to dismiss and granted the private college's request to compel the board to designate the college as a polling place for the general election.[26] The college argued that, after it was used

---

[23] Vasseur v. State, 260 A.3 1126, 396 Educ. L. Rep. 266 (Vt. 2021).
[24] Sewell v. Racine Unified Sch. Dist. Bd. of Canvassers, 972 N.W.2d 155. 401 Educ. L. Rep. 1146 (Wis. 2022).
[25] Lay v. City of Lowell, 188 N.E.3d 115, 403 Educ. L. Rep. 928 (Mass. App. Ct. 2022).
[26] Bard Coll. v. Dutchess Cnty. Bd. of Elections, 157 N.Y.S.3d 57, 398 Educ. L. Rep. 420 (N.Y. App. Div. 2021).

as a polling place for many years, the board arbitrarily decided to make a local church the sole polling location. When the board fails to designate a polling place by a majority vote, it must use the previously designated polling location. Because the college was most recently designated as a polling place along with the church, the court indicated that it was arbitrary and capricious for the board to revert to the polling places used multiple years ago instead of the most recent election.

In Texas, a school board published instructions for filing applications for a place on the ballot for election to its board of trustees.[27] A specific email address designated for candidates' applications was included in the instructions. The board election coordinator denied the application of a candidate who sent his application materials to the coordinator's official email address. An appellate court granted the candidate's petition for a writ of mandamus seeking to compel the coordinator to accept his application because he complied with the state's Election Code.

Board Operations and Authority Issues

Three state courts issued decisions on complaints about board operations and limits of authority. One state supreme court heard a case concerning the limits of the authority of boards. Two lower state courts examined the right of a particular employee to challenge a board rule and a challenge to the authority of the state commissioner to intervene before a local board reached a decision concerning detachment and annexation.

A school board entered an agreement with the parish sheriff's office concerning fines levied against motorists who attempted to overtake or pass a school bus while visual signs indicated that the bus was preparing to stop to allow students to get on or off.[28] The school board purchased and installed monitoring equipment on each bus and then provided video recordings to the sheriff's department for decision and collection of fines. The plaintiffs protesting the fines brought a class action against the parish, seeking reimbursement of the fines paid and the declaration of the law as unconstitutional. The Supreme Court of Louisiana held that the state constitution was unambiguous in limiting the legislative bodies in home rule charter parishes from controlling or affecting school boards.

---

[27] In re Miller, 641 S.W.3d 924, 401 Educ. L. Rep. 1186 (Tex. App. 2022).
[28] Mellor v. Par. of Jefferson, 338 So.3d 1138, 404 Educ. L. Rep. 387 (La. 2022).

In Florida, a school custodian was suspended without pay after he was charged with grand theft and other offenses.[29] The reason for the suspension was a "disqualifying offense" under state law. The custodian challenged the suspension, but the Administrative Law Judge upheld it. The union representing the board's non-instructional employees joined the custodian in challenging his suspension by the board and the validity of the state law that allowed the suspension. An appellate court found that neither the custodian nor the union showed real and immediate injury, which would be required for establishing standing to challenge the state's Administrative Procedure Act and the school board rule.

An appellate court in Texas addressed a state commissioner's authority in a detachment and annexation dispute between two boards and a land developer.[30] State law requires that a petition for detachment and annexation of land must be approved in an open meeting by the boards of both districts. If both boards do not agree, the law permits the petitioner to request a review by the commissioner. One board approved the petition, but the other did not act. The petitioner sought the commissioner's approval for the detachment and annexation, citing "constructive denial" by the non-acting board as the trigger that placed the matter at his discretion. The non-acting board appealed the commissioner's decision, challenging his jurisdiction to review the petition without a conflicting decision. The court entered a judgment in favor of the board on the point of law.

Taxation

Eight state cases involved disputes on taxation, five of which were resolved in state supreme courts on points of law and jurisdiction, procedural matters on public notice requirements, and a taxation scheme's relationship to equal educational opportunities.

When county commissioners refused to comply with a local law requiring the distribution of proceeds from a Simplified Sellers Use Tax to the county and city boards of education, local education officials and other education-related plaintiffs sued the commissioners in their individual and official capacities.[31] A trial court upheld local law. On appeal by the commissioners, the Supreme Court of Alabama affirmed that the local law did not

---

[29] Escambia Cnty. Sch. Bd. v. Warren, 337 So. 3d 496, 403 Educ. L. Rep. 341 (Fla. Dist. Ct. App. 2022).
[30] Lampasas Indep. Sch. Dist. v. Morath, 644 S.W.3d 866, 403 Educ. L. Rep. 967 (Tex. Ct. App. 2022).
[31] Barnett v. Jones, 338 So. 3d 757, 404 Educ. L. Rep. 362 (Ala. 2021).

violate the state constitution's statute prohibiting local laws that dealt with matters pertaining to a general law.

In a second case from the Supreme Court of Alabama, it affirmed a grant of summary judgment in favor of a city in response to a suit by a county board of education and its employees to avoid an occupational tax.[32] The tax at issue imposed a 1% tax on anyone who works within the city and does not otherwise pay a license fee to work there. The plaintiffs argued that they should be exempt from the occupational tax because they provide an essential government service. The court affirmed that, regardless of how important the roles of state employees are, they still must pay the occupational tax.

A recall committee distributed a petition to stop a proposed tax increase by challenging the legality of the board's public notice.[33] The county clerk certified some electronic signatures on the petition even though there had been no security procedures in place during their collection. The Supreme Court of Kentucky affirmed that the school board's failure to include the general tax rate of the previous year in its notice of a proposed tax increase was not a substantive violation of the notice requirement.

The Supreme Court of Nevada affirmed a motion for summary judgment in favor of the state when parents, a scholarship organization, and businesses' claims challenged the constitutionality of legislation eliminating future increases in the amount of tax credits available.[34] The court decided that the appellants had standing under the public-importance exception which requires the involvement of an issue with significant public importance, the involvement of a challenge to a legislative expenditure or appropriation on a state constitutional basis, and no other person who is in a better position to and capable of bringing the claim. Still, the court rejected the claim because the legislation was not subject to the state constitutional provision requiring two-thirds of the members' votes in each legislative house.

A student, a taxpayer, and a town sued the state alleging deprivation of equal educational opportunities for the student, disproportional tax contribution for education by the taxpayer, and the town being forced to collect an unconstitutional tax.[35] A lower court granted the state's motion for summary judgment. On appeal, the Supreme Court of Vermont affirmed that the statewide education funding taxation scheme did not deprive the student of her

---

[32] Jefferson Cnty. Bd. of Educ. v. City of Irondale, 331 So.3d 597, 399 Educ. L. Rep. 1090 (Ala. 2020).
[33] Freidmann v. Jefferson Cnty. Bd. of Educ., 1647 3.W.3d 181, 405 Educ. L. Rep. 1198 (Ky. 2022).
[34] Morency v. Dep't of Educ., 496 P.3d 584, 395 Educ. L. Rep. 1141 (Nev. 2021).
[35] Boyd v. State, 275 A.3d 155, 404 Educ. L. Rep. 201 (Vt. 2022).

right to equal educational opportunities, nor did the taxation scheme require the taxpayer to pay a disproportionate contribution to the funding of education. The court added that the town had no standing to bring action against the state.

An appellate court in Arizona reversed and remanded the lower court's grant of summary judgment in favor of the taxpayer and its order for the state to pay.[36] The taxpayer, a county and school board, sued the state and the Department of Revenue seeking payment of the disputed tax funds as additional state aid for educational purposes. The issue arose from a state constitutional provision capping ad valorem taxes on residential property at 1% of the full cash value of the property, with three exceptions, and the state reimbursed the additional primary property tax amounts as "additional state aid for education" to any school boards that were affected. The panel disagreed with the tax court in holding that the desegregation expenses were "secondary property taxes," and that the removal of the desegregation expenses as "additional state aid for education" from the reimbursement calculation did not render it unworkable. The court concluded that the state's refusal to pay excess desegregation expenses did not render the reimbursement calculation unworkable.

In Florida, an appellate court affirmed the grant of a temporary injunction to construction entities' to prevent the collection of school impact fees while litigation was pending.[37] The entities involved in the construction of residential property argued that the imposition of impact fees on a countywide basis was unconstitutional and invalid. For impact fees to be a valid exercise of authority, "they must be true impact fees and not taxes." To make this determination, courts use the dual rational nexus test, which requires local government to "demonstrate a reasonable connection...between the need for additional capital facilities and the growth in population generated by the subdivision." Additionally, the fees must grant some kind of special benefit to only those who pay the fee. Here, the court found that flaws in the school board's testimony and reports indicated a substantial likelihood of success on the merits. Further, the court observed that irreparable harm is assumed when a constitutional violation likely occurred.

In Illinois, a Montessori school with tax-exempt status operated on property owned by the local school board.[38] The Montessori school

---

[36] Pima Cnty. v. State, 497 P.3d 1012, 396 Educ. L. Rep. 808 (Ariz. App. Ct. 2021).
[37] Bd. of Cnty. Comm'rs, Santa Rosa Cnty. v. Home Builders Ass'n of W. Fla., 325 So. 3d 981, 396 Educ. L. Rep. 344 (Fla. Dist. Ct. App. 2021).
[38] Keystone Montessori Sch. v. Vill. of River Forest, 187 N.E.3d 1167, 403 Educ. L. Rep. 898 (Ill. App. Ct. 2021).

and the village government agreed that the school would waive its property tax exemption. That arrangement was in effect from 1998 until 2018 when the school applied for the exemption. The school's case was removed to federal court, where two counts were dismissed, and the case was remanded. An appellate court rejected the original agreement as invalid because, under state law, school officials cannot waive a school's tax-exempt status. Because the court did not think that village authorities acted in bad faith, it rejected school officials' request for sanctions based on unjust enrichment.

Finance

All five finance issues that were litigated reached state supreme courts. In the first, California's Greene Act provides state funding to assist in construction projects from two funding streams: new construction and hardship funding. Generally, the state share and local funding of construction projects is targeted at 50% each. The state can adjust that proportion. One school board received over $35 million but contributed approximately $200,000 of local funds, thereby saving approximately $3 million. The State Allocation Board presented the board with a bill of over $3 million to be returned to the state, leading the latter to seek writ of administrative mandamus claiming it was entitled to keep the savings from unused hardship funding. An appellate court affirmed that the board could keep the funds because the Greene Act allowed it to retain savings "achieved by the district's efficient and prudent expenditure"[39] of the funds. The court further recognized the conflict between the Greene Act and other state regulations about returning unused funds.

School boards sued the governor and the state educational establishment, seeking a declaration that the defending parties had a constitutional obligation to provide them with adequate funding to meet the learning standards set by the state board of education.[40] The Supreme Court of Illinois affirmed that the boards' request for adequate funding did not present an actual controversy required for a declaratory judgment.

A taxpayer advocacy group in Michigan sued state authorities requesting enforcement of a state constitutional amendment, the Headlee Amendment, that required a specified percentage of state spending to be allocated to local government.[41] The state's high court

---

[39] San Bernadino City Unified Sch. Dist. v. State Allocation Bd., 294 Cal. Rptr.3d 348, 350, 403 Educ. L. Rep. 275 (Cal. Ct. App. 2022).
[40] Cahokia Unit. Sch. Dist. No. 187 v. Pritzker, 184 N.E.3d 233, 401 Educ. L. Rep. 1094 (Ill. 2021).
[41] Taxpayers for Mich. Const. Gov't v. Dep't of Tech. Mgmt. and Budget, 972 N.W.2d 738, 402 Educ. L. Rep. 361 (Mich. 2021).

held that the "Proposal A" funds cited by the advocacy group should be counted in the required state spending allocation, that public school academies were not considered "school districts" within the provisions of the Headlee Amendment, and that state funding for all units of local government was counted toward compliance with the Amendment.

A group of parents in three counties brought action against all levels of the state educational establishment.[42] The complaint was far-reaching but centered on continued low academic achievement, as evidenced by the state's low state education rankings and standardized test scores. The combined failures allegedly violated the state constitution's requirement to provide sufficient, basic education. A trial court dismissed the complaint as a nonjusticiable political question. Pointing out that the state constitution provides a clear textual commitment of public education to the state legislature, the Supreme Court of Nevada affirmed that public education funding is a nonjusticiable political question.

A second case from Nevada tested the state's commitment to school tuition vouchers.[43] The trial court enjoined an advocacy group's petition circulation and the corresponding initiative for education savings accounts on the ballot for an election to amend the state constitution. On appeal, the state's high court determined that the proposed initiative to establish a private school voucher system, an education freedom account, was an unfunded mandate. The published explanatory literature in the initiative's proposal was deceptive and misleading.

The Tennessee governor and state education officials defended a pilot program that directly funded students through the Education Savings Account Act. City and county governments opposed the pilot program and sought a declaratory judgment as Home Rule entities under the state constitution. To qualify for application of the Home Run Amendment, three requirements must be met: "1) the statute in question must be local in form or effect; 2) it must be applicable to a particular county or municipality; and 3) it must be applicable to the particular county or municipality in either its governmental or proprietary capacity." The lower courts agreed with the city and county, finding them to be Home Rule entities. On further review, the state's supreme court vacated and remanded on the basis that there was sufficient injury for standing but that, because the Act did

---

[42] Shea v. State, 510 P.3d 148, 403 Educ. L. Rep. 300 (Nev. 2022).
[43] Educ. Freedom PAC v. Reid, 512 P.3d 296, 404 Educ. L. Rep. 924 (Nev. 2022).

not apply to the city or county, it did not implicate the Home Rule Amendment.[44]

Charter Schools

Administration

The single case concerning the administration of a charter school came from an appellate court in Texas and dealt with various aspects of charter school governance, clarifying the validity of three rules.[45] A district or campus identified as low performing over time faces sanctions from the state agency. One way to avoid sanctions was to partner with a charter company under the state administrative code. There were three rules at issue here: the Consultation Rule required the protection of the contractual rights of existing school staff only in contracts with open-enrollment charter schools; the Local Policy Rule required a partnership with a charter school to identify the specific local rules and policies that were not excluded; and the Final Decision Rule prohibited appeals of the commissioner's decisions to approve or deny board authorized charter partnerships. Two teacher organizations challenged the commissioner and the Texas Education Agency seeking a declaratory judgment on the validity of these rules. After a trial court invalidated all three rules, an appellate panel observed that the Consultation and Local Policy Rules were not invalid. Still, the Final Decision Rule granting ultimate authority on approving or denying charter school partnerships to the commissioner's discretion was invalid.

Funding

In California, an appellate court reversed and remanded a grant of a school board's motion for judgment on the pleadings seeking a determination of the amounts due for facilities costs that the school board was authorized to charge the charter school. Under the relevant regulations, "charter schools are responsible for ongoing operations and maintenance at facilities they use; school districts are responsible for major maintenance and capital improvements; and a district may charge a charter school a pro rata share of its 'facilities costs.'"[46] The court maintained that there were significant discrepancies between what the charter school considered to be its

---

[44] Metro. Gov't of Nashville and Davidson Cnty. v. Tenn. Dep't of Educ., 645 S.W.3d 141, 404 Educ. L. Rep. 301 (Tenn. 2022).
[45] Morath v. Tex. Am. Fed'n of Tchrs., 646 S.W.3d 40, 404 Educ. L. Rep. 345 (Tex. App. 2022).
[46] Mt. Diablo Unified Sch. Dist. v. Clayton Vall. Charter High Sch., 284 Cal.Rptr.3d 850, 852, 395 Educ. L. Rep. 1024 (Cal. Ct. App. 2021).

pro rata share and what the board thought the charter school owed for its share, explaining that the ambiguity stemmed from a provision of the regulation regarding a charter school's payment of facilities costs. The court held that the facilities costs excluded any contributions made by the board to its ongoing and major maintenance account that were ultimately dispersed to pay the types of costs paid by the charter school.

Five charter schools in Florida sued to compel their county school board to share referendum funds proportionally with the charter schools.[47] The city operated two of the charter schools, and three had private operators. The lower court consolidated the cases and granted the board's motion for summary judgment. An appellate court reversed and remanded, holding that the county board was required to share referendum funds proportionally so that the students in the charter schools were funded "the same as" those in the public schools. The remand was to determine when the board was required to begin sharing funds.

Officials of a charter school in Pennsylvania sought a refund of real estate taxes that the local board collected in error.[48] The trial court cited a lack of subject matter jurisdiction and sustained the board's preliminary objections. On further review, an appellate court remarked that charter school officials did not waive their right to challenge the county board's erroneous tax assessment notice by paying the taxes. Reversing and remanding, the court rejected the dismissal as improper and, instead, held that the proper solution was to transfer the issue to the county board of assessment appeals.

Other Charter School Cases

An appellate court in Ohio affirmed in part and reversed and remanded in part findings that a superintendent was strictly liable for conflicted transactions, that all family members should relinquish wages, and that the contracts between the school and the superintendent's husband's company constituted a pattern of corrupt activity.[49] This case was initiated by the Attorney General against the superintendent of a charter school, her husband who served as project manager, and her daughter who worked in various roles, based on allegations that they violated state law by possessing a personal interest in the charter school's transactions. The appellate court affirmed that the superintendent and her husband

---

[47] Archimedean Acad. v. Sch. Bd. of Miami-Dade Cnty., 338 So. 3d 1032, 404 Educ. L. Rep. 382 (Fla. Dist. Ct. App. 2022).
[48] Circle of Seasons Charter Sch. v. Nw. Lehigh Sch. Dist., 273 A.3d 23, 402 Educ. L. Rep. 295 (Pa. Commw. Ct. 2022).
[49] Sun Bldg. Ltd. P'ship v. Value Learning & Teaching Acad., 175 N.E.3d 10, 395 Educ. L. Rep. 1107 (Ohio Ct. App. 2021).

had an interest in the charter school's contracts with the husband's corporation, that the superintendent and husband should forfeit their employment wages, and that the superintendent was strictly liable for the amounts of the charter school's contracts with her husband's corporation and the contract with her daughter. The court reversed the finding that the school's contracts with the husband's corporation constituted a pattern of corrupt activity under the Ohio Corrupt Practice Act because the contracts only represented a single event, not a pattern of corrupt activity.

The last charter school case generated two opinions. State officials rejected an application to operate a Multiple Charter School Organization because of inadequacies related to improving student performance as well as establishing accepted standards of fiscal management and acceptable governance procedures.[50] The school's application failed to meet any of the requirements for these and other areas. As a result, the Charter School Approval Board (CAB) denied the application. For schools or campuses that met none of the requirements, a provision in charter school regulations allowed the consolidation of the failing school with another charter that did meet the requirements.[51] The court was of the opinion that the charter school's amended application to consolidate eight charter schools, all failing to meet threshold school performance profile scores, did not qualify for CAB approval.

Localized Governance Issues

Bidding & Awarding of Contracts

In the only case related to the awarding of a contract, a school board challenged the valuation of a taxpayer's mineral-interest property, alleging that the property was omitted from appraisal for several years.[52] At trial, the taxpayer claimed that the board's contract with the lawyer representing them violated a state tax code provision banning "tax ferret" contracts incorporating contingency fee arrangements for collecting taxes. Ruling on the taxpayer's motion to dismiss, the trial court declared that the lawyer lacked authority to represent the board based on the allegedly void contract.

---

[50] Propel Charter Schs. v. Sch. Dist. of Pittsburgh (State Charter Sch. Appeal Bd.), 271 A.3d 1, 401 Educ. L. Rep. 970 (Pa. Commw. Ct. 2021).
[51] Propel Charter Schs. v. Pa. Dep'. of Educ. (State Charter Sch. Appeal Bd.), 271 A.3d 17, 401 Educ. L. Rep. 970 (Pa. Commw. Ct. 2021).
[52] Iraan-Sheffield Indep. Sch. Dist. v. Pecos Cnty. Appraisal Dist., 645 S.W.3d 827, 404 Educ. L. Rep. 328 (Tex. App. 2022).

On further review, an appellate court in Texas reversed and remanded, stating that although the board's contract with the attorney was partly a tax ferret contract, the specific provisions were permissible under the tax code. Therefore, the court noted that the attorney had the authority to file the property tax valuation petition on behalf of the board. Because the contract was, in fact, valid, the panel concluded that the trial court erred in granting the property owner's motion to dismiss.

Breach of Contract

An appellate court in Connecticut affirmed a judgment in favor of a school board on its claims for breach of contract against the contractor who performed repair work on an outdoor stairway.[53] The board argued that the contractor breached the contract because the concrete replacement and stairway repair were defective and unworkmanlike. The contractor argued that the trial court erred in finding that his work proximately caused the defects without expert testimony and improperly calculated the damages awarded to the board based on the replacement of the stairs instead of repair. While expert testimony is generally required when the issue goes beyond a lay person's ordinary knowledge and experience, it is not required "when there is such gross want of care or skill as to afford, of itself, an almost conclusive inference of negligence." The court affirmed that the issue fell within this exception to the expert witness requirement due to the extent of the evidence showing the work was performed in an unworkmanlike fashion. In concluding there was insufficient evidence to reject the replacement as unnecessary, the court upheld the damages award.

Another breach of contract case concerned the actions of the estate of a philanthropist in Florida to deny creditor claims filed by an educational foundation attached to a charter school in Detroit.[54] The charter school foundation claimed that, before his death, the philanthropist pledged donations and guaranteed loans totaling several million dollars. To resolve the case, the parties executed a settlement agreement. Still, the probate court did not include the settlement agreement document in its final order closing the case. When a subsequent dispute resulted in the estate ceasing payments to the foundation, the trial court ruled in favor of the foundation's motion to enforce the settlement agreement. Agreeing with the

---

[53] Reg'l Sch. Dist. 8 v. M & S Paving and Sealing, 261 A.3d 153, 396 Educ. L. Rep. 714 (Conn. Ct. App. 2021).
[54] Pulte v. New Common Sch. Found., 334 So.3d 677, 401 Educ. L. Rep. 1192 (Fla. Dist. App. Ct. 2022).

estate, an appellate panel reversed and remanded because the probate court lacked continuing jurisdiction over the settlement agreement insofar as its final approval order did not explicitly retain the probate court's jurisdiction to enforce its terms.

In the first of three breach of contract claims involving construction, a school board in Georgia hired a general contractor to build a new wrestling facility.[55] When both parties failed to pay a construction materials supplier for steel used in the project, the supplier sued both parties. The board, claiming that it paid the general contractor in full, expecting that the general contractor would pay the supplier, received a default judgment order with damages awarded. In response, the general contractor petitioned the court to vacate the order and enjoin the execution and collection of the damages. An appellate panel reversed the trial court's denial of injunctive relief for the general contractor and remanded the case to the trial court. Because the trial court order did not contain language terminating the proceedings, the panel reasoned that the default judgment order was not a final judgment because it only established liability, not a determination of damages awarded.

A company alleged that a school board breached its contract by impeding its work through excessive and untimely change order requests and requiring the performance of additional work without compensation.[56] The board countered that any delays were due to unforeseen site conditions that they could not have reasonably anticipated. An appellate court in New York affirmed the order denying the board's motion to dismiss because including a no-damages-for-delay clause in the contract was an insufficient defense for it as a matter of state law.

At issue in a second case from New York, a school construction authority awarded nine contracts to a construction company.[57] Over the course of the work related to these contracts, the company twice served notices of claims seeking allegedly unpaid monies related to change order requests. Because the board failed to pay for the work outlined in the change orders, the construction company filed suit to recover the costs for the disputed charges. An appellate court affirmed the dismissal, pointing out that many of the claims were untimely as they exceeded the statutory limitation of three months for filing claims. Additionally, the court indicated that because the two notice of claims documents served on the construction authority

---

[55] Larkin v. Madison Cnty. Sch. Dist., 873 S.E.2d 471, 404 Educ. L. Rep. 280 (Ga. Ct. App. 2022).
[56] BCI Constr., v. Bd. of Educ., Washingtonville Cent. Sch. Dist., 164 N.Y.S.3d 632, 401 Educ. L. Rep. 1091 (N.Y. App. Div. 2022).
[57] One Ten Restoration, v. N.Y.C. Sch. Const. Auth., 163 N.Y.S.3d 562, 401 Educ. L. Rep. 540 (N.Y. App. Div. 2022).

lacked the required fully-executed verification page, they were not valid.

Copyright Infringement

To promote reading achievement among their students, a school board in Texas implemented a reading incentive program with a theme related to becoming a millionaire.[58] On learning of the program, a company producing educational resources for reading instruction filed a complaint against the board for trademark infringement under the Lanham Act, alleging that its reading program used symbols and branding confusingly similar to their trademarked products. The Fifth Circuit affirmed that the Lanham Act's prohibitions against trademark infringement relied on the likelihood of consumer confusion between the trademarks in question and that the chances of such confusion in this case were minimal given that sophisticated school board purchasers could easily distinguish between the goods and services marketed by the company and those implemented by another board.

In another case involving copyright infringement, the Fifth Circuit affirmed a federal trial court in Texas' dismissal of an author's copyright infringement claim against a public school board.[59] The issue here arose after a school board official tweeted a one-page passage from the plaintiff's sports psychology book on the official microblog websites for the school's softball team and color guard. In response to the author's copyright infringement claim, the board claimed the affirmative defense of fair use. In evaluating a claim of fair use, courts consider four factors: "(1) the purpose and character of the use, ... (2) the nature of the copyrighted work; (3) the amount and sustainability of the portion used in relation to the copyrighted work as a whole; and (4) the effect of the use upon the potential market for or value of the copyrighted work." The court wrote that because factors one and four favored the board, two favored the author, and three was neutral, the tweets were protected under the fair use defense.

Insurance

After a former student in Illinois sued a school board alleging that one of it its officials sexually abused him multiple times, its

---

[58] Springboards to Educ. v. Pharr-San Juan-Alamo Indep. Sch. Dist., 33 F.4th 747, 402 Educ. L. Rep. 115 (5th Cir. 2022).
[59] Bell v. Eagle Mtn. Saginaw Indep. Sch. Dist., 27 F.4th 313, 400 Educ. L. Rep. 46 (5th Cir. 2022).

insurance carrier denied coverage for the claim.[60] The board and the insurance carrier disagreed about whether, under the terms of the policy, the student complaint was part of a "single claim" against the board because it shared related facts, circumstances, and situations with three student lawsuits concerning the same official that were filed before the implementation of the insurance policy. The trial court denied the insurer's motion to dismiss, granted the board's motion for summary judgment, and ordered the insurer to indemnify the board for approximately $1.2 million. However, an appellate court reversed in part, vacated in part, and remanded with directions to dismiss the claims with prejudice. The court based its order on clearly defining a single claim in the policy as incorporating all claims with related facts and events. It, therefore, concluded that all claims related to the administrator in question were part of a single claim predating the implementation of the insurance policy.

Property Rights

In a case addressing the purchase of property, a Catholic diocese sought to sell a property they rented to one of its high schools and its educational foundation as part of a bankruptcy proceeding.[61] After a third-party developer offered substantially more for the property, the diocese renegotiated with the high school officials who agreed to pay the higher price. The diocese then approved procedures allowing the high school foundation to buy the property as negotiated without a higher third-party bid. The Official Committee of Unsecured Creditors objected, stating that the proposed bidding procedures did not withstand the strict scrutiny applied to insider negotiations and were designed to chill bidding on the property rather than maximize the property's value. A federal bankruptcy court in New York denied the diocese's motion without prejudice, holding that the procedures proposed were designed to discourage competitive bidding and did not incorporate the degree of transparency required for a bankruptcy proceeding. The court noted that it would consider a hearing on an amended motion that adequately addressed these concerns.

A school board in Louisiana filed suit against an oil and gas company claiming negligence, strict liability, and breach of contract due to damage to their property from company operations under

---

[60] Freeburg Cmty. Consol. Sch. Dist. No. 70 v. Country Mut. Ins. Co., 183 N.E.3d 1020, 401 Educ. L. Rep. 622 (Ill. App. Ct. 2021).
[61] In re Diocese of Buffalo, N.Y., 637 B.R. 701, 401 Educ. L. Rep. 956 (Bankr. W.D.N.Y. 2022).

long-standing oil and gas leases.[62] The company countered that the board did not meet the statute of limitations for filing a strict liability claim. The oil and gas company appealed after a jury returned a strict liability verdict in favor of the board while imposing a significant damages award for land remediation. An appellate panel vacated the trial court's decision and remanded the case for a new trial. Both parties appealed to the state supreme court, which affirmed the appellate court decision and granted a re-hearing at the request of both parties. The court noted that state law only allows for recovery of excess remediation damages when specified by contract; if the contract is silent on the matter, the standard returns the land to its original condition. The court also affirmed that the board's hiring of counsel to investigate the matter did not constitute actual or constructive knowledge of harm sufficient to apply the statute of limitations for strict liability claims.

In a second case involving the purchase of property, a school board sought to purchase a parcel of land from a development company to build two new schools.[63] To avoid a threatened condemnation action from the board, the development company negotiated a sale of the property. A decade later, the board elected to sell the property rather than use it to build schools. The original owner sought declaratory relief, arguing that they should have had the first right of refusal to re-purchase the land. An appellate court found in favor of the board, stating that no actual condemnation action was filed, so the sale did not occur under the threat of condemnation. On further review, the Supreme Court of Utah disagreed, reversing and remanding because, although the board did not specifically file an eminent domain action, it did notify the developer that they intended to acquire the parcel of land through eminent domain if necessary. Because the board specifically authorized condemnation to acquire the property, the developer met the burden of demonstrating that the property was sold under threat of condemnation.

In a local zoning law dispute, Maryland property owners of pipestem lots adjacent to a private school had granted a non-exclusive easement to the private school to use the twenty-two twelve-inch pipestem strips for property maintenance.[64] Years later, officials at the private school filed a proposed zoning amendment that would allow them to build on the easement area without

---

[62] State of La. v. La. Land and Exploration Co., 339 So. 3d 1163, 405 Educ. L. Rep. 542 (La. 2022).
[63] Cardiff Wales v. Wash. Cnty. Sch. Dist., 511 P.3d 1155, 404 Educ. L. Rep. 270 (Utah 2022).
[64] Howard Cnty. v. McClain, 270 A.3d 1062, 401 Educ. L. Rep. 961 (Md. Spec. App. 2022).

permission of the land owners; the county council amended this proposal to make it applicable only to private academic schools. The property owners filed a complaint for declaratory judgment against the county, alleging that the changed zoning requirements were a special law to benefit the private school and, therefore, unconstitutional. In the county's appeal of the trial court's decision to grant summary judgment to the property owners, an appellate court held that the zoning regulation was unconstitutional because it was designed to benefit the private school in question, violating the state constitution.

Public Records and Freedom of Information Act (FOIA)

After a former school police officer in California requested to view his personnel records, he uncovered a document detailing sustained findings of an internal affairs investigation that concluded after he left the district.[65] The officer was aware of the investigation but received no notice of the conclusions sustained. Over a year later, board officials notified him that they had received multiple open records requests relating to the investigation and discipline of school officers and that documents in his file were responsive to the requests. The officer filed for a writ of mandamus and temporary restraining order to prevent school officials from releasing the records, stating that he never received an official notice of findings or opportunity for administrative appeal. On further review, an appellate court affirmed in part and reversed in part. Although the panel upheld the injunction against disclosure of the records because the sustained findings were issued after the officer resigned, it required the trial court to limit that injunction to requests filed before the legislature adopted new penal code amendments effective January 1, 2022, that may require disclosure of the records.

Shortly after hiring, a Michigan superintendent requested a closed school board meeting under the Open Meetings Act (OMA) to address complaints lodged against her.[66] The school board president shared a document outlining the complaints at the meeting. Soon after, the superintendent resigned, and the board appointed an interim superintendent at an open meeting. A newspaper filed a FOIA request for the document shared at the closed session, but the board denied the request, claiming that the document was exempt

---

[65] Wyatt v. Kern High Sch. Dist., 296 Cal.Rptr.3d 476, 405 Educ. L. Rep. 1130 (Cal. Ct. App. 2022).
[66] Traverse City Record-Eagle v. Traverse City Area Pub. Sch. Bd. of Educ., 975 N.W.2d 104, 404 Educ. L. Rep. 254 (Mich. Ct. App. 2021).

from disclosure. The newspaper then filed suit, claiming FOIA and OMA violations. The parties cross-filed for summary disposition, resulting in the trial court granting summary disposition for the plaintiffs on the FOIA claim and summary disposition for the defendants on the OMA claim. After a cross-appeal, an appellate court in Michigan affirmed, noting that, although discussions and deliberations of closed meetings are exempt from FOIA requests, documents used at those meetings may be disclosable. Further, although plaintiffs disagreed with the short deliberation period on hiring the interim superintendent, the board complied with the OMA in voting on the hiring and contract at a public meeting.

Plaintiffs in New Jersey filed an Open Records Act (OPRA) request, seeking all special education settlement agreements involving students with an individualized education plan or Section 504 accommodation agreement, final decisions related to those agreements, any evidence of the cost of legal services related to the settlements, and any board resolutions approving the settlements.[67] The school board denied the first request on the grounds of confidentiality and the second request due to vagueness. They produced redacted invoices and board resolutions to meet the third and fourth requests. The trial court ordered the board to provide redacted settlement agreements and final decisions and granted attorneys' fees to the plaintiffs. Subsequently, an appellate court affirmed that settlement agreements adjudicated by the Office of Administrative Law are judicial filings subject to a presumption of public access in redacted form. Additionally, the court explained that OPRA allows the prevailing party to receive reasonable attorneys' fees.

School Boundaries

In the first of two detachment-and-annexation cases, an Illinois family temporarily living with a family member was advised to enroll their children in the family member's school district.[68] When the family moved back to their residence in a neighboring district, the parents petitioned to detach the property from the school district in the boundary area it was located in and annex it to the one where the students attended classes. The Regional Board denied the petition, finding that the parents failed to demonstrate that the educational benefit to the annexing district outweighed the

---

[67] C. E. v. Elizabeth Pub. Sch. Dist., 276 A.3d 662, 405 Educ. L. Rep. 380 (N.J. Super. Ct. App. Div. 2022).
[68] Burle v. Reg'l Bd. of Sch. Trs. of Educ. No. 35, 189 N.E.3d 922, 405 Educ. L. Rep. 512 (Ill. App. Ct. 2021).

detriment to the community losing the detachment area property. The appellate court in Illinois affirmed an administrative hearing supporting the Regional Board's denial of the petition. Noting that the evidence for maintaining the students' educational placement continuity was tenuous, the court rejected the claim that the board's decision was erroneous.

Under New York state law, residents of a property intersected by the boundary lines of more than one school district may choose which system their children will attend class in.[69] On listing the property for sale, a homeowner claimed that the property was intersected by the boundary lines of two districts. Therefore, anyone purchasing the property could choose between the two districts. One of the school boards disagreed, asserting that the entire property lay within its boundaries. An appellate court affirmed that the property is intersected by the boundary lines of both districts, observing that a surveyor's map of the property presented in evidence was more accurate than the one used by the later board to justify its position.

Transportation

In the only case related to the transportation of school students, a not-for-profit corporation in New York objected to a school board policy denying transportation of students to nonpublic schools on days that the public schools were not in session.[70] The board denied such requests, and the corporation filed suit, claiming that it was not providing equitable transportation services. On further review of a grant of a permanent injunction directing the board to provide transportation on days when the nonpublic schools were open but the public schools were not, an appellate court reversed in favor of the board. The court cited state law as permitting, but not requiring, board's to transport nonpublic students on days when the public schools are closed.

Procedural Issues

---

[69] Castaldi v. Syosset Cent. Sch. Dist., 164 N.Y.S.3d 626, 401 Educ. L. Rep. 1087 (N.Y. App. Div. 2022).
[70] United Jewish Cmty. of Blooming Grove v. Washingtonville Cent. Sch. Dist., 169 N.Y.S.3d 401, 404 Educ. L. Rep. 247 (N.Y. App. Div. 2022).

An appellate court in Florida dismissed the county school board's petition for certiorari review after the trial court issued a discovery order requiring an in-camera review process for the production of healthcare records and finding that the board's request for employment histories was overbroad in the underlying action alleging the board violated state civil rights and worker's compensation law.[71] The trial court restricted the board's request for documents from all current and former employers of the injured to their "applications for employment, job descriptions, pay and benefit records, and time and attendance records." The board sought review from this decision, but the appellate court held that it lacked jurisdiction to hear the board's appeal because it failed to establish that it would suffer irreparable material harm absent a grant of certiorari.

COVID-19

The Supreme Court of Pennsylvania affirmed a grant summary relief for parents and school officials who challenged the commonwealth's mask mandate that required individuals to wear a facial covering inside of schools in an effort to control the spread of COVID-19. The court held that disease control measures available to the Department of Health under its non-emergency powers are limited to those adopted by a formal rule or regulation. The law allows discrete mitigation efforts triggered once a report of a communicable disease is received; then, the department must assess whether the disease "is subject to isolation, quarantine, or any other control measure,"[72] and, if so, it must implement appropriate measures to control the disease. The secretary argued that the mask mandate constituted a "modified quarantine," but the court disagreed, observing that it could not be a modified quarantine without a contact nexus or time limit pursuant to the statutory or regulatory requirements. The court added that the mask mandate could not fall under the regulation's catchall provision as it only applied to the "surveillance" of disease and not control.

An appellate court in Florida granted the state's request to reinstate the automatic stay of the temporary injunction order on the state education association, teachers, parents, and NAACP's claims regarding the reopening plan for schools after closures due to

---

[71] Alachua Cnty. Sch. Bd. v. Barnes, 340 So.3d 567, 405 Educ. L. Rep. 571 (Fla. Dist. Ct. App. 2022).
[72] Corman v. Acting Sec'y of Pa. Dep't of Health, 266 A.3d 452, 463, 399 Educ. L. Rep. 308 (Pa. 2021).

COVID-19.[73] The Commissioner of Education issued an Emergency Order addressing funding issues faced by schools as a result of online learning and required districts to submit a reopening plan allowing students the option to attend in-person for the district to be evaluated under the new funding formula. The plaintiffs argued that this Emergency Order forced districts to offer in-person instruction when it was unsafe to do so by threatening the loss of funds and sought a temporary injunction on the order. The panel was convinced that the trial court abused its discretion in three ways by vacating the automatic stay. First, there were no compelling circumstances that warranted vacating the stay. Additionally, the court indicated that the state was substantially likely to succeed on the merits of its claim on appeal. Finally, the court emphasized that the appellees failed to allege adequately that reinstating the automatic stay would have caused irreparable harm.

In another case from Florida an appellate court dismissed a school board's petition for review of an emergency rule adopted, and later repealed, by the state Department of Health and Surgeon General that required schools to allow parents to opt out of the masking requirement for their student during COVID-19. Department officials argued that dismissal was proper because the rule had been repealed so the issue was moot; the board countered that the court should issue a judgment on the merits due to collateral legal consequences. According to the court, for a repealed rule to be ripe for judicial review, a party must "stand[] to lose property, advantages, or rights as a collateral result of the dismissal."[74] Because the board did not challenge the rule through administrative procedures but instead did so through direct judicial review, the court denied its claim for attorney fees because the question was moot.

Conclusion

Constitutional issues related to the Free Expression Clause of the First Amendment were more numerous than in recent years. In a departure from the previous year, board operations and election issues were fewer. Finance and funding issues centered on legislative responsibility for adequacy. Charter litigation reflected some of the same issues as in public schools.

---

[73] DeSantis v. Fla. Educ. Ass'n, 325 So. 3d 145, 395 Educ. L. Rep. 1167 (Fla. Dist. Ct. App. 2020).
[74] Sch. Bd. of Miami-Dade Cnty. v. Fla. Dep't of Health, 329 So. 3d 784, 787, 398 Educ. L. Rep. 560 (Fla. Dist. Ct. App. 2021).

Unlike in previous years, cases involving contracts predominated litigation involving local governance issues, with five cases addressing some aspect of breach of contract and one addressing the bidding and awarding of contracts. The breach of contract cases were largely construction-related, with three adjudicating disputes over change orders and the responsibility to pay subcontractors. Similarly, property rights were commonly litigated, with four cases addressing property rights in some capacity. Overall, non-board parties were slightly more successful than their district counterparts, with nine decisions favoring the non-district parties, seven favoring the school districts, and three split decisions.

Alphabetical List of Cases

A.C. by Waithe v. McKee
A.H. *ex rel* Hester v. French
Alachua Cnty. Sch. Bd. v. Barnes
Archimedean Acad. v. Sch. Bd. of Miami-Dade Cnty.
Barnett v. Jones
Bard Coll. v. Dutchess Cnty. Bd. of Elections
BCI Constr. v. Bd. of Educ. Sch. Dist.
Bd. of Cnty. Comm'rs, Santa Rosa Cnty. v. Home Builders Ass'n of W. Fla.
Bell v. Eagle Mtn. Saginaw Indep. Sch. Dist.
Boyd v. State
Burle v. Reg'l Bd. of Sch. Trs. of Educ. No. 35
Cahokia Unit Sch. Dist. No. 187 v. Pritzker
Cardiff Wales v. Wash. Cnty. Sch. Dist.
Carson *ex rel.* O.C. v. Makin
Castaldi v. Syosset Cent. Sch. Dist.
C. E. v. Elizabeth Pub. Sch. Dist.
Circle of Seasons Charter Sch. v. Nw. Lehigh Sch. Dist.
Contoocook Vall. Sch. Dist. v. State
Corman v. Acting Sec'y of Pa. Dep't of Health
Davison v. Rose
DeSantis v. Fla. Educ. Ass'n
Diocese of Buffalo, N.Y., In re
Educ. Freedom PAC v. Reid
Escambia Cnty. Sch. Bd. v Warren
Fearrington v. City of Greenville
Freeburg Cmty. Consol. Sch. Dist. No. 70 v. Country Mut. Ins. Co.
Freidmann v. Jefferson Cnty. Bd. of Educ.
Garnier v. O'Connor-Ratliff
Hetherington v. Madden
Howard Cnty. v. McClain
Iraan-Sheffield Indep. Sch. Dist. v. Pecos Cnty. Appraisal Dist.
Jefferson Cnty. Bd. of Educ. v. City of Irondale
Kenny v. Wilson
Keystone Montessori Sch. v. Vill. of River Forest
Krebs v. Graveley
Lampasas Indep. Sch. Dist. v. Morath
Larkin v. Madison Cnty. Sch. Dist.
Lay v. City of Lowell
Marshall v. Amuso
Mellor v. Par. of Jefferson

Metro. Gov't of Nashville & Davidson Cnty. v. Tenn. Dep't of Educ.
Miller, In re
Morath v. Tex. Am. Fed'n of Teachers
Morency v. Dep't of Educ.
Mt. Diablo Unified Sch. Dist. v. Clayton Vall. Charter High Sch.
One Ten Restoration v. N.Y.C. Sch. Const. Auth.
People v. Swenson
Pima Cnty. v. State
Propel Charter Schs. v. Pa. Dep't of Educ. (State Charter Sch. Appeal Bd.)
Propel Charter Schs. v. Sch. Dist. of Pittsburgh (State Charter Sch. Appeal Bd.)
Pulte v. New Common Sch. Found.
Resurrection Sch. v. Hertel (a)
Resurrection Sch. v. Hertel (b)
Riley's Am. Heritage Farms v. Elsasser (a)
Riley's Am. Heritage Farms v. Elsasser (b)
Rivera v. Pasadena
Reg'l Sch. Dist. 8 v. M & S Paving and Sealing
San Bernadino City Unified Sch. Dist. v. State Allocation Bd.
Sch. Bd. of Miami-Dade Cnty. v. Fla. Dep't of Health
Sewell v. Racine Unified Sch. Dist. Bd. of Canvassers
Shea v. State
Springboards to Educ. v. Pharr-San Juan-Alamo Indep. Sch. Dist.
State of La. v. La. Land and Exploration Co.
Sun Bldg. Ldt. P'ship v. Value Learning & Teaching Acad.
Taxpayers for Mich. Const. Gov't v. Dep't of Tech., Mgmt. & Budget
Traverse City Record-Eagle v. Traverse City Area Pub. Sch. Bd. of Educ.
Tyler v. Coeur d'Alene Sch. Dist. #271
United Jewish Cmty. of Blooming Grove v. Washingtonville Cent. Sch. Dist.
U.S. v. Coleman
Vasseur v. State
Victim Rts. Law Ctr. v. Cardona
Wyatt v. Kern High Sch. Dist.

Cases by Jurisdiction

FEDERAL CASES

Supreme Court
Carson *ex rel.* O.C. v. Makin

First Circuit
A.C. by Waithe v. McKee

> *Massachusetts*
> Victims Rts. Ctr. v. Cardona

Second Circuit

> *Vermont*
> A.H. *ex rel* Hester v. French

> *Bankruptcy Court of New York*
> Diocese of Buffalo, N.Y., In re

Third Circuit

> *Pennsylvania*
> Marshall v. Amuso

Fourth Circuit
Davison v. Rose
U.S. v. Coleman

> *South Carolina*
> Kenny v. Wilson

Fifth Circuit
Bell v. Eagle Mtn. Saginaw Indep. Sch. Dist.
Springboards to Educ. v. Pharr-San Juan-Alamo Indep. Sch. Dist.

> *Texas*
> Rivera v. City of Pasadena

Sixth Circuit
Resurrection Sch. v. Hertel (a)

> *Michigan*

Resurrection Sch. v. Hertel (b)

Sevent Circuit
Krebs v. Graveley

Ninth Circuit
Garnier v. O'Connor-Ratliff
Riley's Am. Heritage Farms v. Elsasser (a)
Riley's Am. Heritage Farms v. Elsasser (b)

Idaho
Tyler v. Coeur d'Alene Sch. Dist. #271

11th Circuit

Florida
Hetherington v. Madden

STATE & D.C. COURT CASES

Alabama
Barnett v. Jones
Jefferson Cnty. Bd. of Educ. v. City of Irondale

Arizona
Pima Cnty. v. State

California
Mt. Diablo Unified Sch. Dist. v. Clayton Vall. Charter High Sch.
San Bernadino City Unified Sch. Dist. v. State Allocation Bd.,
Wyatt v. Kern High Sch. Dist.

Connecticut
Reg'l Sch. Dist. 8 v. M & S Paving and Sealing

Florida
Alachua Cnty. Sch. Bd. v. Barnes
Archimedean Acad. v. Sch. Bd. of Miami-Dade Cnty.
Bd. of Cnty. Comm'rs, Santa Rosa Cnty. v. Home Builders Ass'n of
    W. Fla.
DeSantis v. Fla. Educ. Ass'n
Escambia Cnty. Sch. Bd. v. Warren
Pulte v. New Common Sch. Found.

Sch. Bd. of Miami-Dade Cnty. v. Fla. Dep't of Health

Georgia
Larkin v. Madison Cnty. Sch. Dist.

Illinois
Burle v. Reg'l Bd. of Sch. Trs. of Educ. No. 35
Cahokia Unit. Sch. Dist. No. 187 v. Pritzker
Freeburg Cmty. Consol. Sch. Dist. No. 70 v. Country Mut. Ins. Co.
Keystone Montessori Sch. v. Vill. of River Forest
People v. Swenson

Kentucky
Freidmann v. Jefferson Cnty. Bd. of Educ.

Louisiana
Mellor v. Par. of Jefferson
State of La. v. La. Land and Exploration Co.

Maryland
Howard Cnty. v. McClain

Massachusetts
Lay v. City of Lowell

Michigan
Taxpayers for Mich. Const. Govt. v. Dep't of Tech. Mgmt. and Budget
Traverse City Record-Eagle v. Traverse City Area Pub. Sch. Bd. of
    Educ.

Nevada
Educ. Freedom PAC v. Reid
Morency v. Dep't of Educ.

New Hampshire
Contoocook Vall. Sch. Dist. v. State

New Jersey
C. E. v. Elizabeth Pub. Sch. Dist.

New York
Bard Coll. v. Dutchess Cnty. Bd. of Elections
BCI Constr. v. Bd. of Educ., Washingtonville Cent. Sch. Dist.

Castaldi v. Syosset Cent. Sch. Dist.
One Ten Restoration v. N.Y.C. Sch. Const. Auth.
United Jewish Cmty. of Blooming Grove v. Washingtonville Cent. Sch. Dist.

North Carolina
Fearrington v. City of Greenville

Ohio
Sun Bldg. Ldt. P'ship v. Value Learning & Teaching Acad.

Pennsylvania
Circle of Seasons Charter Sch. v. Nw. Lehigh Sch. Dist.
Corman v. Acting Sec'y of Pa. Dep't of Health
Propel Charter Schs. v. Pa. Dep't of Educ. (State Charter Sch. Appeal Bd.)
Propel Charter Schs. v. Sch. Dist. of Pittsburgh (State Charter Sch. Appeal Bd.)

Tennessee
Metro. Gov't of Nashville and Davidson Cnty. v. Tenn. Dep't of Educ.

Texas
Iraan-Sheffield Indep. Sch. Dist. v. Pecos Cnty. Appraisal Dist.
Lampasas Indep. Sch. Dist. v. Morath
Miller, In re
Morath v. Tex. Am. Fed'n of Teachers

Utah
Cardiff Wales v. Wash. Cnty. Sch. Dist.

Vermont
Boyd v. State
Vasseur v. State

Wisconsin
Sewell v. Racine Unified Sch. Dist.

Chapter 2

SCHOOL EMPLOYMENT

Clarissa Bruton, J.D.[75] and Sarah Barber, J.D.[76]

Introduction	39
Discrimination	40
Race and National Origin	40
Gender, Sexual Orientation, and Sexual Harassment	44
Age	46
Disability	47
Religion	48
Hostile Work Environment	48
Procedural Issues	49
Substantive Constitutional Rights	53
First Amendment Claims	53
Dismissal, Nonrenewal, Demotion, and Discipline	54
Dismissal and Nonrenewal	54
Demotion and Reassignment	60
Contractual Disputes	60
Tenure	62
Fee Determinations	67
COVID-19	67
Workers' Compensation	70
Workplace Safety	75
Professional Conduct	76
Compensation and Benefits	77

---

[75] Research Manager of Law and Policy, University of Louisville, Louisville, Ky.
[76] Attorney Advisor at U.S. Department of Justice Executive Office for Immigration Review, Slidell, La.

Miscellaneous 77
Conclusion 78
Alphabetical List of Cases 80
Cases by Jurisdiction 82

Introduction

The area of Employment Law covers a wide range of topics and areas of law. Employment Law encompasses discrimination and retaliation, contracts, termination, demotions, workers' compensation, constitutional rights such as First Amendment rights, and many other areas. Within the context of educational institution employers, there are additional issues that arise, such as tenure and, most recently, the impact of state and federal COVID-19 vaccine mandates.

The Equal Employment Opportunity Commission ("EEOC") is the federal agency responsible for enforcing federal anti-discrimination laws in the workplace for covered employers. Some of these laws include Title VII of the Civil Rights Act of 1964, the Equal Pay Act of 1963, the Age Discrimination in Employment Act of 1967, Titles I and V of the Americans with Disabilities Act of 1990, Sections 501 and 505 of the Rehabilitation Act, and many others. Additionally, many, if not all, states have implemented state-specific protections for employees.

Employment Law also protects employees from wrongful termination. Two major areas of wrongful termination are discrimination and retaliation. Termination based on discrimination occurs when an employer terminates employment with an employee for a discriminatory reason such as race, religion, sex, national origin, disability, or other legally protected class of people. Termination in retaliation is when an employer terminates an employee in retaliation for the employee engaging in certain protected activities including, but not limited to, filing a complaint with the EEOC, filing a workers' compensation claim, whistleblowing, or taking permitted medical leave. The key here is that the employee must show that they engaged in a protected activity and that their termination was in retaliation for them engaging in that activity.

Furthermore, all states have workers' compensation laws. These laws protect employees who sustain an injury during the course and scope of their employment. Workers' compensation claims are extremely fact driven. The likelihood of success on these claims depends strongly on where the injury occurred, what activity the claimant was engaged in during the injury, the scope of the claimant's job responsibilities, and often the terms of the contract between the employer and the insurer who covers the employer's workers' compensation claims. These claims can get particularly tricky in cases involving pre-existing conditions.

Lastly, as the COVID-19 pandemic continues, state governments and the federal government pass more regulations in an attempt to reduce COVID-19 cases. These regulations have generated a large amount of litigation surrounding an individual's rights to bodily autonomy, the practice of their religion and religious beliefs, and their employment interests. While courts have broadly acknowledged that individuals have a property interest in their salaries and benefits tied to their employment, the courts must balance the asserted individual interest against state and federal interests in protecting the health and safety of the public. As with most rights, courts have stated the right to work in a chosen job is not absolute and is subject to infringement based on a balancing of competing interests.

Discrimination

Race and National Origin

The Second Circuit affirmed a New York federal trial court's dismissal of a teacher's claims for discrimination and retaliation based on race and the First Amendment.[77] The plaintiff, an African American male, was a tenured teacher who was terminated for allegedly sending harassing emails. However, he alleged that his termination was the result of discriminatory retaliation based on his race and speech. The court concluded that simply alleging the city's department of education targeted "African-American male teachers 'who speak out' and that these teachers are 'almost always terminated'...whereas two non-African-American teachers received lesser sanctions for similar conduct" was not sufficient to state a claim for discrimination based on race or speech. Thus, the dismissal of his claims was affirmed.

In another case, the Second Circuit, in a case from Connecticut, affirmed in part and vacated in part the federal trial court's rulings in favor of the defendants on the African American principal's claims for race discrimination and retaliation.[78] The court granted summary judgment in favor of the board on the plaintiff's claims stemming from her placement on paid administrative leave during an investigation of alleged physical abuse against students and dismissed her claims relating to her suspension without pay and

---

[77] Green v. Dep't of Educ. of City of N.Y., 16 F.4th 1070, 396 Educ. L. Rep. 56 (2d Cir. 2021).
[78] Perez-Dickson v. Bridgeport Bd. of Educ., 860 F. App'x 753, 395 Educ. L. Rep. 493 (2d Cir. 2017).

board actions upon her return. On appeal, the plaintiff argued that the court erred in concluding that her placement on paid administrative leave was not an adverse employment action. However, this conclusion did not rely on a lack of adverse employment action but instead found that the plaintiff failed to identify a similarly situated comparator. Thus, the grant of summary judgment was affirmed in favor of the board on the plaintiff's claims arising from her placement on paid administrative leave. However, the court vacated the dismissal of the plaintiff's claims stemming from her suspension without pay and the board's actions following her return to work, remanding for a determination of whether the claim was precluded by her earlier complaints.

The Fourth Circuit affirmed a North Carolina federal trial court's partial dismissal and grant of summary judgment in favor of the defendant board of education in the Title VII and § 1981 racial discrimination claims brought by a Black public high school drama teacher.[79] The plaintiff alleged that the school board refused to either pay him an additional supplement or hire another teacher to assist with the technical work he performed for student performances. The teacher also claimed that extra-duty pay for non-theater events at the school was issued discriminatorily. The appellate court affirmed that the failure to pay the plaintiff a second supplement for technical work was not discriminatory as he failed to allege that any teacher in the system received multiple supplements, and there was not a similarly situated comparator receiving more favorable treatment. Additionally, the failure to hire another teacher to assist did not constitute an "adverse employment action" as required to support a showing of racial discrimination. One judge concurred in the grant of summary judgment on the extra-duty pay and staffing claims but dissented as to the dismissal of the additional supplemental pay claim.

A federal trial court in Illinois heard an African American teacher's claims against the board of education for race discrimination and retaliation under Title IV and hostile environment under Title IX.[80] Title IV limits employment discrimination to situations where "(1) providing employment is a primary objective of the federal aid, or (2) discrimination in employment necessarily causes discrimination against the primary beneficiaries of the federal aid." Here, the plaintiff, who taught at an alternative high school for detained juveniles, alleged that the

---

[79] Tabb v. Bd. of Educ. of Durham Pub. Schs., 29 F.4th 148, 401 Educ. L. Rep. 50 (4th Cir. 2022).
[80] Agbefe v. Bd. of Educ. of City of Chi., 538 F.Supp.3d 833, 397 Educ. L. Rep. 619 (N.D. Ill. 2021).

defendant receives federal funding but made no allegations about its "primary objective," which is to educate students. The plaintiff argued the board's discrimination towards her had a discriminatory effect on students but did not plead any nexus between racial discrimination and a substandard educational environment for students. Instead, she argued that the harm to students emerged from the racially preferential treatment of another employee. The court observed that the plaintiff was not the proper party to vindicate the allegations for racially preferential treatment of another employee. Thus, her racial discrimination claim failed. Her Title IX claim was precluded by Title VII since the relief requested under Title IX was available to the plaintiff under Title VII.

In Kentucky, a federal trial court denied the defendant board of education's motion for summary judgment on the basketball coaches' race discrimination claims under Title VII.[81] Here, the plaintiffs were coaches of the girls' high school basketball team who filed suit after two African American assistant coaches were terminated and an African American coach was placed on a performance-expectations plan before being terminated. The defendants argued that, while termination is an adverse employment action, placement on a performance-expectations plan is not. The court found that a performance-expectation plan may constitute an adverse employment action where, as was the case here, "the plaintiff 'suffered, or is in jeopardy of suffering,' because of the performance-expectations plan." Additionally, in a meeting regarding the assistant coaches' terminations, the principal made explicit statements about wanting more White players and coaches. The court ruled that this was sufficient to create a genuine issue of fact as to racial discrimination, thus precluding summary judgment.

A former assistant superintendent brought race discrimination and retaliation claims under Title VII in a federal trial court in Virginia, and the court granted the school board's motion for summary judgment.[82] The plaintiff was Caucasian, but he filed a complaint on behalf of his African American colleagues alleging discrimination. The complaint was followed by the elimination of the plaintiff's position and his demotion to a teaching position. The court found that the plaintiff did state a prima facie case of discrimination under Title VII; he engaged in a protected activity by complaining to the school board, the elimination of his position and his demotion constituted an adverse employment action, and the adverse

---

[81] Johnson v. Bd. of Educ. of Bowling Green Indep. Sch. Dist., 537 F.Supp.3d 922, 397 Educ. L. Rep. 150 (W.D. Ky. 2021).
[82] McClain v. Lynchburg City Schs., 531 F.Supp.3d 1115, 395 Educ. L. Rep. 978 (W.D. Va. 2021).

employment action occurred less than six months after the board became aware of the plaintiff's complaint showing a causal link. However, the school board sufficiently rebutted this prima facia showing by offering a legitimate, nondiscriminatory reason for its actions. Specifically, the board asserted that the elimination of the plaintiff's position was part of a reorganization due to budget constraints. Therefore, the plaintiff's claims under Title VII failed, and the defendant school board was granted summary judgment.

An appellate court in New York affirmed the grant of summary judgment in favor of the defendant state department of education and school board on a former probationary teacher's claim alleging that her termination was motivated by age and race discrimination.[83] The department provided evidence of a nondiscriminatory motive for its actions, so the issue before the court was whether the department sufficiently showed that "'there is no evidentiary route' that could allow a fact-finder to believe that discrimination played a role in plaintiff's dismissal from her position." The court found that the department met this burden with evidence that the plaintiff did not conduct and submit required assessments, did not provide requested lesson plans and conduct records, was not an effective teacher, and was outside the building during class time without arranging adequate supervision for her class. Because the plaintiff failed to show that the department's nondiscriminatory reasons for her dismissal were "false, misleading, or incomplete," the plaintiff's claims failed.

In Ohio, an appellate court affirmed the lower court's grant of summary judgment in favor of the defendant board of education on a teacher's reverse race discrimination and wrongful discharge claims.[84] After a few years of teaching, several students accused the plaintiff of making threatening statements against students. The plaintiff was placed on paid leave during an investigation into her comments. After the investigation, she was notified of the board's intent to terminate her, and she sought review of the decision. The state department of education concluded that there was inadequate evidence of good and just cause to terminate the plaintiff and recommended she not be terminated, but the board terminated her anyway. She alleged that the principal made statements about wanting an all African American teaching staff at the school and criticized Caucasian staff members for disciplining African American students, but she did not offer any admissible evidence of

---

[83] McIntosh v. Dep't of Educ. of City of N.Y., 165 N.Y.S.3d 31, 402 Educ. L. Rep. 338 (N.Y. App. Div. 2022).
[84] Martcheva v. Dayton Bd. of Educ., 179 N.E.3d 687, 398 Educ. L. Rep. 1085 (Ohio Ct. App. 2021).

these statements as she only heard about them from other people. The appellate court affirmed the trial court's finding that the plaintiff did not provide any direct evidence of discrimination.

Gender, Sexual Orientation, and Sexual Harassment

The Seventh Circuit, in a case from Indiana, affirmed a grant of summary judgment in favor of the defendant, a private Catholic school, on the plaintiff former employee's discrimination, retaliation, and hostile work environment claims under Title VII and state tortious interference claims.[85] The plaintiff brought suit after her contract was not renewed due to her being in a same-sex relationship. The defendant argued that the ministerial exception under the First Amendment applied to the Title VII claim. The ministerial exception "ensures that the authority to select and control who will minister to the faithful…is the church's alone" and requires courts to "stay out of employment disputes involving those holding certain important positions with churches and other religious institutions." Here, the plaintiff was the Co-Director of Guidance and a member of the Administrative Council, which made her responsible for supervising the guidance counselors as well as a significant amount of the school's "daily ministry, education, and operations." The court held that the plaintiff was a minister under the First Amendment's ministerial exception, barring her Title VII claims.

In the Connecticut federal trial court, a former substitute teacher sued his employer and various individuals alleging a hostile work environment, disparate treatment, and wrongful termination based on "his status as a white, heterosexual male" under Title VII and state employment law.[86] The plaintiff alleged that he was mocked for dating an "old lady" and called names like "whore," "gay" and "Nazi." The court found these allegations sufficient to state a prima facie case for a hostile work environment under Title VII and denied the defendant's motion to dismiss. For disparate impact, the plaintiff alleged that his classroom preferences were not honored, and he was given "difficult and challenging" students compared to his female coworkers. However, the court found this insufficient to plead an adverse employment action, and his disparate impact claim was dismissed. Lastly, the plaintiff alleged that he was terminated "as the culmination of the hostility and social aggression" by

---

[85] Starkey v. Roman Cath. Archdiocese of Indianapolis, 41 F.4th 931, 405 Educ. L. Rep. 674 (7th Cir. 2022).
[86] Cloutier v. Ledyard Bd. of Educ., 575 F.Supp.3d 276, 405 Educ. L. Rep. 167 (D. Conn. 2021).

management and coworkers, but the complaint alleged facts suggesting a legitimate, nondiscriminatory reason for his termination that the plaintiff failed to rebut, so his claim was dismissed.

A superintendent sued her school board and a board member for sex discrimination and hostile work environment under Title VII, along with state law claims, in an Illinois federal trial court.[87] The female superintendent allegedly had several uncomfortable, inappropriate, and threatening encounters with the male school board member during her two years with the district, many of which were witnessed by others. She ultimately resigned because of the board member's behavior towards her, and she was later denied a position for seemingly related reasons. Regarding her hostile work environment claim, the court found that the plaintiff adequately pled unwelcome harassment based on her sex that was "sufficiently severe or pervasive," as evidenced by the board member's repeatedly asking her out, instructing her to climb a ladder before him while wearing a skirt, and escalated harassment in response to refusing his advances, so the defendants' motion to dismiss was denied. Similarly, in the constructive discharge claim, the court denied the defendants' motion to dismiss because the plaintiff adequately alleged that she gave sufficient opportunities to address the harassment through her complaints to board members and the district attorney prior to her resignation.

An assistant principal filed suit for retaliation and sexual harassment under Title VII and Title IX in the Kansas federal trial court.[88] Here, a female student reported to the plaintiff that a male student in a special education program had sexually assaulted her at school. The principal was upset with the plaintiff for reporting the assault to another administrator before him, and he sent her a formal reprimand. Subsequently, the principal began excluding and harassing the plaintiff, and the plaintiff's numerous complaints about this conduct were ignored. The court first held that Title VII does not preempt Title IX for employment discrimination claims, so the plaintiff could proceed under both theories of liability. Further, the court found that the plaintiff sufficiently alleged retaliation under Title IX; she engaged in a protected activity by reporting the sexual assault, which the defendant was aware of, and the formal reprimand was a materially adverse action that was causally connected to the report. However, the court held that a negative

---

[87] Kibbons v. Taft Sch. Dist. 90, 563 F.Supp.3d 798 402 Educ. L. Rep. 257 (N.D. Ill. 2021).
[88] Kincaid v. Unified Sch. Dist. No. 500, Kansas City, Kan., 572 F.Supp.3d 1081, 404 Educ. L. Rep. 776 (D. Kan. 2021).

performance evaluation was not sufficient to constitute an adverse employment action that could support a retaliation claim under Title VII.

The final sex discrimination claim was brought by a school principal in New York against the school district, board of education, and superintendent alleging sex discrimination and a hostile work environment under Title VII and state law.[89] The plaintiff alleged that the superintendent had excessively scrutinized and criticized her, questioned her competency based on her being a mother, made inappropriate comments about working with women, and given her incomplete and irregular performance evaluations. The board of education ultimately terminated her upon the superintendent's recommendation. A jury found in favor of the plaintiff and awarded nearly $500,000. The defendants moved for judgment as a matter of law, a new trial, and reduction of damages. The court denied these motions and upheld the jury verdict, stating that substantial evidence supported the plaintiff's claim of sex-based discrimination and a hostile work environment.

Age

In Alabama, a federal trial court granted the defendant school board's motion for summary judgment on the plaintiff employee's claims under the ADEA.[90] The plaintiff, age 56, alleged that she was discriminated against when the board failed to hire her for an open position and instead promoted a younger and less qualified candidate. Under the ADEA, employers cannot "refuse to hire or to discharge any individual or otherwise discriminate against any individual with respect to his compensation, terms, conditions, or privileges of employment, because of such individual's age." Here, the plaintiff established that she was a member of a protected class (i.e., age 40-70), subject to adverse employment action (i.e., failure to hire), and that a substantially younger person was hired. The issue was whether she was qualified for the position she sought. Because the plaintiff lacked the required coursework to be qualified for the position and the candidate that was hired had completed all requisite coursework, the court found that she failed to state a prima facie case of age discrimination.

In the federal trial court for New Mexico, an elementary school teacher sued her school district and several employees alleging age

---

[89] Krause v. Kelahan, 575 F.Supp.3d 302, 405 Educ. L. Rep. 181 (N.D.N.Y. 2021).
[90] Jones v. Bessemer Bd. of Educ., 570 F.Supp.3d 1099, 403 Educ. L. Rep. 822 (N.D. Ala. 2021).

discrimination, retaliation, hostile work environment, and constructive discharge under the Age Discrimination in Employment Act (ADEA) and state law.[91] The plaintiff had numerous complaints and conflicts with colleagues and superiors during her employment. The plaintiff ultimately resigned after being given the option to resign or be terminated following an incident involving her physical restraint of a special education student in her classroom during which she left over twenty students unsupervised for forty-five seconds. The plaintiff was fifty-five at the time of her resignation, and the teacher hired to replace her was twenty-nine. The court granted the defendants' motion for summary judgment because the school offered a legitimate, non-discriminatory reason for the plaintiff's forced resignation, and she failed to allege that these offered reasons were mere pretext for age discrimination. Further, there was no evidence that there was a hostile work environment based on the plaintiff's age, and she did not engage in a protected activity for which the school board could have retaliated against her.

Disability

An appellate court in Connecticut affirmed the trial court and Commission on Human Rights and Opportunities' awarding of back pay and emotional distress damages to an employee upon finding that the board of education discriminated against her because of her partial hearing loss which caused her to speak loudly.[92] The disabled employee worked directly for the human resources (HR) assistant in a secretarial role, and the HR assistant encouraged her to apply for his position when he retired. He even trained and supported her for the position, which she was fully qualified for as originally listed. However, another HR employee, who had made comments on the disabled employee's volume, made an unauthorized revision to the job listing that added an additional year of experience and removed preference for applicants with the disabled employee's educational background. The employee was not granted an interview because she did not meet the newly revised qualifications. The court found that the Commission's findings regarding back pay were supported by substantial evidence that the disabled employee would have been

---

[91] DeLopez v. Bernalillo Pub. Schs., 558 F.Supp.3d 1129, 401 Educ. L. Rep. 786 (D.N.M. 2021).
[92] Bd. of Educ. of City of Waterbury v. Comm'n on Hum. Rts. and Opportunities, 276 A.3d 447, 404 Educ. L. Rep. 835 (Conn. App. Ct. 2022).

interviewed for and promoted to HR assistant absent the unlawful discrimination.

Religion

A school corporation was granted summary judgment on a former teacher's claims for religious discrimination and retaliation under Title VII in a federal trial court in Indiana.[93] The teacher claimed he was forced to resign after he refused to refer to transgender students by the names chosen by students, their parents, and their healthcare providers due to religious objections. He attempted to address students by only their last names to avoid the issue, but the school received complaints from students and other teachers that felt this was insulting and disrespectful. The court held that the plaintiff's use of only students' last names created an undue hardship for the school, and the school did not have to offer the teacher alternative accommodations for his religious beliefs. Thus, the school did not fail to accommodate the plaintiff's religious beliefs, and he was not forced to resign or retaliated against in violation of Title VII.

Hostile Work Environment

The First Circuit affirmed the Rhode Island federal trial court's grant of summary judgment in favor of the defendant city, school department, and superintendent on the former principal's claims for a hostile work environment and retaliation under § 1981 and state law.[94] The plaintiff, an African American woman, was a school principal for over a decade before applying to three other positions in the district, including superintendent, which was filled by a white woman. After the plaintiff sued and ultimately settled with the school department for not satisfying commitments to pursue affirmative action hiring practices, she alleges she was subjected to a hostile work environment. As examples, she asserts that her request for classroom-related purchases was denied, she was given a higher percentage of special needs students than other principals, her performance reviews were too close together, and the superintendent transferred her to a position as principal of a new pre-K program despite the plaintiff's resistance. The appellate court affirmed that the principal was not subject to a hostile work

---

[93] Kluge v. Brownsburg Cmty. Sch. Corp., 548 F.Supp.3d 814, 399 Educ. L. Rev. 607 (S.D. Ind. 2021).
[94] Lima v. City of E. Providence, 17 F.4th 202, 396 Educ. L. Rep. 81 (1st Cir. 2021).

environment, and the defendant offered legitimate and nondiscriminatory reasons for her involuntary transfer (i.e., she had extensive experience and already had credentials for pre-K). Thus, her claims failed.

The Fourth Circuit, in a case from Virginia, affirmed the grant of summary judgment in favor of the defendant school board on the plaintiff/special education instructional assistant's Title VII claim alleging a hostile work environment arising from sexual harassment by an eight-year-old student with Down's Syndrome and ADHD.[95] Specifically, the plaintiff alleged that the student frequently put his hands up her dress and touched her inappropriately, and administrators largely ignored her complaints about such behaviors. While the plaintiff sufficiently alleged that the conduct was unwelcome, as required to establish a case under Title VII, she failed to show that the student's conduct was based on sex because he was unable to distinguish between the sexes due to his disabilities, nor could she show that the conduct was "severe or pervasive" or imputable to the school board as the board did respond to the plaintiff's allegations, even if the plaintiff did not feel the response was sufficient.

In New York, an appellate court affirmed the trial court's grant of the defendant city department of education's motion to dismiss the employee's age discrimination, retaliation, and hostile work environment claims.[96] The plaintiff's age discrimination claims failed because she did not provide her age or her coworkers' ages, thus her evidence was insufficient. However, her hostile environment claim could proceed based on the allegations that her supervisor made negative comments about the plaintiff's race, issued several write-ups, and transferred her to another school. Further, as an African American, she was a member of a protected class, and her termination constituted an adverse employment action.

Procedural Issues

A federal trial court in New York denied the plaintiff employee's motion for recusal and dismissed her amended complaint.[97] Here, a school district employee alleged discrimination against various district entities and employees. The plaintiff employee filed a motion

---

[95] Webster v. Chesterfield Cnty. Sch. Bd., 38 F.4th 404, 404 Educ. L. Rep. 450 (4th Cir. 2022).
[96] Campbell v. N.Y. City Dep't of Educ., 160 N.Y.S.3d 12, 399 Educ. L. Rep. 991 (N.Y. App. Div. 2021).
[97] Malcolm v. Assoc. of Supervisors and Admins. of Rochester, 532 F. Supp.3d 114, 396 Educ. L. Rep. 103 (W.D.N.Y. 2021).

for recusal, arguing that the court bullied her by imposing sanctions and through its rulings against the plaintiff. Under federal law, "[a] judge is required to recuse in any proceeding in which his impartiality might reasonably be questioned, and the test to be applied is an objective one which assumes that a reasonable person knows and understands all the relevant facts." The court held that the plaintiff failed to allege any facts showing that the court was impartial, thus, her motion for recusal was denied.

In South Dakota, a federal trial court granted the school board's motion to dismiss the former principal's retaliation, wrongful termination, and breach of contract claims after he was terminated following a dispute over his administration of federal grant funds because the board was entitled to sovereign immunity.[98] In reaching this determination, the court considered the entity's method of creation, purpose and structure, ownership, and management, including the level of tribal control; the tribe's intent to extend its sovereign immunity to the entity; the financial relationship between the tribe and the entity; and whether the purposes of tribal sovereign immunity are served by granting immunity. It found all factors weighed in favor of extending the tribe's sovereign immunity to the board. Additionally, the court found the former principal failed to plead sufficient facts that he engaged in a protected activity for his retaliation claim and that the board had sovereign immunity against this claim. It did not decide the issues of diversity or supplemental jurisdiction over the state law claims based on the board's sovereign immunity. Based on these findings, the court granted the board's motion to dismiss.

The Massachusetts state supreme court held that the defendant's peremptory challenge of a juror was pretextual and inadequate, and the text messages and school policies admitted into evidence did not violate evidentiary rules about hearsay.[99] The defendant was a faculty member at a private PK-12 school who was convicted of indecently touching a thirteen-year-old. At trial, the defense attempted to challenge a juror based on him being a father and uncle, but the judge denied the peremptory challenge. The court affirmed this decision, finding that the justification was inadequate and pretextual. As for the evidentiary issues, the state supreme court held that text messages the defendant sent to the victim that were not admitted for the truth of the matter asserted were not hearsay, the text conversation that allegedly was hearsay was

---

[98] Stathis v. Marty Indian Sch. Bd., 560 F.Supp.3d 1283, 410 Educ. L. Rep. 935 (D.S.D. 2022).
[99] Commonwealth v. Kozubal, 174 N.E.3d 1169, 395 Educ. L. Rep. 1084 (Mass. 2021).

properly admitted as an adoptive admission, and the school's policies regarding child abuse and inappropriate sexual relations were admissible under the business records exception to hearsay.

At issue in a case from Connecticut was a trial court's decision declining to instruct the jury on the Family and Medical Leave Act (FMLA) counts and rendering judgment for the board of education on the remaining counts following the jury's verdict.[100] The plaintiff was a secretary alleging disability discrimination and retaliation under state employment law, retaliation under workers' compensation law, interference with her exercising her rights under FMLA, and FMLA retaliation. The trial court declined to instruct the jury on the plaintiff's FMLA claims because it found that there was no real evidence to support the claim. The appellate court affirmed this holding because there was no evidence that the plaintiff ever actually requested FMLA leave, and the defendant had a policy against the concurrent use of workers' compensation and FMLA leave. Further, the court found no issues with the admission of a letter written by the plaintiff's coworker or the refusal to admit certain medical records offered by the plaintiff.

A licensed physician and faculty member at a medical school appealed the decision of a trial court in North Carolina to grant an insurance provider's motions to dismiss for lack of subject matter jurisdiction and failure to state a claim upon which relief can be granted under the state rules of civil procedure.[101] Her amended complaint alleged breach of contract, unfair and deceptive trade practices, and bad faith refusal to pay health or medical insurance benefits. The physician argued the trial court had jurisdiction, but the appellate court disagreed. It found the case on which the physician relied did not apply because it involved a negligence claim, and this case was stipulated to only raise contract claims. While the physician exhausted her remedies by seeking external review by the independent review organization, she failed to seek review before the Industrial Commission as required. Therefore, the physician, insurance provider, and court are bound by the independent review organization's denial of coverage. The court affirmed the trial court's finding that the physician conceded jurisdiction to the Industrial Commission rather than the trial court and affirmed the grant of the insurance provider's motion to dismiss.

An appellate court in Ohio held that the one-year statute of limitations period for penal statutes did not apply to the state's

---

[100] Monts v. Bd. of Educ. of City of Hartford, 259 A.3d 1256, 395 Educ. L. Rep. 1016 (Conn. App. Ct. 2021).
[101] Birchard v. Blue Cross and Blue Shield of N.C., 873 S.E.2d 635, 404 Educ. L. Rep. 286 (N.C. Ct. App. 2022).

action against the defendant treasurer, but the lower court's denial of the treasurer's laches defense was warranted.[102] The state filed this action against several individuals involved in a community school alleging that the defendants used the school's public funds for their own benefits. The trial court found that the state's claims against the treasurer were time-barred, but the state argues that the state law at issue does not impose a penalty and, therefore, is not subject to the state law imposing a one-year statute of limitations. The appellate court agreed that the statute did not impose a penalty, thus, the claim was not subject to a one-year statute of limitations and was not time-barred. Further, the treasurer argued that she was entitled to summary judgment under the doctrine of laches, which requires evidence of "unreasonable delay or lapse of time in asserting a right" without an excuse, actual or constructive knowledge of the injury, and prejudice. The court affirmed that the treasurer could not assert a laches defense against the state.

A teaching assistant (TA) in Oregon appealed a trial court's grant of summary judgment in favor of a school board.[103] The TA alleged contract and quasi-contract claims based on the fact she worked for years as a solo instructor performing duties in line with a teacher position and not a TA position. The school board argued that the TA's exclusive remedy was under the Collective Bargaining Agreement (CBA) and had been resolved. It also argued jurisdictional issues in a reply memorandum. On appeal, the TA argued that the trial court erred by considering the jurisdictional challenge as it was first made in a reply memorandum. On appeal, the court found the trial court did not err in considering the jurisdictional issue because the board did not raise a factual issue, only a legal issue, in its memorandum. The court stated the CBA gives the Employment Relations Board (ERB) exclusive jurisdiction over claims involving the CBA or unfair labor practices. Here, the appellate court found the nature of the TA's claims are part of the CBA and an employer's alleged breach of a CBA is an unfair labor practice. Therefore, the TA's claims were under the exclusive jurisdiction of the ERB.

In Pennsylvania, a child protective services agency filed two reports naming a teacher as the perpetrator of abuse against two minor students. The teacher appealed the reports and was granted

---

[102] State ex rel. Ohio Att'y Gen. v. Peterson, 182 N.E.3d 41, 400 Educ. L. Rep. 353 (Ohio Ct. App. 2021).
[103] George-Buckley v. Medford Sch. Dist., 509 P.3d 738, 402 Educ. L. Rep. 1184 (Or. Ct. App. 2022).

a hearing.[104] The teacher requested subpoenas *duces tecum* be issued to compel the appearance of witnesses, including school employees, and production of documents. The Administrative Law Judge (ALJ) granted the request and issued subpoenas, but the employees objected, asserting the requested documents were privileged and confidential under HIPAA and FERPA. The employees did not appear at the hearing, and the ALJ granted the teacher leave to seek enforcement of the subpoenas in state court. In doing so, the court granted the teacher's motion. The employees appealed, arguing the trial court lacked jurisdiction and erred in enforcing the subpoenas without ruling on their objections and cross-motions, denying them due process, and the subpoenas were overly broad and unduly burdensome, sought in bad faith, and sought confidential and privileged information. The appellate court found that the court had jurisdiction to enforce the subpoenas. However, the trial court denied the school employees due process by failing to rule on their objections and cross-motion. Thus, the order was vacated and remanded for further proceedings.

Substantive Constitutional Rights

First Amendment Claims

The Tenth Circuit federal appellate court held that the Colorado federal trial court's decision denying summary judgment based on the affirmative defense of the ministerial exception under the First Amendment is not immediately appealable under the collateral order doctrine.[105] A former teacher and chaplain at a religion-based school was terminated after holding a chapel meeting on race and religion. He filed suit against his former employer after receiving a right to sue letter from the EEOC. The employer moved to dismiss based on the ministerial exception and the trial court converted this motion into a motion for summary judgment and denied it. The religious employer appealed. The Tenth Circuit found that orders preliminarily denying religious employers summary judgment on the ministerial exception defense does not fit within the "small, modest, and narrow class of cases capable of satisfying this stringent collateral-order test." It also held that, on appeal, a religious employer may not raise the broader church autonomy doctrine as a

---

[104] In re S.H., 272 A.3d 1000, 402 Educ. L. Rep. 284 (Pa. Commw. Ct. 2022).
[105] Tucker v. First Bible Chapel Int'l, 36 F.4th 1021, 403 Educ. L. Rep. 204 (10th Cir. 2022).

defense when the employer fails to develop an adequate factual basis. The court made no decision on the merits and instead found it lacked jurisdiction to consider the matter before a final judgment is rendered.

The state supreme court of West Virginia affirmed the lower court's denial of the employees' motion for relief from an order granting the media outlets' and law firm's motion to dismiss.[106] The issue stemmed from allegations by public school employees that media outlets and a law firm violated the West Virginia Wiretapping and Electronic Surveillance Act by publishing a recording received from a parent allegedly showing the employees' physical and verbal abuse of students. The first question the court addressed was whether the recording involved a matter of public concern, and the court found that it did. The court next held that the state law at issue was unconstitutional to the extent it permitted a civil action against an innocent third party who published information that was unlawfully obtained relating to a public concern but who did not participate in intercepting the communication. Lastly, the court held that the law firm's publication of the video was not commercial in nature because it was not proposing a commercial transaction, therefore, it was protected by the First Amendment.

Dismissal, Nonrenewal, Demotion, and Discipline

Dismissal and Nonrenewal

In one of two federal cases discussing dismissal and nonrenewal, the federal trial court for Massachusetts heard a case from a former employee alleging failure to accommodate and wrongful termination in violation of the Americans with Disabilities Act (ADA) and state law against the school board.[107] The plaintiff was a paraprofessional for a middle school. She began having vision issues related to diabetes and eventually had surgery. She returned to work but was soon out on medical leave for most of the school year for other diabetes-related issues. Her employment was not renewed for the following school year despite her expressing intent to return, and, after failing to come to a resolution with the board, she filed this suit. The court held that the school board did not fail to provide the plaintiff with reasonable accommodations, so the court granted

---

[106] Yurish v. Sinclair Broad. Grp., 866 S.E.2d 156, 397 Educ. L. Rep. 831 (W. Va. 2021).
[107] Ellis v. N. Andover Pub. Schs., 569 F.Supp.3d 61, 403 Educ. L. Rep. 686 (D. Mass. 2021).

summary judgment on that claim. However, the court denied summary judgment on the wrongful termination claim because the plaintiff presented sufficient evidence to create a fact issue as to whether she was qualified to perform her job duties with or without accommodations.

In another federal case, a trial court in New York granted the defendant school board's motion for summary judgment on the tenured teacher's claim that his termination violated the ADA, state human rights law, and the First Amendment.[108] The plaintiff was terminated after receiving five misconduct charges, and a hearing and subsequent appeal confirmed these charges. He was unable to control his anger and had repeated incidents involving his anger and inappropriate comments, which the plaintiff alleged were due to his PTSD. The plaintiff argued that the defendant withdrew his disability accommodations, but the "accommodations" he referred to involved parts of a Corrective Action Plan and participation in a therapy course at the former principal's direction. The court found that these were not actually accommodations for his PTSD but instead were disciplinary measures. Further, the school board did not owe the plaintiff a duty to engage in the interactive process because he failed to request an accommodation, and his case did not fall within the limited exception when "the employer knew or reasonably should have known that the employee was disabled."

The Supreme Court of Georgia heard an appeal brought by a public teacher after the lower court granted summary judgment in favor of the defendant school district based on the one-year statute of limitation for whistleblower claims.[109] The plaintiff's whistleblower claims were based on her allegations that she was terminated in retaliation for failing to change students' failing grades, reporting complaints, and retaining counsel. Under state law, the "one-year statute of limitation period begins to run on the date that the alleged act of retaliation is discovered by the public employee." The state supreme court disagreed that the written notice of termination was simply formalizing the decision that was made in April and instead held that the May 3, 2017, written notice of termination constituted a separate adverse employment action. Therefore, the one-year statute of limitation had not expired on the plaintiff's claims stemming from the written notice of termination. In an appellate case from Georgia, a teacher appealed the state board of education's decision upholding the local board of education's

---

[108] Geer v. Gates Chili Cent. Sch. Dist., 577 F.Supp.3d 147, 405 Educ. L. Rep. 873 (W.D.N.Y. 2021).
[109] Mimbs v. Henry Cnty. Schs., 872 S.E.2d 685, 403 Educ. L. Rep. 311 (Ga. 2022).

decision to terminate her employment.[110] The plaintiff's contract was not renewed by the local board because of "insubordination, incompetence, willful neglect of duty, and 'other good and sufficient cause.'" The day before her hearing, the plaintiff requested the appointment of a tribunal instead of the local board at her hearing, but this request was denied. The plaintiff claimed this denial violated her due process rights. Under state law, a termination hearing "*shall* be conducted before the local board, *or* the local board *may* designate a tribunal." Thus, the court reversed and remanded the lower court's decision in favor of the plaintiff, instead holding that due process did not require the appointment of a tribunal instead of the local board to determine whether the plaintiff's employment contract should be renewed.

In Illinois, the state supreme court affirmed the lower court's grant of the diocese's motion to dismiss the former principal's claims for retaliatory discharge and violation of the Whistleblower Act arising from her termination after she reported a parent's threatening conduct to police.[111] The court first addressed the retaliatory discharge claim, holding that the plaintiff's employment was governed by a contract and she was not at-will, therefore, she could not bring a retaliatory discharge claim under state law. As for her whistleblower claims, the court first noted that the plaintiff did qualify as a whistleblower, despite the fact that she was reporting the illegal activities of a parent and not an employer. However, the ministerial exception "allows religious organizations to select and control their ministers without judicial review or government interference." The court held that the ministerial exception barred the plaintiff's claim here because there was sufficient evidence to establish that she was a minister based on the requirements that she remain a practicing Catholic and abide by the Diocesan handbook during her employment.

A teacher petitioned for writ of mandamus compelling the defendant school board to offer him a full-time teaching contract, but the Supreme Court of North Dakota affirmed the denial of the teacher's petition.[112] The plaintiff was a teacher at the defendant school district for two school years before he was notified that his contract as a probationary teacher would not be renewed the following year. He argued that he was not a probationary teacher because he had taught in another school district for four years

---

[110] Rabun Cnty. Bd. of Educ. v. Randel, 864 S.E.2d 160, 396 Educ. L. Rep. 338 (Ga. Ct. App. 2021).
[111] Rehfield v. Diocese of Joliet, 182 N.E.3d 123, 400 Educ. L. Rep. 786 (Ill. 2021).
[112] Motisi v. Hebron Pub. Sch. Dist., 968 N.W.2d 191, 398 Educ. L. Rep. 503 (N.D. 2021).

previously, but the trial court held that the statute defining probationary teacher as "any individual teaching for less than two years" meant two years "in that particular district." The state supreme court affirmed this interpretation, thus finding that the teacher was a probationary teacher and was not entitled to a continuing contract.

In a case involving the school board's dismissal of a teacher for good and just cause, the Supreme Court of Wyoming affirmed the lower court's decision reversing the dismissal.[113] The district leadership discovered sexually explicit personal images that had accidentally synced from the teacher's personal cell phone to the school-issued tablet that he kept at home as backup during the school year as both devices used the same Apple ID. After an investigation, during which the plaintiff was placed on administrative leave, the superintendent recommended his termination for violating technology policies and allowing pornographic materials to be stored on a district device. After a hearing, the hearing examiner recommended the board find in favor of the employee and not terminate his employment, but the board terminated him anyway. The court held that the board's policies surrounding technology did not provide the plaintiff with a clear standard of conduct, and the board's finding that this incident related to the teacher's fitness or capacity to teach was contrary to the overwhelming weight of the evidence. Therefore, the plaintiff's termination was improper.

An appellate court in Arkansas heard two cases involving dismissal and nonrenewal. In the first case, it affirmed the board of review's decision denying a substitute teacher's claim for unemployment benefits during summer break.[114] Here, the plaintiff had been a substitute teacher in the district for many years. She did not have a contract with the district but was placed on a "substitute-teacher list" to have her availability confirmed annually and to call her as needed. When the district shut down because of COVID-19, the plaintiff's substitute teaching services were no longer needed, so she filed for unemployment benefits. Her claim for benefits was denied from May 31 to August 15 because, under state law, teachers are ineligible for unemployment benefits during summer breaks "as long as there is a reasonable assurance of performing services in the next academic year." The appellate court affirmed that the plaintiff had a reasonable assurance of employment the following year from

---

[113] Bd. of Trs. of Lincoln Cnty. Sch. Dist. No. 2 v. Earling, 503 P.3d 629, 399 Educ. L. Rep. 1025 (Wyo. 2022).
[114] Johnson v. Dir., Dep't of Workforce Servs., 645 S.W.3d 352, 404 Educ. L. Rep. 321 (Ark. Ct. App. 2022).

the "substitute-teacher list," and the board's denial of unemployment benefits during summer break was not in error. The second appellate case in Arkansas was very similar. The court again affirmed the board of review's denial of a substitute teacher's claim for unemployment benefits.[115] Like in the first case, the court held that the substitute teacher was not entitled to unemployment benefits during summer break when she had a "reasonable assurance of performing services in the next academic year" due to the "substitute-teacher list" that was used to contact her annually.

In New Jersey, an appellate court affirmed the school board's denial of the appellant bus driver's ordinary disability retirement benefits after she was terminated.[116] The plaintiff agreed to irrevocably resign after rear-ending another school bus in the school parking lot while children were on her bus, resulting in her being charged with multiple driving while intoxicated charges. She was subsequently deemed ineligible for accidental disability retirement benefits. The court held that, when a retirement system-eligible employee irrevocably resigns "based upon a negotiated settlement agreement resolving a pending grievance concerning disciplinary charges that do not 'relate to' a disability, such a separation of employment renders the member ineligible for ordinary or accidental disability retirement benefits." Because the plaintiff irrevocably resigned for reasons entirely unrelated to any disability, she was ineligible for disability retirement benefits.

In a termination dispute in New York, the appellate court held in favor of the plaintiff on her claims surrounding her termination as the director of transportation.[117] Here, the plaintiff was first temporarily appointed to the position, then appointed on a provisional basis, and, finally, fully appointed by the board, which began a 26-week probationary period. Exactly 26 weeks later, the plaintiff was terminated and subsequently brought this suit alleging her termination was unlawful, arbitrary, and capricious, and that the board acted retaliatorily in bad faith. The appellate court held that the documentary evidence did not utterly refute the plaintiff's allegation that her termination violated lawful procedure, so her claim should survive dismissal. Further, the court found that evidence supported the plaintiff's allegation that the board terminated her not for poor performance but rather after she tried to enforce vendor and bus monitor compliance with certain laws,

---

[115] Green v. Dir., Ark. Dep't of Workforce Servs., 646 S.W.3d 642, 405 Educ. L. Rep. 537 (Ark. Ct. App. 2022).
[116] Rooth v. Bd. of Trs., Pub. Emps. Retirement Sys., 277 A.3d 26, 405 Educ. L. Rep. 429 (N.J. Super. Ct. App. Div. 2022).
[117] O'Hara v. Bd. of Educ., Yonkers City Sch. Dist., 156 N.Y.S.3d 311, 397 Educ. L. Rep. 1095 (N.Y. App. Div. 2021).

which suggested bad faith. Lastly, the court found that documentary evidence did not utterly refute the plaintiff's allegation that she was terminated in retaliation for engaging in a protected activity. Thus, the plaintiff's claims should survive dismissal.

An appellate court in North Carolina affirmed the state employee's dismissal as an educational development assistant at a deaf school that operated busses to transport students to and from school.[118] Each bus had two educational development assistants, one served as bus driver and the other as bus monitor. One afternoon, the defendant received a call about a school bus driving at a high rate of speed with passengers. The defendant called the bus phone which the bus monitor answered and confirmed the petitioner was driving. The petitioner was placed on paid leave during an investigation. She denied the allegations but did admit to going above the allowed speed to pass a vehicle and was ultimately terminated. The petitioner argued that she was not operating a "school activity bus" under state law because it was white and shorter than most buses, but the court affirmed that the act of transporting students home from school was sufficient to qualify as a "school activity bus." Further, substantial evidence supported the determination that the bus driver violated the state statute governing speed limits for school bus drivers, so her termination was proper.

In Ohio, an appellate court affirmed the grant of the defendant school board's motion for summary judgment on the teacher's claims for the non-renewal of her contract.[119] The plaintiff was given a one-year administrative contract for the position of assistant principal. He was first placed on a professional growth plan then two performance-improvement plans before being investigated for misconduct and a lack of professionalism. At the end of the school year, it was determined that the plaintiff was ineffective as assistant principal, and his contract was not renewed. The plaintiff alleged that he was wrongfully terminated based on age discrimination and in violation of public policy. However, the court affirmed that the plaintiff did not present any evidence that the non-renewal was the result of retaliation. Further, he failed to refute the board's claims that his contract was not renewed based on his ineffective evaluation that was supported by substantial evidence. Therefore, the plaintiff's claim for the nonrenewal of his contract failed.

---

[118] Sharpe-Johnson v. N.C. Dep't of Pub. Instruction, 867 S.E.2d 188, 398 Educ. L. Rep. 1162 (N.C. Ct. App. 2021).
[119] Hammonds v. Beavercreek City Schs., 182 N.E.3d 34, 400 Educ. L. Rep. 346 (Ohio Ct. App. 2021).

Demotion and Reassignment

In Florida, an employee sued the public school board under the Public Sector Whistleblower's Act alleging his demotion from assistant principal to a teaching position was in retaliation for his participation in an Office of Inspector General (IG) investigation concerning the basketball team.[120] A jury returned a verdict in favor of the employee, awarding him $170,000 in damages. The trial court subsequently denied the school board's motion for a directed verdict or for a new trial and the employee's motion for equitable relief. Both parties appealed. The appellate court affirmed the jury verdict in favor of the employee, finding that it was supported by substantial evidence, and the trial court's denial of the school board's motion for a new trial because the board failed to argue any fundamental error. Finally, the appellate court reversed the trial court's denial of the employee's motion for equitable relief, finding that the trial court was required to award him front pay because state law requires the award of either reinstatement or front pay.

An appellate court in Pennsylvania heard a business administrator's appeal after a school board reassigned him to a different position with a substantial salary reduction.[121] The appellant had one satisfactory performance review, but a few months later, he received a letter of reprimand documenting a number of concerns with his job performance and warning him that further issues could lead to disciplinary action including termination. Less than a month later, the appellant received another letter containing several more allegations against him and placing him on administrative leave. Ultimately, the appellant was reassigned to a substantially lower paying position. The trial court affirmed the board's decision, and the employee again appealed. The state appellate court held that the appellant's reassignment was not a removal that would entitle him to a board hearing, and he was not a "professional employee" under the Public School Code so as to entitle him to a board hearing before demotion. Thus, the board's reassignment decision was affirmed.

Contractual Disputes

The dismissal of a former assistant principal's breach of contract claims were affirmed by an appellate court in New York because she

---

[120] Sch. Bd. of Palm Beach Cnty. v. Groover, 337 So.3d 799, 403 Educ. L. Rep. 348 (Dist. Ct. App. Fla. 2022).
[121] Medina v. Harrisburg Sch. Dist., 273 A.3d 33, 402 Educ. L. Rep. 305 (Commw. Ct. Pa. 2022).

failed to serve a timely notice of claim and, regardless, her claims were time-barred.[122] The plaintiff was demoted from probationary assistant principal to a teaching position after receiving an unsatisfactory performance review as assistant principal. In New York, a notice of claim arising from a breach of contract must be served on a school board "within three months from accrual of the claim," and the action "must be commenced within a one-year statute of limitations." Further, breach of contract claims accrue when "payment for the amount claimed was denied." Here, the plaintiff's claim accrued more than three months before she served the board with a notice of claim and more than one year before she commenced this action in court. Thus, the plaintiff's breach of contract claims based on her demotion were barred.

A North Carolina appellate court affirmed the dismissal of two public teachers' claims for breach of contract against the state government department after it reduced their long-term disability benefits.[123] Both plaintiffs received Transitional Disability Benefits from the defendant department. These benefits are reduced based on Social Security Disability eligibility which means that when Social Security benefits increase to account for cost-of-living adjustments, disability payments from the defendant decrease accordingly. The defendant discovered that the plaintiffs had both been overpaid more than $13,000 and $19,000, respectively, over the span of eleven years and reduced their payments to recover the amounts overpaid. The plaintiffs challenged this reduction in their benefits. The court held that the defendants were entitled to recover the overpayments as was mandated by the statute entitling the plaintiffs to long-term disability benefits. Therefore, the plaintiffs' breach of contract claim failed.

In Ohio, an appellate court reversed and remanded the lower court's entry of summary judgment in favor of the defendant board of education on the former employees' claims alleging improper suspension of their contracts after a reduction in force (RIF).[124] Shortly after signing two-year contracts, the plaintiff employees had their contracts suspended due to an RIF affecting about twenty administrators. The plaintiffs also alleged that the board should have recalled them into newly created positions under their contracts. The court found that there was a genuine issue of fact as to whether the plaintiffs' positions were eliminated through an RIF

---

[122] Blaize v. N.Y. City Dep't of Educ., 168 N.Y.S.3d 512, 404 Educ. L. Rep. 242 (N.Y. App. Div. 2022).
[123] Moss v. N.C. Dep't of State Treasurer, 872 S.E.2d 113, 402 Educ. L. Rep. 1196 (N.C. Ct. App. 2022).
[124] State ex rel. Bennet v. Bd. of Educ. of Dayton Pub. Schs., 177 N.E.3d 648, 397 Educ. L. Rep. 719 (Ohio Ct. App. 2021).

at the transportation department because the defendants failed to allege that the factors affecting the school board were also affecting the transportation department, leading to necessary cuts. Even if there was a genuine RIF at the transportation department, there was a genuine issue of material fact as to whether the plaintiffs had recall rights because the defendants did not even know if they were qualified for the new position meaning they were not considered at all. Thus, summary judgment was reversed, and the case was remanded for further proceedings.

Tenure

In 2022, twelve cases involved issues of tenure or tenured employees. Two of these cases were at the federal level, and ten were in state courts. In the only federal appellate case, the Sixth Circuit, in a case from Michigan, affirmed the dismissal of a teacher's procedural due process, wrongful termination, retaliation, and whistleblower claims against the defendant school board.[125] The plaintiff had been a teacher for ten years and alleged that he and the defendant school board "acted with the understanding that he had tenure." Under the Teachers' Tenure Act (TTA), a teacher "'is considered to be on continuing tenure' only '[a]fter the satisfactory completion of the probationary period.'" The court found that, because the plaintiff had been rated ineffective on his previous three annual evaluations, he was not considered to be tenured. Thus, the Sixth Circuit affirmed that the plaintiff lacked a protected property interest in his job to state a procedural due process claim, that the school board did not wrongfully terminate him after he received three consecutive ineffective ratings, and that the school board did not violate the Family Medical Leave Act by terminating him.

In a federal trial court in New York, a former tenured teacher sued the school district and school officials alleging that his termination violated the Americans with Disabilities Act (ADA), state human rights law, and the First Amendment.[126] The plaintiff was a tenured teacher who was terminated after receiving five charges of misconduct, mostly involving anger issues and inappropriate behavior towards students and colleagues. The court found that the school board made multiple efforts to solve issues caused by the plaintiff's misbehavior, thus his termination was not

---

[125] Hasanaj v. Detroit Pub. Schs. Cmty. Dist., 35 F.4th 437, 403 Educ. L. Rep. 66 (6th Cir. 2022).
[126] Greer v. Gates Chili Cent. Sch. Dist., 577 F.Supp.3d 147, 405 Educ. L. Rep. 873 (W.D.N.Y. 2021).

the result of discrimination against him for his post-traumatic stress disorder. Further, the court held that the plaintiff's statements voicing opposition to the principal were not protected by the First Amendment as he was speaking as an employee on matters of private concern.

The Supreme Court of Illinois reversed the appellate court's decision holding that the board did not have the authority to suspend the teacher following her termination hearing.[127] Here, disciplinary proceedings were filed against the tenured teacher which resulted in a termination hearing. At the termination hearing, the board found that a 90-day unpaid suspension was appropriate instead of termination. The teacher sought review in the appellate court, which held that the board's decision to suspend the teacher and reduce her back pay was not legally authorized because, under state law, the only permissible outcomes during a termination proceeding are termination or reinstatement with back pay. The city board of education appealed to the state supreme court. The court held that the state law in question, as a matter of first impression, did not bar the board's implied authority to suspend the tenured teacher without pay, and the decision to suspend the teacher with a reduction in back pay to account for the unpaid suspension was within the board's implied authority to manage public schools. In an appellate case from Illinois concerning the same state law, the court affirmed the city board of education's decision to sanction the teacher for misconduct by reducing her back pay and issuing a warning resolution.[128] Here, the petitioner, a tenured teacher, was suspended without pay pending a dismissal hearing due to misconduct. The hearing officer recommended against dismissal, and the board adopted this recommendation and decided that her misconduct warranted a warning resolution regarding her hostile language and physical altercations with students and a 50% reduction in back pay. The teacher appealed, arguing that the board did not have the authority to reduce her back pay under state law. The appellate court held that the board did have the implied authority to issue an unpaid suspension through a reduction in backpay, and the teacher was given adequate due process. Thus, the board's decision was affirmed.

In a second appellate case from Illinois, the court reversed the decision ordering a tenured teacher be reinstated with back pay and

---

[127] Bd. of Educ. of City of Chi. v. Moore, 182 N.E.3d 94, 400 Educ. L. Rep. 771 (Ill. 2021).
[128] Mohorn-Mintah v. Bd. of Educ. of City of Chi., 178 N.E.3d 254, 398 Educ. L. Rep. 439 (Ill. App. Ct. 2020).

benefits.[129] The plaintiff was a tenured teacher who was suspended with pay during a Department of Children and Family Services (DCFS) investigation of her concerning her children. After the investigation determined that the allegations were unfounded, the plaintiff returned to work, but the board felt the DCFS report was inconsistent with the information the plaintiff had given them. The plaintiff received a warning but continued teaching. After repeatedly leaving her class during class time, the plaintiff was dismissed. The appellate court held that the board's decision to dismiss the teacher for repeatedly leaving her classroom after having a previous warning was not arbitrary, unreasonable, or unrelated to the requirements of service.

The Supreme Court of Missouri vacated the lower court's judgment and affirmed the board's decision to terminate a tenured teacher for violating board confidentiality policies.[130] The plaintiff, a tenured teacher of eleven years, copied documents from the Google Drive assigned to her on the school district's domain to her personal Google account. She claims to have intended to copy only her work files, but the drive also contained files created by other district employees as well as confidential student information. The board ultimately terminated the plaintiff for her unauthorized downloading of confidential student information from the district-provided drive to her personal Google account. The court held that the board did not act improperly in terminating the plaintiff because evidence suggested that the teacher willfully engaged in a "prohibited disclosure" under FERPA and against board policy. Thus, her termination was upheld. In a Missouri appellate court case, the court reversed the decision ordering a tenured teacher be reinstated.[131] The former tenured teacher was proceeding pro se, and her filings had significant deficiencies. Specifically, the appellate court noted that the teacher was the appellant in this case and, therefore, required to file the appellant's brief; however, her pro se brief did not comply with the appellate briefing rule. Further, the burden of proof was on the teacher to show that the board committed a reversible error in her termination, and she failed to do so.

A Kentucky appellate court reversed the trial court's grant of summary judgment in favor of the school board in the teacher's claims following the nonrenewal of his contract.[132] The plaintiff was

---

[129] Kalisz v. Bd. of Educ. of Kildeer Countryside Cmty. Consol Sch. Dist. 96, 189 N.E.3d 439, 404 Educ. L. Rep. 846 (Ill. App. Ct. 2021).
[130] Ferry v. Bd. of Educ. of Jefferson City Pub. Sch. Dist., 641 S.W.3d 203, 401 Educ. L. Rep. 659 (Mo. 2022).
[131] Waldner v. Dexter R-XI Sch. Dist., 647 S.W.3d 321, 405 Educ. L. Rep. 1215 (Mo. Ct. App. 2022).
[132] Smith v. Bennett, 644 S.W.3d 516, 403 Educ. L. Rep. 317 (Ky. Ct. App. 2021).

a tenured teacher in one school district, after which he was employed in a number of other districts. After completing a probationary contract with the district at issue here, the plaintiff and board entered a "Continuing Contract of Employment" to "be continued from year to year." The following year, he was informed that his contract would not be renewed. The plaintiff argued that this was improper as he had a "continuing service contract," or tenure. The appellate court held that the teacher's continuing contract status was portable and remained enforceable, thus the board breached his contract when it informed him of the nonrenewal of his contract.

In New Jersey, an appellate court affirmed the Commissioner of Education's decision finding that the school board violated the petitioner's rights by refusing to allow her to return as a tenured full-time teacher.[133] After six years of full-time employment, the petitioner requested to be transferred to an available part-time position for as long as the position was available or until returning to full-time work was in her family's best interest. Her transfer was approved, but the board failed to inform her that, by voluntarily taking a part-time position, she would not be entitled to return to any full-time position. After taking an extended maternity leave, the petitioner was informed that she had no right to return to a full-time teaching position after voluntarily taking the part-time position. The petitioner appealed to the Commissioner, who held that the petitioner "did not knowingly and voluntarily waive her right to a full-time position." The court affirmed the Commissioner's findings, holding that school boards have a duty to notify tenured full-time teachers who are considering a voluntary transfer to part-time that they may not retain the right to return to a full-time position.

The final three cases involving tenure came from New York appellate courts. In the first case, the court reversed the grant of the teacher's petition to vacate the hearing officer's arbitration award and denial of the state department of education's motions to dismiss and to confirm the arbitration award.[134] The petitioner was a tenured teacher for the state department of education who received disciplinary charges and was ultimately terminated for numerous instances of incompetence, misconduct, and neglect. The hearing officer denied the teacher's motion to dismiss, sustained the department's allegations, and held that the teacher should be dismissed. The petitioner alleged that the hearing officer exceeded his power because the "probable-cause determination" was only

---

[133] Parsells v. Bd. of Educ. of Borough of Somerville, 277 A.3d 33, 405 Educ. L. Rep. 436 (N.J. Super. Ct. App. 2022).
[134] Cardinale v. N.Y. City Dep't of Educ., 168 N.Y.S.3d 90, 403 Educ. L. Rep. 863 (N.Y. App. Div. 2022).

signed by the principal, but the court did not find this to strip the hearing officer of jurisdiction or authority to hear charges. Thus, the case was remanded with instructions to confirm the arbitration award. In a second case, the court affirmed a judgment annulling the school board's decision to terminate the petitioner's employment.[135] The petitioner was a long-term substitute teacher who was covering for a teacher on maternity leave. After the teacher came back, the plaintiff applied for and received a position as a full teacher. The petitioner received good performance evaluations during her four years as a full teacher, though her teaching certificate lapsed for a few months at one point. The petitioner was ultimately terminated with no pre-termination hearing. She commenced an Article 78 proceeding in which she alleged that her termination was improper because "she had acquired tenure by estoppel" based on the board's "acceptance of her teaching services beyond her probationary period without granting or denying her tenure prior to the expiration thereof." The lower court granted her petition, and the appellate court affirmed, holding that "[t]enure may be acquired by estoppel when a school board accepts the continued services of a teacher...but fails to take the action required by law to either grant or deny tenure" before the probationary period expires. A third appellate case from New York affirmed, modified, and remanded in part the lower court's grant of the defendant board of education's motion to dismiss a tenured school secretary's challenge to receiving "no rating" instead of a satisfactory rating and the board's denial of back pay.[136] Here, the teacher was entitled to "per session" employment during summer school. During a summer session, she originally received a satisfactory rating from the principal, but it was later changed to an unsatisfactory rating by another principal due to a disciplinary letter accusing the teacher of time theft during the summer. The principal was instructed to reinstate the satisfactory rating but instead replaced it with "no rating." The court held that the lower court did not consider whether giving the teacher "no rating" instead of a satisfactory rating was arbitrary and capricious, thus they should make that determination on remand. However, she was not entitled to back pay for subsequently being denied an assignment because she cannot prove the denial was because of the unsatisfactory rating.

---

[135] Matter of Sisson v. Johnson City Cent. Sch. Dist., 170 N.Y.S.3d 259, 405 Educ. L. Rep. 498 (N.Y. App. Div. 2022).
[136] Dennis v. Bd. of Educ. of City Sch. Dist. of City of N.Y., 161 N.Y.S.3d 45, 400 Educ. L. Rep. 715 (N.Y. App. Div. 2021).

Fee Determinations

A Florida appellate court affirmed the lower court's dismissal of the appellant superintendent's claims for reimbursement of attorney's fees and costs incurred in challenging her suspension.[137] The superintendent was suspended by the governor and investigated for failure to provide necessary training, supervision, and safety. She was reinstated with the expectation that she would resign immediately, which she did. She then filed suit seeking reimbursement from the school board for the attorney's fees and other costs she incurred in the process of challenging her suspension. The court held that, because only the governor has the power to suspend a public official like the appellant, the separation of powers doctrine prohibited the judiciary from determining whether the superintendent was entitled to reimbursement for her attorney's fees and incurred costs.

COVID-19

Six cases addressed issues surrounding COVID-19 in 2022. In the only federal appellate court case, the employees, contractors, and volunteers of two Head Start programs in Michigan challenged the Department of Health and Human Services' ("HHS") final interim rule mandating vaccination.[138] These individuals challenged the rule under the Administrative Procedure Act, Congressional Review Act, and the Constitution. A federal trial court originally granted a temporary restraining order, but later denied a preliminary injunction and dissolved the restraining order. The employees, contractors, and volunteers appealed. The Sixth Circuit denied the appeal, finding the individuals failed to establish a likelihood of prevailing on the merits. Specifically, the court found that HHS did not violate the Administrative Procedure Act by issuing an interim final rule instead of notice-and-commenting rulemaking and likely has statutory authority to issue the rule mandating vaccination. As such, the Sixth Circuit denied the request for a preliminary injunction.

Four cases involved Department of Education employees in New York, three of which were brought in federal trial courts. In the first case, school employees sought a preliminary injunction against the Department of Education (DOE) regarding the COVID-19 vaccine

---

[137] Jackson v. Sch. Bd. of Okaloosa Cnty., 326 So.3d 722, 396 Educ. L. Rep. 815 (Fla. Dist. Ct. App. 2021).
[138] Livingston Educ. Serv. Agency v. Becerra, 35 F.4th 489, 403 Educ. L. Rep. 104 (6th Cir. 2022).

mandate.[139] The DOE entered into impact arbitrations to provide employees ways to seek religious and medical exemptions, appeal exemption denials, voluntarily separate with benefits, or take extended leave without pay. Employees who did not comply or receive an exemption would be placed on unpaid leave and protected from termination for non-compliance for a period and could then only be terminated through existing procedures. The injunction sought to enjoin the DOE from withholding pay from, disciplining, and terminating non-compliant employees. Parties seeking a preliminary injunction must show a likelihood of success on the merits, a likelihood of irreparable harm absent preliminary relief, the balance of equities is in their favor, and an injunction is in the public interest. Here, the court found the employees failed to establish a clear or substantial likelihood of success on the merits, the employees' harm was not irreparable as money damages would be adequate compensation for loss of income, and the balance of equities and public interest weighed against granting the requested relief. The court denied the employee's motion for a preliminary injunction.

In the second case, New York DOE employees sought a preliminary injunction to enjoin the DOE from enforcing the city's vaccine mandate against employees with sincere religious objections to the vaccine.[140] The court denied the motion, and the employees appealed to the Second Circuit, which entered an interim order requiring the DOE to provide the employees with reconsideration of their religious accommodation. It entered an opinion vacating the denial of the injunction and remanded the cases. The employees requested a preliminary injunction to enjoin the DOE from enforcing the vaccine mandate against any employee who asserts a sincere religious objection to the vaccine pending resolution of the litigation and an order requiring the DOE to immediately reinstate employees to their original positions prior to enforcement of the vaccine mandate. The DOE opposed this request, and the court denied the request, finding that the employees had not demonstrated irreparable harm or a likelihood of success on the merits. It stated that the employees failed to establish that the panel's decision was constitutionally or otherwise suspect because they failed to show the panel's decision was not neutral or generally applicable.

In the third case, and the final case in federal court, New York City DOE employees sought a preliminary injunction against

---

[139] Broecker v. N.Y. City Dep't of Educ., 573 F.Supp.3d 878, 404 Educ. L. Rep. 812 (E.D.N.Y. 2021).
[140] Kane v. de Blasio, 575 F.Supp.3d 435, 405 Educ. L. Rep. 195 (S.D.N.Y. 2021).

enforcement of the order mandating vaccination for COVID-19.[141] The employees claimed the order violated their substantive due process and equal protection rights under the Fourteenth Amendment and was arbitrary and capricious in violation of state law. The court found the employees' substantive due process rights were not violated because they were not absolutely barred from pursuing jobs in education, and they failed to demonstrate the state's actions were so egregious and outrageous to shock the conscience. The court also found that, while the employees would suffer injury because of the mandate, the balance of equity when compared to public interest did not outweigh the interest to protect the public. The employees' equal protection claim failed for the same reason. The court applied a rational basis standard and found the employees did not demonstrate there was no rational basis for the difference in treatment under the mandate as they worked in confined spaces, potentially with children too young to get vaccinated or who were immunocompromised and especially vulnerable to COVID-19. Therefore, the court denied the preliminary injunction.

Florida sought a preliminary injunction to enjoin Executive Order 14042 requiring each employee of a federal contractor or subcontractor to be fully vaccinated against COVID-19, arguing it exceeded legal authority, violated notice and comment requirements, and constituted arbitrary and capricious agency action.[142] It also claimed President Biden acted *ultra vires* and exercised unconstitutionally delegated legislative power, the order violated the APA, and it was an unconstitutional exercise of Congress's spending power. The federal government argued that Florida lacked standing. A federal trial court found Florida sufficiently pleaded a likelihood it would suffer an injury-in-fact traceable to allegedly unlawful conduct and redressable by the requested relief. The court found the order had an expansive application, was invasive, and intruded into a state prerogative into which Congress likely cannot intrude. The court also found that Florida demonstrated irreparable harm because available remedies could not adequately compensate it for loss of federal contracts and irreparable harm to sovereign interests. It found the balance of harms to each party and public interest weighed in favor of a preliminary injunction. The court granted the injunction under claims that President Biden exceeded authorization with his

---

[141] Maniscalco v. N.Y. City Dep't of Educ., 563 F.Supp.3d 33, 402 Educ. L. Rep. 213 (E.D.N.Y. 2021).
[142] State v. Nelson, 576 F.Supp.3d 1017, 405 Educ. L. Rep. 296 (M.D. Fla. 2021).

Executive Order but held the balance of the motion under advisement.

In the only state-level case, the New York Commissioner of Health and Mental Hygiene issued an order mandating COVID-19 vaccinations for all department employees.[143] A group of employees filed an Article 78 petition to vacate the Commissioner's order and sought a preliminary injunction. The court issued a temporary restraining order and the Commissioner issued a new order. A trial court in New York now grants the defendant city's motion to dismiss. To obtain a preliminary injunction, the party seeking relief must establish a "likelihood of ultimate success on the merits," "irreparable injury if the injunction is not granted," and "a balancing of the equities in its favor." The court determined that the plaintiffs were not likely to succeed on the merits of their claims as they would not be able to establish a "fundamental right protected by substantive due process"; they would not be able to establish irreparable harm as money damages and reinstatement would remedy any alleged harms; and the balancing of equities weighs in favor of public health, not the concerns of a few employees. Thus, the claim was dismissed.

Workers' Compensation

In a case out of Missouri, a custodian brought suit against a school board alleging the board fired him in retaliation for him filing a workers' compensation claim.[144] The custodian suffered a hernia while working for the district and initiated a workers' compensation claim. The authorized treatment provider collected a urine sample from the custodian, which came back positive for marijuana. The school board fired the custodian for violation of the drug policy and denied his workers' compensation claim based on the positive results from his drug test. The custodian claimed discrimination under workers' compensation laws. The school board denied the allegations and asserted his claim was barred by governmental sovereignty and/or Eleventh Amendment immunity and filed a motion for summary judgment. The trial court granted the school board's motion and the custodian appealed. The state supreme court indicated that the only issue before it was whether any employee could assert his discrimination claim against the school board under

---

[143] N.Y.C. Mun. Lab. Comm. v. City of N.Y., 156 N.Y.S.3d 681, 397 Educ. L. Rep. 1101 (Sup. Ct. N.Y. 2021).
[144] Poke v. Indep. Sch. Dist., 647 S.W.3d 18 (Mo. 2022).

any circumstances. It found the plain language of the applicable statute and related statutes shows the general assembly expressly waived any immunity the school board might have against such claims and reversed and remanded the trial court.

A cafeteria worker in Oklahoma fell on a piece of broken concrete while returning from her authorized work break.[145] Her injuries required two surgeries and she did not return to work. The cafeteria worker filed a workers' compensation claim, which her employer denied arguing she was not in the course and scope of employment at the time of injury. The ALJ found the cafeteria worker's injuries were compensatory. The employer requested review of the decision and the Workers' Compensation Commission reversed the ALJ's decision, finding the cafeteria worker was not inside of the facility as required to be considered within the course and scope of employment. The cafeteria worker sought review. The Supreme Court of Oklahoma found the Commission's authority to modify or reverse the ALJ's decision was limited to finding that the decision was not supported by the clear weight of the evidence or contrary to law and the Commission exceeded its authority. It upheld the ALJ's decision. There were two dissenting opinions. The first stated the majority opinion applied the wrong standard of review, and the second stated the majority opinion conflated the definition of "on the employer's premises" with "inside the employer's facility."

A special education teacher filed a petition for a hearing with the Department of Labor and Regulation in South Dakota.[146] The school board and its insurer filed a motion for summary judgment regarding coverage for medical expenses, which the Department granted. The teacher appealed to the trial court which affirmed the Department's decision, and she appealed again. After injuring her back at work, the teacher sought treatment; one surgeon determined she was not a surgical candidate, and the insurer denied her request for a second consultation. The teacher had the second surgical consultation anyway and underwent surgery. In the ongoing administrative proceedings, the board/insurer filed a motion for summary judgment stating the second surgeon was an out-of-plan provider and his expenses were not compensable care unless justified by a legal exception. The ALJ considered the exceptions, determined they were not applicable, and granted the board/insurer's motion, which was affirmed and is now on appeal. The state supreme court held that, because the board/insurer denied

---

[145] Johnson v. Midwest City Del City Pub. Schs., 507 P.3d 637, 402 Educ. L. Rep. 401 (Okla. 2021).
[146] Dittman v. Rapid City Sch. Dist., 976 N.W.2d 773, 404 Educ. L. Rep. 913 (S.D. 2022).

compensability of the teacher's claim from the time of its original answer through her referral to the second surgeon and subsequent surgery, the surgeon's expenses were authorized despite being an out-of-network provider.

A school custodian in Connecticut appealed the Compensation Review Board's denial of his motion for articulation or reconsideration on the commissioner's decision, claiming the board improperly denied his request to remand the matter to a different commissioner.[147] The board of education appealed the commission's decision reversing in part the commissioner's approval. The board filed a Form 36 to discontinue or reduce the custodian's workers' compensation benefits because a medical examination revealed he had a work capacity and had reached maximum medical improvement. The commissioner approved the form finding the custodian had reached maximum medical improvement and determined his combined permanent partial disability to be 21%. The custodian appealed and the board partially reversed the decision approving the Form 36. The board of education appealed. The appellate court indicated the role of the court is limited to whether the board's decision resulted from an incorrect application of law to the facts or an inference illegally or unreasonably drawn from them. It found the record supported the board's finding, the board did not err in vacating commissioner's determination, and the board was not required to remand for a de novo ruling by a new commissioner. It affirmed the board's decisions.

An employer and carrier (E&C) appealed the order of the Judge of Compensation Claims (JCC) striking their authorized physician under the one-time-change statute because the physician's fees exceeded the base fee schedule rate.[148] The JCC found the physician is not an authorized treating physician where they charge fees in excess of the maximum amount allowed by law and directed the claimant to receive a one-time change to a physician of her choice. The E&C appealed. An appellate court in Florida reversed the JCC's order for three reasons. First, the court found the JCC's authority did not extend to resolving issues or striking a provider over their fee rates as review and resolution for this is left to DFS. Second, the workers' compensation code expressly allowed for higher-than-fee-schedule arrangements. Lastly, the court stated that the statute did not provide claimants recourse to litigate complaints before a JCC regarding the reimbursements between E&Cs and authorized

---

[147] Arrico v. Bd. of Educ. of City of Stamford, 274 A.3d 148, 403 Educ. L. Rep. 250 (Conn. App. Ct. 2022).
[148] Palm Beach Cnty. Sch. Dist. v. Smith, 337 So.3d 383, 403 Educ. L. Rep. 331 (Fla. Dist. Ct. App. 2022).

treating physicians. In another appellate case from Florida, a teacher filed a workers' compensation claim after falling at work.[149] The teacher was sitting in his chair, and upon attempting to stand, he fell and broke his femur, likely due to his leg falling asleep. The JCC found the teacher's claim was non-compensable because his injury did not arise out of his work as a teacher even though the incident occurred while he was at work and performing work. The teacher appealed. An appellate court affirmed the JCC's determination and clarified that the law requires claimants to show that work performed in the course and scope of employment was a major contributing cause of the injury. The teacher argued that, since he did not have a pre-existing condition, there was a presumption that any exertion connected with his employment was adequate to satisfy the legal causation test. The court disagreed and stated that an idiopathic condition triggers the increased hazard test which requires that, when there is more than one cause of an injury, work must be the preponderant cause compared to any idiopathic cause. Here, the court found the teacher failed to establish his employment was the preponderant cause of his fall and affirmed the JCC.

In Georgia, an employee suffered a compensable injury in 2008 and received temporary total disability (TTD) benefits until May 2016 and permanent partial disability benefits until September 2016.[150] In November 2016, the employee filed an application for a hearing requesting TTD benefits based on the catastrophic nature of the claim. He filed several more requests which were also removed from the docket. After another request, the employer contested the request on the basis of the statute of limitations. An ALJ found the employee's claim was still viable. The appellate division adopted the ALJ's decision, and the superior court adopted and affirmed the appellate division's decision. The employer requested review of the superior court's decision to determine whether the superior court had jurisdiction to review the appellate division's decision. The appellate court found the superior court lacked jurisdiction to review the employer's appeal of the appellate division's decision because an interlocutory appeal is not authorized under the applicable workers' compensation laws. It reversed and remanded the superior court with orders for that court to dismiss the appeal as premature.

An appellate court in Louisiana reversed and remanded the Office of Workers' Compensation's (OWC) decision, finding that the

---

[149] Silberberg v. Palm Beach Cnty. Sch. Bd., 335 So.3d 148, 402 Educ. L. Rep. 500 (Fla. Dist. Ct. App. 2022).
[150] Newton Cnty. Bd. of Educ. v. Nolley, 871 S.E.2d 884, 402 Educ. L. Rep. 884 (Ga. Ct. App. 2022).

OWC had subject matter jurisdiction but that evidence did not support the OWC's decision to equate the claimant's employment as a teacher, coach, and athletic director to clerical work in determining if he suffered an occupational disease.[151] Here, the plaintiff filed a workers' compensation claim for exposure to toxic mold and other contaminants that resulted in immune and neurological issues, but the school board denied his claims and he brought the present suit. To establish that his exposure was covered under workers' compensation, the plaintiff must show that the mold caused him to suffer an occupational disease, defined as a "disease or illness which is due to causes and conditions characteristic of and peculiar to the particular trade, occupation, process, or employment in which the employee is exposed to such disease." The court held that the OWC erred by evaluating the plaintiff the same way it would a clerical worker instead of actually examining the nature of his specific duties. Thus, the case was reversed and remanded to OWC.

The special appellate court's reversal of the grant of summary judgment in favor of the workers' compensation claimant was affirmed by an appellate court in Maryland.[152] The claimant injured her shoulder in an accident while working as a school bus driver. The Workers' Compensation Commission issued a summary denial of her requests for modification of an earlier order denying her request for authorization of shoulder surgery, and the claimant sought judicial review. The appellate court held that summary denials by the Commission were not subject to judicial review, therefore, the defendant was entitled to summary judgment.

A New York public school principal appealed the Workers' Compensation Board's decision finding her ineligible for workers' compensation benefits under the applicable law.[153] The principal claimed multiple work-related physical and psychological injuries. The Workers' Compensation Law Judge disallowed her claim on the basis her role as principal was pedagogical which made her ineligible for benefits and the board affirmed this decision. The principal appealed. A trial court found the principal's employment responsibilities were principally pedagogical in nature and she was not engaged in the instruction of any qualifying subject matter at the time of her injuries. As such, it denied the principal's appeal and affirmed the board's decision.

---

[151] LeCompte v. St. Tammany Par. Sch. Bd., 324 So.3d 1066, 395 Educ. L. Rep. 872 (La. Ct. App. 2021).
[152] Sanders v. Bd. of Educ. of Harford Cnty., 265 A.3d 1083, 399 Educ. L. Rep. 257 (Md. Ct. App. 2021).
[153] Cunningham v. Dep't of Educ., 169 N.Y.S.3d 715, 404 Educ. L. Rep. 843 (N.Y. App. Div. 2022).

In another case from New York, a teacher suffered injuries when she fell after the doorknob of a door she attempted to open broke.[154] She filed for workers' compensation and received TTD payments. The teacher was later evaluated by two physicians. One found she sustained a 60% schedule loss of use (SLU) in her left leg, and the other found a 0% SLU. The Workers' Compensation Law Judge (WCLJ) credited the physician's opinion finding she experienced a 60% SLU. The Workers' Compensation Board rescinded that finding based on guidelines requiring consideration of updated x-rays, which were not considered in that medical opinion. The Board directed the teacher to obtain a third evaluation, after which the WCLJ found it did not provide a permanency assessment and the previously credited opinion was not in compliance, so the WCLJ credited the evaluation finding a 0% SLU. The Board affirmed. The teacher appealed, arguing the medical assessment relied upon in the recent WCLJ determination was also not in compliance with the guidelines as it did not consider updated x-rays. An appellate court in New York agreed and reversed and remanded for a proper determination of the teacher's SLU award in accordance with applicable guidelines.

Workplace Safety

The Supreme Court of Ohio affirmed the lower court's holding that a state statute's training or experience requirement applies to teachers who are authorized by a board of education to carry a firearm while on duty, and the defendant board of education violated that statute by permitting untrained and inexperienced school employees to carry a deadly weapon while on duty.[155] Here, the board granted a resolution that it would "grant written authorization to individuals to be designated by the district's superintendent...to convey into and possess in a school safety zone deadly weapons or dangerous ordnance for the safety of the district's students." Under the resolution, a designated individual must maintain a state concealed carry license, complete "response-to-active-shooter training," and re-certify annually; it did not require designated individuals to satisfy the statutory training or experience requirements. The court held that the statutory training or experience requirements for armed school personnel applied to school employees, including teachers and administrators, and that

---

[154] Strack v. Plattsburgh City Sch. Dist., 163 N.Y.S.3d 272, 401 Educ. L. Rep. 532 (N.Y. App. Div. 2022).
[155] Gabbard v. Madison Loc. Sch. Dist. Bd. of Educ., 179 N.E.3d 1169, 399 Educ. L. Rep. 761 (Ohio 2021).

no exception applied that would allow the board to circumvent the training or experience requirements.

Professional Conduct

The Supreme Court of Ohio ordered the permanent disbarment of an attorney after he engaged in inappropriate sexual relationships with two minors while serving as a teacher.[156] He was also convicted on multiple felony charges of gross sexual imposition and sexual battery. The attorney argued that "the board improperly weighed the relevant aggravating and mitigating factors in his case" and the proper punishment was an indefinite suspension. Specifically, he claims that he accepted responsibility by entering a guilty plea in the criminal case and that his continued attempts to contact his victims were before he was admitted to the bar. The court found that had the attorney disclosed his misconduct or been convicted before he sought admission to the bar, his application would not have been approved. Thus, permanent disbarment was the appropriate sanction.

In Kentucky, an appellate court held that a teacher and athletic trainer were not under a ministerial duty to administer an automated external defibrillator (AED) within a certain timeframe.[157] The teacher was supervising a basketball open gym when a student experienced trouble breathing and went to the athletic trainer's office where he collapsed. The trainer sent two students to retrieve an AED while he administered CPR and the teacher assisted. The trainer delivered one AED shock before first responders arrived, and the student was taken to the emergency room where he passed away. The lower court held that the teacher was not entitled to qualified immunity because he was engaging in ministerial acts and not medical treatment, but the trainer was immune under the Good Samaritan statute. The appellate court affirmed that the trainer was immune. Further, the court held that the school's protocol did not impose a mandatory duty on the teacher to retrieve an AED within a three-minute window, and the teacher made an appropriate judgment call to assist the trainer who had more training and was in control of the situation. Thus, he was not engaged in a ministerial act and was entitled to qualified immunity.

---

[156] Disciplinary Couns. v. Polizzi, 175 N.E.3d 501, 395 Educ. L. Rep. 1128 (Ohio 2021).
[157] Armstrong v. Est. of Ifeacho by and through Ifeacho, 633 S.W.3d 333, 396 Educ. L. Rep. 1062 (Ky. Ct. App. 2021).

Compensation and Benefits

An appellate court in New York affirmed the Unemployment Insurance Appeal Board's decision that the claimant was disqualified from receiving unemployment benefits.[158] The claimant was a probationary teacher for less than two months before quitting with two days notice and no provided reason. When applying for unemployment benefits, the claimant alleged that she quit for safety reasons due to the general misbehavior of students. The Department of Labor found that she was disqualified from receiving benefits because she voluntarily quit without good cause. The Board and appellate court both affirmed this decision.

Similarly, a Pennsylvania appellate court affirmed the Unemployment Compensation Board of Review's denial of the claimant's request for unemployment benefits.[159] Here, the claimant was a school custodian. He received a letter from the school notifying him that he was suspended without pay pending the school board's decision regarding his potential termination after an altercation with another employee. The claimant filed for unemployment benefits, and the school stated that it terminated him "for willful misconduct for violating company policy concerning appropriate behavior, citing Claimant's altercation with the coworker." The claimant was denied benefits because of his willful misconduct and filed this appeal. During a subsequent hearing, the school instead asserted that the claimant voluntarily resigned as part of a workers' compensation settlement. The Board held that the claimant voluntarily resigned as part of the workers' compensation settlement and thus was ineligible for benefits. The appellate court affirmed.

Miscellaneous

A former teacher in New York sued a charter school and educational corporation for violating state labor laws under the anti-kickback provisions.[160] He alleged the charter school coerced him to make payments from his wages to an educational corporation which funneled funds to the Gülen movement. The former teacher alleged six causes of action against the defendants after the school failed to renew his teaching contract, including that they used threats of "unemployment or demotion in employment, portions of [his] wage,

---

[158] Frederick v. Comm'r of Lab., 153 N.Y.S.3d 698, 395 Educ. L. Rep. 1081 (N.Y. App. Div. 2021).
[159] Smith v. Unemployment Comp. Bd. of Rev., 261 A.3d 615, 396 Educ. L. Rep. 739 (Commw. Ct. Pa. 2021).
[160] Konkur v. Utica Acad. of Sci. Charter Sch., 185 N.E.3d 483, 402 Educ. L. Rep. 347 (N.Y. 2022)

salary, and [ ] overtime." The defendants moved to dismiss, which the trial court in New York granted in part but denied as to the labor law claim. They appealed, and the appellate court reversed. The former teacher appealed, and the highest state court held that the state anti-kickback statute did not create a private right of action. It found the former teacher satisfied the first two factors in determining if legislative intent created an implied right to private action, but failed to meet the third because the text and statutory history of the anti-kickback section clearly provided avenues for enforcement and to create a private right of action was inconsistent with the state's already comprehensive enforcement scheme.

In Georgia, a teacher obtained a default judgment against a parent who attacked her at school while the parent walked her child to class for a field trip.[161] The teacher was covered under the County Board of Education's (BOE) agreement with a self-insurance policy (the Fund). The teacher sued the Fund as a judgment creditor for the parent. The trial court denied both parties' summary judgment motions regarding whether the parent was covered by the agreement and granted the teacher's motion finding that a clause in the agreement excluding willful violations of a penal statute was unenforceable as a matter of law. Both parties appealed. The Fund argued the parent was not covered and their criminal violation barred recovery. The teacher argued the parent was covered because a "member" under the agreement included any authorized volunteer. The state appellate court found the parent was not an authorized volunteer at the time, as required by the plain meaning of the agreement language and was not covered. It found the parent was an approved volunteer through the school, but not acting as such at the time. It reversed and remanded the trial court's denial of the Fund's summary judgment motion.

Conclusion

In 2022, the number of cases involving primary and secondary school employees decreased by just over 25%, from 114 in 2021 to 84 in 2022. This is likely due, in part, to COVID-19 litigation waning over the last year after peaking in 2021. The issues that arose were similar to those last year, ranging from civil rights issues like discrimination to tenure, termination, and workers' compensation, among many others. These cases were brought in both state and

---

[161] Ga. Sch. Bds. Assoc. Risk Mgmt. Fund v. Royal, 362 Ga. App. 678, 401 Educ. L. Rep. 650 (Ga. Ct. App. 2022).

federal courts, but most issues were decided by state courts and involved primarily state law. Additionally, the cases presented in this chapter displayed tensions between employees and a variety of opposing parties, including fellow employees, employers, state retirement boards, and state departments of education.

Alphabetical List of Cases

Agbefe v. Bd. of Educ. of City of Chi.
Armstrong v. Est. of Ifeacho by and through Ifeacho
Arrico v. Bd. of Educ. of City of Stamford
Birchard v. Blue Cross and Blue Shield of N.C.
Blaize v. N.Y. City Dep't of Educ.
Bd. of Educ. of City of Chi. v. Moore
Bd. of Educ. of City of Waterbury v. Comm'n on Hum. Rts. and Opportunities
Bd. of Trs. Of Lincoln Cnty. Sch. Dist. No. 2 v. Earling
Broecker v. N.Y. City Dep't of Educ.
Cardinale v. N.Y. City Dep't of Educ.
Cloutier v. Ledyard Bd. of Educ.
Campbell v. N.Y. City Dep't of Educ.
Commonwealth v. Kozubal
Cunningham v. Dep't of Educ.
DeLopez v. Bernalillo Pub. Schs.
Dennis v. Bd. of Educ. of City Sch. Dist. of City of N.Y.
Disciplinary Couns. v. Polizzi
Dittman v. Rapid City Sch. Dist.
Ellis v. N. Andover Pub. Schs.
Ferry v. Bd. of Educ. of Jefferson City Pub. Sch. Dist.
Frederick v. Comm'r of Lab.
Gabbard v. Madison Loc. Sch. Dist. Bd. of Educ.
Geer v. Gates Chili Cent. Sch. Dist.
George-Buckley v. Medford Sch. Dist.
Ga. Sch. Bds. Assoc. Risk Mgmt. Fund v. Royal
Green v. Dep't of Educ. of City of N.Y.
Green v. Dir., Ark. Dep't of Workforce Servs.
Greer v. Gates Chili Cent. Sch. Dist.
Hammonds v. Beavercreek City Schs.
Hasanaj v. Detroit Pub. Schs. Cmty. Dist.
Jackson v. Sch. Bd. of Okaloosa Cnty.
Johnson v. Bd. of Educ. of Bowling Green Indep. Sch. Dist.
Johnson v. Dir., Dep't of Workforce Servs.
Johnson v. Midwest City Del City Pub. Schs.
Jones v. Bessemer Bd. of Educ.
Kalisz v. Bd. of Educ. of Kildeer Countryside Cmty. Consol. Sch. Dist. 96
Kane v. de Blasio
Kibbons v. Taft Sch. Dist. 90
Kincaid v. Unified Sch. Dist. No. 500, Kansas City, Kan.

Kluge v. Brownsburg Cmty. Sch. Corp.
Krause v. Kelahan
Konkur v. Utica Acad. of Sci. Charter Sch.
LeCompte v. St. Tammany Par. Sch. Bd.
Lima v. City of E. Providence
Livingston Educ. Serv. Agency v. Becerra
Malcolm v. Assoc. of Supervisors and Admins. of Rochester
Maniscalco v. N.Y. City Dep't of Educ.
Martcheva v. Dayton Bd. of Educ.
Matter of Sisson v. Johnson City Cent. Sch. Dist.
McClain v. Lynchburg City Schs.
McIntosh v. Dep't of Educ. of City of N.Y.
Medina v. Harrisburg Sch. Dist.
Mimbs v. Henry Cnty. Schs.
Mohorn-Mintah v. Bd. of Educ. of City of Chi.
Monts v. Bd. of Educ. of City of Hartford
Moss v. N.C. Dep't of State Treasurer
Motisi v. Hebron Pub. Sch. Dist.
N.Y.C. Mun. Lab. Comm. v. City of N.Y.
Newton Cnty. Bd. of Educ. v. Nolley
Norris v. Stanley
O'Hara v. Bd. of Educ., Yonkers City Sch. Dist.
Palm Beach Cnty. Sch. Dist. v. Smith
Parsells v. Bd. of Educ. of Borough of Somerville
Perez-Dickson v. Bridgeport Bd. of Educ.
Poke v. Indep. Sch. Dist.
Rabun Cnty. Bd. of Educ. v. Randel
Rehfield v. Diocese of Joliet
Rooth v. Bd. of Trs., Pub. Emps. Retirement Sys.
Sanders v. Bd. of Educ. of Harford Cnty.
Sch. Bd. of Palm Beach Cnty. v. Groover
Sharpe-Johnson v. N.C. Dep't of Pub. Instruction
S.H., In re.
Silberberg v. Palm Beach Cnty. Sch. Bd.
Smith v. Bennett
Smith v. Unemployment Comp. Bd. of Rev.
Starkey v. Roman Cath. Archdiocese of Indianapolis
State ex rel. Bennet v. Bd. of Educ. of Dayton Pub. Schs.
State ex rel. Ohio Att'y Gen. v. Peterson
State v. Nelson
Stathis v. Marty Indian Sch. Bd.
Strack v. Plattsburgh City Sch. Dist.
Tabb v. Bd. of Educ. of Durham Pub. Schs.

Tucker v. First Bible Chapel Int'l
Waldner v. Dexter R-XI Sch. Dist.
Webster v. Chesterfield Cnty. Sch. Bd.
Yurish v. Sinclair Broad. Grp.

Cases by Jurisdiction

FEDERAL CASES

First Circuit
Lima v. City of E. Providence

Massachusetts
Ellis v. N. Andover Pub. Schs.

Second Circuit
Green v. Dep't of Educ. of City of N.Y.
Perez-Dickson v. Bridgeport Bd. of Educ.

Connecticut
Cloutier v. Ledyard Bd. of Educ.

New York
Broecker v. N.Y. City Dep't of Educ.
Greer v. Gates Chili Cent. Sch. Dist.
Kane v. de Blasio
Krause v. Kelahan
Malcolm v. Assoc. of Supervisors and Admins. of Rochester
Maniscalco v. N.Y. City Dep't of Educ.

Fourth Circuit
Tabb v. Bd. of Educ. of Durham Pub. Schs.
Webster v. Chesterfield Cnty. Sch. Bd.

Virginia
McClain v. Lynchburg City Schs.

Sixth Circuit
Hasanaj v. Detroit Pub. Schs. Cmty. Dist.
Livingston Educ. Serv. Agency v. Becerra

Kentucky
Johnson v. Bd. of Educ. of Bowling Green Indep. Sch. Dist.

Michigan
Norris v. Stanley

Seventh Circuit
Starkey v. Roman Cath. Archdiocese of Indianapolis

Illinois
Agbefe v. Bd. of Educ. of City of Chi.
Kibbons v. Taft Sch. Dist. 90

Indiana
Kluge v. Brownsburg Cmty. Sch. Corp.

Eighth Circuit

South Dakota
Stathis v. Marty Indian Sch. Bd.

Tenth Circuit
Tucker v. First Bible Chapel Int'l

Kansas
Kincaid v. Unified Sch. Dist. No. 500, Kansas City, Kan.

New Mexico
DeLopez v. Bernalillo Pub. Schs.

Eleventh Circuit

Alabama
Jones v. Bessemer Bd. of Educ.

Florida
State v. Nelson

STATE & D.C. COURT CASES

Arkansas
Green v. Dir., Ark. Dep't of Workforce Servs.
Johnson v. Dir., Dep't of Workforce Servs.

Connecticut
Arrico v. Bd. of Educ. of City of Stamford
Bd. of Educ. of City of Waterbury v. Comm'n on Hum. Rts. and Opportunities
Monts v. Bd. of Educ. of City of Hartford

Florida
Jackson v. Sch. Bd. of Okaloosa Cnty.
Palm Beach Cnty. Sch. Dist. v. Smith
Sch. Bd. of Palm Beach Cnty. v. Groover
Silberberg v. Palm Beach Cnty. Sch. Bd.

Georgia
Mimbs v. Henry Cnty. Schs.
Ga. Sch. Bds. Assoc. Risk Mgmt. Fund v. Royal
Newton Cnty. Bd. of Educ. v. Nolley
Rabun Cnty. Bd. of Educ. v. Randel

Illinois
Bd. of Educ. of City of Chi. v. Moore
Rehfield v. Diocese of Joliet
Mohorn-Mintah v. Bd. of Educ. of City of Chi.
Kalisz v. Bd. of Educ. of Kildeer Countryside Cmty. Consol. Sch. Dist. 96

Kentucky
Armstrong v. Est. of Ifeacho by and through Ifeacho
Smith v. Bennett

Louisiana
LeCompte v. St. Tammany Par. Sch. Bd.

Maryland
Sanders v. Bd. of Educ. of Harford Cnty.

Massachusetts
Commonwealth v. Kozubal

Missouri
Ferry v. Bd. of Educ. of Jefferson City Pub. Sch. Dist.
Poke v. Indep. Sch. Dist.
Waldner v. Dexter R-XI Sch. Dist.

New Jersey
Parsells v. Bd. of Educ. of Borough of Somerville
Rooth v. Bd. of Trs., Pub. Emps. Retirement Sys.

New York
Konkur v. Utica Acad. of Sci. Charter Sch.
Blaize v. N.Y. City Dep't of Educ.
Campbell v. N.Y. City Dep't of Educ.
Cardinale v. N.Y. City Dep't of Educ.
Cunningham v. Dep't of Educ.
Dennis v. Bd. of Educ. of City Sch. Dist. of City of N.Y.
Frederick v. Comm'r of Lab,
Matter of Sisson v. Johnson City Cent. Sch. Dist.
McIntosh v. Dep't of Educ. of City of N.Y.
O'Hara v. Bd. of Educ., Yonkers City Sch. Dist.
Strack v. Plattsburgh City Sch. Dist.
N.Y.C. Mun. Lab. Comm. v. City of N.Y.

North Carolina
Birchard v. Blue Cross and Blue Shield of N.C.
Moss v. N.C. Dep't of State Treasurer
Sharpe-Johnson v. N.C. Dep't of Pub. Instruction

North Dakota
Motisi v. Hebron Pub. Sch. Dist.

Ohio
Disciplinary Couns. v. Polizzi
Gabbard v. Madison Loc. Sch. Dist. Bd. of Educ.
Hammonds v. Beavercreek City Schs.
Martcheva v. Dayton Bd. of Educ.
State ex rel. Bennet v. Bd. of Educ. of Dayton Pub. Schs.
State ex rel. Ohio Att'y Gen. v. Peterson

Oklahoma
Johnson v. Midwest City Del City Pub. Schs.

Oregon
George-Buckley v. Medford Sch. Dist., 509 P.3d 738 (Or. Ct. App. 2022)

Pennsylvania
S.H., In re.
Medina v. Harrisburg Sch. Dist.
Smith v. Unemployment Comp. Bd. of Rev.

South Dakota
Dittman v. Rapid City Sch. Dist.

West Virginia
Yurish v. Sinclair Broad. Grp.

Wyoming
Bd. of Trs. Of Lincoln Cnty. Sch. Dist. No. 2 v. Earling

Chapter 3

STUDENTS IN K-12 SCHOOLS

Beth Godett, J.D., Ed.D.[162] and Christine Collins-Otto, M.S.[163]

Introduction	89
COVID-19 Challenges	90
Masks	90
Vaccinations	95
COVID-19 Learning Models	96
First Amendment	96
Expression	96
Fourth Amendment	98
Abuse and Harassment	100
Employee-on-Student	100
Student-on-Student	103
Discrimination	106
Racial	106
Sexual	107
School Enrollment	109
Contracts with Private Schools	109
Residency	110
Trespass	110
Truancy	110
Discipline	111
Due Process	111
Criminal Proceedings	112

---

[162] Adjunct Professor of Education Law and Policy at Boston College, Rider University, Fairleigh Dickinson University.
[163] Senior Educational Services and Bridges Director, Multnomah Educational Service District, Portland, Ore.

Injury Damages Under Insurance Law 112
Conclusion 113
Alphabetical List of Cases 115
Cases by Jurisdiction 116

Introduction

This year's cases, which continued some of the themes from prior years, appear in West's *Education Law Reporter,* volumes 395-405. Abuse and harassment, discrimination, First Amendment rights, and discipline all remained important areas of focus. However, two years into the COVID-19 pandemic, a new theme stemming from pandemic response and mitigation efforts emerged as one of the most contested areas in student law. Of the 56 cases highlighted in this chapter, 14 centered on COVID-19-related mask mandates, vaccines, or learning models. Another point of distinction this year is the conspicuous absence of several prior themes, including school resource officers and student protests.

COVID-19 mask mandates dominated dockets in 2022, and in almost every instance, mask mandates won. Students, parents, nonprofit organizations, and states approached challenging mandates from a variety of angles, but nearly all of the challenges failed to sway the courts. As one judge explained when opining in favor of mandates, "No one is forcing plaintiff to send her child to public school or live in New York State, but once she made those decisions, she must comply with their rules. Her authority stops, so to speak, at the schoolhouse door."[164] This general lack of tolerance for objections to pandemic measures carried over to other COVID-19-related challenges including in-person learning models and vaccine requirements.

After mask-related issues, which were involved in fourteen cases, abuse and harassment cases were the most frequent areas of contention, with six cases involving employee-on-student abuse and harassment, and seven cases grounded in student-on-student harassment. Two of the employee-on-student harassment cases and two of the student-on-student harassment cases were appealed beyond the United States federal trial courts to the circuit courts of appeals. Claims were filed under Title IX, Section 1983, and state law. Title IX claims looked at board actions largely through the lens of deliberate indifference. Equal Protection claims examined both whether substantial due process was in order, as well as exceptions for "special relationship" and "state-created danger." State law determined a board's duty under negligence to protect students.

New First Amendment expression cases brought *Tinker's* famous "schoolhouse gate" metaphor and the ramifications of the *Mahanoy* case to the forefront, evoking consideration of the

---

[164] Doe v. Franklin Square Union Free Sch. Dist., 568 F. Supp. 3d 270, 291, 403 Educ. L. Rep. 509 (E.D.N.Y. 2021).

parameters of student speech rights. Similar boundary questions also were raised in cases focused on school negligence, school choice, privacy, and contract mutuality. Defining the world inside that schoolhouse gate and determining when and to whom the gate is open or closed were issues discussed in this year's cases.

Also present were ongoing questions surrounding sexual harassment, bullying, and assault, which continued to beg consideration of where the line is drawn between a school's sensitivity to discrimination and its responsibility to protect students. Are "victims" denied the right to participate in educational opportunities that other students access out of fear, because they are placed in some danger, or because there is a difference in values? Where does duty end and deliberate indifference begin?

COVID-19 Challenges

Masks

COVID-19 related mask mandates were the most significant body of legal challenges, with fourteen cases before the courts, challenging mandates from a range of angles and across the United States. In eleven of the fourteen cases, mask mandates were upheld or re-instituted.

In one of only three cases where mask mandates failed, students with disabilities in Texas contested the governor's executive order prohibiting school boards from mandating masks, expressing concern that it placed them at a higher risk of contracting COVID-19.[165] A federal trial court in Texas sided with the students and placed an injunction on enforcing the order. However, upon appeal, the Fifth Circuit federal appellate court overturned the lower court's injunction, noting that the spread of COVID-19 could not be traced back to enforcing the order, and since none of the students had contracted COVID-19 directly due to the order, the students lacked Article III standing.

Another mask challenge came from a Florida parent on behalf of minor children who filed a series of Section 1983 claims against the children's school district alleging violations of multiple Fifth and Fourteenth Amendment rights, as well as their rights to due process, Equal Protection, the Florida Parents' Bill of Rights, and privacy

---

[165] E.T. v. Paxton, 41 F.4th 709, 405 Ed. L. Rep. 634 (5th Cir. 2022).

under the Florida Constitution.[166] A federal trial court dismissed the case, stating that the parent failed to submit a claim where relief could be granted, and many of the claims were filed in the wrong jurisdiction. The court also referenced other mask challenges, stating that the masking was a legitimate power of the state to curb the spread of COVID-19.

The second case overturning mask mandates occurred in Kentucky. Parents at a Kentucky Catholic school sued the governor over an August 2021 executive order mandating masking in schools and requested emergency injunctive relief.[167] A federal trial court issued a temporary restraining order, and then found that the governor acted in violation of state laws, which required the governor to first acquire General Assembly approval to extend emergency orders. He had not, making the executive order invalid.

Mask challenges were dismissed again by a federal trial court in Missouri when a nonprofit association of parents and concerned citizens contested mandates implemented in seven different school districts and by two municipalities, stating these mandates ignored their expressed concerns with masking and the potential for harm.[168] The association's case was dismissed since no harm had yet occurred, and the association lacked Article III standing.

After the governor of New Jersey issued two executive orders requiring masking in schools, parents of several school-age children filed suit alleging violations of their children's First Amendment freedom of speech and Fourteenth Amendment Equal Protection rights and requested preliminary injunctive relief.[169] The federal trial court in New Jersey denied their motion, noting that the orders were related to the legitimate governmental interest of controlling the spread of COVID-19. Additionally, while the court did agree that masks "muzzled" speech, it did not meet the standard of preventing expressive speech.

A girl with severe asthma requested medical accommodations exempting her from the board's mask mandate.[170] After multiple denials, her mother requested injunctive relief to invalidate the state Department of Public Health (NYPDH) and school board's COVID-19 masking requirements. The Second Circuit, using rational basis review, denied the request asserting the state mask mandates were temporary orders based on Centers for Disease Control (CDC)

---

[166] Lloyd v. Sch. Bd. of Palm Beach Cnty., 570 F. Supp. 3d 1165, 403 Educ. L. Rep. 835 (S.D. Fla. 2021).
[167] Oswald v. Beshear, 555 F. Supp. 3d 475, 401 Educ. L. Rep. 284 (E.D. Ky. 2021).
[168] Northland Parent Ass'n v. Excelsior Springs Sch. Dist. # 40, 571 F. Supp. 3d 1104, 404 Educ. L. Rep. 628 (W.D. Mo. 2021).
[169] Stepien v. Murphy, 574 F. Supp. 3d 229, 405 Educ L. Rep. 93 (D.N.J. 2021).
[170] Doe v. Franklin Square Union Free Sch. Dist., 568 F. Supp. 3d 270, 403 Educ. L. Rep. 509 (E.D.N.Y. 2021).

recommendations, which the court found reasonable, especially given NYPDH's allowance for medical exemptions. The mother countered, alleging violation of the rights to a medical exemption, to refuse medical treatment, and of parents to make educational decisions. The court dismissed all of these as (1) the policy allowed for medical exemptions, the daughter was just denied; (2) states must balance individual rights of treatment and lives of the public; and (3) parents do not have the right to make educational decisions for all children just because they want it for their own children. A federal trial court in New York found no substantive due process violations but recommended the board work with the plaintiff to find a resolution.

In response to the ongoing COVID-19 pandemic, the Nevada governor issued two emergency executive orders mandating masks in schools.[171] Following the executive orders, a school board implemented masking policies as well, without including parents in the decision-making process. In response to the mandates, several parents filed claims alleging their Ninth and Fourteenth Amendment rights had been violated, as it was their right as parents to make medical decisions for their children. As with other parental rights claims about masking, the federal trial court in Nevada dismissed the claims on the basis that parental rights do not trump the legitimate governmental interest of mitigating the spread of the virus.

Claiming masks are unscientific, unsafe, tantamount to slavery, and unfairly restrain children, parents, representing themselves and their children, unsuccessfully brought suit against their local school board for enforcing the Oregon law mandating statewide masking in public schools.[172] The parents alleged violations of their Oregon and United States constitutional rights and expressed concerns that mandatory masks interfered with their parental rights. The federal trial court in Oregon dismissed the parental rights claims, stating the parents were taking issue with the wrong governmental body as masks were a law, not a board policy. The court also dismissed without prejudice the allegations by the students, since they were represented by their parents, and not by an attorney.

In another case challenging the constitutionality of mask mandates, Pennsylvania parents cited violations of their First, Fifth, and Fourteenth Amendment rights when their school board enforced

---

[171] Branch-Noto v. Sisolak, 576 F. Supp. 3d 790, 405 Educ. L. Rep. 279 (D. Nev. 2021).
[172] Gunter v. N. Wasco Cnty. Sch. Dist. Bd. of Educ., 577 F. Supp. 3d 1141, 405 Educ. L. Rep. 974 (D. Or. 2021).

state mask mandates.[173] A federal trial court in Pennsylvania dismissed all of the parent's claims. In their analysis, the court commented that the plaintiffs mistakenly believed their First Amendment liberty right extended to deciding whether their children wear masks during a pandemic; it does not. Likewise, mask requirements do not inhibit students' property interests in an education as they may still access their education when wearing a mask. The court further noted that the existence of a "property interest" does not mean students and parents may dictate the rules of the school. Lastly, the court determined no due process rights were infringed and no irreparable harm was expected to result from masking.

Masking policies were challenged from a completely different angle in a case heard by a federal trial court in Tennessee.[174] In 2021, the governor of Tennessee issued Executive Order 84 giving parents the right to opt out of school board mask mandates. The families of three medically vulnerable students filed suit claiming the opt-out violated the Americans with Disabilities Act's nondiscrimination clause because exposure to maskless students increased their medically vulnerable children's likelihood of contracting COVID-19. While the local school board did have other safety measures in place, none were as effective in providing a fully-masked educational environment. After issuing a temporary restraining order pausing the implementation of the governor's executive order, the federal trial court sided with the families, finding that universal masking was a reasonable accommodation to protect medically vulnerable students, and any non-medical opt-outs undermined that accommodation.

After parents were granted temporary relief from the school board's mask mandate policies, the Supreme Court of Arkansas ultimately found in favor of the board's mask mandates and chided the trial court for issuing the temporary injunction.[175] Parents argued that the board's mask mandates violated their state constitutional liberty interest in the care, custody, and maintenance of their own children. Using the *Jacobson v. Massachusetts* framework, the courts noted that parental rights might be limited by the state when child welfare is in question, and, given ongoing pandemic health threats, the state had that right regarding masks. The court also stated that the parents failed to prove irreparable

---

[173] Oberheim v. Bason, 565 F. Supp. 3d 607, 402 Educ. L. Rep. 706 (M.D. Pa. 2021).
[174] G.S. ex rel. Schwaigert v. Lee, 560 F. Supp. 3d 1113, 401 Educ. L. Rep. 902 (W.D. Tenn. 2021).
[175] Bentonville Sch. Dist. v. Sitton, 643 S.W.3d 763, 402 Educ. L. Rep. 1230 (Ark. 2022).

harm by the mandates, and the board had the right to implement mask policies for its students. In a concurring opinion, one judge reminded the plaintiff that "parents do not have the constitutional right to micromanage the operations of the school," and if they are unhappy with the district, they still have the right to vote.

The Supreme Court of Kansas reversed a lower court's declaration that the legislation governing COVID-19 mitigation measures for school districts was unconstitutional but declined to express an opinion on its constitutionality.[176] The case was filed by parents in the school district who challenged the board's mask mandate during the pandemic. After the lower court's ruling, the Attorney General appealed. The court first held that the lower court should not even have reached the issue of constitutionality as the bill in question was not applicable here. Under the bill at issue, an action must be filed in court within thirty days of the policy adoption; however, the mask policy was adopted before the bill became law. Thus, the bill was not applicable to their challenges. Further, the doctrine of constitutional avoidance required the trial court to refrain from adjudicating the bill's constitutionality.

At the Attorney General's request, the Supreme Court of South Carolina declared that the city's ordinances mandating the use of facemasks in all K-12 public schools in the city were void because they violated the state legislature's appropriations act.[177] The provision at issue here "set forth the intent of the legislature to prohibit mask mandates funded by the 2021-2022 Appropriations Act in K-12 public schools." The court held that the legislature's policy allowing parents to make the decision of whether their child should wear a facemask to school was within its constitutional boundaries and did not violate the one-subject rule of the state constitution. Therefore, the ordinances were preempted by the appropriations act and were void.

In Illinois, an appellate court vacated and remanded the lower court's issuance of a temporary restraining order (TRO) requiring the school board to refrain from enforcing a mask mandate.[178] Here, parents and guardians filed a petition seeking declaratory relief and a writ of injunction against the school board to bar enforcement of the it's requirement for all students to wear a mask indoors at school. The trial court granted the plaintiffs' TRO to prevent the school from requiring students to wear masks on school property. The appellate

---

[176] Butler v. Shawnee Mission Sch. Dist. Bd. of Educ., 502 P.3d 89, 398 Educ. L. Rep. 1135 (Kan. 2022).
[177] Wilson ex rel. State v. City of Columbia, 863 S.E.2d 456, 395 Educ. L. Rep. 1158 (S.C. 2021).
[178] Lurkins v. Bond Cnty. Cmty. Unit No. 2, 175 N.E.3d 680, 396 Educ. L. Rep. 312 (Ill. App. Ct. 2021).

court held that the TRO should be vacated because the plaintiffs failed to name necessary parties, specifically the governor, the Illinois State Board of Education, and the Illinois Department of Public Health.

Vaccinations

Trying to curb future outbreaks, New York banned all non-medical immunization exemptions for school-age students and significantly limited medical exemptions.[179] When several families applied for medical exemptions for their children under the new law, they were denied multiple times, even with medical evidence indicating that an exemption was appropriate. This resulted in several students being expelled and losing access to services. In response to the denials and disciplinary actions, the families, as well as a non-profit advocacy group, filed a class action suit against the state health department and local school districts challenging New York's medical exemptions requirements as violations of Section 1983 due process and the Rehabilitation Act. After their initial claim was dismissed, the Second Circuit federal appellate court reviewed the case and affirmed the dismissal, stating that families do not have a fundamental right to medical exemptions, the board did not discriminate when applying the new regulation, and the state has a legitimate interest in mitigating the spread of preventable illnesses.

After President Biden announced that his government's "patience is wearing thin," the Department of Health and Human Services (DHHS) mandated near-universal COVID-19 vaccination and masking for all Head Start locations across the country as a condition to receive funding.[180] As this mandate ran counter to Texas state orders, adhering to the DHHS requirement would result in the loss of educational access for hundreds of programs and thousands of students in Texas. The State of Texas and several school boards in the state filed suit alleging the DHHS acted illegally as the Department did not have the permission of Congress to initiate this new rule, and the mandates, because they ran counter to state orders, violated Texas's sovereign rights, including the right to serve as *parens partriae*. A federal trial court, in reviewing the evidence, sided with the plaintiffs and issued a preliminary injunction preventing enforcement of the DHHS rule.

---

[179] Goe v. Zucker, 43 F.4th 19, 405 Educ. L. Rep. 800 (2d Cir. 2022).
[180] Tex. v. Becerra, 577 F. Supp. 3d, 527, 405 Educ l. Rep. 906 (N.D. Tex. 2021).

COVID-19 Learning Models

Tired of pandemic-related restrictions, fourteen California families and one student at a private school proactively filed suit after the state issued the "2020-21 Reopening Framework," which provided guidance on when in-person instruction was safe and permissible, stating any further closures violated their children's constitutional and statutory rights, not their parental rights.[181] After a federal trial court in California dismissed the case as moot and an attempt at creating an "insurance policy," the families appealed citing a violation of their Fourteenth Amendment due process rights. The Ninth Circuit federal appellate court reviewed the case and, referencing similar findings by the First, Third, Fourth, and Seventh Circuits, affirmed the case as moot.

In yet another pandemic-related case, parents seeking to compel school boards to offer full-time, in-person instruction in lieu of the current COVID-19 hybrid/remote learning model appealed a judgment denying their requests for a temporary restraining order and preliminary injunction.[182] After the defendant boards withdrew policies pertaining to hybrid/remote learning, the expiration of state executive orders that had formed the basis of the policy, and the replacement of the statutory scheme that initially permitted the governor to issue the order, the appellate court in New York declared the appeal moot and vacated the judgment.

First Amendment

Expression

A middle school student and a high school student in Wisconsin challenged their school board's dress code which prohibited them from wearing t-shirts depicting firearms and a message in support of the right to bear arms.[183] A federal trial court ruled in favor of school administrators, consolidating the cases and applying the most lenient standard, speech in a nonpublic forum, to the restriction. The court admitted an expert witness report on the "weapons effect" theory that images of firearms can encourage aggressive behavior. On appeal, the Seventh Circuit declared the middle school student's challenge moot as the student had moved on to high school. The court

---

[181] Brach v. Newsom, 38 F.4th 6, 404 Educ. L. Rep. 424 (9th Cir. 2022).
[182] Hensley v. Williamsville Cent. Sch. Dist., 170 N.Y.S.3d 412, 405 Educ. L. Rep. 509 (N.Y. App. Div. 2022).
[183] N.J. by Jacob v. Sonnabend, 37 F.4th 412, 403 Educ. L. Rep. 493 (7th Cir. 2022).

applied the *Tinker* "substantial disruption" standard to the high school student's case, likening the student's shirt to the black armbands worn in *Tinker* as an expression of political speech. The court determined that school officials had the burden to show that wearing the t-shirt would have led them to "'forecast substantial disruption of or material interference with school activities' or the invasion of the rights of others." The appellate court vacated the trial court's judgment and remanded for further proceedings.

In Colorado, a high school student posted an anti-Semitic picture and caption on Snapchat while at an off-campus thrift store with friends after school on a Friday.[184] A couple of hours later, he deleted the post but not before at least one person took a picture of the post and shared it with parents, who then notified the school and several community organizations. When the student arrived at school on Monday, he was detained by an administrator and suspended. Two days later, he was recommended for expulsion and ultimately expelled; however, at no point in the process was he given an opportunity to defend himself. The school board contended that the student was able to defend himself during the expulsion hearing. However, the Tenth Circuit federal appellate court found this to be insufficient as the student had not been afforded due process up to that point. In this post-*Mahanoy* ruling, the court also noted that the board could not prove substantial disruption to the school, thereby violating the student's First Amendment right to free speech. The request by the administrator for qualified immunity was remanded to the lower court.

The mother of a Missouri seventh grader, who was suspended from playing volleyball when the school learned that she had violated the school's alcohol policy through Snapchat, claimed that the Snapchat posts of alcohol usage and its effects by both mother and daughter were protected First Amendment speech and requested injunctive relief.[185] Prior to the suspension, the student posted a video of herself on Snapchat consuming alcohol while at home, and her mother posted a subsequent video after finding the student unconscious and taking her to the hospital for treatment for alcohol poisoning. As the suspension was due to the daughter's conduct, not her words, and her conduct was illegal and not expressive in nature, a federal trial court sided with the school board and dismissed the plaintiff's claims. Contrasting the board's policy with the one in *Mahanoy*, the court also found that the board's

---

[184] C1.G ex rel. C.G. v. Siegfried, 38 F.4th 1270, 404 Educ. L. Rep. 516 (10th Cir. 2022).
[185] Cheadle ex rel. N.C. v. N. Platte R-1 Sch. Dist., 555 F. Supp. 3d 726, 401 Educ. L. Rep. 339 (W.D. Mo. 2021).

alcohol policy was reasonable and served the government's interests in deterring underage drinking.

In a third case involving off-campus Snapchat posts, a high school student and self-identified aspiring rapper posted several messages that alluded to threats against his school, and after being suspended for the remainder of the year, he filed suit in federal court.[186] Upon report of the threatening messages, police declined to arrest the student, but the school board suspended him for five days while awaiting a disciplinary hearing. The hearing resulted in a suspension for the remainder of the school year. The student appealed this decision to the state commission and then filed this suit in federal court. The school board, in turn, filed a motion to dismiss citing collateral estoppel and seeking qualified immunity, noting the behavior's substantial disruption to the school. In reviewing the board's motion, a federal trial court in New York found insufficient evidence that the Snapchats posed a substantial disruption but recognized there may be more evidence to support their actions. Regardless, the court denied the board's motion and its request for qualified immunity, noting that free speech is well-litigated. Splitting the decision, the court did grant dismissal of the student's *Monnell* claim since he failed to provide sufficient evidence in his appeal.

Fourth Amendment

The Fifth Circuit, in a case from Texas, reversed the denial of the defendant school resource officer's motion for summary judgment and rendered judgment for the officer.[187] Here, a student and his mother brought a § 1983 excessive force claim against the school district and school resource officer after the officer used a stun gun on the student. The officer claimed qualified immunity, but a plaintiff may overcome qualified immunity if they can show "(1) that the official violated a statutory or constitutional right, and (2) that the right was 'clearly established' at the time of the challenged conduct." The appellate court held that the plaintiff failed to demonstrate a clearly established right because the state law on the Fourth Amendment's role in school discipline is inconsistent at best. Therefore, the officer was entitled to qualified immunity.

---

[186] Casler v. W. Irondequoit Sch. Dist., 563 F. Supp. 3d 60, 402 Educ. L. Rep. 223 (W.D.N.Y. 2021).
[187] J. W. v. Paley, 860 F. App'x 926, 395 Educ. L. Rep. 524 (5th Cir. 2021).

Parents of four children with special needs filed a Section 1983 action against their children's teacher and school administrators alleging deprivation of substantive due process and unreasonable seizure under the Fourth Amendment.[188] The teacher's actions included holding students in a "little room" and "calm-down corner" to discipline them, "pushing a student into a swimming pool, and pinning a student down to strip his clothes off." The teacher moved for summary judgment on the basis of qualified immunity. The federal trial court in South Dakota dismissed the claims against the school administrators and denied the teacher's motion. On appeal, the Eighth Circuit federal appellate court held that the teacher was not entitled to qualified immunity for unreasonable seizures in that the children, through their behaviors, had posed no imminent risk of harm either to themselves or to others. The court also ruled that the physical and verbal abuse the teacher inflicted upon the children did not meet the conscience-shocking standard for violations of substantive due process.

In Ohio, a federal trial court granted summary judgment in favor of the defendant school board, principal, teacher, and classroom aide.[189] The plaintiff, an elementary school student diagnosed with Attention Deficit Hyperactivity Disorder (ADHD), Oppositional Defiance Disorder, and Generalized Anxiety Disorder, brought suit against the defendants alleging violations of the Americans with Disabilities Act (ADA), the Rehabilitation Act, and Section 1983 stemming from an incident where he was physically restrained on the floor in the prone position. The plaintiffs claimed this constituted excessive force and an unlawful seizure in violation of the Fourth Amendment. The defendants argued they were entitled to qualified immunity. Qualified immunity shields government officials "from liability for civil damages insofar as their conduct does not violate clearly established statutory or constitutional rights of which a reasonable person would have known." The court held that educators restraining a student to prevent him from injuring himself or others were not knowingly violating a constitutional right. Thus, the defendants were entitled to qualified immunity.

The juvenile court's adjudication of a juvenile defendant for possessing and intending to distribute marijuana was reversed and remanded by an appellate court in Colorado.[190] The defendant was a student, and the marijuana was discovered during a search of his

---

[188] Doe v. Aberdeen Sch. Dist., 42 F.4th 883, 405 Ed. Law Rep. 773 (8th Cir. 2022).
[189] D.M. v. Bd. of Educ. Toledo Pub. Schs., 575 F.Supp.3d 897, 405 Educ. L. Rep. 206 (N.D. Ohio 2021).
[190] People in Interest of C.C-S., 503 P.3d 152, 399 Educ. L. Rep. 998 (Colo. App. 2021).

backpack at school based on an anonymous tip that he had a firearm a month prior. The defendant refused the search and attempted to leave, but officers did not allow him to leave and searched his backpack. The defendant argued that the evidence of the marijuana should be suppressed because of the illegal seizure of his person and unreasonable search and seizure of his backpack in violation of the Fourth Amendment. The appellate court agreed, finding that an anonymous tip alone was not sufficient to establish reasonable suspicion for the search. Additionally, the information provided in the tip was stale because it was a month old and had been erased. Thus, the evidence of the marijuana found in the search should have been suppressed.

Abuse and Harassment

Employee-on-Student

The mother of a child diagnosed with autism spectrum disorder filed suit against district officials for negligence in failing to report alleged mistreatment by the child's teacher to North Carolina state authorities or to take corrective action to protect the child.[191] The suit was filed after the teacher pled guilty to misdemeanor assault on a disabled person when a therapist lodged a report with the sheriff's office upon learning other students had experienced mistreatment. A district employee who had witnessed the teacher's behavior, which included placing the child in a trashcan and forcing him to stay there, reported the information to school officials. A federal trial court in North Carolina concluded the school board had a ministerial duty to report the abuse; however, the Fourth Circuit federal appellate court reversed the trial court's decision, granting officials latitude in staff supervision and in the operation of district schools. The decision on appeal distinguished between discretionary duties such as employee supervision, where, according to the Fourth Circuit, district officials' actions fell, and ministerial duties, for which there could be exceptions affording immunity based upon district officials' acting with malice. No malicious intent to harm was determined.

A student sued her Wisconsin school district under Title IX alleging she suffered repeated sexual abuse by a school security

---

[191] R.A. v. Johnson, 36 F.4th 537, 403 Educ. L. Rep. 185 (4th Cir. 2022).

assistant.[192] A federal trial court dismissed the suit, noting the assistant, having regular contact with students, was observed by the school's positive behavior support coach discouraging inappropriate plaintiff-initiated physical interaction. Additionally, the evidence speaks to the principal's conversation setting guidelines for the assistant after becoming aware of concerns about his student interactions, the student's silence regarding details of the alleged abuse, and what the student alleged was grooming behavior by the assistant. The Seventh Circuit federal appellate court, acknowledging the school board had not acted with "deliberate indifference" when receiving notice of the alleged abuse, affirmed the lower court's decision, which granted summary judgment for the school board because no reasonable jury would find that the conduct of which the principal had actual knowledge amounted to sexual harassment or discrimination under Title IX. The court further held that districts and circuit courts, when considering Title IX institutional liability, need to apply the "deliberate indifference" framework established in *Gebser* and *Davis* "along clear and workable lines, ever mindful of the delicate educational settings in which facts unfold."

An appellate court in New Jersey affirmed the lower court's grant of summary judgment in favor of the defendant school bus company and township school district on the Law Against Discrimination (LAD) claim.[193] The issue here was whether LAD applied to a claim involving a sexual predator's assault of a young girl on the school bus while employed as a bus aide. LAD bars discrimination based on gender and age, among other protected classes, in various settings. The court found that LAD did not apply here because "there was no evidence that the predator's compulsive and repetitive behavior was the result of any proven intention to discriminate specifically against young women." In other words, the predator's actions were based on compulsion and not the victim's age or gender, thus discrimination was not involved, and LAD was not applicable.

Dating back to December 1966 through October 1977, when the claimant was a minor enrolled at a residential state school for blind students, the now-adult plaintiff alleged sexual abuse and assault by a teacher. This appeal, filed under the Child Victims Act in New York against the state and certain state agencies, concerned tolling

---

[192] C.S. v. Madison Metro. Sch. Dist., 34 F.4th 536, 548, 402 Educ. L. Rep. 578 (7th Cir. 2022).
[193] C.V. by and through C.V. v. Waterford Twp. Bd. of Educ., 277 A.3d 507, 405 Educ. L. Rep. 1058 (N.J. Super. Ct. App. Div. 2022).

the statute of limitations.[194] The court granted the defendant's motion to dismiss the claims in part. Regarding the statute of limitations on cases filed or commenced by childhood victims of sexual abuse, the court noted the statutory deadline had been met by virtue of modifications to state court operations limited during the COVID-19 pandemic. Given the time lapse between filing and the alleged incidents, the court determined it understandable that the claimant might not be able to provide exact dates. The court also found that both the claimant's reference to the abuses having occurred on school premises and the claimant's description of the nature of the alleged sexual abuse were sufficient for the state to proceed with its investigation, and the argument could not be made the teacher was "acting within the scope of his employment" when the abuse took place.

An appellate court in North Carolina dismissed the appeal of the children's home operators after the trial court entered an ex parte order directing the disclosure of non-joined, third-party records of alleged child sexual abuse.[195] Here, the plaintiff alleged that she was sexually abused by operators of the children's home that she lived in as a minor and moved for the production of confidential criminal investigation records regarding alleged child sexual abuse by any employee of the children's home against any minor that lived there. The plaintiff did not serve the defendants with this motion. The trial court entered the proposed order ex parte, and the defendants appealed. The appellate court held that the defendants failed to sufficiently allege that their substantial rights were violated because they were not the subject of any criminal investigation records being sought, therefore, they were not entitled to any notice.

In another case asserting negligence, the mother of an Oregon high school student filed a claim against the school district after her son was sexually assaulted by one of his teachers while at his cousin's home.[196] The teacher was house-sitting at the cousin's house. The mother alleged this would have been preventable if not for the fact that district officials failed to investigate and report rumors about inappropriate relationships between the teacher and male students. The courts disagreed with the mother's claim, with the appellate court in Oregon affirming the decision of the lower court granting summary judgment to the district on the basis that the teacher's sexual assault of the student was not foreseeable. As to

---

[194] M.C. v. State, 163 N.Y.S.3d 741, 401 Educ. L. Rep. 545 (N.Y. Ct. Cl. 2022).
[195] Fore v. W. N.C. Conf. of United Methodist Church, 875 S.E.2d 32, 405 Educ. L. Rep. 1181 (N.C. Ct. App. 2022).
[196] F.T. v. W. Linn-Wilsonville Sch. Dist., 509 P.3d 655, 402 Educ. L. Rep. 1170 (Or. Ct. App. 2022).

the question of where the duty of supervision begins and ends, the court indicated the school's duty would end and the parents' begin at the point when parents resume custodial control beyond the school day, which would include entrusting their child to the supervision of another after school hours.

Student-on-Student

The Fourth Circuit federal appellate court affirmed a federal trial court in Virginia's grant of the plaintiff's motion to proceed under a pseudonym on her Title IX, § 1983, and state law claims for sexual harassment and sexual abuse.[197] The plaintiff is a former student bringing suit against the school, teachers, guidance counselors, school officials, and male students after she was repeatedly "raped, sexually assaulted, sexually harassed, terrorized, extorted, bullied, and threatened with death by other students" while in middle school, and the school refused to take any corrective action. She filed these claims under a pseudonym "to protect her privacy and health," which the lower court allowed, and the defendants appealed. The Fourth Circuit affirmed the lower court's decision, holding that filing a claim under a pseudonym was immaterial to the Article III case or controversy requirement. Thus, the plaintiff was allowed to proceed under the pseudonym.

A consolidated appeal involved the parents of two female students who attended different high schools in the same Tennessee district.[198] The parents filed suit under Title IX and Equal Protection alleging the schools failed to take proper action after other students videotaped their children engaging in unwelcome sexual acts with male students on school premises, and the videos circulated among students. The parents claimed the school board has a responsibility to address harassment both before and after it occurs. Asserting widespread district harassment, the defendants cited past precedent according to the *Kollaritsch* standard requiring a student to suffer more than one incident for the board to take responsibility. The Sixth Circuit vacated a federal trial court's summary judgment for the school board, reasoning that immunizing the board unless a victim is subjected to more than one incident would defeat Title IX's intended purpose and remanded the case back to the trial court to reconsider under the deliberate indifference standard. The trial

---

[197] B.R. v. F.C.S.B., 17 F.4th 485, 396 Educ. L. Rep. 90 (4th Cir. 2021).
[198] Doe ex rel. Doe #2 v. Metro. Gov't of Nashville & Davidson Cnty., Tenn., 35 F.4th 459, 403 Educ. L. Rep. 88 (6th Cir. 2022).

court granted summary judgment to the school board with respect to both girls' "after" claims. In response, the school board filed a petition for rehearing *en banc* by the Sixth Circuit, which was denied.

The parent of a kindergarten student filed Title IX, Section 1983, and state law claims alleging her daughter was sexually assaulted and harassed by a male classmate.[199] After the parent notified the principal, who unsuccessfully put a safety plan in place to separate the child from her alleged offender, the parent ultimately enrolled her child in a private school and sought counseling for the child. A federal trial court in Illinois viewed the school board's failure to properly implement the safety plan as "deliberate indifference," reasoning that merely having a plan without enforcing it is not enough to comply with Title IX's requirement for a school to reasonably respond to the harassment. The court dismissed the parent's equal protection claims on the basis that the facts provided did not reveal any discriminatory intent on the part of the board. The court also dismissed the parent's *Monell* claim on the basis that the school board's action did not demonstrate a failure to act or "deliberate indifference" to the child's constitutional rights. The court allowed the parent to file an amended complaint as to state law claims within a prescribed deadline. In another federal trial court decision from Illinois, parents filed Title IX, Section 1983, and state tort law claims alleging their child, while a kindergartener, had been bullied and physically and sexually assaulted by students in his class and in an after-school supervised care program, as well as by a sixth grader on the bus transporting him to and from the after-school program.[200] School officials intervened once aware, including moving the child to the front of the bus, though parents alleged the interventions exacerbated the problem as the older students, members of the student bus patrol, positioned themselves near their son on the bus, hiding their abuse from the driver's view. The court determined this situation did not merit statutory exceptions under Section 1983 for alleged failure to protect the child. Concerning Title IX, the court determined that after having actual knowledge of the harassment and abuse, school officials were not deliberately indifferent to it, nor was there evidence of any retaliatory motive. The court allowed state negligence claims to proceed based upon the facts established, including the duty to

---

[199] Moore v. Freeport Cmty. Unit Sch. Dist. No. 145, 570 F. Supp. 3d 601, 403 Educ. L. Rep. 786 (N.D. Ill. 2021).
[200] Doe v. Sch. Dist. U-46, 557 F. Supp. 3d 860, 401 Educ. L. Rep. 465 (N.D. Ill. 2021).

protect and the duty to train educators and administrators to prevent sexual assault of students entrusted to their care.

A Maryland school board's potential negligence was the focus of Title IX, Section 1983, and state law claims by parents of a female high school student shot and killed by a male student at school.[201] The male student pressured the female student to engage in sexual activity, harassing her using increasingly violent physical abuse at school and on social media. The plaintiffs allegedly informed their daughter's teacher of concerns, but the board and teacher claimed ignorance. The board also contended a teacher was not an "appropriate official" for reporting purposes. The federal trial court in Maryland disagreed with the plaintiff, finding neither a special relationship between the board and the female student nor a district-created danger to her under Section 1983. However, the court recognized a special relationship based upon *in loco parentis* requiring the board to exercise "reasonable care" to protect students from harm, including assuming a duty to take precautionary measures upon receiving a threat of violence potentially compromising safety on school premises. The state's wrongful death statute leaves the board further responsible for loss of support and/or other benefits to the female student's family since she died by virtue of the board's alleged negligence.

Parents of an elementary student who died by suicide after being bullied for years at school filed Title IX, Section 1983, and wrongful death and survival claims in a Pennsylvania federal trial court.[202] The student, identified as having disabilities, also had a known history of anxiety, depression, and reactive disruptive behavior, which placed him at risk of harming himself. Although the school officials were aware of his history and the physical and verbal abuse, they punished the student for his response to the bullying rather than those accused. Under Section 1983, the court found the board's actions made the child more vulnerable to the toxic environment at school, thus creating the danger resulting in his suicide. Under Title IX, the court found that the plaintiffs successfully demonstrated the board's apparent disregard of on-going gender-stereotyped harassment and deprived their son of educational opportunities and school activities. Regarding the plaintiffs' claims for wrongful death and survival, the court found the board was entitled to immunity, with officials' actions not rising to the level of negligence despite

---

[201] Willey v. Bd. of Educ. of St. Mary's Cnty., 557 F. Supp. 3d 645, 401 Educ. Rep. 436 (D. Md. 2021).
[202] Spruill v. Sch. Dist. of Phila., 569 F. Supp. 3d 253, 403 Educ. L. Rep. 710 (E.D. Pa. 2021).

their intentional and willful handling of the bullying and harassment faced by the child.

The Supreme Court of Alabama reversed and remanded the lower court's dismissal of the plaintiff student's parent's complaint with prejudice.[203] In this case, the parents of a student brought suit against the superintendent, principal, county board of education, and members of the board of education after the student was sexually assaulted at school. The defendants sought and were granted two continuances of the hearing on their motion to dismiss. The plaintiffs requested one continuance, which was ignored, and did not show up when the hearing was held. At this point, the lower court dismissed the complaint with prejudice. The appellate court noted that previous decisions affirming similar dismissals involved flagrant behavior by the plaintiff. Thus, the appellate court held that, because there was not a clear record of delay or willful behavior by the plaintiffs, dismissal with prejudice was improper.

Discrimination

Racial

The Tenth Circuit affirmed the federal trial court in Kansas's denial of the coach's motion for summary judgment on the student's racial discrimination claims under Title VI and the Equal Protection Clause.[204] An African-American student sued her former coach, high school principal, and school district after the coach repeatedly displayed racial prejudice against her and encouraged students on the team to do the same. The coach argued that she was entitled to qualified immunity because she didn't discriminate against the student or cause her to be denied an educational benefit, but the court disagreed. First, the court found that a jury could reasonably find that the coach treated the student differently than similarly situated, non-African-American students. Further, the court concluded that the coach's conduct resulted in the loss of an educational benefit to the student, specifically, the student had to miss classes because of her blatant exclusion from the team. Finally, the student's right to equal protection was clearly established as a constitutional right at the time of the coach's violation. Therefore, the coach was subject to liability for racial discrimination.

---

[203] S.C. v. Autauga Cnty. Bd. of Educ., 325 So.3d 793, 395 Educ. L. Rep. 1176 (Ala. 2020).
[204] Sturdivant v. Fine, 22 F.4th 930, 398 Educ. L. Rep. 49 (10th Cir. 2022).

Since the 1970s, one county in Maryland has attempted different measures to ensure racial integration. Prior attempts have either not produced the desired results or have been challenged in court. In 2019, in another attempt at increased diversity, the county implemented a field test requirement for magnet school admissions. A parent group, the Association for Education Fairness, sued on behalf of its members stating that the field test policy was discriminatory in nature and violated the rights of Asian-American students, as they attended high-achieving magnet schools in greater percentages.[205] Shortly after the lawsuit was filed, Montgomery County again changed its admissions policies followed by a motion to dismiss challenging the Association's standing as well as the ripeness of the suit. The federal trial court, in reviewing the case, found that the Association did have standing as at least one member was affected by the policies and that the case was valid, thus denying the dismissal. It further ordered a review using strict scrutiny as the field test because, while on the surface the policy was race-neutral, it appeared to be implemented in a discriminatory manner. The amended complaint to the case was dismissed as moot in July 2022.

Sexual

Female students at a North Carolina public charter school asserted that the school's dress code, requiring them to wear skirts conforming with the school's "traditional" values, violated Title IX and the Equal Protection Clause by denying them the opportunity to fully participate in their education.[206] A federal trial court held that the skirt requirement violated the Equal Protection Clause, but that dress codes are not subject to Title IX. A panel of the Fourth Circuit federal appellate court reversed the trial court's judgment on both claims. On appeal *en banc*, the appellate court reasserted that charter schools operate as public schools, thus subject to state authority. The court further held that the skirt requirement perpetuated gender stereotypes, thus violating the Equal Protection Clause. Noting that dress is not specifically a Title IX exception, the appellate court remanded the case to the trial court for an evidentiary hearing on this claim. A lengthy dissent challenged the court's reasoning that charter schools are state actors, asserting they should be exempt from statutes and regulations applicable to local school boards when operated by private, non-profit corporations.

---

[205] Ass'n for Educ. Fairness v. Montgomery Cnty. Bd. of Educ., 560 F. Supp. 3d 929, 401 Educ. L. Rep. 874 (D. Md. 2021).
[206] Peltier v. Charter Day Sch., 37 F.4th 104, 120, 403 Educ. L. Rep. 436 (4th Cir. 2022).

A high school's Gay-Straight Alliance sought a preliminary injunction against the school board for its refusal to allow the organization to publicize its activities, including fundraising, or to be listed as an organization in the school's student handbook in the same manner that other school organizations were allowed.[207] A federal trial court in Indiana ruled that the suit was likely to succeed under the Equal Access Act and granted the group's request for a preliminary injunction using the *Mergens* definition of non-curriculum-related student groups. *Mergens* identified four situations where a student group may be directly related to a school's curriculum: when participation is a course requirement, if participation results in academic credit, if the group's subject matter concerns school courses as a whole, and/or if the group's subject matter is or will be taught as a regular course. Observing that another one of the school's clubs, the Outdoor Adventure Club, deemed curriculum-related, actually failed to meet the *Mergens* conditions, and on the basis of overall inconsistencies in the school's classification of student groups, the court found in favor of the Gay-Straight Alliance.

The Supreme Court of Wisconsin determined the right to anonymity was central to an appeal by parents distraught over a board policy they believed interfered with their constitutional right to parent by excluding them from knowing their child may be transitioning to a different gender identity.[208] The parents sought to use pseudonyms for anyone except the court and their own attorneys, fearing leaked information could compromise safety. Determining this request too narrow, the trial court authorized a protective order to disclose for other attorneys and staff to sign. The parents sought an interlocutory appeal, which was granted. Failing to obtain injunctive relief, the parents unsuccessfully appealed to the state supreme court, which determined the parents provided no evidence to support confidentiality fears and agreed that knowing the parents' and students' identities could reveal unique existing circumstances potentially important to resolving policy concerns. The appellate court upheld the order allowing parents to proceed anonymously without withholding their identities from opposing attorneys and remanded to adjudicate the parents' policy claims. The dissent reprimanded the majority for "choosing not to address

---

[207] Pendleton Heights Gay-Straight All. v. S. Madison Cmty. Sch. Corp., 577 F. Supp. 3d 927, 405 Educ. L. Rep. 967 (S.D.Ind. 2021).
[208] Doe 1 v. Madison Metro. Sch. Dist., 976 N.W.2d 584, 404 Ed. Law Rep. 885 (Wis. 2022).

the critical issue on which this case turns: the constitutional right of parents to raise their children as they see fit"

After their daughter was sexually assaulted by a bus aide while being transported on a school bus, parents of a five-year-old filed suit under New Jersey's Law Against Discrimination (LAD). [209] The aide was criminally charged with aggravated sexual assault and pled guilty as a compulsive and repetitive sex offender. In this appeal, claiming negligence by the school bus company and the school board under the LAD, the court ruled that the LAD did not apply, affirming summary judgment for the defendants. The court's decision was based on the predator's history of abusing both boys and girls, resulting in actions motivated by his pedophilia and not intended against the victim because of her sex.

School Enrollment

Contracts with Private Schools

Parents filed suit against a private boarding school for children with learning disabilities after the school expelled their son determining he was no longer a "fit" with their program.[210] The parents maintained that the contract they signed with the school lacked mutuality and included a substantially unconscionable arbitration clause, making it unenforceable. The trial court found the arbitration clause, but not the contract as a whole, substantively unconscionable and unenforceable on the basis that the contract allowed the school to litigate claims but limited the parents only to arbitration. However, the appellate court in Illinois found that, even if contractual mutuality did not exist regarding arbitration, the parents paying the tuition in full and the school providing specific services for their child provided consideration for the contract. The appellate court remanded the case for the trial court to determine the enforceability of the arbitration clause, allowing that the court "may look beyond the provisions in the arbitration clause to inform its decision" and leaving open the potential for an evidentiary hearing should either party request it.

---

[209] C.V. by and through C.V. v. Waterford Twp. Bd. of Educ., 277 A.3d 507, 405 Ed. Law Rep. 1058 (N.J. Super. Ct. App. Div. 2022).
[210] Hartz v. Brehm Prep. Sch., 183 N.E.3d 172, 401 Educ. L. Rep. 579 (Ill. App. Ct. 2021).

Residency

During a normal review of student residencies, a district business specialist flagged the plaintiff's family address as suspect.[211] After an extensive investigation, including the use of a private investigator who watched the family's movements at night, the school board determined that the family lived in a different school district than where their child attended school. In their suit against the board, the family demanded full disclosure of the board's evidence and supplied some evidence to the contrary, such as mail at the in-district address. In looking at the evidence, the court sided with the board, finding the family's evidence was insufficient and pointing toward an attempt by the family to gain tuition-free access to an education in a district other than the one in which the family resided.

Trespass

A suspended student in Florida contested his trespass charges on the grounds that he did not willfully violate "no trespass" orders.[212] The student had been suspended the day prior and sent home with an exclusion letter requiring his mother to contact the school before he could return. Instead of contacting the school, she dropped him off at school. An appellate court dismissed the student's claim that he did not willfully violate the order, stating that that there was no statutory requirement that the trespass must be intentional to be a violation. Additionally, he did not have a "legitimate business interest" to be on school grounds as he was still under the trespass order.

Truancy

A middle school assistant principal, who served as the attendance manager, filed a Child Requiring Assistance petition with the Massachusetts court after numerous other efforts to improve the attendance of a habitually truant twelve-year-old caught in the middle of a custody battle failed.[213] The youth, represented by an attorney, motioned to dismiss the petition asserting that the assistant principal, who was not an attorney, was illegally practicing law and did not have the authority to file a legal

---

[211] Gwozdz v. Bd. of Educ. of Park Ridge-Niles Sch. Dist. No. 64, 189 N.E.3d 487, 404 Educ. L. Rep. 857 (Ill. App. Ct. 2021).
[212] X.B. v. State, 337 So.3d 99, 402 Educ. L. Rep. 1245 (Fla. Dist. Ct. App. 2021).
[213] Lexington Pub. Sch. v. K.S., 183 N.E.3d 372, 401 Educ. L. Rep. 605 (Mass. 2022).

petition. The juvenile court disagreed, and the state supreme court of Massachusetts affirmed, stating that the truancy procedures can be initiated by anyone, including parents, and requiring schools to engage an attorney for every truant child is an undue burden on school boards trying to meet their legal obligations.

Discipline

Due Process

A New York student and her parent appealed the decision of the trial court to dismiss their case alleging the student was denied procedural due process and subjected to emotional distress in the handling of her suspension from school.[214] The appellate court affirmed the decision of the lower court because the facts revealed that the student, when suspended, had been given a hearing with counsel, including the opportunity to present and cross-examine witnesses, and that the suspension had been cleared from her record after a successful administrative appeal.

In North Carolina, a middle school student took a female classmate's phone, securing a personal photo of her that was on the phone.[215] The student then shared this photo with three male friends, all of whom threatened to further share it if the female classmate did not buy them food and other items. Upon investigation by the school resource officer, the student was charged with and found guilty of extortion. The student appealed, stating the conviction was fatally flawed because the court never named the victim by her legal name, a violation of his rights to be clearly apprised of his charges, and that it was not extortion or a true threat since he did not threaten physical violence. The court rejected his appeal, stating exact identity is unnecessary in cases of extortion as long as there is sufficient explanation of the alleged conduct. The court also dismissed the student's violent true threat claim since that argument was not mentioned during the initial trial. However, the appellate court found the trial court had not provided sufficient written proof of the findings, thus, the case and the adjudication order were vacated and remanded back to the original court.

---

[214] A.R. v. City of N.Y., 170 N.Y.S.3d 180, 405 Educ. L. Rep. 494 (N.Y. App. Div. 2022).
[215] Matter of J.A.D., 872 S.E.2d 374, 402 Educ. L. Rep. 1206 (N.C. Ct. App. 2022).

Criminal Proceedings

An appellate court in California reversed the trial court's findings regarding a juvenile who was adjudicated a ward of the court for allegedly possessing a stun gun on school grounds.[216] During an altercation with another student, the juvenile pulled "a pink rectangular device with two protruding antennas" that produced a spark when turned on from her bag; the other student believed it to be a taser. The principal was notified, and a school resource officer (SRO) confiscated the device. The SRO testified that he identified the device as a stun gun with unknown voltage and originally opined that it likely could not immobilize a person, though he later changed this opinion. The juvenile appealed the lower court's adjudication of her as a ward of the court, arguing that there was insufficient evidence that her device could immobilize a person and no evidence of its charge. The appellate court agreed, finding that there was insufficient evidence to establish that her device was capable of immobilizing a person as required by state law.

In Indiana, a juvenile posted an image to a friend's Snapchat of a cartoon character holding two handguns with text warning people not to come to school on a certain day.[217] An appellate court held that there was sufficient evidence to establish that the juvenile meant to threaten students to engage in conduct against their will and to refrain from attending school using social media, which supported his adjudication for intimidation as a level 6 felony. Specifically, the juvenile argued that the state could not prove, beyond a reasonable doubt, that she acted with the intent to make students engage in conduct against their will because she considered it a joke. However, the court noted that intent does not require the speaker to actually intend to carry out the threat, but "whether he intends it to place the victim in fear of bodily harm or death." Because it could be reasonably inferred that posting such an image would lead students to avoid school on that day in fear of a school shooting, there was sufficient evidence to establish intent.

Injury Damages Under Insurance Law

A high school student sought damages for injuries she allegedly sustained while riding a school bus.[218] When the bus drove over a

---

[216] In re M.S., 285 Cal.Rptr.3d 661, 396 Educ. L. Rep. 273 (Cal. Ct. App. 2021).
[217] Matter of K.Y., 175 N.E.3d 820, 396 Educ. L. Rep. 317 (Ind. Ct. App. 2021).
[218] Tully v. Kenmore-Tonawanda Union Free Sch. Dist., 171 N.Y.S.3d 693, 405 Educ. L. Rep. 1154 (N.Y. App. Div. 2022).

large bump, she was lifted out of her seat and struck her head on a bar located above the emergency exit door. The appellate court in New York ruled that any injuries she allegedly sustained were neither permanent nor serious and did not merit damages under insurance law as she failed to provide objective proof that her activities after the incident were curtailed at school, at home, or at her job.

Conclusion

While some cases this year addressed questions easily settled, as in the truancy and residency cases, others touched on much deeper issues, calling into question societal expectations and beliefs about educational equity and parental involvement. Cases that centered on district racial equity initiatives and on LGBTQIA+ rights and gender equity have not yet been fully settled. Several have been appealed to the Supreme Court or remanded back for further consideration.

One such case, the *Peltier* case, has been appealed to the United States Supreme Court and remains a horizon issue as at least four Supreme Court justices have requested advice from the Solicitor General prior to the Court's granting certiorari. While the Solicitor General's advice is not binding on the Court, such a request is "often a sign that the underlying case has the potential for great impact or the disruption of how the government administers programs – like public education."[219] Regardless of the outcome, further review of *Peltier's* handling of gender discrimination, as well as the issue of charter schools as state actors, will likely resonate with other cases in 2023. As state Educational Savings Accounts and voucher programs gain traction,[220] whether a charter school, when receiving state funding, is a state actor, or whether support from a for-profit corporation grants a license for it to operate as a private school, may become significant. If charter schools are treated differently, would such a distinction release a charter school from statutory obligations applying to traditional public schools, which would include protections afforded, for example, under Title IX and the IDEA?

---

[219] Tressa Pankovits, With Separation of Church and State on the Line, Supreme Court Makes an Unexpected Move, Realclear Educ. (Feb. 6, 2023), https://www.realcleareducation.com/articles/2023/02/06/with_separation_of_church_and_state_on_the_line_supreme_court_makes_an_unexpected_move__110817.html.

[220] Ben Chapman, School Vouchers Gain Momentum as States Look at Learning Options, The Wall Street J. (Feb. 3, 2023), https://www.wsj.com/articles/school-vouchers-gain-momentum-as-states-look-at-learning-options-11675400474.

The *Doe 1 v. Madison Metropolitan School District* case involving a school policy providing protections for students identifying as transgender, non-binary, and gender-expansive, which the summary in this section addresses as the parents' appeal for privacy, is another such case as it was dismissed by the trial court on remand. The dismissal was based on the fact that the only plaintiff remaining in the case could not show evidence that guidance from the board would cause individual harm. However, the questions at the root of the case remain undecided, as the remaining plaintiff's appeal for this dismissal is under consideration by the appellate court of Wisconsin as of January 2023.[221]

As in *Doe 1,* a clear pattern emerged this year of parents' attempting to affirm constitutional protections and guarantees of "parental rights," with courts pushing back when the claim for these rights conflicted with legitimate state action. While the rights of minor students are often arbitrated through parental action, parents in and of themselves do not necessarily maintain rights in the process, as many of the COVID-19 masking cases highlight.

Looking ahead, questions concerning the extent to which parents may assert their influence in determining policies and practices in public schools are likely to continue with an anticipated focus on newly emerging issues related to book bans and curricular topics. Additionally, cases challenging state and local policies relating to the participation of transgender students in athletics and the rights of LGBTQIA+ students and their families, are likely. The future impact on students of recent Supreme Court decisions regarding religion and other culture war issues remains to be seen as well.

---

[221] Doe v. Madison Metropolitan School District, ACLU (Feb. 10, 2023), https://www.aclu.org/cases/doe-v-madison-metropolitan-school-district.

Alphabetical List of Cases

A.R. v. City of N.Y., *et al.*
Ass'n for Educ. Fairness v. Montgomery Cnty. Bd. of Educ.
Bentonville Sch. Dist. v. Sitton
Brach v. Newsom
Branch-Noto v. Sisolak
B.R. v. F.C.S.B.
Butler v. Shawnee Mission Sch. Dist. Bd. of Educ.
C1.G *ex rel.* C.G. v. Siegfried
C.S. v. Madison Metro. Sch. Dist.
C.V. by and through C.V. v. Waterford Twp. Bd. of Educ.
Casler v. W. Irondequoit Sch. Dist.
Cheadle ex rel. N.C. v. N. Platte R-1 Sch. Dist.
D.M. v. Bd. of Educ. Toledo Pub. Schs.
Doe v. Aberdeen Sch. Dist.
Doe v. Franklin Square Union Free Sch. Dist.
Doe v. Sch. Dist. U-46
Doe *ex rel.* Doe #2 v. Metro. Gov't of Nashville & Davidson Cnty., Tenn.
Doe 1 v. Madison Metro. Sch. Dist.
E.T. v. Paxton
Fore v. W. N.C. Conference of the United Methodist Church
F.T. v. W. Linn-Wilsonville Sch. Dist.
Goe v. Zucker
G.S. *ex rel.* Schwaigert v. Lee
Gunter v. N. Wasco Cnty. Sch. Dist. Bd. of Educ.
Gwozdz v. Bd. of Educ. of Park Ridge-Niles Sch. Dist. No. 64
Hartz v. Brehm Prep. Sch.
Hensley v. Williamsville Cent. Sch. Dist.
J.A.D., Matter of
J.W. v. Paley
K.Y., Matter of
Lexington Pub. Sch. v. K.S.
Lloyd v. Sch. Bd. of Palm Beach Cnty.
Lurkins v. Bond Cnty. Cmty. Unit No. 2
M.C. v. State
Moore v. Freeport Cmty. Unit Sch. Dist. No. 145
M.S., In re.
N.J. by Jacob v. Sonnabend
Northland Parent Ass'n v. Excelsior Springs Sch. Dist. #40
Oberheim v. Bason
Oswald v. Beshear

Peltier v. Charter Day Sch.
Pendleton Heights Gay-Straight All. v. S. Madison Cmty. Sch. Corp.
People in Interest of C.C-S
R.A. v. Johnson
S.C. v. Autauga Cnty. Bd. of Educ.
Spruill v. Sch. Dist. of Phila.
Stepien v. Murphy
Sturdivant v. Fine
Tex. v. Becerra
Tully v. Kenmore-Tonawanda Union Free Sch. Dist.
Willey v. Bd. of Educ. of St. Mary's Cnty.
Wilson ex rel. State v. City of Columbia
X.B. v. State

Cases by Jurisdiction

FEDERAL CASES

Second Circuit
Doe v. Franklin Square Union Free Sch. Dist.
Goe v. Zucker

New York
Casler v. W. Irondequoit Sch. Dist.

Third Circuit

New Jersey
Stepien v. Murphy

Pennsylvania
Oberheim v. Bason
Spruill v. Sch. Dist. of Phila.

Fourth Circuit
B.R. v. F.C.S.B.
Peltier v. Charter Day Sch.
R.A. v. Johnson

Maryland
Ass'n for Educ. Fairness v. Montgomery Cnty. Bd. of Educ.

Willey v. Bd. of Educ. of St. Mary's Cnty.

Fifth Circuit:
E.T. v. Paxton
J.W. v. Paley

Texas
Tex. v. Becerra

Sixth Circuit
Doe ex rel. Doe #2 v. Metro. Gov't of Nashville & Davidson Cnty., Tenn.

Kentucky
Oswald v. Beshear

Tennessee
G.S. ex rel. Schwaigert v. Lee

Ohio
D.M. v. Bd. of Educ. Toledo Pub. Schs.

Seventh Circuit
C.S. v. Madison Metro. Sch. Dist.
N.J. by Jacob v. Sonnabend

Illinois
Moore v. Freeport Cmty. Unit Sch. Dist. No. 145

Indiana
Pendleton Heights Gay-Straight All. v. S. Madison Cmty. Sch. Corp.

Eighth Circuit
Doe v. Aberdeen Sch. Dist.

Missouri
Cheadle ex rel. N.C. v. N. Platte R-1 Sch. Dist.
Northland Parent Ass'n v. Excelsior Springs Sch. Dist. #40

Ninth Circuit
Brach v. Newsom
Branch-Noto v. Sisolak

Tenth Circuit
C1.G ex rel. C.G. v. Siegfried
Sturdivant v. Fine

Eleventh Circuit

Florida
Lloyd v. Sch. Bd. of Palm Beach Cnty.

STATE AND D.C. COURT CASES

Alabama
S.C. v. Atauga Cnty. Bd. of Educ.

Arkansas
Bentonville Sch. Dist. v. Sitton

California
M.S., In re.

Colorado
People in Interest of C.C-S

Florida
X.B. v. State

Illinois
Doe v. Sch. Dist. U-46
Gwozdz v. Bd. of Educ. of Park Ridge-Niles Sch. Dist. No. 64
Hartz v. Brehm Prep. Sch.
Lurkins v. Bond Cnty. Cmty. Unit No. 2

Indiana
K.Y., Matter of

Kansas
Butler v. Shawnee Mission Sch. Dist. Bd. of Educ.

Massachusetts
Lexington Public Sch. v. K.S.

New Jersey
C.V. by and through C.V. v. Waterford Twp. Bd. of Educ.

New York
A.R. v. City of N.Y.
Hensley v. Williamsville Cent. Sch. Dist.
M.C. v. State
Tully v. Kenmore-Tonawanda Union Free Sch. Dist.

North Carolina
Fore v. W. N.C. Conference of the United Methodist Church
J.A.D., Matter of

Oregon
F.T. v. W. Linn-Wilsonville Sch. Dist.
Gunter v. N. Wasco Cnty. Sch. Dist. Bd. of Educ.

South Carolina
Wilson ex rel. State v. City of Columbia

Wisconsin
Doe 1 v. Madison Metro. Sch. Dist.

Chapter 4

BARGAINING

Jeffrey S. Greenley, J.D., M.B.A.[222]

Introduction 121
Arbitration 121
Negotiations 122
Fair Share Fees and Union Dues 122
Unfair Labor Practices 123
Interpretation of CBAs and Statutes 124
Standing 125
Conclusion 125
Alphabetical List of Cases 127
Cases by Jurisdiction 127

---

[222] Superintendent, Belpre City Schools, Belpre, Ohio.

Introduction

This chapter will review K-12 collective bargaining cases published during the year 2022. The cases come from both state and federal courts and provide a glimpse of the current state of the ever-changing collective bargaining process. This chapter is divided by subject matter to better organize the various cases and their holdings. The cases in 2022 primarily involved issues of arbitration, negotiation, union fees and dues, unfair labor practices, and collective bargaining agreements (CBAs).

Arbitration

Generally, an arbitrator's decision will be upheld as long as the issue was arbitrable, there was no mistake, and the decision is within the arbitrator's decision. Two New Hampshire educators grieved a decision by the board to delay their early retirement benefits as called for under the CBA.[223] The arbitrator found in favor of the union, holding that the language of the CBA did not support the delay in payment and awarded damages to the educators. The board appealed and argued that the matter was not arbitrable and exceeded the scope of the arbitrator's authority. The Supreme Court of New Hampshire affirmed a lower court decision, which affirmed the original arbitrator's holding that the issue was arbitrable and within the arbitrator's authority. The court also bypassed a board argument of past practice by finding no mutuality of understanding of acceptance of the practice by both sides.

On the contrary, an arbitrator can be overruled if a decision exceeds the scope of his or her power. An Ohio teacher brought a grievance under specific CBA language arguing that he had been nonrenewed from his basketball decision because of protected union activity.[224] The arbitrator found no evidence that the specific language cited in the grievance had been violated but affirmed the grievance because the board acted in an arbitrary and capricious manner. The board appealed the decision, which was granted by a trial court in Ohio. The appellate court affirmed, holding that the arbitrator lacked the power to affirm the grievance on any language not found in the CBA.

---

[223] Keene Sch. Dist. V. Keene Educ. Ass'n., 174 N.H. 796, 403 Educ. Law Rep. 268 (N.H. 2022).
[224] Akron Educ. Ass'n v. Akron City Sch. Dist. Bd. of Educ., 184 N.E.3d 891, 401 Educ. L. Rep. 1140 (Ohio Ct. App. 2022).

Negotiations

An appellate court in New York denied the school board's petition while granting the Public Employment Relations Board's (PERB) cross-petition after the board commenced an Article 78 proceeding to review the PERB's decision that the board engaged in improper practice by failing to negotiate with the union in good faith regarding the termination of union employees and the transfer of their work to nonunion employees.[225] At the district, security aides were union employees who were terminated at the end of the school year and replaced by a third-party service. The administrative law judge (ALJ) dismissed the charges based on the significant difference in services provided by security aids and the third-party company, but the PERB reversed in part, finding that the transfer of property protection tasks previously performed by security aids violated civil service law. The appellate court held that the issue relating to personal protection work was not ripe for review as it was remanded to the ALJ and still awaiting their decision. However, the court noted that PERB's finding that the property protection work performed previously by security aids and now by the third-party company was substantially similar was supported by substantial evidence.

Fair Share Fees and Union Dues

Generally, the recent shift in constitutional jurisprudence around fair share fees does not permit the retroactive refund of dues or fees collected prior to the decision. Four Minnesota state employees, including an educator, sought refunds of fair share fees that were deducted from their paychecks in light of the landmark *Janus* decision abolishing that power.[226] A federal trial court granted summary judgment in favor of the unions, holding that they were protected by their good-faith reliance on then-existing case law and that union members could not leave the union, and their duty to pay dues, until a contractually permitted time frame. The Eighth Circuit federal appellate court agreed. The court also found that although the union had sought to refund the money, an offer rejected by the union members, the rejection of the offer by the members did not render the matter moot.

---

[225] Lawrence Union Free Sch. Dist. v. N.Y. State Pub. Emp. Rels. Bd., 161 N.Y.S.3d 112, 400 Educ. L. Rep. 719 (N.Y. App. Div. 2021).
[226] Hoekman v. Educ. Minn. et. al., 41 F.4th 969, 405 Educ. L. Rep. 691 (8th Cir. 2022).

As noted above, the collection of union dues after a union member has legally joined a union until a specific timeframe agreed to in the agreement does not violate the First Amendment. An Illinois educator agreed to join the union after she believed she was required to do so as part of her employment.[227] After learning that she was not obligated to join, she sought to vacate her membership and avoid paying dues. The union denied her request because, under the agreement, she could only drop her membership during a specific time period that had already passed. A federal trial court rejected the educator's claim and held that requiring her to pay dues after she no longer wanted to did not violate the First Amendment insofar as she had voluntarily entered into a contract with the union that could only be broken during a specific time period. The court also found that although the board and union had sought to refund the money, an offer rejected by the union member, the rejection of the offer by the member did not render the matter moot.

An appellate court in Pennsylvania reversed and remanded the lower court's grant of the Pennsylvania State Education Association's (PSEA) motion for summary judgment on the teachers' declaratory judgment and Section 1983 claims against it.[228] The teachers brought this action to challenge the constitutionality of the PSEA's collection of fair share fees and its implementation of the religious objector provisions under the Fair Share Law. The trial court granted the PSEA's motion for summary judgment, finding the plaintiffs' claims were moot. The teachers argued that their claims were not moot because the issue of attorney's fees was still outstanding. The court found that the issue of attorney's fees was still a ripe case or controversy for the trial court to decide, thus the plaintiff's claims were not moot and the case was reversed and remanded.

Unfair Labor Practices

An appellate court in Oregon affirmed the Employment Relations Board's (ERB) order finding that the public university attempted to influence faculty members' decisions regarding whether to support representation by a union.[229] In response to the faculty's move to organize, the university created a website with FAQs and distributed the link to faculty along with a link for them

---

[227] Baro v. Lake Cnty. Fed. of Tchrs. Loc. 504, 594 F.Supp.3d 1012, 409 Educ. L. Rep. 706 (N.D. Ill. 2022).
[228] Ladley v. Pa. State Educ. Assoc., 269 A.3d 680, 400 Educ. L. Rep. 1043 (Commw. Ct. Pa. 2022).
[229] United Acads. of Or. State Univ. v. Or. State Univ., 502 P.3d 254, 398 Educ. L. Rep. 1154 (Or. Ct. App. 2021).

to submit their own questions. These FAQs covered a range of topics, including several highlighting the potential negative consequences of faculty unionization. The questions submitted by faculty members were also heavily edited in some instances. Due to these concerns, the union brought an unfair labor practice claim before the ERB, which found that the university improperly attempted to subtly influence opinions on whether faculty members should unionize through the FAQ page. The university petitioned for judicial review, arguing that the ERB's conclusions were unreasonable and unsupported by substantial evidence. However, the court affirmed that the ERB's finding that the university attempted to influence the faculty's decision regarding unionization was supported by substantial evidence.

Interpretation of CBAs and Statutes

A CBA is a contract and must be enforced according to the plain meaning of its terms. The Supreme Court of Indiana affirmed the lower court's decision denying the teachers' petition for judicial review after the state ERB affirmed the findings of the compliance officer that their respective CBAs contained provisions contrary to law.[230] The ERB found that the parties violated state law by bargaining over impermissible subjects. The issue here was whether the teachers' unions and schools could collectively bargain over a limitation on or the definition of ancillary duties. The court first concluded that the statutes at issue here prohibit the parties from bargaining over what comprises an ancillary duty. They may bargain over the wages for such ancillary duties, but they cannot bargain over the duties themselves. Only schools have the authority to manage and assign the work of teachers, and CBAs cannot conflict with this right of schools. Thus, because all four of the teachers' CBAs at issue bargained over what was considered an ancillary duty and impeded the school's right to direct its teachers, the relevant provisions were properly struck by the ERB.

A union in New York sought to grieve a board's decision to assign an employee to a certain duty by filing with the office called for under the plain language of the CBA.[231] The board refused to entertain the grievance because it had not been filed with the Office of Labor Relations and Collective Bargaining. The union countered by

---

[230] Culver Cmty. Tchrs. Assoc. v. Ind. Educ. Emp. Rels. Bd., 174 N.E.3d 601, 395 Educ. L. Rep. 813 (Ind. 2021).
[231] Dist. Council 37 v. N.Y. City Dep't of Educ., 164 N.Y.S.3d 556, 401 Educ. L. Rep. 1084 (N.Y. App. Div. 2022).

arguing that the complaint was filed to the director specified in the CBA. An appellate court held that the department's failure to issue a determination on the out-of-title complaint was arbitrary and capricious and that the union's three-month period to serve a notice of claim on the department was not triggered.

An appellate court in Oregon affirmed the ERB's certification of an association's appointment as the exclusive representative of a proposed bargaining unit consisting of several university department chairs.[232] The university argued that the department chairs lacked the right to organize under state law because they were considered supervisory employees. The term at issue here is "head or equivalent position" as included under the definition of a "supervisory employee," and whether that includes a department chair. The ERB's interpretation is not subject to deference because it is not a delegative term. The court ultimately concluded that department chairs are not supervisory employees because they are not "in charge" of the department, and they have an academic, rather than administrative, focus. Therefore, they were barred from organizing a union.

Standing

In some circumstances, taxpayers may have standing to bring claims against public districts for collective bargaining terms. A Wisconsin taxpayer brought two claims (free-speech and public purpose) against his school district related to a CBA provision that allowed employees up to ten days of paid leave each year to engage in union activities.[233] The board removed the action to federal court, arguing that the resident's claims were grounded in federal law. A federal trial court disagreed, holding both that (1) as the action did not solely arise under federal law, but also state constitutional provisions, the court lacked subject matter jurisdiction, and (2) the taxpayer would lack standing to bring such a claim in federal court.

Conclusion

In a pattern seen over the last two years, there were far fewer cases to review this year as a result of concluding the worldwide COVID-19 pandemic that impacted courts across the country. Given

---

[232] Or. Tech Am. Assoc. of Univ. Professors v. Or. Inst. of Tech., 500 P.3d 55, 397 Educ. L. Rep. 797 (Or. Ct. App. 2021).
[233] Sebring v. Milwaukee Pub. Schs., 569 F.Supp.3d 767, 403 Educ. L. Rep. 7490 (E.D. Wis. 2021).

the present atmosphere of labor unrest around the country, this trend is not likely to continue in future editions.

Alphabetical List of Cases

Akron Educ. Ass'n v. Akron City Sch. Dist. Bd. of Educ.
Baro v. Lake Cnty Fed. of Tchrs. Loc. 504
Culver Cmty. Tchrs. Assoc. v. Ind. Educ. Emp. Rels. Bd.
Dist. Council 37 v. N.Y. City Dep't of Educ.
Hoekman v. Educ. Minn. et.al.
Keene Sch. Dist. v. Keene Educ. Ass'n
Ladley v. Pa. State Educ. Assoc.
Lawrence Union Free Sch. Dist. v. N.Y. State Pub. Emp. Rels. Bd.
Or. Tech Am. Assoc. of Univ. Professors v. Or. Inst. of Tech.
Sebring v. Milwaukee Pub. Schs.
United Acads. of Or. State Univ. v. Or. State Univ.

Cases by Jurisdiction

FEDERAL CASES

7th Circuit

Illinois
Baro v. Lake Cnty Fed. of Tchrs. Loc. 504

Wisconsin
Sebring v. Milwaukee Pub. Schs.

Eighth Circuit
Hoekman v. Educ. Minn. et. al.

STATE & D.C. COURT CASES

Indiana
Culver Cnty. Tchrs. Assoc. v. Ind. Educ. Emp. Rels. Bd.

New Hampshire
Keene Sch. Dist. v. Keene Educ. Ass'n

New York
Dist. Council 37 v. N.Y. City Dep't of Educ.
Lawrence Union Free Sch. Dist. v. N.Y. State Pub. Emp. Rels. Bd.

Ohio
Akron Educ. Ass'n v. Akron City Sch. Dist. Bd. of Educ.

Oregon
United Acads. of Or. State Univ. v. Or. State Univ.
Or. Tech Am. Assoc. of Univ. Professors v. Or. Inst. of Tech.

Pennsylvania
Ladley v. Pa. State Educ. Assoc.

Chapter 5

STUDENTS WITH DISABILITIES

Susan C. Bon, J.D., Ph.D.[234] and Allan G. Osborne, Jr., Ed.D.[235]

Introduction	**131**
IDEA - Entitlement to Services	**132**
Eligibility	133
Classification	133
Nonpublic Schools	133
Procedural Safeguards	**134**
Child Find	135
Evaluation	136
Developing Individualized Education Programs	137
Change in Placement	137
Dispute Resolution	**138**
Administrative Hearings	139
Exhausting Complaints Brought under Other Statutes	139
COVID-Related Cases	139
Exhaustion in Other Section 504/ADA Cases	142
Exhausting Complaints Brought under the IDEA	143
Court Procedures	145
Standing to Sue	146
Statute of Limitations	146
Placement	**147**
Appropriate Educational Placement	148
Least Restrictive Environment	150
Private Facilities	151

---

[234] Professor of Education and Law; Affiliate Professor, Joseph F. Rice School of Law; University of South Carolina, Columbia, S.C.
[235] Retired Principal, Snug Harbor Community School, Quincy Mass.; *Education Law Into Practice* Editor, West's *Education Law Reporter*.

Related Services 151
Transition Services 152
Discipline 152
Remedies 154
    Tuition Reimbursement 156
    Compensatory Services 158
    Attorney Fees 158
    Section 1983 159
Discrimination Under Section 504 of the Rehabilitation Act and the Americans with Disabilities Act 160
    Students in Elementary and Secondary Schools 161
        COVID-Related Cases 161
        Other Disability Discrimination Issues 166
Conclusion 169
Alphabetical List of Cases 171
Cases by Jurisdiction 173

Introduction

When Congress passed the statute currently known as the Individuals with Disabilities Education Act (IDEA) in 1975, it altered the way public schools deliver educational services. Prompted in part by litigation,[236] this landmark legislation now requires states to guarantee students with disabilities a free, appropriate public education (FAPE) in the least restrictive environment. Today, school boards are charged with providing necessary educational services and programs for students with a wide array of disabilities. Given the myriad of requirements of the IDEA, school boards face many parental challenges to the services they offer.

Since the law took effect in 1977, much of the litigation has centered around parental challenges to placement decisions. While the core issue in most of the proceedings is whether school boards offered students FAPEs, courts also adjudicate a variety of procedural questions. In addition, hearing officers and judges often must fashion equitable remedies when boards fail to live up to their statutory responsibilities. In this respect, tuition reimbursement, compensatory educational services, and attorney fees remain oft-litigated topics.

The IDEA defines a FAPE as an educational program consisting of any needed special education and related services.[237] Given the emphasis on individualization, the statute does not establish any clear-cut substantive standards by which the adequacy of those services can be easily measured. The IDEA stipulates that students must be given specially designed instruction as outlined in their individualized education programs (IEPs).[238] The Supreme Court has stated that the IDEA obliges school boards to furnish students with disabilities with personalized instruction and support services sufficient for them to benefit from the education provided,[239] consistent with their circumstances.[240] Even so, the Court cautioned lower courts not to impose their views of preferable educational methods on school personnel.[241] Nevertheless, hearing officers and judges must determine the level of services required to meet the IDEA's minimum standards.

---

[236] See, e.g., Penn. Ass'n. for Retarded Child. (PARC) v. Penn., 343 F. Supp. 279 (E.D. Pa. 1972); Mills v. Bd. of Educ. of D.C., 348 F. Supp. 866 (D.D.C. 1972).
[237] 20 U.S.C. §§ 1401(9), 1412(a)(1)(A).
[238] 20 U.S.C. §§ 1401(14), 1401(29), 1414(d).
[239] Bd. of Educ. of Hendrick Hudson Cent. Sch. Dist. v. Rowley, 458 U.S. 176, 5 Educ. L. Rep. 34 (1982).
[240] Endrew F. ex rel. Joseph F. v. Douglas Cnty. Sch. Dist. RE-1, 137 S. Ct. 988 (2017).
[241] Rowley, 458 U.S. 176.

Although most of the litigation covered in this chapter focuses on the IDEA, consistent with previous years, lawsuits were also filed on behalf of students with disabilities under Section 504 of the Rehabilitation Act (Section 504) and the Americans with Disabilities Act (ADA). The plaintiffs in these actions by and large alleged that students were subjected to discriminatory treatment based on their disabilities. Of particular note is that parents in several suits alleged that the arrangements school boards made for instruction in response to the COVID-19 pandemic had a discriminatory effect on children with disabilities.

IDEA - Entitlement to Services

As a condition of receiving federal funds under the IDEA, states, and by delegation school boards, must make a FAPE available to each resident child with disabilities between the ages of three and twenty-one, inclusive.[242] The statute does, however, contain two significant limitations to that requirement. First, states do not have to provide services to students between the ages of three through five and eighteen through twenty-one if doing so would be inconsistent with state law, practice, or court orders concerning the provision of public education to children in those age ranges.[243] Second, states are not mandated to provide special education to youth between the ages of eighteen through twenty-one who are incarcerated in adult facilities if they had not been previously identified as having disabilities and did not have IEPs at the time of their incarceration.[244] Further, students who have graduated from high school with a regular diploma are no longer eligible under the IDEA.[245]

The IDEA defines students with disabilities as those who have at least one of any number of identified impairments and who consequently need special education and related services.[246] The identified disabilities are further defined in the IDEA's implementing regulations.[247] As a group, students attending nonpublic schools are entitled to some benefits of the IDEA, but individual students do not have a right to receive services. Under the IDEA, school boards are required to spend only a proportionate

---

[242] 20 U.S.C. § 1412(a)(1)(A).
[243] 20 U.S.C. § 1412(a)(1)(B)(i).
[244] 20 U.S.C. § 1412(a)(1)(B)(ii).
[245] 34 C.F.R. § 300.102(a)(2)(B) (2017).
[246] 20 U.S.C. § 1401(3).
[247] 34 C.F.R. § 300.8 (2017).

share of their federal special education dollars to provide services to parentally placed nonpublic school students.[248]

Eligibility

In the first of two cases, a federal trial court in Pennsylvania decreed that a child with disabilities did not lose her eligibility under the IDEA when her parents enrolled her in a nonpublic school.[249] The court wrote that she continued to be a child with a disability while enrolled in the nonpublic school and that, under the IDEA, she remained eligible for special education until an evaluation deemed her ineligible. In a second decision, that same court held that a child with autism spectrum disorder was eligible for placement in a typical preschool.[250] The court noted that, under state regulations, children between the ages of three to five were entitled to a FAPE and that the county could not deny a child placement in the least restrictive environment of a typical preschool for administrative convenience or to avoid additional costs.

Classification

In a dispute from Washington, the Ninth Circuit ascertained that school personnel correctly classified a child under the category of specific learning disabilities.[251] The court observed that educators conducted several assessments to evaluate the student's reading and writing skills and did not procedurally violate the IDEA by finding that she was eligible for language-related services under that classification category.

Nonpublic Schools

The Ninth Circuit affirmed that a school board in California was not required to prepare an IEP for a student whose parents enrolled her in a nonpublic school.[252] The court explained that, when parents remove their children from public schools and enroll them in nonpublic schools, school boards must develop IEPs if asked to do so but need to prepare IEPs only when the parents ask for them.

---

[248] 20 U.S.C. § 1412(a)(10)(A).
[249] M.D. v. Colonial Sch. Dist., 539 F. Supp. 3d 380, 397 Educ. L. Rep. 941 (E.D. Pa. 2021).
[250] Montgomery Cnty. Inter. Unit No. 23 v. K.S., 546 F. Supp. 3d 385, 399 Educ. L. Rep. 132 (E.D. Pa. 2021).
[251] Crofts v. Issaquah Sch. Dist. No. 411, 22 F.4th 1048, 398 Educ. L. Rep. 593 (9th Cir. 2022).
[252] Capistrano Unified Sch. Dist. v. S.W., 21 F.4th 1125, 398 Educ. L. Rep. 17 (9th Cir. 2021).

Procedural Safeguards

The IDEA includes a structure of due process safeguards to ensure that students with disabilities are properly identified, evaluated, and placed according to its requirements. The statute mandates that school boards offer parents or guardians of children with disabilities the opportunity to participate in the development of the IEPs for and placement of their children. The IDEA further requires school boards to provide written notice and obtain parental consent before evaluating any children or making any initial placements. Once students have been placed in special education, school boards must give parents proper notice before initiating any changes in placement.[253] At the same time, while administrative or judicial actions are pending, school boards may not change students' placements without parental consent, hearing officers' orders, or court decrees.[254]

Under the IDEA, school boards have an affirmative obligation to identify, locate, and evaluate all children with disabilities who reside within the school district. This includes children who have been placed in nonpublic schools by their parents.[255] However, the IDEA's regulations place the child-find obligation on the boards in the districts where the nonpublic schools are located rather than the boards in the districts where the children reside.[256]

School personnel must conduct initial evaluations before they place students in special education programs. Evaluators need to complete all assessments within sixty days of the date when parents gave their consent for the evaluations.[257] All evaluations must be multidisciplinary, meaning that they should consist of a variety of assessment tools and strategies to obtain relevant information in the suspected areas of disability.[258] Students with disabilities may be entitled to independent evaluations at public expense if their parents disagree with the school boards' evaluations.[259] However, school boards can challenge requests for independent evaluations via administrative hearings, and parents are not entitled to obtain independent evaluations at public expense if the school boards demonstrate that their evaluations were appropriate.[260]

---

[253] 20 U.S.C. §§ 1414-1415.
[254] Honig v. Doe, 484 U.S. 305, 43 Educ. L. Rep. 857 (1988).
[255] 20 U.S.C. § 1412(a).
[256] 34 C.F.R. § 300.131 (2006).
[257] 20 U.S.C. § 1414(a).
[258] 20 U.S.C. § 1414(b)(2), (3).
[259] 20 U.S.C. § 1415(b)(1).
[260] 34 C.F.R. § 300.502(b).

The IDEA stipulates that all IEPs ought to contain statements of students' current educational performance, annual goals, and short-term objectives; specific educational services to be provided; the extent to which each child can participate in general education; the dates of initiation and duration of services; and evaluation criteria to determine if the objectives are being met.[261] IEPs must include statements concerning how students' impairments affect their abilities to be involved in and progress in the general education curriculum along with statements regarding any modifications that may be needed to allow them to participate in the general education program. IEP teams should review the situations of all students who have IEPs at least annually[262] and reevaluate them at least every three years unless the parent and school officials agree that a reevaluation is unnecessary.[263]

Child Find

The Third Circuit, in a case from New Jersey, affirmed that a school board had not violated its child-find obligation by disregarding the results of the severe-discrepancy method in favor of the response-to-intervention (RTI) method for determining eligibility.[264] Commenting that state regulations allowed the use of both approaches, the court pointed out that, by using the RTI method, school personnel determined that the child had benefitted from provided interventions. Further, the court agreed that, in the absence of behavior indicating that the child had autism, school officials did not violate their child-find duty by not evaluating him for that disability.

The Fifth Circuit affirmed that a school board in Texas violated its child-find obligation because it should have been aware of the child's disability when the accommodations it provided under Section 504 failed to improve his reading level.[265] Further, the court noted that school personnel unreasonably delayed an evaluation of the child by at least four months. In another case from Texas, the Fifth Circuit upheld the lower court's finding that a school board did not fail to meet its child-find duty where a parent had not expressed concern or formally requested an evaluation before the student was in the tenth grade.[266] The court was further persuaded by the fact

---

[261] 20 U.S.C. § 1414(d)(1)(A).
[262] 20 U.S.C. § 1414(d)(4)(A).
[263] 20 U.S.C. § 1414(a)(2).
[264] J.M. ex rel. C.M. v. Summit City Bd. of Educ., 39 F.4th 126, 404 Educ. L. Rep. 529 (3d Cir. 2022).
[265] D.C. ex rel. J.C. v. Klein Indep. Sch. Dist., 860 F. App'x 894, 395 Educ. L. Rep. 499 (5th Cir. 2021).
[266] Leigh Ann H. ex rel. K.S. v. Riesel Indep. Sch. Dist., 18 F.4th 788, 397 Educ. L. Rep. 25 (5th Cir. 2021).

that his educational record did not show a consistent pattern of failure that would have put school personnel on notice that he had a disability.

A federal trial court in Georgia was convinced that a school system was impeded in meeting its child-find obligation towards incarcerated students because a practical method of identifying detainees with disabilities did not exist.[267] The court found that the jail lacked a formal process to assist with the identification and evaluation of detainees and that school board personnel did not have access to their identities.

Evaluation

In the latest chapter in an ongoing dispute in the District of Columbia, the federal trial court ascertained that the school board's fee cap on independent evaluations was reasonable.[268] The court noted that the parents' fee request was excessively high because they had asked the evaluator to perform a more expensive neuropsychological evaluation instead of a psychological assessment.

A federal trial court denied a request from parents in Texas for an independent evaluation at public expense after determining that the school board's evaluation was appropriate.[269] The court was satisfied that school personnel assessed the child using a variety of tools and strategies in all areas of suspected disability, including health, vision, hearing, social and emotional status, general intelligence, academic performance, communication skills, and motor abilities.

A Texas state appellate court affirmed the lower court's dismissal of the plaintiff's IDEA claims but reversed its denial of the defendant's plea to jurisdiction.[270] The plaintiff, a mother bringing suit against an open-enrollment charter school, alleged her student's rights were violated when the school labeled the student a problem child and did not test her for cognitive and behavioral performance issues despite the mother's requests. The IDEA requires any claims for the denial of a FAPE to be subject to the IDEA's exhaustion requirements. Here, because the claims could probably not be brought by anyone other than a student at a school, and because the mother invoked the IDEA procedure, this was a denial of a FAPE

---

[267] T.H. ex rel. T.B. v. DeKalb Cnty. Sch. Dist., 564 F. Supp. 3d 1349, 402 Educ. L. Rep. 631 (N.D. Ga. 2021).
[268] B.D. ex rel. Davis v. D.C., 548 F. Supp. 3d 222, 399 Educ. L. Rep. 591 (D.D.C. 2020).
[269] Heather H. ex rel. P.H. v. Nw. Indep. Sch. Dist., 529 F. Supp. 3d 636, 395 Educ. L. Rep. 680 (E.D. Tex. 2021).
[270] Responsive Educ. Sols. v. Kirschner, 629 S.W.3d 581, 395 Educ. L. Rep. 861 (Tex. App. 2021).

claim and thus was subject to the exhaustion requirements. Because the plaintiff did not exhaust the administrative remedies available to her before seeking judicial relief, her claim must be dismissed and the defendant's plea to the jurisdiction should be granted.

Developing Individualized Education Programs

The Ninth Circuit affirmed that although the placement recommendation for a child with disabilities from California was inadequate, the goals of her IEP were appropriate because they addressed her needs.[271] The court observed that in developing the goals, school personnel considered recommendations offered by her parents and their expert and did not infringe on their opportunity to participate. Further, the court noted that the IEP included statements of measurable goals and how progress would be measured.

Parents in the District of Columbia were not denied full participation in the IEP process according to a ruling of the federal trial court in that jurisdiction.[272] The court averred that the parents failed to show that the school board's refusal to reimburse private providers for time spent at IEP meetings impeded the child's right to a FAPE or caused a deprivation of educational benefits.

A federal trial court in Pennsylvania ruled that a school board's delay in offering an IEP without any reasonable justification denied a child with learning disabilities a FAPE.[273] The court found that school personnel failed to seek the child's parents' consent for a reevaluation for three months and did not have an IEP in place at the start of the school year as they were obligated to do.

Change in Placement

In a split decision, the First Circuit ruled that a private school was not the stay-put placement for a child with disabilities from Maine.[274] A hearing officer concluded that the school committee had denied the child a FAPE for a period of time and ordered partial tuition reimbursement but determined that the latest IEP was appropriate. The court explained that, because the hearing officer had not found the private school to be an appropriate placement and had not approved a change in placement, it was not the status quo.

---

[271] Capistrano Unified Sch. Dist. v. S.W, 21 F.4th 1125, 398 Educ. L. Rep. 17 (9th Cir. 2021).
[272] B.D. ex rel. Davis v. D.C., 548 F. Supp. 3d 222, 399 Educ. L. Rep. 591 (D.D.C. 2020).
[273] M.D. v. Colonial Sch. Dist., 539 F. Supp. 3d 380, 397 Educ. L. Rep. 941 (E.D. Pa. 2021).
[274] Doe v. Portland Pub. Schs., 30 F.4th 85, 401 Educ. L. Rep. 144 (1st Cir. 2022).

The dissent, on the other hand, felt that the private school was the child's stay-put placement because the federal trial court had found it to be the last one agreed on by the parents and the state.

The Ninth Circuit, overturning a decision by a federal trial court in Oregon, held that a private school was a child's stay-put placement because an administrative law judge's order clearly required her transfer to a residential facility.[275] In the court's view, the judge's final unappealed order constituted an agreement between the state and parents making the private school the child's legal placement.

Dispute Resolution

In crafting the IDEA, Congress envisioned cooperative efforts to develop IEPs between school personnel and parents, but it recognized that disagreements were possible. Thus, Congress incorporated a detailed mechanism into the statute to resolve disputes between the parties that includes resolution meetings,[276] mediation,[277] administrative due process hearings,[278] and, as a final resort, appeals to the courts.[279]

Parents may file due process complaints if they disagree with any recommendations or decisions made by school personnel regarding proposed IEPs or any aspect of a FAPE. Parties must request hearings within two years of the dates they knew or should have known about the actions upon which the complaints are based.[280] Even so, parents can be excused from meeting this timeline if they can show that school officials misrepresented that the problems complained of had been resolved or withheld required information from the parents.[281] Any party not satisfied with the final decision of the administrative proceedings has the right to appeal to state or federal courts; however, all administrative remedies must be exhausted before resorting to the courts unless it is futile to do so. The IDEA requires aggrieved parties to file judicial appeals within 90 days of final administrative decisions.[282]

---

[275] S.C. ex rel. K.G. v. Lincoln Cnty. Sch. Dist., 16 F.4th 587, 395 Educ. L. Rep. 921 (9th Cir. 2021).
[276] 20 U.S.C. § 1415(f)(1)(B).
[277] 20 U.S.C. § 1415(e).
[278] 20 U.S.C. §§ 1415(f), (g).
[279] 20 U.S.C. § 1415(i)(2)(A).
[280] 20 U.S.C. § 1415(f)(3)(C).
[281] 20 U.S.C. § 1415(f)(3)(D).
[282] 20 U.S.C. § 1415(i)(2)(B).

The Supreme Court, in *Schaffer ex rel. Schaffer v. Weast*,[283] placed the burden of persuasion in administrative proceedings on the parties challenging the IEPs. This ruling effectively puts the burden of proof on parents in most due process hearings since they are the ones who typically challenge IEPs. The IDEA empowers the courts to review the record of the administrative proceedings, hear additional evidence, and "grant such relief as the court determines is appropriate" based on the preponderance of evidence standard.[284] In this regard, the Court has cautioned judges not to substitute their views of proper educational methodology for that of competent school authorities.[285] Parties appealing final administrative decisions have 90 days to do so unless state law dictates otherwise.

Administrative Hearings

Exhausting Complaints Brought under Other Statutes

Plaintiffs may attempt to sidestep the IDEA's exhaustion rule by bringing suit under statutes such as Section 504 or the ADA that do not have an analogous requirement. In 2017, in *Fry v. Napoleon Community Schools* (*Fry*),[286] the Supreme Court clarified that, in such cases, exhaustion is not required when the crux of the suit is something other than a denial of a FAPE but is required if relief is available under the IDEA. Thus, if the gravamen of the complaint seeks relief for the denial of a FAPE, the parties must first exhaust the IDEA's administrative remedies. Despite the Supreme Court's ruling, litigation has continued. Several of the cases discussed here involve complaints brought by parents related to issues arising from school boards' attempts to provide educational services during the COVID-19 pandemic.

COVID-Related Cases. As schools began to return to in-person learning during the COVID-19 pandemic, most instituted precautions such as requiring all staff and students to wear masks. Officials and lawmakers in several states, however, issued orders and passed legislation prohibiting schools from implementing universal mask mandates. Parents of students in these states, who had significant medical issues that increased their risk of serious complications or death from COVID-19, sought restraining orders to

---

[283] 546 U.S. 49, 203 Educ. L. Rep. 49 (2005).
[284] 20 U.S.C. § 1415(i)(2)(C)(iii).
[285] Bd. of Educ. of Hendrick Hudson Cent. Sch. Dist. v. Rowley, 458 U.S. 176, 5 Educ. L. Rep. 34 (1982).
[286] 580 U.S. 154, 340 Educ. L. Rep. 19 (2017).

prevent the implementation of these orders, alleging that they violated their children's rights under Section 504 and the ADA. Although the complaints varied, the essence of the suits was that, because the children could not safely attend school if other students and personnel were not required to wear masks, they were effectively denied access to the schools' programs and services because of their disabilities. As the cases summarized below demonstrate, the outcomes were mixed.

The governor of Texas issued a similar executive order prohibiting school boards from requiring anyone to wear face coverings. In a parental challenge to that order, a federal trial court decreed that the plaintiffs were not required to exhaust the IDEA's administrative remedies because the gravamen of their complaint sought relief for disability discrimination, not the denial of FAPEs.[287] As the court saw it, the parents were not seeking special education services, but instead, alleged that their children had been denied the benefits of the programs, services, and activities of a public entity because of their disabilities. The Fifth Circuit disagreed, however, and issued a stay of the lower court's injunction.[288] Examining *Fry's* questions, the appeals court stated that the essential component of the parents' claims, access to in-person learning, could not be levied against a public facility other than a school and a non-student adult at the school would not be able to bring the same complaint because access to in-person learning would not be applicable.

A nonprofit advocacy agency in Iowa, along with parents of students who had underlying health conditions, filed suit to enjoin the state from enforcing its mask-mandate ban.[289] A federal trial court declared that they did not need to first exhaust the IDEA's administrative remedies because the gravamen of the complaint did not involve FAPEs. In the court's opinion, the plaintiffs' claims were properly brought under Section 504 and the ADA and there was no reason for them to participate in the IDEA's administrative process. The Eighth Circuit affirmed, explaining that the issue was one of access to public facilities and that masks, like wheelchair ramps, made the school building accessible.[290]

---

[287] E.T. v. Morath, 571 F. Supp. 3d 639, 404 Educ. L. Rep. 606 (W.D. Tex. 2021).
[288] E.T. v. Paxton, 19 F.4th 760, 397 Educ. L. Rep. 488 (5th Cir. 2021). In a subsequent decision, the court vacated and remanded the district court's order on other grounds. 41 F.4th 709, 405 Educ. L. Rep. 634 (5th Cir. 2022).
[289] ARC of Iowa v. Reynolds, 559 F. Supp. 3d 861, 401 Educ. L. Rep. 824 (S.D. Iowa 2021).
[290] ARC of Iowa v. Reynolds, 24 4th 1162, 399 Educ. L. Rep. 524 (8th Cir. 2022). The appeals court later vacated the district court's injunction as moot because conditions differed from those that existed when the injunction was issued. 33 4th 1042, 402 Educ. L. Rep. 120 (8th Cir. 2022).

A suit in California challenged how school boards delivered services to students with disabilities during the pandemic.[291] The state assembly passed legislation making independent study the primary avenue for distance learning. Parents and an advocacy organization alleged that because independent study was inaccessible to their children, it forced them to choose between in-person instruction or foregoing their educations. A federal trial court averred that the plaintiffs were not required to exhaust administrative remedies because they were not alleging denial of FAPEs, challenging decisions by their IEP teams, or contesting specific services.

In Colorado, health officials in one county issued an order that effectively loosened mask and quarantine requirements for public school students.[292] A school board and parents of children with health complications filed suit claiming that the order prevented school officials from granting reasonable accommodations that would give the students meaningful access to their schools' programs and services. The federal trial court was satisfied that the plaintiffs did not need to exhaust the IDEA's administrative remedies before seeking an injunction to prevent the implementation of the order. As with courts in other jurisdictions, the Colorado court viewed the issue as one of access, not FAPE.

After the governor of Florida issued an executive order directing the state's health and education departments to promulgate rules protecting parents' rights to make decisions regarding the masking of their children, parents of students with unique health-related concerns filed suit to enjoin enforcement of the order.[293] A federal trial court denied the motion, stating that the plaintiffs' attempt to characterize their suit as one involving a denial of access, and not a denial of FAPE, was untethered to their allegations.

The governor of Tennessee issued an executive order giving parents of K-12 students the right to opt out of any requirement to wear a face covering in school, on school buses, or at school functions. In the first of three cases challenging that order, a federal trial court ruled that parents bringing suit under Section 504 and the ADA were not required to first exhaust administrative remedies under the IDEA because the children's IEPs were not the crux of the lawsuit.[294]

---

[291] E.E. v. Cal., 570 F. Supp. 3d 759, 403 Educ. L. Rep. 799 (N.D. Cal. 2021).
[292] Douglas Cnty. Sch. Dist. RE-1 v. Douglas Cnty. Health Dep't., 568 F. Supp. 3d 1158, 403 Educ. L. Rep. 654 (D. Colo. 2021).
[293] Hayes ex rel. W.H. v. DeSantis, 561 F. Supp. 3d 1187, 402 Educ. L. Rep. 170 (S.D. Fla. 2021).
[294] G.S. ex rel. Schwaigert v. Lee, 558 F. Supp. 3d 601, 401 Educ. L. Rep. 758 (W.D. Tenn. 2021). Subsequently, in an unpublished decision, the Sixth Circuit denied the governor's motion for a stay of the district court's order. 2021 WL 5411218 (6th Cir. 2021).

Rather, the court viewed the gravamen of their complaint, not as one seeking a FAPE, but to gain nondiscriminatory access to their schools by way of reasonable accommodations. In the second decision challenging the same executive order, another federal trial court in Tennessee reached an identical conclusion after ascertaining that the remedy the parents sought was not for the denial of FAPEs but rather for the educational harm caused by the executive order.[295] To make it unanimous, in yet another suit challenging the governor's order, a third federal trial court also saw the issue as one involving a failure to accommodate under Section 504 and the ADA and not a denial of FAPEs.[296]

A state appellate court in Indiana posited that the parents of two high school students had to exhaust their administrative remedies even though they were challenging the implementation of their Section 504 accommodation plans during the pandemic because they were seeking accommodations unique to the classroom setting.[297] The parents contended that under the hybrid model of instruction the high school used, the accommodation plans could not be implemented the three days a week the students received virtual instruction at home.

Exhaustion in Other Section 504/ADA Cases. In an ongoing dispute from California, an en banc Ninth Circuit affirmed that a parent who filed suit alleging violations of the ADA was required to exhaust the IDEA's administrative remedies.[298] Rather than provide the child, who exhibited disability-related behaviors, with a one-on-one aide, school administrators frequently sent the child home. After filing a due process complaint, the mother negotiated a settlement with the school board. Nevertheless, she filed suit under the ADA. A federal trial court dismissed, but a panel of the Ninth Circuit reversed, observing that the complaint focused on the child's exclusion from his classroom, not the inadequacy of his IEP. The full court voted to rehear the case en banc and vacated that decision. On rehearing, in a split decision, the full court found that the crux of the complaint was that the school board failed to provide the required accommodations, aids, and services the child needed to access his education. Even so, the court's majority saw this as a FAPE issue.

---

[295] R.K. v. Lee, 563 F. Supp. 3d 774, 402 Educ. L. Rep. 243 (M.D. Tenn. 2021).
[296] S.B. *ex rel.* M.B. v. Lee, 566 F. Supp. 3d 835, 402 Educ. L. Rep. 803 (E.D. Tenn. 2021). In an unpublished opinion, the Sixth Circuit denied the Tennessee Board of Education's motion for a stay of the district court's preliminary injunction. M.B. v. Lee, 2021 WL 6101486 (6th Cir. 2021).
[297] Reinoehl v. St. Joseph Cnty. Health Dep't, 181 N.E.3d 341, 400 Educ. L. Rep. 323 (Ind. Ct. App. 2021).
[298] D.D. *ex rel.* Ingram v. L.A. Unified Sch. Dist., 18 F.4th 1043, 397 Educ. L. Rep. 47 (9th Cir. 2021) (*cert. granted, vacated and remanded* for further consideration in light of the Supreme Court's intervening decision in *Luna Perez v. Sturgis Pub. Schs.*, 143 S.Ct. 859 (2023)).

The parents of a student with intellectual disabilities from Massachusetts filed suit under Section 504 after she had been sexually assaulted in the restroom. Although the child's IEP called for her to have a one-on-one assistant at all times, she went to the restroom unaccompanied because her aide was at lunch and no substitute was provided. The federal trial court denied the school committee's motion to dismiss on exhaustion grounds finding that the IDEA's exhaustion rule did not apply because the parents were seeking redress for their daughter's injuries.[299]

A state appellate court in Texas affirmed that parents who filed suit against a charter school alleging violations of Section 504 and for breach of contract were required to exhaust administrative remedies.[300] The parent claimed that the school had unfairly labeled the child as a problem without testing her for cognitive or behavioral performance issues. Under the *Fry* analysis, the court ascertained that the gravamen of the complaint concerned the denial of a FAPE.

Exhausting Complaints Brought under the IDEA

The First Circuit, in a dispute from Puerto Rico, was convinced that parents who filed suit to enforce the terms of an administrative law judge's order had to exhaust administrative remedies.[301] In vacating the lower court's judgment, the appeals court pointed out that the parents sought to do more than enforce the order, and the trial court made determinations regarding whether the education department had provided a FAPE without the benefit of administrative findings.

In an appeal of a hearing decision, parents from California attempted to join the state's education department in claiming that a state regulation violated the IDEA.[302] A federal trial court denied the state's motion to dismiss, acknowledging that an administrative law judge did not have the authority to declare the regulation in question unenforceable.

The federal trial court in the District of Columbia insisted that parents who alleged that the board's due process hearing system violated the IDEA's requirement that a hearing officer must be independent and neutral had to exhaust administrative remedies.[303] In the court's view, this was a challenge that could have been brought to a hearing officer.

---

[299] Doe v. Dennis-Yarmouth Reg. Sch. Dist., 578 F. Supp. 3d 164, 405 Educ. L. Rep. 1037 (D. Mass. 2022).
[300] Responsive Educ. Sols. v. Kirschner, 629 S.W.3d 581, 395 Educ. L. Rep. 861 (Tex. Ct. App. 2021).
[301] Valentin-Marrero v. P.R., 24 F.4th 45, 401 Educ. L. Rep. 41 (1st Cir. 2022).
[302] M.C. v. L.A. Unified Sch. Dist., 559 F. Supp. 3d 1112, 401 Educ. L. Rep. 846 (C.D. Cal. 2021).
[303] B.D. *ex rel.* Davis v. D.C., 548 F. Supp. 3d 222, 399 Educ. L. Rep. 591 (D.D.C. 2020).

Parents from Michigan filed a due process complaint against the state's education department and their school board.[304] An administrative law judge dismissed the education department for lack of jurisdiction and the parents settled with the board. Even so, the parents filed suit against the state. A federal trial court determined that since the state had succeeded in convincing the administrative law judge that the administrative process lacked jurisdiction, the parents had exhausted their administrative remedies.

A federal trial court in Texas stipulated that parents who alleged a systemic violation of the IDEA were not required to exhaust administrative remedies because systemic failures could not be solved within the IDEA's structure for individual hearings.[305]

The Supreme Court of Iowa affirmed the lower court's affirmation of the Department of Education's declaratory order determining that the decision of whether to excuse an absence for applied behavioral analysis (ABA) therapy was generally up to school boards and such absence could violate the IDEA if it led to students missing services provided by their IEP.[306] The central issue in this case, brought by an ABA therapy provider, was who determines whether a student may be excused from school to attend ABA therapy, the physician's order or public agencies (i.e., school boards and education agencies). The court first affirmed that the Department of Education had the authority to issue such an order under state law. It then went on to affirm that the school board has the authority to determine whether a student can be excused from school to attend ABA therapy because state law grants the school discretion in determining its attendance policies.

An appellate court in New Jersey affirmed the lower court's finding that the requested records were public records subject to the Open Public Records Act (OPRA), entry of judgment requiring the release of the records, and award of the requestor's attorney fees.[307] Here, individuals requested records of settlements pertaining to students subject to an IEP or accommodation plan, and the defendants denied the request in part, claiming some documents were exempt as confidential student records and others were "vague and [did] not seek identifiable government records." The court begins its discussion by noting that OPRA requests should be "construed in favor of the public's right of access." The court goes on to state that

---

[304] A.B. *ex rel.* K.B. v. Mich. Dep't of Educ., 570 F. Supp. 3d 531, 403 Educ. L. Rep. 775 (W.D. Mich. 2021).
[305] J.R. *ex rel.* Analisa and Joe R. v. Austin Indep. Sch. Dist., 374 F. Supp. 3d 428, 405 Educ. L. Rep. 113 (W.D. Tex. 2021).
[306] Hills & Dales Child Dev. Ctr. v. Iowa Dep't of Educ., 968 N.W.2d 238, 398 Educ. L. Rep. 1123 (Iowa 2021).
[307] C.E. v. Elizabeth Pub. Sch. Dist., 276 A.3d 662, 405 Educ. L. Rep. 380 (N.J. Super. Ct. App. Div. 2022).

under the IDEA, the institution must disclose the de-identified records. Further, the requestors were not required to obtain a court order or parental permission to receive records of previous settlements. Lastly, the court concluded that the requestors were entitled to attorney fees because they prevailed under OPRA.

Court Procedures

In the first of two cases from New Jersey, the Third Circuit decreed that the federal trial court had jurisdiction to hear a suit in which parents contended that they did not knowingly and voluntarily enter into a settlement agreement with their school board.[308] The court insisted that, under the IDEA, jurisdiction arises when an administrative order disposing of a complaint is the subject of a suit. In the present case, an administrative law judge incorporated the terms of the settlement into a final appealable order. In the second suit, the Third Circuit averred that the lower court did not err when it refused to admit additional evidence as requested by parents.[309] The court commented that reports or evidence that did not exist at the time the IEP team made its determination were not relevant to the issue of whether the school board violated its obligations.

The Fourth Circuit affirmed a federal trial court in North Carolina's dismissal of a suit as moot because the children in question were no longer enrolled in the school system and the complaint did not include a request for compensatory services.[310] The appeals court stated that the lower court could not order prospective relief because the students no longer attended school in the district and the parent's failure to request compensatory services deprived the court of an opportunity to exercise its discretion.

In another dispute involving a question of mootness, the Tenth Circuit affirmed a dismissal by the federal trial court in Colorado on those grounds.[311] The lower court ascertained that the expiration of the contested IEP rendered the suit moot. The appeals court agreed, noting that the parents had not shown a reasonable expectation that the specific IDEA violations they alleged would be repeated or that the school board would deny the child a FAPE in the future. The appeals court agreed that the claims the parents initially raised were based on a series of fact-specific disputes over an IEP that had

---

[308] G.W. v. Ringwood Bd. of Educ., 28 F.4th 465, 400 Educ. L. Rep. 447 (3d Cir. 2022).
[309] J.M. *ex rel.* C.M. v. Summit City Bd. of Educ., 39 F.4th 126, 404 Educ. L. Rep. 529 (3d Cir. 2022).
[310] Johnson *ex rel.* A.J. v. Charlotte-Mecklenburg Schs. Bd. of Educ., 20 F.4th 835, 397 Educ. L. Rep. 531 (4th Cir. 2021).
[311] Patrick G. v. Harrison Sch. Dist. No. 2, 40 F.4th 1186, 405 Educ. L. Rep. 45 (10th Cir. 2022).

subsequently been superseded. Further, the court stated that the parents' request for a stay-put injunction was also moot because the placement claim on which it was based was moot.

A federal trial court in North Carolina concluded that a review officer's findings were entitled to deference because she examined the record in detail and discounted an administrative law judge's determinations that were based on factual inaccuracies or that were unsupported.[312] The court added that the reviewing officer explained her reasons for departing from the administrative law judge's decision.

In Texas, a federal trial court declared that a suit brought by the parents of five children and an advocacy agency was not moot because their claims for compensatory education kept the controversy alive.[313] The court added that the issue would not end because it involved structural deficiencies that could harm students in the future, and there was a strong possibility that the violations could further impact the students because of their need for continued IEPs.

Standing to Sue

A federal trial court in Michigan decreed that parents had standing to sue on behalf of their son as a minor child.[314] The parents had alleged that the state's education department had failed to monitor the local school board and allowed it to continue to deny their child a FAPE. The department had found itself in violation but closed the matter without fully addressing the complaint, after which the parents brought discrimination claims under Section 504 and the ADA. To succeed on a discrimination claim under Section 504, the plaintiff must establish either bad faith or gross negligence. The department's failure to maintain sufficient oversight of the school board, allowing it to continue denying a FAPE, and its failure to fully address the parents' complaint barred dismissal on the Section 504 and ADA claims.

Statute of Limitations

The IDEA does not have a time limit for filing claims for attorney fees so one needs to be borrowed from analogous state law. A federal

---

[312] Wake Cnty. Bd. of Educ. v. S.K. *ex rel.* R.K., 541 F. Supp. 3d 652, 398 Educ. L. Rep. 233 (E.D.N.C. 2021).
[313] J.R. *ex rel.* Analisa and Joe R. v. Austin Indep. Sch. Dist., 574 F. Supp. 3d 428, 405 Educ. L. Rep. 113 (W.D. Tex. 2021).
[314] A.B. *ex rel.* K.B. v. Mich. Dep't of Educ., 570 F. Supp. 3d 531, 403 Educ. L. Rep. 775 (W.D. Mich. 2021).

trial court in Virginia ascertained that the state's limitations period of 180 days for seeking judicial review of administrative decisions was most appropriate.[315] The court commented that the application of this statute of limitations did not abridge the parents' rights under the IDEA. Next, the court held that under this limitations period, the parent's suit was untimely and that tolling was not appropriate because the parent and her counsel knew that she should have promptly sought fees.

Placement

The IDEA regulations require school boards to ensure that a "continuum of alternative placements" exists to meet the needs of students with disabilities for special education and related services.[316] The placements chosen for all students must be in the least restrictive environment (LRE) for each child and removal from general education can occur only to the extent necessary to provide special education and related services.[317] All placements have to be made at public expense and need to meet state educational standards.[318] IEP teams ought to review all placements at least annually and revise them when necessary.[319] The Supreme Court, in *Rowley*, defined an appropriate education as one that is developed in compliance with the IDEA's procedures and is reasonably calculated to enable the child to receive educational benefits.[320] In *Endrew F.*, the Court clarified that children's programs should be appropriately ambitious in light of their individual circumstances.[321] Although states, at a minimum, must adopt policies and procedures that are consistent with the IDEA, they may provide greater benefits than those required by federal law. If states do establish higher standards, courts will consider those standards along with the IDEA when evaluating the appropriateness of IEPs.[322]

---

[315] Sanchez v. Arlington Cnty Sch. Bd., 563 F. Supp. 3d 484, 402 Educ. L. Rep. 235 (E.D. Va. 2021).
[316] 34 C.F.R. § 300.115 (2017).
[317] 20 U.S.C. § 1412(a)(5).
[318] 20 U.S.C. § 1401(9).
[319] 20 U.S.C. § 1414(d)(4).
[320] Bd. of Educ. of Hendrick Hudson Cent. Sch. Dist. v. Rowley, 458 U.S. 176, 5 Educ. L. Rep. 34 (1982).
[321] Endrew F. ex rel. Joseph F. v. Douglas Cnty. Sch. Dist. RE-1, 580 U.S. 386 (2017).
[322] See, e.g., David D. v. Dartmouth Sch. Comm., 775 F.2d 411, 28 Educ. L. Rep. 70 (1st Cir. 1985); Geis v. Bd. of Educ. of Parsippany-Troy Hills, 774 F.2d 575, 27 Educ. L. Rep. 1093 (3d Cir. 1985).

Appropriate Educational Placement

The First Circuit affirmed that a school committee in Massachusetts provided a FAPE for a student with learning disabilities.[323] The court saw no error in a hearing officer's reliance on informal assessments that showed that the child had made slow gains under her IEP because this finding was based on her individual circumstances as opposed to how she performed on state-wide tests that are not designed to measure progress without regard to a child's circumstances.

In the first of two cases from Texas decided by the Fifth Circuit, the court agreed with a trial court that a school board's IEP for a child with a reading disability was inappropriate.[324] A hearing officer had determined that the services outlined in the IEP served to accommodate, but not remediate, the child's deficiencies. The court pointed out that under that plan the child's grades did not meaningfully improve, and test results did not demonstrate a meaningful benefit. In the second decision, the court affirmed that the IEP for a high school student was reasonably tailored to his needs even though the services were offered in a general education setting.[325] The court observed that the IEP's goals corresponded with his academic weaknesses.

The Eighth Circuit agreed with a lower court that a school board in Minnesota did not deny a FAPE to a child with autism spectrum disorder.[326] Commenting that the IDEA requires improvement, not mastery, the court explained that the IEP's goals were reasonably calculated to allow the child to make appropriate progress. Further, the court noted that the IEP team continually updated the child's goals, tried new curricula, and increased services.

In affirming that a school board in Washington did not deny a child a FAPE, the Ninth Circuit asserted that, as a matter of law, the board was not required to use the methodology preferred by her parents.[327] Despite the disagreement over methodology, the court agreed that the child's IEPs were reasonably calculated to enable her to make progress, and, although she did not meet all of her IEP goals, she did make progress. Thus, in the court's view, the IDEA's standard was met.

In the latest chapter in an ongoing dispute, the federal trial court in the District of Columbia decreed that the school board's IEPs for

---

[323] G.D. *ex rel.* Jeffrey D. v. Swampscott Pub. Schs., 27 F.4th 1, 400 Educ. L. Rep. 32 (1st Cir. 2022).
[324] D.C. *ex rel.* J.C. v. Klein Indep. Sch. Dist., 860 F. App'x 894, 395 Educ. L. Rep. 499 (5th Cir. 2021).
[325] Leigh Ann H. *ex rel.* K.S. v. Riesel Indep. Sch. Dist., 18 F.4th 788, 397 Educ. L. Rep. 25 (5th Cir. 2021).
[326] Minnetonka Pub. Schs., Indep. Sch. Dist. No. 276 v. M.L.K., 42 F.4th 847, 405 Educ. L. Rep. 765 (8th Cir. 2022).
[327] Crofts v. Issaquah Sch. Dist. No. 411, 22 F.4th 1048, 398 Educ. L. Rep. 593 (9th Cir. 2022).

a student with complex disabilities were appropriate because their goals were based on the child's levels of academic and functional performance.[328] The court acknowledged that the IEPs included behavior intervention plans that targeted many of the behavioral issues the child's parents alleged that the IEPs failed to address.

A federal trial court in Georgia ascertained that two youths were denied FAPEs while incarcerated in the county jail.[329] Although the court was aware that school personnel did not have sufficient access to the students to implement their IEPs because of the sherriff's lack of cooperation, it declared that the board was not relieved of the requirement to provide FAPEs despite those challenges.

The federal trial court in Massachusetts held that a school committee did not offer a high school student with autism an appropriate placement in his junior and senior years.[330] The court ascertained that the child's IEP for his junior year was not adequate because it did not address his severe mental health needs nor account for a crisis the previous summer. As far as his senior year was concerned, the court reasoned that the IEP team's failure to provide a FAPE the previous year rendered that IEP inappropriate because it would have required a transfer of schools.

In a Pennsylvania case, a federal trial court judged that programs proposed by an IEP team for a child with cognitive deficits, brain abnormalities, and difficulty speaking would not have provided a FAPE because they were unlikely to confer educational benefits.[331] The court contended that the offered programs would give her limited vocational alternatives and did not provide appropriate instruction in independent living skills.

In the first of two cases from Texas, a school board offered a FAPE to a student with Asperger syndrome, according to a federal trial court, because his IEP team consistently evaluated, consulted, prescribed, and addressed his individual needs in collaboration with his parents.[332] The court remarked that he received services tailored to his individual needs that were delivered by qualified professionals in coordination with his teachers. Further, the court observed that he passed all of his classes and demonstrated progress toward his IEP goals. In the second decision from Texas, another federal trial court posited that a school board did not deny a FAPE to a child with learning disabilities who occasionally became upset and angry, even

---

[328] B.D. *ex rel.* Davis v. D.C., 548 F. Supp. 3d 222, 399 Educ. L. Rep. 591 (D.D.C. 2020).
[329] T.H. *ex rel.* T.B. v. DeKalb Cnty. Sch. Dist., 564 F. Supp. 3d 1349, 402 Educ. L. Rep. 631 (N.D. Ga. 2021).
[330] Doe v. Newton Pub. Schs., 537 F. Supp. 3d 56, 397 Educ. L. Rep. 111 (D. Mass. 2021).
[331] Perkiomen Valley Sch. Dist. v. R.B., 533 F. Supp. 3d 233, 396 Educ. L. Rep. 419 (E.D. Pa. 2021).
[332] J.B. *ex rel.* Lauren v. Frisco Indep. Sch. Dist., 528 F. Supp. 3d 614, 395 Educ. L. Rep. 631 (E.D. Tex. 2021).

though his teacher failed to follow his behavior intervention plan.[333] The court recognized that school officials took this failure seriously and promptly mitigated it by maintaining his services when his mother removed him from school. The court emphasized that whether a child received benefits must be determined by considering the entirety of the school year and that when the year was viewed as a whole it was clear that his teacher's failure to follow the plan ultimately did not detract from his receipt of a FAPE.

A state appellate court in New York affirmed that a school board denied a child with multiple disabilities, including medical issues, a FAPE because it did not provide her with a one-on-one nurse.[334] The court was cognizant of the board's efforts to secure a nurse but reflected that an impossibility of performance defense was at odds with the purpose of the IDEA.

Least Restrictive Environment

The Fifth Circuit affirmed that a blended placement whereby a student from Texas with Down Syndrome would receive part of her instruction in a special education setting was the least restrictive environment.[335] The court was persuaded by evidence showing that school personnel tried to accommodate the child in the general education setting by implementing a modified curriculum with inclusion support and proposed the blended placement only after making multiple attempts to keep her in that setting. The court stated that the trial court correctly found that she was not making appropriate progress in that setting and that her behavioral issues had a detrimental effect on others.

In an appeal from Missouri, the Eighth Circuit affirmed that a special school for students with severe disabilities was the least restrictive environment for a child who had previously been taught in a segregated special education class.[336] The court found no clear error in the lower court's conclusion that the child had received a minimal benefit from his placement in the less restrictive environment and that the next step on the placement continuum was the special school. In addition, the court noted that he had derived minimal social benefit from placement in his previous special class.

A placement in a class exclusively for students with disabilities was not the least restrictive environment for a kindergarten student

---

[333] Lamar Consol. Indep. Sch. Dist. v. J.T., 577 F. Supp. 3d 599, 405 Educ. L. Rep. 943 (S.D. Tex. 2021).
[334] Elmira City Sch. Dist. v. N.Y. State Educ. Dep't, 166 N.Y.S.3d 710, 402 Educ. L. Rep. 1074 (N.Y. App. Div. 2022).
[335] H.W. *ex rel.* Jennie W. v. Comal Indep. Sch. Dist., 32 F.4th 454, 402 Educ. L. Rep. 48 (5th Cir. 2022).
[336] J.P. ex rel. Ogden v. Belton Sch. Dist. No. 234, 40 F.4th 887, 405 Educ. L. Rep. 36 (8th Cir. 2022).

with autism according to a federal trial court in Tennessee.[337] The court was swayed by evidence showing that he had made progress in an inclusive preschool classroom and felt it indicated that he would benefit from placement in general education in kindergarten with proper support and services. Further, the court saw no evidence that he would be a disruptive influence.

Private Facilities

The federal trial court in Massachusetts was persuaded that a private school was an appropriate placement for a high school student with autism because it offered him the therapeutic support that he needed via experienced staff, counseling, small classes, and the teaching of metacognitive skills.[338] However, the court was not convinced that the school's residential component was appropriate as it was not the least restrictive environment.

In Pennsylvania, a federal trial court concluded that a private residential program was appropriate for a child with intellectual disabilities as it addressed her unique needs and interests.[339] The court was convinced that the residential component was necessary for her to receive a FAPE as her educational needs were not segregable from her medical, social, or emotional needs, and to make meaningful progress she needed to practice independent living skills in a natural environment with appropriate support.

Related Services

School boards are required to provide related, or supportive, services to students with disabilities if such services are needed to assist the students in benefiting from their special education programs.[340] The IDEA specifically mentions transportation and such developmental, supportive, and corrective services as speech pathology, audiology, psychological services, physical therapy, occupational therapy, recreation (including therapeutic recreation), social work services, counseling services (including rehabilitation counseling), orientation and mobility services, medical services (for diagnostic or evaluative purposes only), and early identification and assessment as related services. The Supreme Court has declared

---

[337] Knox Cnty. Tenn. v. M.Q., 535 F. Supp. 3d 750, 396 Educ. L. Rep. 939 (E.D. Tenn. 2021).
[338] Doe v. Newton Pub. Schs., 537 F. Supp. 3d 56, 397 Educ. L. Rep. 111 (D. Mass. 2021).
[339] Perkiomen Vall. Sch. Dist. v. R.B., 533 F. Supp. 3d 233, 396 Educ. L. Rep. 419 (E.D. Pa. 2021).
[340] 20 U.S.C. § 1401(26).

that related services need to be provided only to students receiving special education and only those services that are necessary for the children to benefit from special education must be incorporated into their IEPs.[341] The only limitation placed on what might be considered related services is that medical services are exempted unless they are specifically for diagnostic or evaluative purposes as are medical devices that are surgically implanted or the replacement of such devices.[342]

A federal trial court in Pennsylvania was convinced that a child with autism spectrum disorder who needed to be placed in a typical preschool program to receive a FAPE was entitled to transportation.[343] A hearing officer had ascertained that evaluation data supported placement in the typical preschool.

Transition Services

The IDEA requires school personnel to develop transition services to facilitate students with disabilities in moving from school to post-school activities such as employment, vocational training, or independent living. Transition services include related services, instruction, community experiences, and the acquisition of daily living skills.[344] School personnel must include a statement of needed transition services in students' IEPs before they turn 16 years of age.[345]

In a dispute from Texas, the Fifth Circuit affirmed that the school board provided an appropriate transition plan for a high school student who had a history of mixed academic success checkered with disciplinary problems.[346] The court noted that in developing the student's transition goals, his IEP team relied on his aspirations, reports and recommendations of his teachers, and vocational survey data.

Discipline

Congress has amended the IDEA to add specific provisions outlining disciplinary requirements for students with disabilities.[347]

---

[341] Irving Indep. Sch. Dist. v. Tatro, 468 U.S. 883, 18 Educ. L. Rep. 138 (1984).
[342] 20 U.S.C. § 1401(26).
[343] Montgomery Cnty. Inter. Unit No. 23 v. K.S., 546 F. Supp. 3d 385, 399 Educ. L. Rep. 132 (E.D. Pa. 2021).
[344] 20 U.S.C. § 1401(34).
[345] 20 U.S.C. § 1414(d)(1)(A)(i)(VIII).
[346] Leigh Ann H. ex rel. K.S. v. Riesel Indep. Sch. Dist., 18 F.4th 788, 397 Educ. L. Rep. 25 (5th Cir. 2021).
[347] 20 U.S.C. § 1415(k).

Before the adoption of these amendments, courts applied the IDEA's change in placement and status quo provisions to the disciplinary process. The Supreme Court even emphasized that special education students could not be expelled for disciplinary reasons where their infractions were manifestations of, or caused by, their disabilities.[348] The IDEA's disciplinary amendments codified some of the prior case law and helped to clarify some grey areas that still existed. The current provision allows school administrators to transfer students to interim alternative settings for up to forty-five days for possession of weapons or drugs or infliction of serious bodily injury.[349] The statute also makes it clear that educational services must continue during expulsion periods.[350] Another important section requires school boards to conduct functional behavioral assessments (FBAs) and develop behavior intervention plans (BIPs) under specified circumstances.[351]

Nevertheless, the Supreme Court decision and the current language of the IDEA have not left school authorities without the ability to impose discipline. Special education students may be suspended temporarily and are subject to other normal disciplinary sanctions that do not result in changes in placement. If necessary, school boards may seek hearing officer or court intervention pending completion of administrative due process hearings in situations where it can be shown that students are dangerous and school officials cannot reach an agreement with their parents concerning proper placements.

The Fifth Circuit affirmed that a school board in Texas did not violate the IDEA by not including a high school student in an initial manifestation review meeting.[352] The court pointed out that although the board should have included him in that initial meeting, the error did not result in substantive harm because he attended subsequent meetings and had the opportunity to participate in the decision-making process.

In a second case from Texas, a federal trial court determined that a school board was not required to include a behavior intervention plan in the IEP of a child with Asperger Syndrome.[353] Since the child's IEP adequately identified his behavioral impediments and included several accommodations and supports aimed at helping

---

[348] Honig v. Doe, 484 U.S. 305, 43 Educ. L. Rep. 857 (1988).
[349] 20 U.S.C. § 1415(k)(1)(G).
[350] 20 U.S.C. § 1415(k)(1)(D).
[351] 20 U.S.C. § 1415(k)(1)(D), (E).
[352] Leigh Ann H. ex rel. K.S. v. Riesel Indep. Sch. Dist., 18 F.4th 788, 397 Educ. L. Rep. 25 (5th Cir. 2021).
[353] J.B. ex rel. Lauren v. Frisco Indep. Sch. Dist., 528 F. Supp. 3d 614, 395 Educ. L. Rep. 631 (E.D. Tex. 2021).

him with his behaviors, the court was satisfied that it met the IDEA's requirements.

The Supreme Court of Connecticut reversed and remanded the trial court's conviction of the defendant of risk of injury to a child.[354] The defendant was picking his daughter up from school for therapy, but she did not want to go and an altercation ensued. The primary issues on appeal centered around evidentiary rulings. The defendant attempted to testify about his daughter's aggressive behavior at home and questioned her teacher about her aggressive behavior at school, but the court sustained several of the prosecutor's objections to this testimony, which the defendant argued violated his constitutional right to present his parental justification defense. The court held that the exclusion of the cross-examination of his daughter's teacher about the reasonableness of his actions was outside the scope of the teacher's credibility and the court did not abuse its discretion. However, the defendant's testimony regarding why he felt his actions were reasonable and necessary was relevant and admissible. Further, the lower court's preclusion of the defendant's testimony about his daughter's ongoing aggression, his struggle with managing her aggression, and his attempts to get her urgent mental health care were prejudicial.

Remedies

The IDEA guarantees relief if school boards fail to provide FAPEs through the award of remedies to parents of children with disabilities. Courts typically award prospective relief as well as reimbursement of expenses and costs that parents incur when seeking appropriate special education and related services for their children.[355] If parents are deemed to be prevailing parties and the child's placement is appropriate, the Supreme Court concluded that school boards may be responsible for the costs of special education and related services.[356]

Reimbursement awards may be limited when parents do not provide prior notice regarding placement concerns or intentions to seek private school enrollment opportunities.[357] Yet, courts have required school boards to reimburse parents even though the selected placement was not in a state-approved facility as long as the

---

[354] State v. Mark T., 260 A.3d 402, 396 Educ. L. Rep. 191 (Conn. 2021).
[355] 20 U.S.C. § 1415(i)(2)(C)(iii).
[356] Burlington Sch. Comm. v. Dep't of Educ., Commonwealth of Mass., 471 U.S. 359, 23 Educ. L. Rep. 1189 (1985).
[357] 20 U.S.C. § 1412(a)(10)(C)(iii).

programs were otherwise appropriate.[358] Parents who lack financial means have also sought compensatory education services for their children with disabilities while litigation is ongoing. In many circumstances, courts have granted such awards to provide access to the necessary special education and related services.

The amount of attorney fees awarded is determined by the court and depends on the prevailing party status and reasonableness of the hours, rates, and award amount requested given the nature of the claim. Pursuant to the IDEA, parents qualify as the prevailing party if the relief granted in response to the child or parent's claim materially alters the legal relationship between the parties.[359] Furthermore, courts adhere to the Supreme Court's two-step analysis for determining attorney fees for a prevailing party who attained partial success through (1) consideration of the relationship between the successful and unsuccessful claims, and (2) evaluation of the significance of the relief granted in light of the reasonableness of hours spent on the litigation.[360]

The Supreme Court's decision in *Buckhannon Board and Care Home, Inc. v. West Virginia Department of Health and Human Resources (Buckhannon)* specified guidelines for attorney fees awards.[361] The *Buckhannon* decision applied to a non-education issue, however, the definition of a "prevailing party" applies to IDEA claims. According to the definition, a prevailing party is one who achieves the desired result through a court-ordered judgment on the merits or by a court-approved consent decree.

School boards may seek and be awarded reimbursement of legal fees when parents pursue litigation that is deemed to be frivolous, unreasonable, or without foundation; or that is premised on improper purposes, caused unreasonable delays, or needlessly increased litigation costs.[362] If such awards are granted to boards, the parents' attorneys are responsible for the awards under this provision.

Before seeking a remedy in the courts, individuals are required to exhaust administrative remedies as provided in the IDEA.[363] Exceptions to the exhaustion requirement are addressed earlier in this chapter and most frequently arise when parents of children with disabilities seek relief or remedies available through Section 504 or the ADA, and Section 1983 of the Civil Rights Act of 1871. The IDEA

---

[358] Florence Cnty. Sch. Dist. Four v. Carter, 510 U.S. 7, 86 Educ. L. Rep. 41 (1993).
[359] 20 U.S.C. §1415(i)(3).
[360] Hensley v. Eckerhart, 461 U.S. 424 (1983).
[361] 532 U.S. 598 (2001).
[362] 20 U.S.C. § 1415(i)(3)(B)(i)(II), (III).
[363] 20 U.S.C. § 1415(l).

specifies that parents may pursue additional avenues to compel adherence to the rights of their children with disabilities. As such, the exhaustion remedy is not to be interpreted as impeding Constitutional remedies or rights available under Section 504, the ADA, or Section 1983 of the Civil Rights Act of 1871. This chapter includes a review of Section 504 and ADA-related cases as well as the exhaustion provision of the IDEA illustrating the court's analysis of the potential intersections between these various claims.

Tuition Reimbursement

One of the most frequently sought remedies, tuition reimbursement, may be available to parents who seek an award for the costs incurred when they enrolled their children in private schools. Legal expenses may also be awarded if parents are determined to be a prevailing party as established by the 1986 IDEA amendments.[364] Parents may seek private school tuition reimbursement after pursuing non-public educational services because they believe that the public school failed to provide FAPE for their children. If parents fail to timely inform the IEP team that they reject the school's placement and plan to enroll their child in a private school, a reduction to the amount awarded is appropriate pursuant to the IDEA. In addition, if parents refuse to make their child available for evaluation by the school district, or when their actions were unreasonable, the award amount may be reduced.[365]

Tuition reimbursement claims are often made after parents unilaterally enroll their children in private school placements. In these circumstances, the courts will reject parental claims for tuition reimbursement if such unilateral placements by parents are made without first seeking an evaluation and requesting an IEP from the public school. For example, the Second Circuit, in a case from New York, held that the IDEA did not permit a school board to unilaterally amend a student's IEP during the 30-day resolution period after parents filed a due process complaint.[366] According to the IDEA, school officials are permitted to suggest changes to the child's IEP, but parents have the right to reject a proposed public school placement and to place their child in a suitable private school. In this case, the school board erroneously indicated in the IEP that the child would be placed in a 12-student classroom, which the

---

[364] Handicapped Children's Protection Act, 20 U.S.C. § 1415(i)(3)(B) et seq.
[365] 20 U.S.C. § 1412(a)(10)(C)(iii).
[366] Bd. of Educ. of Yorktown Cent. Sch Dist. v. C.S., 990 F.3d 152, 387 Educ. L. Rep. 105 (2d Cir. 2021).

parents rejected as insufficient, and there was evidence to support the parents' belief that the school board intended to place the child in a 15-student class, which they also believed was inappropriate. In light of this error and the unilateral IEP amendment, the court concluded that the school denied a FAPE to the child because it promised what would not be done, therefore, the court ordered the school board to reimburse the parents for the private school tuition.

The Third Circuit affirmed a federal trial court in Pennsylvania's holding that a general conversation and expression of interest in special education programming by the parent did not qualify as a request for evaluation or intent to reenroll their child in the public school.[367] As such, the school had no duty to evaluate, propose an IEP, or reimburse the parent for private school tuition.[368]

A federal trial court in North Carolina awarded tuition and transportation reimbursement for all four school years requested by the parent of a student with disabilities who sought a private school placement after being denied FAPE by the school board.[369] However, the court denied parental claims for the reimbursement of costs for the before-and-after school care, noting that the IDEA specifies reimbursement awards for tuition and transportation costs and fails to require reimbursement for care provided outside the typical school day.

In the first of three disputes heard by federal trial courts in Pennsylvania, the parents of a child with a disability asserted that the school board was obligated to pay for their child's placement in a typical preschool to meet the LRE requirements. The court agreed and ordered tuition reimbursement even though Pennsylvania does not provide free, universal preschool. According to the court, Pennsylvania adopted the IDEA and regulations in their entirety when they did not specify that they intended to opt out of the three-to-five-year age group.[370] In the second case, the court awarded full reimbursement for tuition, room and board, and transportation to the parents of a child who unilaterally enrolled her in a residential program.[371] The court agreed with a hearing officer that the school board's proposals would not have provided the child with a FAPE and that the residential program was necessary because her educational needs were not segregable from her medical, social, and emotional needs. In the third Pennsylvania case, the court awarded

---

[367] A.B. ex rel. K.B. v. Abington Sch. Dist., 841 F. App'x 392, 388 Educ. L. Rep. 183 (3rd Cir. 2021).
[368] 20 U.S.C. § 1412(a)(10)(A)(i); 34 C.F.R. § 300.137(a) (2007).
[369] Wake Cnty. Bd. of Educ. v. S.K. ex rel. R.K., 541 F.Supp.3d 233, 398 Educ. L. Rep. 233 (E.D.N.C. 2021).
[370] Montgomery Cnty. Intermediate Unit No. 23 v. K.S., 546 F. Supp. 3d 385, 399 Educ. L. Rep. 132 (E.D. Pa. 2021).
[371] Perkiomen Vall. Sch. Dist. v. R.B., 533 F. Supp. 3d 233, 396 Educ. L. Rep. 419 (E.D. Pa. 2021).

tuition reimbursement to parents who had enrolled their child in a private school after the school board failed to meet its obligation to have an IEP in place at the start of the school year.[372] The court found that this procedural violation resulted in a denial of a FAPE. However, the court denied reimbursement for the next school year because the school board proposed an appropriate IEP, but the parents failed to cooperate with the board.

Compensatory Services

As an equitable remedy, courts may award compensatory education when necessary to put children in the position they would have been in absent an IDEA violation by the school board.[373] If a school board denies a FAPE the parents of a child with a disability may seek compensatory education and services under the IDEA.[374] Compensatory educational services awarded to a child who has not been provided appropriate services under the IDEA should be reasonably calculated to provide the educational benefits that likely would have accrued from special education services the school board should have supplied in the first place.[375]

Contrary to a claim by the parent of a student with a disability from Alabama, a procedural IDEA child-find violation does not result in an automatic remedy of compensatory educational services. According to the Eleventh Circuit, substantive relief such as compensatory services, for a procedural violation is only appropriate if the violation causes substantive harm.[376] Accordingly, the court denied the parent's request for compensatory education. Specifically, the court denied parent relief because the IEP team was developing a program before litigation began and the parent failed to show how an earlier IEP would have benefitted the child.

Attorney Fees

A student with disabilities initiated a complaint, without parental involvement, against the New York Department of Corrections and Community Supervision for the denial of a FAPE in violation of the IDEA while he was incarcerated.[377] The hearing officer concluded that the Department violated the IDEA and

---

[372] M.D. v. Colonial Sch. Bd., 539 F. Supp. 3d 380, 397 Educ. L. Rep. 941 (E.D. Pa. 2021).
[373] 20 U.S.C. § 1401(9).
[374] Florence Cnty. Sch. Dist. Four v. Carter, 510 U.S. 7, 15-16, (1993); 20 U.S.C. 1415(i)(2)(C)(iii).
[375] 20 U.S.C.A. § 1415(b)(6)(A); 34 C.F.R. § 300.151(b)(1) (2006).
[376] J.N. v. Jefferson Cnty. Bd. of Educ., 12 F.4th 1355, 395 Educ. L. Rep. 74 (11th Cir. 2021).
[377] J.S. v. N.Y. State Dep't of Corr. and Cmty. Supervision, 557 F.Supp.3d 403, 401 Educ. L. Rep. 429 (W.D.N.Y. 2021).

awarded the student compensatory services. Subsequently, the student sought an award of attorney fees as the prevailing party, which a federal trial court denied pursuant to the clear language permitting parents to recover attorney fees under the IDEA, but not students. Despite referring to the canon against absurdity, the court resisted and cautioned against the risks of questioning Congress' judgment in the IDEA to clearly define the scope of individuals who are entitled to recover attorney fees.

As determined by a federal trial court in North Carolina, an award of attorney fees should not be reduced even when the parent did not prevail on every claim brought forward.[378] If the parents achieved excellent results and were successful on their most significant claims, the court concluded a full fee award for the attorney is appropriate.

Section 1983

Section 1983 is a federal civil rights statute that authorizes remedies, such as monetary, declaratory, or injunctive relief, for federal statutory or constitutional rights violations. Pursuant to Section 1983, individuals may seek monetary damages for civil rights violations by state actors, including public school boards or employees. In order to be successful pursuant to such a claim, individual plaintiffs must prove a violation of a federal constitutional right as a result of state policy or custom.[379] Furthermore, the IDEA's exhaustion requirements may not be circumvented for the purpose of claiming money damages available through a section 1983 claim.[380]

On the other hand, in circumstances that failed to implicate or focus on the denial of FAPE, courts recognized the IDEA exhaustion mandate did not apply. Such was the case in Georgia where a federal trial court maintained that the parents and guardians of a child with disabilities provided sufficient facts that their child's special education teacher and paraprofessional used intentional, rampant, and widespread force, abuse, and restraint.[381] They requested damages pursuant to Section 1983 for the alleged violation of their son's constitutional substantive due process rights. According to the court, the IDEA exhaustion mandate was not implicated by these

---

[378] Wake Cnty. Bd. of Educ. v. S.K. ex rel. R.K., 541 F.Supp.3d 233, 398 Educ. L. Rep. 233 (E.D.N.C. 2021).
[379] Monell v. Dep't of Soc. Servs., 436 U.S. 658 (1978).
[380] 20 U.S.C. 1415(i)(3)(B)(i)(I); 20 U.S.C. 1401(3)(A).
[381] D.D.T. ex rel. S.C. and D.T. v. Rockdale Cnty. Pub. Schs., 580 F. Supp. 3d 1314, 406 Educ. L. Rep. 756 (N.D. Ga. 2021).

facts given the absence of a complaint focused on the denial of a FAPE.

Similarly, in Massachusetts, the parents of a sixteen-year-old female student with significant cognitive impairments sought damages pursuant to Section 1983 under the state-created danger substantive due process doctrine. Specifically, the parents claimed their daughter was assaulted by a male student when she was permitted to use the bathroom unsupervised. A federal trial court dismissed this claim noting that even if the school created a substantial risk of serious harm by failing to provide constant one-on-one supervision, such action is insufficient to shock the conscience of the court as the evidence fails to demonstrate arbitrariness and caprice from bad faith or egregious and extreme actions.[382] In addition, the parents claimed negligent supervision, Section 504, and Title IX violations, which the school board sought to dismiss citing the IDEA's exhaustion requirement. Denying the board's dismissal request, the court noted that the board's actions injured the child in ways unrelated to the FAPE and IEP violations.

Discrimination Under Section 504 of the Rehabilitation Act and the Americans with Disabilities Act

Disability rights and protections are the focus of both Section 504 of the Rehabilitation Act of 1973 (Section 504) and the Americans with Disabilities Act of 1990 (ADA) as amended in 2008. Section 504 prohibits exclusion and discrimination of individuals with disabilities, specifically "[n]o otherwise qualified individual with a disability... shall, solely by reason of her or his disability be excluded from participation in, be denied benefits of, or be subjected to discrimination under any program or activity receiving [f]ederal financial assistance...."[383] These protections apply both to services provided by an agency and to employment by an institution receiving federal funding.

Pursuant to these federal civil rights statutes and accompanying regulations, discrimination and exclusion of individuals with disabilities are prohibited. Section 504 applies to federally funded programs and activities, while the ADA applies to all public entities, regardless of the receipt of federal funds. Originally enacted in 1990, the ADA has greatly impacted both the public and private sectors.

---

[382] Doe v. Dennis-Yarmouth Reg'l Sch. Dist., 578 F.Supp.3d 164, 405 Educ. L. Rep. 1037 (D. Mass. 2021).
[383] 29 U.S.C. § 794.

According to the ADA Amendments Act, the term disability should be broadly interpreted both in the ADA and Section 504.[384] The ADA Amendments Act expressly sought to clarify the meaning of a person with a disability and to make it easier to qualify as a person with a disability. Before the Amendments Act, the Supreme Court ruled that an individual who claimed to be regarded as disabled needed to show that their disability limited a major life activity.[385]

The statutory constructions of Section 504 and the ADA are similar, thus these claims often are reviewed simultaneously in the courts.[386] In order to qualify as an individual with a disability under Section 504 and the ADA, an individual must demonstrate that a physical or mental impairment substantially limits one or more major life activities, has a record of such impairments, or is regarded as having such impairments.[387] The definition of major life activities is broadly interpreted and includes "functions such as caring for oneself, performing manual tasks, walking, seeing, hearing, speaking, breathing, learning, and working."[388]

In two previous Supreme Court cases, the definition of "otherwise qualified" was interpreted as meaning an individual could meet all of the program requirements despite the individual's disability.[389] Once it is determined that an individual is otherwise qualified, an entity receiving federal funds is required to make reasonable accommodations unless this would create an undue hardship.[390] Similarly, the ADA imposes the duty to provide reasonable accommodations for private entities.

Students in Elementary and Secondary Schools

COVID-Related Cases

Although the Office for Civil Rights (OCR) has the authority and responsibility to enforce Section 504 and the ADA, parents typically litigate these claims in the federal courts, seeking relief from alleged discrimination by schools and school employees. Additionally, parents may seek relief in the courts under all three statutes, Section 504, the ADA, and the IDEA. Despite similarity across the three statutes, parental claims under Section 504 and the ADA may

---

[384] P.L. 110-325, 122 Stat. 3553 (2008).
[385] Sutton v. United Air Lines, 527 U.S. 471 (1999), superseded by statute, 42 U.S.C. § 12102(3)(A) (2008).
[386] See 42 U.S.C. §§ 12134(b), 12201(a).
[387] 42 U.S.C. § 12102(1); 34 C.F.R. §104.3(j)(1) (2017).
[388] 34 C.F.R. § 104.3(j)(2)(ii) (2017).
[389] Sch. Bd. of Nassau Cnty. v. Arline, 480 U.S. 273, 37 Educ. L. Rep. 448 (1987); Se. Cmty. Coll. v. Davis, 442 U.S. 397 (1979).
[390] 34 C.F.R. § 104.12(a).

be distinct from the IDEA claims, in which case the IDEA's failure to exhaust mandate may be inapplicable. Specifically, as discussed earlier in this chapter, if parental claims for relief under Section 504 and the ADA were unrelated to FAPE, such claims likely survived school boards' dismissal requests because the courts determined the parents' claims were not subject to exhaustion of administrative remedies under the IDEA.

Beginning in March 2020, a global and deadly pandemic caused by the novel coronavirus, known as COVID-19, disrupted daily life, and caused serious illness resulting in death rates across the United States and the world that were unparalleled in the last 100 years.[391] The Centers for Disease Control and Prevention (CDC) responded with a list of factors regarding individuals at higher risk of severe illness or death from COVID-19, including children with medical complexities, genetic, neurologic, metabolic conditions, or congenital heart disease; and children with obesity, diabetes, asthma or chronic lung disease, sickle cell disease, or immunosuppression.[392] Foreseeably, the COVID-19 pandemic resulted in dramatic disputes between school boards and parents of children with disabilities, particularly children with medical complexities, and especially in states where governors and legislators adopted anti-mask mandates and similar face-covering provisions affecting disabled children's access to schools for in-person learning.

Disability rights advocates initiated a suit against the South Carolina Governor, Attorney General, and Superintendent of Education, as well as several county school boards, challenging a state statutory proviso prohibiting enforcement of mask mandates in the public schools.[393] They claimed the proviso violated Section 504 and the ADA. The advocates moved for a temporary restraining order and preliminary injunction enjoining enforcement of the proviso on behalf of students whose disabilities increased their risk of contracting COVID-19 and/or who had an increased risk of serious complications or death from COVID-19 infections. A federal trial court granted injunctive relief, citing the COVID-19 health emergency and the discriminatory measures that the anti-mask mandate imposed on children with disabilities. According to the court, "This is not a close call. The General Assembly's COVID measures disallowing school districts from mandating masks, as

---

[391] Shannon Sabo & Sandra Johnson, *U.S. Deaths Spiked as COVID-19 Continued*, U.S. CENSUS BUREAU (Mar. 24, 2022), https://www.census.gov/library/stories/2022/03/united-states-deaths-spiked-as-covid-19-continued.html.
[392] *Covid-19: Medical Conditions*, CDC (May 11, 2023), https://www.cdc.gov/coronavirus/2019-ncov/need-extra-precautions/people-with-medical-conditions.html.
[393] Disability Rts. S.C. v. McMaster, 24 F.4th 893, 399 Educ. L. Rep. 482 (4th Cir. 2022).

found in Proviso 1.108, discriminates against children with disabilities." The Fourth Circuit, however, vacated that judgment and remanded with instructions to dismiss on the grounds that the parents and advocacy organization lacked standing.

In Texas, the parents of seven children with disabilities that increased their risk of contracting COVID-19 and suffering severe illness sought to enjoin enforcement of the governor's executive order prohibiting mask mandates by governmental entities, including school districts. They alleged that the order violated Section 504 and the ADA by denying equal access to in-person school and prohibiting consideration of mask mandates as a reasonable accommodation for students. A federal trial court found that the order denied disabled students equal access to the in-person learning benefits provided to other students and excluded them from participation and benefits of the services, programs, or activities of a public entity. The court was convinced that the documented higher risks of contracting COVID-19 as compared to non-impaired peers effectively foreclosed in-person learning or forced parents to unnecessarily assume greater health and safety risks. Thus, the court asserted that the governor's order violated Section 504 and the ADA and permanently enjoined the board from enforcing the order. The Fifth Circuit stayed the injunction pending appeal and eventually vacated the order, reasoning that the plaintiffs had not presented an injury in fact sufficient to satisfy the requirements for an injunction.[394]

In Iowa, parents of children with underlying health conditions making them vulnerable to COVID-19 complications sought a preliminary injunction of a state statute that prohibited mask requirements in schools.[395] The parents claimed the statute violated Section 504 and the ADA by failing to allow the provision of reasonable accommodations that were necessary to enable their children to access schools for in-person learning. A federal trial court issued a temporary restraining order and subsequent preliminary injunction giving the public schools discretion to act in the best interests of public health and permitting the adoption of public school masking mandates. On appeal, the Eighth Circuit affirmed the preliminary injunction but later vacated it as moot because conditions differed from those that existed when it was granted.

A federal trial court in Georgia denied temporary restraining order and preliminary injunction requests by four parents of

---

[394] E.T. v. Paxton, 19 F.4th 760, 397 Educ. L. Rep. 488 (5th Cir. 2021), *vacated* 19 F.4th 709, 405 Educ. L. Rep. 634 (5th Cir. 2022).
[395] ARC of Iowa v. Reynolds, 24 F.4th 1162, 399 Educ. L. Rep. 524 (8th Cir. 2022); *vacated as moot* 33 F.4th 1042, 402 Educ. L. Rep. 120 (8th Cir. 2022).

students with disabilities whose disabilities made them particularly vulnerable to COVID-19.[396] In response to the school board's removal of mask mandates and modification of other COVID restrictions, the parents asserted disparate treatment and failure to accommodate claims pursuant to the ADA and Section 504. The court rejected their claims, finding the school board's policy was facially neutral and that the virtual learning program offered meaningful access to education. As the court remarked, the board had the authority to make operational decisions about students' health and the court refused to second-guess or usurp such authority. The Eleventh Circuit reversed and remanded, stating that the trial court erred by misconstruing the students' argument as a right to education generally, despite the record clearly showing that they were alleging a denial of access to in-person education that the school district provides to all students.[397] On remand, the appellate court instructed the lower court to determine if virtual schooling is a reasonable accommodation for in-person schooling, not education in general.

Students with disabilities, an advocacy organization, and students' families filed a class action suit seeking a temporary restraining order and relief from the imposition of state policy creating a barrier to students with disabilities whose health conditions would pose a serious risk if they were denied access to distance learning and instead required to return to an in-person educational setting during the COVID-19 pandemic.[398] A federal trial court in California granted the temporary restraining order given their likelihood of success on the merits of the Section 504 and ADA claims along with their demonstration of irreparable harm to children with disabilities. In addition, the court rejected the state's claim that administrative exhaustion under the IDEA is required because the students and their families were not seeking relief for the denial of a FAPE.

In a dispute from Colorado, the parents of nine children with disabilities that put them at great risk of health complications from COVID-19 challenged a county health order loosening mask and quarantine requirements.[399] The federal trial court granted their motion for a temporary restraining order finding that the parents were likely to establish that the county's action deprived the children of equal access to their schools' services to the fullest extent possible.

---

[396] L.E. v. Ragsdale, 568 F.Supp.3d 1364, 403 Educ. L. Rep. 664 (N.D. Ga. 2021).
[397] L.E. *ex rel.* Cavorley v. Superintendent of Cobb Cnty. Sch. Dist., 55 F.4th 1296, 410 Educ. L. Rep. 141 (11th Cir. 2022).
[398] E. E. v. Cal., 570 F.Supp.3d 759, 403 Educ. L. Rep. 799 (N.D. Cal. 2021).
[399] Douglas Cnty. Sch. Dist. RE-1 v. Douglas Cnty. Health Dep't, 568 F. Supp. 3d 1158, 403 Educ. L. Rep. 654 (D. Colo. 2021).

On the other hand, a federal trial court in Florida denied a claim by eleven parents seeking a preliminary injunction of the governor's executive order adopting COVID-19-related health protocols in schools.[400] The parents sought injunctive relief, claiming their students, who were enrolled in public school districts throughout the state, had health issues that made attending school without a universal mask mandate difficult or impossible. The Florida Department of Health issued an emergency rule requiring students to wear masks or facial coverings unless a parent or legal guardian requests to opt out; it also prohibited harassment or discriminatory treatment of any students who opted out. Concurrently, the state Department of Education issued an emergency rule adopting transfer procedures for any public school student subjected to COVID-19 harassment at school. The court asserted that the parents failed to adhere to the IDEA's exhaustion requirement, which rendered their request for relief out of line with public interest. Further, they failed to establish irreparable harm because their children had not been denied educational services altogether. The court directed parents to pursue exhaustion, thereby enabling a case-by-case review with effective solutions for each individual child that would not be achieved through a blanket injunction.

Injunctive relief was also denied to five parents of public school students, at least one of whom had a disability, seeking injunctive relief under Section 504, the ADA, Section 1983, the Fifth and Fourteenth Amendments, and the Pennsylvania Constitution to restrain the school boards from endorsing a policy that allowed exceptions to the district's COVID-19 mask-mandate.[401] According to their complaint, the policy permitted students to obtain an exception from mandatory masking without supporting documentation or medical evidence to support the request for an exception. A federal trial court denied injunctive relief after determining that the parents were unlikely to succeed on the merits of their Section 504 and ADA claims given the lack of evidence showing the school board policy discriminated on the basis of disability or that any of the students were deprived of an opportunity to participate in educational programs or services solely on the basis of disability.

In Tennessee, the governor adopted a mask mandate applicable to public schools that contained broad opt-out provisions available for any reason to a student's parent or guardian by simple written

---

[400] Hayes ex rel. W.H. v. DeSantis, 561 F.Supp.3d 1187, 402 Educ. L. Rep. 170 (S.D. Fla. 2021).
[401] Doe #1 v. Del. Vall. Sch. Dist., 572 F.Supp.3d 38, 404 Educ. L. Rep. 660 (M.D. Pa. 2021).

notification.[402] In response to the governor's executive order, students with disabilities and their parents sought relief in the courts, specifically claiming that Tennessee school boards violated the ADA and Section 504 by not providing reasonable accommodations for medically fragile students to access fundamentally safe educational opportunities. In four separate legal actions, parents requested temporary restraining orders and preliminary injunctions on behalf of their children with significant medical conditions increasing the severity of COVID-19 risks. The trial courts granted temporary restraining orders or preliminary injunctions in all four cases.

Another challenge arose in Tennessee shortly after the General Assembly passed additional legislation signed by the governor with a prohibition on mask mandates by school districts.[403] In response, parents of eight children with disabilities that increased the severity of risks from COVID-19 claimed the new law violated Section 504 and the ADA. They sought a temporary restraining order and preliminary injunction, which a federal trial court granted, noting the likelihood of success on the merits of Section 504 and ADA claims, a demonstration of irreparable harm to the children with disabilities, and the reminder that state law must yield to federal law when they conflict.[404]

The parents of two Indiana high school students who received academic accommodations pursuant to Section 504 plans filed suit alleging that the school board's adoption of a hybrid model of instruction during the pandemic violated their rights because their accommodation plans could not be implemented at home.[405] A state trial court granted the school board's motion to dismiss, and an appellate court affirmed. The appellate court agreed that the parents had not alleged facts showing that the school board intentionally discriminated against the children or that the virtual instruction plan disproportionately impacted students with disabilities.

Other Disability Discrimination Issues

In a case from California, the Ninth Circuit rejected a student's claim that the four-factor test established by the 2014 U.S. Department of Education's *Dear Colleague Letter* created a legal

---

[402] R.K. v. Lee, 563 F.Supp.3d 774, 402 Educ. L. Rep. 243 (M.D. Tenn. 2021); S.B. *ex rel.* M.B. v. Lee, 566 F.Supp.3d 835, 402 Educ. L. Rep. 803 (E.D. Tenn. 2021), *motion to amend judgment denied* 567 F. Supp. 3d 850, 402 Educ. L. Rep. 1003 (E.D. Tenn. 2021); G.S. *ex rel.* Schwaigert v. Lee, 558 F. Supp. 3d 601, 401 Educ. L. Rep. 758 (W.D. Tenn. 2021).
[403] TENN. CODE ANN. § 14-1-101 et seq.
[404] R.K. v. Lee, 575 F.Supp.3d 957, 405 Educ. L. Rep. 214 (M.D. Tenn. 2021).
[405] Reinoehl v. St. Joseph Cnty. Health Dep't, 181 N.E.3d 341, 400 Educ. L. Rep. 323 (Ind. Ct. App. 2021).

obligation.[406] Rather, the court applied the *Davis* framework to assess the student's request for damages pursuant to claims of peer-on-peer harassment based on disability. According to the *Davis* framework, the student must show actual knowledge of the harassment and demonstrate deliberate indifference, which sets a high bar requiring the school's response to be clearly unreasonable in light of the known circumstances. Additionally, the legal framework under Section 504 or the ADA sets a much higher bar for awarding damages and requires intentional discrimination on the basis of disability or deliberate indifference to the disability. Finally, *Dear Colleague Letters* do not establish enforceable and distinct legal obligations according to the Ninth Circuit's interpretation.

In another dispute from California, a federal trial court denied a parent's motion for summary judgment after finding that triable issues of material fact existed as to whether the school board's failure to provide remote instruction denied her child, who had health issues, meaningful access to its educational programs.[407] In the court's view, it was unclear as to whether the parent's requested accommodations were reasonable in light of the accommodations the school board did provide.

In Georgia, a federal trial court faced a matter of first impression in determining whether a sheriff could be held liable for IDEA violations experienced by incarcerated and detained students with disabilities.[408] Although the court determined that the sheriff violated child-find with regard to the students' protections under the IDEA, the court denied the students' Section 504 and ADA claims because the Sheriff's actions were not so unreasonable as to constitute intentional discrimination by deliberate indifference.

A student from Louisiana who utilized a wheelchair attended an orientation session at a sectarian high school but was discouraged from applying for admission by school officials who felt they could not accommodate her disability. After the student's mother filed suit, a federal trial court denied the school's motion to dismiss finding that the parent had shown that her daughter suffered an injury in fact even though she had never submitted her application.[409]

In the first of three cases from Pennsylvania, parents of a gifted child with multiple medical conditions affecting physical and behavioral functions alleged that the school board denied an appropriate education and violated the IDEA, Section 504, and the

---

[406] Csutoras v. Paradise High Sch., 12 F.4th 960, 395 Educ. L. Rep. 40 (9th Cir. 2021).
[407] S.T. v. L.A. Unified Sch. Dist., 545 F.Supp.3d 840, 398 Educ. L. Rep. 945 (C.D. Cal. 2021).
[408] T.H. *ex rel.* T.B. v. DeKalb Cnty. Sch. Dist., 564 F.Supp.3d 1349, 402 Educ. L. Rep. 631 (N.D. Ga. 2021).
[409] Beverly R. v. Mt Carmel Acad. of New Orleans, 528 F. Supp. 3d 451, 395 Educ. L. Rep. 584 (E.D. La. 2021).

ADA.[410] The student did not have an approved Section 504 plan, instead having a Gifted Individualized Educational Plan (GIEP), an Individual Health Plan, and an Emergency Care Plan. Soon after the communications between the parents and school personnel became strained, the parents requested full homebound instruction, which the board refused, instead providing homebound services to supplement in-school instruction. After the student threw a remote control striking the homebound instructor, the board discontinued homebound instruction and offered to provide education in a different location. A federal trial court asserted that there are no bright line rules to determine an appropriate education under Section 504, noting that parents must provide specific evidence of educational deprivation to support a violation of the Section 504 FAPE provision.

In the second case, the parents of a student with disabilities alleged discrimination under Section 504 and the ADA after a Pennsylvania school board denied a request for their child to attend school with a service dog.[411] They requested a preliminary injunction permitting the student to attend school with her service dog pending the outcome of the litigation. The court first examined whether the dog qualified as a service animal using the two-part test to determine if the animal was "individually trained to do work or perform tasks for the benefit of an individual with a disability" and if the tasks to be performed by the animal were directly related to the individual's disability. The court granted the parents' request, determining that they met the three-factor preliminary injunction test by showing (1) a substantial likelihood of success on the merits because the dog qualifies as a service animal; (2) evidence of irreparable harm if the preliminary injunction is denied; and (3) the balance of equities reveals benefits to the student and an absence of harm to the district, thus weighing in favor of granting the preliminary injunction.

In the third dispute involving the parents of a child with learning disabilities, a federal trial court ascertained that school officials had not violated Section 504 by failing to offer the student accommodations.[412] The court found that, on at least two occasions, the parents had rejected school officials' offers to discuss accommodations as the school year approached.

---

[410] A.C. and D.C. *ex rel.* C.C. v. Owen J. Roberts Sch. Dist., 554 F. Supp. 3d 620, 400 Educ. L. Rep. 949 (E.D. Pa. 2021).
[411] C.G. ex rel. P.G. v. Saucon Vall. Sch. Dist., 571 F.Supp.3d 430, 404 Educ. L. Rep. 589 (E.D. Pa. 2021).
[412] M.D. v. Colonial Sch. Dist., 539 F. Supp. 3d 380, 397 Educ. L. Rep. 941 (E.D. Pa. 2021).

A federal trial court in Texas found that a student stated a claim for discrimination under the ADA and Rehabilitation Act, and her mother stated a claim for retaliation under the ADA.[413] The student attended a public high school and had multiple IEPs since an accident rendered her disabled when she was younger. Due to the student's disability, she missed substantial amounts of school, which the school failed to adequately accommodate despite numerous doctor's notes and requests from her mother, and she was ultimately disenrolled from the high school unilaterally. The court agreed that the student's allegations regarding the school's unwillingness to follow the medical advice she received or to accommodate the student's disabilities, and its ultimate disenrollment of her, were sufficient to create "an inference of professional bad faith or gross misjudgment" to state a claim of intentional discrimination. Further, the mother was successful in her retaliation claims based on the school's filing of truancy charges against her despite substantial medical documentation for the student's absences.

Conclusion

Litigation over provisions of the IDEA, Section 504, and the ADA continues but at a slower pace than in previous years. In this respect, cases challenging school board decisions regarding the provision of services to students with disabilities during the COVID-19 pandemic were prominent.

Despite the Supreme Court's decision in *Fry*, litigation over when parents asserting claims under other statutes, such as Section 504 and the ADA, must exhaust the IDEA's administrative remedies before filing suit has continued with mixed results. Much of this litigation was COVID-related and centered on the claims of students effectively being denied access to educational programs when schools discontinued mandatory mask mandates. The issue revolved around the question of whether these were FAPE-based complaints or allegations of discriminatory treatment.

Parents continued to seek remedies for school boards' failure to provide FAPEs in the form of tuition reimbursement, compensatory education awards, and attorney fees. Even so, litigation in this area has declined from past years.

Since students with disabilities have rights and protections under Section 504 and the ADA in addition to the IDEA, it is not

---

[413] Round Rock Indep. Sch. Dist. v. Amy M., 540 F.Supp.3d 679, 398 Educ. L. Rep. 114 (W.D. Tex. 2021).

surprising that suits continue to be filed under all three statutes. As in the past, courts are reluctant to find discrimination absent evidence of bad faith or gross negligence on the part of school officials. Again, COVID-related cases were prominent with parents claiming that their medically fragile children were unable to attend school in person on the same basis as their peers because the discontinuation of mask mandates made it unsafe for them to do so. The results in these cases were mixed.

Alphabetical List of Cases

A.B. ex rel. K.B. v. Abington Sch. Dist.
A.B. ex rel. K.B. v. Mich. Dep't of Educ.
A.C. and D.C. ex rel. C.C. v. Owen J. Roberts Sch. Dist.
ARC of Iowa v. Reynolds
B.D. ex rel. Davis v. D.C.
Bd. of Educ. of Hendrick Hudson Cent. Sch. Dist. v. Rowley
Bd. of Educ. of Yorktown Cent. Sch Dist. v. C.S.
Beverly R. v. Mt Carmel Acad. of New Orleans
Burlington Sch. Comm. v. Dep't of Educ., Commwealth of Mass.
Capistrano Unified Sch. Dist. v. S.W.
C.E. v. Elizabeth Pub. Sch. Dist.
Cedar Rapids Cmty. Sch. Dist. v. Garret F.
C.G. ex rel. P.G. v. Saucon Vall. Sch. Dist.
Crofts v. Issaquah Sch. Dist. No. 411
Csutoras v. Paradise High Sch.
David D. v. Dartmouth Sch. Comm.
D.C. ex rel. J.C. v. Klein Indep. Sch. Dist.
D.D. ex rel. Ingram v. L.A. Unified Sch. Dist.
D.D.T. ex rel. S.C. and D.T. v. Rockdale Cnty. Pub. Schs.
Disability Rts. S.C. v. McMaster
Doe #1 v. Del. Vall. Sch. Dist.
Doe v. Dennis-Yarmouth Reg. Sch. Dist.
Doe v. Newton Pub. Schs.
Doe v. Portland Pub. Schs.
Douglas Cnty. Sch. Dist. RE-1 v. Douglas Cnty. Health Dep't
E.E. v. Cal.
Elmira City Sch. Dist. v. N.Y. State Educ. Dep't
Endrew F. ex rel. Joseph F. v. Douglas Cnty. Sch. Dist. RE-1
E.T. v. Morath
E.T. v. Paxton
Florence Cnty. Sch. Dist. Four v. Carter
Forest Grove Sch. Dist. v. T.A.
Fry v. Napoleon Cmty. Schs.
G.D. ex rel. Jeffrey D. v. Swampscott Pub. Schs.
Geis v. Bd. of Educ. of Parsippany-Troy Hills, Morris Cnty.
G.S. ex rel. Schwaigert v. Lee
G.W. v. Ringwood Bd. of Educ.
Hayes ex rel. W.H. v. DeSantis
Heather H. ex rel. P.H. v. Nw. Indep. Sch. Dist.
Hills & Dales Child Dev. Ctr. v. Iowa Dep't of Educ.
Honig v. Doe

H.W. ex rel. Jennie W. v. Comal Indep. Sch. Dist.
Irving Indep. Sch. Dist. v. Tatro
J.B. ex rel. Lauren v. Frisco Indep. Sch. Dist.
J.M. ex rel. C.M. v. Summit City Bd. of Educ.
J.N. v. Jefferson Cnty. Bd. of Educ.
Johnson ex rel. A.J. v. Charlotte-Mecklenburg Schs. Bd. of Educ.
J.P. ex rel. Ogden v. Belton Sch. Dist. No. 234
J.R. ex rel. Analisa and Joe R. v. Austin Indep. Sch. Dist.
J.S. v. N.Y. State Dep't of Corr. and Cmty. Supervision
Knox Cnty. Tenn. v. M.Q.
Lamar Consol. Indep. Sch. Dist. v. J.T.
L.E. ex rel. Cavorley v. Superintendent of Cobb Cnty. Sch. Dist.
Leigh Ann H. ex rel. K.S. v. Riesel Indep. Sch. Dist.
M.B. v. Lee
M.C. v. L.A. Unified Sch. Dist.
M.D. v. Colonial Sch. Dist.
Minnetonka Pub. Schs., Indep. Sch. Dist. No. 276 v. M.L.K.
Mills v. Bd. of Educ. of D.C.
Montgomery Cnty. Inter. Unit No. 23 v. K.S.
Patrick G. v. Harrison Sch. Dist. No. 2
Penn. Ass'n for Retarded Child. (PARC) v. Penn.
Perkiomen Vall. Sch. Dist. v. R.B.
Reinoehl v. St. Joseph Cnty. Health Dep't
Responsive Educ. Sols. v. Kirschner
R.K. v. Lee
Round Rock Indep. Sch. Dist. v. Amy M.
Sanchez v. Arlington Cnty. Sch. Bd.
S.B. ex rel. M.B. v. Lee
S.C. ex rel. K.G. v. Lincoln Cnty. Sch. Dist.
Schaffer ex rel. Schaffer v. Weast
Sch. Bd. of Nassau Cnty. v. Arline
Se. Cmty. Coll. v. Davis
S.T. v. L.A. Unified Sch. Dist.
State v. Mark T.
T.H. ex rel. T.B. v. DeKalb Cnty. Sch. Dist.
Valentin-Marrero v. P.R.
Wake Cnty. Bd. of Educ. v. S.K. ex rel. R.K.

Cases by Jurisdiction

FEDERAL CASES

U.S. Supreme Court

Bd. of Educ. of Hendrick Hudson Cent. Sch. Dist. v. Rowley
Burlington Sch. Comm. v. Dep't of Educ., Commwealth of Mass.
Endrew F. ex rel. Joseph F. v. Douglas Cnty. Sch. Dist. RE-1
Florence Cnty. Sch. Dist. Four v. Carter
Fry v. Napoleon Cmty. Schs.
Honig v. Doe
Irving Indep. Sch. Dist. v. Tatro
Schaffer ex rel. Schaffer v. Weast
Sch. Bd. of Nassau Cnty. v. Arline
Se. Cmty. Coll. v. Davis

First Circuit
David D. v. Dartmouth Sch. Comm.
Doe v. Dennis-Yarmouth Reg. Sch. Dist.
Doe v. Portland Pub. Schs.
G.D. ex rel. Jeffrey D. v. Swampscott Pub. Schs.
Valentin-Marrero v. P.R.

Massachusetts
Doe v. Newton Pub. Schs.

Second Circuit
Bd. of Educ. of Yorktown Cent. Sch Dist. v. C.S.

New York
J.S. v. N.Y. State Dep't of Corr. and Cmty. Supervision

Third Circuit
A.B. ex rel. K.B. v. Abington Sch. Dist.
Geis v. Bd. of Educ. of Parsippany-Troy Hills, Morris Cnty.
G.W. v. Ringwood Bd. of Educ.
J.M. ex rel. C.M. v. Summit City Bd. of Educ.

Pennsylvania
A.C. and D.C. ex rel. C.C. v. Owen J. Roberts Sch. Dist.
C.G. ex rel. P.G. v. Saucon Vall. Sch. Dist.
Doe #1 v. Del. Vall. Sch. Dist.

M.D. v. Colonial Sch. Dist.
Montgomery Cnty. Inter. Unit No. 23 v. K.S.
Penn. Ass'n for Retarded Child. (PARC) v. Penn.
Perkiomen Vall. Sch. Dist. v. R.B.

Fourth Circuit
Disability Rts. S.C. v. McMaster
Johnson ex rel. A.J. v. Charlotte-Mecklenburg Schs. Bd. of Educ.

North Carolina
Wake Cnty. Bd. of Educ. v. S.K. ex rel. R.K.

Virginia
Sanchez v. Arlington Cnty. Sch. Bd.

Fifth Circuit
D.C. ex rel. J.C. v. Klein Indep. Sch. Dist.
E.T. v. Paxton
H.W. ex rel. Jennie W. v. Comal Indep. Sch. Dist.
J.B. ex rel. Lauren v. Frisco Indep. Sch. Dist.
Leigh Ann H. ex rel. K.S. v. Riesel Indep. Sch. Dist.

Louisiana
Beverly R. v. Mt Carmel Acad. of New Orleans

Texas
E.T. v. Morath
Heather H. ex rel. P.H. v. Nw. Indep. Sch. Dist.
J.R. ex rel. Analisa and Joe R. v. Austin Indep. Sch. Dist.
Lamar Consol. Indep. Sch. Dist. v. J.T.
Round Rock Indep. Sch. Dist. v. Amy M.

Sixth Circuit
M.B. v. Lee

Michigan
A.B. ex rel. K.B. v. Mich. Dep't of Educ.

Tennessee
G.S. ex rel. Schwaigert v. Lee
Knox Cnty. Tenn. v. M.Q.
R.K. v. Lee
S.B. ex rel. M.B. v. Lee

Eighth Circuit
ARC of Iowa v. Reynolds
J.P. ex rel. Ogden v. Belton Sch. Dist. No. 234
Minnetonka Pub. Schs., Indep. Sch. Dist. No. 276 v. M.L.K.

Iowa
ARC of Iowa v. Reynolds

Ninth Circuit
Capistrano Unified Sch. Dist. v. S.W.
Crofts v. Issaquah Sch. Dist. No. 411
Csutoras v. Paradise High Sch.
D.D. ex rel. Ingram v. L.A. Unified Sch. Dist.
S.C. ex rel. K.G. v. Lincoln Cnty. Sch. Dist.

California
E.E. v. Cal.
M.C. v. L.A. Unified Sch. Dist.
S.T. v. L.A. Unified Sch. Dist.

Tenth Circuit
Patrick G. v. Harrison Sch. Dist. No. 2

Colorado
Douglas Cnty. Sch. Dist. RE-1 v. Douglas Cnty. Health Dept.

Eleventh Circuit
L.E. ex rel. Cavorley v. Superintendent of Cobb Cnty. Sch. Dist.
J.N. v. Jefferson Cnty. Bd. of Educ.

Florida
Hayes ex rel. W.H. v. DeSantis

Georgia
D.D.T. ex rel. S.C. and D.T. v. Rockdale Cnty. Pub. Schs.
T.H. ex rel. T.B. v. DeKalb Cnty. Sch. Dist.

D.C. Circuit

D.C.
B.D. ex rel. Davis v. D.C.
Mills v. Bd. of Educ. of D.C.

STATE COURTS

Connecticut
State v. Mark T.

Indiana
Reinoehl v. St. Joseph Cnty. Health Dep't

Iowa
Hills & Dales Child Dev. Ctr. v. Iowa Dep't of Educ.

New Jersey
C.E. v. Elizabeth Pub. Sch. Dist.

New York
Elmira City Sch. Dist. v. N.Y. State Educ. Dep't

Texas
Responsive Educ. Sols. v. Kirschner

Chapter 6

TORTS

Erin Biolchino, J.D., Ed.D.[414] and Raquel Muñiz, J.D., Ph.D.[415]

Introduction	**178**
Elementary and Secondary Education	**178**
Student Claims	178
Sexual Misconduct	178
Defamation	179
Negligence	180
Vicarious Liability	187
Immunity from Liability	188
Employee Claims	190
Claims by Other Injured Parties	192
Higher Education	**196**
Vehicle Accidents	196
Sexual Misconduct	197
Defamation	198
Medical Malpractice	199
Racial Profiling	199
Sports Injuries	200
Dangerous Conditions of Campus or Facilities	200
Employees	203
Immunity	203
Conclusion	**204**
Alphabetical List of Cases	**204**
Cases by Jurisdiction	**206**

---

[414] Assistant Professor of Educational Leadership, California State University, Long Beach, Long Beach, Ca.
[415] Assistant Professor, Lynch School of Education & Human Development; Assistant Professor, School of Law, Boston College, Boston, Mass.

Introduction

Of the sixty-four tort liability cases from 2022, forty-six were K-12 cases and eighteen were in higher education. The significant number of K-12 cases underscores the additional legal duties placed on K-12 schools because they serve children.

A majority of the K-12 cases were brought by students and/or their parents and included claims of sexual misconduct, unlawful disclosure of intimate images, defamation, and injuries occurring on school premises. In addition to the student claims, cases were also brought by school employees and other parties. The cases raised questions of state tort law, procedure, the duty to supervise, and state immunity laws for public entities and public employees.

The eighteen cases in a higher education context were also varied in nature. Four of the higher education cases were decided by federal courts, and the other fourteen cases were from state courts. The topic with the most cases was injuries resulting from dangerous conditions of the campus or facilities, with five cases relating to negligence and premises liability claims for unsafe conditions. Other topics at issue in these cases included vehicle accidents, sexual misconduct by college students and instructors, defamation, medical malpractice, racial profiling, and an injury to a student-athlete.

Elementary and Secondary Education

Student Claims

Sexual Misconduct

A federal trial court in California allowed a student's claim for discrimination under respondeat superior but dismissed her claim for disability discrimination under the Rehabilitation Act, holding that the school could not be held vicariously liable under state law.[416] The plaintiff, a twelve-year-old student with a speech impediment, brought this action against her school for direct and vicarious liability under the Rehabilitation Act and state law after she was sexually assaulted by a speech therapist who contracted with the school. The plaintiff's claim under the Rehabilitation Act for direct liability failed because she merely alleged that the school did not adequately supervise and vet the instructors it contracted with. She

---

[416] Doe v. Alameda Cmty. Learning Ctr., 532 F.Supp.3d 867, 396 Educ. L. Rep. 151 (N.D. Cal. 2021).

did not allege it was based on disability. The Ninth Circuit generally applies respondeat superior to any actions brought under a civil rights statute, so her respondeat superior claim under the Rehabilitation Act survived as she plausibly alleged that the speech therapist sexually assaulted her because he believed her speech impediment would prevent her from telling anyone. However, the school could not be vicariously liable for the therapist's actions on the state law claims because the therapist was not acting within the scope of his employment.

The alleged sexual abuse of a minor and grooming that included manipulation by a coach was at issue in a case from Illinois.[417] The school argued that it was entitled to indemnification due to its insurance policy coverage at the time of the alleged abuse. The court disagreed. A federal trial court held that the school's liability policy imposed a duty to provide notice to the insurance company in a case where the school became aware of instances of sexual misconduct between an employee and a student. It held that the school failed to notify the insurance company of the incident as required by the policy. Moreover, there was no coverage because the behavior involved criminal or deceptive acts.

Defamation

Two cases from New York involved issues surrounding defamation. In one case, the parents of a high school student at an all-girls preparatory school brought claims for defamation, breach of contract, and intentional and negligent infliction of emotional distress against the school.[418] The plaintiffs claimed that the defendant breached its own harassment policy by failing to investigate their complaints. The appellate court affirmed the order to dismiss all claims against the defendant, finding that the breach of contract claim was not actionable because the basis of the alleged harassment was not a characteristic protected by law or mentioned in the school's handbook, no defamation occurred because all statements made about the plaintiff were true, and there was a lack of outrageous conduct that would support emotional distress claims.

In the second case from New York, a trial court held that the verified complaint filed by alumnus on consent in federal court was the operative pleading on remand.[419] Alumnus of a private school moved for a confirmation of parties, correction of the caption,

---

[417] Westport Ins. Corp. v. Sycamore Cmty. Unit Sch. Dist. #427, 555 F. Supp. 3d 550, 401 Educ. L. Rep. 289 (N.D. Ill. 2021).
[418] Parker v. Trs. of Spence Sch., 168 N.Y.S.3d 56, 403 Educ. L. Rep. 860 (N.Y. App. Div. 2022).
[419] Fouad v. Milton Hershey Sch. And Sch. Trust, 158 N.Y.S.3d 541, 399 Educ. L. Rep. 382 (Sup. Ct. N.Y. 2021).

confirmation of the operative pleading, and approval of the form of service in their action for defamation and other tort claims against the school and other defendants. The plaintiff asked that the first amended complaint he filed be deemed the operative pleading in this case, but the defendants argued that, because there was no subject matter jurisdiction over the claim, granting him leave to file an amended complaint and the amended complaint itself became a nullity. The court held that the amended complaint was nullified on remand, but the verified complaint he filed in a federal trial court with the intent to file it in state court absent the removal was not nullified. Therefore, the verified complaint was the operative pleading and the defendants' motions to dismiss were meritless.

Negligence

In 2022, nineteen cases involved negligence, with three cases being decided in federal court and the remaining sixteen cases in state courts. In New York, a federal trial court denied the plaintiff former student's motion to disqualify a law firm as counsel for the defendant county department of social services.[420] The former student brought an action against the department alleging it was negligent in its investigation or failure to investigate when she alleged sexual assault by a former teacher. The plaintiff argued that the law firm should be disqualified from representing the department because the firm had represented her and "obtained privileged and confidential information" in a matrimonial action over two decades prior. For disqualification to be appropriate, there must be "a substantial relationship between the subject matter of the counsel's prior representation of the moving party and the issues in the present lawsuit." The court held that information discussed by the student in her prior matrimonial action was irrelevant to her current action against the department, so the substantial relationship test for disqualification was not met.

A federal trial court in Ohio held that the student plaintiffs were entitled to default judgment on their Title IX, sexual assault, and battery claims against the teacher; their negligence claims against the principal and assistant principal survived a motion to dismiss; and their intentional infliction of emotional distress (IIED) claims against the principal and assistant principal were dismissed.[421] The students alleged that they were sexually assaulted and abused by their former teacher with claims spanning more than ten years. The

---

[420] L.D. v. Seymour, 577 F.Supp.3d 85, 405 Educ. L. Rep. 851 (N.D.N.Y. 2022).
[421] Doe 1 v. Cleveland Metro. Sch. Dist. Bd. of Educ., 533 F.Supp.3d 567, 396 Educ. L. Rep. 447 (N.D. Ohio 2021).

plaintiffs' Title IX claim was subject to a twelve-year statute of limitations, thus, it was not time-barred. Further, the plaintiffs adequately alleged negligence against the two officials because they failed to investigate any of the teacher's questionable conduct that they had actual knowledge of. However, the plaintiffs did not adequately allege an IIED claim because they failed to allege extreme mental anguish.

The final federal case took place in Texas where a trial court denied the defendant school board's motion to dismiss the plaintiff's Title IX claim and granted the board and principal's motions to dismiss the plaintiff's intentional infliction of emotional distress (IIED) and gross negligence claims.[422] The plaintiff, a student's mother, alleged that the school admitted a twenty-five-year-old man so he could play on the school's basketball team, and he engaged in a sexual relationship with her fourteen-year-old daughter. The adult student claimed to be seventeen years old and homeless, and the school did not attempt to verify his identity or age in any way. The court held that the plaintiff did state a claim for deliberate indifference under Title IX based on the school's failure to verify the information provided by the twenty-five-year-old student. However, the principal and school were entitled to qualified immunity from the IIED claim under the Tort Claims Act, and the principal was immune from the gross negligence claim. The plaintiffs did not allege gross negligence against the school.

In Alabama, the parents of a third-grade student alleged that their daughter was improperly supervised when the teacher left the classroom to use the restroom.[423] As a result of this alleged lack of supervision, the student fell inside the classroom and suffered facial fractures requiring surgery. The state supreme court affirmed summary judgment in the case, dismissing the parents' claims for negligence. The court found that the teacher and the principal were entitled to immunity, and it clarified that the claims against the teacher and principal in their official capacities as employees of the school are barred because the parents did not present sufficient evidence that the teacher and principal acted beyond their authority or in violation of school policy.

The state supreme court of Pennsylvania affirmed the lower court's grant of the defendant childcare center's motion to transfer for forum non conveniens.[424] The plaintiff parents sued the center

---

[422] Doe on Behalf of Doe v. Dallas Indep. Sch. Dist., 534 F.Supp.3d 682, 396 Educ. L. Rep. 597 (N.D. Tex. 2021).
[423] Moore v. Tyson, 333 So.3d 668, 401 Educ. L. Rep. 667 (Ala. 2021).
[424] Doe v. Bright Horizons Children's Ctr., 261 A.3d 1065, 396 Educ. L. Rep. 789 (Pa. 2021).

for negligence, negligent supervision, negligent hiring and retention, and premises liability, alleging that their child was sexually abused by an employee at the defendant center for two years. The defendant center moved to transfer the case to a closer venue, arguing that they could not maintain the state-required teacher-to-student ratios if teachers had to travel 1.5-2.5 hours to testify at trial. The court agreed with the center, finding that the plaintiffs' selected venue would be oppressive to the center to an extent that there was reasonable evidentiary basis to transfer venue.

In the first of three California appellate cases, a high school student sued the school district for negligence after suffering serious injuries from a stabbing that occurred on school grounds after school.[425] The plaintiff stayed on campus after school ended for track practice. The locker room remained unlocked until 6:00, and campus security left campus each day at 4:00. While the plaintiff was on campus to retrieve her books from the locker room at 5:30, she was stabbed by a former student. The state trial court granted summary judgment in favor of the school district, but the appellate court reversed, finding triable issues of material fact. The appellate court found that the school board owed a duty of care on school grounds after school hours because the plaintiff was participating in a school-related function. The fact that practice ended early and she later returned to collect her belongings was a red herring because it was foreseeable that if practice ended early, students could leave campus and return to retrieve possessions from the open locker room. The court also found that the issue of whether additional security after school would have prevented the injury was a triable issue of material fact.

In the second case, an appellate court denied a former student's petition for a writ of mandamus challenging the lower court's decision allowing the school board to introduce evidence that she had been sexually abused by someone else.[426] The student, along with many others, was molested by her fourth-grade teacher and later sued the school board for negligent hiring and retention, negligent supervision, negligent failure to warn, and negligence per se in failing to report his abuse. During discovery, the school board learned that the student had also been sexually molested by a family friend a couple of years later, which the lower court ruled was admissible. The appellate court held that state law governing the admissibility of prior sexual conduct was also applicable to

---

[425] Achay v. Huntington Beach Union High Sch. Dist., 295 Cal. Rptr. 3d 867, 405 Educ. L. Rep. 1119 (Cal. Ct. App. 2022).
[426] Doe v. Sup. Ct. of L.A. Cnty., 286 Cal.Rptr.3d 204, 396 Educ. L. Rep. 1025 (Cal. Ct. App. 2021).

involuntary sexual conduct, and the trial court did not abuse its discretion in allowing the school board to admit evidence of the student's unrelated sexual abuse for impeachment purposes.

In the third case from California, the appellate court affirmed in part and reversed in part the lower court's grant of summary judgment in favor of the defendant school board on the plaintiff student's negligence and Child Abuse and Neglect Reporting Act (CANRA) claims.[427] The plaintiff here was a middle school student who was sexually abused by a music instructor employed by the school board. The court noted that "school administrators have a duty to protect students from sexual abuse by school employees, even if the school does not have actual knowledge of" an employee's history of or propensity to commit abuse. Therefore, the appellate court reversed the lower court's grant of summary judgment on the plaintiff's negligence claims. However, the court affirmed summary judgment in favor of the defendant school board on the plaintiff's CANRA claim because CANRA requires actual knowledge, and there was no evidence of actual knowledge in this case.

In a case involving bullying, the trial court's consolidation of cases and grant of the defendants' motions were affirmed by an appellate court in Connecticut.[428] Here, two sets of parents with middle school students sued the town, board of education, and school employees for negligence in responding to reports of bullying at school. The court held that the plaintiff parents failed to establish that the board of education and employees acted in bad faith when responding to the bullying reports. Further, the employees did not act recklessly by failing to detect, prevent, investigate, and remediate bullying in accordance with the safe school climate plan or by retaliating against students. Lastly, the court found that the town and board of education were not liable under respondeat superior.

In Florida, parents sued the Catholic Archdiocese for injuries to their daughter, a high schooler at a private Catholic school, that occurred during her participation in a service-learning activity.[429] The high school required students to participate in service learning, and the equestrian center was one of the school's forty-five pre-approved sites. The defendant moved for summary judgment, claiming they did not owe the student a duty at the time she was injured and they did not have authority over the equestrian center.

---

[427] Doe v. Lawndale Elementary Sch. Dist., 72 Cal.App.5th 113, 397 Educ. L. Rep. 673 (Cal. Ct. App. 2021).
[428] Doe 1 v. Bd. of Educ. of Town of Westport, 277 A.3d 164, 405 Educ. L. Rep. 443 (Conn. App. Ct. 2022).
[429] Neff v. Archdiocese of Miami, 338 So. 3d 959, 404 Educ. L. Rep. 377 (Fla. Dist. Ct. App. 2022).

The trial court agreed and explained that, as a matter of law, the service learning was not school-related. The plaintiffs appealed, arguing that the defendant owed them a duty of reasonable care in compiling the list of pre-approved service sites and a duty of supervision because the service learning was school-related. The appellate court affirmed the judgment in favor of the defendant because service learning at the equestrian center was not school-related. The duty to supervise only arises when a school officially sponsors the activity and has reserved authority to control the activity. The school's service-learning requirement did not create an affiliation with the equestrian center that would make the plaintiff's activities at the center school-related.

An appellate court in Louisiana affirmed a trial court's summary judgment order dismissing a parent's claim of negligence by the school and its employees after the parent's son, age six, slipped and fell while climbing a slide ladder on the school's playground structure at recess.[430] The two teachers supervising the playground, who were ten to fifteen feet from the student at the time he fell, did not see the accident but immediately ran to his aid after being notified by other students. One of the teachers picked the student up and carried him to the office, and the school then called the parent, who declined the school's offer to call an ambulance. The parent transported her son to the hospital, where his fractured left femur required surgery. The parent's complaint alleged failure to supervise and negligent treatment by the teachers after the fall. The appellate court emphasized that the law does not require that school employees, such as the teachers on recess duty, provide constant supervision but only adequate, reasonable supervision. The court concluded that the risk of injury was not foreseeable and that the teachers did provide adequate supervision.

In Maryland, parents brought a negligence action against teachers and school administrators on behalf of their daughter who was injured in several physical and verbal altercations with other students.[431] An appellate court affirmed the lower court's grant of the defendant teachers and administrators' motion for summary judgment. The court first affirmed that the individual defendants were entitled to immunity under the federal Paul D. Coverdell Teacher Protection Act because they were acting within the scope of their duties according to the law regarding student discipline, they were licensed teachers, and their acts were not "willful or criminal

---

[430] Hernandez v. Livingston Par. Sch. Bd., 341 So.3d 680, 405 Educ. L. Rep. 1225 (La. Ct. App 2022).
[431] Gambrill v. Bd. of Educ. of Dorchester Cnty., 259 A.3d 144, 395 Educ. L. Rep. 1003 (Md. Ct. Spec. App. 2021).

misconduct, gross negligence, reckless misconduct, or a conscious, flagrant indifference." Further, the parents' claims against the school board regarding student discipline constituted educational negligence claims, and school boards cannot be held liable for claims for damages grounded in educational negligence.

An appellate court in Mississippi held that a school board was not liable for injuries sustained by a high school student who jumped down bleachers inside the school gym.[432] Before school on the morning the injury took place, the student's mother called school administrators to warn them that another high school student had threatened to attack her daughter. Two administrators met both students at their school busses to address the risk, but the administrators did not restrain the student who made the threat and the student immediately broke away in pursuit of the threatened student. The threatened student sustained injuries from climbing up the bleachers and jumping down the bleachers to attempt to escape the aggressive confrontation. The court held that the school has a ministerial duty to use ordinary care and take reasonable steps to minimize foreseeable risks to students; however, the court did not find that the school breached this duty. The court found that the school neither failed to provide the student with a safe environment nor failed to take reasonable steps to minimize foreseeable risks of harm to the student.

In the first of four cases from New York, an elementary school student tripped on the stairs at her school injuring her ankle, and the student's mother filed, and the trial court allowed, a late claim more than one year after the injury.[433] The late filing violated the timely service of notice of claim requirement for tort claims against municipal entities, and the school appealed the allowance of the late claim. The issue on appeal was whether the lower court correctly exercised its discretion under General Municipal Law § 50-e(5) to allow late notice. The appellate court reversed the trial court's earlier decision, finding that the petitioner failed to show that the school had knowledge of the essential facts of the claim. The fact that the school knew about the tripping incident and injury, which happened on school grounds, is not sufficient to constitute the actual knowledge of the essential facts of the claim of negligent supervision. Further, the petitioner did not submit a reasonable excuse for her claim's tardiness.

---

[432] Robertson v. Houston, Miss. Pub. Sch. Dist., 335 So.3d 1082, 402 Educ. L. Rep. 516 (Miss. Ct. App. 2021).
[433] J.G. v. Acad. Charter Elementary Sch., 166 N.Y.S.3d 246, 402 Educ. L. Rep. 1060 (N.Y. App. Div. 2022).

In the second case, a New York appellate court reversed the lower court's denial of the defendant school board's motion for a directed verdict and to set aside the jury verdict.[434] The parent brought a negligence suit against the school board on behalf of their student after the student was injured by a teacher loudly speaking into a microphone in the school auditorium. Despite evidence at trial that no other students were injured by this noise, even though many students were closer to the speaker, the jury found in favor of the plaintiff. The appellate court granted the defendant's motion for a directed verdict and to set aside the jury verdict, holding that there was no evidence that the words were spoken at an "unreasonable" or "foreseeably unsafe" volume, so there was no breached duty of care.

The third case from New York involved a student who was injured during a class demonstration.[435] Here, the appellate court affirmed the denial of the defendant city and city department of education's motion to set aside the jury verdict and for a new trial on damages. The parents brought a negligence suit on behalf of their student who was set on fire during a chemistry demonstration which resulted in burns to 31% of the student's body. A jury awarded the plaintiffs over $29.5 million for past pain and suffering, $29.5 million for future pain and suffering, plus 9% interest. In response to the defendant's challenge to the 9% interest rate, the court noted that the defendants did not seek a lower interest rate until forty-eight days after the plaintiff noticed his judgment for settlement, whereas they should have formally moved for a lower interest rate before the judgment was entered. Thus, their motion was properly denied.

In the final case, a New York appellate court affirmed the lower court's grant of the defendant city and department of education's motion to dismiss the plaintiffs' negligence and vicarious liability claims as well as the teachers' crossclaims and motion for summary judgment as to the department of education.[436] This case was brought after the infant plaintiff was injured during an afterschool program that was approved by the principal despite a number of errors within the permit and failure to verify proper insurance. The court held that the city could not be held liable for the department of education's torts as they were separate legal entities. Further, the department of education established that it was entitled to summary judgment because the principal's grant of the permit for the

---

[434] Joni C. v. Cheektowaga-Sloan Union Free Sch. Dist., 153 N.Y.S.3d 335, 395 Educ. L. Rep. 1078 (N.Y. App. Div. 2021).
[435] Yvonne Y. v. City of N.Y., 158 N.Y.S.3d 60, 399 Educ. L. Rep. 358 (N.Y. App. Div. 2021).
[436] R.K. by Fatmir K. v. City of N.Y., 161 N.Y.S.3d 16, 400 Educ. L. Rep. 711 (N.Y. App. Div. 2021).

afterschool program was a discretionary action, thus it was entitled to governmental immunity.

In North Carolina, a high school student was injured after being struck by a car on a school access road and sued the school district for negligence and negligent infliction of emotional distress.[437] The plaintiff was on the football team and was walking on school property between the football film room and locker room using an access road that was open to pedestrians and vehicles. By his own admission, the plaintiff had his back to oncoming traffic, was listening to music using headphones, and was dancing in the road. The trial court granted summary judgment in favor of the district, and the appellate court affirmed. The plaintiff's own admission of contributory negligence as the proximate cause of his injury meant that there was no genuine issue of material fact that required a trial.

An appellate court in Ohio affirmed the lower court's denial of the defendants' motion to dismiss based on statutory immunity.[438] The plaintiffs were public high school students who were injured after a bottle of isopropyl alcohol caught on fire and exploded during a class science experiment. The students brought suit against the city board of education, science teacher, and principal. The appellate court held that the lower court did not have to issue findings of fact and conclusions of law in its ruling, so the court did not err by failing to address whether the principal, teacher, and school board were entitled to immunity. Additionally, the court affirmed that the principal and teacher had sufficient notice regarding the students' allegation of reckless or wanton conduct.

Vicarious Liability

In Louisiana, the mother of a fifth-grade student filed a claim against the school board for negligent hiring and supervision after a special education teacher had inappropriate conversations with the fifth grader and took him off campus for breakfast without his mother's knowledge.[439] The school filed a motion for summary judgment, claiming that they could not be held liable for negligence because the teacher's actions were not reasonably foreseeable. In her response to the school's motion, the petitioner raised a claim of vicarious liability. In response, the school argued that the original petition did not include the vicarious liability claim and that they could not be liable for both negligence and vicarious liability since

---

[437] Archie v. Durham Pub. Sch. Bd. of Educ., 283 N.C.App. 472, 405 Educ. L. Rep. 530 (N.C. Ct. App. 2022).
[438] Doe v. Greenville City Schs., 174 N.E.3d 917, 395 Educ. L. Rep. 827 (Ohio Ct. App. 2021).
[439] J.C. ex rel. N.C. v. St. Bernard Par. Sch. Bd., 336 So.3d 92, 402 Educ. L. Rep. 529 (La. Ct. App. 2022).

those claims were mutually exclusive. The trial court granted the school's motion for summary judgment, and the petitioner appealed. The appellate court reversed the summary judgment order and remanded the case for further proceedings. The court reasoned that the Petitioner presented sufficient evidence—her own testimony, notes from the child's therapist, and emails from the teacher—to support the claim of vicarious liability.

Immunity from Liability

In California, the parents of a high school student shot by another student during his first period class sued the school board, including administrators who were members of the threat assessment team.[440] In the months preceding the shooting, several school staff and other students had reported threatening words, drawings, and gestures by the student, which prompted the school to conduct a threat assessment. The threat assessment ranked the student's threat level as a four out of five with "insufficient evidence of violence potential," and he was allowed to return to school with weekly counseling check-ins for one month. Part of the court's opinion is unpublished; however, the court stated that they chose to publish the opinion because the school board's argument that members of a threat assessment team are immune from liability had not been addressed in any prior published opinions. The court held that conducting a threat assessment falls outside the scope of qualified immunity under California Government Code Section 855.6, so members of a threat assessment team can be held liable for acts or omissions that occurred during the threat assessment of a potentially violent student.

A mother sought to sue the state of Connecticut for violations of federal and state rights to a free public education in a safe school setting, arguing that the school was decrepit and caused respiratory problems for her two children, who subsequently had to enroll in private schools.[441] The appeals court held that the state's legislative body did not waive its sovereign immunity regarding the claimants' legislative negligence claim. The claims commissioner dismissed the claim because it was filed outside the statute of limitations. The claimants sought review from the legislature who approved a joint resolution vacating the decision of the claims commissioner and allowed the claimants to bring suit. The trial court dismissed the case on the grounds that the resolution was an unconstitutional

---

[440] Cleveland v. Taft Union High Sch. Dist., 291 Cal. Rptr. 3d 759, 401 Educ. L. Rep. 1017 (Cal. Ct. App. 2022).
[441] State v. Avoletta, 275 A.3d 716, 404 Educ. L. Rep. 214 (Conn. App. Ct. 2022).

public emolument in violation of the state constitution. The claimants subsequently filed a second claim with the claims commissioner for legislative negligence, arguing that they were harmed by the legislature's failure to articulate a public purpose in their joint resolution. The appellate court found the argument unpersuasive.

In Indiana, parents of a first-grade student sued the school board for breaching its duty of reasonable care after the student was mistakenly released from school and instructed to walk home on the second day of the school year.[442] The student was supposed to take the bus and was waiting in the bus line when a teacher instead instructed him to walk home. While trying to walk the 1.2 miles home, the student walked a mile in the wrong direction and encountered several hardships, including crossing a major highway, being chased by dogs, and being approached by a homeless man in an alley. A stranger found the student and called the police. The court held that the school board was not immune from liability under state law because a school cannot claim immunity when it is being sued for matters related to its compliance with laws or school policies.

Parents of two high school students in New Jersey sued their school board and the township for negligence after the students were struck by a car while walking home from school.[443] At the time, in accordance with state law, the board had a policy of providing mandatory free bus transportation to all high school students living more than 2.5 miles from school; the plaintiffs lived less than 2.5 miles from their school. As part of its transportation policy, the board determined hazardous routes for students walking to school, and the plaintiffs' route was deemed safe. The board and township claimed immunity under state tort law, and the trial court granted summary judgment in favor of the board and township. The plaintiffs appealed, and the appellate court affirmed the trial court's summary judgment order in favor of the township. The court found that the township owed no duty to the plaintiffs beyond the duty to work with the board to designate hazardous routes, which the township did. However, the court overturned the trial court's summary judgment order for the board because it was not entitled to immunity, and there were several unresolved material factual disputes related to the negligence claim.

---

[442] Hopkins v. Indianapolis Pub. Schs., 183 N.E.3d 308, 401 Educ. L. Rep. 596 (Ind. Ct. App. 2022).
[443] T.B. v. Novia, 275 A.3d 47, 404 Educ. L. Rep. 189 (N.J. Super. App. Div. 2022).

Employee Claims

A federal trial court in Ohio granted the defendant board of education's motion for judgment on the pleadings on the teacher's constructive discharge, breach of contract, and negligent and intentional infliction of emotional distress claims (NIED/IIED).[444] The plaintiff taught for nine years without accommodations. Upon request, the board provided her with accommodations for severe anxiety and depression for roughly another nine years. After the plaintiff had surgery, the board allegedly refused to continue providing her with accommodations, and the plaintiff claims she was forced to resign. The court dismissed her constructive discharge claim because it is not an independent cause of action in Ohio and her breach of contract claim because the plaintiff failed to identify an actionable contract. As for her emotional distress claims, the court found that the plaintiff did not allege that "she was a bystander to a serious accident," as is required to state a NIED claim. Further, the plaintiff did not allege that the denial of her requested accommodations was extreme or outrageous, as is required to state a claim for IIED.

The state supreme court of Maine vacated and remanded with directions the lower court's grant of the defendant parents' special motion to dismiss pursuant to the anti-SLAPP statute.[445] Here, an assistant principal brought a defamation action against a student's parents after they sent a letter to school officials accusing him of misconduct relating to issues their student faced with bullying at school. SLAPP lawsuits "are filed with the goal 'to stop citizens from exercising their political rights or to punish them for having done so'" and must be dismissed if the opposing party presents prima facie evidence that the moving party's petitioning activities were devoid of any reasonable factual support or arguable basis in law, causing actual injury. The court found that the parents' letter constituted a petitioning activity, the letter was devoid of any factual support or arguable basis in law, and the assistant principal suffered an actual injury.

In Louisiana, a former maintenance employee filed a tort claim against a school for damages, alleging that his workplace exposure to lead-based paint over a twenty-year period caused chronic medical conditions, especially chronic kidney disease.[446] As part of his job duties, the petitioner was required to scrape and sand lead-based

---

[444] Ritter v. Bd. of Educ. of Arcadia Loc. Schs., 535 F.Supp.3d 690, 396 Educ. L. Rep. 931 (N.D. Ohio 2021).
[445] Thurlow v. Nelson, 263 A.3d 494, 397 Educ. L. Rep. 656 (Me. 2021).
[446] Jackson v. Jefferson Par. Sch. Bd., 336 So.3d 561, 402 Educ. L. Rep. 550 (La. Ct. App. 2022).

paint from school buildings, and his doctor informed him that his chronic kidney disease and other conditions were likely caused by exposure to toxic levels of lead. The school argued it was immune from tort liability because the Louisiana Workers' Compensation Act (LWCA) lists lead poisoning as a compensable occupational disease; accordingly, petitioner would be entitled to remedies under LWCA but not under tort law. The trial court agreed with the defendant. However, the appellate court vacated the trial court's decision and remanded the case for further proceedings. The court reasoned that a determination of whether the petitioner's medical conditions were covered under LWCA or tort law were fact-intensive inquiries that must be explored by the trial court on a case-by-case basis.

In the first of three appellate cases from New York, a teacher at a public elementary school brought a suit against the City of New York and the state department of education claiming that the defendants breached their duty to maintain the school premises in a reasonably safe condition, which resulted in the plaintiff's injury sustained by falling ice on school grounds.[447] The trial court granted the defendants' motion for summary judgment, and the plaintiff appealed. The appellate court overturned the dismissal of the plaintiff's complaint against the DOE because, as the property owner, the DOE failed to offer evidence that they did not have notice of the alleged dangerous condition at the school. The court found that triable issues of fact existed relating to the DOE's inspection of exterior fixtures on the school campus.

An assistant principal in New York brought suit against a state legislator alleging defamation, tortious interference, and intentional infliction of emotional distress.[448] In this case, the appellate court affirmed all three orders of the trial court. First, the trial court denied the plaintiff's motion to compel nonparty witnesses to comply with subpoena requests on procedural grounds, and the appellate court affirmed because the plaintiff failed to provide a reason for his delay in moving to compel the witnesses to comply. Second, the court affirmed the denial of the plaintiff's motion to amend his complaint because the defendant would be prejudiced if the amendment were allowed at such a late stage in the litigation. Finally, the denial of the plaintiff's motion to compel nonparty witnesses to comply with discovery was affirmed because the information sought by the plaintiff was available from other sources.

---

[447] Marazita v. City of N.Y., 163 N.Y.S.3d 219, 401 Educ. L. Rep. 527 (N.Y. App. Div. 2022).
[448] Verdi v. Dinowitz, 168 N.Y.S.3d 24, 403 Educ. L. Rep. 297 (N.Y. App. Div. 2022).

In the third appellate case from New York, the court held that the defendant city was not liable for tortious interference when the statements at issue were substantially true.[449] A former president of a charter school sued the city and the mayor for defamation and tortious interference with a contract, alleging that statements made by the mayor about the school's refusal to let its first African American valedictorian speak at graduation forced him to resign. One of the elements of tortious interference requires the plaintiff to show that the defendant "acted with the sole purpose of harming the plaintiff[ ] or by using unlawful means." The court held that, because the mayor's statements were substantially true and did not mention the plaintiff by name, there is no evidence that she "acted solely out of malice." Thus, the tortious interference claim was dismissed.

In South Carolina, an appellate court reversed a jury verdict and damages award in favor of a retired athletic director on his wrongful termination and defamation claims.[450] The plaintiff was a high school teacher and athletic director for over twenty years before the school board removed reassigned him to serve as a middle school guidance counselor. He completed the school year and then retired. After he was reassigned, the athletic trainer emailed coaches and administrators about potential issues with the eligibility files for student-athletes, the upkeep of which had been the plaintiff's responsibility. The plaintiff sued for defamation based on this email. The court noted that, because the plaintiff was considered a public official, he was required to prove actual malice to succeed in his defamation claim. However, he failed to show any actual malice by the athletic trainer or the school board. Thus, the jury verdict was improper, and the appellate court reversed the lower court's denial of the district's motion for a directed verdict.

Claims by Other Injured Parties

A company's motion to dismiss the school boards' negligence, gross negligence, and state law consumer claims was denied by a federal trial court in California.[451] The plaintiffs, consisting of government entities and school boards, sued an E-cigarette company and individual officers and directors, alleging they acted with the goal of growing nicotine addiction. Specifically, the plaintiffs alleged that the company released deceptive advertisements that did not

---

[449] Munno v. City of Rochester, 153 N.Y.S.3d 309, 395 Educ. L. Rep. 1075 (N.Y. App. Div. 2021).
[450] Cruce v. Berkeley Cnty. Sch. Dist., 865 S.E.2d 391, 397 Educ. L. Rep. 404 (S.C. Ct. App. 2021).
[451] In re JUUL Labs, Mktg, Sales Pracs., and Prod. Liab. Litig., 533 F.Supp.3d 858, 396 Educ. L. Rep. 469 (N.D. Cal. 2021)

reference any nicotine content in its products and, eventually, started targeting their advertisements toward teenagers. The school board plaintiffs argued that "corporate officers and directors may be liable in negligence where they 'authorized, directed or participated in the allegedly tortious conduct.'" The court agreed, finding that, while liability to corporate officers and directors had mostly been extended in cases involving physical injury, it was not necessarily barred in the case of pecuniary harm. The court also found that the individual defendants were sufficiently involved in the violations of New York and Florida's consumer protection laws to be held liable. Thus, dismissal was inappropriate.

The Supreme Court of Texas addressed a claim from an automobile insurance company against a school district for a golf cart accident that occurred on a high school campus.[452] A female high school student was injured when she was thrown from a golf cart driven by the school's athletic trainer. In separate litigation, the student sued the school district and received a $100,000 judgment for her injuries. The school board then sued their insurance company, and the trial court determined that the district's insurance policy requires the insurance company to defend and indemnify the district. The court ordered the insurance company to pay the district for the costs of the student's injury case, including the $100,000 judgment. The state supreme court reversed the trial court's decision, reasoning that the evidence presented did not establish that the golf cart was an automobile designed for travel on public roads that was covered by the insurance policy.

In West Virginia, the highest state court found that the landowner defendants were liable for flooding the plaintiff school's baseball field.[453] The defendants constructed an embankment and built a bridge on the right of way along the southern boundary of the school's property. The improvements were not an issue until Hurricane Ivan led to regional flooding, including of the school's baseball field. The defendants argued that they were not the cause of the flooding. However, the court found that several witnesses and expert testimony proved that the flooding began at the embankment and bridge. Therefore, the embankment and bridge were the proximate cause of the field's flooding.

The lower court's dismissal of the plaintiff's personal injury claims against the school district and employee was reversed by an

---

[452] Pharr–San Juan–Alamo Indep. Sch. Dist. v. Tex. Pol. Subdivisions Prop./Casualty Joint Self Ins. Fund, 642 S.W.3d 466, 402 Educ. L. Rep. 458 (Tex. 2022).
[453] Reilley v. Bd. of Educ. of Cnty. of Marshall, 874 S.E.2d 333, 404 Educ. L. Rep. 966 (W. Va. 2022).

appellate court in California after the plaintiff sustained injuries in a traffic accident involving a school district vehicle.[454] Under the Government Claims Act, an "employee of a public entity is liable for his torts to the same extent as a private person and the public entity is vicariously liable for any injury its employee causes to the same extent as a private employer."

An appellate court in Florida denied a party's claim that the school board was self-insured for purposes of qualifying as uninsured under state law.[455] The plaintiff suffered injuries when the board's bus collided with his employer's work vehicle where the plaintiff was a passenger. He sued the board and his own employer's insurance carrier. He settled the lawsuit with the board and the claim was dismissed. He subsequently sought to collect damages from his employer's insurance carrier under the uninsured motorist statute, a statute designed to provide a remedy when the tortfeasor is uninsured or underinsured. The court found that the board, however, was not self-insured or underinsured, because it regularly made payments to their insurance company and had a cap on settlements greater than the amount for which the plaintiff settled. Moreover, the court found that the plaintiff failed to exhaust all avenues to collect from the board under their insurance. Therefore, the plaintiff was not entitled to further remedies from their employer's insurance company.

In a second appellate case from Florida, the defendant's school board's request for a certiorari review of a trial court order was denied.[456] The plaintiff filed a suit against the board, alleging discrimination and retaliation. During discovery, the trial court issued an order stating that it would review *in camera* responsive documents to the board's request for medical and psychiatric records and that the plaintiff would have an opportunity to review, inspect, and propose redactions to such documents. Moreover, the trial court found that the board's request for documents from current and former employees was overbroad. The board next sought certiorari review, arguing that the trial court's order departed from essential requirements of law and that the board would suffer irreparable harm if the request for certiorari was not granted. The appellate court disagreed, reasoning that providing *in camera* review and an opportunity for the board to revise its requests did not prevent the board from defending itself.

---

[454] Cavey v. Tualla, 284 Cal.Rptr.3d 377, 395 Educ. L. Rep. 788 (Cal. Ct. App. 2021).
[455] White v. Ascendant Com. Ins., 337 So.3d 1264, 403 Educ. L. Rep. 973 (Fla. Dist. Ct. App. 2022).
[456] Alachua Cnty. Sch. Bd. v. Barnes, 340 So.3d 567, 405 Ed. Law. Rep. 571 (Fla. Dist. Ct. 2022).

An appellate court in Louisiana reversed and remanded the lower court's dismissal of the driver's claims and its decision to maintain the school system's peremptory exception of res judicata.[457] A driver sued a parish school system and its insurer to recover for injuries sustained in an accident involving a school bus driven by a school system employee. Res judicata bars the court from rehearing a matter involving the same parties that has already been adjudicated in court. The school system here alleged that res judicata precluded this case based on a compromise it had entered into with the plaintiff driver. However, the school did not introduce a copy of the Release of All Claims at the hearing on the exception, and the court is unable to consider exhibits attached to the memorandum in support of its exception, so the lower court erred in maintaining the school's exception.

In New Jersey, a ten-year old child was shot during a high school football game and died from his injuries five days later. Eighty-six days after the child's death, but ninety-one days after the shooting, the child's mother emailed a notice of a tort claim to the school board, asserting wrongful death, survivor claims, and negligent infliction of emotional distress. The school board alleged that they did not receive timely notice of the claim, but the court ruled that the claim was timely and fell within the ninety-day deadline under state law because the time to file a claim was tolled until the date the child died.[458]

A plaintiff in Ohio suffered an injury while riding a bike after encountering a rope the school had strung across the bike trail.[459] The plaintiff argued that, because the school had placed the rope for a sports event, the trail became closed to the public and, therefore, the school was not immune from liability under state law. The appellate court found that a rope placed across on a school bike trail was legally considered a condition of the premises. However, the court found that the trail remained open to the public for recreational purposes after the rope was added. The rope did not change the essential character of the trail, and, therefore, the school qualified for immunity per state law.

An appellate court in Oregon affirmed the lower court's grant of summary judgment in favor of the school district.[460] Here, the plaintiff was a piano tuner, who provided tuning services to the school district and aided in the production of concerts in district

---

[457] Cyprian v. Tangipahoa Par. Sch. Sys., 332 So.3d 689, 400 Educ. L. Rep. 366 (La. Ct. App. 2021).
[458] Est. of Dunmore v. Pleasantville Bd. of Educ., 269 A.3d 1172, 401 Educ. L. Rep. 486 (N.J. Super. App. Div. 2022).
[459] Stone v. Northmont City Schs., 187 N.E.3d 54, 402 Educ. L. Rep. 1113 (Ohio Ct. App. 2022).
[460] Lowell v. Medford Sch. Dist. 549C, 497 P.3d 797, 396 Educ. L. Rep. 332 (Or. Ct. App. 2021).

facilities. He brought suit against the school district, the school theater technician, the technician's supervisor, and the district support services assistant based on their alleged statements that the plaintiff was intoxicated while working on school grounds. The school board filed a motion for summary judgment, arguing that the statements "were made by public employees in the performance of their official duties," thus entitling them to absolute privilege and immunity. The court agreed, finding that the school district was entitled to absolute immunity.

In Washington D.C., an appellate court held that a charter school did not have third-party standing to bring an intentional infliction of emotional distress claim on behalf of its students and parents.[461] Over a period of time, students and parents were accosted daily by protesters who denounced a Planned Parenthood clinic being built next to the charter school. The school brought suit on behalf of the students and their parents for the emotional distress the protesters caused. The court found that the school did not have standing to do so. Although the school could have plausibly claimed to be harmed by the protestors and had a close relationship with the families, it failed to show that the students and parents had some hindrance to protect their own interests.

Higher Education

Vehicle Accidents

An appellate court in New York held that the bank that leased a vehicle to a university could not be held vicariously liable for the harm resulting from a car accident.[462] While driving a vehicle leased by the university, a driver rear-ended a stopped vehicle. Under state law, the plaintiff made a prima facie case of negligence based on these facts. The bank that leased the vehicle to the university argued that it could not be held vicariously liable for the accident because the university was under the lease during the time of the accident and was also responsible for car maintenance and repairs. The court agreed with the bank and found that the bank was entitled to summary judgment.

A case was remanded to the trial court for further proceedings after holding that the plaintiff did not have to satisfy due diligence

---

[461] Nicdao v. Two Rivers Pub. Charter Sch., 275 A.3d 1287, 404 Educ. L. Rep. 234 (D.C. 2022).
[462] Kalair v. Fajerman, 164 N.Y.S.3d 106, 401 Educ. L. Rep. 576 (N.Y. App. Div. 2022).

in service of process because due diligence was not a statutory prerequisite to a suit under the Texas Tort Claims Act (TTCA).[463] The plaintiff filed suit against a state university system, state university, and individual employees after sustaining injuries as a passenger in a golf cart when she was thrown from the cart. In compliance with the TTCA, she provided service of process to all defendants on different dates. The university responded that the plaintiff provided an untimely service of process and therefore was required to prove diligence in service efforts. On appeal, the court held that due diligence was not a requirement under the TTCA and remanded the case for further proceedings.

Sexual Misconduct

The Ninth Circuit federal appellate court found that the certification of a question to the Washington Supreme Court was warranted in a negligence case that raised an unresolved question of law.[464] The plaintiff, a freshman student, sued the university alleging it owed the student a duty of care. The student was repeatedly raped at a party by another student who had a history of sexual misconduct on campus. The university argued that it was not responsible for student-on-student assault incidents such as the one in the case. The circuit court found that, though the state has not recognized a duty in such cases, the question of duty remains open and has implications for public policy (e.g., protecting young people from sexual abuse). Thus, the court certified the question for the state supreme court's consideration.

In Connecticut, an appellate court held that the trial court properly rendered summary judgment in favor of the defendant university in a case where the plaintiffs, minors at the time of the incidents, were sexually assaulted by a head resident of a residential area on campus.[465] The perpetrator was a member of the university basketball team and used the facilities to lure children between the ages of thirteen and fifteen years old. The plaintiffs argued that the perpetrator lured children under the pretense of instructing them in plyometrics, stretching, and other physical activities. However, this was a ruse to sexually assault them. Nonetheless, the court found that the plaintiffs failed to present any evidence that the university

---

[463] Tanner v. Tex. State Univ., 644 S.W.3d 747, 403 Educ. L. Rep. 324 (Tex. App. 2022).
[464] Barlow v. State, 38 F.4th 62, 404 Educ. L. Rep. 444 (9th Cir. 2022).
[465] Salamone v. Wesleyan Univ., 270 A.3d 172, 401 Educ. L. Rep. 492 (Conn. App. Ct. 2022).

was aware or should have known that the perpetrator would assault the plaintiffs in his dorm room.

A former student of a ballet company in New York brought a claim against the company and its former employees for disclosure of intimate images without consent, negligent hiring, and intentional and negligent infliction of emotional distress.[466] The plaintiff was in an intimate relationship with her instructor, and during that time he took sexually explicit pictures and videos of her despite her objections. The instructor later shared these images with other male employees of the company without the plaintiff's permission. The plaintiff alleges the sharing of these images caused her emotional distress and ruined her reputation at the company. An appellate court affirmed the lower court's decision as modified, dismissing the plaintiff's claims against the company and all individuals except the claim against her instructor for unlawful disclosure of an intimate image.

Defamation

A federal trial court in Pennsylvania denied a plaintiff's defamation claim because it found it did not have merit.[467] Following a long-standing rivalry between allopathic and osteopathic medicine in the United States, the main accreditation body agreed to combine its residency programs into a single system. A few years later, a prominent board of medicine issued a statement that it would only accept attestations from directors of residency programs who were certified in allopathic medicine. Plaintiffs representing the osteopathic community sued the board of medicine for defamation. The court explained that courts only dismiss claims for lack of defamatory meaning when the statement can only reasonably be interpreted as nondefamatory. The court found that the statement (i.e., the announcement that communicated that osteopathic medicine certified directors will now be unqualified to serve as program directors) did not imply they were inferior and can only be read as nondefamatory. The court reasoned that the statement only shared a new policy and did not suggest the reasons for adopting the policy. The court declined the invitation to expand liability in such cases.

In a state-level case from Pennsylvania, an appellate court affirmed the grant of summary judgment in favor of the defendant

---

[466] Waterbury v. N.Y.C. Ballet, 168 N.Y.S.3d 417, 403 Educ. L. Rep. 878 (N.Y. App. Div. 2022).
[467] Am. Osteopathic Ass'n v. Am. Bd. of Internal Med., 555 F. Supp. 3d 142, 401 Educ. L. Rep. 231 (E.D. Pa. 2021).

university and supervisor on the plaintiff's tortious interference with contract claim.[468] The plaintiff was employed as a tax accountant for the defendant and received mostly positive performance reviews. She was promoted to tax compliance manager, at which point her relationship with the defendant supervisor began to deteriorate, and the plaintiff was ultimately terminated. The plaintiff brought suit, alleging that her supervisor intentionally interfered with contractual relations between her and the university. The parties dispute whether the plaintiff's at-will employment status precludes her claim for intentional interference with that employment. The court held in favor of the defendant, finding that the plaintiff could not state a claim for intentional interference with existing contractual relations.

Medical Malpractice

An appellate court in New York found that a defendant psychiatrist's disclosure of a plaintiff patient's medical condition to university personnel did not constitute medical malpractice.[469] The plaintiff was in a residency program at the university. She was placed on a three-month probationary period after poor performance and subsequently took a seven-week leave of absence upon recommendation of her psychiatrist. After returning from her leave, she participated in a meeting to evaluate her performance, and according to her supervisors, she engaged in erratic and concerning behavior. Her supervisors contacted her psychiatrist, who disclosed that her mental health was deteriorating. The supervisors met and ultimately voted not to renew her appointment. She sued her psychiatrist for disclosing private information (i.e., medical malpractice). The court held that the disclosure did not constitute malpractice because in disclosing, the psychiatrist was not engaging in the practice of examining, diagnosing, and treating or providing care for the plaintiff as his patient.

Racial Profiling

In Ohio, an appellate court found that a college's actions were sufficiently severe and outrageous to support the plaintiff bakery

---

[468] Salsberg v. Mann, 262 A.3d 1267, 397 Educ. L. Rep. 224 (Sup. Ct. Pa. 2021).
[469] Bonner v. Lynott, 166 N.Y.S.3d 325, 402 Educ. L. Rep. 1064 (N.Y. App. Div. 2022).

owner's claims for intentional infliction of emotional distress.[470] The plaintiffs owned and worked for a local bakery located near the college, and the bakery provided baked goods for an on-campus bakery. Students alleged that the bakery had a history of racial profiling dating back decades. Protests re-emerged when the plaintiffs tackled a student of color they suspected of shoplifting. Students created a flyer that called attention to the racialized incidents, and the student government body voted on a resolution denouncing the incidents. The college told the on-campus bakery to stop their ongoing business with the local bakery, which it did. The plaintiffs sued the college, alleging an intentional infliction of emotional distress. The court reasoned that, through private messages and public discussions, the college expressed greater concern about the students than about the local bakery's ongoing business with the on-campus bakery. Thus, the court agreed that the college's behavior was sufficiently severe and outrageous to support a remedy in favor of the local bakery.

Sports Injuries

An appellate court in Pennsylvania held that a series of procedural errors rendered a student-athlete's appeal deficient and, therefore, the lower court's opinions were affirmed.[471] The student-athlete suffered a knee injury during his tenure as a football player for the university. After undergoing surgery, he continued to experience pain and eventually contracted an infection. He sued the university and its employees pro se, alleging negligent infliction of emotional distress and ordinary negligence. After losing the claims in the lower court, he raised multiple issues on appeal, including denial of relief and judicial bias. The court held that the plaintiff failed to conform to procedural timelines and processes and thus lost on appeal.

Dangerous Conditions of Campus or Facilities

On appeal from Nebraska, the Eighth Circuit found that a plaintiff failed to plausibly allege her negligence claim against the defendants because she could not establish that her injury was

---

[470] Gibson Bros. v. Oberlin Coll., 187 N.E.3d 629, 402 Educ. L. Rep. 1134 (Ohio Ct. App. 2022).
[471] Jordan v. Pa. State Univ., 276 A.3d 751, 405 Educ. L. Rep. 390 (Pa. Super. 2022).

reasonably foreseeable.[472] The plaintiff sued after a member of an on-campus fraternity entered her dorm room without permission and slashed her throat with a pocketknife. The assault occurred during the initiation week of the fraternity, and the perpetrator was "blackout" drunk. The federal trial court dismissed the case after finding that the defendants could not have foreseen the injuries of the plaintiff, in relevant part, because the fraternity had no knowledge that the perpetrator had a propensity to assault strangers. The appellate court found that the victim failed to state a claim under state negligence law.

In the first of two cases involving the Maine Tort Claims Act decided by the state supreme court, the court held that an industrial kitchen mixer did not fall within the Act's exception to immunity in negligence cases.[473] The plaintiff was employed as a baker by a third-party company that provided food and dining services for the university system. The plaintiff severely injured their finger while using an industrial, motorized kitchen mixer supplied and owned by the university. He sued the university which, in turn, argued immunity under the Tort Claims Act. The plaintiff countered that the case fell within the Act's immunity exceptions, specifically, that the ownership of the industrial kitchen mixer fell under the statutory "other machinery or equipment, whether mobile or stationary" category. The court disagreed and reasoned that the category is narrow and does not include items such as the kitchen mixer. Thus, the university was entitled to immunity. In the second case, the court affirmed that the defendant university had immunity where the plaintiff fell in the parking lot adjacent to a university building.[474] The plaintiff parked her vehicle and walked across the street to enter the library. After a few hours, she walked back to the parking lot. She fell on an untreated patch of ice and sustained injuries. She sued the university, arguing that it was liable for maintaining and operating the parking lot. The university argued that it had immunity under the Maine Tort Claims Act because the parking lot did not qualify as an "appurtenance." The court agreed and upheld the defendant's immunity.

An appellate court in Louisiana affirmed the trial court's grant of summary judgment in favor of the defendant university on the contractor's employee's claims stemming from an injury sustained

---

[472] Spagna v. Phi Kappa Psi, 30 F.4th 710, 401 Educ. L. Rep. 177 (8th Cir. 2022).
[473] Badler v. Univ. of Me. Sys., 277 A.3d 379, 405 Educ. L. Rep. 480 (Me. 2022).
[474] Klein v. Univ. of Me. Sys., 271 A.3d 777, 401 Educ. L. Rep. 1004 (Me. 2022).

while working.[475] The employee was performing debris cleanup work on the university's campus when he fell into a large hole. He sought and received workers' compensation benefits from the contractor then brought this suit against the university for damages. The court found that the contract between the university and the contractor established the university as the statutory employer of the contractor's employees, so the employee had to show that the work he was doing at the time of his injury was not part of the university's "trade, business, or occupation." The employee argued that the university's business was teaching and creating opportunities for a diverse student body, but he did not provide any evidence to support that debris removal was not a regular part of university business. Thus, the university was the employee's statutory employer and was entitled to tort immunity.

A defendant university's contractual and common law indemnification claims against a third-party employer were denied by an appellate court in New York.[476] The plaintiff worked at the university as a general manager of food services for a third-party contractor. The plaintiff fell down a concrete staircase that led from the kitchen to the loading dock. Alleging negligence, he sued the university, who in turn sued the third-party contractor. The court found that, under contract law, the third party would be liable only if the third-party employer was solely negligent. However, the defendant university was solely negligent in this case. The court held that the claim also failed under common law doctrine because the plaintiff's claim was based upon the university's negligence, not the third party's, and the university failed to prove that there was any scenario demonstrating that the university could be held liable for the negligence of the third party.

In Pennsylvania, an appellate court held that the defendant college's affirmative actions gave rise to a duty of care to protect members of the college's club crew team from unreasonable risks.[477] The team practiced at a boathouse approximately two miles from campus, and the road from campus to the boathouse was poorly lit, narrow, and had no sidewalk. The college did not provide transportation for team members. Finding no parking space in the usual lot during one of the practices, the plaintiff parked in a remote parking lot down the road from the boathouse, and as she returned to her car, she was hit by a drunk driver and suffered lifelong

---

[475] Preston v. S. Univ. *ex rel.* Bd. of Supervisors of S. Univ. Agric. & Mech. Coll., 328 So.3d 1194, 397 Educ. L. Rep. 1130 (La. Ct. App. 2021).
[476] O'Toole as Tr. for Charafeddine v. Marist Coll., 170 N.Y.S.3d 264, 405 Educ. L. Rep. 503 (Sup. Ct. N.Y. 2022).
[477] Baumbach v. Lafayette Coll., 272 A.3d 83, 402 Educ. L. Rep. 275 (Pa. Super. 2022).

injuries. Her parents sued the college for negligence. The court found that the college acted in a manner that raised an expectation for them to protect the students on the crew team from certain risks. More specifically, the college entered into an agreement with the boathouse that specified required safety procedures, parking, and that the college provided coaches who instructed students on the risks of vehicular accidents nearby. This gave rise to a duty of care to protect the team members.

Employees

The Third Circuit, on appeal from Pennsylvania, affirmed in part and reversed in part a federal trial court's grant of the defendant's motion to dismiss the plaintiff's claims.[478] A former materials scientist for the Department of Energy brought suit against his former employer for violations of the Privacy Act and Federal Tort Claims Act after the department disclosed records to state prosecutors, negligence in conducting an internal investigation into alleged inappropriate and abusive behavior by the former employee towards a student-intern, and its refusal to return his personal property. The court held that the Civil Service Reform Act (CSRA) barred the former employee's claims based on the internal investigation because it was considered a personnel action, so that claim was properly dismissed. However, the CSRA did not bar his claims regarding the disclosure of his records to prosecutors or his conversion claim as neither of those claims constituted a personnel or employment action. Thus, his claims based on the department's cooperation with prosecutors and conversion were reversed and remanded.

Immunity

An appellate court in Michigan affirmed in part and reversed in part the grant of summary disposition in favor of the university and the dismissal of the operator's claims because he did not comply with the notice requirements under the Court of Claims Act.[479] The plaintiff, the operator of a coffee shop in the university's student union, sued a state university for breach of contract, violation of the anti-lockout statute, unjust enrichment, and constructive eviction after the university terminated its commercial lease agreement. The

---

[478] Manivannan v. U.S. Dep't of Energy, 42 F.4th 163, 405 Educ. L. Rep. 743 (3d Cir. 2022).
[479] Elia Cos. v. Univ. of Mich. Regents, 966 N.W.2d 755, 397 Educ. L. Rep. 733 (Mich. Ct. App. 2021).

operator argued that, while the university would generally be entitled to governmental immunity, the proprietary-function exception applied here. The proprietary-function exception applies to "any activity" with the primary "purpose of producing a pecuniary profit for the governmental agency," unless the activity is "normally supported by taxes or fees." The court found that the proprietary-function exception did not apply here because the primary purpose of leasing commercial spaces in the student union was not to earn profit but to provide services for students with as little loss as possible. The court also found that the operator's claims under the anti-lockout statute sounded in tort and, therefore, were barred by governmental immunity.

Conclusion

In K-12 schools, the 2022 cases show that most tort liability cases involving schools are resolved in the state court systems and involve state tort statutes. Disputes continue about what does and does not constitute a school-related or school-sponsored event or location over which the school exercises control; the outcomes of these controversies are highly dependent on the particular facts of individual cases. Additionally, the cases illustrated that public schools and public employees are not always immune from tort liability under state law. Several cases also reinforced that schools are not guarantors of students' absolute safety and that reasonable and adequate supervision—not constant supervision—is the legal standard required of schools and school employees.

In the higher education cases, the courts' decisions were highly dependent on the facts of the individual cases with the exception of two of the U.S. Circuit Court of Appeal cases, which seemed to articulate broader legal principles related to the standard of liability for on-campus harms perpetuated by students. The Eighth Circuit did not hold a university responsible for the violent actions of a fraternity member because the student's propensity for violence was not known and therefore the incident was not foreseeable. The Ninth Circuit opened the door for a potential university duty to protect students from student-on-student sexual misconduct, even though the court has not previously recognized such a duty, due to a public policy interest in protecting young people from sexual assault.

Alphabetical List of Cases

Achay v. Huntington Beach Union High Sch. Dist.
Alachua Cnty. Sch. Bd. v. Barnes
Am. Osteopathic Ass'n v. Am. Bd. of Internal Med.
Archie v. Durham Pub. Sch. Bd. of Educ.
Badler v. Univ. of Me. Sys.
Barlow v. State
Baumbach v. Lafayette Coll.
Bonner v. Lynott
Cavey v. Tualla
Cleveland v. Taft Union High Sch. Dist.
Cruce v. Berkeley Cnty. Sch. Dist.
Cyprian v. Tangipahoa Par. Sch. Sys.
Doe 1 v. Bd. of Educ. of Town of Westport
Doe 1 v. Cleveland Metro. Sch. Dist. Bd. of Educ.
Doe on behalf of Doe v. Dallas Indep. Sch. Dist.
Doe v. Alameda Cmty. Learning Ctr.
Doe v. Bright Horizons Children's Ctr.
Doe v. Greenville City Schs.
Doe v. Lawndale Elementary Sch. Dist.
Doe v. Sup. Ct. of L.A. Cnty.
Elia Cos. v. Univ. of Mich. Regents
Est. of Dunmore v. Pleasantville Bd. of Educ.
Fouad v. Milton Hershey Sch. and Sch. Trust
Gambrill v. Bd. of Educ. of Dorchester Cnty.
Gibson Bros. v. Oberlin Coll.
Hernandez v. Livingston Par. Sch. Bd.
Hopkins v. Indianapolis Pub. Schs.
Jackson v. Jefferson Par. Sch. Bd.
J.C. ex rel. N.C. v. St. Bernard Par. Sch. Bd.
J.G. v. Acad. Charter Elementary Sch.
Joni C. v. Cheektowaga-Sloan Union Free Sch. Dist.
Jordan v. Pa. State Univ.
JUUL Labs v. Marketing, Sales Practices, and Products Liability
    Litigation, In re.
Kalair v. Fajerman
Klein v. Univ. of Me. Sys.
L.D. v. Seymour
Lowell v. Medford Sch. Dist. 549C
Manivannan v. U.S. Dep't of Energy
Marazita v. City of N.Y.
Moore v. Tyson
Munno v. City of Rochester
Neff v. Archdiocese of Miami

Nicdao v. Two Rivers Pub. Charter Sch.
O'Toole as Tr. For Charafeddine v. Marist Coll.
Parker v. Trs. of Spence Sch.
Pharr–San Juan–Alamo Indep. Sch. Dist. v. Tex. Pol. Subdivisions Prop./Casualty Joint Self Ins. Fund
Preston v. S. Univ. ex rel. Bd. of Supervisors of S. Univ. Agric. & Mech. Coll.
Reilley v. Bd. of Educ. of Cnty. of Marshall
Ritter v. Bd. of Educ. of Arcadia Loc. Schs.
R.K. by Fatmir K. v. City of N.Y.
Robertson v. Houston, Miss. Pub. Sch. Dist.
Salamone v. Wesleyan Univ.
Salsberg v. Mann
Spagna v. Phi Kappa Psi
State v. Avoletta
Stone v. Northmont City Sch.
Tanner v. Tex. State Univ.
T.B. v. Novia
Thurlow v. Nelson
Verdi v. Dinowitz
Waterbury v. N.Y.C. Ballet
Westport Ins. Corp. v. Sycamore Cmty. Unit Sch. Dist. #427
White v. Ascendant Com. Ins.
Yvonne Y. v. City of N.Y.

Cases by Jurisdiction

FEDERAL CASES

Second Circuit

New York
L.D. v. Seymour

Third Circuit
Manivannan v. U.S. Dep't of Energ

Pennsylvania
Am. Osteopathic Ass'n v. Am. Bd. of Internal Med.

Fifth Circuit

Texas
Doe on behalf of Doe v. Dallas Indep. Sch. Dist.

Sixth Circuit

Ohio
Doe 1 v. Cleveland Metro. Sch. Dist. Bd. of Educ.
Ritter v. Bd. of Educ. of Arcadia Loc. Schs.

Seventh Circuit

Illinois
Westport Ins. Corp. v. Sycamore Cmty. Unit Sch. Dist. #427

Eighth Circuit
Spagna v. Phi Kappa Psi

Ninth Circuit
Barlow v. State

California
Doe v. Alameda Cmty. Learning Ctr.
JUUL Labs v. Mktg, Sales Pracs, and Prods. Liab. Litig., In re.

STATE & D.C. COURT CASES

Alabama
Moore v. Tyson

California
Achay v. Huntington Beach Union High Sch. Dist.
Cavey v. Tualla
Cleveland v. Taft Union High Sch. Dist.
Doe v. Lawndale Elementary Sch. Dist.
Doe v. Sup. Ct. of L.A. Cnty.

Connecticut
Doe 1 v. Bd. of Educ. of Town of Westport
Salamone v. Wesleyan Univ.
State v. Avoletta

District of Columbia
Nicdao v. Two Rivers Pub. Charter Sch.

Florida
Neff v. Archdiocese of Miami
White v. Ascendant Com. Ins.
Alachua Cnty. Sch. Bd. v. Barnes

Indiana
Hopkins v. Indianapolis Pub. Schs.

Louisiana
Cyprian v. Tangipahoa Par. Sch. Sys.
Hernandez v. Livingston Par. Sch. Bd.
Jackson v. Jefferson Par. Sch. Bd.
J.C. ex rel. N.C. v. St. Bernard Par. Sch. Bd.
Preston v. S. Univ. ex rel. Bd. of Supervisors of S. Univ. Agric. & Mech. Coll.

Maine
Badler v. Univ. of Me. Sys.
Klein v. Univ. of Me. Sys.
Thurlow v. Nelson

Maryland
Gambrill v. Bd. of Educ. of Dorchester Cnty.

Michigan
Elia Cos. v. Univ. of Mich. Regents

Mississippi
Robertson v. Houston, Miss. Pub. Sch. Dist.

New Jersey
Est. of Dunmore v. Pleasantville Bd. of Educ.
T.B. v. Novia

New York
Bonner v. Lynott
Fouad v. Milton Hershey Sch. and Sch. Trust
Joni C. v. Cheektowaga-Sloan Union Free Sch. Dist.
J.G. v. Acad. Charter Elementary Sch.
Kalair v. Fajerman
Marazita v. City of N.Y.
Munno v. City of Rochester

O'Toole as Tr. for Charafeddine v. Marist Coll.
Parker v. Trs. of Spence Sch.
R.K. by Fatmir K. v. City of N.Y.
Verdi v. Dinowitz
Waterbury v. N.Y.C. Ballet
Yvonne Y. v. City of N.Y.

North Carolina
Archie v. Durham Pub. Sch. Bd. of Educ.

Ohio
Doe v. Greenville City Schs.
Gibson Bros. v. Oberlin Coll.
Stone v. Northmont City Sch.

Oregon
Lowell v. Medford Sch. Dist. 549C

Pennsylvania
Baumbach v. Lafayette Coll.
Doe v. Bright Horizons Children's Ctr.
Jordan v. Pa. State Univ.
Salsberg v. Mann

South Carolina
Cruce v. Berkeley Cnty. Sch. Dist.

Texas
Pharr–San Juan–Alamo Indep. Sch. Dist. v. Tex. Pol. Subdivisions
    Prop./Casualty Joint Self Ins. Fund
Tanner v. Tex. State Univ.

West Virginia
Reilley v. Bd. of Educ. of Cnty. of Marshall

Chapter 7

SPORTS

Gillian P. Foss, Ph.D.[480] and Joy Blanchard, Ph.D.[481]

Introduction	211
Discrimination	211
Title IX and Sex Discrimination	211
Race-Based Discrimination	214
Negligence	214
First Amendment Issues	216
Tort	218
COVID-19	220
Employment Issues	221
Discipline	222
Procedural Issues	222
Conclusion	223
Alphabetical List of Cases	224
Cases by Jurisdiction	224

---

[480] Lutrill and Pearl Payne School of Education, Louisiana State University, Baton Rouge, La.
[481] Associate Professor, Higher Education, Lutrill and Pearl Payne School of Education, Louisiana State University, Baton Rouge, La.

Introduction

This chapter reviews litigation from 2022 addressing issues in sports in K–12 schools and higher education. In both the K–12 and higher education sectors, the legal issues covered reflect litigation patterns of negligence claims, tort disputes, Title IX discrimination, and First Amendment challenges. The cases in this chapter comprise appellate court judgments, trial court actions, and a Supreme Court ruling, and some may also appear in other chapters due to intersecting topics (e.g., students in higher education, employees, and torts).

Discrimination

Title IX and Sex Discrimination

The First Circuit affirmed the Rhode Island federal trial court's decision to overrule the objections against a negotiated revised settlement that eliminated certain varsity sports more than twenty years after a Title IX class action settlement between the university and student-athletes.[482] Here, the university decided to downgrade five women's and six men's teams from varsity status to club status in order to upgrade the women's and co-ed sailing teams to varsity status. After mediation, the university and the class reached a new agreement. Twelve class members objected to the new settlement, arguing the named class representatives were inadequate and the settlement was not "fair, reasonable, and adequate." The court disagreed, holding that the named representatives could still adequately represent the class despite no longer participating in the university's athletic program and the revised agreement was fair, reasonable, and adequate.

The Sixth Circuit, on appeal from Michigan, vacated and remanded a federal trial court's denial of the plaintiffs' motion for a preliminary injunction.[483] The plaintiffs were members of the university's women's swimming and diving team suing the university for violating Title IX after it eliminated the men's and women's swimming and diving teams. The plaintiffs argued that allowing the university to eliminate the women's swimming and

---

[482] Cohen v. Brown Univ., 16 F.4th 935, 396 Educ. L. Rep. 37 (1st Cir. 2021).
[483] Balow v. Mich. State Univ., 24 F.4th 1051, 399 Educ. L. Rep. 505 (6th Cir. 2022).

diving team would fail to provide women with "substantially proportionate athletic opportunities, as required by Title IX." The appellate court held that the trial court erred by failing to focus on the number of participation opportunities, as opposed to the participation gap as a percentage of the athletic program's size, and it was required to compare the participation gap to the size of a viable team as opposed to the average team.

A group of female student-athletes in Minnesota sued the university and university officials for sex discrimination under Title IX after the university decided to disband certain women's sports teams.[484] The Eighth Circuit reversed and remanded the grant of judgment in favor of the plaintiff student-athletes. The court affirmed the trial court's finding that the university operated its athletics based on a three-tier system. However, the appellate court found that the trial court erred by requiring the university to provide equitable treatment and benefits "among the tiers of support." Thus, the court affirmed that the university failed to comply with Title IX in its allocation of athletic participation opportunities, but the court reversed and remanded as to the trial court's findings about equitable treatment and benefits.

Members of a high school varsity water polo team in Hawai'i pursued a Title IX claim against the state department of education and an interscholastic sports association.[485] Among their claims of gender-based discrimination were (a) unequal treatment, including disparate access and quality of the male athletes' locker room and equipment compared to the female athletes' resources; (b) unequal opportunity for participate in athletics, alleging a notable gap between female student–athletes and total female student enrollment; and (c) school administrator retaliation efforts to quash early concerns brought up by the plaintiffs. Despite a loss in the federal trial court, the Ninth Circuit reversed and remanded in favor of the female student-athletes. Based on the argument pertaining to the percentage of female student-athletes to total current and future female student enrollment, the court held that the trial court likely improperly applied the numerosity argument from *Jordan v. County of Los Angeles*. Moreover, the court argued that the overall treatment of water polo players was suggestive of systemic discrimination that would plausibly extend and impact future female student-athletes if left unaddressed.

---

[484] Portz v. St. Cloud State Univ., 16 F.4th 577, 395 Educ. L. Rep. 911 (8th Cir. 2021).
[485] A. B. v. Haw. State Dep't of Educ., 30 F.4th 828, 401 Educ. L. Rep. 188 (9th Cir. 2022).

Due to alleged budget constraints, a university eliminated the women's rowing team along with two men's sports teams.[486] A federal trial court in Connecticut granted the plaintiff students' motion for a temporary restraining order (TRO) to maintain the status quo pending a ruling on their preliminary injunction motion to prevent the university from eliminating the women's rowing team, alleging Title IX violations. To be granted a TRO, the party seeking it must show that they are "likely to succeed on the merits," "likely to suffer irreparable harm in the absence of preliminary relief," "the balance of equities tips in his [or her] favor," and "an injunction is in the public interest." The court found that the university was noncompliant with Title IX's effective-accommodation mandate and that eliminating the women's rowing team only worsened the noncompliance by increasing the participation gap between men and women's sports, so the plaintiffs were likely to succeed on the merits of their claim. Further, the loss of the health and social benefits the rowing team provided its members could not be repaired by monetary damages. The court also found that the balancing of equities and public interest weighed in favor of granting the TRO.

In Texas, a federal trial court heard a case involving a student who was allegedly physically assaulted by her boyfriend, a football player, and who was suing the university for Title IX and negligence, the city for due process violations, and the former football coach for negligence.[487] The coach filed motions to compel further discovery from the university, and the court held that the university's documents dated before and after the student attended university and information regarding the coach's steps to conceal reports of sexual assault or domestic violence against players were relevant. However, the court also held that information about the university's actions in response to on-campus safety, whether the university implemented a policy to respond to sexual assault or dating violence, and when the university issued or withdrew policies of sexual assault or dating violence were not relevant.

A number of student-athletes at a public university sued based on New Jersey's anti-discrimination law, claiming to have been subject to a "hostile educational environment, disparate treatment, and retaliation" in the women's basketball program based on sex and sexual orientation.[488] The university's interim head women's basketball coach allegedly made disparaging remarks about the

---

[486] Lazor v. Univ. of Conn., 560 F. Supp.3d 674, 401 Educ. L. Rep. 857 (D. Conn. 2021).
[487] Lozano v. Baylor Univ., 339 F.R.D. 447, 397 Educ. L. Rep. 1068 (W.D. Tex. 2020).
[488] Morris v. Rutgers-Newark Univ., 277 A.3d 13, 16, 405 Educ. L. Rep. 416 (N.J. Super. Ct. App. Div. 2022).

student-athletes based on sexual orientation and engaged in a series of actions to prohibit the team captain from playing after she complained to university administrators about his actions. A trial court dismissed the claims brought by the other players party to the suit, but the appellate court reversed and remanded, citing that those words "spoken to one member of the small group were the functional equivalent of saying those words to all" and could have served to create a hostile environment among the entire team.

Race-Based Discrimination

A former student-athlete sued a private institution after he allegedly experienced years of race-based harassment from his teammates and coaches.[489] The student based his claims on Title VI of the Civil Rights Act of 1964 and asserted that both coaches and athletic administrators were deliberately indifferent to the student's numerous complaints. Based on an application of the one-year statute of limitations per the District of Columbia Human Rights Act, the federal trial court dismissed all claims as time-barred. The university argued that the claim was mostly time-barred by a one-year statute of limitations, while the plaintiff argued that a three-year statute of limitations should apply to all claims. In Washington D.C., courts generally apply the three-year statute of limitations for personal injury claims to claims under Title VI, since it does not have an express statute of limitations itself; however, this court found the one-year statute of limitations under the D.C. Human Rights Act to be more appropriate. The plaintiff's more recent claims were also dismissed because the court found that the university responded appropriately to those claims of harassment.

Negligence

The Fifth Circuit, in a case from Texas, affirmed in part and remanded in part a negligence claim that emerged after an assistant high school football coach urged two members of his team to physically assault a game official for supposedly making inappropriate comments and adverse calls in favor of the opposing team.[490] The players' assault went viral and the official filed suit for negligence, yet had little success due to the players' status as private

---

[489] Stafford v. The George Wash. Univ., 578 F.Supp.3d 25, 405 Educ. L. Rep. 997 (D.D.C. 2022).
[490] Watts v. Northside Indep. Sch. Dist., 37 F.4th 1094, 404 Educ. L. Rep. 175 (5th Cir. 2022).

actors and the school's lack of a role in orchestrating the issue. Where the plaintiff had success was with a revised substantive due process claim against the assistant coach specifically; with this shift, the appellate court identified the coach as a public official engaged in state action and remanded the case back to the trial court to determine the extent of the negligence claim.

A federal trial court in Indiana granted the NCAA's motion to dismiss the former and current collegiate athlete's negligence and breach of contract claims for failing to create regulatory safeguards to protect the student-athletes from sexual abuse by coaches.[491] The court first held that the current student, who had not been sexually assaulted by her coaches, lacked standing. The former students' claims failed because they exceeded the statute of limitations. The court held that the repression of one athlete's memories of the sexual abuse did not toll the statute of limitations, nor did fraudulent concealment apply to any of the athlete's claims which would estop the statute of limitations.

A school district in California had greater success with a summary judgment motion after negligence claims arose from a former junior varsity football player who sustained a traumatic head injury during a game.[492] The appellate court affirmed that the plaintiff had voluntarily signed a pre-season waiver to participate in football that covered both risk of injury and potential negligence on the part of all relevant stakeholders at the school (e.g., coaches, trainers, athletic director). Additionally, evidence from the defendants suggested coaching staff had undergone substantive concussion protocol training and had extended information on brain injuries to parents and their student-athletes in addition to the preseason waiver. These protective efforts and the release were sufficient to satisfy the assumption of risk doctrine and preclude the school board from liability.

In a similar ruling under the assumption of risk doctrine, an appellate court in Indiana reversed and remanded a trial court's ruling and held that summary judgment should be considered as part of a school board's argument that they were not liable for a high school cheerleader's injuries.[493] The injury occurred during a warmup session at a school basketball game, which involved the cheerleader falling to the ground and seriously injuring her mouth during a routine. Although coaching and school staff testified there

---

[491] Aldrich v. Nat'l Collegiate Athletic Assoc., 565 F.Supp.3d 1094, 402 Educ. L. Rep. 722 (S.D. Ind. 2021).
[492] Brown v. El Dorado Union High Sch. Dist., 292 Cal. Rptr. 3d 72, 401 Educ. L. Rep. 1057 (Cal. Ct. App. 2022).
[493] Tippecanoe Sch. Corp. v. Reynolds, 187 N.E.3d 213, 402 Educ. L. Rep. 1125 (Ind. Ct. App. 2022).

could have been improved protective measures in place (e.g., mats on the ground), the appellate court ruled that none of the actions or omissions during the event extended beyond the "ordinary" scope of the cheerleading sport. To present this argument, the appellate court cited an earlier ruling by the Supreme Court of Indiana, *Pfenning v. Lineman*, that had further defined standards of recklessness and intent when deliberating over otherwise "ordinary" practices of the sport.

After a member of a high school soccer team faced alleged physical attacks from players of the opposing team resulting in a traumatic brain injury, she filed a negligence suit against her school district and, more specifically, against the security guard for the high school.[494] The school board and the security guard defendant countered with motions to dismiss based on sovereign immunity and official immunity, respectively, and the appellate court affirmed the trial court's prior decision to grant these motions. The court noted that, although the situation could possibly have been handled differently, "there is no dispute… [that the security official] is a public employee whose actions were within the scope of her official duties and there is no allegation she acted with malice."

An appellate court in New York reversed and remanded a trial court ruling that granted summary judgment to the host school of a high school swim meet after a participating athlete sustained injuries from the event.[495] The female swimmer, who vehemently argued their status as a novice with insufficient training and expertise on a starting block, endured head and neck injuries after diving into the shallow end of the pool. The appellate court maintained that although student-athletes do carry an assumption of risk when participating in athletics, the defendants were not immune from liability due to a lack of factual clarity on (a) the absence of safety-related guidance for the inexperienced swimmer, and (b) whether keeping the starting blocks in the shallow end of the pool during the meet was suggestive of negligence.

First Amendment Issues

The U.S. Supreme Court reversed prior trial and appellate court decisions in favor of a public high school football coach in Washington who was suspended for inviting players to pray with

---

[494] Gray-Ross v. St. Louis Pub. Schs., 643 S.W.3d 665, 402 Educ. L. Rep. 1221 (Mo. Ct. App. 2022).
[495] A. L. v. Chaminade Mineola Soc'y of Mary, 166 N.Y.S.3d 186, 402 Educ. L. Rep. 340 (N.Y. App. Div. 2022).

him on the 50-yard line of the football field after games.[496] The defendant school board undertook several attempts to persuade the coach to adjust his prayer practice so as not to violate the Establishment Clause of the First Amendment, yet the coach continued to pray on the 50-yard line immediately after games. The board ultimately pursued disciplinary action. Although lower court rulings dismissed the coach's complaint, arguing that "his speech was made in his capacity as a public employee, not a private citizen," the Supreme Court disagreed, ruling that the coach's "midfield prayer practice did not violate the Establishment Clause." The Court also held that the lower courts should have interpreted the Free Exercise and Free Speech clauses together to expand protections for religious expression, largely overturning the three-pronged test developed in *Lemon v. Kurtzman* to identify Establishment Clause violations.

In Oklahoma, a federal trial court granted the university's motion to dismiss and granted in part and denied in part the coaches' motions to dismiss the student-athlete's claim for First Amendment retaliation.[497] The student-athlete alleged she was retaliated against based on her political beliefs and her reaction to claims of racism by others. The university did not consent to suit and was entitled to Eleventh Amendment immunity. The coaches, on the other hand, were not entitled to immunity. The court found the plaintiff had engaged in constitutionally protected speech when she posted a "somewhat ambiguous emoji on a third-party website" and expressed skepticism about whether a song was racist. The court also found that the plaintiff suffered an adverse action through evidence of a coach ordering her to remove a post, pressuring her to apologize to university personnel, hosting team meetings involving the diversity and inclusion office that focused on the plaintiff's opinions, restricting the plaintiff from practice and ignoring her questions, and ultimately forcing her to leave the program. Finally, the court found that the coaches' actions were due to disagreement with her political views. Thus, the plaintiff sufficiently alleged that the coaches violated her First Amendment rights.

After a Louisiana football coach was fired from a private high school in response to a racially explicit locker room video of his players that went viral, the coach faced further media condemnation, with one headline titled "High School Football Coach Fired After Using Racial Slur in Pre-Game Chant," which did not

---

[496] Kennedy v. Bremerton Sch. Dist., 142 S. Ct. 2407, 404 Educ. L. Rep. 43 (2022).
[497] McLaughlin v. Bd. of Regents of Univ. of Okla., 566 F.Supp.3d 1204, 402 Educ. L. Rep. 862 (W.D. Okla. 2021).

accurately reflect the circumstances of the issue.[498] The plaintiff unsuccessfully sued for defamation of character against two media outlets and appealed both outcomes. The appellate court found that the trial court erred in dismissing the complaint against the media outlet with the aforementioned title, given the basis of the platform's "public issue" defense was based on the inaccurate report that the coach's firing stemmed from his own speech in a public forum. The court upheld the dismissal against the other media outlet based on its lack of jurisdiction in Louisiana and remanded any other unresolved questions to the trial court.

Tort

A federal trial court in Connecticut denied the defendants' motion to dismiss the student-athlete's negligent misrepresentation and breach of contract claims under state law but granted dismissal as to the student-athletes' and managers' claims for constructive fraud and breach of the contract to sponsor Division I athletics for the duration of their enrollment.[499] The plaintiffs, student-athletes and student-managers for the university's intercollegiate athletic teams, brought this suit after the board voted to transition the university's athletic programs from Division I to Division II. The court found that one student-athlete plausibly alleged negligent misrepresentation because he was told that he would be "held to the expectations of a Division I athlete" for the four years he attended university. The court further held that the plaintiffs' breach of contract claim failed because, aside from the one student who successfully claimed negligent misrepresentation, there was no promise from the university to sponsor Division I athletics for the entirety of the plaintiffs' enrollment.

A student-athlete's father brought a claim for personal injury after the cross country coach allowed the student-athlete to race after being stung by a wasp and failing to provide proper medical care to the student-athlete when he fell and hit his head during the race.[500] The Supreme Court of Mississippi affirmed the lower court's grant of summary judgment in favor of the school board. While this case was being decided, the state supreme court had restored a two-part public policy function test to determine "if an allegedly tortious activity involved the exercise of a discretionary function and thus

---

[498] Jones v St. Augustine High Sch., 336 So.3d 470, 402 Educ. L. Rep. 541 (La. Ct. App. 2022).
[499] Bell v. Univ. of Hartford, 577 F. Supp.3d 6, 405 Educ. L. Rep. 819 (D. Conn. 2021).
[500] Strickland on Behalf of Strickland v. Rankin Cnty. Sch. Dist., 341 So.3d 941, 405 Educ. L. Rep. 1234 (Miss. 2022).

was entitled to sovereign immunity." However, before reaching the public policy function test, the plaintiff must identify an alleged tort, which the plaintiff here failed to do. Specifically, the court found that the plaintiff failed to allege a breach of a duty of care by any school employee that proximately caused the student-athlete's injuries.

In Indiana, the state supreme court was asked to decide whether the apex doctrine could be applied to a series of concussive head injury cases brought against a national athletic association by former student-athletes.[501] The plaintiffs in these cases were seeking to depose the president, chief operating officer, and chief medical officer of the association—none of whom were in their respective positions at the time of the injuries. The apex doctrine "shields high-level executives from depositions unless the requesting party shows (1) the executive possesses unique or personal knowledge relevant to the issues being litigated and (2) the information cannot be obtained through a less intrusive discovery method." The court declined to adopt the apex doctrine and remanded the case to the lower court to review whether good cause existed to limit or prohibit the deposition of these national association officials.

A former high school student in California sued the school board, arguing it was obligated to indemnify him for his defense costs in a negligence action brought against him by a referee for injuries sustained during an "away" football game.[502] An appellate court affirmed the lower court's grant of the school board's demurrer without leave to amend and dismissal of the plaintiff's claims. The plaintiff argued that the school board was required to ensure his participation on the football team was free, and they failed to do that by refusing to pay for his legal defense. The court held that the state constitution did not impose a mandatory duty on the school board to provide students a free legal defense, and the board's refusal to defend the student did not result in the student incurring a statutorily prohibited charge for an extracurricular activity.

An appellate court in Louisiana affirmed the trial court's grant of summary judgment in favor of the high school and head coach on the plaintiff child's claims following injuries he received in a physical altercation with another football training camp attendee in the high school locker room.[503] The child alleged that there was a genuine dispute of material fact as to whether the high school assumed an enhanced duty to supervise the locker room. A school and teachers

---

[501] Nat'l Coll. Athletic Ass'n v. Finnerty, 191 N.E.3d 211, 405 Educ. L. Rep. 1160 (Ind. 2022).
[502] Srouy v. San Diego Unified Sch. Dist., 290 Cal.Rptr.3d 606, 400 Educ. L. Rep. 675 (Cal. Ct. App. 2022).
[503] Dean v. De La Salle of New Orleans, 334 So.3d 425, 401 Educ. L. Rep, 678 (La. Ct. App. 2021).

are generally only liable for "damages caused by students under their supervision when the school board, the teacher, or other school authorities 'might have prevented the act which caused the damages and have not done so.'" Here, the child and his parents failed to identify any specific imminent threat or to show that there was a hostile history between the students involved; instead, the fight was spontaneous and unforeseeable. Therefore, the school did not owe a higher duty of supervision.

A basketball recruit sued after incurring a knee injury while on a visit to a state university in Oregon.[504] The plaintiff notified coaches that he had both knees "scoped" after the previous basketball season, and, despite that knowledge, the coaches had him perform a series of aggressive contact drills. A trial court granted summary judgment to the university, citing that the injuries stemmed from the plaintiff's normal assumption of risk while participating in athletic activities. The appellate court reversed and remanded for trial, noting that it was for a jury to decide if the coaches acted with reasonable care and if the injuries were foreseeable in light of the knowledge that the plaintiff had suffered from knee issues prior to the injury.

COVID-19

The Sixth Circuit denied the defendant's motion for a stay pending appeal after a federal trial court in Michigan granted the plaintiffs' preliminary injunction.[505] Here, a group of student-athletes sued the board of trustees for constitutional and statutory violations after the university denied their requests for a religious exemption from the COVID-19 vaccine requirement for student athletes. The trial court issued a preliminary injunction, preventing the university from enforcing the vaccine mandate against the plaintiffs. The appellate court held that, because the plaintiffs established that the vaccine policy burdened their free exercise of religion and they had a strong likelihood of success on the merits, the preliminary injunction was not inappropriate. Therefore, the defendant's motion to stay the preliminary injunction pending appeal was denied.

---

[504] Clark v. Univ. of Or., 512 P.3d 457, 404 Educ. L. Rep. 938 (Or. Ct. App. 2022).
[505] Dahl v. Bd. of Trs. Of W. Mich. Univ., 15 F.4th 728, 395 Educ. L. Rep. 484 (6th Cir. 2021).

Employment Issues

In the first of two employment cases from Pennsylvania, a federal trial court denied the NCAA's motion to dismiss but granted the non-attended universities' motion to dismiss the student-athletes' claims for violations of the Fair Labor Standards Act (FLSA), Pennsylvania Minimum Wage Act, New York Labor Law, and Connecticut Minimum Wage Act.[506] The student-athletes brought this claim arguing that they are employees and should be paid minimum wage for their time spent related to athletic activities. The NCAA argued that it could not be a joint employer as it merely regulated the student-athletes' participation in intercollegiate athletics. The court considered four factors in its joint employer test: the ability to hire and fire the alleged employees; the ability to set conditions of employment, including compensation, benefits, and scheduling; the involvement in day-to-day supervision; and the actual control of alleged employee records. The court found that the student-athletes did not adequately allege any of the four elements as to the non-attended universities, but all four factors weighed in favor of finding that the NCAA was a joint employer. Therefore, the non-attended universities' motion to dismiss was granted while the NCAA's was denied. In a related lawsuit, a federal trial court in Pennsylvania considered the student-athlete's claims under the same laws against their own universities and colleges; it denied the institutions' motion to dismiss in this case.[507] The court did not find the "amateurism" of NCAA interscholastic athletics or the fact that the students "played" on a team sufficient to establish that the student-athletes were not employees under the FLSA. The court also held that the Department of Labor's field operations handbook did not exclude NCAA interscholastic athletics from a potential employer-employee relationship for FLSA purposes. Instead, the court applied the primary beneficiary test, which analyzes seven factors to determine who the primary beneficiary of the relationship is. The court found that four of the factors weighed in favor of the plaintiffs, with two factors being neutral and one weighing in favor of the institutions. Thus, the student-athletes plausibly alleged that they were employees of the colleges and universities they attended.

A high school football coach brought claims against the school board and board of education for violations of the Open Meetings

---

[506] Johnson v. Nat'l Collegiate Athletic Assoc., 561 F. Supp.3d 490, 402 Educ. L. Rep. 135 (E.D. Pa. 2021).
[507] Johnson v. Nat'l Collegiate Athletic Assoc., 556 F. Supp.3d 491, 401 Educ. L. Rep. 370 (E.D. Pa. 2021).

Law following a closed session that resulted in the non-renewal of his appointment.[508] An appellate court in New York reversed the trial court's grant of partial summary judgment declaring that the executive session violated the Open Meetings Law, making action taken during the session void. The Open Meetings Law generally requires "every meeting of a public body shall be open to the general public," but there is an exception when "communications [are] made pursuant to an attorney-client relationship." Because that exception applied here, the matter was exempted from the Open Meetings Law. The court further noted that, even if there was a violation of the Open Meetings Law, it did not require voiding the board's action during the session.

Discipline

In Pennsylvania, an appellate court held that the state's interscholastic athletic association's (PIAA) decision prohibiting the student from participating in postseason basketball for the academic year was arbitrary and capricious.[509] Under PIAA bylaws, a student is ineligible to compete in the postseason unless they can show "that [a school] transfer was necessitated by exceptional and unusual circumstances beyond the reasonable control of the student's family." The student attended the same district for 8th-10th grade before transferring to another district closer to his father's work to avoid termination. The PIAA found that, because the father had not changed employment, the move was not necessary. The appellate court found this reasoning to be arbitrary and capricious, especially considering the PIAA deliberated for less than 16 minutes on the issue and did not offer the father an opportunity to testify as to why the move was necessary to his employment.

Procedural Issues

The Supreme Court of Texas reversed in part and remanded the trial court's rendering of judgment finding the manufacturer breached its warranty and awarding the school district $175,000 in damages.[510] The school board brought suit against the contractor who installed turf on the football field for breach of warranty and the

---

[508] Sindoni v. Bd. of Educ. of Skaneateles Cent. Sch. Dist., 163 N.Y.S.3d 343, 401 Educ. L. Rep. 536 (N.Y. App. Div. 2022).
[509] K.H. v. Pa. Interscholastic Athletic Assoc., 277 A.3d 638, 405 Educ. L. Rep. 1070 (Commw. Ct. Pa. 2022).
[510] FieldTurf USA v. Pleasant Grove Indep. Sch. Dist., 642 S.W.3d 829, 402 Educ. L. Rep. 488 (Tex. 2022).

manufacturer of the turf for fraud and breach of warranty after the school officials discovered issues with field degradation roughly five years after it was installed. The contractor objected to the introduction of the G-Max report, which tests shock absorption, arguing that it did not document that a proper testing device was used or that the device had been calibrated and the authenticity of the report was not established. The court held that the appellate court erred in relying on the report because the trial court had not included it as a part of the summary judgment proof. Because there was no alternative basis on which to affirm the appellate court, the state supreme court remanded.

Conclusion

In this chapter, litigation from 2022 involved student-athletes, coaches, and governing organizations in K–12 and higher education. The adjudication suggests patterns of affirmation of broad First Amendment protections for students and coaches; school officials' widespread protection from liability for athlete injury under the negligence doctrine; and somewhat successful student-athlete claims of inequitable systemic practices in athletics, particularly from a gender discrimination standpoint. Such outcomes indicate stakeholders at both K–12 and higher education levels must balance student-athlete and staff autonomy of expression and self-advocacy with continual efforts to pursue equity in the sports arena.

Alphabetical List of Cases

A. B. v. Haw. State Dep't of Educ.
A. L. v. Chaminade Mineola Soc'y of Mary
Aldrich v. Nat'l Collegiate Athletic Assoc.
Balow v. Mich. State Univ.
Bell v. Univ. of Hartford
Brown v. El Dorado Union High Sch. Dist.
Clark v. Univ. of Or.
Cohen v. Brown Univ.
Dahl v. Bd. of Trs. Of W. Mich. Univ.
Dean v. De La Salle of New Orleans
FieldTurf USA v. Pleasant Grove Indep. Sch. Dist.
Gray-Ross v. St. Louis Pub. Schs.
Johnson v. Nat'l Collegiate Athletic Assoc. (a)
Johnson v. Nat'l Collegiate Athletic Assoc. (b)
Jones v. St. Augustine High Sch.
Kennedy v. Bremerton Sch. Dist.
K.H. v. Pa. Interscholastic Athletic Assoc.
Lazor v. Univ. of Conn.
Lozano v. Baylor Univ.
McLaughlin v. Bd. of Regents of Univ. of Okla.
Morris v. Rutgers-Newark Univ.
Nat'l Coll. Athletic Ass'n v. Finnerty
Portz v. St. Cloud State Univ.
Sindoni v. Bd. of Educ. of Skaneateles Cent. Sch. Dist.
Srouy v. San Diego Unified Sch. Dist.
Stafford v. The George Wash. Univ.
Strickland on Behalf of Strickland v. Rankin Cnty. Sch. Dist.
Tippecanoe Sch. Corp. v. Reynolds
Watts v. Northside Indep. Sch. Dist.

Cases by Jurisdiction

FEDERAL CASES

U.S. Supreme Court
Kennedy v. Bremerton Sch. Dist.

D.C. Circuit
Stafford v. The George Wash. Univ.

First Circuit
Cohen v. Brown Univ.

Second Circuit

Connecticut
Bell v. Univ. of Hartford
Lazor v. Univ. of Conn.

Third Circuit

Pennsylvania
Johnson v. Nat'l Collegiate Athletic Assoc. (a)
Johnson v. Nat'l Collegiate Athletic Assoc (b)

Fifth Circuit
Watts v. Northside Indep. Sch. Dist.

Texas
Lozano v. Baylor Univ.

Sixth Circuit
Balow v. Mich. State Univ.
Dahl v. Bd. of Trs. Of W. Mich. Univ.

Seventh Circuit

Indiana
Aldrich v. Nat'l Collegiate Athletic Assoc.

Eighth Circuit
Portz v. St. Cloud State Univ.

Ninth Circuit
A. B. v. Haw. State Dep't of Educ.

Tenth Circuit

Oklahoma
McLaughlin v. Bd. of Regents of Univ. of Okla.

STATE & D.C. COURT CASES

California
Brown v. El Dorado Union High Sch. Dist.
Srouy v. San Diego Unified Sch. Dist.

Indiana
Nat'l Coll. Athletic Ass'n v. Finnerty
Tippecanoe Sch. Corp. v. Reynolds

Louisiana
Dean v. De La Salle of New Orleans
Jones v. St. Augustine High Sch.

Mississippi
Strickland on Behalf of Strickland v. Rankin Cnty. Sch. Dist.

Montana
Gray-Ross v. St. Louis Pub. Schs.

New Jersey
Morris v. Rutgers-Newark Univ.

New York
A. L. v. Chaminade Mineola Soc'y of Mary
Sindoni v. Bd. of Educ. of Skaneateles Cent. Sch. Dist.

Oregon
Clark v. Univ. of Or.

Pennsylvania
K.H. v. Pa. Interscholastic Athletic Assoc.

Texas
FieldTurf USA v. Pleasant Grove Indep. Sch. Dist.

Chapter 8

HIGHER EDUCATION ADMINISTRATION & FACULTY

Jeffrey C. Sun, J.D., Ph.D.[511] and Jesse Hagan, J.D.[512]

Introduction	229
Admissions	229
Discrimination and Harassment	230
Race	230
Sex/Sexual Orientation	232
Disability	235
Age	237
Retaliation	238
First Amendment	239
Whistleblowing	241
COVID-19 Policy	242
Due Process	243
Contracts	244
Tenure	247
Labor Relations	247
Workers' Compensation	248
Procedural Issues	250
Jurisdiction	250
Privilege	251

---

[511] Professor of Higher Education and Law, Distinguished University Scholar, Associate Dean for Innovation and Strategic Partnerships, and Director of the SKILLS Collaborative at the University of Louisville, Ky. He is also Counsel at Manley Burke.
[512] Assistant County Attorney, Louisville, KY.

    Attorney Fees 251
    Standing 252

Environmental Protections 252

Intellectual Property 254
    Trademark 254
    Misappropriation of Information 254

Property-Related Issues 255

Safety 256

Crime-Related Issues 256

Consumer Protection 258

Policy Changes 259

Conclusion 259

Cases by Alphabetical 261

Cases by Jurisdiction 262

Introduction

This chapter includes summaries of cases reported in 2022 that involved issues affecting higher education institutions (HEIs) and their administrators, staff, faculty, students, and families. The issues within this period included admissions, discrimination and harassment, First Amendment, whistleblowing, challenged policies in light of COVID-19, due process, contracts, tenure, labor relations, workers' compensation, procedural issues in the law, environmental protections, intellectual property, property-related issues, safety, crime-related matters, consumer protection concerns, and academic policy change implications.

When discussing discriminatory matters and constitutional violations, this chapter presented several short-form references. For instance, when raising issues around Title VI, these cases are referring to Title VI of the Civil Rights Act of 1964, those cases pertain to alleged discriminatory matters based on race, color, or national origin either due to the university denying participation or benefits associated with a university program. Similarly, Title VII refers to that part of the Civil Rights Act of 1964 prohibiting discrimination based on race, color, or national origin in the employment context. Also, when referencing Section 1981 or Section 1983, these short forms of the law refer to allegations of nongovernmental discrimination or governmental-sourced discrimination, respectively.

Collectively, the cases covered in this chapter summarize the key cases in 2022 addressing higher education matters involving faculty or administration. Accordingly, these cases will be instructive to administrators, scholars, and policymakers involved in various issues affecting HEIs.

Admissions

The Fifth Circuit reversed a federal trial court's grant of summary judgment in favor of the university in a suit for declaratory and injunctive relief under Sections 1983 and 1981, the Equal Protection Clause, and Title VII.[513] A nonprofit organization brought this suit based on the university's consideration of race in admissions. The defendants claimed, and the trial court agreed, that because the organization's directors were involved in previous cases

---

[513] Students for Fair Admissions v. Univ. of Tex. at Austin, 37 F.4th 1078, 404 Educ. L. Rep. 162 (5th Cir. 2022).

for the same matter, they were precluded from making the claim *res judicata*. The appellate court held that the organization cannot be precluded from bringing this lawsuit merely because a director, in her individual capacity, sued for similar reasons while acting in a different capacity. Further, the appellate court determined that the operative facts were not the same as initially raised. The organization alleged that the admissions policy had changed since the previous case, *Fisher*, and therefore the case was technically challenging a new and different policy. Accordingly, the court reversed the trial court's judgment regarding standing and the *res judicata* ruling and remanded the case.

In a case from North Carolina, the plaintiff alleged that the university's consideration of race in its admissions policy violated the Equal Protection Clause of the Fourteenth Amendment and constituted Title VI discrimination.[514] A federal trial court ruled in favor of the university based on alleged violations under Title VI, Section 1983, and the Civil Rights Act of 1964. The court found that the admissions policy survived strict scrutiny under the Equal Protection Clause because it had a compelling interest in pursuing the educational benefits of diversity; the university used race as a "plus factor," and it was narrowly tailored to pursue the above interest; and the university clearly established that there were not viable race-neutral alternatives as required to survive strict scrutiny. After this case was decided, the U.S. Supreme Court reversed the decision, holding that the university's race-conscious admissions violated the Equal Protection clause.[515]

Discrimination and Harassment

Race

In Indiana, a Black lecturer brought a Title VII racial discrimination claim alleging that the university paid him less than one of his white colleagues and did not provide him with an early promotion.[516] On appeal, the Seventh Circuit dismissed the claim because it exceeded the statute of limitations, requiring suits for an unlawful employment practice be brought within 300 days. This suit

---

[514] Students for Fair Admissions v. Univ. of N.C., 567 F. Supp. 3d 580, 402 Educ. L. Rep. 908 (M.D.N.C. 2021).
[515] Students for Fair Admissions v. President and Fellows of Harvard Coll., 143 S. Ct. 2141 (2023) (ruling against the university in a consolidated case with Harvard University).
[516] Palmer v. Ind. Univ., 31 F.4th 583, 401 Educ. L. Rep. 720 (7th Cir. 2022).

was filed several years after the alleged unlawful employment practice, so even equitable tolling could not save the claim. As for the unequal pay claim, the court made clear that the plaintiff and his chosen comparator, another lecturer in his department, were not equal in all factors except race because the comparator taught more classes, had more leadership roles, and did substantially more work than the plaintiff. Because there were more justifications for unequal pay besides race, the appellate court affirmed the dismissal of this case.

A federal trial court in Georgia granted summary judgment in favor of a university's board of regents on an employee's disparate impact, segregation, and disparate treatment claims under Title VII and Section 1981.[517] The employee's claims were based on alleged salary disparities between the university in question and another university for a similar position. Contesting the two positions at-issue, one university filled with individuals of one racial group and the other university filled those positions with another racial group; neither racial group reflected the plaintiff. The trial court stated that each university was governed separately, and the Supreme Court did not allow for the sort of comparison the plaintiff was making. Further, the court stated that neither the *McDonnell Douglas* theory nor the Convincing Mosaic theory, both approaches asserted by the plaintiff, could be upheld because there were legitimate reasons for the disparity (i.e., lack of funding) and the Convincing Mosaic theory did not relate to the plaintiff's claims.

An African-American male hired as part of an internship established to offer students opportunities to learn from diverse faculty in New York alleged that, after over two years of discrimination based on race, his "all white chain of command" replaced him with a "token" African-American from another department to avoid a race discrimination claim.[518] The EEOC found insufficient evidence to establish a statutory violation, and the plaintiff brought this suit in federal court for failure to employ, failure to promote, and retaliation based on race. A federal trial court partially granted and denied the college and faculty association's motion to dismiss the plaintiff's claims under Title VII and state law. The court found that the plaintiff plausibly pled race discrimination and retaliation based on allegations that he was not allowed to teach certain classes, he was by-passed for two full-time teaching positions, and his courses were moved to days that he was unable to

---

[517] Andrews v. Bd. of Regents of Univ. Sys. of Ga., 565 F. Supp. 3d 1343, 402 Educ. L. Rep. 746 (M.D. Ga. 2021).
[518] Felton v. Monroe Cmty. Coll., 528 F.Supp.3d 122, 395 Educ. L. Rep. 564 (W.D.N.Y. 2021).

teach. However, he did not plausibly allege a hostile work environment.

In Texas, a federal trial court both granted and denied in part the university's motion to dismiss the African-American employee's discrimination claims under Section 1983, Title VII, and the Family Medical Leave Act (FMLA).[519] The magistrate judge recommended the Section 1983 claims against defendants in their individual capacities be dismissed based on qualified immunity. The judge also recommended that the Section 1983 claims based on the plaintiff's requests for reinstatement/rehire, Title VII claims, and FMLA claims survive dismissal. The plaintiff objected to the dismissal based on qualified immunity, arguing he demonstrated that the individuals' conduct violated a clearly established law. Specifically, he alleged that his direct supervisors and an administrator were responsible for a violation of the FMLA Compliance Policy. However, the plaintiff did not present any case law supporting this objection. Thus, the court adopted the magistrate judge's recommendation in dismissing the Section 1983 claims against the defendants acting in their individual capacities and allowing the remaining claims to proceed.

A state appellate court in Missouri reversed and remanded a decision from the trial court dismissing claims of race-based discrimination, gender-based discrimination, and retaliation under the Missouri Human Rights Act.[520] The main issue addressed by the appellate court was the Missouri Commission on Human Rights' initial issuance to plaintiff a right-to-sue letter then rescinding the letter after recognizing the defendant's exemption for religious reasons. The trial court essentially used this occurrence to dismiss the claims. The appellate court held, however, that the trial court should have limited the scope of its analysis to the petition of the plaintiff and not outside information. The trial court should have only relied on the plaintiff's statements and take them as true at this point of the proceeding.

Sex/Sexual Orientation

The Second Circuit affirmed and vacated in part the district court's ruling brought by a former assistant professor against a private university for discrimination in violation of Title IX and Title

---

[519] Berry v. Tex. Woman's Univ., 528 F.Supp.3d 579, 395 Educ. L. Rep. 596 (E.D. Tex. 2021).
[520] Gomoletz v. Rockhurst Univ., 642 S.W.3d 745, 402 Educ. L. Rep. 473 (Mo. Ct. App. 2022).

VI.[521] The former assistant professor claimed that the university discriminated against him by disciplining him for having an inappropriate relationship with a student. As for the federal defendants, he claims that the guidance documents provided by the Department contributed to the gender discrimination. The appellate court disagreed with the trial court on the Title IX claim, stating that Title IX does afford a private right of action for a university's intentional gender-based discrimination, and the complaint asserted such a claim. However, the appellate court affirmed the dismissal of the remaining claims.

In Louisiana, a female associate professor brought a gender discrimination claim against the administrators at a private university's medical school alleging disparate treatment, retaliation, and a hostile work environment under Title VII.[522] This suit arose from a series of contentious interactions between the associate professor and her supervisor and the eventual nonrenewal of her contract. The Fifth Circuit affirmed a federal trial court's grant of summary judgment in favor of the administrators. On the disparate treatment claim, the court stated that the professor failed to offer nearly identical comparators to establish a prima facie case where her male colleagues had different workloads. The retaliation claim also failed. Although the professor alleged gender-based discrimination, she could not point to any protected activity she engaged in triggering the university's non-renewal of her contract. The plaintiff's hostile work environment claim was stronger, but it still failed. Although the plaintiff did allege some harassment and the record appeared to show some level of harassment, the court was not convinced that this harassment was based on her gender but rather a more general harassment that did not fall under the claims she made.

In a Sixth Circuit decision, a male scientist applied for a job at a state university and the search committee recommended him overwhelmingly ahead of the other two applicants who were female.[523] Questions arose about pressures from the dean and department chair to hire the two females over a qualified male and the search chair's prior interactions with the leading male candidate, so the dean canceled the search in its entirety. The Sixth Circuit reversed a federal trial court in Ohio's decision to dismiss the Title IX and Section 1983 claims for gender discrimination. While the trial

---

[521] Vengalattore v. Cornell Univ., 36 F.4th 87, 403 Educ. L. Rep. 156 (2d Cir. 2022).
[522] Saketkoo v. Adm'rs of Tulane Educ. Fund, 31 F.4th 990, 402 Educ. L. Rep. 33 (5th Cir. 2022).
[523] Charlton-Perkins v. Univ. of Cincinnati, 35 F.4th 1053, 403 Educ. L. Rep. 140 (6th Cir. 2022).

court stated that there was no prima facie case under Title VII because no one with similar qualifications got the job, the Sixth Circuit found that the plaintiff's de facto injury was still present and the cancellation which resulted in no one at all getting the job was possibly a concealment of a discriminatory reason to hire no one. Thus, the appellate court ruled that the plaintiff pled a prima facie case for employment discrimination based on gender.

A federal trial court in Illinois granted the university's motion to dismiss the plaintiff psychologist and clinic's claims alleging that the university violated Title IX when it terminated its professional services agreement (PSA) with the clinic along with breach of contract, indemnification, defamation, and false light claims.[524] The PSA was terminated after the clinic reported abuse by the head softball coach against players and staff. The university argued that the plaintiffs, as independent contractors providing mental health services for students, lacked statutory standing to bring a Title IX retaliation claim. The court agreed, stating that statutory standing is only granted to "employees of an education program or activity" and "those who are denied access to an 'education program or activity,'" and the plaintiffs were indisputably independent contractors. Regardless, the court noted that the university's decision to terminate the PSA was not causally linked to the clinic's reports of abuse.

In West Virginia, the state supreme court reversed the lower court's dismissal and grant of immunity to the college in a case involving a former instructor's suit against a community and technical college for illegal age and sex discrimination under the West Virginia Human Rights Act.[525] While the petitioner raised factual questions about the motivation of her adverse employment action, the more important issue for the court was whether the complaint pled sufficient facts to survive a motion to dismiss. The appellate court disagreed with the lower court, stating that immunity did not apply to the college because it was acting within its discretion against a clear statute. In addition, the court ruled that the plaintiff pled sufficient facts to bolster her claim.

A New York appellate court affirmed the trial court's dismissal of a complaint asserting violations of New York State and New York City Human Rights Laws and intentional infliction of emotional distress.[526] A former adjunct faculty member commenced this action

---

[524] Conviser v. DePaul Univ., 532 F.Supp.3d 581, 396 Educ. L. Rep. 112 (N.D. Ill. 2021).
[525] Judy v. E. W. Va. Cmty. & Tech. Coll., 874 S.E.2d 285, 404 Educ. L. Rep. 955 (W. Va. 2022).
[526] Russell v. N.Y. Univ., 167 N.Y.S.3d 471, 403 Educ. L. Rep. 282 (N.Y. App. Div. 2022).

against the university and its officials due to harassment she was receiving based on her age, gender, and sexual identity. Putting aside these harassment claims, the court concluded that the human rights laws were estopped, under the doctrine of collateral estoppel, as she had brought the same claims in a prior action against many of the same defendants. Further, the plaintiff failed to allege facts sufficient to support a claim for intentional infliction of emotional distress as the stated harassment did not meet the standards required for such a claim.

In a case from Texas, the plaintiff alleged that she was unfairly disciplined and harassed after expressing her intent to become pregnant, and, when she complained about this treatment to a supervisor, she was terminated.[527] An appellate court affirmed the denial of the college's plea to the jurisdiction on the former employee's sex discrimination claim under state human rights law. The college argued that the Texas Commission on Human Rights Act (TCHRA) only prohibited discrimination based on pregnancy, but "attempting to get pregnant" was not protected. The court held that the TCHRA's provisions afford the same protection as the analogous Title VII provisions, which protect women who intend to become pregnant. Therefore, the plaintiff belonged to a protected class under the TCHRA denying the college's dismissal plea to the jurisdiction.

Disability

The Eighth Circuit affirmed a federal trial court in Minnesota's grant of summary judgment for the university in an ADA discrimination case.[528] An employee was unable to continue working full-time at her current job due to a disability which affects her ability to speak without pain. Given non-accommodations and job demands, she was forced to quit her job. She sued, claiming that the university did not accommodate her or try to find her a replacement position. The appellate court held that determining whether reassignment was available as a reasonable accommodation depended on whether the employee could show that she satisfied the legitimate prerequisites for an alternative position. The court stated that, while she listed eight jobs she could work at the school, she failed to show any job postings or position descriptions. Reassignment is not possible for jobs that are not available, even if she was qualified. Finally, the university did engage in an

---

[527] S. Tex. Coll. v. Arriola, 629 S.W.3d 502, 395 Educ. L. Rep. 853 (Tex. App. 2021).
[528] Ehlers v. Univ. of Minn., 34 F.4th 655, 402 Educ. L. Rep. 593 (8th Cir. 2022).

interactive process with the former employee when she made it clear that she needed accommodations. The university tried to help her find a new job and put-forth a good faith effort to accommodate her.

In a case from Alabama, the plaintiff, who has spastic cerebral palsy, was terminated after an investigation found his conduct with a student violated Title IX and the university's intimate relations policy.[529] A federal trial court granted the university's motion for summary judgment on the plaintiff instructor's claims for disability discrimination and failure to accommodate under the Rehabilitation Act and the ADA. The court first found that the ADA claims were barred by Eleventh Amendment immunity. It then held that the discrimination claim under the Rehabilitation Act failed because the plaintiff did not present evidence that his termination was the result of anything other than his policy violations. Further, the plaintiff was unable to show that the university's legitimate, nondiscriminatory reason for his termination was pretextual. On his failure to accommodate claim, the plaintiff requested and was denied an interpreter, proxy, or translator to speak for him during meetings with the Office of Affirmative Action/Equal Employment Opportunity. However, the court held that the university did not have to provide this accommodation under the Rehabilitation Act because such meetings were not an essential function of his job.

A former counselor sued a university in Michigan for failing to accommodate her disability and terminating her because of her disability after the university made changes to its mental health program to better serve students and decrease wait times.[530] These changes included turning part-time positions into full-time positions. The plaintiff could not work full-time due to a disability, and, after failed efforts to find a replacement position, the university terminated her. A federal trial court granted summary judgment in favor of the university on the plaintiff's claims for violation of the Rehabilitation Act and disability-based discrimination. The plaintiff's Rehabilitation Act claim failed primarily because she is no longer "otherwise qualified" for the position as it required a full-time employee, a requirement she could not satisfy. The same reasoning precluded her claim that she was terminated based on her disability. The court found that the plaintiff was terminated because she was no longer qualified for the position. Finally, the plaintiff was not owed a reasonable interactive process to determine appropriate

---

[529] Peebles v. Auburn Univ., 532 F.Supp.3d 1201, 396 Educ. L. Rep. 176 (M.D. Ala. 2021).
[530] Saroki-Keller v. Univ. of Mich., 568 F. Supp. 3d 860, 403 Educ. L. Rep. 595 (E.D. Mich. 2021).

accommodations because she could not perform the job with any accommodations since she could not work full-time.

An appellate court in Texas affirmed a trial court's denial of summary judgment for the employer, a university health center, stemming from allegations of disability discrimination in violation of the Texas Commission on Human Rights Act.[531] A former employee sued the university after being terminated from a residency program due to her disability of morbid obesity. The appellate court agreed that morbid obesity can be considered an impairment under the statute, though the court stated that it could not be considered an "actual disability" but rather a "regarded as" disability. Because morbid obesity is considered a disability and the university took an adverse employment action based on this impairment, the appellate court ruled that the plaintiff provided sufficient evidence to support her claim for disability discrimination.

Age

On appeal from Texas, the Fifth Circuit affirmed a federal trial court's grant of the university's motion for summary judgment on the plaintiffs' claims for age discrimination in the hiring process and retaliatory termination.[532] One of the plaintiffs applied for, but did not receive, a job with the university. The second plaintiff, an employee involved in the hiring process who reported alleged age-based discrimination, was terminated as part of a reduction-in-force. The court held that the hiring committee's comments about the plaintiff-applicant's methods being "old school" did not constitute pretext for age discrimination where the applicant was runner-up for the position out of over 100 applicants. The court further held that the plaintiff-employee failed to establish a causal link between her opposition to age-based comments in the hiring process and her termination due to a reduction-in-force, which was decided three days before the applicant's interview.

In Indiana, a sixty-year-old African American woman alleged that a university discriminated against her by taking away her supervisory duties and eventually eliminated her position sometime after the employee raised concerns about diversity at the university.[533] The plaintiff brought claims under Section 1981, Title VII, and the Age Discrimination in Employment Act (ADEA). A

---

[531] Tex. Tech Univ. Health Sci. Ctr. - El Paso v. Niehay, 641 S.W.3d 761, 401 Educ. L. Rep. 1153 (Tex. App. 2022).
[532] Oldenburg v. Univ. of Tex. at Austin, 860 F. App'x 922, 395 Educ. L. Rep. 520 (5th Cir. 2021).
[533] Lewis v. Ind. Wesleyan Univ., 36 F.4th 755, 403 Educ. L. Rep. 196 (7th Cir. 2022).

federal trial court in Indiana granted summary judgment in favor of the university on the retaliation claims, concluding that the plaintiff waived the age discrimination claim without addressing the race discrimination claim. The Seventh Circuit affirmed in part, vacated in part, and remanded for consideration. The appellate court agreed that the age discrimination claim had been waived when the plaintiff failed to present any evidence of eliminating her position based on age. Further, the court affirmed the trial court's summary judgement on the retaliation claim as the position elimination was due to structural changes and unrelated to plaintiff's comments about diversity at the university. However, the court concluded that the trial court failed to explain the rationale behind granting summary judgment in favor of the university for the plaintiff's racial discrimination claim, so it remanded that issue.

Retaliation

A jury in Arizona awarded a professor $300,000 in damages on his retaliation claim.[534] The professor alleged that he was passed over for the dean position because of his statements made about the lack of a pro-diversity culture at the university. Following the state court verdict, the defendants sought relief from the federal trial court in Arizona via a judgment as a matter of law, a new trial, or remittitur. The court found that the plaintiff established a prima facie case for a Title VII retaliation claim as the professor participated in a protected activity and was subjected to adverse employment action by not getting the deanship that was causally linked to the protected activity expressing the lack of diversity culture. However, the federal trial court did take issue with the amount of damages awarded and granted remittitur.

A federal trial court in Washington D.C. granted summary judgment in favor of a university and dean for a professor's retaliation claims under Section 1981, the District of Columbia Human Rights Act, the First Amendment, and the False Claims Act.[535] The professor's retaliation claim consisted of several actions: depressing performance evaluations, declining to appoint her to leadership positions, overloading her with teaching duties without appropriate compensation, and creating a hostile work environment. The court considered the depressed performance evaluations as adverse, but the university showed that its reasons for the depressed

---

[534] Alozie v. Ariz. Bd. of Regents, 562 F. Supp. 3d 203, 402 Educ. L. Rep. 194 (D. Ariz. 2021).
[535] Harris v. Trs. of Univ. of D.C., 567 F. Supp. 3d 131, 402 Educ. L. Rep. 878 (D.D.C. 2021).

evaluations were valid based on the professor's lack of research and published materials. The same justification was accepted by the court for the lack of leadership appointments. The third point, overloading her with teaching duties, was justifiable as the court recognized the university had experienced legitimate staffing issues and all professors were required to teach more. Finally, the court found no evidence of the university creating a hostile work environment out of retaliation. The First Amendment retaliation claims also failed because the court stated that, in all complained instances, the professor was complaining as an employee and not as a citizen on matters of public concern.

First Amendment

The U.S. Supreme Court granted a federal trial court in Texas its petition for certiorari in a case that the trial court dismissed, but the Fifth Circuit court reversed and remanded back to the trial court.[536] The plaintiff, a member of the board of trustees for a public community college district, sued under Section 1983 claiming a violation of his First Amendment free speech rights when the college censured him for criticizing other board members and filing lawsuits against the board's actions. The plaintiff sought declaratory and injunctive relief, along with damages, punitive damages, and attorney fees. The Supreme Court held that a public censure of an elected official by another elected official of the same body is not an infringement of First Amendment rights. Elected officials are expected to get criticized, and the expectation is that they will continue to exercise their rights when that criticism comes. The Court noted, however, that its holding was narrow and only to be understood for censures, not any other sort of punishment.

A professor in Texas was disciplined by the university after numerous reports of him making inappropriate, sexually harassing comments to students during class time and rehearsals.[537] The university disciplined him including a written reprimand, loss of merit pay, and ineligibility to teach the following summer. The Fifth Circuit affirmed a federal trial court's dismissal of the professor's claims for retaliation in violation of Title IX and the First Amendment. For a public university employee to succeed on a claim for retaliation under the First Amendment, the complaining party

---

[536] Hous. Cmty. Coll. Sys. v. Wilson, 142 S. Ct. 1253, 401 Educ. L. Rep. 29 (U.S. 2022).
[537] Trudeau v. Univ. of N. Tex., By and Through its Bd. of Regents, 861 F. App'x 604, 395 Educ. L. Rep. 529 (5th Cir. 2021).

must establish an adverse action for "speech that is a matter of public concern" and that the employee's "interest in the speech outweighed the university's interest in regulating the speech." Matters of public concern may involve issues of social, political, or other interest to a community. Here, the professor failed to plausibly allege that his comments about students' sex lives and mental health were on a matter of public concern.

The Eleventh Circuit affirmed a summary judgment decision of a federal trial court in Alabama favoring the university in a Section 1983 action for free speech and due process violations.[538] A traveling evangelist brought this suit, alleging that the university's ground-use policy requiring permits for non-affiliates to speak violated his First Amendment rights and due process protections. The appellate court stated that the permit requirement was a reasonable restriction of speech within a limited public forum. Further, there were no due process violations. The evangelist had alleged that the exceptions to the permit-use policy for "casual recreation and social activities" was unconstitutionally vague, thus violating due process. However, the court ruled that this was not vague and that the requirement and its language satisfied due process.

In Illinois, a federal trial court heard a case dealing with a former faculty counselor at a community college who sued the college, its president, the executive director of human resources, and the president's assistant for First Amendment retaliation, defamation, false light invasion of privacy, intentional infliction of emotional distress, and negligent infliction of emotional distress.[539] These claims arose from allegations that she was forced to accept a lesser role after speaking out about a perceived waste of taxpayer dollars. The college moved to dismiss for failure to state a claim. The court granted the motion in part and denied in part. The counselor's claims of First Amendment retaliation and invasion of privacy under state law were the only claims that survived dismissal. The First Amendment claim survived because the counselor sufficiently alleged that she was forced to take a non-faculty position because she voiced concerns as a private citizen over the college's use of taxpayer funds. The court further held that the plaintiff sufficiently alleged an invasion of privacy placing the plaintiff in a false light by having her arrested, and the defendants acted with actual malice because they knew the statements were false and caused her harm.

---

[538] Keister v. Bell, 29 F.4th 1239, 401 Educ. L. Rep. 120 (11th Cir. 2022), *cert. denied*, 143 S. Ct. 1020 (2023).
[539] Marsden v. Kishwaukee Cmtty Coll., 572 F.Supp.3d 512, 404 Educ. L. Rep. 735 (N.D. Ill. 2021)

Whistleblowing

In Florida, a compliance officer was terminated while investigating billing practices that allegedly overbilled Medicare for unnecessary services.[540] A federal trial court denied the private university's motion to dismiss retaliation claims under the False Claims Act. The court found that the plaintiff sufficiently alleged the conduct he was fired for was protected and raised at least a reasonable inference that the acts were lawful and he attempted to stop the violation of the False Claims Act. Further, compliance professionals must give more notice to an employer about their plan to pursue a suit based on a protected activity, such as "alleging that his employer was aware of either his 'lawful acts ... in furtherance of' a False Claims Act suit or his 'other efforts to stop 1 or more violations of' the Act." Because the plaintiff sent an email with the required notice twelve days before the firing, the court found the notice was sufficient. Finally, the defendants state that the plaintiff's actions did not cause him to be fired, but the court found that the plaintiff's allegations were sufficient to allege the university feared the harm of investigations and terminated the compliance professional for wanting to investigate further.

An appellate court in California reversed and remanded the grant of summary judgment in favor of the defendants regarding claims of whistleblowing retaliation.[541] The claims were brought by the Chief Administrative Officer (CAO) after he reported that the board of regents was poorly managing the medical school on several different levels. He had begun trying to come up with ways to problem solve these issues along with ensuring that any violations were properly reported. Shortly after these efforts began, he was terminated. The notice of termination from the university listed several reasons other than retaliation for the termination, such as increasingly subpar performance. However, the previous year's performance evaluations showed complete satisfaction with the CAO. The appellate court ruled that, although the employer listed several non-retaliatory justifications for the adverse employment action, the evidence to the contrary raised a question as to whether the reasons listed were pretextual, and that question should be left to the fact finder.

---

[540] Lord v. Univ. of Miami, 571 F. Supp. 3d 1299, 404 Educ. L. Rep. 641 (S.D. Fla. 2021).
[541] Scheer v. Regents of Univ. of Cal., 291 Cal. Rptr. 3d 822, 401 Educ. L. Rep. 1043 (Cal. Ct. App. 2022).

COVID-19 Policy

In Florida, a federal trial court granted the state's motion for a preliminary injunction against enforcement of President Biden's executive order implementing a COVID-19 vaccine mandate for employees of federal contractors and subcontractors.[542] The state argued that the order was in excess of the Presidential power, the President exercised unconstitutionally delegated legislative power, and agency guidance and notices exceeded legal authority, violated notice and comment requirements, and constituted arbitrary and capricious agency action. The court held that the mandate exceeded the authorization of the Federal Property and Administrative Services Act (FPASA). Further, the court found that the mandate was too expansive and invasive based on its inclusion of private employees that worked "in connection with a covered contract" or at a contractor- or federal government-controlled location. Based on these determinations, along with the court's findings that the mandate likely intruded into the state's police power without the constitutional authorization to do so, the mandate was likely to cause irreparable harm to the state, and the balance of harms and public interest, the court granted the state's preliminary injunction.

A federal trial court in Michigan denied an injunction of a university's COVID-19 vaccine mandate.[543] The trial court was required to consider four factors: the moving party's likelihood of success on the merits, whether the harm suffered by the moving party would be irreparable, whether the order would cause substantial harm to others, and whether the public interest was served by the order. The court primarily focused on addressing the first two factors. First, the court found that the plaintiff did not have a high likelihood of success on the merits as the vaccine mandate was rationally related to the legitimate government interest of preventing the spread of COVID-19. Second, the court held that there was no irreparable harm as, even if the plaintiff was terminated and a court found that termination to be wrongful, the plaintiff would be compensated monetarily by order of the court. The court quickly disposed of the final two factors by stating that keeping people safe was the goal of the mandate. Therefore, the injunction was denied.

In the only state-level case addressing COVID-19 safety measures, an appellate court in Virginia affirmed the decision of the

---

[542] State v. Nelson, 576 F. Supp.3d 1017, 405 Educ. L. Rep. 296 (M.D. Fla. 2021).
[543] Norris v. Stanley, 567 F. Supp. 3d 818, 402 Educ. L. Rep. 996 (W.D. Mich. 2021).

trial court, which affirmed the decision to terminate a law enforcement officer for not following the COVID-19 protocols.[544] The officer had come to work while feeling ill. He said he would take a COVID-19 test but did not. After he was sent home by his supervisor, he tested positive for the virus and was terminated. The officer argued that the hearing officer should have resolved all factual issues, and because some issues were left unaddressed, the administration was unfairly prejudiced in their decision. Further, the officer argued that the limiting of thirty minutes for oral arguments in the trial court breached his due process rights. However, the appellate court stated that each level of appeal had looked at the facts of the case and had determined that there were sufficient facts to show that the university's decision was justified.

Due Process

A doctor employed by a public university in Kentucky brought suit for alleged procedural and substantive due process violations, First Amendment retaliation, breach of contract, violations of state wage and hour law, violations of Kentucky's Whistleblower Act, and defamation.[545] A federal trial court granted summary judgment in favor of the public university, which rendered all claims dismissed except his due process claim for deprivation of a property interest in his employment through constructive discharge and the issue of whether the process he received after being denied the ability to treat patients at the VA hospital was sufficient. The court found that the doctor had no property interest in his employment, and, although he did have an interest in the clinical work and income, he was afforded due process. The court also refused to grant summary judgment for his wage and hour claims as there was a genuine issue of material fact as to whether the wages sought by the doctor were agreed upon.

In Michigan, a federal trial court dismissed all claims against the administrating college of a police academy, which included claims under Section 1983 and libel claims under state law.[546] The adjunct instructor was accused of inappropriate touching of students, including striking students in the groin, tickling, and inappropriate sexual comments. On his due process claim, the instructor claimed that any state actor even partially responsible for

---

[544] Morris v. George Mason Univ., 871 S.E.2d 231, 402 Educ. L. Rep. 427 (Va. Ct. App. 2022).
[545] Cunningham v. Blackwell, 568 F. Supp. 3d 799, 403 Educ. L. Rep. 564 (E.D. Ky. 2021).
[546] Bowles v. Macomb Cmty. Coll., 558 F. Supp. 3d 539, 401 Educ. L. Rep. 730 (E.D. Mich. 2021).

the deprivation of a property right must provide the employee with a full evidentiary hearing. The plaintiff argued that each agency remotely involved in his termination owed a separate and independent hearing to the plaintiff. The court found that there was no due process violation because the plaintiff did receive a hearing from the university, though not all investigatory agencies, and, further, he did not have any protected property interest as the benefit received, being a certified adjunct, was purely discretionary. The libel claim arose from an employee in the investigatory agency communicating the findings of misconduct to the proper authority, the university. The court held that this individual had a qualified privilege to defame because he owed a duty to a person having a corresponding interest or duty.

A Michigan appellate court affirmed the denial of a preliminary injunction and temporary restraining order and issued a summary disposition in favor of the board of governors' voting members.[547] Board members boycotted a university board meeting and sued the university, university president, and board for violation of the Open Meetings Act (OMA) after the board determined a quorum when there was not one and held a closed session without approval. Nonvoting members sought to prohibit the acquisition of a sublease by boycotting, but the board allowed the president to count as a member to establish a quorum and voted for the sublease. The plaintiffs claimed this violated the OMA by moving into a closed executive session without holding a roll-call or three-quarter majority vote. Regarding the preliminary injunction, the court stated it is a form of equitable relief to maintain the status quo pending a final hearing. The appellate court agreed that the OMA cannot be asserted against the board as a matter of law and could not serve as the basis of injunctive relief. Further, because the president was a member of the board due to the virtue of his office, he could be counted to establish a quorum.

Contracts

A federal trial court in Georgia granted in part and denied in part a marketing company's motion for summary judgment on the institute's third-party claims for indemnification and breach of contract.[548] The plaintiff brought a putative class action against the

---

[547] Busuito v. Barnhill, 976 N.W.2d 60, 404 Educ. L. Rep. 869 (Mich. Ct. App. 2021).
[548] Person v. Tech. Educ. Servs., 542 F. Supp.3d 1355, 398 Educ. L. Rep. 364 (N.D. Ga. 2021).

technical institute under the Telephone Consumer Protection Act (TCPA), and the institute filed a third-party complaint against the marketing company. The marketing company argued that it did not owe the institute a duty to indemnify it because there was no evidence that it violated the TCPA, and it is not responsible for the institution's independent violations of the TCPA. The court agreed, finding the marketing company owed no duty to indemnify. However, the marketing company's motion for summary judgment focused almost exclusively on the indemnification claim. Thus, the court allowed the breach of contract claim to survive based on the assumption that the institute may be a third-party beneficiary to the order and may enforce the provision at issue.

A former football coach at a state university in Mississippi brought a breach of contract claim and later filed a Chapter 13 bankruptcy petition without disclosing the breach-of-contract lawsuit.[549] After winning a jury verdict, the coach dismissed the bankruptcy petition. However, the trial court granted a motion for judgment notwithstanding the verdict in favor of the university, which caused the coach to again pursue bankruptcy proceedings without disclosing the suit. The appellate court reversed and remanded the case, and the trial court ruled for summary judgment under the doctrine of judicial estoppel. The Supreme Court of Mississippi affirmed the judgment of the trial court granting summary judgment for the university because the coach failed to meet his burden of showing that his contradictory representations were inadvertent, failed to identify an abuse of discretion in the trial court's decision, and failed to set forth a genuine dispute of material fact.

In Kentucky, an appellate court affirmed the trial court's grant of summary judgment in favor of the university on its claim challenging the state retirement systems' determination that former university employees whose positions were privatized were still employees for purposes of the state retirement systems.[550] The court held that the retirement systems improperly used the IRS test to determine whether the employees were "still" employees of the university. Further, the university was operating well within its authority when it privatized the maintenance workers' jobs by outsourcing.

---

[549] Jones v. Alcorn State Univ., 337 So. 3d 1062, 403 Educ. L. Rep. 360 (Miss. 2022).
[550] Ky. Ret. Sys., by and through the Bd. of Trs. of Ky. Ret. Sys. v. W. Ky. Univ., 640 S.W.3d 62, 400 Educ. L. Rep. 841 (Ky. Ct. App. 2021).

An employee in New Mexico brought suit for breach of contract and breach of the implied covenant of good faith and fair dealing after she was laid off from the public television station staffed by university employees and was not rehired.[551] The state appellate court affirmed the trial court's dismissal of the former employee's claims holding that the university did not breach an implied contract with the employee by failing to reinstate her eighteen months after she was laid off. The court found that the terms of the contract were ambiguous as to when a laid-off employee must be reinstated, but, based on the evidence provided, it determined that the right to reinstatement was available for one year. Thus, the plaintiff was no longer entitled to reinstatement when her position was restored 18 months after she was laid off. Further, the court dismissed the breach of the implied covenant of good faith and fair dealing claim because the university did not act in bad faith; the layoffs were solely due to a loss of funds.

An Ohio appellate court affirmed the dismissal of a complaint by an electricity supplier seeking the return of its electrical equipment installed on a community college campus.[552] The claims court dismissed the complaint after determining that the contracts between the college and the supplier were void because of a failure to obtain certification by the college's fiscal officer. The appellate court held that the lower court did have subject-matter jurisdiction over the action because the supplier was asking for equitable restitution or protection of the court because, due to the court's ruling, the possessor does not own the electrical equipment via a legal transaction. Additionally, because the relief is only equitable and not monetary damages, the lower court could decide this case. The appellate court stated that the claims court did not err by dismissing the complaint because the supplier did not state a claim upon which relief could be granted. To allow the supplier to obtain restitution for the equipment even though the rest of the transaction created no rights would frustrate the policy which required the college's fiscal officer to approve purchases.

In Oregon, the purported owner of a student loan issued by a bank made a claim against the borrower for failing to make monthly payments under the terms of the loan agreement.[553] The state appellate court affirmed the trial court's grant of summary judgment in favor of the defendant on a cross-motion for summary judgment

---

[551] Bachmann v. Regents of Univ. of N.M., 496 P.3d 604, 395 Educ. L. Rep. 1150 (N.M. Ct. App. 2021).
[552] Duke Energy One v. Cincinnati State Tech. & Cmty. Coll., 187 N.E.3d 28, 402 Educ. L. Rep. 1105 (Ohio Ct. App. 2022).
[553] Nat'l Coll. Student Loan Tr. 2006-2 v. Gimple, 508 P.3d 561, 402 Educ. L. Rep. 420 (Or. Ct. App. 2022).

in a breach of contract and quantum meruit claim. The opinion focused on whether two pieces of evidence should have been admitted, as the plaintiff asserts. The plaintiff sufficiently showed that the defendant failed to pay but could not show that the plaintiff was the person to whom the money was owed. The plaintiff tried to introduce evidence showing that it had bought the loan from the issuer, but the trial court ruled that the evidence was hearsay because it was without a competent foundation and was not a business record. The appellate court affirmed, stating there was no showing of personal knowledge that the record was based on first-hand observations, and the evidence should be excluded. As such, the appellate court agreed that there was no evidence proving that the loan was between the plaintiff and defendant, and summary judgment for the defendant was appropriate.

Tenure

The Supreme Court of Arkansas affirmed a trial court's dismissal of a complaint by tenured faculty.[554] The faculty alleged that the threat of a unilateral adoption of a policy regarding the promotion and tenure of faculty would expand the grounds for dismissal and violate the state constitution and state contract law. However, the court ruled that there was not a justiciable controversy as the appellants failed to plead facts sufficient to establish an actual controversy regarding both the state constitution and state contract law.

Labor Relations

A state university petitioned for administrative review of an opinion from the board which stated that the university violated the Educational Labor Relations Act when it failed to comply with a finding that it violated a collective bargaining agreement and its remedies by laying off tenured faculty members at the university.[555] The Supreme Court of Illinois reversed the appellate court's decision regarding an opinion of the Education Labor Relations Board. The appellate court vacated the board's decision and remanded the claim. The state supreme court held that it was the exclusive duty of the board to make a review of compliance with a binding award. Because

---

[554] Palade v. Bd. of Trs. of Univ. of Ark. Sys., 645 S.W.3d 1, 404 Educ. L. Rep. 292 (Ark. 2022).
[555] W. Ill. Univ. v. Ill. Educ. Lab. Rels. Bd., 184 N.E.3d 249, 401 Educ. L. Rep. 1110 (Ill. 2021).

of this, the court reversed the appellate court's holding. Importantly, the court noted that state courts normally have the right to review compliance with an arbitration agreement, however, the statutory language for arbitration within public education placed arbitration compliance review exclusively within the board's jurisdiction.

In Washington, a state appellate court reversed and remanded a lower court's decision to grant motions for declaratory and summary judgment in favor of the plaintiff unions under the Address Confidentiality Program.[556] Labor unions sued for declaratory judgment against state agencies, universities, and community colleges asserting that releasing the personal information of survivors of domestic violence, stalking, and sexual assault under the Public Records Act would violate their constitutional rights. They further sought summary judgment and a permanent injunction against the release of information about such individuals and the birthdates of public employees. The lower court granted the motions in favor of the unions under the Address Confidentiality Program. The appellate court reversed and remanded because the Address Confidentiality Program was not sufficient to protect against the release of the information. The court essentially found that there was not enough evidence to show that the release of the requested information under the Public Records Act would pose a threat to those whose information was being released.

Workers' Compensation

The Supreme Court of Connecticut reversed and remanded the appellate court's reversal of the Workers' Compensation Review Board's (WCRB) decision.[557] The WCRB decision affirmed the Workers' Compensation Commissioner's ruling in favor of the employer after the claimant suffered injuries from an idiopathic fall at work. The plaintiff argued that the WCRB erred in finding that the injury suffered from her fall did not arise out of her employment because it was caused by a personal medical condition. She alleged that her "injury arose out of her employment because it occurred on the premises of her employer when she hit her head on the ground before the start of her morning shift." The court agreed with the WCRB's decision finding that the fall and resulting injury did not arise out of her employment because it was not "caused by a hazard

---

[556] Wash. Fed'n of State Emps., Council, 28 v. State, 511 P.3d 119, 403 Educ. L. Rep. 940 (Wash. Ct. App. 2022).
[557] Clements v. Aramark Corp., 261 A.3d 665, 396 Educ. L. Rep. 747 (Conn. 2021).

unique or distinctive to the employment." Therefore, her injury was not compensable.

A police officer in Arkansas was stopping a domestic disturbance when he was pushed down onto the concrete.[558] After being pushed down, he suffered severe pain and underwent surgeries to fix the issue. When it was discovered that he had a bulging disc requiring emergency surgery sometime after the initial injury, he continued claiming benefits, which was challenged by the university. The university argued that he used the improper form to claim the benefits and that the injury to his spine was not work-related. An appellate court affirmed the Workers' Compensation Commission's decision finding that the claimant sustained a compensable injury to his thoracic spine. The court heavily relied on the medical records to determine that the injury was work-related, was specifically related to the incident where he was pushed down, and that the time between the injury and the emergency surgery was reasonable. Further, the statutory language does not bar a claim for the use of a wrong form if the university is aware of the injury, which it was. Therefore, the appellate court affirmed the Commission's decision.

An appellate court affirmed a decision by the Illinois Workers' Compensation Board which denied a claim of benefits to a temporary administrative assistant employed by a state university.[559] The claim arose from an incident in which the employee fell while trying to hop a fence while taking her timecard to the required drop location before work began. The court stated that, because the employee hopped over the fence, she exposed herself to unnecessary danger entirely separate from her employment responsibilities and did so only for her benefit and not the university's. Therefore, the accident did not arise out of her employment. The court also found that the employee could not be considered a travelling employee because she was not required to travel as part of her daily activities. Thus, the employee could not recover for her injuries.

---

[558] Univ. of Ark. for Med. Scis. v. Barton, 644 S.W.3d 818, 403 Educ. L. Rep. 961 (Ark. Ct. App. 2022).
[559] Purcell v. Ill. Workers' Comp. Comm'n, 184 N.E.3d 373, 401 Educ. L. Rep. 1131 (Ill. App. Ct. 2021).

Procedural Issues

Jurisdiction

A federal trial court in Illinois denied a social media user's motion to dismiss for lack of personal jurisdiction in a suit brought by a professor at a public university in a different state.[560] The social media user made repeated posts about the professor being a sexual predator of students, calling her abusive and other derogatory terms in Hindi and Urdu. The court denied the motion to dismiss for two reasons. First, the court stated that the defendant created minimum contacts with the plaintiff's state because the state was the focal point of the story and of the harm suffered. Illinois is where the reputation of the professor was most hurt, and it was reasonable for the court to infer that the intent behind the posts was to turn people from Illinois against the plaintiff. Second, the court found that the forum state's interest in adjudicating the dispute, the plaintiff's interest in obtaining convenient and effective relief, and the interstate judicial system's interest in obtaining an efficient resolution of controversies weighed in favor of the plaintiff. Therefore, the court's exercise of personal jurisdiction over the plaintiff is consistent with the principles of fair play and substantial justice.

A professor in Pennsylvania brought suit against an author for libel, defamation per se, and false light invasion of privacy based on a series of Tweets by the author.[561] A federal trial court denied the professor's motion to remand and the author's motion to dismiss the professor's claims for lack of personal jurisdiction and failure to state a claim. The court noted that it had original subject matter jurisdiction over this case based on diversity of citizenship because the parties were citizens of different states and the amount in controversy exceeded $75,000. Next, the court found that it had specific personal jurisdiction over the defendant based on his five Tweets about the plaintiff, who was a resident of Pennsylvania, and the medical school in Pennsylvania where he taught. Finally, the court addressed the merits of the complaint, finding that the plaintiff sufficiently alleged his claim of libel based on the defendant's defamatory Tweets, defamation based on four of the Tweets, defamation per se because the Tweets could be interpreted as

---

[560] Majumdar v. Fair, 567 F. Supp. 3d 901, 402 Educ. L. Rep. 1014 (N.D. Ill. 2021).
[561] Goldfarb v. Kalodimos, 539 F.Supp.3d 435, 397 Educ. L. Rep. 961 (E.D. Pa.).

imputing business misconduct, and false light invasion of privacy based on the Tweets.

Privilege

In Washington D.C., the federal trial court affirmed its prior ruling that all but one student-employee of a university waived attorney-client privilege by emailing their attorneys with university-issued email accounts.[562] The student-employees sued the university alleging violations of the District of Columbia's Human Rights Act, negligent training, supervision, and retention, and Title IX. Because the university was clear that there was no right to personal privacy with respect to email messages on their university-issued accounts and the plaintiffs accepted these terms and conditions, the plaintiffs were on notice of the university's policy and there could be no objectively reasonable expectation of privacy. The students presented three arguments for reconsideration: new evidence showing their use of employer-issued email accounts was reasonable, the emails are not relevant under Federal Rules of Civil Procedure, and the court did not consider the work-product privilege assertion. The court ruled that the new evidence did not change the fact that the students were adequately put on notice of the policy; the rules did not apply to the emails because they were already in the school's possession; and the work-product assertion did not apply because the emails were already in the university's possession and not discoverable.

Attorney Fees

An appellate court in Louisiana affirmed as amended the trial court's rendering of judgment in favor of the college for over $65,000 in attorney fees and costs after the college's president emeritus petitioned to annul the consent judgment confirming an arbitration award between him and the college and was denied.[563] The president emeritus argued that the college could only be awarded attorney fees if the court found his action was "frivolous, filed in bad faith, and/or misrepresented relevant facts," while the college argued that it only had to be the prevailing party. The court agreed with the college, finding that because the college prevailed on president emeritus's nullity action, it was entitled to reasonable attorney fees. The court

---

[562] Doe 1 v. George Wash. Univ., 573 F. Supp. 3d 88, 404 Educ. L. Rep. 795 (D.D.C. 2021).
[563] Aguillard v. La. Coll., 326 So.3d 314, 396 Educ. L. Rep. 350 (La. Ct. App. 2021).

further held that the amount of $66,829.36 for the original suit, plus $5,000 for the appeal, was reasonable.

Standing

An association of professors brought an adversary proceeding to challenge the certification of a fiscal plan for the university by the Financial Oversight and Management Board, which the association alleged made reforms to the university retirement system to the detriment of the vested rights of retirees, participants, and beneficiaries.[564] The federal trial court in Puerto Rico granted the defendant's motion to dismiss based on lack of subject matter jurisdiction. The court found that the plaintiffs lacked constitutional standing because no reduction in benefits had occurred nor had any modifications been made that would reduce benefits. Further, the court found that the board's actions surrounding its certification of the fiscal plan were not subject to judicial review, so it lacked jurisdiction. This decision was later affirmed by the First Circuit federal appellate court.

Environmental Protections

The Fourth Circuit, on appeal from West Virginia, affirmed the grant of the university's motion to remand its case against past and present operators of a chemical manufacturing plant and wastewater treatment unit on adjacent property.[565] The university brought this suit alleging several state and common law claims and requesting operators adopt remedial measures beyond those required by the EPA to address groundwater contamination of the university's property. The defendant removed the case to federal court. The court held that removal was improper for three reasons. First, the operators were not acting under the guidance or control of the EPA, so removal pursuant to the federal officer removal statute was not proper. Further, the university's claims did not challenge a "cleanup" as defined by the Comprehensive Environmental Response, Compensation, and Liability Act (CERCLA). Lastly, the claims were not preempted by the Resource Conservation and Recovery Act to support removal based on federal question jurisdiction.

---

[564] In re Fin. Oversight and Mgmt. Bd. for P.R., 632 B.R. 1, 395 Educ. L. Rep. 996 (D.P.R. 2021), aff'd 60 F.4th 9, 411 Educ. L. Rep. 980 (1st Cir. 2023).
[565] W. Va. State Univ. Bd. of Governors v. Dow Chem. Co., 23 F.4th 288, 398 Educ. L. Rep. 615 (4th Cir. 2022).

In California, the board of trustees at a university sued a contractor for violation of the CERCLA and other state law claims.[566] The board and contractor cross-claimed for summary judgment for assessment and evaluation costs relating to the hazardous substances identified on the property. A federal trial court denied summary judgment for both the plaintiff and the defendant. Two elements for a private claim under CERCLA were discussed in this case: that there was a disposal during the defendant's control of the property, and a plaintiff seeking private party response costs may only recover the necessary costs of response that are consistent with the national contingency plan. In this case, the court found that there was a genuine factual dispute as to whether there was a disposal, and the plaintiff did not show compliance with the national contingency plan.

The government sued private companies for response and enforcement costs under CERCLA alleging they operated sites where hazardous substances were released and disposed of.[567] The companies sought contribution against the town, community college, the college's endowment, and the county and contractual indemnification against the town. Both parties and the third-party defendants moved for summary judgment. A federal trial court in North Carolina granted summary judgment in favor of the plaintiffs and partially granted the defendant's motions for summary judgment for third-party claims. The court held that summary judgment against the companies was appropriate because they are owners of the sites under CERCLA, which makes any person who owned or operated a facility where hazardous substances were disposed of liable. The defendant's motion against the town was granted as the town was the record owner of the facility and, therefore, strictly liable. The motions against the community college and its endowment failed because they did not arrange for the waste to be dumped and encouraged the companies to properly remove waste. The court also dismissed the indemnification claim against the city and contribution claims against the community college and affiliates.

---

[566] Bd. of Trs. of Leland Stanford Jr. Univ. v. Agilent Tech., 573 F. Supp. 3d 1371, 404 Educ. L. Rep. 827 (N.D. Cal. 2021).
[567] U.S. v. Godley, 572 F. Supp. 3d 171, 404 Educ. L. Rep. 707 (W.D.N.C. 2021).

Intellectual Property

Trademark

The federal trial court in Arizona denied a board of regents' motion for default judgment against a student on its claims for trademark infringement, false designation of origin, and false advertising under the Lanham Act.[568] These claims arose from a student's use of Instagram to promote university parties during the COVID-19 pandemic. The defendant's answer to the complaint was stricken for litigation misconduct, after which he stopped participating in the proceedings. The court acknowledged that, although the plaintiff's motivations for suing were understandable, there was no establishment by the plaintiff that the defendant's conduct implicates the trademark doctrines identified in the complaint. While many of the factors weighed in favor of granting default judgment, the court essentially found that there could be no confusion regarding the "source of origin" from the posts and messages of the social media account promoting COVID-19 parties. Because the posts were explicitly averse to the university, it was clear that consumers would not think that the university was making these posts. Therefore, the motion was denied, and the case was dismissed. The Ninth Circuit later affirmed this decision.

Misappropriation of Information

On appeal from Utah, the Tenth Circuit affirmed the grant of summary judgment in favor of a state university research foundation in a suit dealing with misappropriation of proprietary information in connection with proposed construction and deployment of satellite systems.[569] The appeal mostly dealt with due process concerns about the legal standards used when determining damage causation. The appellate court decided that all legal standards were properly used when the trial court determined damage causation, including the distinction between inferences and speculation as it relates to damage causation. Further, the foundations under the university and the university's vice president were entitled to sovereign immunity. Finally, the university's

---

[568] Ariz. Bd. of Regents v. Doe, 555 F. Supp. 3d 805, 401 Educ. L. Rep. 353 (D. Ariz. 2021), aff'd No. 21-16525, 2022 WL 1514649 (9th Cir. May 13, 2022).
[569] GeoMetWatch Corp. v. Behunin, 38 F.4th 1183, 404 Educ. L. Rep. 464 (10th Cir. 2022).

advanced systems foundation was entitled to recover the costs it incurred after the execution of the agreement.

A doctor in Pennsylvania brought suit under the Defend Trade Secrets Act claiming that a colleague used the doctor's pig model for his own studies and that the university and his colleague filed patent applications using that model.[570] The colleague and university filed motions to dismiss, which a federal trial court granted in part and remanded in part. A claim under the Defend Trade Secrets Act (DTSA) requires the existence of a trade secret (i.e., information with independent economic value that the owner has taken reasonable measures to keep secret), that the information is related to a product or service used in interstate or foreign commerce, and that the information was misappropriated (i.e., a knowing improper acquisition, use, or disclosure of the secret). This case found that all claims against the colleague should be dismissed due to the statute of limitations. The claims against the university were remanded for fact finding as to the university's invention ownership policy to determine who owned the pig model of research.

Property-Related Issues

The Supreme Court of Arizona affirmed in part and remanded in part the appellate court's grant of summary judgment and dismissal of claims made by the state's Attorney General.[571] The Attorney General sued the board of regents of a state university for injunctive relief and relief under the quo warranto statute related to an agreement between the board of regents and a hotel operator to build and operate a hotel on the board's property. The Attorney General alleged that the project violated the state constitution's gift clause and was an illegal payment of public money. The trial court agreed, granting summary judgment on the gift clause claim and dismissing the remaining claims. The attorney general appealed. The state supreme court held that the Attorney General lacked the authority to bring claims about the board abusing its tax-exempt status, improperly diverting property tax revenues, and bringing a quo warranto action to avoid taxes. The tax evasion claims were granted summary judgment because there were no tax statutes to enforce. However, the attorney general's quo warranto action alleging that the board violated a statute and the non-delegation

---

[570] Houser v. Feldman, 569 F. Supp. 3d 216, 403 Educ. L. Rep. 694 (E.D. Pa. 2021).
[571] State v. Ariz. Bd. of Regents, 507 P.3d 500, 402 Educ. L. Rep. 391 (Ariz. 2022).

doctrine in the lease provision was remanded for further consideration.

Safety

A board of regents sought declaratory relief in the form of a statement that the statute prohibiting the board from enforcing certain firearms restrictions was unconstitutional.[572] The Supreme Court of Montana affirmed the trial court's grant of summary judgment in favor of the board against the state. The court ruled that the statute, which limited the board's ability to regulate firearm possession and transportation on campus, was unconstitutional. The board had been constitutionally vested with the management of the campus, and the court stated that when legislative action infringes upon constitutionally granted powers, the legislative power must yield.

Crime-Related Issues

The Third Circuit affirmed the federal trial court in Delaware's denial of a motion to dismiss an indictment in a prosecution for cyberstalking.[573] The defendant first challenged the cyberstalking statute as being overbroad as to the definitions of harassment and intimidation. However, the court stated that the intent and harassment elements of the statute should be narrowly read and enforced to preserve the statute. Thus, the court held that "intent" means to put the victim in fear of death or bodily injury, and to "harass" is to distress the victim by threatening, intimidating, or the like. Therefore, the conviction of the defendant was upheld. The court noted in its conclusion that cyberstalking laws generally must be read narrowly to avoid punishing protected speech. People are legally allowed to annoy other people, so the line must be drawn with a narrow reading of "intent" in these statutes.

In Illinois, victims brought a claim for violation of the Racketeer Influenced and Corrupt Organizations Act (RICO) based on alleged conspiring to cover up sexual assaults of teenagers by the church and college.[574] The Seventh Circuit affirmed as modified the dismissal of the victims' complaint against the church, affiliated college, and

---

[572] Bd. of Regents of Higher Educ. v. State ex rel. Knudsen, 512 P.3d 748, 404 Educ. L. Rep. 946 (Mont. 2022).
[573] U.S. v. Yung, 37 F.4th 70, 403 Educ. L. Rep. 421 (3d Cir. 2022).
[574] Ryder v. Hyles, 27 F.4th 1253, 400 Educ. L. Rep. 441 (7th Cir. 2022).

alleged perpetrator based on repeated sexual assaults. RICO makes it "unlawful for any person employed by or associated with any enterprise…to conduct or participate, directly or indirectly, in the conduct of such enterprise's affairs through a pattern of racketeering activity," and anyone "injured in his business or property" may recover damages. The court held that, while personal injuries are horrific, they did not amount to "injuries to any business or property."

In the first of two appellate cases from Oregon, the court reversed and remanded a trial court's conviction of the defendant for identity theft, second-degree burglary, second-degree theft, and interfering with a police officer.[575] The issue on appeal was whether the office in the university building where the briefcase was stolen constituted a separate building. It was argued that the office should be considered a separate building because it had a locking door. If the office was found to be a separate building, the burglary charge would remain. If it was considered a part of the larger building, the defendant would receive the lesser charge of theft. The appellate court ruled that the office was simply a part of the larger building and not a separate one, thus, the case was reversed and remanded. In another case, the appellate court affirmed the conviction of a defendant for giving false information to a peace officer, resisting arrest, interfering with a police officer, and second-degree trespass.[576] The defendant was found on university-owned property, and an officer arrested and charged him with the above convictions. The defendant failed to attend a pretrial conference, and the state issued a warrant. The defendant was arrested on the warrant two years later, after which he was convicted. The defendant alleged untimely prosecution and untimely trial, which the appellate court denied because the prosecutors and police had very little information available to find the defendant. The defendant also argued that evidence from his interaction with the arresting officer should have been suppressed as the officer did not have the requisite suspicion to make the arrest. The appellate court disagreed with this claim as well, finding there was reasonable suspicion that the defendant was trespassing because he was on property not generally open to the public. The defendant also made a motion of acquittal on inadequacy of evidence grounds which the appellate court denied.

In Pennsylvania, a defendant was convicted by the trial court in a non-jury trial after being denied a motion to suppress evidence

---

[575] State v. Haley, 511 P.3d 440, 404 Educ. L. Rep. 265 (Or. Ct. App. 2022).
[576] State v. Melecio, 507 P.3d 764, 402 Educ. L. Rep. 412 (Or. Ct. App. 2022).

discovered during a warrantless search of his home.[577] The issue was whether the campus officers had exigent circumstances to enter the home at the time they chose to enter. An appellate court vacated the sentence and remanded the case, reasoning that the individual, who had been spotted driving erratically before entering his home, did not provide the police with any exigent circumstances which would make a warrantless entry reasonable. There was no immediate threat to police or other persons, and the individual was not a fleeing felon.

An appellate court in Virginia reversed a conviction of grand larceny.[578] The issues on appeal were whether the Commonwealth presented sufficient evidence that the defendant committed the crime and what the value of the stolen property was. The defendant allegedly stole tools at a construction site at the medical school, but the only evidence available was a video depicting the defendant putting items from the box into a bag. However, it was not clear what tools were put in the bag, and it was stated that the defendant had permission to access the tools. The court found that this evidence was not sufficient to prove the defendant committed the crime. Because there was insufficient evidence to prove the crime, the court did not need to determine the value of the stolen tools.

Consumer Protection

An Attorney General alleged that a business violated the Colorado Consumer Protection Act (CCPA) and Colorado's Uniform Consumer Credit Code (UCCC) through its efforts to recruit consumers and enroll them as students.[579] An appellate court affirmed in part and reversed in part the trial court's entry of judgment against the business after the Attorney General brought an action against the business and its principals. The court noted that the CCPA claims were not barred by the educational malpractice doctrine because they did not pertain to the quality of education provided. Further, the business's use of national wage data in its advertisements did not shield it from liability under the CCPA. As for the UCCC claim, the court was required to look beyond the terms of the loan to the circumstances of the consumer based on the probability of repayment factor. Lastly, the two year and nine month delay in the trial court's entry of its judgment constituted a

---

[577] Commonwealth v. Edgin, 273 A.3d 573, 402 Educ. L. Rep. 1038 (Pa. Super. Ct. 2022).
[578] Goldman v. Commonwealth, 871 S.E.2d 243, 402 Educ. L. Rep. 435 (Va. Ct. App. 2022).
[579] State *ex rel.* Weiser v. Ctr. for Excellence in Higher Educ., 499 P.3d 1081, 397 Educ. L. Rep. 757 (Colo. App. 2021).

significant delay that constituted an "extreme circumstance" and required a new judge to hear the case on remand.

Policy Changes

In Pennsylvania, a federal trial court granted the private university's motion for a preliminary injunction and declaratory relief to stop the Commission on Graduates of Foreign Nursing Schools (CGFNS) from instituting an English-language proficiency requirement for certain nurses pursuing work in the United States and to compel CGFNS to issue certified statements to graduates meeting the statutory criteria.[580] The court held that, while CGFNS does have certain statutorily-provided discretionary authorities, it does not have the authority to restrict the phrase "nursing program" to exclude graduate-level programs. Further, CGFNS lacked the authority to implement the policy change requiring certain foreign nurses meet English-language proficiency requirements in order to receive their certificate. Lastly, the court ordered that foreign nurses who have graduated from either an entry-level or graduate-level program be able to receive a certified statement from CGFNS.

Conclusion

Among the cases presented, a handful latch onto ongoing political and cultural concerns and movements. The Supreme Court held that race-conscious admissions policies were unconstitutional, affecting the admissions process at institutions across the United States. The Arizona case concerning a student's use of social media to anonymously promote parties during the COVID-19 pandemic using the university's logo was appealed to the Ninth Circuit. The federal appellate court affirmed the lower court's denial of the university's motion for default judgment on its Lanham Act claims as it was unlikely consumers would believe the social media account was run or endorsed by the university. The Eleventh Circuit case from Alabama concerning the traveling evangelist's unsuccessful challenge to a university's grounds-use policy requiring unaffiliated persons to obtain a permit to speak publicly on campus resulted in a denial of certiorari. We presented three cases concerning COVID-19 policies implemented by HEIs, though the ongoing and often

---

[580] Franklin Univ. v. CGFNS Int'l, 534 F. Supp.3d 457, 396 Educ. L. Rep. 560 (E.D. Pa. 2021).

changing nature of the virus and uncertain future of the pandemic response mean challenges yet remain, and cases have continued into the 2023-2024 academic year as lower court decisions find their way into the appellate level. As task forces devoted to COVID-19 responses know all too well, much is still unknown about emerging variants and how they will move through populations over the coming semesters. So, the hot buttons do not all burn at the same temperature, but underlying issues remain inflamed.

Cases by Alphabetical

Aguillard v. La. Coll.
Alozie v. Ariz. Bd. of Regents
Andrews v. Bd. of Regents of Univ. Sys. of Ga.
Ariz. Bd. of Regents v. Doe
Bachmann v. Regents of Univ. of N.M.
Berry v. Tex. Woman's Univ.
Bd. of Regents of Higher Educ. v. State ex rel. Knudsen
Bd. of Trs. of Leland Stanford Jr. Univ. v. Agilent Tech.
Bowles v. Macomb Cmty. Coll.
Busuito v. Barnhill
Charlton-Perkins v. Univ. of Cincinnati
Clements v. Aramark Corp.
Commonwealth v. Edgin
Conviser v. DePaul Univ.
Cunningham v. Blackwell
Doe 1 v. George Wash. Univ.
Duke Energy One v. Cincinnati State Tech. & Cmty. Coll.
Ehlers v. Univ. of Minn.
Felton v. Monroe Cmty. Coll.
Fin. Oversight and Mgmt. Bd. for P.R., In re
Franklin Univ. v. CGFNS Int'l
GeoMetWatch Corp. v. Behunin
Goldfarb v. Kalodimos
Goldman v. Commonwealth
Gomoletz v. Rockhurst Univ.
Harris v. Trs. of Univ. of D.C.
Houser v. Feldman
Hous. Cmty. Coll. Sys. v. Wilson
Jones v. Alcorn State Univ.
Judy v. E. W. Va. Cmty. & Tech. Coll.
Keister v. Bell
Ky. Ret. Sys., by and through the Bd. of Trs. of Ky. Ret. Sys. v. W. Ky. Univ.
Lewis v. Ind. Wesleyan Univ.
Lord v. Univ. of Miami
Majumdar v. Fair
Marsden v. Kishwaukee Cmty. College
Morris v. George Mason Univ.
Nat'l Coll. Student Loan Tr. 2006-2 v. Gimple
Norris v. Stanley
Oldenburg v. Univ. of Tex. at Austin

Palade v. Bd. of Trs. of Univ. of Ark. Sys.
Palmer v. Ind. Univ.
Peebles v. Auburn Univ.
Person v. Tech. Educ. Servs.
Purcell v. Ill. Workers' Comp. Comm'n
Russell v. N.Y. Univ.
Ryder v. Hyles
Saroki-Keller v. Univ. of Mich.
Saketkoo v. Adm'rs of Tulane Educ. Fund
Scheer v. Regents of Univ. of Cal.
S. Tex. Coll. v. Arriola
State ex rel. Weiser v. Ctr. for Excellence in Higher Educ.
State v. Ariz. Bd. of Regents
State v. Haley
State v. Melecio
State v. Nelson
Students for Fair Admissions v. Univ. of Tex. at Austin
Students for Fair Admissions v. Univ. of N.C.
Students for Fair Admissions v. President and Fellows of Harvard Coll.
Tex. Tech Univ. Health Sci. Ctr. - El Paso v. Niehay
Trudeau v. Univ. of N. Tex., By and Through its Bd. of Regents
Univ. of Ark. for Med. Scis. v. Barton
U.S. v. Godley
U.S. v. Yung
Vengalattore v. Cornell Univ.
Wash. Fed'n of State Emps., Council, 28 v. State
W. Ill. Univ. v. Ill. Educ. Lab. Rels. Bd.
W. Va. State Univ. Bd. of Governors v. Dow Chem. Co.

Cases by Jurisdiction

FEDERAL CASES

U.S. Supreme Court
Hous. Cmty. Coll. Sys. v. Wilson
Students for Fair Admissions v. President and Fellows of Harvard Coll.

First Circuit

Puerto Rico
Fin. Oversight and Mgmt. Bd. for P.R., In re

Second Circuit
Vengalattore v. Cornell Univ.

New York
Felton v. Monroe Cmty. Coll.

Third Circuit
U.S. v. Yung

Pennsylvania
Franklin Univ. v. CGFNS Int'l
Goldfarb v. Kalodimos
Houser v. Feldman

Fourth Circuit
W. Va. State Univ. Bd. of Governors v. Dow Chem. Co.

North Carolina
Students for Fair Admissions v. Univ. of N.C.
U.S. v. Godley

Fifth Circuit
Oldenburg v. Univ. of Tex. at Austin
Saketkoo v. Adm'rs of Tulane Educ. Fund
Students for Fair Admissions v. Univ. of Tex. at Austin
Trudeau v. Univ. of N. Tex., By and Through its Bd. of Regents

Texas
Berry v. Tex. Woman's Univ.

Sixth Circuit
Charlton-Perkins v. Univ. of Cincinnati

Kentucky
Cunningham v. Blackwell

Michigan
Bowles v. Macomb Cmty. Coll.

Norris v. Stanley
Saroki-Keller v. Univ. of Mich.

Seventh Circuit
Lewis v. Ind. Wesleyan Univ.
Palmer v. Ind. Univ.
Ryder v. Hyles

Illinois
Conviser v. DePaul Univ.
Majumdar v. Fair
Marsden v. Kishwaukee Cmty. Coll.

Eighth Circuit
Ehlers v. Univ. of Minn.

Ninth Circuit

Arizona
Alozie v. Ariz. Bd. of Regents
Ariz. Bd. of Regents v. Doe

California
Bd. of Trs. of Leland Stanford Jr. Univ. v. Agilent Tech.

Tenth Circuit
GeoMetWatch Corp. v. Behunin

Eleventh Circuit
Keister v. Bell

Alabama
Peebles v. Auburn Univ.

Georgia
Andrews v. Bd. of Regents of Univ. Sys. of Ga.
Person v. Tech. Educ. Servs.

Florida
Lord v. Univ. of Miami
State v. Nelson

D.C. Circuit

D.C.
Doe 1 v. George Wash. Univ.
Harris v. Trs. of Univ. of D.C.

STATE & D.C. COURT CASES

Arizona
State v. Ariz. Bd. of Regents

Arkansas
Palade v. Bd. of Trs. of Univ. of Ark. Sys.
Univ. of Ark. for Med. Scis. v. Barton

California
Scheer v. Regents of Univ. of Cal.

Colorado
State ex rel. Weiser v. Ctr. for Excellence in Higher Educ.

Connecticut
Clements v. Aramark Corp.

Illinois
Purcell v. Ill. Workers' Comp. Comm'n
W. Ill. Univ. v. Ill. Educ. Lab. Rels. Bd.

Kentucky
Ky. Ret. Sys., by and through the Bd. of Trs. of Ky. Ret. Sys. v. W. Ky. Univ.

Louisiana
Aguillard v. La. Coll.

Michigan
Busuito v. Barnhill

Mississippi
Jones v. Alcorn State Univ.

Missouri
Gomoletz v. Rockhurst Univ.

Montana
Bd. of Regents of Higher Educ. v. State ex rel. Knudsen

New Mexico
Bachmann v. Regents of Univ. of N.M.

New York
Russell v. N.Y. Univ.

Ohio
Duke Energy One v. Cincinnati State Tech. & Cmty. Coll.

Oregon
Commonwealth v. Edgin
Nat'l Coll. Student Loan Tr. 2006-2 v. Gimple
State v. Haley
State v. Melecio

Texas
S. Tex. Coll. v. Arriola
Tex. Tech Univ. Health Sci. Ctr. - El Paso v. Niehay

Vermont
Morris v. George Mason Univ.

Virginia
Goldman v. Commonwealth

Washington
Wash. Fed'n of State Emps., Council, 28 v. State

West Virginia
Judy v. E. W. Va. Cmty. & Tech. Coll.

Chapter 9

STUDENTS IN HIGHER EDUCATION

Elizabeth T. Lugg, J.D., Ph.D.,[581] Joy Blanchard, Ph.D.,[582] and Gillian P. Foss, Ph.D.[583]

Introduction	269
Academic and Curricular Matters	269
Authority over Curricular Requirements	269
Challenges to Managerial Authority	269
Student Misconduct	270
Academic Misconduct	270
Non-Academic Misconduct	271
Admissions	274
Torts	274
COVID-19-Related	276
Discrimination	282
Disability Discrimination	284
Gender and Sexual Harassment	285
Race/National Origin Discrimination	292
Tuition and Student Financial Aid	293
First Amendment	297
Civil Procedure Issues	297
Conclusion	301
Alphabetical List of Cases	302

---

[581] Associate Professor, Educational Law, Illinois State University, Normal, Ill.
[582] Associate Professor, Higher Education, Lutrill and Pearl Payne School of Education, Louisiana State University, Baton Rouge, La.
[583] Lutrill and Pearl Payne School of Education, Louisiana State University, Baton Rouge, La.

Cases by Jurisdiction 304

Introduction

This chapter reviews cases reported in 2022 involving student-related matters in higher education. These cases dealt with academic and curricular issues; misconduct on academic and non-academic grounds; admissions; torts; crimes; discrimination claims involving race, gender, and disability; and financial aid.

Academic and Curricular Matters

Authority over Curricular Requirements

The Supreme Court of Vermont upheld a ruling granting summary judgment to a university medical center after staff opted not to renew a medical resident's fellowship beyond the standard one-year duration.[584] The medical resident had been plagued by a myriad of physical and mental health challenges throughout the course of their fellowship, resulting in considerable absences from training. The plaintiff argued that the university's decision to deny their request for a six-month extension to catch up on their education was discrimination and violated Vermont's Fair Employment Practices Act. The court dismissed these claims, however, noting that the resident was permitted to carry out their initial fellowship period, thereby still receiving the same contractual pay and benefits as any other fellow—the fellow was simply not offered an extension based on academic concerns, which failed to satisfy the accommodation claim under the Fair Employment Practices Act.

Challenges to Managerial Authority

In a case that reached the Second Circuit, a former university student, embattled by sexual assault allegations since 2015, pursued a defamation and tortious interference claim against the university and the student who made the accusation.[585] The plaintiff was acquitted of all charges in Connecticut's criminal court but was expelled based on the institution's use of the preponderance standard of evidence for the allegations. Specifically, the plaintiff argued that the quasi-judicial immunity bestowed by the state of Connecticut does not extend to non-governmental entities like a

---

[584] Kelly v. Univ. of Vt. Med. Ctr., 280 A.3d 366, 407 Educ. L. Rep. 186 (Vt. 2022).
[585] Khan v. Yale Univ., 27 F.4th 805, 400 Educ. L. Rep. 411 (2d Cir. 2022).

private university. The appellate court ruled this claim too ambiguous to predict the state supreme court's outcome; thus, they certified a series of five questions and related sub-questions to determine whether the student-accuser's prior immunity status would shield them from the plaintiff's claims in a non-governmental setting.

In Colorado, a university student sued her institution's director of student conduct for a First Amendment violation after the director allegedly set parameters disallowing the student to interact with a former professor, along with restricting them from talking about the professor with peers from those classes.[586] The student's heated interactions with the professor in question escalated to the point where she dropped the course and attempted to persuade her former classmates, via email, to leave critical teaching evaluations. Based on these facts, a trial court initially ruled that the director of student conduct was entitled to qualified immunity, but the Tenth Circuit reversed and remanded this judgment. The court held that the director violated the student's constitutional right to free speech, rendering his qualified immunity claim moot as a public employee. The Tenth Circuit held that the student's criticisms of their professor and subsequent email to classmates did not constitute a substantial disruption to the course and reaffirmed that "student critiques of faculty members are widely recognized as a useful mechanism for improving college teaching."

Student Misconduct

Academic Misconduct

The Supreme Court of Utah affirmed the lower court's grant of summary judgment in favor of the state on the plaintiff student's breach of contract, breach of the covenant of good faith and fair dealing, and negligence claims.[587] The plaintiff was a state university graduate student who was dismissed from the university's neuroscience program for alleged dishonesty and research misconduct. She alleged that this breached a contract between her and the university, which was "established in various documents memorializing her status or relationship in the [u]niversity or the program." The court held that not all university

---

[586] Thompson v. Ragland, 23 F.4th 1252, 399 Educ. L. Rep. 45 (10th Cir. 2022).
[587] Rossi v. Univ. of Utah, 496 P.3d 105, 395 Educ. L. Rep. 838 (Utah 2021).

policies form a contractual relationship, and the question became "whether the terms of the document can be shown to amount to a legally enforceable promise made in exchange for a promise or performance by a student." The policies at issue here were found insufficient to arise to a contract, and the lower court properly granted summary judgment in favor of the state.

A medical resident in California brought forth a gender discrimination and retaliation claim following their dismissal from an internal medicine residency program.[588] The appellate court reversed the prior judgment dismissing the suit based on the standard of academic deference to the residency location and affirmed that the plaintiff's status as a medical resident was more reflective of an "employee–employer" relationship than an expressly academic program. Many of the criticisms of the plaintiff's performance were valid, but they were more reflective of her insufficient employment role of patient care rather than the explicitly academic parts of the residency; as such, the court remanded the case for a subsequent trial.

Non-Academic Misconduct

In the first of two cases from the federal trial court in Massachusetts, the court denied a student's motion for partial summary judgment and the university's cross-motion for summary judgment on the student's claim for violations of Title IX, state law, breach of contract, and negligent hiring following the sexual misconduct claims brought against the student by his ex-girlfriend and the related disciplinary proceedings.[589] The court held that the college was not deliberately indifferent to any discrimination against him, there was no evidence that the complainant filed her complaint based on the plaintiff's gender, and the absence of live testimony at the disciplinary proceeding did not breach its obligations of basic fairness. Therefore, the student's motion for summary judgment was denied. However, the court did find that a genuine issue of material fact existed as to whether administrators interfered with the hearing panel's deliberations and whether the investigator's report about the allegations prevented the student from receiving a fair adjudication. Thus, the university's motion for summary judgment was dismissed as well. In the second case, the court granted summary judgment in favor of the college on the former student's claims under the

---

[588] Khoiny v. Dignity Health, 291 Cal. Rptr. 3d 496, 401 Educ. L. Rep. 502 (Cal. Ct. App. 2021).
[589] Doe v. Williams Coll., 530 F.Supp.3d 92, 395 Educ. L. Rep. 929 (D. Mass. 2021).

Americans with Disabilities Act (ADA) and Rehabilitation Act.[590] The issues arose from the plaintiff's expulsion for verbal abuse, violent or endangering behavior, and personal conduct after numerous instances of him engaging in threatening speech and behavior. The ADA and Rehabilitation Act both protect against discrimination based on an individual's disability status. The plaintiff argued that the university discriminated against him by treating him differently than it did other similarly situated students who did not share the plaintiff's disability and by failing to offer him accommodations. However, the court held that the plaintiff's claims regarding disparate treatment were not supported by evidence, and he failed to allege that his dismissal was due to his disability or the university's failure to accommodate.

A cadet in New York was disenrolled following a disciplinary hearing finding him responsible for the sexual assault of a fellow midshipman.[591] A federal trial court denied the cadet's motion for a preliminary injunction and granted judgment in favor of the defendant United States and marine academy in the plaintiff cadet's Administrative Procedure Act (APA) and due process claims. The cadet argued that his disciplinary hearing violated the APA and the Due Process Clause of the Fifth Amendment and sought a preliminary injunction for the academy to immediately reinstate him. The court denied his motion for a preliminary injunction, finding that he failed to establish a likelihood of success on the merits because the board's finding of violation was not arbitrary and capricious as required under the APA, and his disciplinary hearing followed the academy's procedures and involved adequately trained hearing officers. Further, the court noted that public interest weighed against granting the preliminary injunction because "it is in the national interest that only [officers] of the highest moral character serve and defend the United States."

Three non-academic disciplinary cases were decided in California appellate courts. In the first, the court affirmed the denial of a student's petition for a writ of mandate to set aside his two-year suspension from the university following his violation of the university's sexual assault policy.[592] The plaintiff alleged that he was denied fair process in the university's investigation and adjudication of the sexual assault allegations. Specifically, he argued that he was denied a live hearing and an opportunity to cross-examine witnesses;

---

[590] Joseph M. v. Becker Coll., 531 F.Supp.3d 383, 395 Educ. L. Rep. 961 (D. Mass. 2021).
[591] N.B. v. U.S., 552 F.Supp.3d 387, 400 Educ. L. Rep. 525 (E.D.N.Y. 2021).
[592] Doe v. Regents of Univ. of Cal. (c), 285 Cal.Rptr.3d 513, 395 Educ. L. Rep. 1039 (Cal. App. Ct. 2021).

the investigator did not conduct a fair, thorough, and impartial investigation; and the findings were not supported by substantial evidence. The court found that the plaintiff was not denied adequate process because a live hearing where he could cross-examine witnesses was not required; the investigator was fair, thorough, and impartial in his investigation; and evidence supported the finding that the victim lacked the capacity to consent to the sexual encounter with the plaintiff because she was intoxicated. In another decision from the same day, the court affirmed the denial of the plaintiff's petition for a writ of administrative mandate seeking to set aside his suspension for dating violence.[593] The plaintiff argued that the university failed to provide a fair process and the factual findings were not supported by sufficient evidence. The court held that fair process did not require personal observation or cross-examination of witnesses if their credibility was not in dispute, the plaintiff's lack of access to the complainant's statements during her debrief interview was not unfair, the review committee followed university policy regarding an appeal hearing, and substantial evidence supported the finding of bodily injury to the complainant.

Two non-academic misconduct-related cases yielded different outcomes. In the first, following a California student's expulsion from law school, the student pursued a violation of due process claim against their former institution.[594] Specifically, the student had been expelled after a department of student conduct hearing determined him responsible for accessing fellow students' email accounts to print and send lewd correspondence to members of the campus community on two separate occasions. However, the student argued that student conduct officials violated a basic tenet of due process after denying him the ability to cross-examine witnesses as part of the disciplinary proceedings, and the appellate court agreed, reversing and remanding the case in favor of the student.

In the second case, an appellate court in New York ruled in favor of the disciplining institution after student conduct officials expelled the student for sexually assaulting of a fellow student.[595] The court reexamined the overwhelming evidence supporting the accusing student's claim and affirmed the institution's decision to expel them based on student code of conduct parameters. Additionally, the court ruled that the disciplinary proceedings adhered to all standards of due process in arriving at this outcome.

---

[593] Doe v. Regents of Univ. of Cal. (d), 285 Cal.Rptr.3d 532, 395 Educ. L. Rep. 1058 (Cal. App. Ct. 2021).
[594] Tchr. v. Cal. W. Sch. of Law, 292 Cal.Rptr.3d 343, 402 Educ. L. Rep. 315 (Cal. Ct. App. 2022).
[595] Alexander M. v. Cleary, 168 N.Y.S.3d 162, 403 Educ. L. Rep. 869 (N.Y. App. Div. 2022).

Admissions

A student originally from Missouri enrolled as an out-of-state student in Florida but later pursued the reclassification process three separate times to benefit from in-state tuition rates.[596] The university denied these applications, positing that the student had yet to establish proof of a "bona fide domicile" in Florida beyond their status as an enrolled university student. The appellate court agreed, while also holding that university's process of reviewing and deciding on the student's applications was procedurally sound.

Torts

A student whose degree was withheld from an Ivy League university in Massachusetts while awaiting the outcome of a Title IX deliberation successfully argued to the First Circuit, in part, a breach of contract claim against the university.[597] The student, who had secured postgraduate employment contingent on degree conferral, was accused of sexual misconduct by three female students at a private university in early May, which kickstarted an institutional fact-finding mission about the alleged events. Amid these proceedings, which extended into the following fall, the plaintiff participated in all graduation events, but the institution never conferred his degree. The student argued breach of contract on four counts, and although the appellate court upheld the dismissal of three, it ruled the student's claim regarding the ambiguity of the investigative process timeline, along with a lack of promised confidentiality about the proceedings, possibly constituted a breach of contract.

In Illinois, sorority members were sued in a wrongful death action after a pledge committed suicide.[598] A federal trial court granted the sorority members' counterclaim for a declaration of the sorority's commercial general liability insurer's duty to defend them. The sorority members argued that the sorority's commercial general liability insurer owes them a duty to defend, but the insurer argued that they were not insured under the policy and that the policy's "hazing exclusion" barred coverage. The court discounted the first argument, finding that, as long as the complaint alleged that the individual defendants are within a category of individuals defined as

---

[596] Porras v. Univ. of Fla., 337 So.3d 471, 403 Educ. L. Rep. 337 (Fla. Dist. Ct. App. 2022).
[597] Sonoiki v. Harvard Univ., 37 F.4th 691, 404 Educ. L. Rep. 90 (1st Cir. 2022).
[598] Admiral Ins. Co. v. Anderson, 529 F.Supp.3d 804, 395 Educ. L. Rep. 710 (N.D. Ill. 2021).

"an insured" by the policy and does not negate the possibility that they are within that definition, the insurer must defend. The insurer's second argument failed as well because it was not clear whether the pledge's death was solely caused by an act excluded by the policy's hazing exclusion.

The Supreme Court of New Hampshire affirmed the lower court's grant of summary judgment in favor of the former students in their claim seeking a determination that they were implied coinsureds under the policy through defendant insurance company.[599] The plaintiffs started a fire in their dormitory by using a charcoal grill. The insurance company paid over $4 million in damages, then brought a subrogation claim against the plaintiffs to recover. The plaintiffs brought the current action seeking a declaratory judgment that they are implied coinsureds under the defendant's policy. The defendant argued that the trial court erred in finding that the plaintiffs had a possessory interest in their dorm rooms. The court affirmed that the plaintiffs had sufficient control over their dorms for it to be comparable to a tenant's right to control the leased premises, thus, the plaintiffs had a possessory interest. Further, the court found that the handbook did not amount to an express agreement negating anti-subrogation.

A Kansas student sued the university and an administrator for violating the Family Educational Rights and Privacy Act (FERPA) and for defamation and negligence after the administrator disclosed his student records to his new college.[600] An appellate court affirmed the lower court's grant of the university's motion to strike the student's petition and dismiss his case. The trial court found that the defendants were protected by the anti-SLAPP act, which protects a party's "exercise of the right of free speech, right to petition or right of association." The plaintiff argued that two exceptions applied: the act does not protect FERPA disclosures and the act does not protect information that is false and defamatory. The court found that FERPA did not protect the plaintiff's claims because FERPA does not create a private right of action, nor does it prohibit the disclosure of information. Further, the act did not require the defendants to establish that the information disclosed was true. Therefore, the defendants did not violate FERPA.

An appellate court in Louisiana affirmed the dismissal of a community college student's detrimental reliance claim.[601] The

---

[599] Ro v. Factory Mut. Ins. Co. as Trs. of Dartmouth Coll., 260 A.3d 811, 396 Educ. L. Rep. 218 (N.H. 2021).
[600] Doe v. Kan. State Univ., 499 P.3d 1136, 397 Educ. L. Rep. 779 (Ct. App. Kan. 2021).
[601] Harris v. Bd. of Supervisors of Cmty. and Tech. Colls., 340 So.3d 1121, 405 Educ. L. Rep. 589 (La. Ct. App. 2022).

student allegedly evaded the directives of a campus safety officer in haste to get to an exam and was later detained by police officers after refusing to comply with their efforts to issue a traffic citation. However, the student maintained that she relied on the original officer's promise to only issue a traffic citation when going with him to the police department building and instead was later issued another citation for physically and verbally resisting officers' attempts to detain her. The court ruled that the reliance argument was far too ambiguous and lacked evidence to grant the appeal.

COVID-19-Related

Several legal challenges were filed by students in response to institutional responses to the COVID-19 pandemic, primarily seeking partial refunds for tuition and fees for the time converted to online instruction following nationwide lockdowns.

Some suits in 2022 challenged the vaccination and medical requirements imposed on students seeking to return to campus. In one case, a group of plaintiffs filed a suit protesting a public university's mandate regarding COVID-19 vaccinations and requested an injunction.[602] A federal trial court in Indiana denied the request for an injunction, and the Seventh Circuit upheld that ruling because all but one of the plaintiffs was eligible for the religious exemption to the vaccine, and the other withdrew from the university with no intent to return, making the issue moot.

Other cases centered around institutional decisions to transition to online learning in light of the pandemic. In the Fifth Circuit, a student filed suit for contract claims after her classes were moved online at the start of the pandemic.[603] Her suit hinged on the language in the university's "Financial Responsibility Agreement" (FRA), which students signed when they registered for classes and paid tuition and fees. The plaintiff argued that the university had a separate tuition and fee structure for courses advertised as online, and the university failed to reimburse her for fees related specifically to on-campus services, activities, and facilities. A federal trial court in Texas granted the university's motion to dismiss, finding that the contract between the plaintiff and the university did not explicitly promise in-person instruction. The appellate court affirmed that a contract existed, but reversed and remanded the issue to determine

---

[602] Klaassen v. Trs. of Ind. Univ., 24 F.4th 638, 399 Educ. L. Rep. 103 (7th Cir. 2022).
[603] King v. Baylor Univ., 46 F.4th 344, 407 Educ. L. Rep. 69 (5th Cir. 2022).

the meaning of the ambiguous term "educational services" referenced in the university's FRA. In another case from the Fifth Circuit, a group of students filed a putative class action lawsuit against a private institution in Louisiana for failing to reimburse tuition and fees after classes moved online as a result of the COVID-19 pandemic.[604] A federal trial court granted the university's motion to dismiss the claim, finding that the students' contention that online instruction was not comparable to on-campus instruction related to a complaint regarding educational quality and educational malpractice suits are not justiciable. On appeal, the appellate court reversed that judgment, finding that, although no express contract existed between the students and the university, certain statements from the university website may have created promises for an on-campus experience via implied contracts, and the court remanded the issue for further consideration.

In Illinois, two students filed suit against a public university claiming violations of Section 1983 via the Takings Clause of the Fifth Amendment and the Due Process Clause of the Fourteenth Amendment after the university remitted some but not all mandatory fees after classes were moved online.[605] The university argued that portions of the fee included expenses required to maintain the institution regardless of how instruction was delivered. A federal trial court dismissed the suit, noting that the claims stemmed from a contractual dispute, not a constitutional claim. The students, on appeal to the Seventh Circuit, countered that the institution's promises were specific enough to create a property interest. The Seventh Circuit upheld the prior ruling, finding that any potential dispute would be via a contract claim in state court. In another case from Illinois that reached the Seventh Circuit, a group of students filed a putative class action lawsuit claiming breach of contract and unjust enrichment after their on-campus classes were moved online in response to the pandemic.[606] The plaintiffs sought partial reimbursement of tuition and fees. A federal trial court dismissed their claims, but, on appeal, the appellate court found that the students had sufficiently stated a breach of contract claim to survive the dismissal stage. The court found that certain statements from the university regarding how it advertised courses—particularly the fact that it denoted in its registration bulletin whether a class required in-person attendance—created an implied

---

[604] Jones v. Admin'rs of Tulane Educ. Fund, 51 F.4th 101, 408 Educ. L. Rep. 680 (5th Cir. 2022).
[605] Thiele v. Bd. of Trs. of Ill. State Univ., 35 F.4th 1064, 403 Educ. L. Rep. 151 (7th Cir. 2022).
[606] Gociman v. Loyola Univ. of Chi., 41 F.4th 873, 405 Educ. L. Rep. 654 (7th Cir. 2022).

contract that instruction would be on-campus and that students would have access to certain on-campus services.

The D.C. Circuit considered appeals from two different cases alleging breach of contract and unjust enrichment against private institutions that moved instruction online at the start of the pandemic and failed to refund students for portions of their tuition and fees.[607] A federal trial court in Washington D.C. granted the universities' motion to dismiss the claims, and, on appeal, the D.C. Circuit affirmed that no express contract existed. However, the appellate court remanded for further proceedings to determine whether the universities promised in-person instruction via implied contracts.

In the first of three cases from California, law students argued that the university's course catalog specifically promised "in-person educational services, experiences, opportunities, and other related services."[608] A federal trial court granted the university's motion to dismiss the law students' claims for breach of an implied-in-fact contract, violation of the Unfair Competition Law, and unjust enrichment after it switched to remote learning during the COVID-19 pandemic. The court did not find that any statements in the course catalog promised on-campus instruction during a global pandemic. At most, the court found a general promise, but no specific promises as required to state a claim for breach of contract. The plaintiffs' unfair competition claim was premised on the breach of contract claim, so it failed as well. Finally, California does not recognize a cause of action for unjust enrichment. In another case, the same federal trial court granted the university's motion to dismiss the students' unjust enrichment and conversion claims but denied the motion as to their breach of contract claims.[609] The students filed a class action lawsuit against a private university alleging breach of contract, unjust enrichment, and conversion based on the university's decision to transition to online learning during the COVID-19 pandemic. The university argued that the Enrollment Agreement it entered with each student governed the dispute, and the agreement does not promise to provide on-campus instruction. However, the plaintiffs countered that the agreement was only part of a student's contract with the university and that the university's "marketing, advertisements, and other public representations" promised in-person learning and on-campus experiences. The court

---

[607] Shaffer v. George Wash. Univ., 27 F.4th 754, 400 Educ. L. Rep. 394 (D.C. Cir. 2022).
[608] Abuelhawa v. Santa Clara Univ., 529 F.Supp.3d 1059, 395 Educ. L. Rep. 761 (N.D. Cal. 2021).
[609] Nguyen v. Stephens Inst., 529 F.Supp.3d 1047, 395 Educ. L. Rep. 749 (N.D. Cal. 2021).

found this sufficient for the plaintiffs' breach of contract claims to survive.

In a third federal trial court decision in California, a plaintiff sought certification in a putative class action lawsuit for herself and others who paid tuition and fees at a private institution during the semester in which classes were moved online as a response to the COVID-19 pandemic, citing breach of contract and unjust enrichment.[610] The court granted the motion for certification as a class, noting that the plaintiff met the four requirements for certification: "(1) numerosity, (2) commonality, (3) typicality, and (4) adequacy of representation."

In Connecticut, students and parents brought claims for breach of contract and unjust enrichment against a university following the transition to online learning during the pandemic.[611] The federal trial court dismissed the parents' claims, finding that they lacked standing. The students' claims, on the other hand, were far more successful. The students not only point to language on the university's website about the on-campus experience, but they also allege that the university charges significantly less per credit for online degree programs. The court found this sufficient to infer that the students and the university entered an agreement for on-campus instruction. Further, the court found that it could be inferred that the university accrued more funds by moving its classes online, so there was a remaining issue of fact as to whether the university was unjustly enriched. The court did dismiss the students' conversion claims, holding that the claims for a tuition refund sounded in breach of contract and not a conversion action. In another case, the federal trial court in Connecticut granted the university's motion to dismiss the students' class action suit against it for breach of contract, unjust enrichment, and violation of state consumer protection law after the university switched to online learning due to the COVID-19 pandemic.[612] The plaintiffs alleged that the university breached its contract by promising and failing to provide in-person education for the entire semester by pointing to a school policy that states, "[i]n the unlikely event that public health…concerns cause the [u]niversity temporarily to suspend…operations…The decision to suspend programs shall be made at the discretion and judgment of the [u]niversity." However, this provision specifically reserves the right for the university to

---

[610] Arredondo v. Univ. of LaVerne, 341 F.R.D. 47, 402 Educ. L. Rep. 1029 (C.D. Cal. 2022).
[611] Metzner v. Quinnipiac Univ., 528 F.Supp.3d 15, 395 Educ. L. Rep. 541 (D. Conn. 2021).
[612] Michel v. Yale Univ., 547 F.Supp.3d 179, 399 Educ. L. Rep. 205 (D. Conn. 2021).

suspend operations in response to an emergency, and the plaintiffs cannot successfully claim breach of contract when the university was exercising its express authority. Further, the plaintiffs failed to show that the university breached its duty of good faith and fair dealing by refusing to issue refunds. Finally, the plaintiffs' unjust enrichment claim failed because they failed to establish a distinct, alternative cause of action from the breach of contract claim.

A student filed a claim against a private institution in Florida after classes had been moved online after the start of the pandemic.[613] A year later, the Florida legislature passed a law immunizing colleges and universities via the Florida Immunity Statute for Educational Institutions for Actions Related to the COVID-19 Pandemic. A federal trial court denied the university's motion to dismiss the student's claim pursuant to the immunity statute, finding that doing so retroactively would violate the student's due process in enforcing his vested interest in a cause of action.

After a group of students challenged the requirement to be vaccinated against COVID-19, a consent judgment was entered which would allow them to attend the institution but with reasonable safety measures imposed upon them.[614] Later, the students filed another claim, alleging that the institution was in contempt for violating the consent judgment by requiring them to wear masks and submit to weekly COVID testing. A federal trial court in Louisiana rejected the plaintiffs' motion, finding that the new requirements did not violate the consent judgment's provision related to reasonable safety measures nor did it conflict with state law.

The federal trial court in Massachusetts granted the university's motion to dismiss the plaintiff students' class action for failure to provide refunds after the university switched to online learning during the COVID-19 pandemic.[615] The students claimed breach of express and implied contracts, unjust enrichment, and conversion. The court first noted that the claims were not impermissible claims for educational malpractice but, ultimately, the students failed to state a claim for breach of contract, and the unjust enrichment and conversion claims were barred under state law because the relationship was governed by contract. Specifically, the court found that the plaintiffs failed to identify specific terms from promotional

---

[613] Ferretti v. Nova Se. Univ., 586 F.Supp.3d 1260, 407 Educ. L. Rep. 811 (S.D. Fla. 2022).
[614] Magluilo v. Edward Via Coll. of Osteopathic Med., 582 F.Supp.3d 373, 406, Educ. L. Rep. 878 (W.D. La. 2022).
[615] Barkhordar v. Pres. And Fellows of Harvard Coll., 544 F.Supp.3d 203, 398 Educ. L. Rep. 675 (D. Mass. 2021).

or other materials promising in-person instruction. In another decision by the federal trial court in Massachusetts, the university's motion to dismiss was denied as to the students' claims for breach of contract and unjust enrichment after the university transitioned to online learning during the COVID-19 pandemic.[616] The plaintiffs argued that the university promised an in-person experience through publications, payment of tuition and fees, and the students' registration for and attendance at on-campus classes. The university argued that the alleged promises in its publications were "too 'vague' and 'generalized' to form an implied-in-fact-contract." However, the court disagreed, finding that the representations in publications combined with the plaintiffs' payment of fees and tuition and registration for and attendance of on-campus classes was sufficient to state an implied-in-fact contract. Further, the court found that the plaintiffs stated a claim for unjust enrichment because the students alleged that they conferred a benefit on the university (i.e., tuition and fees), the university provided in-person experiences the first half of the semester but virtual the second half, and it was reasonable for students to expect an on-campus experience for the entire semester, which the university failed to deliver.

In New York, a group of students brought a putative class action lawsuit against a private university after its decision to move classes online, claiming breach of contract and unjust enrichment.[617] A federal trial court dismissed the case, finding no evidence that the university made promises to supply only in-class instruction.

A federal trial court in Pennsylvania granted a university's motion to dismiss claims for breach of contract and unjust enrichment stemming from a putative class action lawsuit following the conversion of on-campus courses to online courses after the start of the COVID-19 pandemic.[618] The students argued that the quality of the education was inferior to what they had paid for and had been promised. In its ruling, the court noted that educational malpractice and any claims related to the quality of education were not justiciable; rather, any claims would have to be considered under a contract theory. Finding the university made no contractual promise as to whether courses would be delivered online or in-person, the court dismissed the suit.

In the first of two appellate cases from Florida, students filed a class action lawsuit against a public college for breach of contract

---

[616] Durbeck v. Suffolk Univ., 547 F.Supp.3d 133, 399 Educ. L. Rep. 187 (D. Mass. 2021).
[617] Morales v. N.Y. Univ., 585 F.Supp.3d 610, 407 Educ. L. Rep. 689 (S.D.N.Y. 2022).
[618] Brezinski v. Widener Univ., 582 F.Supp.3d 257, 406 Educ. L. Rep. 865 (E.D. Pa. 2022).

when instruction was moved online during the pandemic.[619] A trial court rejected the state's claim that it was immune from suit, finding that the list of fees charged to students for various services constituted an express contract. However, on appeal, the court reversed, noting that only an express contract can override the state's sovereign immunity and that the language in the registration materials did not create an express promise that instruction would be delivered on campus. In another case, the appellate court ruled differently.[620] The court upheld a trial court's denial of the public university's motion to dismiss a class action lawsuit for breach of contract for not returning tuition and fees when course instruction moved online during the pandemic. The appellate court noted the language in the registration bulletin whereby students must check a box indicating that they have read all policies related to registration regulations and acknowledge that they were entering a "legal, binding contract" with the university. The court found that a trial must determine if the registration policies provided any specific guarantees in exchange for student fees.

Students in Indiana brought a class action lawsuit against two public universities in Indiana, requesting a pro-rated refund of tuition and fees related to activities, food, and housing costs after the university switched to remote learning due to the pandemic.[621] The plaintiffs claimed that the universities were unjustly enriched by keeping these funds after classes were moved online. The universities appealed a trial court's decision to not grant summary judgment, and the appellate court affirmed, finding that the plaintiffs' breach of contract claims were sufficient to proceed to trial.

Discrimination

A federal trial court in Arizona decided a case that alleged both racial discrimination and a violation of the plaintiff's First Amendment right to free speech.[622] The question before the court was whether the former student's claims were timely. The lawsuit arose out of incidents that occurred on campus in 2017, all revolving around the student's right to be on campus and the alleged disparate treatment of the student on the basis of his race. The former student

---

[619] Dist. Bd. of Trs. of Miami Dade Coll. v. Verdini, 339 So.3d 413, 404 Educ. L. Rep. 979 (Fla. Dist. Ct. App. 2022).
[620] Univ. of S. Fla. Bd. of Trs. v. Moore, 347 So.3d 545, 408 Educ. L. Rep. 1144 (Fla. Dist. Ct. App. 2022).
[621] Trs. of Ind. Univ. v. Spiegel, 186 N.E.3d 1151, 402 Educ. L. Rep. 1092 (Ind. Ct. App. 2022).
[622] Belli v. Grand Canyon Univ., 28 F.4th 948, 400 Educ. L. Rep. 469 (9th Cir. 2022).

filed suit in 2020, three years after the incidents occurred, asserting five causes of action against the university. The trial court found his claims untimely and dismissed the complaint with prejudice. On appeal, the Ninth Circuit held that the claims were time-barred because they were brought more than two years after he was injured and delayed accrual did not apply.

The next two cases involved the same plaintiff, a national religious student group with chapters at many universities. In the first case, the question before the court was whether the student organization's leaders were qualified ministers and, therefore, entitled to the First Amendment's ministerial protections.[623] A federal trial court in Michigan found that the leaders were qualified ministers, and the organization was entitled to ministerial protections. When the Supreme Court established the ministerial exception, it stated that the ministerial exception is founded on a larger and deeply ingrained right of religious organizations to select their leaders and messengers. Moreover, the university's anti-discrimination policy requiring the organization to amend its leadership requirements violated the organization's freedom of internal management rights under the First Amendment. The court found in favor of the plaintiffs finding that, as a matter of law, the university had violated the organizations First Amendment rights and the Establishment Clause. Although university officials were granted qualified immunity on the claim for violation of freedom of assembly, qualified immunity was denied on all other charges as the law was clearly established.

The second case was a request for reconsideration of the previous decision which was brought against a state university alleging violation of both state and federal constitutional provisions when it revoked the local chapter's standing as a registered student organization on grounds that its criteria for leadership positions violated the university's non-discrimination policy.[624] The court, as a matter of law, violated the group's constitutional rights to free speech, freedom of association, and freedom of assembly and enjoined the university from rescinding the group's RSO status. Although the student group did not move for summary judgment, the court said it would consider *sua sponte* summary judgment and gave the university a chance to respond. The university's motion for

---

[623] Intervarsity Christian Fellowship/USA v. Bd. of Governors of Wayne State Univ. (a), 534 F.Supp.3d 785, 396 Educ. L. Rep. 610 (E.D. Mich. 2021).
[624] Intervarsity Christian Fellowship v. Bd. of Governors of Wayne State Univ. (b), 542 F.Supp.3d 621, 398 Educ. L. Rep. 345 (E.D. Mich. 2021).

reconsideration was unsuccessful, and a federal trial court in Michigan entered summary judgment in favor of the student group.

Disability Discrimination

Four cases dealt with claims of disability discrimination in 2022. In the Fifth Circuit, a graduate student diagnosed with attention-deficit hyperactivity disorder (ADHD) was dismissed from two graduate nursing-studies program and subsequently filed suit alleging violation of the Americans with Disabilities Act (ADA), Rehabilitation Act, and Due Process Clause.[625] The plaintiff first enrolled in both the Doctor of Nursing program (DNP) and the Family Nurse Practitioner program (FNP). She requested and was granted accommodation in the FNP but did not request the same accommodations for the DNP until two years later. While she progressed well with the FNP, the plaintiff claimed that when she requested accommodations in the DNP, she faced hostility and not all the accommodations due were provided. The university's motion to dismiss was denied by a federal trial court in Texas, and an interlocutory appeal on the question of qualified immunity followed. On appeal, the Fifth Circuit found that it lacked jurisdiction to make the determinations requested because the court did not have appellate jurisdiction over the Fourteenth Amendment claims. The question of due process was not before the court on appeal, and the case was dismissed.

Plaintiffs in Georgia alleged that police officers responding to a suspicious person report encountered a student in a mental health crisis, and the encounter ended with a police officer fatally shooting the student.[626] The plaintiffs alleged that the university failed to properly train the police and that if they had been properly trained, the student would not have been killed. A federal trial court held that the plaintiffs, who brought this suit on behalf of the deceased student's estate, had not identified any university official with the requisite knowledge of the university police's alleged discrimination or that had the ability to change police policy such that the university could be held liable under the ADA or the Rehabilitation Act. The plaintiffs failed to establish that the failure to train officers in mental health crisis intervention amounted to deliberate indifference, which is required to be held liable under the ADA or

---

[625]Pickett v. Tex. Tech Univ. Health Scis. Ctr., 37 F.4th 1013, 404 Educ. L. Rep. 136 (5th Cir. 2022).
[626] Est. of Schultz v. Bd. of Regents of Univ. Sys. of Ga., 554 F.Supp.3d 1274, 400 Educ. L. Rep. 996 (N.D. Ga. 2021).

the Rehabilitation Act. The defendant's motion to dismiss was granted.

A federal trial court in Tennessee addressed the claims of a medical student who suffered from major depressive disorder and was dismissed for poor performance after he suffered a relapse of his condition.[627] Prior to the relapse, his performance was excellent, but the relapse had a profound effect on his ability to succeed. The student sued under the ADA and the Rehabilitation Act in addition to state law claims for breach of contract, breach of the implied covenant of good faith and fair dealing, promissory estoppel, negligent misrepresentation, and negligent infliction of emotional distress. The university moved to dismiss for failure to state a claim, which was granted. The court held that the federal claims were time-barred under the applicable statute of limitations, and the plaintiff failed to adequately state his claims under state law.

An emergency medicine resident in Texas brought this action against the university health center alleging that she was wrongfully terminated from the residency program based on a perceived disability of morbid obesity.[628] The university moved for summary judgment. The motion was denied, and an appeal followed. On appeal, the court found that there was a genuine issue of material fact as to whether the program's associate director had sufficient influence such as to ultimately determine whether an employee would be dismissed. Moreover, the court found that morbid obesity was considered an impairment, and there was evidence that the plaintiff was being dismissed because of that disability. Therefore, summary judgment would be inappropriate, and the decision of the lower court was affirmed.

Gender and Sexual Harassment

An expelled male student sued his university alleging discrimination on the basis of sex during a Title IX investigation of claims filed by a female student.[629] The case was dismissed by the federal trial court in New Jersey, and the student appealed. On appeal, the Third Circuit held that the lower court had impermissibly taken as true the findings in the university's investigative report, even though they were disputed in the complaint. In his complaint, the plaintiff plausibly alleged that sex

---

[627] Evans v. Vanderbilt Univ. Sch. of Med., 589 F.Supp.3d 870, 408 Educ. L. Rep. 295 (M.D. Tenn. 2022).
[628] Tex. Tech Univ. Health Scis. Ctr. v. Niehay, 641 S.W.3d 761, 401 Educ. L. Rep. 1153 (Tex. App. 2022)
[629] Doe v. Princeton Univ., 30 F.4th 335, 401 Educ. L. Rep. 157 (3d Cir. 2022).

was a motivating factor in the investigation, thus, the plaintiff stated a plausible claim for relief under Title IX. The plaintiff also plausibly stated that the university had been influenced by external pressure in making its decision and the university had not adhered to its own disciplinary procedures. The court acknowledged that discovery may prove that those allegations are false, but at the inception of the case, plausibility is the standard. These facts, combined with plausible claims of breach of contract and bad faith, made dismissal inappropriate. The decision of the lower court was vacated and remanded.

In another case from the Third Circuit, the court found that the university had sufficient notice that its deliberate indifference to sexual harassment by a non-student guest could result in Title IX liability.[630] The parents of a student murdered in her dorm room by her non-student guest filed suit alleging deliberate indifference to known sexual harassment by the guest in violation of Title IX. A federal trial court in Pennsylvania granted summary judgment to the university, holding that the university lacked notice that it could face liability under Title IX for the actions of a non-student guest. In reversing the trial court's decision, the appellate court found that the plain terms of Title IX give notice to institutions that it is an intentional violation of Title IX to show deliberate indifference to known sexual harassment occurring in a location over which the university has substantial control, even if the harasser is a third party.

On appeal from Texas, the Fifth Circuit put forth the theory of erroneous outcome and selective enforcement based on procedural irregularities.[631] The university disciplined a male student for violation of university policies prohibiting sexual abuse and dating violence, and the student sued alleging claims of selective enforcement and erroneous outcome in violation of Title IX as well as deprivation of due process. On appeal, the court held that, in order for it to decide the Title IX claims, it must determine whether the alleged facts raise a plausible inference that the student was discriminated against on the basis of his sex. Gender bias by the university, in connection with the disciplinary hearing in the instant case, could not be inferred as required. In addition, the court held that due process did not require that students accused of sexual assault be permitted attorney-led direct cross-examination of the alleged victim during the disciplinary hearings.

---

[630] Hall v. Millersville Univ., 22 F.4th 397, 398 Educ. L. Rep. 33 (3d Cir. 2022).
[631] Overdam v. Tex. A&M Univ., 43 F.4th 522, 406 Educ. L. Rep. 65 (5th Cir. 2022).

A case alleging deliberate indifference dealt with the harassment of a student by an instructor at the university.[632] The plaintiff alleged that a faculty member made inappropriate comments in class, subjected her to unwanted touching, and sent her text messages to which she did not respond. A report was made to the university, and the plaintiff declined to be interviewed out of fear of retaliation. The university closed the investigation only to open another several months later resulting in a recommendation for termination of the faculty member. The plaintiff filed a Title IX action claiming that the university's deliberate indifference caused the delay and its harmful effects. A federal trial court in Ohio dismissed the action, holding that deliberate indifference exists only if university action was clearly unreasonable in light of the circumstances. On appeal, the Sixth Circuit found that the facts alleged were sufficient to allow the inference that the plaintiff's fear of retaliation was objectively reasonable and the delay resulted in the deprivation of educational opportunities as required to sustain the claim. The trial court erred in failing to construe the complaint in the light most favorable to the plaintiff, therefore, the trial court's dismissal was reversed.

Alleged victims of repeated sexual assault as teenagers filed suit against the church, the affiliated college, and the alleged perpetrators, asserting a civil claim for violation of the Racketeer Influenced and Corrupt Organization Act (RICO).[633] Their theory was based on an alleged conspiracy among the defendants to cover up the sexual assaults by conducting sham investigations years later. A federal trial court in Illinois dismissed the complaint for failure to show injury to business or property as required by the RICO statute. Recovery for personal injuries is not allowed under RICO. On appeal, the Seventh Circuit found that, even though the allegations were horrific, the nature of the alleged personal injuries does not transform them into injuries to business or property.

The Ninth Circuit heard a case involving an alleged violation of Title IX resulting from the university's use of the erroneous outcome and selective enforcement theories.[634] The plaintiff was suspended based on misconduct allegations but before a Title IX investigation. Five months later, the suspension was made permanent based on the university's finding that the plaintiff violated the university's dating violence policy. As a result, the plaintiff lost his housing, his

---

[632] Wamer v. Univ. of Toledo, 27 F.4th 461, 300 Educ. L. Rep. 60 (6th Cir. 2022).
[633] Ryder v. Hyles, 27 F.4th 1253, 400 Educ. L. Rep. 441 (7th Cir. 2022).
[634] Doe v. Regents of Univ. of Cal. (a), 23 F.4th 930, 398 Educ. L. Rep. 663 (9th Cir. 2022).

job as a teaching assistant, his ability to complete his Ph.D., and his student visa. A federal trial court in California dismissed the complaint by concluding that the plaintiff's allegations were insufficient to state a Title IX claim under either the erroneous outcome or selective enforcement theory. On appeal, the court reversed, stating that the issue on such a motion is whether the alleged facts, if true, raise a plausible inference that the university discriminated against the plaintiff based on sex. The appellate court held that the complaint met that standard finding that, taken together, the plaintiff's allegations of external pressure and an internal pattern and practice of bias were sufficient to give rise to a plausible inference that he was discriminated against because of sex.

In a second case brought to the Ninth Circuit, a female student sued under Title IX for physical harassment by a university football player, who was her ex-boyfriend, which occurred at his private off-campus residence.[635] She alleged that the university had shown deliberate indifference by failing to respond to the prior reports of his domestic abuse. On appeal from the federal trial court of Arizona's dismissal, the appellate court held that, because the assault occurred at an off-campus residence over which the university had no substantial control, the university did not exhibit deliberate indifference in not acting on reports of previous assaults by that student. The court cited Supreme Court precedent that Title IX liability exists where an educational institution exercises substantial control over both the harasser and the location. Therefore, although the university had control over the alleged harasser, it did not have control over the place where the harassment occurred. Therefore, the Title IX claim failed.

A Title IX case in the Eleventh Circuit considered whether there was a defensible claim of erroneous outcome or selective enforcement.[636] A student was found responsible for sexual assault, and the university suspended him for five years. On a consolidated appeal from a federal trial court in Alabama, two issues were before the court: whether the student stated a Title IX claim based on the decision of the university, which the plaintiff claimed to be erroneous and based on sex, and whether the student is entitled to proceed under a pseudonym. On the first issue, the court stated that the U.S. Supreme Court has not established a framework for analyzing Title IX challenges to university disciplinary proceedings. The student advanced two theories – erroneous outcome and selective

---

[635] Brown v. State of Ariz., 23 F.4th 1173, 399 Educ. L. Rep. 22 (9th Cir. 2022).
[636] Doe v. Samford Univ., 29 F.4th 675, Educ. L. Rep. 89 (11th Cir. 2022).

enforcement. The court chose a third theory – whether the facts raise a plausible inference of a Title IX violation. On that theory, the court found that neither the alleged procedural irregularities nor the alleged public pressure and public statements made sex discrimination plausible. Once the first issue was addressed and no claim under Title IX was found, the second issue of proceeding under a pseudonym became moot.

The plaintiff, while a student at a California state university, was sexually assaulted, and she alleged that the university systematically failed to educate its students about sexual assault and what constituted a healthy relationship.[637] The alleged assailant had been aggressive and sexually inappropriate earlier. The plaintiff alleged that the failure to educate on the part of the institution constituted a Title IX violation; specifically, it constituted deliberate indifference to sexual harassment thus creating a risk that led to her assault. She reasoned that if the university had provided appropriate education on what constitutes sexual misconduct, she would not have engaged with her alleged attacker. The university moved to dismiss. A federal trial court in California decided that, although this idea is new and evolving, the plaintiff had plausibly pled a claim sufficient to overcome a motion to dismiss. Another federal trial court in California dealt with the religious exception to Title IX.[638] Students who were expelled from the seminary for violating school policies against same-sex marriage and extramarital sexual activity brought a Title IX claim and a claim under the California Equity in Higher Education Act. The court held that, because the school was controlled by a religious organization, the seminary was excepted from the application of Title IX's prohibition of discrimination on the basis of gender. To apply such would have violated the institution's religious tenets, so the defendant's motion to dismiss was granted.

A former student of a college in Iowa brought a claim alleging discrimination on the basis of sex and breach of the covenant of good faith and fair dealings.[639] The plaintiff, during his time as a student, was expelled for violation of the college's sexual misconduct policy and subsequently filed suit. The former student alleged four claims against the college, two of which were that sex was a motivating factor in the college's decision to discipline him, and the college exhibited sex bias against him during the investigation through its

---

[637] Karasek v. Regents of Univ. of Cal., 534 F. Supp.3d 1136, 396 Educ. L. Rep. 665 (N.D. Cal. 2021).
[638] Maxon v. Fuller Theological Seminary, 549 F. Supp.3d 1116, 399 Educ. L. Rep. 722 (C.D. Cal. 2020)
[639] Moe v. Grinnell Coll.(a), 556 F.Supp.3d 916, 401 Educ. L. Rep. 392 (S.D. Iowa 2021).

investigators and adjudicator. The college moved for summary judgment. A federal trial court in Iowa found sufficient evidence to create genuine issues of material fact on the Title IX and breach of contract claims and denied summary judgment on those counts. Summary judgment was granted on all other counts. Additionally, there was an earlier case between these same parties that presented a very narrow issue.[640] In this case, the plaintiff brought an action seeking damages from the college after his expulsion for violating the college's sexual misconduct policy. He presented expert forensic economic testimony that calculated the plaintiff's lost earning and hedonic damages. The college moved to strike the testimony regarding hedonic damages stating that it was unreliable and thus inadmissible. The motion to strike was granted. A federal trial court in Iowa held that the hedonic damages calculation was not sufficiently reliable for admission at trial because the method was not testable, has not been peer-reviewed, lacks governing standards, and is not generally accepted by economists.

A student-athlete brought an action against a Maryland state university alleging discrimination and retaliation in violation of Title IX.[641] The suit arose out of the university's handling of her report of sexual assault and sexual harassment by another member of the university track team. In its analysis, the court listed the four elements necessary for a Title IX claim based on sexual harassment or assault: that the educational institution receives federal funds; that harassment was based on the sex of the alleged victim; that the harassment was sufficiently severe or pervasive to create a hostile environment; and that there is a basis for imputing liability to the institution. In the instant case, the federal trial court found that there was no issue of material fact regarding the first three elements. As to the fourth element, the question of whether the response of the institution showed deliberate indifference presented a question of material fact as did the question of retaliation. The court granted portions of plaintiff's motion for summary judgement and denied the defendants' motion for summary judgment.

A New York student filed suit against his private college after being expelled for sexually assaulting a female classmate.[642] The charges in his complaint included violation of Title IX, breach of contract, negligence, and promissory estoppel. In 2014, the defendant college was on a list of colleges compiled by the

---

[640] Moe v. Grinnell Coll. (b), 547 F.Supp.3d 841, 399 Educ. L. Rep. 235 (S.D. Iowa 2021).
[641] Doe v. Morgan State Univ., 544 F.Supp.3d 563, 398 Educ. L. Rep. 710 (D. Md. 2021).
[642] Doe v. Hobart and William Smith Colls., 546 F.Supp.3d 250, 399 Educ. L. Rep. 106 (W.D.N.Y. 2021).

Department of Education which were under investigation for possibly violating federal rules aimed at preventing sexual harassment. The investigation caused the college to receive a great deal of bad press about how it handled sexual harassment. The plaintiff alleged that the policy revisions made focused on victim advocacy rather than due process. More specifically, he alleged that the investigation against him was affected by the altered policies that he claimed were biased based on sex. A federal trial court ultimately upheld dismissal of all counts of negligence and promissory estoppel, but the court did not dismiss the plaintiff's breach of contract claim or the claim for a Title IX violation. It further held that the plaintiff alleged sufficient facts to support a minimal plausible inference of sex bias as required to state a claim of discrimination in violation of Title IX. In another federal trial court case from New York, a student brought a Title IX action alleging that the university discriminated against him based on his gender after he was expelled for e-mail hacking and subsequently violating the university's gender-based misconduct policy.[643] He put forth the claims of erroneous outcome and selective enforcement. The court found that the plaintiff had alleged sufficient facts to state a Title IX erroneous outcome claim based on his interim suspension and disciplinary proceedings. The plaintiff alleged procedural defects that may have affected the outcome of the disciplinary proceedings both regarding his interim suspension and complaints of sexual misconduct. As to his selective enforcement claim, however, the court split, stating that he had alleged a plausible claim for selective enforcement regarding the disciplinary proceedings but not for his interim suspension and harassment claims because of his independent suspension for hacking.

In an appellate case from California, Title IX disciplinary actions were taken against a student plaintiff in response to an alleged sexual assault of a fellow student, and the disciplined student brought suit alleging a violation of due process under Title IX.[644] After the accused student's writ of mandate was granted, the alleged victim moved to vacate the order on the grounds that she did not receive any notice related to the writ of mandate proceeding or an opportunity to participate. The motion was denied, and she appealed. The appellate court found the appellant to be a party to the case whose interests were affected by the mandate proceeding, but she was determined not to be a necessary party. Therefore, the

---

[643] Doe v. Columbia Univ., 551 F.Supp.3d 433, 400 Educ. L. Rep. 181 (S.D.N.Y. 2021).
[644] Doe v. Regents of Univ. of Cal. (b), 295 Cal.Rptr.3d 625, 405 Educ. L. Rep. 625 (Cal. Ct. App. 2022).

order of the lower court was affirmed. The court also held that even if the appellant had been a necessary party, she did not establish that her absence would be grounds to void a judgment.

In a Georgia case, the issue was the determination of the proper definition of "school" and "teacher" within the applicable statute.[645] A sixteen-year-old was enrolled at a technical college for on-the-road driving lessons, and, during her driving lesson, the instructor inappropriately touched the student. The instructor was found guilty of sexual assault of a student under Georgia law. On appeal, the appellant instructor argued that the technical college was not a "school" and he was not a "teacher" under the statute, and, therefore, he could not have been found guilty of sexually assaulting a student. The court disagreed and held that, under strict construction of the statute, the technical college was a school, and the instructor was a teacher. The court acknowledged that he did not fulfill all usual teaching tasks like assigning class work or homework, lecturing, or grading exams. However, at the time in question, his job description included managing student behavior, and he was in a specialized driving instruction vehicle with the student, instructing her on driving and correcting her behavior at the time of the sexual assault. Therefore, the instructor had supervisory authority over the student.

A former student in New York was suspended for two semesters after being found in violation of the code of student conduct's prohibition of sexual assault.[646] He filed a complaint asserting claims for breach of contract, violation of Title IX, and violation of state human rights laws. The trial court dismissed his claims holding that they were properly reviewable in an Article 78 proceeding, not a plenary action, and, therefore, were time-barred. On appeal, the court upheld the dismissal stating that regardless of how a plaintiff styles his or her claims, it is the duty of the court to examine whether the claims could be addressed in an Article 78 proceeding. Had the claims not been time barred, the court could have converted the plenary action into an Article 78 proceeding, but the time for that was long past.

Race/National Origin Discrimination

The Ninth Circuit affirmed the federal trial court in Idaho's entry of judgment in favor of the university on the student's claims

---

[645] Huggins v. State, 868 S.E.2d 840, 400 Educ. L. Rep. 827 (Ga. Ct. App. 2022).
[646] Doe v. State Univ. of N.Y., Binghamton Univ., 162 N.Y.S.3d 173, 400 Educ. L. Rep. 747 (N.Y. App. Div. 2022).

for disparate treatment under Title VI.[647] The plaintiff was a Chinese international student who alleged intentional discrimination based on race and national origin upon his dismissal from the doctoral program in clinical psychology after he failed to complete the required internship. The plaintiff argued that the trial court erred based on a comment by the judge regarding the unconscious bias of an expert witness. However, the judge still admitted the expert witness's testimony and deemed her a qualified expert. He also argued that supervisors' comments on his English fluency supported his discrimination claim, but the court found these comments insufficient because all of the referenced comments were made in the context of his ability to perform in a clinical setting and to communicate with patients. Thus, the appellate court found that substantial evidence supported the trial court's finding that the university dismissed the student due to his poor clinical performance and not because of his race or national origin.

An African American student in Illinois alleged that his instructors treated him negatively based on his race and religion.[648] A federal trial court granted the university's motion to dismiss and denied the student's motion to file an amended complaint in his claims for slander, conspiracy and harassment, misrepresentation, negligence, and racial and religious discrimination under Title IV and Title VI of the Civil Rights Act. The court first held that the plaintiff's Title IV claims must fail as a matter of law because Title IV does not provide a private right of action. His religious discrimination claims under Title VI must also fail because Title VI does not protect against religious discrimination. Finally, while race discrimination claims under Title VI are valid, the plaintiff's allegations were too conclusory, and the court found that he failed to state a claim for religious discrimination. Specifically, the court found that the plaintiff failed to establish causation between his race and any adverse treatment by his instructors.

Tuition and Student Financial Aid

The U.S. Court of Federal Claims granted summary judgment to the Internal Revenue Service (IRS), the central defendant in a plaintiff's complaint regarding their 2019 federal income tax return being offset to cover a partial amount of their defaulted student

---

[647] Yu v. Idaho State Univ., 15 F.4th 1236, 395 Educ. L. Rep. 898 (9th Cir. 2021).
[648] Beaulieu v. Ashford Univ., 529 F. Supp.3d 834, 395 Educ. L. Rep. 726 (N.D. Ill. 2021).

loans.[649] The plaintiff had previously defaulted on $170,000 in student loans but engaged in a federal student loan rehabilitation plan to mitigate this issue, only to fall behind once more after a new lender took over his loans. The court ruled the consistent and clear messaging from the federal loan servicer and IRS alike was procedurally sound in accordance with the Treasury Offset Program (TOP).

The Third Circuit similarly affirmed a federal trial court in Pennsylvania's holding that a student loan servicer was acting legally under the parameters of the Telephone Consumer Protection Act (TCPA) following periodic calls and automatic dialing messages to the relatives of a student who had defaulted on student loan payments.[650] The appellate court held that the loan servicer's calls to the plaintiffs were not randomly generated, but rather were a result of the plaintiffs being listed on the student's promissory notes and other student loan documentation.

In a federal bankruptcy case from Alabama, the court discharged the Chapter 7 debtor's $112,000 in student loan debt.[651] The debtor here was forty-four years old, a single mother to two children, and a public school teacher seeking discharge of her student loans based on undue hardship. Considering the totality of the circumstances, the court first held that, based on the debtor's current income and expenses, she would be unable to maintain a minimal standard of living for herself and her children if required to fully repay her loans, even under an income-contingent repayment plan. Next, the court found that based on the debtor's age, the age of her children, her occupation, education, and physical health concerns, her financial situation was unlikely to improve in the foreseeable future. Finally, the court noted that the debtor had made good faith efforts to repay the loans because, despite not enrolling in an income-contingent repayment plan, she made close to $10,000 in payments and had applied for partial forgiveness, forbearances, and deferment on multiple occasions. Thus, the court discharged the debtor's loans.

The former Secretary of Education's motion to quash a subpoena to be deposed was denied by a federal trial court in California based on a finding that extraordinary circumstances warranted her deposition.[652] This case was brought by a putative class of student-loan borrowers seeking to compel the restarting of the adjudicative process of student-loan borrower-defense applications. Following an

---

[649] Seto v. U.S., 160 Fed. Cl. 37, 404 Educ. L. Rep. 180 (Fed. Cl. 2022).
[650] Panzarella v. Navient Sols., 37 F.4th 867, 404 Educ. L. Rep. 117 (3d Cir. 2022).
[651] In re Acosta-Conniff, 632 B.R. 322, 396 Educ. L. Rep. 686 (M.D. Ala. 2021).
[652] In re DeVos, 540 F. Supp.3d 912, 398 Educ. L. Rep. 166 (N.D. Cal. 2021).

eighteen-month pause in issuing final decisions for student-loan borrower-defense applications, which the Secretary justified based on the time required to make decisions, the Department of Education resumed issuing decisions with an alarming rate of form-denial letters. All other officials that had been deposed in this case indicated that the Secretary authorized such conduct. The court found that the Secretary was personally involved based on the testimony of other officials, her credibility was called into question by the discovery of pretext for the cursory and unexplained form-denial letters, and there were material gaps in the administrative record the Secretary submitted to the court. Therefore, the subpoena to depose the Secretary was proper.

A federal bankruptcy court in Iowa discharged $230,000 in student loan debt for the plaintiff debtor.[653] The debtor, age fifty, was a dental assistant who incurred significant student loans while completing her undergraduate and master's degrees. In determining whether a debt imposes an undue hardship on the debtor and their dependents, the court looked at the totality of the circumstances. This inquiry considers "(1) the debtor's past, present, and reasonably reliable future financial resources; (2) a calculation of the debtor's and her dependent's reasonable and necessary living expenses; and (3) any other relevant facts and circumstances." The court found that, based on the debtor's status as a single mother maximizing her earning potential, her already frugal lifestyle, and the tax bill she would incur following an income-based repayment plan, the debtor sufficiently proved that repaying her student loans imposed an undue hardship. Thus, the loans should be discharged.

A consumer alleged that the Department of Education incorrectly reported its credit account on her credit report as an "account in dispute."[654] A federal trial court in Michigan denied the Department's motion to dismiss the consumer's claim alleging violations of the Fair Credit Reporting Act (FCRA). The Department argued that sovereign immunity protected it from liability, but the court held that the FCRA waived sovereign immunity by defining "person" as including "any...government or governmental subdivision or agency." Nonetheless, the department argued that the FCRA's definition of "person" would lead to absurd results and was insufficiently explicit. The court disagreed with both arguments, holding that the definition of "person" including the government and

---

[653] In re Ashline, 634 B.R. 799, 398 Educ. L. Rep. 961 (N.D. Iowa 2021).
[654] Hatch v. Equifax Info. Servs., 539 F. Supp.3d 763, 397 Educ. L. Rep. 990 (E.D. Mich. 2021).

governmental entities was not absurd and that the waiver was clearly discernable.

A guarantor was granted summary judgment on a borrower's claim against the guarantor of his student loan debt that paid the default claim of the lender, claiming violations of the Fair Debt Collection Practices Act (FDCPA) and the state's Unfair, Deceptive, or Unreasonable Collection Practices Act (UDUCPA) based on the guarantor's attempts to collect the debt.[655] The guarantor first argued that it did not qualify as a debt collector under the FDCPA and that, if it did, it was exempted based on its collection activities being merely incidental to its fiduciary obligations to the Department of Education. The federal trial court in New Hampshire agreed that the guarantor was not a debt collector based on its agreement with the Department to act as a guaranty agency. Additionally, the court agreed that the guarantor was not acting on a debt owed to another entity but on a debt owed to the guaranty agency based on its repayment of the lender's default claim. Further, the guarantor was exempt under the FDCPA because its primary function was to guarantee the borrower's promise to repay, and any actions to collect from the borrower were incidental to this primary function.

A federal bankruptcy court in Ohio granted the United States' motion for summary judgment on behalf of the Department of Education on the Chapter 7 debtor's claim seeking discharge of his educational debts.[656] The debtor argued that his loans were not "qualified educational loans." The Department countered by arguing that the debt at issue was educational and fell under the exception for educational debt, making it non-dischargeable. To succeed, the Department must show that an educational loan was "either (a) made, insured, or guaranteed by a governmental unit, or (b) made under a program wholly or partially funded by a governmental unit or nonprofit." The court held that, where the debtor took out loans under two federal student loan programs, there was no issue of fact that the loans were educational. The court further held that the debtor's Direct Loans were "made by a governmental unit" and the FFELP loans were "insured, or guaranteed by a governmental unit" or "made under any program funded in whole or in part by a governmental unit or nonprofit institution." Therefore, the debt was non-dischargeable.

---

[655] Estes v. ECMC Group, 565 F. Supp.3d 244, 402 Educ. L. Rep. 663 (D.N.H. 2021).
[656] In re Latson, 632 B.R. 632, 396 Educ. L. Rep. 983 (N.D. Ohio 2021).

First Amendment

The plaintiff, a Trump supporter, alleged that her professor, a well-known anti-Trump blogger, gave her a "D" in his class, intentionally lowered her grade because of her political beliefs, graded her exams unfairly and unethically, and coordinated with other professors to have her academically dismissed.[657] A federal trial court in Florida dismissed the plaintiff law student's First Amendment claims against the defendant professor. The court first noted that the defendant "was acting within the scope of his discretionary authority," so the burden shifted to the plaintiff to establish that he clearly violated her established constitutional rights. The plaintiff raised two arguments. First, she argued that the defendant's actions had a chilling effect on her free speech rights, but the court found her subjective discomfort was not a constitutional violation. Second, the plaintiff argued that the professor retaliated against her for her political beliefs by grading her using non-academic standards; however, her claims were entirely conclusory, and she did not provide any factual support. Thus, her First Amendment claims against the defendant professor were dismissed.

Civil Procedure Issues

A new category for this edition of the Yearbook is cases where the issues present a civil procedure question. While this category may be of greater interest to attorneys, it can also provide guidance to educational administration regarding available arguments that can determine the survival of a lawsuit. In 2022, there were eight civil procedure cases dealing with certification of class actions, motions in limine, standing, injunctions, and immunity.

In a federal trial court case from Washington D.C., student employees sued the university alleging violations of the District of Columbia's Human Rights Act, violation of Title IX, and negligent training, supervision and retention.[658] The students communicated with their attorneys through university email, and, because of university policy stating that university emails were monitored by the institution, it was found that the students had waived attorney-client privilege. The students moved for reconsideration of this decision. On review, the court found that the students were on notice

---

[657] McLaughlin v. Fla. Int'l Univ. Bd. of Trs., 533 F.Supp.3d 1149, 396 Educ. L. Rep. 493 (S.D. Fla. 2021).
[658] Doe 1 v. George Wash. Univ., 573 F.Supp.3d 88, 404 Educ. L. Rep. 795 (D.D.C. 2021).

that university emails were monitored. Moreover, these emails were not entitled to work-product protection, and the policy of monitoring the emails was not an adhesion contract. The students' motion was denied.

In Georgia, a plaintiff was charged with interstate stalking, and he moved in limine to exclude from trial evidence of past college Title IX proceedings against him as well as a parallel Illinois court proceeding where the victim sought to obtain a stalking no-contact order.[659] A court will grant a motion in limine only if the evidence in question is clearly inadmissible. A federal trial court found that the evidence of the parallel proceedings, videos on cell phones seized, and 205 pages of computer searches could be admitted as evidence of prior bad acts; the evidence was not outweighed by any unfair prejudice.

College and graduate students brought anti-trust claims against three textbook publishers and two on-campus bookstores alleging that they conspired to eliminate competition by convincing institutions that students must buy textbooks and accompanying course materials in a digital format.[660] This requirement limited competition and increased costs for students. Ultimately, the question before the court was whether the students had standing under the Sherman Anti-Trust Act. A federal trial court in New York held that the students had standing against the bookstores, but they were found to lack standing as to the publishers. The difference stemmed from the fact that the students directly purchased textbooks from the bookstores but only indirectly from the textbook publishers. Because of this fact, the students, as indirect purchasers, could not hold the publishers liable under the Sherman Act. Moreover, the students failed to plausibly allege a horizontal conspiracy among the three publishers or the two bookstores. The case was dismissed.

A Texas statute regarding tuition was the topic of the next lawsuit.[661] A student group filed a claim alleging that a Texas law compelled United States citizens to pay higher tuition than some non-citizens. The group also claimed that the state law was preempted by a section of the Illegal Immigration Reform and Immigrant Responsibility Act, which forbids non-citizens from receiving any postsecondary education benefit unless the same benefit is made available to citizens. The university moved to

---

[659] U.S. v. Oury, 568 F.Supp.3d 1380, 403 Educ. L. Rep. 670 (S.D. Ga. 2021).
[660] In re Inclusive Access Course Materials Antitrust Litig., 544 F.Supp.3d 420, 397 Educ. L. Rep. 690 (S.D.N.Y).
[661] Young Conservatives of Tex. Found. v. Univ. of N. Tex., 569 F.Supp.3d 484, 403 Educ. L. Rep. 724 (E.D. Tex. 2021).

dismiss for lack of standing and failure to state a claim on which relief could be granted. A federal trial court held that, since some of the students in the student organization had standing to bring their own individual action, the group then had associational standing. In addition, the organization sought injunctive relief as required to state a claim, therefore, the motion was denied.

Another case from Texas questioned the class certification of a claim.[662] A class action suit was brought against the university claiming fraud and unjust enrichment after enrolling in online professional graduate/certification programs that were not accredited in the state in which she and other members of the class resided.The plaintiff claimed that the assurances given by the institution that she could become a certified teacher in Texas where she resided were false, and had she known, she would not have enrolled. The university responded that the plaintiff was dismissed from the program after failing to pass a required criminal background check. The question before the court was whether the plaintiff had satisfied the four threshold requirements under Federal Rule of Civil Procedure 23(a) for class certification. A federal court denied her motion to certify based on the failure to show commonality within the class, typicality, and predominance, as is required. In other words, the plaintiff failed to show that all of the class members' claims depended on a common issue or law or fact, that members suffered the same or similar injury, and that common questions predominated over any questions affecting only individual members.

In Washington, the plaintiff had completed 75% of his nursing degree when he was banned from campus with an interim trespass order issued because of homicidal ideations about three of his professors.[663] The student suffered from medical issues throughout his studies, but they escalated, causing a need for inpatient counseling. The student unsuccessfully appealed his interim no trespass order. Subsequently, it was decided that the conditions required prior to his return to campus were to successfully re-enroll in the nursing program, participate in counseling, and complete a mental health evaluation. The plaintiff filed a Section 1983 claim for violation of his free speech rights and requested an injunction of various sanctions, including the trespass order and order to provide regular reports of his medical treatment. The institution requested partial summary judgment on the injunction, stating that it is

---

[662] Miller v. Grand Canyon Univ., 540 F.Supp.3d 625, 398 Educ. L. Rep. 100 (N.D. Tex. 2021).
[663] R.W. v. Columbia Basin Coll., 572 F.Supp.3d 1010, 404 Educ. L. Rep. 757 (E.D. Wash. 2021).

immune from suit and asserting that the sanctions were no longer in place since the student never re-enrolled. A federal trial court held that, while immunity did exist, the claim that no sanctions exist was in error because negative information remained on his transcripts. Therefore, for defendants other than the institution itself, the injunction was granted.

A federal trial court in Wisconsin held that the state chapter of a nonprofit voter-rights organization had standing to bring a declaratory judgment action against a state election commission's members challenging the constitutionality of voter-identification requirements for the use of student ID cards, but the national organization failed to show an injury-in-fact, as required to establish standing.[664] In Wisconsin, student ID cards may be used as voter identification so long as it meets certain statutory requirements, such as displaying an issuance date, an expiration date not more than two years after the issuance date, and a signature, which the organization alleged was unconstitutional. The court found that the local chapter established standing because its mission included protecting voters' rights and it had to allocate resources to educating students on voter identification requirements and obtaining a compliant ID, and having to divert resources to this purpose constituted an injury in fact. However, the national organization did not claim to devote any resources to educating students in Wisconsin nor do they identify any other injuries, therefore, it lacked standing.

In the only state court case involving procedural issues, an appellate court in Indiana heard the question of whether a class action suit was allowed in a breach of contract and unjust enrichment claim based on the retention of tuition and fees after in-person classes were canceled due to COVID-19.[665] The plaintiff filed a putative class-action suit, but after the suit was filed, the Indiana General Assembly passed a new law that barred class-action suits in situations like that of the plaintiffs. The state university filed a motion for relief, and the plaintiff was given leave to file an amended complaint removing the class allegations. The plaintiff appealed, and the question before the court was whether the new law or the procedural rule took precedent. The appellate court held that it was a fundamental rule of Indiana law that when a procedural statute conflicts with state supreme court procedural rule, the latter shall take precedent. The new law was a procedural statute as it did not establish rights and responsibilities but only prescribed the way

---

[664] Common Cause v. Thomsen, 574 F.Supp.3d 634, 405 Educ. L. Rep. 124 (W.D. Wis. 2021).
[665] Mellowitz v. Ball State Univ., 196 N.E.3d 1256, 408 Educ. L. Rep. 1008 (Ind. Ct. App. 2022).

such rights and responsibilities could be exercised. Therefore, the procedural rule took precedent, and a class action claim was an appropriate remedy.

Conclusion

Cases involving students in higher education continued to occupy both state and federal courts. This chapter illustrated the balance courts strike in weighing students' rights and those of the institution and other governing bodies.

Alphabetical List of Cases

Abuelhawa v. Santa Clara Univ.
Acosta-Conniff, In re
Admiral Ins. Co. v. Anderson
Alexander M. v. Cleary
Arredondo v. Univ. of LaVerne
Ashline, In re
Barkhordar v. Pres. And Fellows of Harvard Coll.
Beaulieu v. Ashford Univ.
Belli v. Grand Canyon Univ.
Brezinski v. Widener Univ.
Brown v. State of Ariz.
Common Cause v. Thomsen
DeVos, In re
District Bd. of Trs. of Miami Dade Coll. v. Verdini
Doe v. Columbia Univ.
Doe v. Hobart and William Smith Colls.
Doe v. Kan. State Univ.
Doe v. Morgan State Univ.
Doe v. Princeton Univ.
Doe v. Regents of Univ. of Cal. (a)
Doe v. Regents of Univ. of Cal. (b)
Doe v. Regents of Univ. of Cal. (c)
Doe v. Regents of Univ. of Cal. (d)
Doe v. Samford Univ.
Doe v. State Univ. of N.Y., Binghamton University
Doe v. Williams Coll.
Doe 1 v. George Wash. Univ.
Durbeck v. Suffolk Univ.
Est. of Schultz v. Bd. of Regents of Univ. Sys. of Ga.
Evans v. Vanderbilt Univ. Sch. of Med.
Estes v. ECMC Group
Ferretti v. Nova Southeastern Univ.
Gociman v. Loyola Univ. of Chi.
Hall v. Millersville Univ.
Harris v. Board of Supervisors of Cmty. and Tech. Colls.
Hatch v. Equifax Info. Servs.
Huggins v. State
Inclusive Access Course Materials Antitrust Litig., In re
InterVarsity Christian Fellowship/USA v. Bd. of Governors of Wayne State Univ. (a)

InterVarsity Christian Fellowship/USA v. Bd. of Governors of Wayne State Univ. (b)
Jones v. Administrators of Tulane Educational Fund
Joseph M. v. Becker Coll.
Karasek v. Regents of Univ. of Cal.
Kelly v. Univ. of Vt. Med. Ctr.
Khan v. Yale Univ.
Khoiny v. Dignity Health
King v. Baylor Univ.
Klaassen v. Trs. of Indiana Univ.
Latson, In re
Magluilo v. Edward Via Coll. of Osteopathic Medicine
Maxon v. Fuller Theological Seminary
McLaughlin v. Fla. Int'l Univ. Bd. of Trs.
Mellowitz v. Ball State Univ.
Metzner v. Quinnipiac Univ.
Michel v. Yale Univ.
Miller v. Grand Canyon Univ.
Moe v. Grinnell Coll. (a)
Moe v. Grinnell Coll. (b)
Morales v. New York Univ.
N.B. v. U.S.
Nguyen v. Stephens Inst.
Overdam v. Texas A&M Univ.
Panzarella v. Navient Sols.
Pickett v. Tex. Tech Univ. Health Scis. Ctr.
Porras v. Univ. of Fla.
Ro v. Factory Mut. Ins. Co. as Trs. of Dartmouth Coll.
Rossi v. Univ. of Utah
R.W. v. Columbia Basin Coll.
Ryder v. Hyles
Seto v. U.S.
Shaffer v. George Wash. Univ.
Sonoiki v. Harvard Univ.
Tchr. v. Cal. W. Sch. of Law
Texas Tech Univ. Health Scis. Ctr. v. Niehay
Thiele v. Bd. of Trs. of Illinois State Univ.
Thompson v. Ragland
Trs. of Indiana Univ. v. Spiegel
Univ. of S. Fla. Bd. of Trs. v. Moore
U.S. v. Oury
Wamer v. Univ. of Toledo
Young Conservatives of Tex. Found. v. Univ. of N. Tex.

Yu v. Idaho state Univ.

Cases by Jurisdiction
FEDERAL CASES

First Circuit
Sonoiki v. Harvard Univ.

Massachusetts
Barkhordar v. Pres. And Fellows of Harvard Coll.
Doe v. Williams Coll.
Durbeck v. Suffolk Univ.
Joseph M. v. Becker Coll.

New Hampshire
Estes v. ECMC Group

Second Circuit
Khan v. Yale Univ.

Connecticut
Metzner v. Quinnipiac Univ.
Michel v. Yale Univ.

New York
Doe v. Columbia Univ.
Doe v. Hobart and William Smith Colls.
Inclusive Access Course Materials Antitrust Litig., In re.
Morales v. New York Univ.
N.B. v. U.S.

Third Circuit
Doe v. Princeton Univ.
Hall v. Millersville Univ.
Panzarella v. Navient Sols.

Pennsylvania
Brezinski v. Widener Univ.

Fourth Circuit

Maryland
Doe v. Morgan State Univ.

Fifth Circuit
Jones v. Administrators of Tulane Educational Fund
King v. Baylor Univ.
Overdam v. Texas A&M Univ.
Pickett v. Tex. Tech Univ. Health Scis. Ctr.

Louisiana
Magliulo v. Edward via Coll. of Osteopathic-Medicine

Texas
Miller v. Grand Canyon Univ.
Young Conservatives of Tex. Found. v. Univ. of N. Tex.

Sixth Circuit
Wamer v. Univ. of Toledo

Michigan
Hatch v. Equifax Info. Servs.
InterVarsity Christian Fellowship/USA v. Bd. of Governors of Wayne State Univ. (a)
InterVarsity Christian Fellowship/USA v. Bd. of Governors of Wayne State Univ. (b)

Ohio
Latson, In re

Tennessee
Evans v. Vanderbilt Univ. Sch. Of Med.

Seventh Circuit
Gociman v. Loyola Univ. of Chi.
Thiele v. Board of Trustees of Illinois State Univ.
Klaassen v. Trustees of Indiana Univ.
Ryder v. Hyles

Illinois
Admiral Ins. Co. v. Anderson
Beaulieu v. Ashford Univ.

Wisconsin
Common Cause v. Thomsen

Eighth Circuit

Iowa
Ashline, In re
Moe v. Grinnel Coll. (a)
Moe v. Grinnel Coll. (b)

Ninth Circuit
Belli v. Grand Canyon Univ.
Brown v. State
Doe v. Regents of Univ. of Cal. (a)
Yu v. Idaho State Univ.

California
Abuelhawa v. Santa Clara Univ.
Arredondo v. Univ. of LaVerne
DeVos, In re
Karasek v. Regents of Univ. of Cal.
Maxon v. Fuller Theological Seminary
Nguyen v. Stephens Inst.

Washington
R.W. v. Columbia Basin Coll.

Tenth Circuit
Thompson v. Ragland

Eleventh Circuit
Doe v. Samford Univ.

Alabama
Acosta-Conniff, In re

Florida
Ferretti v. Nova Southeastern Univ.
McLaughlin v. Fla. Int'l Univ. Bd. of Trs.

Georgia
Est. of Schultz v. Bd. of Regents of Univ. Sys. of Ga.

U.S. v. Oury

D.C. Circuit
Shaffer v. George Wash. University

D.C.
Doe 1 v. George Wash. Univ.
United States Court of Federal Claims
Seto v. U.S.

STATE & D.C. COURT CASES

California
Doe v. Regents of Univ. of Cal. (b)
Doe v. Regents of Univ. of Cal. (c)
Doe v. Regents of Univ. of Cal. (d)
Khoiny v. Dignity Health
Tchr. v. Cal. W. Sch. of Law

Florida
District Board of Trustees of Miami Dade College v. Verdini
Porras v. Univ. of Fla.
Univ. of S. Fla. Bd. of Trs. v. Moore

Georgia
Huggins v. State

Indiana
Mellowitz v. Ball State Univ.
Trs. of Ind. Univ. v. Spiegel

Kansas
Doe v. Kan. State Univ.

Louisiana
Harris v. Bd. of Supervisors of Cmty. and Tech. Colls.

New Hampshire
Ro v. Factory Mut. Ins. Co. as Trs. of Dartmouth Coll.

New York
Alexander M. v. Cleary
Doe v. State Univ. of N.Y., Binghamton Univ.

Texas
Texas Tech Univ. Health Sciences Ctr. v. Niehay

Utah
Rossi v. Univ. of Utah

Vermont
Kelly v. Univ. of Vt. Med. Ctr.

Chapter 10

FEDERAL AND STATE LEGISLATION

Amy L. Dagley, Ph.D.[666] and David L. Dagley, Ph.D., J.D.[667]

Introduction	310
Federal Legislation	311
State Legislation	312
Accountability and School Reform	312
Athletics	316
Attendance, Promotion, and Graduation	319
Buildings and Grounds	325
Curricular Requirements	328
Employment	335
Finance and School Business	352
Governance and School Leadership	357
Parental and Student Rights	374
Program Development	382
School Choice	391
School Safety	393
Students with Disabilities	405
Technology	409
Transportation	410
Higher Education	412
Conclusion	**439**

---

[666] Associate Professor, Educational Leadership, University of Alabama at Birmingham, Birmingham, Ala.
[667] Professor Emeritus, Educational Leadership, University of Alabama, Tuscaloosa, Ala.

Introduction

This chapter documents and categorizes education-related legislation passed during the 2022 calendar year by the United States Congress and legislatures and general assemblies of the fifty states.[668] The acts recorded in this chapter comprise those impacting schools, both public and private, serving students from early childhood ages through postsecondary and professional schools.

The acts described in these materials tend to provide some policy direction, therefore, general government-wide appropriations acts,[669] appropriations for the state board of education or department of education,[670] appropriations for the K-12 public schools,[671] appropriations for special schools,[672] appropriations for university or community colleges,[673] or appropriations for individual colleges or universities[674] are not included. Resolutions, which reflect the sentiments of the legislature without providing a policy direction, are not usually reported, nor are commemorations, recognitions, and memorials. Legislative changes in the state teacher retirement system, such as changing retirement formulae or altering health insurance programs, are not included, unless the change, such as allowing retired teachers to return to service for a time, addresses a present policy concern.

The authors of this chapter have provided the research for this chapter since the 1998 legislative year, when the federal Congress produced five bills and the individual state legislative bodies passed only 248 acts. Last year, Congress passed ten education-related acts, and the number of acts adopted across the states skyrocketed to 1,307 acts. In the early years of producing this chapter, the existing sources recording legislative activity were physical resources in law libraries, particularly legislative service bulletins and the annotations within statutory codes. In recent years, online resources, including individual state legislative websites, websites for state associations for school boards and for school administrators, and websites such as Legiscan.com and TheLAW.net have provided lists of acts which can be sifted for education-related bills. Compared to earlier years, the ease of finding enrolled acts is unfortunately

---

[668] In Wisconsin's 2021-2022 regular legislative session, all acts were begun in 2021 but were not adopted until 2022. These acts are cited as 2021 acts in these materials.
[669] *See, e.g.*, 2022 Ark. Acts 1, H.B. 1013; 2022 Ark. Acts 1, H.B. 1013.
[670] *See, e.g.*, 2022 Mo. Laws HB 3002.
[671] *See, e.g.*, 2022 Ohio Laws Sub. H.B. No. 583.
[672] *See, e.g.*, 2022 Ark. Acts 202, H.B. 1080.
[673] *See, e.g.*, 2022 Miss. Laws S.B. No. 3002; 2022 Miss. Laws S.B. No. 3011.
[674] *See, e.g.*, 2022 Ark. Acts 164, S.B. 100.

offset by the sheer mass of legislative activity now affecting, if not crippling, schools.

Federal Legislation

In its second session, the 117th Congress passed four acts related to the provision of educational benefits to military veterans. The Student Veteran Emergency Relief Act of 2022 gave permanent authority to the Secretary of Veterans Affairs to assist veterans with their educational assistance benefits during emergency situations. The Secretary may continue to provide educational assistance, including monthly housing stipends or subsistence allowances, for programs converted to distance learning due to an emergency or health-related situation. The act prevents an educational assistance payment from being charged against a veteran's entitlement because the individual was unable to complete a course or program due to an emergency situation.[675] The Veterans Eligible to Transfer School (VETS) Credit Act was adopted to improve the method by which the Secretary determines the effects of a closure or disapproval of an educational institution on individuals who do not transfer credits from the institution. The act concerned eligibility for education assistance for persons who want to transfer credits from an educational program facing closure or disapproval for payments.[676]

The Ensuring the Best Schools for Veterans Act of 2022 was passed to improve the process by which the Secretary determines whether an educational institution meets requirements relating to the percentage of students who receive educational assistance.[677] The Veterans Rapid Retraining Assistance Program Restoration and Recovery Act of 2022 was passed to address the restoration of entitlement to financial assistance to veterans in cases of closure of an educational institution or a disapproval of a program of education. The act asserted that any payment of retraining assistance shall not be charged against any entitlement to retraining assistance if the Secretary determines that an individual was unable to complete a course or program of education as a result of closure or disapproval.[678]

Two federal acts were enrolled in 2022, and signed shortly thereafter, to provide support for the preservation of Native

---

[675] Pub. L. 117-333, H.B. 7939 (Jan. 5, 2023).
[676] Pub. L. 117-297, H.B. 6604 (Dec. 27, 2022).
[677] Pub. L. 117-174, S.B. 4458. (August 26, 2022).
[678] Pub. L. 117-138, S.B. 4089. (June 7, 2022).

American languages as a central feature of culture. In one act, Congress amended the Native American Languages Act to ensure the survival and continuing vitality of native American languages.[679] In the second act, Congress created a Native American language resource center in furtherance of the policy objectives provided by the Native American Languages Act.[680]

Two federal acts commemorated sites distinguished by educational and cultural significance. In one act, Congress redesignated the *Brown v. Board of Education* National Historic Site in Kansas as the *Brown v. Board of Education* National Historic Park, thereby placing it under the supervision of the National Park System.[681] In a second commemorative act, Congress established the Blackwell School National Historic Site in Marfa, Texas, which was associated with the period of racial segregation in Marfa public schools, and the only extant property directly associated with Hispanic education in Marfa since 1965, when the other buildings were torn down after the school closed.[682]

Two other federal education-related acts were adopted in 2022. The Suicide Training and Awareness Nationally Delivered for Universal Prevention (STANDUP) Act was carried over from 2021. The act amended the Public Health Service Act to identify best practices on student suicide awareness and prevention training to state, local, and tribal educational agencies, and to establish and implement school-based student suicide awareness and prevention training policy.[683] The second federal education-related act adopted last year was one which amended the Higher Education Act of 1965, to allow borrowers to separate consolidation loans that had been joined together.[684]

State Legislation

Accountability and School Reform

The legislative activity related to accountability and school reform in 2022 reflected great uncertainty about how to proceed. Directions regarding student assessment and transparency in reporting dominated, yet there was some ambiguity about

---

[679] Pub. L. 117-337. S.B. 1402 (Jan. 5, 2023).
[680] Pub. L. 117-335. S.B. 989 (Jan. 5, 2023).
[681] Pub. L. 117-123, S.B. 270 (May 12, 2022).
[682] Pub. L. 117-206, S.B. 2490. (Oct. 17, 2022).
[683] Pub. L. 117-100, S.B. 1543 (March 15, 2022).
[684] Pub. L. 117-200, S.B. 1098 (October 11, 2022).

consequences for failure. This section describes accountability and school reform-related legislation from the last calendar year.

Virginia directed the state board of education and the superintendent of public instruction to convene a group of stakeholders to make recommendations to the general assembly regarding several goals, including: promoting excellence in instruction and student achievement in mathematics; expanding the advanced studies diploma; increasing transparency of performance measures for public schools; ensuring that performance measures for public schools prioritize the attainment of grade-level proficiency and growth in reading and math for all students from year-to-year; ensuring that proficiency on standards of learning assessments in reading and mathematics are maintained; and ensuring a strong accreditation system for accountability.[685]

In nine states, thirteen bills were enacted related to assessment. Illinois prohibited the state board of education from developing, purchasing, or requiring a school district to administer, develop, or purchase a standardized assessment for students enrolled or preparing to enroll in prekindergarten through grade two, other than for diagnostic purposes.[686] In the first of two laws from Indiana, the state directed the state department of education to apply to the federal department of education for flexibility in assessments.[687] Also, Indiana amended a requirement related to family-friendly assessment of schools, so that if at least 10% of parents request an assessment, the department of education must determine the manner in which the requests are submitted.[688] Kentucky deleted the tenth-grade college admissions examination and added postsecondary readiness indicators to the statewide accountability program.[689] Louisiana amended provisions for literacy screening to require three screenings each school year for students in grades K through three.[690] New Jersey required the state board of education to administer the state graduation proficiency assessment as a field test for the class of 2023.[691]

Oregon required the department of education to ensure that standardized summative assessments are administered to the minimum extent practicable, while still appropriately and effectively assessing the academic achievement of students in the state.[692] In a

---
[685] 2022 Va. Acts Ch. 99, H. 938.
[686] 2022 Ill. Laws Pub. Act 102-0875, SB 3986.
[687] 2022 Ind. Acts Pub. Law 168, HB 1251.
[688] 2022 Ind. Acts Pub. Law 75, HB 1223.
[689] 2022 Ky. Acts Ch. 137, SB 59.
[690] 2022 La. Acts No. 520, HB No. 911.
[691] 2022 N.J. Laws P.L. c. 60, A. 3196.
[692] 2022 Or. Laws Ch. 104, SB 1583.

second law passed in Oregon, the state department of education was required to conduct a survey regarding assessments administered to students by school districts and to develop recommendations and best practices related to assessments.[693] Tennessee authorized the administration of the Tennessee Comprehensive Assessment Program (TCAP) tests to students in a timed format and required the state department of education to establish the required time limit for each TCAP test.[694] Virginia directed the secretary of education and the superintendent of public instruction to convene a work group to revise standards of learning summative assessments of proficiency that require students to demonstrate that they possess the skills, knowledge, and content necessary for success and to develop a plan for implementation of the revised assessments.[695] Further, Virginia required the state board of education, in implementing the through-year growth assessment system for the administration of reading and mathematics assessments in grades three through eight, to seek input and suggestions from each interested local school division regarding the ways in which the administration of such assessments and the reporting of results can be improved.[696] Finally, Wyoming updated provisions regarding reading assessment and intervention to require department approval of assessment and screening instructions.[697]

Seven states enacted eight bills to support data sharing and transparency in accountability reporting. California required the state department of education to annually publish on its website test results showing English language acquisition status and disability.[698] California required the inclusion of data from preschools for the longitudinal pupil achievement data system.[699] Colorado continued the work of the Education Data Advisory Committee, which was set to expire July 1, 2022, and directed the committee to designate requested data as mandatory or voluntary to provide.[700] Missouri required that for any public school, charter school, or school district scoring in the bottom 5% of scores on the annual performance report, each entity must mail a letter to parents and guardians of each student informing them of the rating and any options available to the student as a result of the rating.[701] Nebraska

---

[693] 2022 Or. Laws Ch. 71, HB 4124.
[694] 2022 Tenn. Pub. Acts Ch. No. 978, S.B. No. 2363, Sub. H.B. No. 2461.
[695] 2022 Va. Acts Ch. 760, H. 585.
[696] 2022 Va. Acts Ch. 156, H. 197.
[697] 2022 Wyo. Sess. Laws Ch. No. 56, S.F. 32.
[698] 2022 Cal. Stat. Ch. 907, A.B. No. 1868.
[699] 2022 Cal. Stat. Ch. 901, A.B. No. 22.
[700] 2022 Colo. Sess. Laws HB 22-1265.
[701] 2022 Mo. Laws SB 681 & 662; § 162.084.

changed reporting requirements for the statewide workforce and education reporting system to require an electronic report every December first.[702] Oregon required the state board of education to suspend any reporting requirements that are not required by federal law and those that are not essential, as determined by the board.[703] Tennessee required a local education agency (LEA) or the state department of education to provide testing materials or proposed testing materials in the LEAs or state department's possession to a member of the general assembly upon the member's request to inspect and review the material.[704] Utah reduced reporting requirements for LEAs with respect to a literacy proficiency plan and for a grant program for digital teaching and learning.[705]

Three states passed bills regarding data management. Maryland required the Montgomery County Board of Education to adopt a data disaggregation policy that applies to any data collection, reports, or internal documents and includes a category for each racial and ethnic group that constitutes at least 5% of the student population.[706] Utah moved back one year, to 2024, a requirement for LEAs to implement a school information management system.[707] Vermont paused the implementation of the shared school district data management system until January 1, 2022.[708]

Four states addressed their school report cards. Alabama exempted academic performance of designated English language learner (ELL) students from the state report card. However, beginning the 2021-2022 school year, a student not showing proficiency on ACCESS for ELL or other state-approved English proficiency measures may not be considered in assigning an academic achievement grade to a school or system for the first five years of enrollment.[709] Georgia added to the definition of a charter school to include a requirement that the school is subject to a report card prepared and distributed by the office of student achievement, and it removed a provision reducing the funding for a charter school that deploys virtual instruction.[710] Tennessee allowed the results from TCAP tests administered to students in the 2020-2021 school year to be used in the Tennessee Value-Added Assessment System (TVAAS) and to set annual measurable objectives for schools and

---

[702] 2022 Neb. Laws LB 1130.
[703] 2022 Or. Laws Ch. 116 § 13, HB 4030.
[704] 2022 Tenn. Pub. Acts Ch. No. 1032, S.B. No. 2299, Sub. H.B. No. 2312.
[705] 2022 Utah Laws H.B. 481.
[706] 2022 Md. Laws Ch. 589, HB 812.
[707] 2022 Utah Laws S.B. 79.
[708] 2022 Vt. Laws Act 66, S. 115, § 16. Note that this act was signed in 2021, but cited as a 2022 act.
[709] 2022 Ala. Acts 374, S.170.
[710] 2022 Ga. Laws Act 769, HB 1215.

LEAs for the 2021-2022 school year. TVAAS data may also be used to assign letter grades to schools in the accountability program.[711] Wisconsin required the department of public instruction to include data from a juvenile detention facility or secured residential care center in the school report card.[712]

Four states addressed consequences for failing schools. Colorado permitted the designation of a public school as a community school if it fails to meet turnaround goals.[713] Rhode Island revised the procedures for state intervention and support for failing public schools, as well as chronically under-performing schools, based upon a 2020 action plan incorporating sixteen factors and updated by the commissioner of education.[714] Tennessee established a grading scale that must be used to assign letter grades to students enrolled in grades nine through twelve, for purposes of reporting student grades for postsecondary financial assistance.[715] Utah amended the school turnaround program, by requiring the state board of education to identify the lowest-performing non-Title I schools and to provide targeted support and improvement activities for at least six schools each year.[716]

Other accountability-related acts are described as follows. Alabama adopted the Alabama Numeracy Act, which required proficiency in math by the fifth grade.[717] Maine approved a major substantive rule change of the state department of education regarding parameters for essential instruction.[718] Maine also amended a provision regarding public school restructuring, referring to "innovation" instead of "restructuring."[719]

Athletics

This section describes acts adopted last year regarding athletics. A leading concern was transgender girls participating in girls' sports, with eight states passing nine acts on the topic.

Indiana required any athletic team or sport organized, sanctioned, or sponsored by a school corporation or public school to be expressly designated as one of the following: a male, men's, or boys' team; a female, women's, or girls' team; or a coeducational or

---

[711] 2022 Tenn. Pub. Acts Ch. No. 782, S.B. No. 2321, Sub. H.B. No. 2138.
[712] 2021 Wis. Act 212, 2021 S.B. 235.
[713] 2022 Colo. Sess. Laws SB 54.
[714] 2022 R.I. Laws H. 8094.
[715] 2022 Tenn. Pub. Acts Ch. No. 1080, S.B. No. 388, Sub. H.B. No. 324.
[716] 2022 Utah Laws S.B. 245.
[717] 2022 Ala. Act 249, S.171.
[718] 2022 Me. Acts Ch. 140, H.P. 1441, L.D. 1932.
[719] 2022 Me. Acts Ch. 571, H.P. 1366, L.D. 1845.

mixed team sport. Based upon biological sex at birth, a male may not participate on a sport or team designated as a female, women's, or girl's sport or team. The governor vetoed the bill, but the veto was overridden.[720] In an act generally-identical to Indiana's, Iowa declared transgender females to be ineligible for girls' sports.[721] Kentucky required state activity associations to identify sports as girls', coed, or boys' sports, and prohibited students whose biological sex, based upon a birth certificate and an affidavit by a medical professional, is male from participating in girls' sports in grades six through twelve.[722]

Oklahoma prohibited athletic teams designated for "females," "women," or "girls" to be open to students of the male sex, based upon the biological sex at birth.[723] South Carolina required the designation of gender-based or coeducational teams for public secondary and postsecondary school sports teams and allowed sports teams designated for males to be open to female student participants, but it directed that teams designated for females may not be open to male participants, with gender determined by biological gender statements on an official birth certificate. The act was entitled the "Save Women's Sports Act."[724] South Dakota required teams and sports at the college and scholastic levels, as well as associations governing teams and sports, to designate the activities based upon the biological sex at birth of participating students. Only female students may participate in any team, sport, or athletic event designated as being for females, women, or girls. Failure to comply with this provision is a limited waiver of sovereign immunity for relief authorized in an added section, which provides students a private cause of action for relief against the school, college, or association.[725] Tennessee required the commissioner of education to withhold a portion of state education finance funds for an otherwise-eligible LEA if the LEA fails or refuses to determine a student's gender for participation in sports. The act specifies that the provision does not apply if the LEA is complying with a court order.[726] Utah required schools and LEAs to designate athletic activities by sex, as defined by birth certificate, and prohibited a male student from participating on a team designated for female students.[727] Utah also provided for defense and indemnification

---

[720] 2022 Ind. Acts Pub. Law 177, HB 1041.
[721] 2022 Iowa Acts HF 2416.
[722] 2022 Ky. Acts Ch. 198, SB 83.
[723] 2022 Okla. Sess. Laws SB 2.
[724] 2022 S.C. Acts 193, H. 4608.
[725] 2022 S.D. Laws S.B. 46.
[726] 2022 Tenn. Pub. Acts Ch. No. 909, H.B. No. 1895, Sub. S.B. No. 1861.
[727] 2022 Utah Laws H.B. 11.

regarding actions challenging decisions regarding participation of students in sports designated for female students.[728]

Three states legislated to allow student athletes to receive compensation for use of their name, image, or likeness (NIL). Illinois permitted student athletes to retain an agent for any matter or activity relating to compensation for the use of the name, image, likeness, or voice of the student athlete.[729] Kentucky provided protections for student athletes seeking compensation for their name, image, or likeness.[730] Oregon required the producer of an intercollegiate sports team jersey, video game, or trading card for profit to make a royalty payment to the student athlete for the use of the student athlete's name, image, or likeness.[731]

Three states articulated parental and student rights connected with decisions about wearing team athletic uniforms. Under the first law, also discussed in the section devoted to Parental and Student Rights, Maryland required the state athletic association, county school boards, and boards of community college trustees to allow student athletes to modify an athletic or team uniform to make the attire more modest to conform to the requirements or preferences of the student athlete's religion or culture, or the student's own preferences for modesty.[732] Ohio prohibited any public or nonpublic school, school district, interscholastic conference, or organization that regulates interscholastic athletics to adopt a rule, bylaw, or other regulation that prohibits or creates any obstruction to wearing religious apparel when competing or participating in interscholastic athletics or extracurricular activities. The act provided an exception if a legitimate danger to participants is identified due to wearing the religious apparel. The act defines "wearing religious apparel" as the wearing of headwear, clothing, jewelry, or other coverings while observing a sincerely held religious belief.[733] Under another law that is also discussed in the Parental and Student Rights section, Utah encouraged public and private schools supporting athletic teams and activities to revise internal policies and allow all children and youth participating in athletic activities to wear religious clothing or headwear or to modify their uniforms to accommodate religious beliefs and personal values of modesty.[734]

---

[728] 2022 Utah Laws H.B. 3001 (Spec. Sess.).
[729] 2022 Ill. Laws Pub. Act 102-0892, HB 1175.
[730] 2022 Ky. Acts Ch. 12, SB 6.
[731] 2022 Or. Laws Ch. 20, SB 1505.
[732] 2022 Md. Laws Ch 556, HB 515. 2022 Md. Laws Ch. 557, SB 951.
[733] 2022 Ohio Laws S.B. No. 181.
[734] 2022 Utah Laws H.C.R. 16. Note that Utah deployed a concurrent resolution to encourage recognition of this right.

Two other athletics-related acts were adopted as follows. Pennsylvania required school districts to adopt a policy to permit a home-schooled student to participate, on the same basis as other students enrolled in the school district, in any cocurricular activity that merges extracurricular activities with a required academic course, including, but not limited to, band or orchestra. The provision also required the policy to permit a home-schooled student to participate in academic courses equaling up to at least one-quarter of the school day for full-time students.[735] South Dakota adjusted the general state aid formula to support students attending public schools while in the care and custody of the social services department, corrections, or other state agencies to participate in interscholastic athletics.[736]

Attendance, Promotion, and Graduation

Legislation about attendance, promotion, and graduation includes such topics as compulsory attendance and truancy, school calendars, school schedules, enrollment, progress through the grades, graduation requirements, and diplomas. This section describes bills enacted in 2022 regarding those topics.

Ten states enrolled twelve acts regarding enrollment and admission for students who are not connected to the military. California limited the eligibility for admission to the state summer school for mathematics and science to students from California schools.[737] Colorado allowed enrollment preference plans for charter schools for children with disabilities.[738] Colorado also provided in-state residence for students who attended a high school in Colorado for at least one year prior to graduation.[739] Iowa abandoned a March first deadline for parents to seek open enrollment for their child in the next school year; instead, the parent can seek enrollment in another school setting at any time, if the receiving school consents.[740] Louisiana added, as a prerequisite to enrollment in the first grade of a public school, that a child must have attended a full-day public or nonpublic kindergarten for a full school year before the 2022-2023 school year.[741]

---

[735] 2022 Pa. Laws Act No. 55, HB 1642, Section 13.
[736] 2022 S.D. Laws H.B. 1119.
[737] 2022 Cal. Stat. Ch. 334, S.B. No. 1299.
[738] 2022 Colo. Sess. Laws HB 1294.
[739] 2022 Colo. Sess. Laws HB 1155.
[740] 2022 Iowa Acts HF 2518.
[741] 2022 La. Acts No. 414, SB No. 177.

New Hampshire amended provisions for dual and concurrent enrollment for career and technical education center students to authorize access to non-residential, nonpublic schools which opt to participate.[742] Tennessee added a provision that, if the parent of a school-age child is employed by an LEA outside the LEA of the parent's residence, then the employee's child may attend a school within the LEA that employs the nonresident parent, subject to that LEA's tuition requirements.[743] Utah allowed charter schools to give enrollment preferences to siblings of students already enrolled, foster children living with students already enrolled, and students who withdrew from a charter school to enroll in an online school or home school during the COVID-19 pandemic.[744] Utah also moved the early enrollment period for nonresident students to begin two weeks earlier, on December first.[745]

Vermont required the agency of education to issue a written report for legislative committees on education regarding the impact of standardizing the entrance age threshold for public school kindergarten attendance.[746] Virginia required each local school board that jointly manages and controls a regional academic year Governor's school to ensure that each public middle school that is eligible to send students to attend a Governor's school offers coursework, curriculum, and instruction that is comparable in content and rigor to provide each student in a middle school with the opportunity to gain admission and excel academically at a Governor's school.[747] West Virginia delayed deadlines for executing contracts, student enrollment applications, lottery preferences, and enrollment for charter schools for the school year beginning July 1, 2022, only.[748]

Three states adopted acts concerning enrollment for students connected to the military. Alabama permitted children of military families residing out of state to enroll immediately upon receiving orders to relocate to the state and provided the same opportunity for school assignment, course selection, and athletic participation as other resident students.[749] Alaska provided school district residency for students whose parents or guardian are on active duty in the armed forces or a member of the National Guard.[750] North Carolina

---

[742] 2022 N.H. Laws Ch. 240, SB 421.
[743] 2022 Tenn. Pub. Acts Ch. No. 709, S.B. No. 2314, Sub. H.B. No. 2086.
[744] 2022 Utah Laws H.B. 294.
[745] 2022 Utah Laws H.B. 380.
[746] 2022 Vt. Laws Act 166, S. 283, § 5.
[747] 2022 Va. Acts Ch. 485, H. 127.
[748] 2022 W. Va. Acts Ch. 101, H.B. 4019.
[749] 2022 Ala. Acts 90, S.116.
[750] 2022 Alaska Sess. Laws 6/16 Ch. 7 SLA 22, H.B. 53.

provided the same enrollment transfer protections that children of non-military families receive for children of members of the National Guard or Reserve not in active-duty status but forced to move to perform military service.[751]

Three states adopted the Purple Star Schools Program, which provides a more comprehensive support structure for military-connected students beyond enrollment prior to residency. Maryland established the Purple Star Schools Program to recognize public schools that provide strong services and support for military-connected students and their families.[752] New Jersey adopted the Purple Star Schools Program in the department of education to recognize schools which emphasize the importance of assisting children of military families.[753] Pennsylvania also adopted the Purple Star Schools Program.[754]

Nine states added twelve provisions articulating excused absences under compulsory attendance law. California added an excused absence for middle school and high school students to participate in a civic or political event as long as that permission is obtained ahead of the absence.[755] Georgia provided an excused absence for students participating in 4-H sponsored activities or programs.[756] Illinois amended its compulsory attendance law to permit school absences for a civic event, and inserted the adjective "reasonable" in a requirement for advance notice of absence.[757]

Kentucky required each local school district's attendance policy to provide an exemption for absences due to a student's mental or behavioral health status.[758] Kentucky also directed that a public-school student shall not have his or her perfect attendance record negated by participating in a page program with the General Assembly, and students applying for an excused absence for attendance at the state fair must be granted one day of excused absence.[759] In a third act, Kentucky waived fifteen student attendance days for school district closures due to a tornado disaster in western Kentucky.[760] Finally, Kentucky provided up to ten days of remote instruction per school for school districts to use at the

---

[751] 2022 N.C. Sess. Laws Ch. 71, H.B. 159.
[752] 2022 Md. Laws Ch. 65, HB 277; 2022 Md. Laws Ch. 66, SB 234.
[753] 2022 N.J. Laws 2022, P.L. c. 108, A. 3694.
[754] 2022 Pa. Laws Act No. 69, HB 1867.
[755] 2022 Cal. Stat. Ch. 921, S.B. No. 955.
[756] 2022 Ga. Laws Act 772, HB 1292.
[757] 2022 Ill. Laws Pub. Act 102- 0981, HB 5488.huiuhuiuhui
[758] 2022 Ky. Acts Ch. 228, HB 44.
[759] 2022 Ky. Acts Ch. 168, HB 517.
[760] 2022 Ky. Acts Ch. 65, HB 397.

school, classroom, grade, or group level for the 2021-2022 school year.[761] Louisiana amended home study provisions to specify that public school systems are not responsible for collecting and maintaining school attendance data for children enrolled in an approved home study program until the child is enrolled in a public school.[762] Maryland directed the state department of education and each county school board to adopt an attendance policy for public school students that treats an absence due to a student's behavioral health needs the same as an absence due to illness of another nature.[763] Virginia provided any student who is a member of a state- or federally-recognized tribal nation headquartered in the commonwealth and who is absent from school to attend the tribal nation's pow wow gathering must be granted one excused day of absence each academic year.[764] Washington provided excused absences from school for mental health reasons, including for illness, health condition, or medical appointment.[765] West Virginia exempted from compulsory school attendance a child who participates in a learning pod or micro school.[766]

Three states withdrew an excused absence provision or required more truancy monitoring. Rhode Island directed that public schools are responsible for attendance data monitoring and detection of emerging truant behavior.[767] Virginia required that students missing a partial or full day of school while participating in a 4-H educational program or activity must be counted absent for purposes of calculating average daily membership, but the student must receive course credit in the same manner as for a school field trip.[768] Wyoming increased compulsory attendance enforcement by providing that a child subject to willful absenteeism is neglected under child protection law.[769]

Three states adopted school-calendar related requirements, while two more required observation of Juneteenth in the calendar. Louisiana decreed that all public-school governing authorities may determine their school-year calendars without state board or state department intervention or approval.[770] Tennessee permitted LEAs

---

[761] 2022 Ky. Acts Ch. 4, SB 25.
[762] 2022 La. Acts No. 677, SB No. 124.
[763] 2022 Md. Laws Ch. 554, HB 118.
[764] 2022 Va. Acts Ch. 233, H. 1022.
[765] 2022 Wash. Laws Ch. 31, H.B. 1834.
[766] 2022 W. Va. Acts Ch. 96, S.B. 268.
[767] 2022 R.I. Laws H. 8348, S. 2281.
[768] 2022 Va. Acts Ch. 58, H. 246; 2022 Va. Acts Ch. 59, S. 596.
[769] 2022 Wyo. Sess. Laws Ch. No. 4, S.F. 31.
[770] 2022 La. Acts No. 323, HB No. 244.

to provide up to two days each semester of the required 180 days of classroom instruction through remote instruction due to weather, outbreaks of illness, or end-of-course assessments.[771] Vermont required the agency of education to issue a written report for legislative committees on education regarding a proposed statewide uniform school calendar, particularly with respect to its impact on attendance at regional career and technical education centers.[772] Maryland established Juneteenth National Independence Day as a state legal holiday and state employee holiday.[773] Washington clarified the state legal holidays which are also school holidays, particularly to identify Juneteenth as both.[774]

Two states passed three acts about promotion or retention. Alabama prohibited retaining a third-grade student more than once, but allowed English language learner (ELL) students a good cause exemption with less than three years of ELL instruction.[775] Also, Alabama delayed the Alabama Literacy Act's third grade retention provision for two years, beginning with the 2023-24 school year; at that point third grade students must demonstrate sufficient reading skills for promotion to fourth grade.[776] Missouri deleted a former section about reading instruction and adopted a new section requiring assessment of deficiencies in reading, and then required a discussion between parents and school staff about whether a student with a significant deficiency in reading should be retained at the third grade.[777]

Thirteen states added fifteen graduation-related acts, with some changing graduation requirements, some addressing the timeline for graduation, and some adding recognitions to be affixed to the diploma. Alabama created a state seal of biliteracy to recognize students showing proficiency in two languages. One of the two languages may be American Sign Language.[778] Arizona required youth committed to the juvenile justice system who have not graduated or received a GED to be able to test for the GED or a practice test before release.[779] California allowed a pupil who has transferred into a high school to be allowed a fifth year of high school in order to graduate.[780] Illinois harmonized conflicting provisions

---

[771] 2022 Tenn. Pub. Acts Ch. No. 897, S.B. No. 1887, Sub. H.B. No. 1912.
[772] 2022 Vt. Laws Act 166, S. 283, § 6.
[773] 2022 Md. Laws Ch. 64, HB 227.
[774] 2022 Wash. Laws Ch. 198, H.B. 1617.
[775] 2022 Ala. Acts 392, H.220.
[776] 2022 Ala. Acts 391, S.200.
[777] 2022 Mo. Laws SB 681 & 662; § 167.645.
[778] 2022 Ala. Acts 200, H.46.
[779] 2022 Ariz. Sess. Laws Ch. 363, S.B. 1682.
[780] 2022 Cal. Stat. Ch. 918, S.B. No. 532.

about prerequisites for receiving a high school diploma from three previously-passed acts.[781]

Kentucky allowed students enrolled in a district-operated alternative education program to be eligible for a high school equivalency diploma.[782] Kentucky also deleted the end-of-course examination and ACT benchmark requirements for early high school graduation programs.[783] Louisiana required geometry as a course for high school students in the career major program.[784] Michigan added a provision to the statutory requirements for high school graduation to specify that the requirements do not prohibit a student from exceeding the credit requirements for the merit standard through advanced studies such as accelerated course placement, advanced placement, dual enrollment in a postsecondary institution, or participation in an international baccalaureate program.[785]

Missouri directed the department of elementary and secondary education to establish the Show-Me Success Diploma Program as an alternative pathway to graduation for high school students that may be earned at any point between the end of a student's tenth grade year and the conclusion of the student's twelfth grade year. The program permits a student to continue after the time for completing twelfth grade has passed.[786] Missouri established a workforce diploma program within the department of elementary and secondary education to assist students with obtaining a high school diploma and developing employability and career technical skills. The act detailed eleven pages of direction in establishing and operating the program.[787] Oklahoma permitted the state board of education to develop rules to determine if courses on aviation are eligible for non-elective academic credit toward meeting graduation requirements.[788]

Rhode Island required all high school seniors to complete the Free Application for Federal Student Aid (FAFSA) or the equivalent state-level application offered through the Community College of Rhode Island in order to graduate high school.[789] Tennessee directed that, until July 1, 2023, high school students who complete an early high school graduation program be counted as enrolled in the LEA from which the student graduated for the remainder of the school

---

[781] 2022 Ill. Laws Pub. Act 102-0864, SB 3902.
[782] 2022 Ky. Acts Ch. 78, HB 194.
[783] 2022 Ky. Acts Ch. 54, SB 61.
[784] 2022 La. Acts No. 447, HB No. 207.
[785] 2022 Mich. Pub. Acts 105, HB 5190.
[786] 2022 Mo. Laws SB 681 & 662; § 160.560.
[787] 2022 Mo. Laws SB 681 & 662; § 173.831.
[788] 2022 Okla. Sess. Laws SB 1147.
[789] 2022 R.I. Laws S. 3015, H. 7974.

year.[790] Under a law also discussed in the Parental and Student Rights Washington permitted a school district, at the request of the parent, guardian, or custodian, to issue a posthumous high school diploma for a deceased student.[791] Wyoming created seals of biliteracy and authorized conferral of the seals by school districts as part of high school graduation records.[792]

Two states spoke about transcripts and proof of graduation. Pennsylvania amended the section guiding keystone examinations and graduation requirements to provide a definition for an "industry-recognized credential" and require that an industry-recognized credential attained by a student must be included on the student's transcript no later than the beginning of the 2022-2023 school year.[793] Utah required the state board of education to create a repository for immigrant students' and foreign exchange students' transcripts and amended requirements regarding situations when a students' birth certificate is not available or does not accurately reflect the student's age.[794]

Other attendance, promotion, and graduation-related acts passed in 2022 are described as follows. Hawaii changed the definition of "private schools" in its compulsory attendance law to require unlicensed but accredited private schools to annually submit health and safety documentation to the council of private schools or the various religious-oriented private school associations.[795] Tennessee included students who fulfill the requirements for the work ethic distinction program to also receive recognition as a Tri-Star scholar.[796] West Virginia required the state board of education to establish, develop, and maintain a program whereby students can earn elective course credit for extended learning opportunities that take place outside of the traditional classroom setting.[797]

Buildings and Grounds

This section details buildings and grounds-related legislation passed in 2022. The largest grouping of acts in this section involved planning, property conveyance, and environmental concerns regarding water and air quality. These acts are described as follows.

---

[790] 2022 Tenn. Pub. Acts Ch. No. 943, H.B. No. 2300, Sub. S.B. No. 2328.
[791] 2022 Wash. Laws Ch. 224, S.B. 5498.
[792] 2022 Wyo. Sess. Laws Ch. No. 100, S.F. 78.
[793] 2022 Pa. Laws Act No. 55, HB 1642, Sec. 1.
[794] 2022 Utah Laws H.B. 230.
[795] 2022 Haw. Sess. Laws Act 61, HB 2248.
[796] 2022 Tenn. Pub. Acts Ch. No. 702, S.B. No. 1776, Sub. H.B. No. 1840.
[797] 2022 W. Va. Acts Ch. 4, S.B. 2009 (2nd Spec. Session).

Five states enacted six bills about planning. Delaware created an evaluation and assessment system within the state department of education to determine whether school facilities are in satisfactory condition for use.[798] Illinois amended the public-school code for Chicago to require the department of school demographics and planning to evaluate enrollment patterns in existing schools at least once every five years.[799] Maryland required county boards of education seeking state funds for the construction of a new school to file a pedestrian safety plan in high-density counties.[800] Maryland also extended through fiscal year 2028 the requirement that the governor include an amount in the state budget for increasing the number of green schools in the state.[801] Vermont began the development of a statewide school construction program with a needs assessment and direction to create a ranking system for priorities for school construction. The opening paragraphs of the act acknowledged that Vermont is the only northeast state without a statutory school building program.[802] Virginia required the department of education to develop or adopt and maintain a data collection tool to assist school boards to determine the relative age of each public-school building in the local school division and the amount of maintenance reserve funds necessary to restore each building.[803]

Six states added acts regarding property conveyance or making property available for use. California set conditions to allow a housing development project on real property owned by a local education agency.[804] Connecticut conveyed state land to the town of Cheshire for a school bus depot.[805] Massachusetts authorized the division of capital asset management and maintenance to convey a parcel of land to the school department in the city of Westfield.[806] Mississippi authorized the Meridian Public School District to transfer property to the Meridian Housing Authority.[807] Rhode Island provided for the repurposing of vacant and unused school and other municipal buildings for affordable housing projects.[808]

---

[798] 2022 Del. Laws SB 270.
[799] 2022 Ill. Laws Pub. Act 102-0777, HB 4580.
[800] 2022 Md. Laws Ch. 553, HB 19.
[801] 2022 Md. Laws Ch. 524, SB 383.
[802] 2022 Vt. Laws Act 72, H. 426.
[803] 2022 Va. Acts Ch. 8, H. 563; 2022 Va. Acts Ch. 9, S. 473 (1st Spec. Session).
[804] 2022 Cal. Stat. Ch. 652, A.B. No. 2295.
[805] 2022 Conn. Acts 22-19, S.B. No. 490.
[806] 2022 Mass Acts Ch. 249, H. 5156.
[807] 2022 Miss. Laws S.B. No. 3211.
[808] 2022 R.I. Laws S. 3048, H. 7943.

Tennessee adopted conditions for the transfer of surplus personal property to a local government entity such as a public school.[809]

Three states passed four acts separate from appropriations bills for funding school buildings. Mississippi created a revolving fund for improving educational facilities.[810] New Mexico permitted the state finance authority to receive and review applications for charter school facility loans.[811] Also, New Mexico adjusted the amounts to be used in calculating state distributions to school districts that impose a public-school capital improvements tax and to charter schools within those school districts.[812] Virginia created a school construction fund and program.[813]

Six states created seven acts regarding water quality. California required the incorporation of water bottle filling stations in new construction or modernization projects for public schools.[814] California also required school districts, county offices of education, and charter schools seeking funding for school modernization for school facilities constructed before 2012 to include faucet aerators and water-conserving plumbing fixtures in all bathrooms.[815] Missouri passed the Get the Lead Out of School Drinking Water Act, which remediated water contamination and provides potable water for schools.[816]

New Hampshire required the installation of touchless water bottle filling stations in public schools.[817] New York allowed the commissioner of education to grant a waiver from the testing requirements for potable water for certain school buildings if the school district has substantially completed the testing requirements and has been found to be below lead levels required by regulation.[818] Utah required testing water for lead at schools and child care centers.[819] West Virginia required newly constructed public schools, as well as public schools undergoing major improvements, to have water bottle filling stations.[820]

Three states addressed air quality in school buildings. California required school districts, county offices of education, charter schools, and private schools to ensure that facilities have heating,

---

[809] 2022 Tenn. Pub. Acts Ch. No. 713, S.B. No. 2420, Sub. H.B. No. 2170. See, TENN. CODE ANN. § 12-2-407 for the applicable conditions.
[810] 2022 Miss. Laws S.B. No. 2430.
[811] 2022 N.M. Laws Ch. 19, HB 43.
[812] 2022 N.M. Laws Ch. 22, HB 119.
[813] 2022 Va. Acts Ch. 8, H. 563; 2022 Va. Acts Ch. 9, S. 473 (1st Spec. Session).
[814] 2022 Cal. Stat. Ch. 793, A.B. No. 2638.
[815] 2022 Cal. Stat. Ch. 434, A.B. No. 1867.
[816] 2022 Mo. Laws SB 681 & 662; § 160.077.
[817] 2022 N.H. Laws Ch. 149, SB 233.
[818] 2022 N.Y. Laws Ch. 130, S. 7840.
[819] 2022 Utah Laws H.B. 21.
[820] 2022 W. Va. Acts Ch. 199, S.B. 427.

ventilation, and air conditioning systems that meet minimum ventilation rate requirements.[821] Iowa required radon testing and mitigation in public schools.[822] Oregon made public education providers and federally-recognized tribes eligible for grants related to cleaner air spaces and smoke filtration systems.[823]

Maryland adopted two provisions regarding waste disposal. First, Maryland required the interagency commission on school construction to adopt regulations for county boards of education to include waste disposal infrastructure in design documents.[824] Second, Maryland created a grant program to reduce and compost school waste, with grant awards going to public schools and county boards of education.[825]

Other buildings and grounds-related 2022 acts are described as follows. Alabama increased the threshold amount for projects not subject to approval by the division of construction management, from $500,000 to $750,000, including HVAC and roofing, Americans with Disabilities Act, and fire and safety issues.[826] Illinois amended the counties code to provide that 1% of the school facility occupation taxes collected shall be distribute to the regional superintendent of schools.[827] Maine allowed a school administrative district to lease a former administrative building for a term of not more than twenty years.[828]

Curricular Requirements

This section describes curricular requirements added or changed in the last legislative year, with many of them representing politically-charged beliefs about what happens in classrooms and what it means to be a patriot or good citizen.

Five states introduced prohibitions against the discussion of certain topics in the classroom. Alabama prohibited classroom discussion and instruction on sexual orientation or gender identity in grades K through five.[829] Under a law also presented in the section entitled Parental and Student Rights, Arizona prohibited teaching with the use of sexually-explicit instructional materials without serious educational value; without serious literary, artistic, political,

---

[821] 2022 Cal. Stat. Ch. 777, A.B. No. 2232.
[822] 2022 Iowa Acts HF 2412.
[823] 2022 Or. Laws Ch. 85, SB 1533.
[824] 2022 Md. Laws Ch. 550, HB 566.
[825] 2022 Md. Laws Ch. 205, SB 124.
[826] 2022 Ala. Acts 367, H.419.
[827] 2022 Ill. Laws Pub. Act 102-1062, HB 4326.
[828] 2022 Me. Acts Ch. 23, H.P. 1475, L.D. 1989.
[829] 2022 Ala. Acts 290, H.322.

or scientific value, which describe an explicit list of prohibited sexually-explicit acts; or without parental consent. Students without parental consent must be provided an alternative assignment.[830] Florida added provisions to reinforce the right of parents to control the upbringing of their children, including, for example, a prohibition against discussing sexual orientation in grades K through third. The act also directed the appointment of a special magistrate to bring action against a school district violating the provisions of this act.[831] Georgia passed the Protect Students First Act, which prohibited teaching divisive concepts related to race, including the idea that the United States is fundamentally racist.[832] Utah prohibited sensitive material in public schools, with "sensitive material" defined as an instructional material that is pornographic or indecent material as defined in Utah Code § 76-10-1235.[833]

Seven states addressed enhancement of instruction about the Holocaust. Missouri amended a provision requiring education about the Holocaust, providing further direction about what must be included in the instruction.[834] Nebraska required the state board of education to adopt standards for education on the Holocaust and other acts of genocide.[835] New Hampshire amended the statutory definition of an adequate education, by adding the topics of civics, government, economics, geography, history, and Holocaust and genocide education to the social studies curriculum; wellness to the health education curriculum; music and visual arts to the arts education curriculum; and personal finance literacy to the list.[836] New York authorized the commissioner to conduct a survey regarding instruction on the Holocaust within the state and provide a report to the general assembly.[837] Oklahoma required the state department of education to develop and make available resources related to Holocaust education, and required Holocaust education to be taught to students in grades six through twelve in public schools.[838] Tennessee required a state governmental entity or LEA receiving a complaint alleging that antisemitism has occurred on the premises of a public school serving any grades kindergarten through grade twelve, or through electronic outreach from a public school, to

---

[830] 2022 Ariz. Sess. Laws Ch. 380, H.B. 2495.
[831] 2022 Fla. Laws Ch. 2022-22, HB 1557.
[832] 2022 Ga. Laws Act 719, HB 1084.
[833] 2022 Utah Laws H.B. 374.
[834] 2022 Mo. Laws SB 681 & 662; § 161.700.
[835] 2022 Neb. Laws LB 888.
[836] 2022 N.H. Laws Ch. 273, HB 1671.
[837] 2022 N.Y. Laws Ch. 490, A. 472.
[838] 2022 Okla. Sess. Laws SB 1671.

take into consideration the working definition of antisemitism adopted by the International Holocaust Remembrance Alliance (IHRA) in determining whether the alleged act was motivated by antisemitic intent.[839] Vermont required the agency of education to issue a written report to legislative committees on education regarding the status of Holocaust education in the public schools, as well as recommendations to ensure that Holocaust education is included in the educational programs.[840]

Six states inserted requirements on the teaching of civics, capitalism, or both. Arizona required the social studies curriculum in civics to have a comparative discussion of political ideologies, e.g., communism and totalitarianism, that conflict with principles of freedom and democracy that are essential to the founding principles of the U.S. and civic education standards.[841] Georgia created a commission on civics education to promote and enhance the education of students on the importance of civic involvement in a constitutional republic.[842] Indiana permitted historical and educational documents to be displayed on state property, despite their religious nature.[843] Michigan encouraged the addition of a program of instruction in free enterprise and entrepreneurship in school districts and public-school academies.[844] Tennessee required high school students to be taught about the virtues of capitalism and the constitutional republic form of government in the United States and Tennessee, as compared to other political and economic systems, such as communism and socialism.[845] Utah created a pilot grant program to support LEAs in implementing innovative approaches to civics education.[846]

Three states promoted the adoption of pledges or mottos, and three more states required observance of September 11. Georgia added the principle of "Courage" to its pledge of allegiance to the state flag, so that it now reads "I pledge allegiance to the Georgia Flag and to the principles for which it stands: Wisdom, Justice, Moderation, and Courage."[847] Michigan required the text of section 1 of article VIII of the state constitution (1963) and section 10, as added by 1995 Michigan Public Act 289, to be prominently posted and maintained in school board meeting rooms and in the office of

---

[839] 2022 Tenn. Pub. Acts Ch. No. 1075, H.B. No. 2673, Sub. S.B. No. 2864, § 1.
[840] 2022 Vt. Laws Act 175, H. 716, § 2.
[841] 2022 Ariz. Sess. Laws Ch. 303, H.B. 2008.
[842] 2022 Ga. Laws Act 723, SB 220.
[843] 2022 Ind. Acts Pub. Law 39, SB 11.
[844] 2022 Mich. Pub. Acts 54, HB 4074.
[845] 2022 Tenn. Pub. Acts Ch. No. 959, H.B. No. 2742, Sub. S.B. No. 2728.
[846] 2022 Utah Laws H.B. 273.
[847] 2022 Ga. Laws Act 788, SB 152.

superintendents and principals. That section reads: "Religion, morality and knowledge being important to good government and the happiness of mankind, schools and the means of education shall forever be encouraged."[848] South Carolina authorized the state board of education to make rules and regulations requiring the display of the official mottos of the United States of American and South Carolina.[849]

Arizona required September 11 to be recognized in the curriculum as 9/11 education day, which must be observed on a preceding or following day if it does not fall on a school day.[850] Wisconsin added September 11 to the list of special observance days applying to general school operations.[851] Louisiana required each public school to observe Celebrate Freedom Week each September, in conjunction with Constitution Day and Constitution Week.[852]

Tennessee added two acts regarding teaching about the civil rights movement in social studies. Tennessee required that students in grades five through eight receive a curriculum regarding black history and culture.[853] Additionally, Tennessee urged the standards recommendation committee to include events of the Civil Rights Movement during the time period of 1954 to 1968 in the final recommendation of academic standards in social students in grades nine through twelve.[854]

Three states adopted legislation regarding textbooks. Alabama required the state board of education and state superintendent to establish review criteria for textbooks keyed to standards, with publishers to provide evidence on forms provided by the state department of education.[855] Louisiana prohibited public schools from using textbooks or instructional materials that employ the three-cueing system model of reading, visual memory as the primary basis for teaching word recognition, or the three-cueing system model of reading based on meaning, structure and syntax, and visual, which is also known as "MSV," in reading instruction.[856] Tennessee required all math, science, and social studies textbooks and instructional materials to be aligned with state academic standards

---

[848] 2022 Mich. Pub. Acts 213, HB 5703.
[849] 2022 S.C. Acts 177, S. 969.
[850] 2022 Ariz. Sess. Laws Ch. 244, H.B. 2325.
[851] 2021 Wis. Act 213, 2021 S.B. 398.
[852] 2022 La. Acts No. 370, HB No. 88.
[853] 2022 Tenn. Pub. Acts Ch. No. 938, H.B. No. 2106, Sub. S.B. No. 2501.
[854] 2022 Tenn. Pub. Acts Ch. No. 1063, H.B. No. 2291, Sub. S.B. No. 2508.
[855] 2022 Ala. Acts 80, S.15.
[856] 2022 La. Acts No. 517, HB No. 865.

and prohibited the state board of education from granting waivers for this requirement.[857]

Six states enacted eight bills about online instruction. Missouri required that synchronous instruction connecting students to a live class conducted in a state adult high school must be treated the same as in-person instruction.[858] New Jersey directed the department of education to develop student learning standards in information literacy.[859] Pennsylvania enacted an educational online course initiative, which required the establishment over the next few years of a central clearinghouse for online courses to be used by students in various schools including home schools.[860]

Tennessee clarified that an adult high school may provide virtual instruction in accordance with the Virtual Public Schools Act.[861] Tennessee also allowed alternative schools and programs to provide remote instruction to students.[862] In a third act related to online learning, Tennessee directed LEAs to conduct remote learning drills.[863] Vermont directed the agency of education to issue a written report for legislative committees on education with recommendations for a statewide remote learning policy, with a focus on student attendance, school days, and cumulative instructional hours.[864] Wisconsin permitted service providers to administer the online early learning pilot program to school districts during the 2022-2023 school year, other than those originally designated in an earlier act.[865]

Four states adopted acts regarding computer science instruction. Louisiana added two units of computer science to the core curriculum for students to receive opportunity, performance, or honors awards in the Taylor scholarship program.[866] Missouri required all public high schools and charter high schools to offer at least one computer science course in an in-person setting or by a virtual option. The act also required collection of data about students taking computer science courses.[867] Nebraska required each school district to include computer science and technology education in the elementary and middle schools of the state, and added a one-semester course requirement of computer science and technology for

---

[857] 2022 Tenn. Pub. Acts Ch. No. 990, H.B. No. 2108, Sub. S.B. No. 2154.
[858] 2022 Mo. Laws SB 681 & 662; § 160.2700.
[859] 2022 N.J. Laws P.L. c. 138, S. 588.
[860] 2022 Pa. Laws Act No. 55, HB 1642, Section 29.
[861] 2022 Tenn. Pub. Acts Ch. No. 838, H.B. No. 2553, Sub. S.B. No. 2441.
[862] 2022 Tenn. Pub. Acts Ch. No. 960, H.B. No. 2760, Sub. S.B. No. 2590.
[863] 2022 Tenn. Pub. Acts Ch. No. 936, H.B. No. 1964, Sub. S.B. No. 2369.
[864] 2022 Vt. Laws Act 166, S. 283, § 7.
[865] 2021 Wis. Act 215, 2021 S.B. 838. The earlier act was 2019 Wis. Act 170.
[866] 2022 La. Acts No. 502, SB No. 191.
[867] 2022 Mo. Laws SB 681 & 662; § 170.018.

high school graduation.[868] West Virginia encouraged the addition of more computer science education in public schools.[869]

Three states added acts about reading instruction. Delaware required the state department of education to maintain and publish a list of evidence-based, reading instruction curricula for grades K through third.[870] Idaho adopted the content standards for English language arts and literacy, mathematics, and science prepared by a standards-review committee working in prior years.[871] Kentucky specified the state department of education's role in helping local school districts with respect to reading instruction, supports, and interventions.[872]

Three states added acts about driver education. Illinois allowed the national learning standards to be adapted to meet state licensing and educational requirements with respect to driver's education.[873] Tennessee required the office of research and education accountability to study providing driver's education in Title I public high schools.[874] Virginia required the state board of education to include an additional minimum 90-minute parent and student driver education component as part of the classroom portion of the driver education curriculum.[875]

Three states passed physical education-related acts. Georgia required each elementary school to schedule recess for all students in kindergarten and grades one through five every school day, except for days when a student has had physical education or a structured activity time.[876] New Hampshire repealed and reenacted a provision requiring that school boards provide instruction in physical education and wellness.[877] Virginia required that any physical education class offered to students in grades seven and eight must include at least one hour of personal safety training per school year in each grade level that is developed and delivered in partnership with the local law-enforcement agency.[878]

Two states adopted bills about their family life curriculum. Tennessee required each local education agency to develop and adopt a family life curriculum in compliance with standards adopted by the

---

[868] 2022 Neb. Laws LB 1112.
[869] 2022 W. Va. Acts Ch. 98, S.B. 529.
[870] 2022 Del. Laws SB 4.
[871] 2022 Idaho Sess. Laws Ch. 175, HB 716.
[872] 2022 Ky. Acts Ch. 40, SB 9.
[873] 2022 Ill. Laws Pub. Act 102-0951, HB 4716.
[874] 2022 Tenn. Pub. Acts Ch. No. 1090, S.B. No. 1508, Sub. H.B. No. 1325.
[875] 2022 Va. Acts Ch. 708, S. 78.
[876] 2022 Ga. Laws Act 841, HB 1283.
[877] 2022 N.H. Laws Ch. 112, HB 1263.
[878] 2022 Va. Acts Ch. 168, H. 1215.

state board of education.[879] Virginia required the family life curriculum offered in a high school to include prevention, recognition, and awareness of human trafficking of children.[880]

Two states enacted bills about cardiac arrest. Louisiana required instruction about cardiac health in high schools.[881] Wisconsin required distribution of information about sudden cardiac arrest during youth athletic activities.[882]

Two states promoted hunter safety in their curriculum. Colorado permitted schools to provide a hunter education course for seventh graders.[883] West Virginia permitted the division of natural resources to teacher hunter safety courses in schools.[884]

Other curriculum-related requirements are detailed as follows. Florida added requirements for financial literacy standards for receipt of a high school diploma,[885] and identified those requirements as "state academic standards."[886] Kentucky required that the superintendent, instead of the school council, determine the curriculum after consulting with the principal and school council and after a stakeholder response period.[887] Louisiana required instruction in water safety for public school students.[888] Louisiana also required instruction for high school students regarding information about adoption awareness, including the benefits of adoption to society, the types of adoption available, and resources available to support adoption.[889] In a third act, Louisiana required public schools to develop a mixed provider delivery model for prekindergarten instruction.[890] The final act from Louisiana directed the governing authority for each public high school to adopt policies regarding attendance, breastfeeding, and child care for students who are pregnant or parenting.[891]

Missouri required high school students to receive mental health awareness training.[892] Rhode Island required all public elementary and secondary schools to provide at least one unit of instruction on Asian American, Native Hawaiian, and Pacific Islander history and culture.[893] Virginia required public schools to provide instruction

---

[879] 2022 Tenn. Pub. Acts Ch. No. 1085, S.B. No. 918, Sub. H.B. No. 757, §§ 1 and 2.
[880] 2022 Va. Acts Ch. 459, H. 1023.
[881] 2022 La. Acts No. 385, HB No. 400.
[882] 2021 Wis. Act 210, 2021 A.B. 82.
[883] 2022 Colo. Sess. Laws HB 1168.
[884] 2022 W. Va. Acts Ch. 102, H.B. 4065.
[885] 2022 Fla. Laws Ch. 2022-17, SB 1054.
[886] 2022 Fla. Laws Ch. 2022-16, SB 1048.
[887] 2022 Ky. Acts Ch. 196, SB 1.
[888] 2022 La. Acts No. 722, HB No. 963.
[889] 2022 La. Acts No. 456, HB No. 274.
[890] 2022 La. Acts No. 532, SB No. 47.
[891] 2022 La. Acts No. 472, HB No. 516.
[892] 2022 Mo. Laws SB 681 & 662; § 170.048.4.(2).
[893] 2022 R.I. Laws S. 2910, H. 7272.

concerning gambling and its addictive potential.[894] Washington required school districts with more than 200 enrolled students to offer regular instruction in at least one visual art or at least one performing art throughout the school year.[895] Washington also established a statewide grant program and corresponding outdoor education experience program to foster universal outdoor education.[896] West Virginia required schools to provide self-harm and eating-disorder prevention instruction for teachers and students.[897]

Employment

This is the fifth year in a row in which the dominant legislative concern in the area of employment was in addressing an accelerating shortage of teachers. States attempted to decrease or waive certification requirements, offered higher placement on salary schedules, bonuses, housing, loan forgiveness, and other incentives for teachers to stay or relocate to new locations. More states last year allowed retired teachers to return to work without negatively impacting their retirement income.

Seventeen states approved thirty-two acts attempting to speed new teachers into placement by decreasing certification requirements, normalizing alternative certificates, and speeding approval of certificates bureaucratically. Alabama decreased the time to work under an alternative teaching certificate from three years to one year and allowed the issuance of a certificate for those in an approved alternative teacher education program.[898] Alabama also required the state board of education to issue a license or certificate to an eligible individual within 30 days of application.[899] The first of two laws from Alaska created a preliminary teacher certificate to allow a teacher with a valid certificate in another state who moves to Alaska to quickly begin teaching while completing missing coursework for a regular Alaska teaching certificate.[900] Additionally, Alaska created a limited language immersion teacher certificate, for teaching a non-English language to students in a language immersion program, with the certificate initially valid for one year.[901]

---

[894] 2022 Va. Acts Ch. 192, H. 1108.
[895] 2022 Wash. Laws Ch. 250, S.B. 5878.
[896] 2022 Wash. Laws Ch. 112, H.B. 2078.
[897] 2022 W. Va. Acts Ch. 103, H.B. 4074.
[898] 2022 Ala. Acts 239, H. 307.
[899] 2022 Ala. Acts 92, S.141.
[900] 2022 Alaska Sess. Laws 9/4 Ch. 69 SLA 22, S.B. 20.
[901] 2022 Alaska Sess. Laws 9/12 Ch. 73 SLA, H.B. 19.

Arizona established a high-quality teacher professional development certification program using scholarships and grants in order to develop teachers ready to work in high-need areas.[902] A second Arizona law provided alternative certification for six years for persons to begin teaching with a bachelor's degree and in a classroom-based preparation program with a certified teacher.[903] California directed the commission on teacher credentialing to waive the basic skills proficiency requirement for the issuance of an emergency 30-day substitute permit until 2024.[904] California also amended requirements for verification of employment for renewal of an emergency teaching certificate to make the verification easier in terms of timing and supplying the verification for substitute teachers working in a consortium of school districts.[905]

Connecticut increased the timeframe of validity for a professional educator certificate, from five years to ten years.[906] Delaware provided alternative measures besides a passing score on a Praxis test to show competency to receive a standard teaching certificate.[907]

The first of six acts in Illinois reduced the number of professional development hours required for certificate renewal by 20%.[908] Second, Illinois waived the application fee for a short-term substitute teaching license during a public health emergency.[909] Next, Illinois changed the minimum requirement for a substitute teaching license from a bachelor's degree to an accredited institution of higher education to allow an applicant to be enrolled in an approved education preparation program in the state and have earned at least ninety credit hours.[910] Additionally, Illinois allowed an individual holding a short-term substitute teaching license to teach up to fifteen consecutive days per licensed teacher who is under contract, instead of five consecutive days.[911] Illinois allowed a paraprofessional educator endorsement to be issued to an applicant who is at least eighteen years of age, rather than nineteen, who otherwise meets the criteria for endorsement.[912] Finally, Illinois

---

[902] 2022 Ariz. Sess. Laws Ch. 353, S.B. 1328.
[903] 2022 Ariz. Sess. Laws Ch. 337, S.B. 1159.
[904] 2022 Cal. Stat. Ch. 335, S.B. No. 1397.
[905] 2022 Cal. Stat. Ch. 113, A.B. No. 1876.
[906] 2022 Conn. Acts 22-38, S.B. No. 226.
[907] 2022 Del. Laws HB 441.
[908] 2022 Ill. Laws Pub. Act 102-0852, SB 3663.
[909] 2022 Ill. Laws Pub. Act 102-0867, SB 3915.
[910] 2022 Ill. Laws Pub. Act 102-711, HB 4798.
[911] 2022 Ill. Laws Pub. Act 102-0712, SB 3907.
[912] 2022 Ill. Laws Pub. Act 102-0713, SB 3988.

allowed a lapsed professional educator license to be reinstated for a fee of $50 instead of $500.[913]

Indiana removed a requirement of achieving the age of twenty-six for application for an initial teaching license through an alternative program.[914] The first of three acts in Louisiana removed testing for proficiency with the English language as a prerequisite for obtaining a teaching certificate.[915] Louisiana also permitted nonpublic, parochial schools to hire teachers who are trained at nationally-accredited postsecondary institutions, even if the institution is not regionally accredited.[916] Third, Louisiana allowed persons with master's degrees who meet all other requirements for certification and scored within 10% of a passing score on a subject test to receive a teacher certificate for five years.[917] Missouri created a path for full certification for teachers with the two-year nonrenewable provisional certification by a qualifying score on a designated exam, or by successfully achieving an acceptable score on the state-approved teacher evaluation system from seven walk-through evaluations, two formative evaluations, and one summative evaluation, for each of the two probationary years.[918]

New Jersey prohibited the state board of education from requiring the completion of a performance-based assessment as a condition of eligibility for a certificate with advanced standing.[919] Oklahoma removed a requirement to pass the general education portion of the competency examination as a condition of receiving a teacher certificate.[920] Oregon directed the teacher standards and practices commission to review its process for licensing educators from other states and recommend measures to provide more efficient reciprocity for teachers moving into the state.[921] Pennsylvania extended the deadline for a professional educator's and a paraprofessional educator's current continuing professional development compliance requirement by one year.[922] Pennsylvania also repealed a provision regarding certification of out-of-state teachers and replaced it with similar provisions with the addition of acceptance of persons with national policy board certification.[923]

---

[913] 2022 Ill. Laws Pub. Act 102-710, HB 4246.
[914] 2022 Ind. Acts Pub. Law 134, SB 356.
[915] 2022 La. Acts No. 707, HB No. 546.
[916] 2022 La. Acts No. 566, HB No. 455.
[917] 2022 La. Acts No. 244, SB No. 377.
[918] 2022 Mo. Laws SB 681 & 662; § 168.021.
[919] 2022 N.J. Laws P.L. c. 129, S. 896.
[920] 2022 Okla. Sess. Laws HB 3658.
[921] 2022 Or. Laws Ch. 116 § 2, HB 4030.
[922] 2022 Pa. Laws Act No. 55, HB 1642, Section 7.
[923] 2022 Pa. Laws Act No. 55, HB 1642, Section 11.

Tennessee specified requirements for a person to receive a teaching certificate for a qualified occupational instructor, and the commissioner of education may provide a temporary certificate if a qualified person is not available.[924] Additionally, Tennessee allowed a teacher holding a second or third teaching permit to apply to the state department of education for a limited license to continue teaching the course or subject area being taught pursuant to a current temporary permit.[925] It should be pointed out that, though Tennessee joined sixteen other states in easing certification requirements, there were three areas in which the trend went the other direction: where Tennessee prohibited the state board of education from granting a temporary permit to teach a physical education course, a special education course, or a course for which an end-of-course examination is required.[926]

Virginia permitted the state board of education to provide for the issuance of a provisional license, valid for a period of not more than three years, to an individual who has held an officially-issued and recognized license or certificate to teach issued by an entity outside of the U.S. within the last five years, but does not meet the requirements for a renewable license under current state board regulations.[927] Virginia also allowed local school boards to employ, under a provisional license issued by the state department of education for three school years (with a possible two-year extension), any professional counselor, social worker, or psychologist licensed by a state board, and others working on such licensure.[928] Lastly, Virginia permitted the state board of education to grant a two-year extension of the license of any individual licensed by the board per Code of Virginia § 22.1-298.1 Subsection B and whose license expires in 2022 to provide sufficient time to complete requirements for licensure or renewal.[929] Wisconsin made minor grammatical changes in a provision requiring the state superintendent to grant substitute teacher permits to individuals meeting listed requirements.[930]

Six states added legislation to speed up certification for members of the military and their spouses. Delaware eased restrictions on the timeframe for renewing a teaching certificate for members of the military returning from active deployment.[931] Florida authorized the state department of education to issue a temporary certificate to

---

[924] 2022 Tenn. Pub. Acts Ch. No. 1141, S.B. No. 2442, Sub. H.B. No. 2455.
[925] 2022 Tenn. Pub. Acts Ch. No. 1093, S.B. No. 1864, Sub. H.B. No. 1899.
[926] 2022 Tenn. Pub. Acts Ch. No. 932, H.B. No. 1901, Sub. S.B. No. 1863.
[927] 2022 Va. Acts Ch. 657, H. 979; 2022 Va. Acts Ch. 657, S. 68.
[928] 2022 Va. Acts Ch. 205, H. 829.
[929] 2022 Va. Acts Ch. 104, H. 236.
[930] 2021 Wis. Act 236, 2021 A.B. 975.
[931] 2022 Del. Laws HB 318.

military service members meeting gateway criteria.[932] New Hampshire provided a temporary license to a member of the armed forces or their spouse who holds a current, valid, unencumbered occupational or professional license in good standing issued in another state.[933] South Dakota required the rapid issue of a certificate to qualified active-duty members of the military or their spouses.[934] Tennessee clarified that an assistant principal license is included in reciprocal agreements with other states and to military spouses licensed in other states.[935] Virginia required the state board of education to provide military spouses with teacher licensure by reciprocity with other states.[936]

Thirteen states adopted incentive programs to address teacher and other educator shortages, including scholarships, loan forgiveness, and housing. Alabama increased the loan repayment award for qualified math and science teachers in the Alabama Math and Science Teacher Education Program (AMSTEP), a federal loan program, from $5,000 to $7,500 per year, for $30,000 total.[937] California created a program to allow community college districts to secure affordable housing for college faculty and employees. The program is similar to the program created by the Teacher Housing Act of 2016, which assisted in filling housing needs for teachers and school district employees.[938] Colorado created a stipend program to provide financial assistance for student teachers who might otherwise not be able to afford entering the teaching profession.[939] Delaware established a public education compensation committee to review educator compensation and its ability to compete for employees.[940]

Illinois broadened a loan repayment program to address the shortage of school social workers to include municipal social workers.[941] Iowa created a mental health professional loan repayment program within the college student aid commission.[942] Kentucky created a student loan forgiveness program for teachers obtaining certification through an expedited certification process with a residency component.[943] Louisiana funded scholarships for

---

[932] 2022 Fla. Laws Ch. 2022-186, SB 896.
[933] 2022 N.H. Laws Ch. 310, HB 1653.
[934] 2022 S.D. Laws S.B. 167.
[935] 2022 Tenn. Pub. Acts Ch. No. 692, H.B. No. 2449, Sub. S.B. No. 2475.
[936] 2022 Va. Acts Ch. 545, S. 154; 2022 Va. Acts Ch. 546, H. 230.
[937] 2022 Ala. Acts 396, H.435.
[938] 2022 Cal. Stat. Ch. 640, A.B. No. 1719. The Teacher Housing Act of 2016 was cited as 2016 Cal. Stat. Ch. 732, S.B. No. 1413.
[939] 2022 Colo. Sess. Laws HB 1220.
[940] 2022 Del. Laws SB 100.
[941] 2022 Ill. Laws Pub. Act 102-1022, SB 3761.
[942] 2022 Iowa Acts HF 2549.
[943] 2022 Ky. Acts Ch. 161, HB 277.

students enrolled in high-need teacher preparation programs.[944] New Hampshire specified that, for the purpose of eligibility for state or federal teacher loan forgiveness programs, teachers for grades seven through twelve are considered teachers of secondary school.[945] New Jersey made minor amendments to the educator grant program for the STEM (science, technology, engineering, and mathematics) subject areas.[946] Oklahoma directed the regents for higher education to establish a teacher employment incentive scholarship program funding $1,000 per academic year the first three years and $2,500 for the final academic year.[947] Utah amended an incentive program to attract effective teachers in high-poverty schools by making special education teachers and kindergarten teachers eligible for the program.[948] Washington created a nurse educator loan repayment program to provide incentive for nurses to obtain credentials to teach in nurse educator programs.[949]

Nine states attempted to address teacher shortages by allowing retired school employees to return to work. Georgia permitted a retired teacher, certified in a high-need area, to return to service without interrupting the person's retirement benefit until 2026.[950] Louisiana allowed the reemployment of retirees in the state teacher retirement system in critical shortage positions.[951] Maryland exempted reemployment earnings offsets for retirees in the teacher retirement system to allow school employees to be rehired from July 1, 2022, through June 3, 2024.[952] Missouri permitted retired teachers to be employed as a substitute teacher on a part time or temporary substitute basis without impacting their retirement stipend nor requiring payments to the system as a result of the substitute teaching.[953]

New Mexico allowed retired teachers to return to work with limited impact on their retirement stipends.[954] Vermont permitted a retired educator to resume service as an interim school educator for a period not to exceed one school year without interrupting retirement benefits.[955] Washington permitted individuals retired from the teachers' retirement system to work for a school district for

---

[944] 2022 La. Acts No. 463, HB No. 346.
[945] 2022 N.H. Laws Ch. 150, SB 236, part 6.
[946] 2022 N.J. Laws P.L. c. 119, S. 2563.
[947] 2022 Okla. Sess. Laws HB 3564.
[948] 2022 Utah Laws H.B. 315.
[949] 2022 Wash. Laws Ch. 267, H.B. 2007.
[950] 2022 Ga. Laws Act 724, HB 385.
[951] 2022 La. Acts No. 601, HB No. 1021.
[952] 2022 Md. Laws Ch. 558, HB 743.
[953] 2022 Mo. Laws SB 681 & 662; § 168.036.
[954] 2022 N.M. Laws Ch. 20, HB 73.
[955] 2022 Vt. Laws Act 173, H. 572.

up to 1,040 hours per school year while in receipt of pension benefits until July 1, 2025.[956] Rhode Island temporarily suspended the cap on the number of days retired educators can work without penalty.[957] Tennessee permitted a teacher retired for at least sixty days to be reemployed as a K thorugh twelve teacher, substitute teacher, or bus driver without loss of benefits until 2025.[958]

Michigan added two acts seeking data regarding the practice of allowing retirees to return to work. Michigan amended a provision concerning the office of retirement services making reports to legislative leadership about the number of retired teachers who have returned to teacher employment to specify when reports are to be delivered.[959] Michigan also required reporting units to pay the unfunded actuarial accrued liability associated with the employment of a retired substitute teacher.[960]

Eight states tried other means of addressing shortages of teachers and other educators. Delaware provided funding for full-time employees to be hired as permanent substitute teachers in state schools.[961] Illinois allowed a substitute teacher to teach up to 120 school days, instead of 90, for any one licensed teacher under contract in the same school year.[962] Michigan created and funded a student mental health apprenticeship retention and training (SMART) internship grant program.[963] Minnesota amended a provision allowing a school employee to continue employment when elected to the school board if the expected amount earned will not be more than $20,000. Before the amendment, the maximum earnings were $8,000.[964]

New Mexico authorized public postsecondary educational institutions and tribal colleges to offer a teacher residency program which allowed persons in teacher preparation programs to concurrently work in a guided apprenticeship in a classroom.[965] Oklahoma removed a limitation of 270 clock hours of classroom teaching per semester for adjunct teachers.[966] Oregon required the teacher standards and practices commission to adopt rules that reduce or suspend professional development requirements for

---

[956] 2022 Wash. Laws Ch. 110, H.B. 1699.
[957] 2022 R.I. Laws H. 7825.
[958] 2022 Tenn. Pub. Acts Ch. No. 821, H.B. No. 2783, Sub. S.B. No. 2702.
[959] 2022 Mich. Pub. Acts 185, HB 5536.
[960] 2022 Mich. Pub. Acts 184, HB 4375.
[961] 2022 Del. Laws HB 315.
[962] 2022 Ill. Laws Pub. Act 102-0717, SB 3893.
[963] 2022 Mich. Pub. Acts 180, SB 1012.
[964] 2022 Minn. Laws Ch. 78, S.F. 3107.
[965] 2022 N.M. Laws Ch. 17, HB 13.
[966] 2022 Okla. Sess. Laws SB 1119.

license renewal.[967] Oregon also required the state board of education to adopt rule requirements for the department of education to distribute grants for recruiting and retaining personnel in education, with a priority on personnel in high-need specialties and personnel who are licensed or classified.[968] Pennsylvania directed that an individual employed by a school district prior to January 1, 2012, and serving in the position of a mental health specialist, behavioral specialist, or similar locally-titled position may continue to serve in that position under the direct supervision of a certified school social worker, as long as the individual remains in the position with the same school district.[969]

Four states directed certain bodies to study or survey the shortage of teachers and other education employees. California required the commission on teacher credentialing and the state department of education to survey teachers of local educational agencies resigning their positions or electing to not accept a teaching assignment for the upcoming school year, as well as data regarding their intentions to leave the profession.[970] Missouri required the department of elementary and secondary education to create and maintain a web-based survey for collecting anonymous information from substitute teachers in public schools throughout the state.[971] New Hampshire created a committee to study state teacher shortages and recruitment incentives.[972] Ohio established a committee to study the shortage of substitute teachers and examine the temporary substitute licensing provision in Section 3, H.B. 409 of the 133rd General Assembly and Section 4 of S.B. 1 of the 134th General Assembly.[973]

Two states adopted acts to address teacher shortages through a "grow your own" program. Delaware established a "grow your own" educator program through a competitive grant program administered by the state department of education.[974] Utah made changes to a program entitled the "Grow Your Own Teacher and School Counselor Pipeline Program" to open more scholarship opportunities and allow scholarship money to be used for stipends for school counselor assistants.[975]

---

[967] 2022 Or. Laws Ch. 116 § 4, HB 4030.
[968] 2022 Or. Laws Ch. 116 § 7, HB 4030.
[969] 2022 Pa. Laws Act No. 55, HB 1642, Section 6.
[970] 2022 Cal. Stat. Ch. 924, S.B. No. 1487.
[971] 2022 Mo. Laws SB 681 & 662; § 168.037.
[972] 2022 N.H. Laws Ch. 150, SB 236, part 1.
[973] 2022 Ohio Laws Sub. H.B. No. 583, Section 11.
[974] 2022 Del. Laws HB 430.
[975] 2022 Utah Laws S.B. 251.

Eleven states passed fourteen acts to increase salaries, which may have been meant to assuage employee shortages. Alabama provided a 4% pay increase for public education employees, beginning with the new fiscal year of October 1.[976] Delaware specified a higher salary schedule placement for school-based physical therapists holding advanced graduate degrees.[977] Idaho allowed instructional staff or pupil service staff entering their first year on the career ladder, but with prior certificated experience in an accredited private or parochial school, to be placed higher on the career ladder.[978] Louisiana prohibited uncompensated training burdens on professional teachers, so that additional teacher training shall occur only if provision is made for teachers to receive the training at a time when they are being compensated and not participating in local professional development activities.[979] Louisiana also adopted new salary schedules for school bus operators.[980] Lastly, Louisiana required teachers whose employment has been interrupted by military service to be moved to the place on the salary schedule where they would have been without the interruption.[981]

Maine permitted employees of a school in an unorganized territory to be paid over a twelve-month period, the same as employees of school administrative units.[982] Additionally, Maine funded full payment of the state's salary supplement obligation for teachers with national policy board certification.[983] Maryland authorized the payment of a $500 bonus for noncertificated education support professionals.[984] Missouri amended provisions about career plans for teachers by requiring that career plans, and thus career ladders, must recognize additional responsibilities and volunteer efforts by teachers.[985] New Mexico amended provisions related to level one and two licenses for teachers, to increase the minimum pay for a beginning teacher at $50,000.[986] Rhode Island required school lunch service contracts to provide for payment to school-lunch workers and aides for 180 days or the length of the contract for the school year, whichever is longer.[987] Tennessee

---

[976] 2022 Ala. Acts 285, H.135.
[977] 2022 Del. Laws HB 336.
[978] 2022 Idaho Sess. Laws Ch. 83, HB 656.
[979] 2022 La. Acts No. 569, HB No. 510.
[980] 2022 La. Acts No. 449, HB No. 215.
[981] 2022 La. Acts No. 373, HB No. 131.
[982] 2022 Me. Acts Ch. 699, H.P. 1331, L.D. 1780.
[983] 2022 Me. Acts Ch. 694, H.P. 1271, L.D. 1716.
[984] 2022 Md. Laws Ch. 531, HB 1349; 2022 Md. Laws Ch. 532, SB 831.
[985] 2022 Mo. Laws SB 681 & 662; § 168.500.
[986] 2022 N.M. Laws Ch. 28, SB 1.
[987] 2022 R.I. Laws H. 7488, S. 2411.

deleted a requirement that teachers in the special school district for correctional institutions must receive annual compensation at a rate of one-tenth times twelve of the annual compensation in the county in which an individual correctional teacher works.[988] Utah authorized extra payment to educators for hours involved in professional development.[989]

Four states enacted five bills regarding creating and maintaining data to track workforce issues in K-12 schools. Delaware directed the state department of education to annually study the workforce of early childhood professionals.[990] Maryland directed each county school board and the school board for Baltimore to collect and report data on the number of noncertificated education support professionals in their employ.[991] Oregon directed the teacher standards and practices commission to work with the University of Oregon to establish a workforce data system for gathering data on the needs of the education workforce serving students in kindergarten through grade twelve.[992] Washington required the office of the superintendent of public instruction to report to legislative committees every odd-number year regarding the physical, social, and emotional support staff in school districts, including nurses, social workers, psychologists, counselors, classified staff providing student and staff safety, and parental involvement coordinators.[993]

Three states added to their anti-discrimination employment law. Florida made it an unlawful employment practice to subject an individual, as a condition of employment, membership, certification, licensing, credentialing, or passing an examination, to training, instruction or any other required activity that espouses, promotes, advances, inculcates, or compels such individual to believe any of the listed concepts constitute discrimination based on race, color, sex, or national origin under this section. The act then listed prohibited beliefs, such as that members of one race, color, sex, or national origin are morally superior to members of another race, color, sex, or national origin.[994] Mississippi prohibited a state agency, public official, state institution of higher learning, public community or junior college, county, municipality or other political subdivision of the state from refusing services, health care access, or employment

---

[988] 2022 Tenn. Pub. Acts Ch. No. 1047, H.B. No. 846, Sub. S.B. No. 1599.
[989] 2022 Utah Laws H.B. 396.
[990] 2022 Del. Laws HB 377.
[991] 2022 Md. Laws Ch. 531, HB 1349.
[992] 2022 Or. Laws Ch. 116 § 16, HB 4030.
[993] 2022 Wash. Laws Ch. 109, H.B. 1664.
[994] 2022 Fla. Laws Ch. 2022-72, HB 7.

opportunities to a person, or otherwise discriminate against a person, based upon his or her COVID-19 vaccination status. An exemption was maintained to allow health care agencies to make reasonable accommodations for persons not vaccinated or presumed to be not vaccinated to protect the health of others in that setting.[995] New York added citizenship or immigration status as protected classes in the state anti-discrimination law.[996]

Ten states adopted twelve other acts about certification, without a clear intent to address teacher shortages. Idaho amended teacher certification provisions to award a charter school-specific teaching certificate, with the minimum requirement of a bachelor's degree and teacher training designed by the charter school.[997] Illinois required the state board of education to provide a model program of study to the department of human services for persons to serve as a direct support professional.[998] Louisiana required candidates for teacher certification in elementary education to pass a test on reading instruction.[999] Maine provided final adoption to proposed teacher certification rules brought by the state board of education with changes directed by the legislative body.[1000] Massachusetts authorized the provisional licensure for speech-language pathologists, setting minimum requirements to include the minimum hours of supervised training required by a national certifying body for speech-language pathology.[1001] New Mexico directed the department of education to issue a Native American language and culture certificate to a person proficient in a tribal or pueblo language and culture, who must be paid the same as a level one licensed teacher when working as a full-time instructor. A baccalaureate degree is not required for an applicant for the certificate.[1002]

Pennsylvania directed that an individual employed by a school district prior to January 1, 2012, and serving in the position of a mental health specialist, behavioral specialist, or similar locally-titled position may continue to serve in that position under the direct supervision of a certified school social worker, as long as the individual remains in the position with the same school district.[1003] Pennsylvania also directed the state department of education to

---

[995] 2022 Miss. Laws H.B. No. 1509.
[996] 2022 N.Y. Laws Ch. 748, A. 6328.
[997] 2022 Idaho Sess. Laws Ch. 192, SB 1291.
[998] 2022 Ill. Laws Pub. Act 102-0874, SB 3972.
[999] 2022 La. Acts No. 448, HB No. 214.
[1000] 2022 Me. Acts Ch. 144, H.P. 1442, L.D. 1933.
[1001] 2022 Mass. Acts Ch. 263, H. 5094.
[1002] 2022 N.M. Laws Ch. 40, HB 60.
[1003] 2022 Pa. Laws Act No. 55, HB 1642, Section 6.

develop an instructional certificate in prekindergarten through grade twelve dance instruction.[1004] Tennessee required the state department of education to design and adopt a certificate of licensure for issuance to educators who have met the requirements for licensure established by the state board of education, with seven items detailed to be present on the certificate, including type of license, endorsement areas, and highest level of education attained by the educator as of the date of issuance.[1005] Utah required special education directors at charter schools to receive commensurate certification as other special education directors.[1006] Wyoming exempted after-school programs from child care facility certification requirements.[1007] Additionally, Wyoming required licensure of persons practicing behavior analysis.[1008]

Three states enacted four bills related to certificate denial or revocation. South Dakota amended provisions describing the causes for revocation of teacher and administrator certificates.[1009] New Hampshire prohibited persons charged or convicted of first-degree assault or controlled drug possession violations from employment in public schools or being granted teaching credentials.[1010] New Hampshire added human trafficking to the list of crimes for which teacher credentials shall not be granted to a candidate.[1011] West Virginia amended a provision regarding revocation of school personnel certificates to permit the state superintendent to immediately suspend certificates for certain serious causes.[1012]

Seven states passed eight acts regarding the discipline of school district employees. California prohibited the suspension without pay, suspension, or demotion with a reduction in pay, or dismissal of a permanent employee of a school district who timely requests a hearing on charges against the employee, unless the employer demonstrated by a preponderance of the evidence that the employee engaged in criminal misconduct, misconduct that presents a risk of harm to pupils or students, staff or property, or committed habitual violations of the district's policies or regulations.[1013] Illinois required local school superintendents to notify the state superintendent if the superintendent has reasonable cause to believe that a license holder

---

[1004] 2022 Pa. Laws Act No. 55, HB 1642, Section 11.
[1005] 2022 Tenn. Pub. Acts Ch. No. 1145, S.B. No. 2583, Sub. H.B. No. 2703.
[1006] 2022 Utah Laws S.B. 103.
[1007] 2022 Wyo. Sess. Laws Ch. No. 71, S.F. 85.
[1008] 2022 Wyo. Sess. Laws Ch. No. 47, H.B. 110.
[1009] 2022 S.D. Laws S.B. 167.
[1010] 2022 N.H. Laws Ch. 259, HB 1311.
[1011] 2022 N.H. Laws Ch. 36, HB 1234.
[1012] 2022 W. Va. Acts Ch. 261, S.B. 535.
[1013] 2022 Cal. Stat. Ch. 913, A.B. No. 2413.

has committed an act of sexual misconduct resulting in dismissal or resignation.[1014] Illinois allowed a pause in adverse employment action hearings during a public health emergency, except those charged with particular acts such as physical abuse, grooming, or sexual misconduct.[1015] Indiana required the report of misdemeanors as well as felonies for reports of misconduct by school employees to the state department of education.[1016]

Maryland repealed a prerequisite that certain public-school employees must exhaust administrative remedies before instituting a civil action.[1017] Tennessee required LEAs to include in their written notice to a teacher who is dismissed or whose contract is not renewed that the only reason for the teacher's dismissal or nonrenewal was due to a loss of funding when that is the cause.[1018] Vermont prohibited a teacher, administrator, or other employee of a school district or supervisory union who testifies before the general assembly, its committees, or the state board of education from being subject to discipline by the school district or supervisory union for testifying.[1019] West Virginia amended provisions related to the suspension and dismissal of school personnel by school board process. For example, it requires that upon beginning an investigation involving conduct alleged to jeopardize the welfare of students, the affected must be placed separately from students; it makes a duty of all school personnel to report employee conduct alleged to jeopardize student welfare; and it requires the dismissal cause of incompetency to be supported by a teacher evaluation instrument.[1020]

Ten states accepted eleven acts regarding professional development. Colorado required evidence-based training in the science of reading designed for school administrators in grades K through third.[1021] Oklahoma added to a professional development requirement for dyslexia, to include the study of dysgraphia.[1022] Oregon directed the state board of education to adopt rules by which the department of education may reimburse substitute teachers and instructional assistants for costs personally incurred for required training.[1023] Pennsylvania required the state department of

---

[1014] 2022 Ill. Laws Pub. Act 102-0702, HB 4316.
[1015] 2022 Ill. Laws Pub. Act 102-0708, HB 4690.
[1016] 2022 Ind. Acts Pub. Law 125, SB 115.
[1017] 2022 Md. Laws Ch. 576, HB 468.
[1018] 2022 Tenn. Pub. Acts Ch. No. 678, H.B. No. 1687, Sub. S.B. No. 2100.
[1019] 2022 Vt. Laws Act 111, S. 162, § 2.
[1020] 2022 W. Va. Acts Ch. 264, H.B. 4562.
[1021] 2022 Colo. Sess. Laws SB 4.
[1022] 2022 Okla. Sess. Laws HB 2768.
[1023] 2022 Or. Laws Ch. 116 § 9, HB 4030.

education to establish a program of professional development and applied practice in structured literacy for school personnel that includes in-class demonstration, modeling, and coaching support to improve reading and literacy outcomes.[1024] Pennsylvania enacted a professional development online course initiative, which required the establishment over the next few years of a central clearinghouse for online courses to be used by school employees for professional development.[1025]

Rhode Island moved back one year, to the 2025-2026 school year, a requirement that all teachers employed in a position requiring elementary certification must demonstrate proficiency in knowledge and practices of scientific reading and structured literacy instruction, while all other teachers must demonstrate an awareness of knowledge and practices of scientific reading and structured literacy instruction.[1026] Tennessee required all LEA employees who work directly with students, and not just teachers, to be trained at least once every three years on the detection, intervention, prevention, and treatment of human trafficking.[1027] Vermont required the agency of education to provide professional development learning modules for teachers in methods of teaching literacy in the five key areas of literacy instruction: phonics, phonemic awareness, vocabulary, fluency, and reading comprehension.[1028] Washington established a grant program to provide assistance to school districts for the purpose of integrating financial literacy education into professional development for certified staff.[1029] West Virginia provided a supplemental appropriation for strategic staff development to the state department of education.[1030] Wyoming updated provisions regarding reading assessment and intervention, to require professional development for education professionals.[1031]

Four states passed six acts about teacher evaluation. Colorado suspended the use of student performance measures and student academic growth measures for the purpose of teacher evaluation during the pandemic.[1032] Louisiana amended provisions regarding teacher evaluations to require each person being evaluated and the evaluator to meet for the purpose of discussing the student learning

---

[1024] 2022 Pa. Laws Act No 55, HB 1642, Section 9.
[1025] 2022 Pa. Laws Act No. 55, HB 1642, Section 29.
[1026] 2022 R.I. Laws S. 2169, H. 7164.
[1027] 2022 Tenn. Pub. Acts Ch. No. 1021, S.B. No. 1670, Sub. H.B. No. 2341.
[1028] 2022 Vt. Laws Act 28, S. 114.
[1029] 2022 Wash. Laws Ch. 238, S.B. 5720.
[1030] 2022 W. Va. Acts Ch. 30, S.B. 716.
[1031] 2022 Wyo. Sess. Laws Ch. No. 56, S.F. 32.
[1032] 2022 Colo. Sess. Laws SB 69.

targets of each student and directed that student learning targets not discussed in a meeting between a person and the evaluator shall not be used in the person's evaluation.[1033] New York amended a provision requiring performance reviews before receiving tenure to permit individuals who did not receive an annual performance review rating during the 2019-2020, 2020-2021, and 2021-2022 school years to receive tenure if the individual would have been qualified had they received a performance review.[1034] Tennessee changed a requirement that 50% of a teacher's evaluation score must be based upon achievement data, making the proportion 60%, and increased from 15% to 25% the proportion of a teacher's evaluation score that can be based on other measures of student growth.[1035] Tennessee directed that if a teacher does not have access to individual growth data representative of student growth, then the teacher's evaluation may include substituted data regarding student growth.[1036] Tennessee allowed teachers to use results from benchmark assessments or a universal screener approved by the state board of education to measure student achievement.[1037]

Four states adopted bills regarding unions and collective bargaining. Illinois amended notice requirements for the educational labor relations board to allow other means of providing notice for subpoena, notice of hearing, or other process of notice, rather than personal service.[1038] Indiana changed the language on forms for payroll deductions for paying teacher union dues to more directly state the nature of the deduction and the means of revocation.[1039] Maine suspended an obligation to meet within ten days of written notice of a request to collectively bargain between school administrative units and bargaining agents for teachers during a period between a referendum approving a new regional school unit and the operational date of the regional school unit.[1040] Vermont amended collective bargaining provisions for teachers to clarify that the nonrenewal, suspension, and dismissal of teachers does not apply to a collective bargaining agreement and such a decision must be made by the school board.[1041]

Three states passed bills about leaves of absence. Louisiana expanded the use of sick leave for school employees, to include

---

[1033] 2022 La. Acts No. 333, HB No. 363.
[1034] 2022 N.Y. Laws Ch. 201, S. 8276.
[1035] 2022 Tenn. Pub. Acts Ch. No. 991, H.B. No. 2116, Sub. S.B. No. 2155.
[1036] 2022 Tenn. Pub. Acts Ch. No. 1096, S.B. No. 1986, Sub. H.B. No. 2000.
[1037] 2022 Tenn. Pub. Acts Ch. No. 914, S.B. No. 1890, Sub. H.B. No. 1860.
[1038] 2022 Ill. Laws Pub. Act 102-797, HB 5093.
[1039] 2022 Ind. Acts Pub. Law 22, SB 297.
[1040] 2022 Me. Acts Ch. 752, H.P. 325, L.D. 449.
[1041] 2022 Vt. Laws Act 111, S. 162, § 1.

special circumstances. The act appeared to give the local superintendent the authority to define special circumstances.[1042] Maine extended family medical leave to hourly school employees.[1043] Maine also amended provisions providing paid leave for public school employees affected by COVID-19, particularly to limit paid leave to fifteen days.[1044] Oklahoma allowed a school district board of education to approve a request from a school district employee to take a leave without pay to serve as an officer of a national, statewide, or school district employee association.[1045]

Two states addressed insurance coverage. Arkansas provided coverage for the diagnosis and treatment of morbid obesity under the state and public-school life and health insurance program.[1046] New York permitted the Candor Central School District to establish an insurance reserve fund.[1047] New York also permitted the Canastota Centra School District to establish an insurance reserve fund.[1048]

Five states moved to reimburse teacher purchases for their classrooms, or to provide a means of purchase beforehand. Hawaii created a one-year school supply subsidy pilot program for Title I-eligible schools.[1049] Kansas provided tax credits for school and classroom supplies purchased by teachers, among other education-related activities which can gain tax credits.[1050] Mississippi directed that the procurement card for classroom teachers to purchase supplies must be issued on August 1 of each year.[1051] Maryland established a school arts fund named after Maggie McIntosh to provide grants for public schools in Baltimore City to purchase art supplies for classrooms.[1052] Virginia provided an income tax deduction for 2022, 2023, and 2024 for the lesser of $500 or actual expenses incurred by educators for: participation in professional development courses; the purchase of books, supplies, computer equipment, software, and services; and the purchase of other educational and teaching equipment and supplementary materials.[1053]

Other employment-related acts adopted in 2022 are described as follows. Illinois required a special education cooperative that

---

[1042] 2022 La. Acts No. 648, HB No. 977.
[1043] 2022 Me. Acts Ch. 690, H.P. 668, L.D. 912.
[1044] 2022 Me. Acts Ch. 614, H.P. 1384, L.D. 1874.
[1045] 2022 Okla. Sess. Laws SB 1579.
[1046] 2022 Ark. Acts 109, S.B. 87.
[1047] 2022 N.Y. Laws Ch. 338, S. 8706.
[1048] 2022 N.Y. Laws Ch. 251, A. 8295.
[1049] 2022 Haw. Sess. Laws Act 142, SB 2893.
[1050] 2022 Kan. Sess. Laws HB 2239.
[1051] 2022 Miss. Laws S.B. No. 2422.
[1052] 2022 Md. Laws Ch. 15, HB 1469.
[1053] 2022 Va. Acts Ch. 6, H. 103 (1st Spec. Session).

dissolves or reorganizes to follow a prior-existing provision concerning the continued employment of educational support personnel employees caught up in a reorganization.[1054] Maryland established that professional personnel and staff employed by the state school for the deaf are in the professional and skilled services section of the state personnel management system.[1055] Oklahoma added statutory requirements guiding contracts for teachers at the state schools for the deaf or the blind to have the contract begin on August 1 and end on July 31 of the subsequent calendar year, with a maximum of 1,200 working hours for the duration of the contract.[1056]

Oregon established conditions which could not be used for dismissal of superintendents but permitted the board to terminate the superintendent without cause with twelve months prior notice if the school board and superintendent mutually agree to include a termination-without-cause provision in the contract.[1057] Additionally, Oregon set a state goal that the percentage of diverse employees employed by the state department of education reflects the percentage of diverse students in public schools.[1058]

South Carolina amended a provision regarding duty-free lunch periods to require the state board of education to adopt a policy requiring each local school board to provide at least thirty minutes of unencumbered time on each regular school day to all full-time teachers teaching in grades K through fifth and the same amount of unencumbered time for teachers responsible for instructing in a special education class for more than 20% of the school day with students removed from the general education setting.[1059] Vermont suspended two rules until July 1, 2022, (2362 and 2362.2.5) from the state board of education to allow educators and staff time to adequately prepare for the delivery of special education services.[1060]

Utah amended provisions regarding school nurses to provide a definition of a school nurse and to set a minimum level of nursing services for schools.[1061] Virginia required the employment of one principal full time in each elementary school, replacing a previous permission to hire a half-time principal for elementary schools with less than 300 students.[1062] West Virginia required county boards of

---

[1054] 2022 Ill. Laws Pub. Act 102-0854, SB 3709.
[1055] 2022 Md. Laws Ch. 489, HB 374.
[1056] 2022 Okla. Sess. Laws HB 3888.
[1057] 2022 Or. Laws Ch. 36, SB 1521.
[1058] 2022 Or. Laws Ch. 44, HB 4031.
[1059] 2022 S.C. Acts 176, S. 946.
[1060] 2022 Vt. Laws Act 175, H. 716, § 3.
[1061] 2022 Utah Laws H.B. 114.
[1062] 2022 Va. Acts Ch. 21, S. 490 (1st Spec. Session).

education to post all available positions on the state-wide job bank.[1063] West Virginia also changed the titles of school food service personnel, including custodian, aide, maintenance, office, and school lunch service person, along with their employment terms.[1064]

Finance and School Business

This section describes finance and school business-related legislation adopted in 2022. The largest number of bills addressed school funding formulae, with eight states passing fourteen changes to school finance provisions. California extended an exclusion relevant to San Diego City School District to also include Los Angeles Unified School District regarding the reporting of both teachers who work with pupils and teachers who provide coaching or professional development for other teachers in calculating the administrator to teacher ratio for school funding purposes.[1065] California defined a "frontier school district" in provisions guiding school funding as a school district that meets either of the following conditions: the total number of pupils in average daily attendance at all the schools served by the school district is fewer than 600, or each county in which a school operated by the school district is located has a total population density fewer than ten persons per square mile.[1066]

The first of three laws from Indiana required the reporting of the number of students in dedicated virtual schools or charter schools for the purpose of calculating average daily membership and school funding.[1067] Next, Indiana directed that the amount a school corporation expends for full-time teacher salaries shall include the amount a school corporation expends for participation in special education cooperatives or career technical education cooperatives.[1068] Finally, Indiana required the higher education commission to create a funding formula each year prior to a budget session.[1069]

Maine directed the department of education to study the impacts of the regional adjustment component of the school funding formula and to submit a report to the joint standing legislative committee having jurisdiction over education matters.[1070] Pennsylvania reconstituted the special education funding commission and

---

[1063] 2022 W. Va. Acts Ch. 263, H.B. 4489.
[1064] 2022 W. Va. Acts Ch. 265, H.B. 4829.
[1065] 2022 Cal. Stat. Ch. 908, A.B. No. 2038.
[1066] 2022 Cal. Stat. Ch. 83, A.B. No. 2337.
[1067] 2022 Ind. Acts Pub. Law 148, SB 2.
[1068] 2022 Ind. Acts Pub. Law 132, SB 331.
[1069] 2022 Ind. Acts Pub. Law 66, SB 366.
[1070] 2022 Me. Acts Ch. 155, S.P. 121, L.D. 270.

required the commission to issue a report recommending changes to the special education funding formula.[1071]

The first of three acts in Tennessee enacted the Tennessee Investment in Student Achievement Act (TISA) to put in place a new funding formula designed to prepare each student to read proficiently by third grade and each grade thereafter; prepare each high school graduate to succeed in the postsecondary program or career of the graduate's choice; and provide each student with the resources needed to succeed, regardless of the student's individual circumstances.[1072] Tennessee also changed the definition of an elementary school as a school serving any combination of pre-kindergarten through grade six, for purposes of federal funding.[1073] Further, Tennessee required the coordinated school health program to submit a mid-year report to the state department of education, to assist in determining if program funds should be redistributed.[1074]

As part of a long-term effort to respond to its school finance equity case, Vermont adopted a new weighted school funding formula.[1075] Vermont also created a legislative task force to study further pupil weighting factors in its school finance formula.[1076] To provide more funding, Washington required school districts to group public schools as a means of maximizing, at least to the 40% threshold, the number of public schools eligible to participate in the community eligibility provision of the federal school breakfast and lunch programs.[1077] Wyoming changed its school finance funding formula by modifying its education resource block grant model.[1078]

Five states allowed the issuance of bonded debt as follows. Hawaii authorized the issuance of special revenue bonds for the Saint Joseph School educational facilities.[1079] Illinois permitted six school districts to issue bonds with an aggregate principal amount that was higher than previously allowed.[1080] Rhode Island authorized the town of Warwick to issue up to $350 million general obligation bonds to replace two high schools.[1081]

The first of seven laws from Rhode Island authorized the town of Middletown to issue up to $235 million general obligation bonds, notes, and other marks of indebtedness in construction, renovation,

---

[1071] 2022 Pa. Laws Act No. 55, Section 3, HB 1642, Section 3.
[1072] 2022 Tenn. Pub. Acts Ch. No. 966, H.B. No. 2143, Sub. S.B. No. 2396.
[1073] 2022 Tenn. Pub. Acts Ch. No. 795, S.B. No. 2563, Sub. H.B. No. 1890.
[1074] 2022 Tenn. Pub. Acts Ch. No. 913, S.B. No. 1888, Sub. H.B. No. 1891.
[1075] 2022 Vt. Laws Act 127, S. 287. The school equity case was Brigham v. State, 166 Vt, 246 (1997).
[1076] 2022 Vt. Laws Act 59, S. 13.
[1077] 2022 Wash. Laws Ch. 7, H.B. 1878.
[1078] 2022 Wyo. Sess. Laws Ch. No. 14, H.B. 30.
[1079] 2022 Haw. Sess. Laws Act 199, SB 3280.
[1080] 2022 Ill. Laws Pub. Act 102-0949, HB 4688.
[1081] 2022 R.I. Laws S. 3008, H. 8328.

and furnishing new school facilities throughout the town.[1082] Rhode Island authorized the city of East Providence to issue bonds and notes in an amount not exceeding $148 million to finance the construction, renovation, and furnishing of school facilities.[1083] Rhode Island also authorized the city of Pawtucket to issue not more than $330 million general obligation bonds, notes, and other evidences of indebtedness to finance the acquisition, construction, improvement, and furnishing of a new high school.[1084] Rhode Island authorized the town of Westerly to issue bonds and notes in an amount not exceeding $50 million to finance the construct, renovation, improvement, and furnishing of school facilities.[1085] Rhode Island authorized the town of Scituate to issue not more than $750,000 bonds and notes to improve schools in the town.[1086] Lastly, Rhode Island authorized the town of Johnston to issue bonds and notes in an amount not exceeding $215 million to finance construction, additions, renovation, repair, and furnishing of school facilities.[1087]

Tennessee permitted the McKenzie special school district to issue bonds or notes in the amount of $4 million or less and to issue bond anticipation notes in the amount of $4 million or less.[1088] West Virginia codified current procedures for county boards of education to partner with the school building authority as a funding source in support of local capital improvement bond levies.[1089]

Three states directed four provisions regarding purchasing. Alabama prohibited state agencies or institutions from purchasing a U.S. or state flag that was manufactured outside of the U.S.[1090] Additionally, Alabama allowed school boards to purchase goods or services for child nutrition programs without advertising or bidding.[1091] Illinois reinserted limits on contracts for goods, services, or management in the operation of a school's food service in the list of items which may be purchased by preference following the bidding procedure.[1092] Tennessee set the minimum contract amount required by competitive bidding for board of education purchases at $25,000 or more.[1093]

[1082] 2022 R.I. Laws H. 8257.
[1083] 2022 R.I. Laws H. 8274.
[1084] 2022 R.I. Laws H. 8228, S. 2926.
[1085] 2022 R.I. Laws H. 8218, S. 2927.
[1086] 2022 R.I. Laws S. 2928.
[1087] 2022 R.I. Laws S. 2020.
[1088] 2022 Tenn. Pub. Acts Pr. Ch. No. 51, H.B. No. 2897, Sub. S.B. No. 2914.
[1089] 2022 W. Va. Acts Ch. 106, H.B. 4466.
[1090] 2022 Ala. Acts 113, S.77.
[1091] 2022 Ala. Acts 264, S. 72.
[1092] 2022 Ill. Laws Pub. Act 102-1101, HB 4813.
[1093] 2022 Tenn. Pub. Acts Pr. Ch. No. 60, H.B. No. 2909, Sub. S.B. No. 2926.

355

Georgia renewed homestead exemptions on two types of ad valorem taxes in Georgia. First, Georgia renewed a homestead exemption on ad valorem taxes for educational purposes for Fulton County School District.[1094] Georgia also renewed general homestead exemptions for the following county school districts: Fulton County,[1095] Rockdale County,[1096] Taylor County,[1097] Macon County,[1098] Bartow County,[1099] Hart County,[1100] Early County,[1101] Clarke County,[1102] and Upson County.[1103]

Two states provided state impact aid for school districts. New Jersey appropriated state military impact aid to affected school districts.[1104] Oregon directed the state department of education to award grants to wildfire-impacted school districts in amounts to cover the funding decreases resulting from average daily membership losses caused by wild fires.[1105]

Other finance and school business acts adopted in 2022 are described as follows. Arizona required an evaluation by the county treasurer regarding a school district's application to assume accounting responsibility, including an analysis of computer programming required for a county to manage school district monies.[1106] Florida appropriated $3.5 million to compensate a thirteen-year-old student who was injured due to negligent supervision during a wrestling practice.[1107] Hawaii increased the purposes for which indirect costs from federal grants may be incurred by the department of education and the charter school commission.[1108]

Louisiana authorized tuition increases at the K-12 laboratory schools at LSU and Southern University.[1109] Louisiana also added private nonprofit elementary or secondary schools, as well as public elementary or secondary schools, to the list of organizations which may hold games of chance for fund-raising activities.[1110] Maine directed the department of education and the department of health and human services to develop a support system for "MaineCare"

[1094] 2022 Ga. Laws Act 677, HB 1556.
[1095] 2022 Ga. Laws Act 675, HB 1551.
[1096] 2022 Ga. Laws Act 710, SB 632.
[1097] 2022 Ga. Laws Act 701, HB 1607.
[1098] 2022 Ga. Laws Act 678, HB 1561.
[1099] 2022 Ga. Laws Act 601, HB 604.
[1100] 2022 Ga. Laws Act 623, HB 1196.
[1101] 2022 Ga. Laws Act 619, HB 1101.
[1102] 2022 Ga. Laws Act 605, HB 797.
[1103] 2022 Ga. Laws Act 631, HB 1328.
[1104] 2022 N.J. Laws P.L. c. 19, S. 1929.
[1105] 2022 Or. Laws Ch. 43, HB 4026.
[1106] 2022 Ariz. Sess. Laws Ch. 192, H.B. 2179.
[1107] 2022 Fla. Laws Ch. 2022-264, House Claim 6513.
[1108] 2022 Haw. Sess. Laws Act 225, SB 3090.
[1109] 2022 La. Acts No. 521, HB No. 927.
[1110] 2022 La. Acts No. 387, HB No. 620.

reimbursement for school districts intermediate education units and special-purpose private schools for children from birth to grade twelve.[1111]

Massachusetts authorized the treasurer of the town of Middleborough to pay Middleborough High School students, parents, or guardians amounts paid but not reimbursed for the costs of the 2020 senior trip.[1112] The first of three laws from New Hampshire directed the audit division of the legislative budget assistant to complete a performance audit of the department of education's education freedom account program. The freedom account program allows scholarship funds to follow the student to the educational pathway chosen by the student.[1113] New Hampshire also established an extraordinary need grant for schools, in addition to regular adequate education grants and relief grants, and increased the household income level to qualify as an eligible student under the education tax credit program.[1114] Lastly, New Hampshire added another extraordinary need grant for schools in one of the closing sections of another act.[1115]

New York directed that state lands within the Eastport-South Manor Central School District are subject to taxation for school purposes.[1116] Oklahoma required the direct deposit of lottery proceeds into the teacher empowerment revolving fund.[1117] Rhode Island exempted from taxation the real and tangible personal property of Sophia Academy, San Miguel Education Center, and Community Preparatory School, Inc., which are located in the city of Providence.[1118]

South Carolina suspended requirements for the limit on cash reserves for the Dorchester County School District 4 in the 2021- 2022 fiscal year.[1119] Tennessee required the compensation of county school board members to be included in the school district budget submitted to the county legislative body, rather than being fixed by the county legislative body.[1120]

Vermont created a committee within the legislative bodies to study and make recommendations regarding the creation and implementation of an income-based education tax system to replace

---

[1111] 2022 Me. Acts Ch. 167, H.P. 1326, L.D. 1775.
2022 Me. Acts Ch. 167, H.P. 1326, L.D
. 1775.
. Laws Ch. 297, HB 1135.
[1114] 2022 N.H. Laws Ch. 318, SB 420.
[1115] 2022 N.H. Laws Ch. 272, HB 1661, part XXIX.
[1116] 2022 N.Y. Laws Ch. 692, A. 4217.
[1117] 2022 Okla. Sess. Laws HB 4388.
[1118] 2022 R.I. Laws S. 3062, H. 7957.
[1119] 2022 S.C. Acts 254, S. 912.
[1120] 2022 Tenn. Pub. Acts Ch. No. 670, H.B. No. 1848, Sub. S.B. No. 2003.

the homestead property tax system for funding education in the state.[1121] Vermont permitted school districts, in lieu of taking a personal bond from a collector or treasurer, to choose to provide suitable crime insurance covering the collector or treasurer, or both.[1122] Virginia removed reading recovery from the list of programs for which school boards may use at-risk add-on funds.[1123] Wisconsin directed payments to an independent charter school authorized by a tribal college.[1124]

Governance and School Leadership

This section details 2022 acts concerned with governance and school leadership, beginning with state-level governance entities, including state boards of education, state departments of education, professional standards boards, and the like. Arizona set the termination of the school facilities oversight board for 2025 and set conditions for retiring its debt.[1125] Arkansas created a governing body for the state and public-school life and health insurance program.[1126] Louisiana changed election districts for the state board of elementary and secondary education.[1127] Louisiana also re-created the state department of education.[1128] Maryland changed the composition of the professional standards and teacher education board by adding a member from the state association of nonpublic special education facilities.[1129] New Hampshire clarified the criteria for persons who may be appointed to the professional standards board, allowed for three consecutive terms for appointees, and required reports to be maintained for 25 years.[1130]

Tennessee changed the process for seating members of the state board of education, with the governor appointing all 9 appointive members until June 30, 2022, and beginning July 1, 2022, successor members representing congressional districts will be appointed by the governor, the speaker of the house, and the speaker of the senate, with three each.[1131] Additionally, Tennessee extended the life of the state department of education to June 30, 2026.[1132] The third act

---

[1121] 2022 Vt. Laws Act 175, H. 716, § 5.
[1122] 2022 Vt. Laws Act 166, S. 283, § 11.
[1123] 2022 Va. Acts Ch. 61, H. 418.
[1124] 2021 Wis. Act 219, 2021 S.B. 420.
[1125] 2022 Ariz. Sess. Laws Ch. 165, H.B. 2352.
[1126] 2022 Ark. Acts 114, H.B. 1100.
[1127] 2022 La. Acts No. 3, HB No. 3 (1st Spec. Session).
[1128] 2022 La. Acts No. 133, HB No. 201.
[1129] 2022 Md. Laws Ch. 210, HB 512.
[1130] 2022 N.H. Laws Ch. 315, SB 353.
[1131] 2022 Tenn. Pub. Acts Ch. No. 987, H.B. No. 1838, S.B. No. 1838.
[1132] 2022 Tenn. Pub. Acts Ch. No. 724, S.B. No. 1706, Sub. H.B. No. 1787.

from Tennessee authorized the executive director of the higher education commission to appoint a designee to serve in the executive director's stead on the state board of education.[1133] Vermont directed the agency of education and the state board of education to study the roles and responsibilities of both entities and recommend how those roles should be restructured to meet state educational goals.[1134] Vermont added requirements for the appointment by the governor of members of the state board of education to require a diversity, not only of geographic location, but also of gender, racial, and ethnic background.[1135]

Of the nine state school board members appointed by the governor, Virginia required the governor to consider one member with expertise in local government leadership or policymaking, one member with expertise in career and technical education, and one member with expertise in early childhood education.[1136] Washington made student members of the state board of education members who may vote, except they must recuse themselves from voting on matters directly related to graduation requirement changes that apply to the student member's school or graduating class.[1137] Washington also moved the election of state board of education members by school directors and private school board members from the office of the superintendent of public instruction to the state school directors' association.[1138]

Seven states adopted nine acts changing advisory commissions, councils, boards, and other bodies without the power of governance, but with power to recommend. California increased the number of members for its advisory commission on special education, an entity of state government providing advice to the state board of education, from 17 members to 19 members, and the commission must appoint two pupils with exceptional needs, 16 to 22 years of age, to the commission for one year.[1139] Missouri required that membership on the state advisory board for educator preparation must include both classroom teachers and faculty members from teacher education programs.[1140] Missouri directed the commissioner of education to establish a literacy advisory council, to provide recommendations to the commissioner and the state board of education regarding any identified improvements to literacy instruction and policy for

---

[1133] 2022 Tenn. Pub. Acts Ch. No. 737, S.B. No. 2120, Sub. H.B. No. 1875.
[1134] 2022 Vt. Laws Act 66, S. 115, § 18.
[1135] 2022 Vt. Laws Act 66, S. 115, § 19.
[1136] 2022 Va. Acts Ch. 770, H. 879.
[1137] 2022 Wash. Laws Ch. 44, S.B. 5497.
[1138] 2022 Wash. Laws Ch. 79, H.B. 1974.
[1139] 2022 Cal. Stat. Ch. 917, S.B. No. 291.
[1140] 2022 Mo. Laws SB 681 & 662; § 161.097.

students.[1141] New York increased the number of board members on the autism spectrum disorders advisory board from 19 to 24 members.[1142]

Oklahoma created an education commission with seventeen members, and empowered the commission to engage with multiple stakeholders in research, evaluation, and information sharing to conduct a study on how to improve the quality of instruction and learning through distance and remote modalities.[1143] Tennessee expanded membership on the state textbook and instructional materials quality commission and required the commission to issue guidance for school districts and public charter schools to use when reviewing materials in a library collection to assure the materials are age-appropriate and suitable for the mission of the school.[1144] Virginia directed the superintendent of public instruction to establish and appoint up to twelve members to an advisory council for digital citizenship, internet safety, and media literacy.[1145] Additionally, Virginia established a student advisory board to provide student perspectives on matters before the state board of education.[1146] Washington added measures to promote inclusion of tribal viewpoints in delivery of education services, through consultation with tribal leadership, the office of the superintendent of public instruction, and the education directors' association, and authorized the use of virtual meetings for those purposes.[1147]

Three states changed the identity of the state-level administrator over particular programs. Connecticut designated the executive director of the office of higher education as a department head within state government.[1148] New Hampshire created the position of program administrator for the education freedom account program within the department of education.[1149] Virginia made the school for the deaf and blind subject to the direction and supervision of the governor.[1150]

A fourth state sought greater collaboration between schools and various tribal councils in the state. California established the California Indian Act and encouraged school districts, county offices of education, and charter schools to form task forces with state tribes

---

[1141] 2022 Mo. Laws SB 681 & 662; § 186.080.
[1142] 2022 N.Y. Laws Ch. 453, S. 8647.
[1143] 2022 Okla. Sess. Laws HB 2693.
[1144] 2022 Tenn. Pub. Acts Ch. No. 1137, S.B. No. 2247, Sub. H.B. No. 2666.
[1145] 2022 Va. Acts Ch. 776, H. 1026.
[1146] 2022 Va. Acts Ch. 778, H. 1188.
[1147] 2022 Wash. Laws Ch. 9, S.B. 5252.
[1148] 2022 Conn. Acts 22-122, S.B. No. 105.
[1149] 2022 N.H. Laws Ch. 309, HB 1627.
[1150] 2022 Va. Acts Ch. 389, S. 723.

local to their regions or tribes historically located in the region. The purposes of the task forces include the discussion of issues of mutual concern and to undertake work to support Indian education.[1151]

Twelve states adopted legislation regarding school or school district creation or dissolution. Alaska authorized the state board of education and early development to negotiate a demonstration state-tribal education compact with federally-recognized tribes and tribal organizations, for the purpose of establishing demonstration state-tribal education compact schools. The act authorized up to five such schools, with authority to operate for up to five years. The state board and the education department were charged with reporting to the legislative body including proposed funding legislation by 2026.[1152] Arizona removed the provision for a common school district that is not within a high school district.[1153]

Louisiana created a French immersion school in the community of Pointe-au-Chien in Terrebonne Parish.[1154] Maine directed the creation of reorganization plans for the formation of regional school units to require comprehensive programming for all students from kindergarten to grade twelve and to include at least one publicly supported secondary school. However, the plan may provide programming for K through eighth via separate administrative units or contractual arrangements with other units.[1155] Mississippi authorized the Vicksburg-Warren School District and the Claiborne County Board of Education to apply to the state development authority for the approval of entering a memorandum of understanding with a nuclear facility for the operation of an Energy High School Academy. The purpose of the academy is to provide qualified students in grades eight through twelve with career education, potential student internships, and continuing education for careers in the energy industry.[1156]

Missouri established four pilot recovery high schools, geographically located in metropolitan areas of the state, to serve students with substance use disorder or dependency.[1157] For smaller school districts (designated Class III), Nebraska raised the threshold of student numbers for the point at which the school district is obligated to form a plan to reorganize with neighboring school districts. The threshold number was raised from thirty-five to forty-

---

[1151] 2022 Cal. Stat. Ch. 477, A.B. No. 1703.
[1152] 2022 Alaska Sess. Laws 7/8 Ch. 43 SLA 22, S.B. 34.
[1153] 2022 Ariz. Sess. Laws Ch. 168, H.B. 2672.
[1154] 2022 La. Acts No. 454, HB No. 261.
[1155] 2022 Me. Acts Ch. 537, H.P. 1343, L.D. 1802.
[1156] 2022 Miss. Laws S.B. No. 2885.
[1157] 2022 Mo. Laws SB 681 & 662; § 167.850.

five students, but the relevant applicable grade levels were raised from ninth through twelfth grades to kindergarten through grade twelve.[1158] North Carolina authorized the creation of remote academies, a public school whose instruction is provided primarily online through a combination of synchronous and asynchronous instruction delivered to students in a remote location outside of the school facility and which may include any combination of grade levels. The act included a prior approval process and an annual evaluation report.[1159]

Pennsylvania added a process for a school district of the third class that is located within a county of the fourth or sixth class to change its name, beginning with a two-thirds vote of the local board of the school district and the approval of the department of education.[1160] Rhode Island authorized the city of Newport and the town of Middletown to establish a regional school district.[1161] Tennessee prohibited a county local education agency from operating a school located within the geographic boundaries of a municipal local education agency, unless the parties enter into a written agreement addressing the circumstances requiring the agreement.[1162] Vermont added an act designed to encourage and support the creation of union school districts and unified union school districts through the merger of regular school districts.[1163]

California changed the application of rules that were dependent upon a school district's size. California changed rules related to single-gender classes, the use of property, and terms of employment for school employees and governing board members applying to school districts with average daily attendance of 400,000 or more pupils to make the rules applicable to school districts with average daily attendance of 250,000 or more pupils.[1164]

After the reconstruction period following the Civil War, the former States of the Confederacy adopted state constitutions in which the state governments exerted unique and direct control over local government entities, including county commissions, road and bridge commissions, and school boards. Among the pieces of legislation adopted in 2022 were a multitude of individual acts directing the size of local school boards, the terms of school board members, their compensation, whether the members are elected or

---

[1158] 2022 Neb. Laws LB 1057.
[1159] 2022 N.C. Sess. Laws Ch. 59, S.B. 671.
[1160] 2022 Pa. Laws Act No. 11, HB 232.
[1161] 2022 R.I. Laws H. 8267, S. 2961.
[1162] 2022 Tenn. Pub. Acts Ch. No. 1087, H.B. No. 2430, Sub. S.B. No. 2315.
[1163] 2022 Vt. Laws Act 176, H. 727.
[1164] 2022 Cal. Stat. Ch. 920, S.B. No. 913.

appointed, and whether the members represent separate education districts or the school district at large. Uniquely occurring were the actions in Georgia to "reconstitute" (to constitute again or anew) nearly all of the state's 181 school districts, which is a legislative action the second author of this chapter has not encountered before in the 24 years he has helped to prepare this chapter. The following entries exemplify continuing control over local school boards in certain southern states.

Florida introduced a term limit of 12 years for school board members.[1165] In the first of many related acts from Georgia in 2022, Georgia changed the membership of the school board for the City of Savannah and Chatham County to be composed of a president and eight board members, with the eight members elected to eight election districts.[1166] Georgia also changed the membership of the school board for Carrollton Independent School System, so that two members will be elected at large and the other members will be elected by an election district described as a "ward."[1167]

As noted above, Georgia reconstituted a significant portion of its school districts. Georgia reconstituted the school board for the City of Commerce Independent School District with five education districts,[1168] the City of Jefferson with five education districts,[1169] Quitman County with two education districts and two posts elected in each of the two districts,[1170] and Stephens County with three education districts.[1171] Georgia reconstituted the school board for the following county school districts with four members elected to four education districts: Twiggs County,[1172] Lamar County,[1173] and Wilkinson County.[1174] Georgia reconstituted the school board for the following county school districts with five members elected to five education districts: Atkinson County,[1175] Camden County,[1176] Coffee County,[1177] Crisp County,[1178] Dade County,[1179] Henry County,[1180]

[1165] 2022 Fla. Laws Ch. 2022-21, HB 1467.
[1166] 2022 Ga. Laws Act 585, HB 1510.
[1167] 2022 Ga. Laws Act 576, SB 547.
[1168] 2022 Ga. Laws Act 426, HB 1115.
[1169] 2022 Ga. Laws Act 473, HB 1206.
[1170] 2022 Ga. Laws Act 495, HB 1249.
[1171] 2022 Ga. Laws Act 572, HB 1471.
[1172] 2022 Ga. Laws Act 554, SB 489.
[1173] 2022 Ga. Laws Act 542, HB 1230.
[1174] 2022 Ga. Laws Act 559, SB 476.
[1175] 2022 Ga. Laws Act 525, HB 1315.
[1176] 2022 Ga. Laws Act 529, HB 1247.
[1177] 2022 Ga. Laws Act 532, HB 1365.
[1178] 2022 Ga. Laws Act 570, HB 1430.
[1179] 2022 Ga. Laws Act 595, HB 1567.
[1180] 2022 Ga. Laws Act 536, SB 463.

Houston County,[1181] Irwin County,[1182] Macon County,[1183] Meriwether County,[1184] McIntosh County,[1185] Treutlen County,[1186] Walker County,[1187] and Warren County.[1188] Georgia reconstituted the school board for two county school districts, Bibb County[1189] and Pike County,[1190] with six members elected to six education districts. Georgia reconstituted the school board for three county school districts with seven members elected to seven education districts, as follows: Cobb County,[1191] Harris County,[1192] and Thomaston-Upson County.[1193] Georgia reconstituted the school board for one system, Muscogee County School District, with eight members elected to eight education districts.[1194] Georgia reconstituted the school board for two county school districts with nine members elected to nine education districts, as follows: Clarke County[1195] and Clayton County.[1196] Georgia reconstituted the school board for Richmond County School District with ten members elected to ten education districts.[1197] Georgia reconstituted the school board for Gwinnett County School District with all members elected to education districts pursuant to the Georgia Election Code but without otherwise specifying the number of members.[1198] Georgia reconstituted the school boards for the following county school districts with four internal education districts: Dawson County,[1199] Hall County,[1200] Jones County,[1201] Lanier County,[1202] Lumpkin County,[1203] and Marion County.[1204] Georgia reconstituted the school boards for the following county school districts with four education districts and a fifth member elected at large: Catoosa County,[1205] Columbia County,[1206] Early County,[1207] Pierce County,[1208] Schley

---

[1181] 2022 Ga. Laws Act 538, HB 1124.
[1182] 2022 Ga. Laws Act 569, HB 1362.
[1183] 2022 Ga. Laws Act 543, HB 1363.
[1184] 2022 Ga. Laws Act 547, SB 387.
[1185] 2022 Ga. Laws Act 545, HB 1126.
[1186] 2022 Ga. Laws Act 578, SB 554.
[1187] 2022 Ga. Laws Act 556, HB 1367.
[1188] 2022 Ga. Laws Act 557, SB 446.
[1189] 2022 Ga. Laws Act 526, SB 454.
[1190] 2022 Ga. Laws Act 551, HB 1341.
[1191] 2022 Ga. Laws Act 561, HB 1028.
[1192] 2022 Ga. Laws Act 575, SB 522.
[1193] 2022 Ga. Laws Act 555, HB 1314.
[1194] 2022 Ga. Laws Act 548, HB 1285.
[1195] 2022 Ga. Laws Act 523, HB 1142.
[1196] 2022 Ga. Laws Act 530, HB 1214.
[1197] 2022 Ga. Laws Act 520, SB 458.
[1198] 2022 Ga. Laws Act 516, SB 369.
[1199] 2022 Ga. Laws Act 325, HB 943.
[1200] 2022 Ga. Laws Act 318, HB 889.
[1201] 2022 Ga. Laws Act 513, HB 1070.
[1202] 2022 Ga. Laws Act 388, SB 425.
[1203] 2022 Ga. Laws Act 400, SB 367.
[1204] 2022 Ga. Laws Act 492, HB 1254.
[1205] 2022 Ga. Laws Act 323, HB 936.
[1206] 2022 Ga. Laws Act 369, SB 385.
[1207] 2022 Ga. Laws Act 340, HB 980.
[1208] 2022 Ga. Laws Act 424, HB 1112.

County,[1209] and Whitfield County.[1210] Georgia reconstituted the school boards for the following county school districts with four education districts and the chairperson elected by the county at large: Greene County,[1211] Jefferson County,[1212] Washington County,[1213] White County,[1214] Wilkes County,[1215] and Worth County.[1216] Georgia reconstituted the school board for the following county school districts with five education districts: Appling County,[1217] Baldwin County,[1218] Banks County,[1219] Bartow County,[1220] Bleckley County,[1221] Burke County,[1222] Butts County,[1223] Calhoun County,[1224] Candler County,[1225] Charlton County,[1226] Chattooga County,[1227] Clay County,[1228] Clinch County,[1229] Cook County,[1230] Crawford County,[1231] Crisp County,[1232] Effingham County,[1233] Elbert County,[1234] Forsyth County,[1235] Grady County,[1236] Griffin-Spalding County,[1237] Gwinnett County,[1238] Haralson Count,[1239] Heard County,[1240] Jackson County,[1241] Jasper County,[1242] Johnson County,[1243] Laurens County,[1244] Lee County,[1245] Lincoln County,[1246] Long County,[1247] Madison County,[1248] Miller County,[1249]

[1209] 2022 Ga. Laws Act 491, HB 1255.
[1210] 2022 Ga. Laws Act 432, HB 1128.
[1211] 2022 Ga. Laws Act 475, HB 1209.
[1212] 2022 Ga. Laws Act 377, SB 402.
[1213] 2022 Ga. Laws Act 514, HB 1286.
[1214] 2022 Ga. Laws Act 401, SB 368.
[1215] 2022 Ga. Laws Act 330, HB 948.
[1216] 2022 Ga. Laws Act 394, SB 431.
[1217] 2022 Ga. Laws Act 497, HB 1240.
[1218] 2022 Ga. Laws Act 480, HB 1239.
[1219] 2022 Ga. Laws Act 453, HB 1140.
[1220] 2022 Ga. Laws Act 470, HB 1190.
[1221] 2022 Ga. Laws Act 397, SB 336.
[1222] 2022 Ga. Laws Act 501, HB 1212.
[1223] 2022 Ga. Laws Act 328, HB 946.
[1224] 2022 Ga. Laws Act 409, HB 982.
[1225] 2022 Ga. Laws Act 338, HB 957.
[1226] 2022 Ga. Laws Act 433, HB 1129.
[1227] 2022 Ga. Laws Act 493, HB 1252.
[1228] 2022 Ga. Laws Act 460, HB 1161.
[1229] 2022 Ga. Laws Act 390, SB 427.
[1230] 2022 Ga. Laws Act 420, HB 1105.
[1231] 2022 Ga. Laws Act 345, HB 1006.
[1232] 2022 Ga. Laws Act 408, HB 956.
[1233] 2022 Ga. Laws Act 378, SB 406.
[1234] 2022 Ga. Laws Act 334, HB 952.
[1235] 2022 Ga. Laws Act 483, HB 1246.
[1236] 2022 Ga. Laws Act 490, HB 1258.
[1237] 2022 Ga. Laws Act 509, HB 1109.
[1238] 2022 Ga. Laws Act 406, HB 872.
[1239] 2022 Ga. Laws Act 385, SB 411.
[1240] 2022 Ga. Laws Act 314, HB 874.
[1241] 2022 Ga. Laws Act 425, HB 1114.
[1242] 2022 Ga. Laws Act 329, HB 947.
[1243] 2022 Ga. Laws Act 457, HB 1157.
[1244] 2022 Ga. Laws Act 415, HB 1099.
[1245] 2022 Ga. Laws Act 449, HB 1166.
[1246] 2022 Ga. Laws Act 337, HB 954.
[1247] 2022 Ga. Laws Act 374, SB 415.
[1248] 2022 Ga. Laws Act 357, HB 1026.
[1249] 2022 Ga. Laws Act 488, HB 1262.

Montgomery County,[1250] Morgan County,[1251] Newton County,[1252] Oglethorpe County,[1253] Peach County,[1254] Putnam County,[1255] Randolph County,[1256] Stewart County,[1257] Talbot County,[1258] Taliaferro County,[1259] Tatnall County,[1260] Terrell County,[1261] Turner County,[1262] Wayne County,[1263] Whitfield County,[1264] and Wilcox County.[1265] Georgia reconstituted the school board for Bryan County with five education districts and the chair and vice chair elected at large.[1266] Georgia reconstituted two county school boards, Coweta County[1267] and Jeff Davis County,[1268] with five education districts and two more members elected at large. Georgia reconstituted the following county school boards with six education districts: Cherokee County,[1269] Decatur County,[1270] Dougherty County,[1271] Evans County,[1272] Paulding County,[1273] and Wheeler County.[1274] Georgia reconstituted the following county school boards with seven education districts: Barrien County,[1275] Ben Hill County,[1276] Brooks County,[1277] Carroll County,[1278] Dodge County,[1279] Emanuel County,[1280] Fulton County,[1281] Glynn County,[1282] Gordon County,[1283] Lowndes County,[1284] McDuffie County,[1285] Monroe County,[1286] Polk County,[1287] Screven County,[1288] Sumter County,[1289] Telfair

---

[1250] 2022 Ga. Laws Act 352, HB 1017.
[1251] 2022 Ga. Laws Act 467, HB 1174.
[1252] 2022 Ga. Laws Act 370, SB 451.
[1253] 2022 Ga. Laws Act 332, HB 950.
[1254] 2022 Ga. Laws Act 417, HB 1079.
[1255] 2022 Ga. Laws Act 481, HB 1242.
[1256] 2022 Ga. Laws Act 464, HB 1266.
[1257] 2022 Ga. Laws Act 361, HB 1067.
[1258] 2022 Ga. Laws Act 354, HB 1023.
[1259] 2022 Ga. Laws Act 448, HB 1167.
[1260] 2022 Ga. Laws Act 506, HB 1201.
[1261] 2022 Ga. Laws Act 486, HB 1268.
[1262] 2022 Ga. Laws Act 447, HB 1168.
[1263] 2022 Ga. Laws Act 496, HB 1241.
[1264] 2022 Ga. Laws Act 383, SB 409.
[1265] 2022 Ga. Laws Act 499, HB 1238.
[1266] 2022 Ga. Laws Act 363, HB 1074.
[1267] 2022 Ga. Laws Act 471, HB 1135.
[1268] 2022 Ga. Laws Act 371, SB 392.
[1269] 2022 Ga. Laws Act 427, HB 1118.
[1270] 2022 Ga. Laws Act 428, HB 1122.
[1271] 2022 Ga. Laws Act 489, HB 1260.
[1272] 2022 Ga. Laws Act 477, HB 1227.
[1273] 2022 Ga. Laws Act 549, SB 482.
[1274] 2022 Ga. Laws Act 450, HB 1165.
[1275] 2022 Ga. Laws Act 380, SB 417.
[1276] 2022 Ga. Laws Act 430, HB 1125.
[1277] 2022 Ga. Laws Act 392, SB 429.
[1278] 2022 Ga. Laws Act 343, HB 986.
[1279] 2022 Ga. Laws Act 462, HB 1163.
[1280] 2022 Ga. Laws Act 494, HB 1251.
[1281] 2022 Ga. Laws Act 404, HB 991.
[1282] 2022 Ga. Laws Act 429, HB 1123.
[1283] 2022 Ga. Laws Act 384, SB 410.
[1284] 2022 Ga. Laws Act 437, SB 423.
[1285] 2022 Ga. Laws Act 373, SB 399.
[1286] 2022 Ga. Laws Act 444, HB 1171.
[1287] 2022 Ga. Laws Act 387, SB 413.
[1288] 2022 Ga. Laws Act 442, SB 433.
[1289] 2022 Ga. Laws Act 581, SB 570.

County,[1290] Thomas County,[1291] Tift County,[1292] Troup County,[1293] Walton County,[1294] and Ware County.[1295] Finally, Georgia reconstituted the school board for Bulloch County with eight education districts.[1296]

Georgia also amended the membership and structure of the school board in three instances. Georgia changed the membership of the school board for DeKalb County, electing seven members from seven education districts.[1297] Georgia amended the structure of the school board for Liberty County School District so that it has seven members elected within seven education districts.[1298] Likewise, Georgia amended the structure of the school board for Mitchell County School District with seven members elected with seven education districts.[1299]

Other states made changes regarding school board membership, numbers, eligibility, boundaries, and dealing with vacancies as follows. Maryland, in the first of five laws, changed the means of becoming a school board member for Harford County, with six elected members, three appointed members, one student member, and the county superintendent of school serving as an ex officio non-voting member. The three appointed members are to be appointed by the county executive, subject to the advice and consent of the county council, by a vote of at least five members of the county council.[1300] Maryland changed the boundaries of school board districts for election of the members of the Prince George's County Board of Education.[1301] Maryland changed the method for filling a vacancy on the Frederick County Board of Education so that if there is a vacancy occurring thirty days or less before the candidate registration deadline for the next primary election, the county executive shall appoint, subject to confirmation of the county council, a qualified individual to fill the vacancy.[1302] Maryland changed the boundaries for residence districts for the Montgomery County Board of Education to change the district in which the Ken Gar neighborhood is located.[1303] Lastly, Maryland created a workgroup

---

[1290] 2022 Ga. Laws Act 461, HB 1162.
[1291] 2022 Ga. Laws 511, HB 1077.
[1292] 2022 Ga. Laws Act 502, HB 1207.
[1293] 2022 Ga. Laws Act 315, HB 880.
[1294] 2022 Ga. Laws Act 317, HB 882.
[1295] 2022 Ga. Laws Act 484, HB 1259.
[1296] 2022 Ga. Laws Act 313, HB 871.
[1297] 2022 Ga. Laws Act 574, SB 466.
[1298] 2022 Ga. Laws Act 568, HB 1397.
[1299] 2022 Ga. Laws Act 571, HB 1465.
[1300] 2022 Md. Laws Ch. 569, HB 603.
[1301] 2022 Md. Laws Ch. 454, HB 1473; 2022 Md. Laws Ch. 455, SB 444.
[1302] 2022 Md. Laws Ch. 368, SB 952.
[1303] 2022 Md. Laws Ch. 105, HB 503.

to study and make recommendations regarding implementation of an electoral process for an all-elected board for the Prince George's County Board of Education.[1304]

Massachusetts implemented changes in representation for election of school committee members in Worcester in concert with a consent decree lodged in the U.S. District Court of Massachusetts in *Worcester Interfaith, Inc. v. City of Worcester*, Case No. 4:21-cv-40015-TSH.[1305] Massachusetts also `amended the charter for the city of Haverhill to require that a district school committee member that moves from one district to another during the first eighteen months of an elected term shall be deemed to have vacated their seat.[1306] Missouri adopted a measure to allow school boards to divide a school district to create voting districts for school board members.[1307] New Hampshire amended a provision authorizing one student non-voting member for the school board to specify that there must be one student member for each high school in the school district.[1308] New York reduced the signature requirement for petitions for candidates for the school board of the city of Buffalo from 1,000 voters to 400 voters.[1309]

South Carolina also made several changes to school districts and school boards in 2022. South Carolina reapportioned election districts from which school board members must be elected in 2022 for the Greenville County School District.[1310] Additionally, South Carolina reapportioned the election districts for school board members in Clover School District 2 in York County[1311] as well as for the members of the governing board for the following school districts: Cherokee County School District 1,[1312] Abbeville County School District,[1313] Union County School District,[1314] Pickens County School District,[1315] and Colleton County School District.[1316]

South Carolina consolidated Bamberg Ehrhardt School District One and Denmark Olar School District Two into one school district, to be known as the Bamberg County School District.[1317] South Carolina consolidated two school districts in Hampton County into a

---

[1304] 2022 Md. Laws Ch. 217, HB 355.
[1305] 2022 Mass. Acts Ch. 208, H. 4326.
[1306] 2022 Mass. Acts Ch. 195, H. 4636.
[1307] 2022 Mo. Laws SB 681 & 662; § 162.563.
[1308] 2022 N.H. Laws Ch. 195, HB 1381.
[1309] 2022 N.Y. Laws Ch. 495, A. 9423.
[1310] 2022 S.C. Acts 257, H. 5159.
[1311] 2022 S.C. Acts 265, S. 1270.
[1312] 2022 S.C. Acts 252, S. 1271.
[1313] 2022 S.C. Acts 247, S. 1263.
[1314] 2022 S.C. Acts 264, S. 1299.
[1315] 2022 S.C. Acts 261, S. 1220.
[1316] 2022 S.C. Acts 253, S. 1235.
[1317] 2022 S.C. Acts 249, H. 5098.

single Hampton County School District, with seven single-member election districts,[1318] and two school districts into the Sumter School District, with nine nonpartisan board members elected to serve in nine reapportioned member districts.[1319] South Carolina set the stage for the fiscal management for the consolidation of two school districts into the Hampton County School District, with funds for the separate school districts deposited into the account for the consolidated school district beginning July 1, 2021, and the consolidated county district achieving full fiscal autonomy by 2025.[1320] South Carolina also ratified the state superintendent's emergency declaration on the subject and consolidated two school districts in Florence County to a single Florence County School District.[1321]

South Carolina clarified the terms for incumbent members of school boards after the consolidation of Barnwell County School Districts 29 and 19 into one school district.[1322] South Carolina changed the representational composition of the nine school board members for the Berkeley County School District, with eight members elected in non-partisan elections from single-member districts in which they are residents, and one member elected from the county at large.[1323] South Carolina revised the boundaries of the seven single-member election districts from which members of the school board are elected for the Fairfield County School District.[1324] South Carolina added two non-voting members to the nine regular voting members of the Aiken County Commission for Technical Education.[1325] Finally, South Carolina allowed the governor to remove school district board members (trustees) who are guilty of malfeasance, misfeasance, incompetency, absenteeism, conflicts of interest, misconduct, persistent neglect of duty in office, or incapacity.[1326]

Tennessee increased the number of persons serving on the school board for Polk County, from nine to ten members, subject to local approval;[1327] shortened the terms of school board members for the Tenth Special School District of Wilson County, from six years to four years;[1328] and increased the membership of the school board in

---

[1318] 2022 S.C. Acts 259, S. 1264.
[1319] 2022 S.C. Acts 262, H. 5288.
[1320] 2022 S.C. Acts 258, S. 862.
[1321] 2022 S.C. Acts H. 256, H. 5339.
[1322] 2022 S.C. Acts 250, S. 1157.
[1323] 2022 S.C. Acts 251, S. 910.
[1324] 2022 S.C. Acts 255, S. 1292.
[1325] 2022 S.C. Acts 169, S. 449.
[1326] 2022 S.C. Acts 138, S. 203.
[1327] 2022 Tenn. Pub. Acts Pr. Ch. No. 64, H.B. No. 2911, Sub. S.B. No. 2929.
[1328] 2022 Tenn. Pub. Acts Pr. Ch. No. 57, H.B. No. 2905, Sub. S.B. No. 2921.

Hamilton County, from nine members to eleven members.[1329] Utah raised the number of school board members representing LEAs as LEAs grow larger, for example, from seven to nine members when the LEA serves more than 100,000 students.[1330] Virginia directed that the terms of office of the nine school board members for Loudon County must be staggered so that members of four are elected for four-year terms and the remaining five or elected for two-year terms.[1331]

Six states enacted seven bills regarding school board elections. California changed the timeline for holding a special election for school districts and community college districts so they may be held 88-125 days following the order of the election, but the election may be conducted within 180 days to be consolidated with a regularly-scheduled election.[1332] Georgia added school districts to the parties of interest in a disputed municipal annexation.[1333] Indiana limited the number of school board members that may reside in the same school election district.[1334] New York extended provisions related to absentee ballots for school district elections during a declared disaster emergency to January 1, 2023.[1335] South Carolina moved the date for the school board election for Marion County, from April 12, 2022, to the second Tuesday of May 2022.[1336] South Carolina also specified that only successors to those trustees in the Union County School District whose terms expire in 2022 must be elected in that year's school district elections.[1337] Virginia changed provisions for school board elections in the city of Waynesboro.[1338]

Three states changed school board member compensation as follows. Georgia changed the compensation for school board members in Warren County to $200 per meeting, and to $250 per meeting for the chairperson;[1339] in Bryan County to $750 per month, and $875 for the chairperson;[1340] in Taylor County to $200 per diem for each day of attendance at board meetings;[1341] in Haralson County to $250 per month for meetings of the board;[1342] in Lincoln County

---

[1329] 2022 Tenn. Pub. Acts Pr. Ch. No. 50, H.B. No. 2894, Sub. S.B. No. 2910.
[1330] 2022 Utah Laws S.B. 78.
[1331] 2022 Va. Acts Ch. 798, H. 1138.
[1332] 2022 Cal. Stat. Ch. 831, S.B. No. 1061.
[1333] 2022 Ga. Laws Act 785, HB 1461.
[1334] 2022 Ind. Acts Pub. Law 169, HB 1285.
[1335] 2022 N.Y. Laws Ch. 172, S. 7619.
[1336] 2022 S.C. Acts 260, S. 948.
[1337] 2022 S.C. Acts 264, S. 1299.
[1338] 2022 Va. Acts Ch. 332, H. 1311; 2022 Va. Acts Ch. 571, S. 699.
[1339] 2022 Ga. Laws Act 712, SB 636.
[1340] 2022 Ga. Laws Act 609, HB 897.
[1341] 2022 Ga. Laws Act 603, HB 775.
[1342] 2022 Ga. Laws Act 612, HB 989.

to $200 for each meeting of the board;[1343] and in Meriwether County to $300 per diem for each day of attendance at board meetings.[1344]

Maryland changed the annual compensation of the president of the school board in Carroll County from $9,000 to $13,000, and the compensation for voting members of the board from $8,000 to $12,000;[1345] increased by $7,000 the annual compensation of the president, vice president, and other members of the Anne Arundel County school board;[1346] and altered the scholarship award for the student member of the Montgomery County school board to the costs of annual tuition, mandatory fees, and room and board.[1347] Virginia repealed salary amounts for various county school board members, and substituted instead language that any elected or appointed school board may pay each of its members an annual salary that is consistent with the salary procedures and no more than the salary limits provided for local governments in Article 1.1 (§15.2-1414.1 et seq.) of Chapter 14 of Title 15.2, or as provided by charter.[1348]

Ten states modified the state's open meetings laws regarding school boards. California amended its open meetings act to authorize the presiding member of a local legislative body conducting a meeting to remove, or cause the removal of, an individual for disrupting the meeting.[1349] Colorado amended its open meetings law to allow school boards to interview and negotiate with finalists for the superintendency.[1350] Connecticut permitted public agencies to continue to hold public meetings by means of electronic equipment under its freedom of information act.[1351] Delaware amended its open meetings act to require that open meetings must include an opportunity for community comment.[1352] Indiana amended its open meetings act to require school boards to receive public comment on any topic before taking final action on the topic.[1353]

Kentucky amended provisions in the open meetings law regarding virtual meetings, to require prior announcement of the physical location of the main meeting, and to require participants to be visible at all times during the meeting.[1354] Maine amended its freedom of access (open meeting) act to permit limiting public

---

[1343] 2022 Ga. Laws Act 616, HB 1036.
[1344] 2022 Ga. Laws Act 610, HB 987.
[1345] 2022 Md. Laws Ch. 580, SB 436.
[1346] 2022 Md. Laws Ch. 579, SB 510.
[1347] 2022 Md. Laws Ch. 566, HB 243.
[1348] 2022 Va. Acts Ch. 662, H. 18.
[1349] 2022 Cal. Stat. Ch. 171, S.B. No. 1100.
[1350] 2022 Colo. Sess. Laws HB 1110.
[1351] 2022 Conn. Acts 22-3, H.B. No. 5269.
[1352] 2022 Del. Laws HB 293.
[1353] 2022 Ind. Acts Pub. Law 116, HB 1130 and 2022 Ind. Acts Pub. Law 124, SB 83.
[1354] 2022 Ky. Acts Ch. 37, HB 453.

attendance when there is an emergency or urgent situation that requires the public body to meet only by remote methods.[1355] Nebraska amended its open meeting act to allow virtual conferencing for any public body if the purpose of the virtual meeting is to discuss items that are scheduled to be discussed or acted upon at a subsequent non-virtual open meeting, and no action is taken by the public body at the virtual meeting.[1356] Utah amended a provision in its open meetings law that permitted a public body to hold an electronic meeting to require the public body to adopt a resolution, rule, or ordinance to establish the conditions under which a remote member is included in calculating a quorum.[1357] Vermont temporarily amended its open meeting law to allow safer methods to conduct business, including electronic meetings, during the COVID-19 pandemic.[1358]

Seven states amended their open records acts, as follows. Idaho amended its public records law to remove reference to an "independent public body corporate and politic" from the list of agencies covered by the law and required public records requests to specify that the request is made for a public record.[1359] Louisiana amended its public records law to specify that electronically stored information and databases are included in the law.[1360] Minnesota changed educational records law to define a "parent" as a natural parent, a guardian, or an individual acting as a parent in the absence of a parent or guardian. The revised record law also added provisions to account for school-issued devices and to specify that data on them belong to the school and not the technology company.[1361] Nebraska struck down permission for minutes of the meetings of school boards to be kept as an electronic record, but in another provision added that minutes shall be written or kept as an electronic record and must be made available for inspection within ten working days.[1362] Oklahoma made information on a document provided to a state agency that contains a person's personal address, personal phone number, personal electronic mail address, or other contact information protected from disclosure under the state open records law.[1363] Tennessee extended protection from disclosure of adverse

---

[1355] 2022 Me. Acts Ch. 666, H.P. 1323, L.D. 1772.
[1356] 2022 Neb. Laws LB 908.
[1357] 2022 Utah Laws H.B. 22.
[1358] 2022 Vt. Laws Act 78, S. 222.
[1359] 2022 Idaho Sess. Laws Ch. 306, HB 811.
[1360] 2022 La. Acts No. 770, SB No. 478.
[1361] 2022 Minn. Laws Ch. 69, H.F. 2353.
[1362] 2022 Neb. Laws LB 742.
[1363] 2022 Okla. Sess. Laws SB 970.

childhood experiences in the open records act.[1364] Virginia amended its open records act to make scholastic records disclosable under federal law (Family Educational Rights and Privacy Act 20 U.S.C. 1232g) not subject to a charge for copying.[1365]

Two states added exemptions which impact both open records and open meetings law. Florida provided an exemption from public records and public meetings requirements for portions of a campus emergency response which addresses a response to an act of terrorism, specifically the identify of students and others impacted by the terrorism.[1366] Illinois exempted from disclosure any threat assessment procedures under the requirements for school safety drills from the state freedom of information act.[1367]

Seven states adopted eight acts regarding ethics. Alabama prohibited public employees from expending public funds to advocate in favor of or against statewide and local ballot measures. However, expenditures may be used to inform members of the public as to services that would be cut if ad valorem taxes are not passed or renewed.[1368] California included in the definition of "local agency" in the state ethics law a school district, county office of education, and charter school to clarify their inclusion in training requirements.[1369] Colorado set limits on campaign donations for candidates for school board (director) positions, beginning at $2,500.[1370] Louisiana amended the date for disclosure by any school board member or superintendent whose immediate family member is employed by the school board to the state board of ethics, from within thirty days of the beginning of the school year to September 15.[1371] Louisiana also provided a minimum time period of at least one year that an immediate family member of a local school board member or superintendent must be employed before being promoted to an administrative position.[1372]

Oklahoma added persons appointed as a cabinet secretary or a director of a state agency to the list of state officers who must file financial disclosure statements under the state ethics law.[1373] Oregon required school board members for common school districts or union high school districts to file verified statements of economic

---

[1364] 2022 Tenn. Pub. Acts Ch. No. 740, S.B. No. 2268, Sub. H.B. No. 2089.
[1365] 2022 Va. Acts Ch. 756, H. 307.
[1366] 2022 Fla. Laws Ch. 2022-133, SB 7006.
[1367] 2022 Ill. Laws Pub. Act 102-0791, HB 4994.
[1368] 2022 Ala. Acts 428, S.313.
[1369] 2022 Cal. Stat. Ch. 279, A.B. No. 2158.
[1370] 2022 Colo. Sess. Laws HB 1060.
[1371] 2022 La. Acts No. 50, HB No. 475.
[1372] 2022 La. Acts No. 47, HB No. 411.
[1373] 2022 Okla. Sess. Laws SB 1695.

interest with the state government ethics commission.[1374] West Virginia prohibited county and district officers, superintendents, principals, and teachers in public schools to be pecuniarily interested in the proceeds of any contract or service of the furnishing of any supplies.[1375]

Two states enacted bills regarding public comment opportunities on school board agendas. Georgia required local school boards to provide a public comment section on the agenda of regular monthly meetings. The required time for notice of comment is limited to 24 hours, and the chairperson of the board may impose reasonable time limits on the speech.[1376] Kentucky required each regular meeting of a school board to include a fifteen minute public comment period.[1377]

Two states passed acts regarding appointment of superintendents. Florida repealed a resolution providing for an appointed superintendent in Lee County and reprised a referendum for an elected superintendent.[1378] Missouri added funding to a prior provision permitting two school districts to share a superintendent to make the arrangement more attractive to school districts.[1379]

Other governance and school leadership acts passed in 2022 are described as follows. Alaska determined that Rampart School is located within the Yukon-Koyukuk School District regional area.[1380] Idaho amended the membership for each school district's curricular materials adoption committee so that one-half of the members must be persons who are not educators and are parents of a child or children attending a school or schools within the school district.[1381] Illinois amended a provision regarding the transaction of business by the trustees of schools in a school district representing Township 38, Range 12 East, so that business may be transacted by four elected trustees and three appointed trustees.[1382] Illinois changed the number of days, from twenty-eight days to forty, after the regular election of directors, when the directors must meet and organize by appointing one of their number as a president and another as the clerk.[1383]

Maryland allowed the school board in Baltimore County to retain counsel to represent it in legal matters affecting the board and

---

[1374] 2022 Or. Laws Ch. 66, HB 4114.
[1375] 2022 W. Va. Acts Ch. 83, H.B. 4642.
[1376] 2022 Ga. Laws Act 721, SB 588.
[1377] 2022 Ky. Acts Ch. 92, HB 121.
[1378] 2022 Fla. Laws Ch. 2022-233, HB 4097.
[1379] 2022 Mo. Laws SB 681 & 662; § 168.205.
[1380] 2022 Alaska Sess. Laws 6/20 Ch. 9 SLA 22, S.B. 198.
[1381] 2022 Idaho Sess. Laws Ch. 288, HB 650.
[1382] 2022 Ill. Laws Pub. Act 102-0924, HB 4173.
[1383] 2022 Ill. Laws Pub. Act 102-0798, HB 5127. School board members in Illinois are called "directors" under the school code (105 ILCS 5/10-1).

to contract for the payment of a reasonable fee to the counsel.[1384] Missouri provided a statement of qualified immunity for school employees, including a school nurse, school bus driver, or school bus aide, for any action taken by a school employee trained in good faith by the school nurse.[1385] New York provided for the automatic creation of a vacancy in a public office upon entering a guilty plea in federal court to a felony or a crime involving a violation of an oath of office.[1386] New York also extended provisions authorizing political subdivisions to permit any public body to hold meetings remotely and without in-person access during the COVID-19 state disaster emergency.[1387] Tennessee prohibited an LEA or public charter school from knowingly entering into an agreement with an individual or entity that performs abortions, induces abortions, provides abortion referrals, or provides funding, advocacy, or other support for abortions.[1388]

Parental and Student Rights

This section details the rights and privileges legislatures and general assemblies recognized or granted to parents and students in 2022. The dominant right that was articulated was the right of parents to control the upbringing of their children. Alabama directed school districts to adopt a policy requiring parents to opt-in for mental health services, including counseling.[1389] In a law also discussed in the Curricular Requirements section of this chapter, Arizona prohibited teaching with the use of sexually-explicit instructional materials without serious educational value; without serious literary, artistic, political, or scientific value, which describe an explicit list of prohibited sexually-explicit acts; or without parental consent. Students without parental consent must be provided an alternative assignment.[1390] Arizona required schools to adopt procedures for giving parents access to the school library collection of available books and materials, but exempted schools without a full-time librarian or school libraries under a county or municipal contract from the requirement.[1391]

Florida added provisions to reinforce the right of parents to control the upbringing of their children, including, for example, a

---

[1384] 2022 Md. Laws Ch. 591, SB 55
[1385] 2022 Mo. Laws SB 681 & 662; § 167.625.
[1386] 2022 N.Y. Laws Ch. 757, A. 10144.
[1387] 2022 N.Y. Laws Approval Memo 1, A. 8591.
[1388] 2022 Tenn. Pub. Acts Ch. No. 950, H.B. No. 2557, Sub. S.B. No. 2158.
[1389] 2022 Ala. Acts 442, H.123.
[1390] 2022 Ariz. Sess. Laws Ch. 380, H.B. 2495.
[1391] 2022 Ariz. Sess. Laws Ch. 205, H.B. 2439.

prohibition against discussing sexual orientation in grades K through third. The act also directed the appointment of a special magistrate to bring action against a school district violating the provisions of this act.[1392] Georgia added provisions detailing the right of parents to direct the education of their children, including the right to attend various types of schools including home schools, the right to student records, and the right to review instructional materials[1393] Iowa prohibited school districts and charter schools from administering or conducting an invasive physical examination of a student, or a student health screening that is not required by state or federal law, without written consent of the student's parent or guardian.[1394] Louisiana required public schools and their governing authorities to post laws regarding parental access to instructional materials and the Parents' Bill of Rights on their websites.[1395] Missouri prohibited pupils from being subject to corporal punishment outlined in the discipline and corporal punishment policy without a parent or guardian being notified and providing written permission for the corporal punishment.[1396] Tennessee adopted the "Age-Appropriate Materials Act of 2022," which required each school operated by an LEA and each public charter school to maintain a current list of materials in the school's library and post the list on its website. The act required the development of a procedure to review materials to assure they are age-appropriate when placed, and a procedure for reviewing parental feedback regarding materials.[1397] Virginia required the department of education to develop and make available to each school board model policies for ensuring parental notification of any instructional material that includes sexually explicit content and include information, guidance, procedures, and standards regarding parental notification, directly identifying the specific instructional material in question, parental review of the material, and providing alternative instructional materials.[1398] Virginia also permitted parents to elect for their child to not wear a mask while on school property, with the measure passing on April 27, 2022.[1399] West Virginia allowed parents, guardians, and grandparents to inspect instructional materials used in the classroom.[1400] Wyoming updated

---

[1392] 2022 Fla. Laws Ch. 2022-22, HB 1557.
[1393] 2022 Ga. Laws Act 718, HB 1178.
[1394] 2022 Iowa Acts SF 2080.
[1395] 2022 La. Acts No. 466, HB. No. 369.
[1396] 2022 Mo. Laws SB 681 & 662; § 160. 261.
[1397] 2022 Tenn. Pub. Acts Ch. No. 744, S.B. No. 2407, Sub. H.B. No. 2154.
[1398] 2022 Va. Acts Ch. 100, S. 656.
[1399] 2022 Va. Acts Ch. 2, S. 739; 2022 Va. Acts Ch. 780, H. 1272.
[1400] 2022 W. Va. Acts Ch. 99, S. B. 704.

provisions regarding reading assessment and intervention to require parental or guardian notification.[1401]

Seven states adopted acts prohibiting various categories of discrimination. Louisiana prohibited hair discrimination in education, employment, public accommodations, and housing options.[1402] Maine prohibited discrimination in employment and schools based upon hair texture or hairstyle.[1403] Maryland prohibited discrimination by an educational institution, county board, nonpublic prekindergarten program, or nonpublic school against any person because of the individual's race, ethnicity, color, religion, sex, age, national origin, marital status, sexual orientation, gender identity, or disability.[1404] Tennessee enacted the "CROWN Act: Create a Respectful and Open World for Natural Hair," which prohibited an employer from adopting a policy that does not permit an employee to wear the employee's hair in braids, locs, twists, or another manner that is part of the cultural identification of the employee's ethnic group or that is a physical characteristic of the employee's ethnic group.[1405]

Utah required LEAs to review information on harassment and discrimination within the LEA, adopt a plan to reduce harassment and discrimination, and provide a report of the plan.[1406] Vermont prohibited discriminatory school branding in mascots, nicknames, logos, letterheads, team names, slogans, mottos, or other identifiers, that directly or indirectly references or stereotypes the likeness, features, symbols, traditions, or other characteristics of the race, creed, color, national origin, sexual orientation, or gender identity of any person or groups of persons, or organizations associated with the repression of others.[1407] Virginia prohibited an academic year Governor's school or its leadership and employees to discriminate against any individual or group on the basis of race, sex, color, ethnicity, or national origin in the admission process for students to the school.[1408]

Three states passed four acts taking opposing positions on gender transition and other aspects of LGBTQ+ rights. Alabama prohibited doctors from performing procedures or prescribing medications to alter a minor child's gender or delay puberty. The act also prohibited school personnel from encouraging or coercing a

---

[1401] 2022 Wyo. Sess. Laws Ch. No. 56, S.F. 32.
[1402] 2022 La. Acts No. 529, HB No. 1083.
[1403] 2022 Me. Acts Ch. 643, S.P. 237, L.D. 598.
[1404] 2022 Md. Laws Ch. 739, HB 850.
[1405] 2022 Tenn. Pub. Acts Ch. No. 1078, S.B. No. 136, Sub. H.B. No. 204.
[1406] 2022 Utah Laws H.B. 428.
[1407] 2022 Vt. Laws Act 152, S. 139.
[1408] 2022 Va. Acts Ch. 485, H. 127.

minor to withhold from the minor's parent or guardian that the minor's gender identity does not match biological sex and required school personnel to inform the parent or guardian of that difference in perception.[1409] Alabama also required all K-12 public schools to designate multiple occupancy restrooms and changing areas to be used based upon biological sex, based upon birth certificate.[1410] Oklahoma required public school students to use multiple occupancy restrooms or changing areas based upon the individual's sex as recorded on the original birth certificate. School districts may not depart from this policy, or suffer a 5% decrease in state funding, and a parent or guardian may bring a civil suit to enforce the policy.[1411] Vermont permitted persons, irrespective of their gender, to amend the marker on a birth certificate to reflect the individual's gender identity, including a third non-binary marker.[1412]

Five states supported making feminine hygiene products available in the school setting. Alabama created a grant program for school districts receiving Title I funds to provide feminine hygiene products to enrolled students at no cost.[1413] Delaware expanded, from grades six through twelve to grades four through twleve, the availability of free feminine hygiene products for students.[1414] Hawaii directed the department of education to provide menstrual products for public school students beginning at age ten free of charge.[1415] Utah required schools to provide feminine hygiene products free of charge in each female or unisex restroom in all schools.[1416] Vermont required that students attending public schools and approved independent schools have menstrual products available at no cost in the nurse's office or in restrooms that are gender-neutral or designated for female students and generally used by students age eight years of age or older.[1417]

Seven states fostered special support for students needing targeted assistance, especially for students who have experienced learning losses. California provided a foster child's educational rights holder, attorney, social worker, or tribal social worker the same rights as a parent of a pupil facing suspension or expulsion procedures.[1418] Colorado created the position of foster care education

---

[1409] 2022 Ala. Acts 289, S.184.
[1410] 2022 Ala. Acts 290, H.322.
[1411] 2022 Okla. Sess. Laws SB 615.
[1412] 2022 Vt. Laws Act 88, H. 628.
[1413] 2022 Ala. Acts 380, H.50.
[1414] 2022 Del. Laws SB 205.
[1415] 2022 Haw. Sess. Laws Act 113, SB 2821.
[1416] 2022 Utah Laws H.B. 162.
[1417] 2022 Vt. Laws Act 66, S. 115, § 11.
[1418] 2022 Cal. Stat. Ch. 400, A.B. No. 740.

coordinator within the department of education and required the coordination of programming to address the educational needs of foster care children.[1419] Pennsylvania directed the operation of a process to assist students who have experienced education instability, beginning with the identification of an individual person as a point of contact to assist the student.[1420] Rhode Island required schools, in developing alternative-learning plans, to consider the difficulties and interruptions students experienced because of the COVID-19 pandemic.[1421] Tennessee required each LEA to designate a foster care liaison to address barriers for students in foster care.[1422] Utah amended provisions related to parent engagement with the education process and required LEAs to adopt a policy facilitating assistance to students learning English and their parents.[1423] Washington required the public schools to provide students and their parents or guardians with a description of the services available through the office of the education ombuds and the contact person for the office of the education ombuds in the governor's office at the time of initial enrollment or admission.[1424]

Three states secured the right of tribal members to wear indigenous regalia at graduation ceremonies. Alaska prohibited school boards from adopting dress codes prohibiting students from wearing hairstyles associated with race, wearing a natural hairstyle, or wearing traditional tribal regalia or objects of cultural significance at a graduation ceremony.[1425] South Dakota prohibited the state or any of its political subdivisions to prohibit a Native American student from wearing an eagle feather, eagle plume, or a beaded graduation cap at a school honoring or graduation ceremony.[1426] Utah permitted students enrolled as a member of a tribe to wear tribal regalia during a high school graduation.[1427]

Five states adopted bills with respect to child nutrition programs. Illinois required school districts to provide a plant-based school lunch option to students who submit a prior request for such an option.[1428] Kentucky allowed school administrators over schools participating in the federal school breakfast program to authorize up to fifteen minutes of the student attendance day to provide the

---

[1419] 2022 Colo. Sess. Laws HB 1374.
[1420] 2022 Pa. Laws Act No. 1, SB 324.
[1421] 2022 R.I. Laws S. 2572, H. 7062.
[1422] 2022 Tenn. Pub. Acts Ch. No. 951, H.B. No. 2621, Sub. S.B. No. 2309.
[1423] 2022 Utah Laws H.B. 302.
[1424] 2022 Wash. Laws Ch. 222, S.B. 5376.
[1425] 2022 Alaska Sess. Laws 9/8 Ch. 71 SLA 22, S.B. 174.
[1426] 2022 S.D. Laws H.B. 1185.
[1427] 2022 Utah Laws H.B. 30.
[1428] 2022 Ill. Laws Pub. Act 102-0761, HB 4089.

opportunity for children to eat breakfast during the instruction day.[1429] Vermont created a task force to study and develop a universal school lunch program.[1430] Vermont also required each school board to provide universal school meals, so that the same school breakfast and school lunches provided to students under federal law are provided to all students.[1431] Virginia directed public elementary and secondary schools to process web-based or paper-based applications for participation in the school breakfast or school lunch program within six working days after the date of receipt of the completed application.[1432] Washington required the use of an electronic option for the submission of household income information required for participation in school breakfast and lunch programs.[1433]

Two states added protections for students who are in debt to the child nutrition program. South Carolina prohibited public schools to use debt collection agencies to collect or attempt to collect outstanding debts on student school lunch or breakfast accounts, and those schools may not collect interest or any other monetary penalty for outstanding debts for student lunch and breakfast accounts.[1434] Virginia prohibited school boards or any school board employee from denying any student the opportunity to participate in any extracurricular school activity because the student cannot pay for a meal at school or owes a school meal debt.[1435]

Four states added acts regarding child care subsidies. Illinois required the student assistance commission to annually include information about the child care assistance program in the same languages that schools are required to provide to students who are eligible for grants under the monetary award program.[1436] Indiana permitted a child care program operated by a private or public school on its premises to provide child care for students and employees.[1437] Maryland required the state department of education to establish a process for granting presumptive eligibility for a subsidy under the child care scholarship program.[1438] Also, Maryland directed the state department of education to administer, in fiscal years 2022 and 2023, child care stabilization grants to provide financial support to

---

[1429] 2022 Ky. Acts Ch. 41, SB 151.
[1430] 2022 Vt. Laws Act 67, H. 106.
[1431] 2022 Vt. Laws Act 151, S. 100.
[1432] 2022 Va. Acts Ch. 424, H. 587.
[1433] 2022 Wash. Laws Ch. 111, H.B. 1833.
[1434] 2022 S.C. Acts 182, H. 3006.
[1435] 2022 Va. Acts Ch. 686, H. 583.
[1436] 2022 Ill. Laws Pub. Act 102-00829, SB 3149.
[1437] 2022 Ind. Acts Pub. Law 81, HB 1318.
[1438] 2022 Md. Laws Ch. 525, HB 995; 2022 Md. Laws Ch. 526, SB 920.

child care providers that have faced financial hardship or suffered operational burden during the COVID pandemic.[1439] Virginia directed the board of education to determine the feasibility of amending its regulations to permit all active-duty members of the U.S. armed forces who serve as caregivers to dependents to apply for the child care subsidy program and report to the legislative committees on education.[1440]

Three states enacted bills regarding privacy. California prohibited a business providing proctoring services in an educational setting from collecting, retaining, using, or disclosing personal information, except to the extent necessary to provide proctoring services.[1441] Louisiana permitted local secondary schools to collect social security numbers of students pursuing a diploma and being prepared for postsecondary education, workforce training, and employment, if parents or guardians provide consent and the social security numbers are disclosed only to the company with which the state has contracted to develop unique student identifiers for the state workforce commission.[1442] To an existing provision directing the use of a random number generator for unique pupil identification numbers, New Hampshire added chartered public schools, scholarship organizations, and adult education programs to the list of entities which must use that numbering system.[1443]

Three states moved to assist students in securing a driver's license. Alabama exempted homeless children and youth from some of the fees associated with receiving a driver's license and required a designated school staff member to verify a student's qualification.[1444] Colorado provided funding to allow teen parents to attend driving school without cost.[1445] West Virginia repealed a provision that conditioned progress by students toward receiving a motor vehicle license on school attendance and satisfactory academic progress.[1446]

Two states changed requirements regarding immunization. New Hampshire removed the requirement that a parent's request for a religious exemption to immunizations required for school attendance must be notarized.[1447] Tennessee removed the COVID-19 vaccine

---

[1439] 2022 Md. Laws Ch. 206, HB 89.
[1440] 2022 Va. Acts Ch. 23, H. 994; 2022 Va. Acts Ch. 24, S. 529.
[1441] 2022 Cal. Stat. Ch. 720, S.B. No. 1172.
[1442] 2022 La. Acts No. 567, HB No. 470.
[1443] 2022 N.H. Laws Ch. 271, HB 1626.
[1444] 2022 Ala. Acts 300, H.385.
[1445] 2022 Colo. Sess. Laws HB 1042.
[1446] 2022 W. Va. Acts Ch. 185, H.B. 4535.
[1447] 2022 N.H. Laws Ch. 55, HB 1035.

mandate requirements for schools and LEAs, effective July 1, 2023.[1448]

Two states supported making accommodations to religious viewpoint or personal modesty in athletic uniforms and accessories; both laws are also discussed in the Athletics section. Maryland required the state athletic association, county school boards, and boards of community college trustees to allow student athletes to modify an athletic or team uniform to make the attire more modest to conform to the requirements or preferences of the student athlete's religion or culture, or the student's own preferences for modesty.[1449] Utah encouraged public and private schools supporting athletic teams and activities to revise internal policies and allow all children and youth participating in athletic activities to wear religious clothing or headwear or to modify their uniforms to accommodate religious beliefs and personal values of modesty.[1450]

Two states enacted bills regarding the creation of a limited public forum. Louisiana provided "patriotic organizations" access to school facilities for student recruitment, with the term meaning a youth group listed as a patriotic society in Title 36 of the U.S. Code.[1451] Mississippi noted that students in public schools may engage in political activities or political or philosophical expression before, during, and after the school day, in the same manner and to the same extent that students may engage in nonpolitical activities or expression. The act also built upon the potential for recognition of a limited open forum under the federal Equal Access Act.[1452]

Other parental and student rights legislated in 2022 are described as follows. Arizona amended a declaration of parental rights, particularly in expressing that with state constitutional rights, the government has the burden of proof and must show strict scrutiny in impairment of rights.[1453] Additionally, Arizona required charter schools to develop policies to allow for visitors, tours, and observations of all classrooms by parents with children enrolled or those wishing to enroll their child.[1454] Illinois required all school boards to waive fees assessed by the school district for each student with a parent who is a veteran with an income at or below 200% of the federal poverty level.[1455]

[1448] 2022 Tenn. Pub. Acts Ch. No. 896, S.B. No. 1884, Sub. H.B. No. 1960.
[1449] 2022 Md. Laws Ch 556, HB 515; 2022 Md. Laws Ch. 557, SB 951.
[1450] 2022 Utah Laws H.C.R. 16.
[1451] 2022 La. Acts No. 485, HB No. 618.
[1452] 2022 Miss. Laws H.B. 1416. The Equal Access Act is codified at 20 U.S.C. § 4071.
[1453] 2022 Ariz. Sess. Laws Ch. 200, H.B. 2161.
[1454] 2022 Ariz. Sess. Laws Ch. 237, H.B. 2025.
[1455] 2022 Ill. Laws Pub. Act 102-1032, SB 3867.

Louisiana required public school officials to provide high school seniors the opportunity to vote.[1456] Louisiana also required persons removing a minor from a school into protective custody to supply information about the minor to the school's administrator. This provision does not apply for minors arrested for which there is probable cause.[1457] Further, Louisiana amended and reenacted the Blind Persons' Literacy Rights and Education Act to update the definition of a "blind student" and describe the types of vision assessments which must be performed.[1458] Missouri required school districts and charter schools, after receiving community input, to implement a community engagement policy that provides residents with methods of community engagement with a school board or governing board of the charter school. The act also detailed specific items which must be included in the community engagement policy.[1459]

New Jersey established a sales tax holiday for the first Monday in September each year for retail sales of computers, school computer supplies, school art supplies, school instructional materials, and sport or recreational equipment.[1460] Utah required the state board of education to provide an online school comparison tool to facilitate parent access to data comparing public school performance.[1461] Under a law also discussed in the Attendance, Promotion, and Graduation section, Washington permitted a school district, at the request of the parent, guardian, or custodian, to issue a posthumous high school diploma for a deceased student.[1462]

Program Development

This section chronicles 2022 acts in which legislative bodies created new programs or strengthened existing ones. "Pathways" may be the legislative buzzword for 2022, but it first appeared in legislation in 2019. The term is taken to describe the creation and recognition of alternative paths for students to take, through the "regular" path of schooling through university to a career, or through the alternative path from "regular" schooling through career and technology training, internships, and apprenticeships to a career. Note that "pathways" in the K-12 setting are included in this section,

---

[1456] 2022 La. Acts No. 624, HB. No. 423.
[1457] 2022 La. Acts No. 324, HB No. 245.
[1458] 2022 La. Acts No. 302, SB No. 176.
[1459] 2022 Mo. Laws SB 681 & 662; § 162.058.
[1460] 2022 N.J. Laws P.L. c. 21, A. 1522.
[1461] 2022 Utah Laws H.B. 270.
[1462] 2022 Wash. Laws Ch. 224, S.B. 5498.

while "pathways" in higher education are included in the chapter section for higher education.

Twenty states passed twenty-six bills urging the creation or recognition of "pathways" for students, beginning earlier in the K-12 setting and extending into higher education. Arizona directed the state board of education to establish a continuing high school and workforce training program that provides adult learners with an alternative study learning program leading to a high school diploma and industry-recognized certification. The act also required a similar community college and adult learning program.[1463] Connecticut directed the department of education to develop best practices for local and regional school boards to implement a successful pathways program and identify obstacles or prohibitions that may limit the ability of a school board to build partnerships with local businesses.[1464]

Hawaii passed four related acts creating a project to support commercial enterprise tied into internships and industry-credentialing programs. In the first act, Hawaii created a commercial enterprise revolving fund in the department of education for funds to operate commercial enterprises within the department.[1465] Hawaii also established a career development success program within the department of education to provide financial incentives for participating high schools to encourage students enrolled in grades nine through twelve in public high schools to enroll in and successfully complete qualified industry-credential programs.[1466] In a third act, Hawaii considered student interns engaging in commercial enterprises to be state employees and permitted the department of education to use revenue generated from commercial enterprises to pay interns.[1467] Finally, Hawaii allowed profit-making operations that students may be engaged in at schools to include commercial enterprises, with a requirement that commercial enterprises must be related to the educational purpose of the school and potential career path for students.[1468]

Idaho allowed a cooperative service agency to establish a career technical school.[1469] Illinois allowed school counseling services to include the promotion of career and technical education, by assisting each student to determine an appropriate postsecondary plan based

---

[1463] 2022 Ariz. Sess. Laws Ch. 317, H.B. 2866.
[1464] 2022 Conn. Acts 22-125, S.B. No. 228.
[1465] 2022 Haw Sess. Laws Act 145, SB 2081.
[1466] 2022 Haw. Sess. Laws Act 143, SB 2826.
[1467] 2022 Haw. Sess. Laws Act 149, SB 3092.
[1468] 2022 Haw. Sess. Laws Act 148, SB 3091.
[1469] 2022 Idaho Sess. Laws Ch. 14, SB 1247.

upon student skills, strengths, and goals.[1470] Indiana required the department of education to establish a career coaching pilot program, a grant program to support career coaching for students in school corporations.[1471] Indiana also permitted an entity that has entered into a memorandum of understanding with the department of education to provide a work-based learning environment to have employer liability and workers' compensation insurance coverage for employers involved with work-based learning.[1472]

Kansas promoted career technical education credentialing and a pilot program to support students' transition to employment success.[1473] Kentucky created a virtual computer science career academy to expand access to accelerated, early college career pathways for state high school students and to prepare them for careers in computing.[1474] Louisiana required the state board of elementary and secondary education to develop an advisement policy for middle and high school grades to inform and assist students and their parents in the selection and scheduling of advanced courses and early college opportunities, such as dual enrollment, advanced placement, Cambridge, or international baccalaureate courses.[1475] Maryland created a workgroup to study the fiscal and operational viability of public-private partnerships for Charles County Public Schools.[1476]

Michigan required all school districts, academies, and nonpublic schools to provide information packets for all students enrolled in grades eight to twelve, which contain data and information to assist students and their parents and guardians in planning for career paths and postsecondary education choices. The requirements of the act included such data as school rankings, tuition costs, and employment data.[1477] Subject to a vote of citizens living within three school administrative districts, Maine authorized the creation of a grade nine to sixteen pilot project, in which a career and technical education center will operate.[1478] Mississippi directed the office of workforce development to pilot a career coaching program to support middle schools and high schools as students are exposed, prepared, and connected to career avenues within and beyond the classroom

---

[1470] 2022 Ill. Laws Pub. Act 102-0876, SB 3990.
[1471] 2022 Ind. Acts Pub. Law 130, SB 290.
[1472] 2022 Ind. Acts Pub. Law 140, HB 1094.
[1473] 2022 Kan. Sess. Laws HB 2466.
[1474] 2022 Ky. Acts Ch. 227, HB 680.
[1475] 2022 La. Acts No. 209, HB No. 333.
[1476] 2022 Md. Laws Ch. 425, HB 739; 2022 Md. Laws Ch. 426, SB 916.
[1477] 2022 Mich. Pub. Acts 88, HB 4953.
[1478] 2022 Me. Acts Ch. 22, H.P. 129, L.D. 176.

setting.[1479] Ohio required information documents provided to students for career counseling to include information regarding career fields that require an industry-recognized credential, certificate, associate's degree, bachelor's degree, graduate degree, or professional degree, and information about ways to defray the costs of education.[1480] Oklahoma created the center for an intern partnership program to supplement the STEM workforce pipeline.[1481] Rhode Island directed school committees and superintendents to establish policies governing the incorporation of career and technical education programs into the kindergarten through grade twelve curricula, including knowledge of careers, types of employment opportunities, and apprenticeships.[1482]

Tennessee required the state board of education to create an industry diploma and a graduation pathway for high school students with a provision for students participating in work-based learning.[1483] Tennessee further directed each state college of applied technology to establish partnerships with each LEA located in the county of the state college's main campus to provide early-postsecondary opportunities for high school students.[1484] The third act from Tennessee continued the authorization for state colleges and universities to contract with local boards of education to provide teaching for public school age students in higher education dual-credit programs.[1485]

Virginia required the department of education to annually collect and compile information, distribute it to each high school student, and place it on a website to help high school students plan for future occupations and training paths to achieve those occupations.[1486] Washington created a career and college pathways innovation challenge program, which must develop local and regional partnerships to increase postsecondary enrollment and completion for students, and eliminate opportunity gaps for students of color, English language learners, students with disabilities, and foster and homeless youth.[1487] Wisconsin provided grants for teaching college courses in high schools.[1488]

[1479] 2022 Miss. Laws H.B. No. 1388.
[1480] 2022 Ohio Laws Sub. S.B. No. 135.
[1481] 2022 Okla. Sess. Laws HB 4362.
[1482] 2022 R.I. Laws S. 2841, H. 8294.
[1483] 2022 Tenn. Pub. Acts Ch. No. 946, H.B. No. 2429, Sub. S.B. No. 2498.
[1484] 2022 Tenn. Pub. Acts Ch. No. 884, S.B. No. 2370, Sub. H.B. No. 1959.
[1485] 2022 Tenn. Pub. Acts Ch. No. 760, S.B. NO. 2017, Sub. H.B. No. 2088.
[1486] 2022 Va. Acts Ch. 343, H. 1299.
[1487] 2022 Wash. Laws Ch. 244, S.B. 5789.
[1488] 2021 Wis. Act 217, 2021 S.B. 833.

Five states approved eight acts supporting library programs. Missouri directed the office of childhood to establish a nonprofit entity to work with school districts in participating in Dolly Parton's Imagination Library.[1489] Oklahoma permitted school districts, charter schools, virtual charter schools, state agencies, public libraries and universities to offer digital or online library database resources to students in grades K-12, provided that there are filters to block access to pornography or obscene materials.[1490] Oklahoma required library media programs to be reflective of community standards when acquiring materials, resources, and equipment.[1491] Tennessee expanded membership on the state textbook and instructional materials quality commission and required the commission to issue guidance for school districts and public charter schools to use when reviewing materials in a library collection to assure the materials are age-appropriate and suitable for the mission of the school.[1492] Tennessee adopted the "Age-Appropriate Materials Act of 2022," which required each school operated by an LEA and each public charter school to maintain a current list of materials in the school's library and post the list on its website. The act required the development of a procedure to review materials to assure they are age-appropriate when placed and a procedure for reviewing parental feedback regarding materials.[1493] Vermont created a working group to study the status of libraries in the state.[1494] Vermont also directed the secretary of education to coordinate with the state librarian in the arrangement of conferences, summer schools, and other meetings, as well as to provide cooperation with the board of libraries.[1495] Virginia adopted an act to repeal obsolete provisions involving education and libraries.[1496]

Four states enrolled acts regarding reading instruction. Idaho designated a portion of its public-school educational support program appropriation bill so that a set percentage will pay for funding for reading literacy in grades K through third.[1497] Missouri directed the state board of education to develop a plan to establish a comprehensive system of services for reading instruction, to create an office of literacy, and to align literacy and reading instruction

---

[1489] 2022 Mo. Laws SB 681 & 662; § 178.694.
[1490] 2022 Okla. Sess. Laws HB 3702.
[1491] 2022 Okla. Sess. Laws HB 3092.
[1492] 2022 Tenn. Pub. Acts Ch. No. 1137, S.B. No. 2247, Sub. H.B. No. 2666.
[1493] 2022 Tenn. Pub. Acts Ch. No. 744, S.B. No. 2407, Sub. H.B. No. 2154.
[1494] 2022 Vt. Laws Act 66, S. 115, § 1.
[1495] 2022 Vt. Laws Act 66, S. 115, § 4.
[1496] 2022 Va. Acts Ch. 355, S. 421.
[1497] 2022 Idaho Sess. Laws Ch. 235, HB 790.

coursework for teacher education programs. Missouri also created a program fund to support these literacy initiatives.[1498] Louisiana initiated a book delivery program for students who are falling behind their grade level on reading achievement.[1499] Virginia required "evidence-based literacy instruction," defined as structured instructional practices including sequential, systematic, explicit, and cumulative teaching, that: (i) are based on reliable, trustworthy, and valid evidence consistent with science-based reading research; (ii) are used in core or general instruction, supplemental instruction, or intervention services; (iii) have a demonstrated record of success in adequately increasing students' reading competency, vocabulary, oral language, and comprehension as well as in building mastery of the foundational reading skills of phonological and phonemic awareness, alphabetic principle, phonics, spelling, and text reading fluency; and (iv) are able to be differentiated in order to meet the individual needs of students.[1500]

Four states passed provisions regarding English language learner (ELL) programs. Iowa amended references to students who are limited English proficient to refer to them as English learners and provided a definition in the statute for an "English learner."[1501] Rhode Island directed the department of education to create a model policy and timeline to assist local education agencies in implementing a dual language immersion program.[1502] Vermont authorized school districts and municipalities to jointly fund services for one or more cultural liaisons to support students and families who have limited English proficiency.[1503] Washington addressed providing meaningful, equitable language access to students and their family members who have language access barriers and required public schools to implement a language access plan and program for culturally-responsive, systemic family engagement developed through meaningful stakeholder engagement. The act featured the use of technical assistance and appointment of liaison personnel within the schools.[1504]

Four states passed five acts supporting child nutrition programs. California required the state department of education, in consultation with the state department of social services, to develop and post on its internet website guidance for local educational

---

[1498] 2022 Mo. Laws SB 681 & 662; § 161.241.
[1499] 2022 La. Acts No. 395, HB No. 852.
[1500] 2022 Va. Acts Ch. 549, S. 616; 2022 Va. Acts Ch. 550, H. 319.
[1501] 2022 Iowa Acts SF 2128.
[1502] 2022 R.I. Laws H. 8347.
[1503] 2022 Vt. Laws Act 66, S. 115, § 8.
[1504] 2022 Wash. Laws Ch. 107, H.B. 1153.

agencies participating in the federal school breakfast program that maintain kindergarten or any of grades first to sixth, inclusive, on how to serve eligible non-school-aged children breakfast or a morning snack at a local educational agency school site.[1505] Also discussed in the section on Higher Education, Hawaii set incremental goals for the percentage of fresh local foods purchased by the department of education, the university system, and other state agencies in each five years until 2050.[1506] Maine sought to expand the offering of free or reduced-price school meals, by requiring all public schools to accept data and applications through an internet-based application.[1507] New Jersey required schools to provide free school breakfasts and lunches to students from working class and middle-income families.[1508] New Jersey also required school food authorities to engage in public education campaigns and develop promotional materials to educate parents and guardians of students about existing and expanding school meals program options.[1509]

Two states enacted bills supporting science, technology, engineering, and mathematics (STEM) programs. California amended provisions establishing partnership academies to require the superintendent of public instruction to place in priority proposals for new academies for students who are historically underrepresented in career technical education or STEM programs or professions.[1510] New York changed the frequency of updates on the report of a study regarding assistance needed to encourage women and minorities to pursue careers in STEM to every two years.[1511]

Two states adopted mastery learning programs. Idaho created the designation of a self-directed learner who demonstrates mastery of content knowledge through grades, assessments, or mastery-based learning rubrics.[1512] Missouri created a program fund to support the development of competency-based educational programs as an alternative way for students to earn course credit upon demonstration of mastery, including through early high school graduation.[1513]

Two states provided for alternative delivery of a school leadership program. Arizona authorized the delivery of a locally-

---

[1505] 2022 Cal. Stat. Ch. 905, A.B. No. 558.
[1506] 2022 Haw. Sess. Laws Act 144, HB 1568.
[1507] 2022 Me. Acts Ch. 719, S.P. 540, L.D. 1679.
[1508] 2022 N.J. Laws P.L. c. 104, A. 2368.
[1509] 2022 N.J. Laws P.L. c. 103, A. 2365.
[1510] 2022 Cal. Stat. Ch. 114, A.B. No. 1923.
[1511] 2022 N.Y. Laws Ch. 46, A. 8764.
[1512] 2022 Idaho Sess. Laws Ch. 12, SB 1238.
[1513] 2022 Mo. Laws SB 681 & 662; § 161.380.

based school leadership program.[1514] Colorado continued a school leadership program which was previously a pilot program and funded the program for at least $250,000.[1515]

Other program development-related acts passed in 2022 are detailed as follows. Alabama directed school districts to employ a mental health service coordinator.[1516] Arkansas funded a school safety grant program in the state department of education.[1517] California authorized governing boards of school districts and other public-school entities to enter into an agreement with other local educational agencies to offer individual courses to pupils from other local educational agencies who have been impacted by disruptions, cancellations, or teacher shortages in science, technology, engineering, or mathematics courses, or dual language immersion programs.[1518] California authorized up to two local education agencies to provide extended school year programs for migratory pupils whose early education has been interrupted due to family agricultural migratory movement.[1519]

Delaware extended the timeframe for review and action by the state board of education for participation in a consortium for educational equity.[1520] Georgia transitioned a pilot program for elementary agricultural education to an ongoing program.[1521] Illinois permitted students eligible for remote learning to complete their education while incarcerated through alternative learning opportunities programs.[1522] Maine allocated grant funds for an innovative instruction and tutoring grant program to address learning loss or unfinished learning.[1523] Maryland required the state department of education to study and make recommendations regarding the home and hospital teaching program for students, instructional services, and transition plans for students in the program.[1524]

Missouri required school districts who have identified 3% or more of its students as gifted to establish a state-approved gifted program.[1525] Missouri established a computer science education task force within the department of elementary and secondary education

---

[1514] 2022 Ariz. Sess. Laws Ch. 337, S.B. 1159.
[1515] 2022 Colo. Sess. Laws HB 1248.
[1516] 2022 Ala. Acts 442, H.123.
[1517] 2022 Ark. Acts 3, SB 2 (1st Spec. Session).
[1518] 2022 Cal. Stat. Ch. 711, S.B. No. 941.
[1519] 2022 Cal. Stat. Ch. 483, A.B. No. 1777.
[1520] 2022 Del. Laws HB 436.
[1521] 2022 Ga. Laws Act 599, HB 1303.
[1522] 2022 Ill. Laws Pub. Act 102-0966, HB 5016.
[1523] 2022 Me. Acts Ch. 632, S.P. 700, L.D. 1962.
[1524] 2022 Md. Laws Ch. 211, HB 1327.
[1525] 2022 Mo. Laws SB 681 & 662; § 162.720.

to develop a state strategic plan for expanding a statewide computer science education program.[1526] Ohio required the state department of education to compile a list of tutoring programs that it considers to be of high quality and to have the potential to accelerate learning for students in the areas of English language arts, mathematics, science, and social studies. For this purpose, the department must request the qualifications of public and private entities that provide tutoring programs for students, establish a rubric to evaluate the programs, and determine a minimum score for inclusion on the department's list.[1527] Oklahoma directed the commission for educational quality and accountability to establish a mentor teacher pilot program.[1528] Tennessee closed a pre-kindergarten pilot program and instead provided for a voluntary pre-kindergarten program for at-risk four-year olds.[1529]

The first of five laws from Utah clarified that kindergarten remained optional but provided funding for the "optional enhanced" (i.e., full-time) kindergarten grant program.[1530] Utah required LEAs to provide dropout prevention and recovery services by contracting with a third party for creating a dropout prevention and recovery plan.[1531] Utah removed a repeal date for the student intervention early warning program.[1532] Utah amended innovative program provisions to allow LEAs to adopt alternative classroom schedules and alternative curricula,[1533] and a separate Utah act expanded innovative program offerings with more regulatory requirements.[1534]

Vermont required the agency of education, in collaboration with the school boards association and an advisory council on wellness, to update and distribute to school districts a model wellness program policy.[1535] Vermont provided funding for the implementation of community school programs that provide students with equitable access to a high-quality education.[1536] Virginia created a school health services committee in the legislative branch, to review and provide advice regarding proposals that require school boards to provide health services in school settings.[1537]

[1526] 2022 Mo. Laws SB 681 & 662; § 170.036.
[1527] 2022 Ohio Laws Sub. H.B. No. 583.
[1528] 2022 Okla. Sess. Laws SB 1631.
[1529] 2022 Tenn. Pub. Acts Ch. No. 957, H.B. No. 2709, Sub. S.B. No. 2595.
[1530] 2022 Utah Laws H.B. 193.
[1531] 2022 Utah Laws H.B. 251.
[1532] 2022 Utah Laws H.B. 103.
[1533] 2022 Utah Laws H.B. 386.
[1534] 2022 Utah Laws S.B. 191.
[1535] 2022 Vt. Laws Act 66, S. 115, § 10.
[1536] 2022 Vt. Laws Act 67, H. 106.
[1537] 2022 Va. Acts Ch. 707, S. 62; 2022 Va. Acts Ch. 749, H. 215.

School Choice

This section describes school choice-related legislation passed by general assemblies and legislatures during the last calendar year. Six states adopted acts supporting educational choice scholarships, supported usually by tax credits. Alabama increased the tax credit from 50% to 100% of the tax liability of a taxpayer for contributions to a scholarship granting organization for educational scholarships, with a three-year limit of application. Scholarships under this program pay for income-eligible public-school students to attend private schools.[1538] Arizona amended several provisions related to its empowerment scholarships to pay for students to attend private schools, including: decreasing the required hours of online instruction which varies by grade level; permitting participation of a student at a nonpublic school in a prior year under an IEP; setting an age range for participation by kindergarten students; authorizing expenditures for transport services and computer technology; and requiring participants to withdraw from a school district or charter school before receiving scholarship monies.[1539] Maine reinstated and increased the income tax deduction for contributions made to education savings plans.[1540] Ohio included siblings of previous recipients of an educational choice scholarship as an "eligible student" to receive a scholarship.[1541] Oklahoma changed the reporting dates for obtaining or continuing tax credits in the Oklahoma Equal Opportunity Education Scholarship Act.[1542] Utah amended the Special Needs Opportunity Scholarship Program to make siblings of scholarship students eligible for the program.[1543]

Five states passed six acts changing charter school law. Kentucky allowed an applicant for a public charter school to request technical assistance from the state department of education and indicated that a failure to act on a charter application within sixty days of the established application submission deadline shall be deemed an approval by the authorizer.[1544] New Hampshire made minor adjustments to provisions for access to public-school programs by nonpublic or public chartered schools, or home educated pupils, including making it mandatory, rather than permissive, for public schools to have policies regarding access and to indicate that the

---

[1538] 2022 Ala. Acts 390, S.261.
[1539] 2022 Ariz. Sess. Laws Ch. 388, H.B. 2853.
[1540] 2022 Me. Acts Ch. 707, S.P. 31, L.D. 23.
[1541] 2022 Ohio Laws Sub. H.B. No. 583.
[1542] 2022 Okla. Sess. Laws SB 1659.
[1543] 2022 Utah Laws S.B. 62.
[1544] 2022 Ky. Acts Ch. 213, §§5 and 6, HB 9.

portfolio created for a home-schooled student to provide information to the public school belongs to the parent, not the public school.[1545] North Carolina entitled a charter school to automatically extend any deadline to begin operations or commence the term of its charter until the next school year if it notifies the state board of education by June 30 that it is seeking land use or development approvals for its selected site or facilities, or if it is challenging the denial of any requested land use or development approvals. The term of the charter issued by the state board shall be tolled during the period of any extension or extensions issued under the relevant section.[1546] North Carolina also extended charter school enrollment priority to grandchildren of employees or charter board members, and not just their children.[1547] Oklahoma amended provisions guiding charter schools to delete a requirement of physical location for charter schools for students served by a contract with the office of juvenile affairs.[1548] Tennessee authorized the commission allowing charter schools to require a charter school to delay opening for up to one school year through the charter agreement.[1549]

Three states made changes to provisions for open enrollment. Delaware amended its school choice provisions to clarify that all students in all types of school districts, including reorganized school districts and vocational technology school districts, follow the same procedures for obtaining choice in school attendance.[1550] Louisiana created public high schools of choice, which allow a student to concurrently pursue a high school diploma and either a postsecondary degree, credential, or certificate or a state-registered apprenticeship or pre-apprenticeship, without regard to attendance zones.[1551] Oklahoma gave discretion to a receiving school district to allow a student to transfer to the school district, regardless of capacity, if the student has attended as a resident student for at least three years prior to becoming eligible to apply as a transfer student. In the same act, siblings may be given preference for attending a receiving school district.[1552] Oklahoma also permitted a student who transfers from the student's resident district to another school district under the open transfer act from enrolling in a full-

---

[1545] 2022 N.H. Laws Ch. 131, HB 1663.
[1546] 2022 N.C. Sess. Laws Ch. 75, H.B. 911.
[1547] 2022 N.C. Sess. Laws Ch. 71, H.B. 159.
[1548] 2022 Okla. Sess. Laws HB 3872.
[1549] 2022 Tenn. Pub. Acts Ch. No. 1085, S.B. No. 918, Sub. H.B. No. 757, § 7.
[1550] 2022 Del. Laws HB 270.
[1551] 2022 La. Acts No. 533, SB No. 50.
[1552] 2022 Okla. Sess. Laws HB 3038.

time virtual education program offered by the receiving school district.[1553]

Two states altered provisions about home schools. Louisiana amended home study provisions to specify that public school systems are not responsible for collecting and maintaining school attendance data for children enrolled in an approved home study program, until the child is enrolled in a public school.[1554] Pennsylvania required school districts to adopt a policy to permit a home-schooled student to participate, on the same basis as other students enrolled in the school district, in any cocurricular activity that merges extracurricular activities with a required academic course, including, but not limited to, band or orchestra. The provision also required the policy to permit a home-schooled student to participate in academic courses equaling up to at least one-quarter of the school day for full-time students.[1555]

One state, Missouri, permitted the identification of school innovation teams in single schools or in aligned schools to obtain a waiver from various statutory requirements for schools in the school code.[1556]

School Safety

School safety is a topic area that is perennially one of the most active education-related areas of legislative activity, and that was again the case in 2022. This section describes school safety-related acts adopted in the last calendar year. Planning for school safety elicited the largest grouping of school safety-related legislation, with nine states passing twelve such acts, as follows.

California added to requirements for comprehensive school safety plans by directing the state department of education to develop model content informing parents or guardians about safe storage of firearms and to require school officials who perceive a threat involving firearms to coordinate with local law enforcement or school resource officers to conduct a threat assessment, including the availability of firearms to the student causing the threat.[1557] Colorado continued the working group on school safety[1558] and renewed funding for the school safety program.[1559] Illinois exempted

---

[1553] 2022 Okla. Sess. Laws SB 1238.
[1554] 2022 La. Acts No. 677, SB No. 124.
[1555] 2022 Pa. Laws Act No. 55, HB 1642, Section 13.
[1556] 2022 Mo. Laws SB 681 & 662; § 161.214.
[1557] 2022 Cal. Stat. Ch. 144, S.B. No. 906.
[1558] 2022 Colo. Sess. Laws HB 1274.
[1559] 2022 Colo. Sess. Laws HB 1120.

from disclosure under the state freedome of information act any threat assessment procedures under the requirements for school safety drills.[1560]

Michigan required critical incident mapping data to be included in school safety response plans.[1561] New Hampshire repealed and reenacted a new provision regarding school emergency operations plans to include multiple types of situations, such as acts of violence, biological incidents, civil unrest, cyber incidents, drought, earthquakes, extreme temperatures, floods, hurricanes and severe storms, internal and external hazardous materials releases, medical emergencies, structural fire, threats, tornadoes, wildfire, winter storm, or any other hazard deemed necessary by school officials and local emergency authorities.[1562] New Jersey required public and nonpublic schools to submit critical incident mapping data to local law enforcement officials.[1563] New Jersey also required the board of education of each school district and the board of trustees of each charter school or renaissance school to develop and adopt a policy for the establishment of a threat assessment team at each school.[1564]

New York allowed school boards to include information regarding the installation of a panic alarm system in any school in the district in the district-wide school safety plan.[1565]

Virginia required each local school board to create a detailed and accurate floor plan for each school as part of an annual school safety audit.[1566] Virginia also required local school boards to collaborate with the chief law enforcement officer of the locality, or the chief officer's designee, when conducting the required annual school safety audit.[1567] Washington prohibited the incorporation of active shooter scenarios in school safety lockdown drills.[1568]

Five states supported funding for safety training. Arkansas funded a school safety grant program in the state department of education.[1569] Maine amended a prior provision creating a school safety center to add a list of purposes for the center and a list of services to be provided by the center to the schools.[1570] Ohio created the mobile training team in the department of public safety, which must be administered by a chief mobile training officer, to provide

---

[1560] 2022 Ill. Laws Pub. Act 102-0791, HB 4994.
[1561] 2022 Mich. Pub. Acts 257, HB 6042.
[1562] 2022 N.H. Laws Ch. 187, HB 1125.
[1563] 2022 N.J. Laws P. L. c. 122, S. 2426.
[1564] 2022 N.J. Laws P.L. c. 83, A. 4075.
[1565] 2022 N.Y. Laws Ch. 227, S. 7132.
[1566] 2022 Va. Acts Ch. 57, H. 741.
[1567] 2022 Va. Acts Ch. 21, S. 600; 2022 Va. Acts Ch. 22, H. 1129.
[1568] 2022 Wash. Laws Ch. 77, H.B. 1941.
[1569] 2022 Ark. Acts 3, SB 2 (1st Spec. Session).
[1570] 2022 Me. Acts Ch. 542, H.P. 1380, L.D. 1870.

services to public and nonpublic schools regarding school safety and security, especially in training personnel. School districts are authorized to modify the training as long as key aspects required in the act are covered.[1571] Pennsylvania required that the chief school administrator of a school entity must appoint a school safety and security coordinator charged with providing training to school staff.[1572] Rhode Island required schools to implement trauma-informed practices throughout the state.[1573]

Four states enacted six bills regarding discipline policy. California required the state department of education to develop evidence-based best practices for restorative justice practice implementation on a school campus and to make those best practices available on the department's internet website on or before June 1, 2024.[1574] New York removed the term "incorrigible" from sections of the school code related to student discipline.[1575] Tennessee authorized local school boards or charter schools to implement holistic programs of positive behavior reinforcement and reward-based behavior modification as part of the school's discipline policy.[1576] Tennessee also allowed public school discipline policies to authorize a teacher to withhold a student's phone from a student for the duration of instructional time if the student's phone is a distraction to the class or student.[1577] Vermont directed the Building Bright Futures Council to collaborate with the agency of human services and the agency of education to define suspension, expulsion, and exclusionary practices in early childhood education settings and to establish best practices for supporting children who face such measures.[1578] In a second act, Vermont created a task force on equitable and inclusive school environments to make recommendations to end suspensions and expulsions for all but the most serious student behaviors and to compile data regarding school discipline in public and approved independent schools.[1579]

Two states limited or prohibited corporal punishment. Missouri prohibited pupils to be subject to corporal punishment outlined in the discipline and corporal punishment policy without a parent or guardian being notified and providing written permission for the

---

[1571] 2022 Ohio Laws H.B. No. 99.
[1572] 2022 Pa. Laws Act No. 55, HB 1642, section 19.
[1573] 2022 R.I. Laws H. 6667.
[1574] 2022 Cal. Stat. Ch. 914, A.B. No. 2598.
[1575] 2022 N.Y. Laws Ch. 181, A. 7981.
[1576] 2022 Tenn. Pub. Acts Ch. No. 934, H.B. No. 1930, Sub. S.B. No. 1958.
[1577] 2022 Tenn. Pub. Acts Ch. No. 707, S.B. No. 1995, Sub. H.B. No. 2028.
[1578] 2022 Vt. Laws Act 166, S. 283, § 4.
[1579] 2022 Vt. Laws Act 35, S. 16.

corporal punishment.[1580] New Hampshire prohibited all forms of corporal punishment for children in state agency programs.[1581]

Two states limited the use of restraints, the first of which is also discussed in the Students with Disabilities section. Florida prohibited school personnel from using a mechanical restraint on students with disabilities.[1582] Maryland prohibited public agencies, including schools, from using physical restraint and nonpublic schools from using physical restraint or seclusion as a behavioral health intervention for a student.[1583]

Eight states passed ten acts promoting mental health. California required each school site serving pupils in grades six to twelve to create a poster that identifies approaches and shares resources regarding pupil mental health to be conspicuously displayed in appropriate public areas.[1584] Also, California urged the governing board of each school district to provide access to a comprehensive educational counseling program for all pupils enrolled in the school district. Additionally, the act recast educational counseling to include some postsecondary services.[1585] Colorado continued funding for a youth mental health services program.[1586]

Delaware phased in, over a three-year timeframe, the funding of mental health services at a ratio of 250 students per professional in middle schools.[1587] Delaware required mandatory instruction in age- and developmentally-appropriate social emotional learning and mental health content in all public schools no later than the 2023-2024 school year.[1588] Kentucky required local school superintendents to report information on school based mental health service providers in the district to the state department of education.[1589] Louisiana required instruction on mental health to be provided to students in grades K-12.[1590]

Oklahoma directed school districts to maintain a protocol for responding to students in mental health crisis.[1591] Oklahoma also made it permissible for a parent or legal guardian, prior to enrollment of a student, to disclose if the student has received inpatient or emergency outpatient mental health services from a

---

[1580] 2022 Mo. Laws SB 681 & 662; § 160. 261.
[1581] 2022 N.H. Laws Ch. 2, HB 427.
[1582] 2022 Fla. Laws Ch. 2022-20, HB 235.
[1583] 2022 Md. Laws Ch. 562, SB 705; 2022 Md. Laws Ch. 31, HB 1255.
[1584] 2022 Cal. Stat. Ch. 431, A.B. No. 748.
[1585] 2022 Cal. Stat. Ch. 153, A.B. No. 2508.
[1586] 2022 Colo. Sess. Laws HB 1243.
[1587] 2022 Del. Laws HB 300.
[1588] 2022 Del. Laws HB 301.
[1589] 2022 Ky. Acts Ch. 234, SB 102.
[1590] 2022 La. Acts No. 650, HB No. 981.
[1591] 2022 Okla. Sess. Laws HB 4106.

mental health facility in the previous twenty-four months.[1592] Pennsylvania provided grants to support services for mental health, suicide prevention, and bullying and harassment prevention. The act also expanded telemedicine delivery of school-based mental health services.[1593] Utah directed the mental health institute at the University of Utah to develop a youth behavioral health curriculum.[1594]

Seven states enacted legislation with respect to suicide prevention. California required local education agencies to review and update policies on pupil suicide prevention and revise training materials to incorporate best practices in the materials and training.[1595] Delaware required public schools serving pupils in grades seven through twelve that issue pupil identification cards to have printed on the cards the telephone or text numbers for the national suicide prevention hotline.[1596] Louisiana required age- and grade-appropriate instruction in public schools regarding suicide prevention, student safety, and violence and isolation prevention.[1597] Missouri required at least two hours of in-service training for all practicing teachers regarding suicide prevention.[1598] Additionally, Missouri required students in grades seven to twelve, if they have school identification cards, to have printed on one side of the card the three-digit dialing code for the suicide and crisis lifeline.[1599]

Oklahoma required schools distributing identification cards and serving students in grades seven to twelve to print contact information for the national suicide prevention lifeline and the crisis text line.[1600] Tennessee required LEAs that issue student identification cards in grades six to twelve to include on the cards contact information for suicide prevention resources.[1601] West Virginia amended provisions creating a core behavioral health crisis services system to tie the system in with the national suicide prevention lifeline.[1602]

Six states added acts related to management of seizure disorders. Arizona required all schools to have seizure management treatment plans.[1603] California required the superintendent of public

---

[1592] 2022 Okla. Sess. Laws SB 626.
[1593] 2022 Pa. Laws Act No. 55, HB 1642, Section 18.
[1594] 2022 Utah Laws S.B. 171.
[1595] 2022 Cal. Stat. Ch. 428, A.B. No. 58.
[1596] 2022 Del. Laws HB 254.
[1597] 2022 La. Acts No. 643, HB No. 495.
[1598] 2022 Mo. Laws SB 681 & 662; § 170.047.
[1599] 2022 Mo. Laws SB 681 & 662; § 170.048.4.(1).
[1600] 2022 Okla. Sess. Laws SB 1307.
[1601] 2022 Tenn. Pub. Acts Ch. No. 748, S.B. No. 2510, Sub. H.B. No. 2062.
[1602] 2022 W. Va. Acts Ch. 222, S.B. 181.
[1603] 2022 Ariz. Sess. Laws Ch. 210, S.B. 1654.

instruction to establish minimum standards of training for the administration of emergency anti-seizure medication and to provide training for volunteers in the school to improve care for pupils with seizure disorders.[1604] Florida required the development and implementation of an individualized seizure disorder action plan for students with epilepsy or seizure disorders.[1605] Louisiana directed the department of education to develop and make available two courses of instruction regarding treating students with seizure disorders, seizure recognition, and related first aid. The act included a provision regarding the submission of a seizure management plan by parents or guardians of students with a seizure disorder.[1606] Maryland required county boards of education and allowed nonpublic schools to require at least two school personnel to complete paid professional development training to teach other school personnel how to recognize and respond to student seizures.[1607] Utah required LEAs to provide training on seizures and seizure disorders to teachers and other school professionals.[1608]

Three states passed four measures for dealing with the assault of children. Louisiana required instruction on child assault awareness and prevention in public schools.[1609] Tennessee required all employees working directly with students of an LEA or charter school to complete an annual child abuse training program.[1610] Tennessee also required LEAs and public charter schools to provide contact information for each of their child abuse coordinators and alternative child abuse coordinators to the department of children's services at the beginning of each school year.[1611] West Virginia made it a felony for a "person in a position of trust" to assault, batter, or verbally abuse a disabled child or to neglect to report abuse they witness. The definition included persons working in education.[1612]

Two states provided definitions for the sexual assault of child. Rhode Island defined any act of sexual penetration or contact perpetrated by an individual with a position of authority upon a person over the age of fourteen and under the age of eighteen as third-degree sexual assault.[1613] South Dakota revised the definition of sexual contact with a child under the age of eighteen by a person

---

[1604] 2022 Cal. Stat. Ch. 906, A.B. No. 1810.
[1605] 2022 Fla. Laws Ch. 2022-19, HB 173.
[1606] 2022 La. Acts No. 562, HB. No. 914.
[1607] 2022 Md. Laws Ch. 78, SB 299.
[1608] 2022 Utah Laws H.B. 241.
[1609] 2022 La. Acts No. 180, SB No. 94.
[1610] 2022 Tenn. Pub. Acts Ch. No. 841, H.B. No. 2021, Sub. S.B. No. 2815.
[1611] 2022 Tenn. Pub. Acts Ch. No. 781, S.B. No. 2239, Sub. H.B. No. 2582.
[1612] 2022 W. Va. Acts Ch. 82, H.B. 4600.
[1613] 2022 R.I. Laws H. 8230, S. 2219.

in authority over the child, including teachers and coaches, to make it applicable to a 120-day period immediately preceding the sexual contact.[1614]

Three states altered provisions regarding hazing and bullying. Arizona criminalized hazing in public schools.[1615] California amended a provision requiring a social medial platform to disclose cyberbullying on its system to provide civil penalties or injunctive relief against social media platforms violating the provision.[1616] Louisiana added a definition for "bullying" in a requirement for public schools to have an anti-bullying policy to include written, electronic or verbal communication, gestures, physical acts, and shunning behaviors.[1617]

Six states passed nine acts regarding criminal background checks of persons in schools. Arizona added all charter school representatives, governing board members, officers, directors, and holders of the charter to undergo criminal background checks.[1618] Kentucky allowed school districts to accept a background check for a student teacher which has been completed by an accredited teacher education institution.[1619] Louisiana added to procedures for criminal background checks for educator credentials or authorization to teach through the state board of elementary and secondary education[1620] and required criminal background checks in private training or driving instructor training schools or agencies.[1621]

Missouri added provisions for a substitute teaching certificate, with a required background check, for individuals who have at least thirty-six semester hours at an accredited institution of higher education and online training developed by the department of elementary and secondary education.[1622] New Hampshire amended the authority given to the state board of education in conducting criminal background checks for school personnel, to allow checks to be done through the National Association of State Directors of Teacher Education and Certification (DASDTEC) database and through other state databases.[1623] New Hampshire established a committee to study the feasibility of centralized criminal history checks in education.[1624] New Hampshire allowed substitute teachers

---

[1614] 2022 S.D. Laws S.B. 81.
[1615] 2022 Ariz. Sess. Laws Ch. 202, H.B. 2322.
[1616] 2022 Cal. Stat. Ch. 700, A.B. No. 2879.
[1617] 2022 La. Acts No. 697, SB No. 358.
[1618] 2022 Ariz. Sess. Laws Ch. 201, H.B. 2177.
[1619] 2022 Ky. Acts Ch. 160, HB 283.
[1620] 2022 La. Acts No. 745, HB No. 156.
[1621] 2022 La. Acts No. 347, HB No. 669.
[1622] 2022 Mo. Laws SB 681 & 662; § 168.036.6.
[1623] 2022 N.H. Laws Ch. 222, SB 350.
[1624] 2022 N.H. Laws Ch. 198, HB 1398.

who have undergone a criminal record check to work within the same school administrative unit without undergoing an additional record check.[1625]

Oregon modified criminal background check requirements to remove the requirement for persons who move from one school district to another, received a background check for the prior employer, and remained continuously licensed or registered with the standards and practices commission.[1626] Oregon also required the department of education and the teacher standards and practices commission to review the application process for persons seeking jobs in education in the state, including licensed and classified staff, and to develop a common portal for job listings, receipt of applications, and performance of a common background check.[1627]

Two states enacted changes regarding video cameras. Louisiana added to pre-existing provisions requiring public schools to adopt policies about installation and operation of cameras in classrooms to force a timeline for adoption and submission of a copy of the policy to the state department of elementary and secondary education.[1628] New York amended the hours of operation of a school zone speed camera demonstration program in New York City.[1629]

Two states adopted provisions to promote digital safety. Louisiana required the department of education to develop and distribute health and safety guidelines regarding best practices for the use of digital devices in public schools.[1630] Tennessee made changes to the internet acceptable use policy that LEAs are required to adopt and redefined "obscene" to include material that has educational value.[1631]

Five states enacted bills creating requirements to report health and safety information. Connecticut repealed the listing of mandatory reporters for acts of sexual misconduct against children and produced a new list, including teachers, coaches, administrators, medical professionals, police officers, probation and parole officers, counselors, and other mental health professionals.[1632] Hawaii required unlicensed but accredited private schools to annually submit health and safety documentation to the council of private schools or the various religious-oriented private school

---

[1625] 2022 N.H. Laws Ch. 170, SB 352.
[1626] 2022 Or. Laws Ch. 116 § 1, HB 4030.
[1627] 2022 Or. Laws Ch. 116 § 5, HB 4030.
[1628] 2022 La. Acts No. 588, SB No. 45.
[1629] 2022 N.Y. Laws Ch. 229, S. 5602.
[1630] 2022 La. Acts No. 222, HB No. 548.
[1631] 2022 Tenn. Pub. Acts Ch. No. 1002, H.B. No. 2454, Sub. S.B. No. 2292.
[1632] 2022 Conn. Acts 22-87, H.B. No. 5243.

associations.[1633] In a provision requiring reportable offenses to be reported to the state department of education, Maryland altered the definition of "reportable offense" to include only offenses that occurred off school premises, that did not occur at events sponsored by the school, and that involved certain crimes of violence.[1634] Rhode Island required the governing body of a charter or private school to submit the identity of any teacher terminated for cause to the state department of education.[1635] Virginia amended provisions regarding the duty of school principals to report wrongdoing so that principals must now also report incidents involving controlled substances or injury-causing assaults and batteries on school property or at school events, felony offenses to law enforcement, and, to parents, when their child is the object of misdemeanor or felony offenses requiring reports to the superintendent or law enforcement.[1636]

Six states approved acts regarding school resource officers. Indiana amended provisions regarding school resource officers to allow newly-hired officers 365 days to receive specialty training.[1637] Iowa added school resource officers to the operational functions which may be shared by school districts.[1638] Kentucky required the assignment of a school resource officer for every school building in the school district.[1639] Ohio created an exception for a requirement for armed persons in a school zone to have undergone basic peace officer training to expressly overrule the decision of the Ohio Supreme Court in *Gabbard v. Madison Local School District Board of Education*.[1640] Rhode Island required the department of education and attorney general to publish data on school resource officers, including the number of officers, instances of use of force, number and types of other disciplinary actions taken, and referrals to court services.[1641] Virginia added a school resource officer to a school threat assessment team required by previous law, to serve as a liaison to the school administrator.[1642]

Three states altered provisions regarding firearms in schools. Alabama struck down the requirement for a permit to conceal carry a firearm but continued restrictions on carrying firearms in schools or at school activities.[1643] Hawaii removed a reporting requirement

---

[1633] 2022 Haw. Sess. Laws Act 61, HB 2248.
[1634] 2022 Md. Laws Ch. 742, HB 146.
[1635] 2022 R.I. Laws S. 3040, H. 7274.
[1636] 2022 Va. Acts Ch. 793, H. 4; 2022 Va. Acts Ch. 794, S. 36.
[1637] 2022 Ind. Acts Pub. Law 139, HB 1093.
[1638] 2022 Iowa Acts HF 2080.
[1639] 2022 Ky. Acts Ch. 189, HB 63.
[1640] 2022 Ohio Laws H.B. No. 99. The Gabbard case is cited as Slip Opinion No. 2021-Ohio-2067.
[1641] 2022 R.I. Laws S. 2578, H. 6649.
[1642] 2022 Va. Acts Ch. 769, H. 873.
[1643] 2022 Ala. Acts 133, H.272.

to the federal department of education regarding the number of students excluded because of possession of firearms and the types of firearms found in their possession, with the report still going to the state department of education.[1644] Illinois permitted school boards to provide instruction in safe gun storage.[1645]

Two states made three changes in traffic fines related to school bus transportation. Illinois increased the fines for speeding in a school zone to $250 for a first offense, instead of $150, which is also discussed in the Transportation section.[1646] Illinois also added community service as a penalty for failing to stop before meeting or overtaking a school bus that is stopped for receiving or discharging students.[1647] Tennessee raised the fine from $50 to $200 for the first violation of passing a stopped school bus, even if the evidence comes from the bus safety video.[1648]

Four states adopted six acts regarding the storage and administration of medications. Iowa permitted school districts to obtain opioid antagonist prescriptions.[1649] Iowa permitted the self-administration and storage of bronchodilators, bronchodilator canisters, and bronchodilator canisters and spacers in schools.[1650] Louisiana required schools to store epinephrine in the classrooms of students who may require access to the epinephrine.[1651] Louisiana also allowed early learning centers to stock a supply of auto-injectable epinephrine.[1652] Maine approved a change in rules for medication administration in state schools proposed by the department of education, to the extent the changes are only grammatical, formatting, punctuation, and other technical, non-substantive editing changes to the rules.[1653] Virginia required the state board of education to amend its regulations to require each early childhood care and education entity to implement policies for the possession and administration of epinephrine.[1654]

Two states altered requirements for training in cardiopulmonary resuscitation (CPR).

New York allowed coaches who cannot be certified in CPR to be able to coach high school sports if there is another coach or staff

---

[1644] 2022 Haw. Sess. Laws Act 224, SB 2817.
[1645] 2022 Ill. Laws Pub. Act 102-0971, HB 5193.
[1646] 2022 Ill. Laws Pub. Act 102-0978, HB 5328.
[1647] 2022 Ill. Laws Pub. Act 102-0859, SB 3793.
[1648] 2022 Tenn. Pub. Acts Ch. No. 792, S.B. No. 2512, Sub. H.B. No. 2550.
[1649] 2022 Iowa Acts HF 2573.
[1650] 2022 Iowa Acts HF 771.
[1651] 2022 La. Acts No. 315, SB No. 407.
[1652] 2022 La. Acts No. 335, HB No. 417.
[1653] 2022 Me. Acts Ch. 139, H.P. 1440, L.D. 1931.
[1654] 2022 Va. Acts Ch. 695, H. 1328; 2022 Va. Acts Ch. 696, S. 737.

member present at the sporting activity who is certified in CPR.[1655] Utah required the state board of education to make rules to develop and implement CPR training as part of the health curriculum in schools, and required LEAs to offer CPR training for students.[1656]

Two states enacted bills designed to protect student athletes from heat stroke. Maryland required each middle and high school to develop a venue-specific emergency action plan for a heat acclimatization emergency for all athletic facilities.[1657] Virginia required the state department of education to develop guidelines on policies to inform and educate coaches and student athletes and their parents or guardians of the dangers of heat-related illness.[1658]

Two states passed acts regarding automatic external defibrillators. Maryland required each middle and high school to develop a venue-specific emergency action plan for the operation and use of automatic external defibrillators.[1659] Tennessee encouraged schools to offer automated external defibrillator device training to school bus drivers.[1660]

Other school-safety related legislation passed in 2022 is described as follows. California permitted local education agencies to enter into a memorandum of understanding with a nonprofit eye examination provider to provide noninvasive eye examinations to schoolchildren.[1661] California authorized school governing boards to provide time and facilities to local law enforcement for bicycle, scooter, electric bicycle, motorized bicycle, or motorized scooter safety instruction. The provision previously required local law enforcement to supply the facilities.[1662] California required a school district, county office of education, or charter school to report any cyberattack impacting more than 500 pupils or personnel to the state cybersecurity integration center.[1663] California authorized the department of public health to provide testing programs for COVID-19 in public schools and charter schools, consistent with guidance from the department.[1664]

Colorado funded a study of the amendments to the Title IX regulations issued by the U.S. Department of Education's Office for Civil Rights regarding best practices for responding to sex-based

---

[1655] 2022 N.Y. Laws Ch. 519, A. 9534.
[1656] 2022 Utah Laws S.B. 192.
[1657] 2022 Md. Laws Ch. 212, HB 836.
[1658] 2022 Va. Acts Ch. 428, S. 161.
[1659] 2022 Md. Laws Ch. 212, HB 836.
[1660] 2022 Tenn. Pub. Acts Ch. No. 948, H.B. No. 2530, Sub. S.B. No. 2824.
[1661] 2022 Cal. Stat. Ch. 911, A.B. No. 2329.
[1662] 2022 Cal. Stat. Ch. 116, A.B. No. 2028.
[1663] 2022 Cal. Stat. Ch. 498, A.B. No. 2355.
[1664] 2022 Cal. Stat. Ch. 850, S.B. No. 1479.

discrimination and harassment in the public schools.[1665] Delaware required each school district and charter school to adopt a policy about appropriate relationships between school employees, contractors, coaches, volunteers, and students.[1666] Florida amended its school safety awareness program to provide criminal penalties for making false school safety tips and also appropriated funds for "hardening" schools.[1667] Hawaii permitted the department of education to provide optional asthma education instruction to students and asthma training to teachers and other school employees who interact with students.[1668]

Louisiana directed public schools to provide age and grade-appropriate instruction relative to eating disorder awareness and prevention.[1669] Louisiana also required each public-school authority to either establish a uniform policy for student check-out for each school in its jurisdiction or require each school principal to establish such a policy, to be reviewed by the superintendent.[1670] Ohio designated the month of October as "Ohio School Safety Month" to increase public awareness of school safety programs and to encourage citizens in their role in keeping schools a safe place for students to learn and grow.[1671]

New York required nonpublic schools to follow the same rules and regulations as public schools with regard to a pupil who suffers a concussion and with regard to training on concussion management.[1672] Second, New York permitted schools with the technical ability to batch download sets of statewide immunization records in the department of health to do so.[1673] Lastly, New York provided an exemption for the statutory prohibition against the sale of alcoholic beverages within a certain distance of a school for an identified parcel of land in Manhattan.[1674] Oklahoma permitted optometrists and ophthalmologists to perform vision screening services in schools.[1675] Virginia directed the state department of education to recommend options for isolation and quarantine for students and employees at public schools who contract or are

---

[1665] 2022 Colo. Sess. Laws SB 207.
[1666] 2022 Del. Laws SB 291.
[1667] 2022 Fla. Laws Ch. 2022-174, HB 1421.
[1668] 2022 Haw. Sess. Laws Act 147, SB 2822.
[1669] 2022 La. Acts No. 626, HB No. 440.
[1670] 2022 La. Acts No. 325, HB No. 263.
[1671] 2022 Ohio Laws Sub. H.B. No. 583 Section 1.
[1672] 2022 N.Y. Laws Ch. 617, S. 973.
[1673] 2022 N.Y. Laws Ch. 44, A. 8762.
[1674] 2022 N.Y. Laws Ch. 356, S. 9385.
[1675] 2022 Okla. Sess. Laws HB 3823.

exposed to COVID-19 and to develop and recommend guidelines for schools to use as an alternative to quarantine.[1676]

Students with Disabilities

This section details laws enrolled in the last legislative year regarding students with disabilities. Six states enacted bills setting age ranges for services. To conform with federal law, Delaware required that a child with a disability is eligible for services beginning on the child's third birthday, or earlier if otherwise provided in this title of the law.[1677] New Hampshire changed the definition of a child with a disability under special education laws and thereby provided funding for special education services for students over age twenty-one until their twenty-second birthday.[1678] New York required that a student enrolled in an individualized education program (IEP) during certain school years may continue to receive educational services until the student completes the services pursuant to the IEP or turns twenty-three years old, whichever is sooner.[1679] Pennsylvania required disabled students who have reached twenty-one years of age during the 2022-2023 school year to continue being served until the end of that school year.[1680] Rhode Island directed that special education services would include speech-language pathology services and would not stop because a child has reached nine years of age.[1681] Vermont permitted a state resident who is enrolled in an interstate school district, is on an IEP, is twenty-one years of age or younger, and who is not entitled to receive special education services through the interstate school district due to an age limitation, to be entitled to enroll in a state public high school and receive special education services through the age of twenty-one.[1682]

Four states altered statutes about deaf students. Maine amended provisions regarding the state educational center for the deaf and hard of hearing, the state school for the deaf, and the preschool program at Mackworth Island.[1683] Michigan required the department of education to develop a resource for use by a parent or legal guardian of a child who is age 5 or under and deaf or hard of hearing regarding language developmental milestones and modes of

---

[1676] 2022 Va. Acts Ch. 692, S. 431.
[1677] 2022 Del. Laws HB 454.
[1678] 2022 N.H. Laws Ch. 264, HB 1513; 2022 N.H. Laws Ch. 230, SB 394.
[1679] 2022 N.Y. Laws Ch. 223, A. 8610.
[1680] 2022 Pa. Laws Act No. 55, HB 1642, Section 16.
[1681] 2022 R.I. Laws H. 7273, S. 2570.
[1682] 2022 Vt. Laws Act 166, S. 283, § 12.
[1683] 2022 Me. Acts Ch. 646, H.P. 1216, L.D. 1632.

communication.[1684] Tennessee replaced the phrase "deaf and dumb" with "deaf or hard of hearing" throughout the state code.[1685] Virginia required the state department of education, with two other agencies, to provide assessment resources for parents and educators for children who are deaf or hard of hearing and to identify milestones for language development for children who are deaf or hard of hearing.[1686]

Three states made changes regarding students on the autism spectrum. Colorado required school districts to develop policies to assure provision for medically-necessary services in schools for students. The provision seems to be directed at providing applied behavior analysis services for students with an autism spectrum disorder diagnosis.[1687] Iowa changed the definition of autism spectrum disorder to conform with the most recent edition of the diagnostic and statistical manual of mental disorders and to affirm coverage from health insurance programs.[1688] New York directed the state board of education to publish the autism mapping study, with its discussion on the screening and detection of autism, completed by the State and City Universities of New York in the Journal of Neurodevelopmental Disorders.[1689]

Two states added requirements for students with dyslexia. Indiana required public schools to provide dyslexia screening and intervention.[1690] Louisiana moved back the due date for a report on public school students with dyslexia, from October 31 to December 15, annually, and required an exact number of dyslexic students if the number is more than zero and not more than ten students.[1691]

Two states passed three acts regarding students with disabilities and charter schools. Colorado allowed enrollment preference plans for charter schools for children with disabilities.[1692] New Hampshire required a chartered public school to enter into a memorandum of understanding with a school district of residence for a student attending the charted public school concerning special education services.[1693] New Hampshire also directed a child's resident school district to provide prior notice to the chartered public school for meetings of the child's individualized education program team.[1694]

[1684] 2022 Mich. Pub. Acts 256, HB 5777.
[1685] 2022 Tenn. Pub. Acts Ch. No. 642, S.B. No. 1752, Sub. H.B. No. 1670.
[1686] 2022 Va. Acts Ch. 240, S. 265; 2022 Va. Acts Ch. 238, H. 649.
[1687] 2022 Colo. Sess. Laws HB 1260.
[1688] 2022 Iowa Acts HF 2167.
[1689] 2022 N.Y. Laws Ch. 20, A. 8690.
[1690] 2022 Ind. Acts Pub. Law 126, SB 123.
[1691] 2022 La. Acts No. 622, HB No. 416.
[1692] 2022 Colo. Sess. Laws HB 1294.
[1693] 2022 N.H. Laws Ch. 313, SB 238.
[1694] 2022 N.H. Laws Ch. 24, HB 1074.

Two states altered the definition and eligibility determination for students who are developmentally disabled. New York replaced the term "mentally retarded" with the term "developmentally disabled" in the school code.[1695] Washington eliminated the use of intelligence quotient scores in determining the eligibility for programs and services for individuals with developmental disabilities.[1696]

Other acts adopted in 2022 related to students with disabilities are described as follows. California required the state department of education to publish data related to federal measures of least restrictive environment for pupils with disabilities.[1697] Additionally, California required the state board of education to include fetal alcohol spectrum disorder in the definition of "other health impairment" for purposes of deciding eligibility for special education services.[1698] As was discussed in the School Safety section above, Florida prohibited school personnel from using mechanical restraint on students with disabilities.[1699] Illinois required school districts to provide informational material about the Achieving a Better Life Experience (ABLE) account program to the parent or guardian of a student at a special education student's annual individualized education program review meeting.[1700]

Iowa created a task force regarding special education support for students at nonpublic schools.[1701] Kansas amended provisions regarding vision screening services, particularly to require them to be performed by a trained vision screener, and created a commission for children's vision health and school readiness.[1702] Kentucky made students with intellectual disabilities enrolled in comprehensive transition and postsecondary programs eligible for the Work Ready scholarship program.[1703] Maryland required local school systems to provide equivalent access to digital tools for students with disabilities, including the development, purchase, and provision of certain digital tools that directly connect to student instruction.[1704]

Mississippi authorized state-supported university-based or college-based programs to serve students with disabilities so severe that a local school placement may not be appropriate for them, and

---

[1695] 2022 N.Y. Laws Ch. 479, A. 7882.
[1696] 2022 Wash. Laws Ch. 277, H.B. 2008.
[1697] 2022 Cal. Stat. Ch. 919, S.B. No. 692.
[1698] 2022 Cal. Stat. Ch. 611, S.B. No. 1016.
[1699] 2022 Fla. Laws Ch. 2022-20, HB 235.
[1700] 2022 Ill. Laws Pub. Act 102-0841, SB 3474.
[1701] 2022 Iowa Acts SF 2197.
[1702] 2022 Kan. Sess. Laws SB 62.
[1703] 2022 Ky. Acts Ch. 42, SB 94.
[1704] 2022 Md. Laws Ch. 215, SB 617.

permitted persons with certificates in related fields, such as audiologists, speech-language pathologists, and special and early childhood educators, to serve as the lead teacher for students in these placements.[1705] Missouri adopted the Blind Students' Rights to Independence, Training, and Education (BRITE) Act, which provided direction in providing accessible assistive technology devices, an expanded core curriculum, and appropriate instruction for visually disabled students.[1706]

In the first of three laws from New Hampshire regarding students with disabilities, New Hampshire created the office of the advocate for special education within the department of administrative services and independent from the department of education to serve as an advocate, coordinator, and point of contact for parents, guardians, and caretakers of students with disabilities when dealing with school districts regarding services provided to the students.[1707] New Hampshire also provided for students with an individualized education program or accommodation under Section 504 of the Rehabilitation Act of 1973 to discuss including voter registration in the student's plan.[1708] Finally, New Hampshire acknowledged that schools are required to provide accommodations for disabled students who must take the U.S. naturalization examination to pass the high school government and civics course.[1709] New Jersey extended the period of time for filing special education due process petitions related to COVID-19 school closures and periods of virtual, remote, hybrid, or in-person instruction.[1710]

Rhode Island authorized a licensed physical therapist to perform physical therapy services to a student while in school without prescription or referral, in accordance with the student's IEP or IFSP.[1711] Tennessee added the category of specific learning disability to extend eligibility for the individualized education account program to a child with that disability.[1712]

Tennessee also authorized licensed healthcare providers to provide services in a school setting pursuant to a child's individualized education program.[1713] Utah clarified rules about delivery of special education services in public schools, for example, to require an LEA to use state special education funds for special

---

[1705] 2022 Miss. Laws H.B. No. 881.
[1706] 2022 Mo. Laws SB 681 & 662; § 167.225.
[1707] 2022 N.H. Laws Ch. 316, SB 381.
[1708] 2022 N.H. Laws Ch. 209, HB 1594.
[1709] 2022 N.H. Laws Ch. 116, HB 1367.
[1710] 2022 N.J. Laws P.L. c. 2, S. 905.
[1711] 2022 R.I. Laws H. 6669, S. 2328.
[1712] 2022 Tenn. Pub. Acts Ch. No. 1019, S.B. No. 1158, Sub. H.B. No. 751.
[1713] 2022 Tenn. Pub. Acts Ch. No. 695, S.B. No. 503, Sub. H.B. No. 753.

education, even if doing so provides an incidental benefit to students without a disability.[1714] West Virginia required the placement of video cameras in self-contained classrooms in which a majority of students regularly attending are receiving special education services.[1715]

Technology

This section describes technology-related legislation enacted in 2022. Kansas promoted advancement in computer science education in state schools.[1716] Louisiana adopted a computer science education act to ensure that citizens have the expertise to perform the technology skills embedded in most professions, to meet ever-increasing workforce demands in the technology sector, and to grow the next generation of technology education.[1717] Missouri required all public high schools and charter high schools to offer at least one computer science course in an in-person setting or by a virtual option. The act also required collection of data about students taking computer science courses.[1718] Nebraska adopted the Computer Science and Technology Education Act, which required each school district to include computer science and technology education in the elementary and middle schools of the state, and added a one-semester course requirement of computer science and technology for high school graduation.[1719]

Other technology-related acts passed last calendar year are as follows. To ease development of its computer science programs, Idaho created a grant program of up to $1,000 per student, to assist students in purchasing necessary educational expenses, such as computer hardware, internet access, or other instructional materials.[1720] Louisiana amended its public records law to specify that electronically stored information and databases are included in the law.[1721] South Dakota appropriated funds for high performance computing and data storage systems at South Dakota State University.[1722] Virginia required each school board, through the 2025 school year, to annually report to the state department of education and the state department of housing and community

---

[1714] 2022 Utah Laws S.B. 134.
[1715] 2022 W. Va. Acts Ch. 95, S.B. 261.
[1716] 2022 Kan. Sess. Laws HB 2466.
[1717] 2022 La. Acts No. 541, SB No. 190.
[1718] 2022 Mo. Laws SB 681 & 662; § 170.018.
[1719] 2022 Neb. Laws LB 1112.
[1720] 2022 Idaho Sess. Laws Ch. 13, SB 1255.
[1721] 2022 La. Acts No. 770, SB No. 478.
[1722] 2022 S.D. Laws H.B. 1137.

development each student's 9-1-1 address that does not have broadband access.[1723]

Transportation

This section details transportation-related legislation enrolled in 2022. Five states supported the change to electric buses. Arizona permitted contracts for electric school bus services and charging infrastructure.[1724] Maine allowed electric-powered school buses to have distinctively-colored bumpers, wheels, and rub rails, and allowed public service vehicles to be equipped with a flashing green auxiliary light.[1725] Maryland created an electric school bus pilot program under the supervision of the public service commission.[1726] Mississippi permitted school boards to purchase, own, and operate electric vehicles for the transportation of children to and from public schools.[1727] New Jersey directed the department of environmental protection to implement a three-year electric school bus program to determine the operational reliability and cost effectiveness of replacing diesel-powered school buses with electric school buses for the daily transportation of students.[1728] A sixth act supported the change to clean buses. Idaho created an exception allowing transportation contracts receiving funding under the federal clean school bus program to exceed five years but not to exceed ten years. A clean school bus was defined in the program as having a gross vehicle weight greater than 14,000 pounds, powered by a heavy-duty engine, and operated solely on an alternative or ultra-low sulfur diesel fuel.[1729]

Three states adopted six acts promoting school bus safety through the use of fines and employment training or discipline. Illinois added community service as a penalty for failing to stop before meeting or overtaking a school bus that is stopped for receiving or discharging students[1730] and increased the fines for speeding in a school zone to $250 for a first offense, instead of $150, as was mentioned in the section on School Safety.[1731] Louisiana amended provisions prohibiting bus operators from loading or unloading students to clearly state that it is prohibited in a lane of

---

[1723] 2022 Va. Acts Ch. 211, S. 724.
[1724] 2022 Ariz. Sess. Laws Ch. 347, S.B. 1246.
[1725] 2022 Me. Acts Ch. 582, H.P. 1476, L.D. 1990.
[1726] 2022 Md. Laws Ch. 570, HB 696.
[1727] 2022 Miss. Laws S.B. No. 2887.
[1728] 2022 N.J. Laws P.L. c. 86, A. 1282.
[1729] 2022 Idaho Sess. Laws Ch. 87, SB 1319. The federal clean school bus program is codified at 42 U.S.C. § 16091.
[1730] 2022 Ill. Laws Pub. Act 102-0859, SB 3793.
[1731] 2022 Ill. Laws Pub. Act 102-0978, HB 5328.

traffic.[1732] Louisiana amended a provision regarding bus operators being disciplined to begin the appeals process within twenty days after the superintendent's interim disciplinary report.[1733] Tennessee encouraged schools to offer automated external defibrillator device training to school bus drivers.[1734] Tennessee also raised the fine from $50 to $200 for the first violation of passing a stopped school bus, even if the evidence comes from the bus safety video.[1735]

Two states changed rules regarding school bus driver permits. In provisions for the issuance of a school bus driver permit, Illinois required that if an applicant's driver's license has been suspended within the three years immediately prior to the date of application for the sole reason of failure to pay child support, that suspension shall not bar the applicant from receiving a school bus driver permit.[1736] Rhode Island allowed school bus drivers to pass written state examinations once every ten years, rather than annually.[1737]

Louisiana made two changes regarding bus driver salaries. First. Louisiana adopted a new salary schedule for school bus operators.[1738] Then, Louisiana amended compensation tables for student transportation programs, and added provision for payment for supplemental equipment for transporting students with disabilities, and for air conditioning.[1739]

Two states adopted acts allowing the operation of other vehicles besides regular school buses. Missouri gave school districts the authority to use motor vehicles other than school buses for the purpose of transporting school children.[1740] West Virginia amended requirements allowing service employees to drive county school board-owned vehicles with a seating capacity of 10 persons, including the driver.[1741]

Other transportation-related acts passed in 2022 are described as follows. Maryland required Montgomery County to annually compile and make publicly available a report for the previous fiscal year on each school bus monitoring system operated by a local jurisdiction.[1742] New Hampshire changed the definition of "school activities" in a provision permitting the use of school transportation

---

[1732] 2022 La. Acts No. 640, HB No. 1081.
[1733] 2022 La. Acts No. 332, HB No. 349.
[1734] 2022 Tenn. Pub. Acts Ch. No. 948, H.B. No. 2530, Sub. S.B. No. 2824.
[1735] 2022 Tenn. Pub. Acts Ch. No. 792, S.B. No. 2512, Sub. H.B. No. 2550.
[1736] 2022 Ill. Laws Pub. Act 102-0726, HB 4230.
[1737] 2022 R.I. Laws S. 2901.
[1738] 2022 La. Acts No. 449, HB No. 215.
[1739] 2022 La. Acts No. 661, SB No. 57.
[1740] 2022 Mo. Laws SB 681 & 662; § 304.060.
[1741] 2022 W. Va. Acts Ch. 105, H.B. 4380.
[1742] 2022 Md. Laws Ch. 216, HB 813.

to specify that the activities are approved by the school district.[1743] New Jersey provided a temporary one-year extension of the service life of school buses for the 2022-2023 school year and authorized the chief administrator to allow a one-year extension in the subsequent two school years.[1744]

Virginia permitted local school boards to enter into an agreement with a third-party logistics company to use school buses, but the company cannot use the school buses to provide transportation of passengers for compensation or for residential delivery of products for compensation.[1745] West Virginia amended the eligibility requirements of school bus operators diagnosed with diabetes mellitus requiring insulin and stipulated that the school bus operator must remain in compliance with eligibility stipulations.[1746]

Higher Education

Higher education-related legislation is the category with the most acts in most years. This is the first year in recent years that the higher education-related acts were surpassed, with the most acts occurring in the category of governance and school leadership due to the intervention in state governments over local school boards among two states of the old Confederacy. This section categorizes and describes legislation concerning higher education in 2022.

Ten states enacted eleven bills about higher education governing boards and commissions. Connecticut increased by one person, to twenty-two members, the number of members of the board of regents for higher education.[1747] Connecticut also required the board of regents for higher education and the board of trustees of the University of Connecticut to each adopt a policy requiring that any newly-appointed board member must receive instruction and training in areas touching upon their function as board members.[1748] Kentucky directed the postsecondary education nominating committee to submit names to the governor and the governor to nominate persons to replace members of the board of regents of Kentucky State University.[1749] Mississippi extended a provision

---

[1743] 2022 N.H. Laws Ch. 66, HB 1202.
[1744] 2022 N.J. Laws P.L. c. 41, A. 3990.
[1745] 2022 Va. Acts Ch. 241, S. 774.
[1746] 2022 W. Va. Acts Ch. 262, H.B. 4420.
[1747] 2022 Conn. Acts 22-126, Subs. S.B. No. 279.
[1748] 2022 Conn. Acts 22-16, S.B. No. 18.
[1749] 2022 Ky. Acts Ch. 30, SB 265.

automatically repealing governance and control of the board of trustees of state institutions of higher education to 2025.[1750] North Carolina changed the appointment method for the members of the board of trustees of Rockingham Community College by decreasing from four to two members elected by the board of education of the public-school administrative unit located in the area of the college, and increasing from four to six members elected by the board of commissioners of the county in which the college is located.[1751] Rhode Island modified the appointment and removal process for the board of trustees of the University of Rhode Island with all appointments by the governor for three-year terms, with advice and consent of the senate.[1752] Tennessee extended the life of the higher education commission to June 30, 2026.[1753] Virginia added the president of Virginia State University and removed the presidents of Averett University and Mary Baldwin College to the board of trustees for the Roanoke Higher Education Authority.[1754] Washington required that a faculty member must serve on the board of regents for research universities.[1755] West Virginia amended provisions giving authority to the higher education policy commission regarding legislative rules for the research trust fund program and the reauthorization of degree-granting institutions and giving authority to the council for community and technical college education regarding business, occupational, and trade schools.[1756] Wyoming altered the election schedule for members of community college district boards.[1757]

Three acts addressed other governance entities besides boards of trustees or higher education commissions. California repealed a provision requiring the board of trustees for Compton Community College District to assume the duties of its personnel commission until 2029, to instead allowing it to assume duties annually beginning in 2023. Apparently, this provision was part of fiscal oversight concerning emergency apportionment to the college.[1758] California allowed a student to be elected to serve as an officer in a student government in community colleges if the student is enrolled in an adult education program offered by the community college

---

[1750] 2022 Miss. Laws S.B. No. 2700.
[1751] 2022 N.C. Sess. Laws Ch. 10, S.B. 256.
[1752] 2022 R.I. Laws S. 2747, H. 8124.
[1753] 2022 Tenn. Pub. Acts Ch. No. 728, S.B. No. 1734, Sub. H.B. No. 1815.
[1754] 2022 Va. Acts Ch. 611, S. 395.
[1755] 2022 Wash. Laws Ch. 12, H.B. 1051.
[1756] 2022 W. Va. Acts Ch. 152, H.B. 4291.
[1757] 2022 Wyo. Sess. Laws Ch. No. 58, S.F. 43.
[1758] 2022 Cal. Stat. Ch. 529, A.B. No. 2359.

district or if the student is disabled.[1759] Oregon amended qualifications for membership on the transfer council, which is appointed by the higher education coordinating commission, so that the serving public high school teacher may be employed by a public high school or by an education service district.[1760]

Four states adopted provisions regarding open meeting acts in higher education. Maryland required the higher education commission to make each open meeting to be publicly available through live video streaming.[1761] Rhode Island allowed trustee members of the University of Rhode Island to remotely participate in meetings, without excuse, and to have them considered as the meeting quorum.[1762] South Carolina required meetings of the Coastal Carolina University board of trustees to provide mandatory notice of board meetings, sent either electronically or through the U.S. mail, to each trustee not less than five days before each meeting.[1763] Tennessee extended video streaming and archiving requirements to meetings of standing committees for the board of regents, in addition to meetings of the board, to 2026.[1764]

An open records exemption was granted when Florida exempted from public records requirements any personal identifying information of an applicant for president of a state university.[1765]

Six states enacted bills changing college or university names. California directed that the Hastings College of Law within the University of California is to be designated as the College of the Law, San Francisco.[1766] Colorado changed the name of Pikes Peak Community College to Pikes Peak State College.[1767] New Hampshire passed an act to reflect the merger of Granite State College into the University of New Hampshire.[1768] Pennsylvania named the institution created by consolidating Bloomsburg University of Pennsylvania, Lock Haven University of Pennsylvania, and Mansfield University of Pennsylvania into the Commonwealth University of Pennsylvania.[1769] Tennessee established the University of Tennessee Southern as a new campus of the University

---

[1759] 2022 Cal. Stat. Ch. 79, A.B. No. 1736.
[1760] 2022 Or. Laws Ch. 81, SB 1522.
[1761] 2022 Md. Laws Ch. 639, HB 1030; 2022 Md. Laws Ch. 640, SB 501.
[1762] 2022 R.I. Laws S. 2372, H. 7817.
[1763] 2022 S.C. Acts 130, H. 4944.
[1764] 2022 Tenn. Pub. Acts Ch. No. 755, S.B. No. 1724, Sub. H.B. No. 1805.
[1765] 2022 Fla. Laws Ch. 2022-15, SB 520.
[1766] 2022 Cal. Stat. Ch. 478, A.B. No. 1936.
[1767] 2022 Colo. Sess. Laws HB 1280.
[1768] 2022 N.H. Laws Ch. 35, HB 1218.
[1769] 2022 Pa. Laws Act No. 55, HB 1642, Section 33.

of Tennessee in Giles County.[1770] West Virginia changed the name of Glenville State College to Glenville State University.[1771]

Nine states adopted ten acts to increase course and degree offerings within their institutions of higher education. California authorized institutions in the state university system to award the Doctor of Public Health degree.[1772] Colorado permitted community colleges to offer a bachelor of science degree in nursing.[1773] Maryland established an institute for public leadership at the College Park Campus of the University of Maryland to provide students with experiential learning, enhance the teaching of public leadership, and support students in underrepresented populations.[1774] Nebraska broadened the award of masters' degrees at Peru State College to include subject areas at the discretion of the governing board and the coordinating commission for postsecondary education.[1775] In considering approval of a new degree program, Ohio required the chancellor for a state institution of higher education to take into account the extent to which a degree or degree program aligns with the state's workforce development priorities.[1776]

Oklahoma permitted the board of career and technology education to establish courses in the area of hydrogen energy basics, equipment manufacturing and maintenance, infrastructure, and safety.[1777] South Dakota appropriated funds to the board of technical education to purchase simulation equipment for a health sciences clinical simulations center at Southeast Technical College.[1778] South Dakota also expanded the cyber program at Dakota State University.[1779] Tennessee established an institute of American civics at the University of Tennessee.[1780] Washington provided funds to increase the availability of sexual assault nurse examiner education in rural and underserved areas.[1781]

Nine states added ten acts to provide greater oversight over the functions of private proprietary schools. California extended regulatory control over private postsecondary educational institutions to out-of-state programs offered through distance education.[1782] Delaware expanded the powers of the higher

---

[1770] 2022 Tenn. Pub. Acts Ch. No. 648, S.B. No. 1980, Sub. H.B. No. 2019.
[1771] 2022 W. Va. Acts Ch. 151, H.B. 4264.
[1772] 2022 Cal. Stat. Ch. 936, S.B. No. 684.
[1773] 2022 Colo. Sess. Laws SB 3.
[1774] 2022 Md. Laws Ch. 637, HB 511.
[1775] 2022 Neb. Laws LB 887.
[1776] 2022 Ohio Laws Sub. S.B. No. 135.
[1777] 2022 Okla. Sess. Laws SB 1190.
[1778] 2022 S.D. Laws S.B. 61.
[1779] 2022 S.D. Laws S.B. 54.
[1780] 2022 Tenn. Pub. Acts Ch. No. 963, S.B. No. 2410, Sub. H.B. No. 2157.
[1781] 2022 Wash. Laws Ch. 118, H.B. 1622.
[1782] 2022 Cal. Stat. Ch. 544, S.B. No. 1433.

education office to increase consumer protections for students enrolled in private postsecondary institutions.[1783] Georgia required a financial assessment of a private postsecondary institution that applies to the commission on higher education to operate and renewed a requirement for a surety bond while removing references to agency for the institution.[1784] Iowa widened the definition of for-profit schools required to register with the college student aid commission to schools offering a course of applicable instruction, not just those offering such a program.[1785] Kentucky set up structures, licensing requirements, and procedures to provide protection for student loan borrowers from fraudulent practices.[1786]

Mississippi gave the department of finance and administration control of the association of independent colleges and universities with respect to rules and regulations regarding the application of eligible colleges and universities for grant funds and the award of such grants.[1787] New Jersey required the secretary of higher education to establish performance quality standards for career-oriented programs of study offered by institutions of higher education degree-granting proprietary institutions and private career schools.[1788] New Jersey also required the financial aid award letter provided by institutions of higher education and proprietary schools to be consistent with the financial aid shopping sheet.[1789] New York prohibited discrimination, intimidation, and retaliation against students of proprietary schools who file a written complaint or exercise their right of private action against a proprietary school.[1790] Tennessee revised provisions regarding the regulation of proprietary institutions, such as inserting a statement regarding the authority of an oversight commission to establish minimum standards concerning the provision of education, ethical business practices, and fiscal responsibility to protect against substandard, transient, unethical, deceptive, or fraudulent institutions and practices.[1791]

Five states adopted acts providing for the conversion of university property to an open forum for the enhancement of free speech. Georgia enacted the Forming Open and Robust University Minds (FORUM) Act, which permits any person who wishes to

---

[1783] 2022 Del. Laws HB 481.
[1784] 2022 Ga. Laws Act 789, SB 333.
[1785] 2022 Iowa Acts SF 2130.
[1786] 2022 Ky. Acts Ch. 88, HB 494.
[1787] 2022 Miss. Laws S.B. No. 2700.
[1788] 2022 N.J. Laws 2022, P.L. c. 76, A. 1695.
[1789] 2022 N.J. Laws P.L. 2022, c. 127, A. 1189.
[1790] 2022 N.Y. Laws Ch. 182, S. 6529.
[1791] 2022 Tenn. Pub. Acts Ch. No. 1044, S.B. No. 2843, Sub. H.B. No. 2606.

engage in noncommercial expressive activity in an unrestricted outdoor area of campus to be permitted to do so freely, so long as the person's conduct is not unlawful and does not materially and substantially disrupt the function of the public institution of higher education.[1792] Indiana prohibited state institutions of higher education from designating an outdoor area on campus as an area where protected expression is prohibited.[1793] Louisiana amended provisions regarding expressive activities at public postsecondary institutions of higher education, to allow institutions to require a permit as a condition of granting exclusive control of a location for expressive activity at a reserved time, to allow institutions to require a security fee, and to define a "material and substantial disruption" for identifying authority to control expressive activities.[1794]

Ohio amended provisions related to student and faculty speech in the environment of a public institution of higher education to elucidate the constitutional rights at stake and require each board of trustees to establish a policy and a process under which a student, student group, or faculty member may submit a complaint about alleged violation by an employee of the institution of its policy.[1795] Oklahoma created a free speech committee within the office of the regents for higher education and charged the commission to review free speech policies at public universities, review complaints filed with the committee, review university training on free speech for improvements, and make recommendations to universities on improvements to free speech policies and training.[1796]

Three states adopted "divisive concepts law" to prohibit speech that is proscribed by the legislature. Mississippi directed that no public institution of higher learning, community/junior college, school district or public school, including public charter schools, shall direct or otherwise compel students to personally affirm, adopt, or adhere to any of the following tenets: (a) that any sex, race, ethnicity, religion, or national origin is inherently superior or inferior; or (b) that individuals should be adversely treated on the basis of their sex, race, ethnicity, religion, or national origin.[1797] South Dakota adopted an act describing as its purpose to protect students and employees at institutions of higher education from divisive concepts. The act described "divisive concepts" as follows:

[1792] 2022 Ga. Laws Act 818, HB 1.
[1793] 2022 Ind. Acts Pub. Law 145, HB 1190.
[1794] 2022 La. Acts No. 727, HB No. 185.
[1795] 2022 Ohio Laws Sub. S.B. No. 135.
[1796] 2022 Okla. Sess. Laws HB 3543.
[1797] 2022 Miss. Laws S.B. No. 2113.

For the purpose of this Act, the term, divisive concepts, means:

> That any race, color, religion, sex, ethnicity, or national origin is inherently superior or inferior;
> That individuals should not be discriminated against or adversely treated because of their race, color, etc.
> That an individual's moral character is inherently determined by their race, color, religion, sex, ethnicity, or national origin.
> That an individual, by virtue of their race, color religion, sex, ethnicity, or national origin is inherently racist, sexist, or oppressive, whether consciously or subconsciously;
> That individuals, by virtue of race, color, religion, sex, ethnicity, or national origin, are inherently responsible for actions committed in the past by other members of the same race, etc.;
> An individual should feel discomfort, guilt, anguish, or any other form of psychological distress on account of the individual's race, etc.;
> Meritocracy or traits such as a strong work ethic are racist or sexist or were created by members of a particular race or sex to oppress members of another race or sex.[1798]

Tennessee adopted a "divisive concepts" act very similar to the act adopted in South Dakota. The Tennessee act prohibited public institutions of higher education from penalizing, discriminating against, or causing adverse treatment due to a student's or employee's refusal to support, believe, endorse, embrace, confess, act upon, or otherwise assent to one or more of the divisive concepts identified in the body of the act.[1799]

Five states passed twenty acts to pay for the construction of various university buildings. California required monies appropriated to the university system to directly support campus expansion projects or climate initiatives, or both, at the University of California, Riverside, and the University of California, Merced.[1800] California also required community colleges and state universities,

---

[1798] 2022 S.D. Laws H.B. 1012.
[1799] 2022 Tenn. Pub. Acts Ch. No. 818, H.B. No. 2670, Sub. S.B. No. 2290.
[1800] 2022 Cal Stat. Ch. 526, A.B. No. 2046.

but requested the university system, to ensure that facilities have heating, ventilation, and air conditioning systems that meet minimum ventilation rate requirements.[1801] New York authorized the state university trustees to contract without bidding to make available a portion of the lands of Farmington State University to the university development corporation for the purpose of developing, constructing, maintaining, and operating a multi-purpose athletic facility.[1802] Rhode Island authorized the University of Rhode Island board of trustees to make small procurements up to $50,000 for construction and $10,000 for other purchases.[1803]

South Dakota passed thirteen laws involving construction of university buildings. South Dakota authorized the board of regents to contract for the demolition of Briscoe Hall and Lincoln Hall, and the construction of a new Lincoln Hall, at Northern State University.[1804] South Dakota appropriated funds for multimedia lab equipment at Black Hills State University.[1805] South Dakota appropriated funds to the board of technical education to construct an agriculture and diesel power laboratory and multi-purpose space at Mitchell Technical College.[1806] South Dakota authorized the board of regents to contract for the design, renovation, and construction of an addition for a health sciences center at Black Hills State University-Rapid City.[1807] South Dakota appropriated funds to the board of technical education to build an advanced manufacturing laboratory space and classrooms at Lake Area Technical College.[1808] South Dakota authorized the board of regents to construct an applied research laboratory at Dakota State University.[1809] South Dakota upgraded an education lab and purchased resources for Black Hills State University.[1810]

South Dakota authorized the board of regents to contract for the design and construction of an addition to the wellness center at the University of South Dakota.[1811] South Dakota authorized the board of regents to acquire the incubator building on the campus of South Dakota School of Mines and Technology and contract for its design and renovation.[1812] South Dakota appropriated funds to the board of

---

[1801] 2022 Cal. Stat. Ch. 777, A.B. No. 2232.
[1802] 2022 N.Y. laws Ch. 538, S. 8859.
[1803] 2022 R.I. Laws S. 2755, H. 8123.
[1804] 2022 S.D. Laws S.B. 44.
[1805] 2022 S.D. Laws S.B. 132.
[1806] 2022 S.D. Laws H.B 1032.
[1807] 2022 S.D. Laws S.B. 43.
[1808] 2022 S.D. Laws H.B. 1031.
[1809] 2022 S.D. Laws S.B. 130.
[1810] 2022 S.D. Laws S.B. 133.
[1811] 2022 S.D. Laws S.B. 42.
[1812] 2022 S.D. Laws S.B. 97.

regents for a new biomedical facility at the research park in Sioux Falls.[1813] South Dakota authorized the board of regents to construct an athletics events center at Dakota State University.[1814] South Dakota authorized the board of regents to design and renovate and construct an addition to the Stanley J. Marshall Center at South Dakota State University.[1815] South Dakota appropriated funds to the department of education to renovate the Cultural Heritage Center.[1816]

Tennessee required the higher education commission to comply with the policies of the state building commission concerning capital projects affecting public institutions of higher education.[1817] Tennessee also required Tennessee State University to annually submit a report regarding progress in improving facilities and infrastructure identified in a prior needs assessment.[1818]

Four states prohibited the withholding of transcript requests for students with debt to the institution. Colorado prohibited postsecondary institutions from requiring payment of an outstanding balance on a student's account as a condition of issuing the student's documents.[1819] Illinois prohibited institutions of higher education from refusing to provide an official transcript to a current or former student on the grounds that the student owes a debt.[1820] Maine required 2-year and 4-year postsecondary educational institutions to provide current or former students with a transcript notwithstanding a debt of less than $500 for 2-year schools and $2,500 for 4-year schools. For debt above those levels, the institutions must provide the transcript if the parties have agreed upon a repayment plan.[1821] New York prohibited practices such as withholding a transcript or charging higher fees against students by a degree-granting institution or licensed private career schools.[1822]

Four states enacted bills speaking to finance and business management practices. Arizona imposed a claw-back of state aid for community colleges, with the claw-back graduated in severity based upon excessive spending above a statutory limit.[1823] Kentucky required the president of each state postsecondary or independent institution and the chair of their governing boards to sign certain

---

[1813] 2022 S.D. Laws H.B. 1210.
[1814] 2022 S.D. Laws H.B. 1021.
[1815] 2022 S.D. Laws H.B. 1022.
[1816] 2022 S.D. Laws H.B. 1047.
[1817] 2022 Tenn. Pub. Acts Ch. No. 967, S.B. No. 532, Sub. H.B. No. 650.
[1818] 2022 Tenn. Pub. Acts Ch. No. 836, H.B. No. 2293, Sub. S.B. No. 2216.
[1819] 2022 Colo. Sess. Laws HB 1049.
[1820] 2022 Ill. Laws Pub. Act 102-0998, SB 3032.
[1821] 2022 Me. Acts Ch. 538, S.P. 656, L.D. 1838.
[1822] 2022 N.Y. Laws Ch. 180, A. 6938.
[1823] 2022 Ariz. Sess. Laws Ch. 367, H.B. 2017.

financial disclosure attestations, include statements of financial stability and completion of an audit.[1824] Maryland increased the bonding authority for the university system, from $1.4 to $1.7 billion, for the acquisition, development, and improvement of academic facilities.[1825] Oklahoma permitted the board of regents of an eligible two-year college to adopt a resolution creating a higher education funding district, which has taxing power for raising additional revenue for two-year colleges.[1826]

Five states passed acts controlling relationships with other entities. California limited the real estate investment trusts that could be invested in by the state university system to those that are publicly traded and registered with the U.S. Securities and Exchange Commission.[1827] Tennessee prohibited public entities, including schools and universities, from entering into a contract of a value of $250,000 or more without a written certification that the party is not currently engaged in, and will not be engaged in, a boycott of Israel.[1828] Utah restricted institutions of higher education from seeking or accepting funding support from a restricted foreign entity, as defined as a company, affiliate of a company, or a country that the U.S. Secretary of Defense is required to list under federal national defense authorization acts.[1829] Washington fostered collaborative arrangements between institutions of higher education and nonprofit entities providing comprehensive cancer care.[1830] West Virginia designated the forensic analysis laboratory at Marshall University Science Center as a criminal justice agency, to allow its participation in the state DNA database.[1831]

Nine states enacted eleven bills creating scholarships favoring members of the military and their dependents. Arizona funded tuition scholarships for spouses of military veterans.[1832] California required postsecondary educational institutions to craft regulations about providing information to the agency that awards scholarships to military veterans as part of their application for approval or renewal.[1833] California also required the state university system, and requested the university system, to electronically transmit personal information regarding students whose tuition or fees are paid using

---

[1824] 2022 Ky. Acts Ch. 170, HB 663.
[1825] 2022 Md. Laws Ch. 233, SB 1007.
[1826] 2022 Okla. Sess. Laws HB 2046.
[1827] 2022 Cal. Stat. Ch. 530, A.B. No. 2422.
[1828] 2022 Tenn. Pub. Acts Ch. No. 775, S.B. No. 1993, Sub. H.B. No. 2050.
[1829] 2022 Utah Laws H.B. 346.
[1830] 2022 Wash. Laws Ch. 71, H.B. 1744.
[1831] 2022 W. Va. Acts Ch. 245, S.B. 593.
[1832] 2022 Ariz. Sess. Laws Ch. 315, H.B. 2864.
[1833] 2022 Cal. Stat. Ch. 380, A.B. No. 1731.

GI Bill educational benefits.[1834] Idaho amended scholarship requirements for armed forces and public safety officers and their dependents to include eligibility for those who die or become totally and permanently disabled by injuries or wounds sustained during active duty or inactive duty training.[1835]

Illinois amended a higher education scholarship program for veterans to require an applicant to receive an honorable discharge after leaving federal active-duty service.[1836] Illinois also amended the school code to broaden the number of persons eligible for the MIA-POW scholarship to include adopted children and children under court-ordered guardianship.[1837] Nebraska deleted a provision for tuition assistance for members of the National Guard, which allowed the adjutant general the authority to extend the 10-year entitlement period for members who were deployed during that period.[1838] New Hampshire added a college tuition waiver for the semester for students whose parent was a disabled military veteran and who was a resident of the state at the time of the parent's death.[1839]

North Carolina clarified the criteria of disabled veterans eligible for a scholarship program to include that the veteran incurred traumatic injuries or wounds or sustained a major illness, receiving compensation for at least a 50% disability, and is a state resident.[1840] Pennsylvania created a program which assists National Guard members with tuition during simultaneous training through the National Guard and an ROTC program at a military college.[1841] Virginia added provisions to guide the tuition grant program for members of the National Guard to attend institutions of higher education.[1842]

Eleven states added fourteen scholarships for persons other than those with military connections. Colorado funded a scholarship for descendants of Aurarians displaced by the development of the Auraria higher education center. Auraria is a neighborhood in Denver, which was a mining camp in territorial days.[1843] Idaho amended provisions in a postsecondary credit scholarship to clarify

---

[1834] 2022 Cal. Stat. Ch. 174, A.B. No. 1633.
[1835] 2022 Idaho Sess. Laws Ch. 29, HB 461.
[1836] 2022 Ill. Laws Pub. Act 102-0800, HB 5175.
[1837] 2022 Ill. Laws Pub. Act 102-0855, SB 3762.
[1838] 2022 Neb. Laws LB 779.
[1839] 2022 N.H. Laws Ch. 28, HB 1575.
[1840] 2022 N.C. Sess. Laws Ch. 71, H.B. 159.
[1841] 2022 Pa. Laws Act No. 160, SB 1194.
[1842] 2022 Va. Acts Ch. 604, S. 71; 2022 Va. Acts Ch. 605, H. 857.
[1843] 2022 Colo. Sess. Laws HB 1393.

the amounts could be less than the highest amount of the scholarship.[1844]

Indiana required that college scholarship awards must include in their calculation the factor of the federal need requirement.[1845] Michigan provided financial aid for higher education students through the Reconnect Grant Recipient Act.[1846] Nebraska adopted an act which provided scholarships of up to $15,000 for students in the community college system or at the University of Nebraska.[1847]

New Mexico adopted a scholarship for state residents not yet awarded a baccalaureate degree and enrolled for six hours of credit in a public postsecondary institution or tribal college.[1848] South Carolina established a workforce industry needs scholarship made available to students attending a two-year technical college.[1849] Tennessee made a student eligible for a Promise scholarship if the student graduates early from an eligible high school, completes high school at an eligible home school early, or obtains a GED or HiSET diploma before the spring semester and is admitted early to a postsecondary program.[1850] Tennessee also increased the amount awarded each semester to a full-time student receiving the middle-college scholarship, from $1,250 to $2,000.[1851]

Washington amended provisions concerning the opportunity scholarship program, to raise the family income level for graduate students and include registered apprenticeship programs in the types of programs for which the scholarship may be used.[1852] Washington required that the scholarships awarded for students in approved apprenticeship programs must be the same amount as the maximum college grant for students attending two-year institutions of higher education.[1853] Washington created a state student loan program designed by the student achievement council in consultation with the office of the state treasurer and the state investment board for the purpose of increasing the number of students able to afford postsecondary education.[1854] West Virginia provided tuition and fee waivers at state institutions of higher education for volunteers who have completed service in AmeriCorps

---

[1844] 2022 Idaho Sess. Laws Ch. 158, HB 685.
[1845] 2022 Ind. Acts Pub. Law 52, SB 89.
[1846] 2022 Mich. Pub. Acts 252, HB 6130.
[1847] 2022 Neb. Laws LB 902.
[1848] 2022 N.M. Laws Ch. 42, SB 140.
[1849] 2022 S.C. Acts 204, H. 3144.
[1850] 2022 Tenn. Pub. Acts Ch. No. 1125, S.B. No. 2631, Sub. H.B. No. 2436.
[1851] 2022 Tenn. Pub. Acts Ch. No. 1101, S.B. No. 2081, Sub. H.B. No. 2226.
[1852] 2022 Wash. Laws Ch. 211, H.B. 1805.
[1853] 2022 Wash. Laws Ch. 166, S.B. 5764.
[1854] 2022 Wash. Laws Ch. 206, H.B. 1736.

programs in the state.[1855] Wyoming created the tomorrow scholarship program, which provides funds for students age twenty-four or older and who may use the scholarship for degree or certification programs.[1856]

Two states passed acts designed to provide rules for scholarships. California prohibited each public and private institution of higher education that receives state-funded financial assistance from reducing students' institution-based gift aid below their financial need, with limited exceptions.[1857] To prevent "scholarship displacement," Washington required postsecondary institutions participating in the state student financial aid program to have a gift equity packaging policy, allowing for a student who receives a private scholarship to receive up to 100% of the student's unmet need, as determined by the U.S. Department of Education's federal need analysis methodology before any of the student's federal, state, or institutional financial aid is reduced under the institution's gift equity packaging policy.[1858]

Two states adopted acts requiring use of the free application for federal student aid (FAFSA) to qualify for scholarships. Indiana required each high school and charter school to use the model FAFSA notice prepared by the higher education commission for uniformity in access to student aid.[1859] Washington established an outreach initiative for the state college grant, as well as an outreach and completion initiative FAFSA and the comparable state financial aid application, to help students succeed in transitioning to postsecondary education or training.[1860]

Seven states provided resident tuition status for members of the military and/or their dependents. Louisiana provided in-state residency status for public postsecondary tuition fees for members and veterans of the military.[1861] Massachusetts provided in-state resident tuition status to postsecondary institutions for members of the military stationed in the commonwealth, for their spouses, and for unemancipated dependents.[1862] Oklahoma provided resident tuition status for spouses and dependent children of members of the armed forces.[1863] Oklahoma provided in-state residency status for

---

[1855] 2022 W. Va. Acts Ch. 147, S.B. 228.
[1856] 2022 Wyo. Sess. Laws Ch. No. 52, H.B. 31.
[1857] 2022 Cal. Stat. Ch. 925, A.B. No. 288.
[1858] 2022 Wash. Laws Ch. 138, H.B. 1907.
[1859] 2022 Ind. Acts Pub. Law 51, SB 82.
[1860] 2022 Wash. Laws Ch. 214, H.B. 1835.
[1861] 2022 La. Acts No. 421, SB No. 317.
[1862] 2022 Mass. Acts Ch. 154, S. 3075.
[1863] 2022 Okla. Sess. Laws HB 1800.

tuition purposes to current members of the National Guard.[1864] Tennessee granted resident status for tuition purposes at public institutions of higher education to veterans or military-affiliated individuals.[1865] Vermont granted resident tuition status for members of the National Guard attending state college institutions or the University of Vermont and State Agricultural College.[1866] Washington provided resident tuition status for students and their spouses, domestic partners, and dependents when military members have been reassigned out-of-state.[1867] Wisconsin provided resident tuition status at university institutions and technical colleges for relocated service members, children, and spouses.[1868]

Three states added five acts to provide resident tuition status for others who are not connected to the military. California provided resident tuition status for Team USA students who train in the state for the Olympics and Paralympics.[1869] California also added an exception to the requirement for payment of nonresident tuition for an English as a second language course for nonresident students enrolled in community college courses.[1870] Third, California allowed the board of governors for community college districts to enter into the Western Undergraduate Exchange through the Western Interstate Commission for Higher Education (WICHE) to exempt out-of-state students covered by the exchange from nonresident tuition charges.[1871] Maryland awarded in-state resident tuition status for Peace Corps volunteers who are domiciled in the state.[1872] Vermont provided resident tuition status to the community college for certain identified immigrants, including refugees pursuant to 8 U.S.C. § 1101(a)(42), those granted parole to enter the U.S. pursuant to 8 U.S.C. § 1182(d)(5), and those issued a special visa pursuant to the Afghan Allies Protection Act of 2009 (Pub. L. 111-8, as amended by Pub. L. 117-328).[1873]

Two states added legislation to provide tuition waivers to certain students. New York extended tuition waivers for police officer students of the City University of New York to 2024.[1874] Tennessee added students enrolled in a middle college program to the types of

---

[1864] 2022 Okla. Sess. Laws SB 1416.
[1865] 2022 Tenn. Pub. Acts Ch. No. 791, S.B. No. 2486, Sub. H.B. No. 2710.
[1866] 2022 Vt. Laws Act 140, H. 517.
[1867] 2022 Wash. Laws Ch. 249, S.B. 5874.
[1868] 2021 Wis. Act 159, 2021 S.B. 605.
[1869] 2022 Cal. Stat. Ch. 972, A.B. No. 2747.
[1870] 2022 Cal. Stat. Ch. 512, A.B. No. 1232.
[1871] 2022 Cal. Stat. Ch. 495, A.B. No. 1998.
[1872] 2022 Md. Laws Ch. 75, SB 50; 2022 Md. Laws Ch. 76, HB 87.
[1873] 2022 Vt. Laws Act 166, S. 283, § 1.
[1874] 2022 N.Y. Laws Ch. 280, A. 9970.

students eligible for the work-based learning student grant program.[1875]

Three states provided direction regarding student fees. Louisiana required that fee requirements must be included in the compensation package of each graduate student serving as a teaching assistant, research assistant, or curatorial assistant.[1876] Ohio prohibited state institutions of higher education from charging more for general and instructional fees for an online course than for a course taught in an in-person, classroom setting.[1877] West Virginia expanded the uses which are permissible for fees paid by students at higher education institutions, apparently to pay for instructional technology.[1878]

Two states added loan forgiveness programs. Idaho required that students who attend medical school through the regional medical school program, or who are in an Idaho slot at the University of Utah, shall commit to practicing in Idaho or reimburse the state for supporting the cost of education.[1879] Oregon amended the definition of an "education employer" for purposes of the state loan forgiveness program to include community colleges and public universities, and not just school districts and public charter schools.[1880]

Three states passed acts regarding college textbooks. Mississippi removed a requirement that any textbook supplier with whom the state board of education has contracted to provide all the state's textbooks must maintain a depository in the state.[1881] New York extended the sunset date for a provision requiring publishers or manufacturers to provide printed instructional materials for college students with disabilities from 2022 to 2025.[1882] West Virginia required state institutions of higher education to provide information to students regarding textbooks and digital courseware as a means of limiting textbook costs.[1883]

Four states enacted seven bills to fight hunger on university and college campuses. California required each campus of the state university system and each community college district to use FAFSA data to identify students who meet the income requirements to participate in the CalFresh program (the state name for the federal

---

[1875] 2022 Tenn. Pub. Acts Ch. No. 625, H.B. No. 211, Sub. S.B. No. 520.
[1876] 2022 La. Acts No. 664, SB No. 76.
[1877] 2022 Ohio Laws Sub. S.B. No. 135.
[1878] 2022 W. Va. Acts Ch. 148, S.B. 546.
[1879] 2022 Idaho Sess. Laws Ch. 278, HB 718.
[1880] 2022 Or. Laws Ch. 100, SB 1572.
[1881] 2022 Miss. Laws S.B. No. 2431.
[1882] 2022 N.Y. Laws Ch. 283, A. 9976.
[1883] 2022 W. Va. Acts Ch. 153, H.B. 4355.

supplemental nutrition assistance program (SNAP)).[1884] Further, California directed the department of social services to post on its information regarding college student eligibility for the CalFresh program and to convene a work group to identify the steps necessary to establish a CalFresh application submission process that accommodates the large influx of applications during the beginning of a school term.[1885] Third, California prohibited education activity participants in the CalWORKS program from being required to participate in orientation and appraisal more than once to participate in welfare-to-work activities to satisfy instructional hours during semester or quarter breaks.[1886] Finally, California required the student aid commission to determine a student's CalFresh eligibility and to provide students written notice of their eligibility for benefits.[1887]

Louisiana required the board of regents to establish a "hunger-free" campus designation program for postsecondary education institutions, through a grant program.[1888] Tennessee directed the higher education commission to submit a report on issues of food insecurity among students at public institutions of higher education.[1889] Virginia required public institutions of higher education to ensure that all students have access to accurate information about the Supplemental Nutrition Assistance Program (SNAP) and SNAP benefits.[1890]

Two states adopted healthy food initiatives. California initiated a pilot program to require the state university system and community colleges to identify five campuses with at least one vending machine that dispenses wellness products.[1891] Under a law also discussed in the section on PProgram Development, Hawaii set incremental goals for the percentage of fresh local foods purchased by the department of education, the university system, and other state agencies in each five years until 2050.[1892]

Seven states approved eleven acts to improve student access to college, as well as structures to increase the likelihood of their success in completing college. The first of four statutes in California required the state university system and each community college district, for each campus that administers a priority enrollment

---

[1884] 2022 Cal. Stat. Ch. 934, A.B. No. 2810.
[1885] 2022 Cal. Stat. Ch. 874, S.B. No. 641.
[1886] 2022 Cal. Stat. Ch. 447, S.B. No. 768.
[1887] 2022 Cal. Stat. Ch. 167, S.B. No. 20.
[1888] 2022 La. Acts No. 719, HB No. 888.
[1889] 2022 Tenn. Pub. Acts Ch. No. 829, H.B. No. 1669, Sub. S.B. No. 1825.
[1890] 2022 Va. Acts Ch. 483, H. 582.
[1891] 2022 Cal. Stat. Ch. 933, A.B. No. 2482.
[1892] 2022 Haw. Sess. Laws Act 144, HB 1568.

system to grant priority in that system for registration for enrollment to a student parent.[1893] California amended a 2012 act (the Seymour-Campbell Student Success Act, CAL. EDUC. CODE § 78211.5), which was adopted to increase community college student access and success. The updated act required community colleges to maximize the probability that students will enter and complete transfer-level coursework in English and mathematics within a one-year timeframe of their initial attempt in the discipline. Also, if the community college places and enrolls a student into a transfer-level mathematics or English course that does not satisfy a requirement for the student's intended certificate or associate degree, the college must verify the benefit of the coursework to the student.[1894] California required the state university system, and requested the university system, to compel each campus to grant students the right to reenroll in their baccalaureate degree program after withdrawing if the student was in good academic standing with the university.[1895] Lastly, California deleted a requirement for community college students that attendance in credit courses cannot exceed two years of full-time attendance.[1896]

Maine directed the public higher education systems coordinating committee to convene a stakeholder group to study equity in and access to early college programs.[1897] Maryland required each public institution of higher education to develop and implement policies and procedures for awarding academic credit for prior learning examinations.[1898] New Hampshire required the higher education system to allow community college students who wish to earn baccalaureate degrees in the state's public higher education system to pursue curricular transfer pathways to a degree.[1899] New York permitted the electronic submission of certificates of residence by enrollees for community college.[1900] Ohio required state institutions of higher education to accept and provide credit for coursework in the same manner across all instructional models, except in the case of courses which may require in-person observations and experiences, such as laboratories and clinicals.[1901] Ohio also directed each community college and state university to enter into agreements establishing joint academic programming and dual

---

[1893] 2022 Cal. Stat. Ch. 935, A.B. No. 2881.
[1894] 2022 Cal. Stat. Ch. 926, A.B. No. 1705.
[1895] 2022 Cal. Stat. Ch. 323, A.B. No. 1796.
[1896] 2022 Cal. Stat. Ch. 490, S.B. No. 1141.
[1897] 2022 Me. Ch. Acts 169, H.P. 1390, L.D. 1880.
[1898] 2022 Md. Laws Ch.143, HB 966.
[1899] 2022 N.H. Laws Ch. 80, HB 1530.
[1900] 2022 N.Y. Laws Ch. 542, S. 8994.
[1901] 2022 Ohio Laws Sub. S.B. No. 135.

enrollment opportunities to assist students completing their degrees in a timely and cost-effective manner.[1902] Oklahoma placed an income qualification for applicants for the higher learning access program based upon the number of dependent children.[1903]

Six more states added acts designed to increase the likelihood of success in college, through the award or transfer of academic credit. Louisiana allowed the transfer of academic credit from public postsecondary education institutions that grant bachelor's degrees to institutions that grant associate's degrees.[1904] Missouri required each in-state public community college, college, or postsecondary institution offering freshmen courses to have a policy to grant undergraduate course credit for advanced placement courses taken in high school.[1905] New Jersey authorized a student attending an institution of higher education to earn credit toward graduation for serving as a poll worker.[1906] North Carolina permitted local community colleges to collaborate with local high school administrative units to offer cooperative innovative high school programs, subject to the approval of the state board of community colleges.[1907] Rhode Island permitted high school students receiving a silver or gold seal of biliteracy to earn two to four semesters of college credit in languages at a college or university if requested within three years after high school graduation.[1908] Virginia directed public institutions of higher education to map education, experience, training, and credentials gained from service in the armed forces of the U.S.[1909]

In the section for Program Development, above, the creation of student pathways at the K-12 levels was a dominant feature. The notion of pathways as a dominant feature continues into this section of Higher Education. Thirteen states passed fifteen acts to support funding, components, infrastructure, and relationships to continue pathways through higher education. California provided that supervised tutoring for foundational skills and for degree-applicable and transfer-level courses in community colleges is eligible for extra funding through state apportionment.[1910] California also authorized county offices of education to enter into college and career access pathways (CCAP) partnership agreements with the governing

---

[1902] 2022 Ohio Laws Sub. S.B. No. 135.
[1903] 2022 Okla. Sess. Laws SB 1673.
[1904] 2022 La. Acts No. 205, HB. No 231.
[1905] 2022 Mo. Laws SB 681 & 662; § 173.1352.
[1906] 2022 N.J. Laws P.L. c. 40, A. 3733.
[1907] 2022 N.C. Sess. Laws Ch. 71, H.B. 159.
[1908] 2022 R.I. Laws S. 2953, H. 7607.
[1909] 2022 Va. Acts Ch. 330, H. 1277.
[1910] 2022 Cal. Stat. Ch. 927, A.B. No. 1187.

boards of community colleges and removed the statewide limit for full-time equivalent students claimed as special "admits."[1911] Colorado directed the leadership of the K-12 system, higher education, and the work force development council to convene a secondary, postsecondary, and work-based learning integration program development task force to develop and recommend policies, laws, and rules to support the equitable and sustainable expansion and alignment of programs.[1912] Connecticut directed the board of regents for higher education to study workforce development issues in the state.[1913]

Georgia directed the state board of the technical college system to create and expand registered apprenticeship programs in the state.[1914] Louisiana required the statewide articulation and transfer council to oversee the development, implementation, and maintenance of statewide transfer pathways for public postsecondary schools and to develop statewide transfer agreements to govern the granting and transfer of credit awarded through competency-based and prior learning assessment.[1915] Maine created a labor and community education center at the University of Southern Maine. The center must focus on providing lifelong community-based labor education, research and outreach, and must offer workshops, symposia, skills-based learning, and opportunities to conduct applied research.[1916] Maine reestablished a task force to study the creation of a comprehensive career and technical education system in the state.[1917] Maryland required the governor to include a $5 million appropriation in fiscal year 2024 for the Shady Grove Regional Higher Education Center, to support a workforce development program.[1918] New Jersey provided project grants for career and technical education at county colleges.[1919]

Oklahoma required each educational institution within the state system of higher education to make available on its website an electronic link to the state regents employment outcomes dashboard, which provides information on employment and earnings outcomes.[1920] Tennessee removed geographic or programmatic considerations in admissions when the higher education commission

---

[1911] 2022 Cal. Stat. Ch. 902, A.B. No. 102.
[1912] 2022 Colo. Sess. Laws HB 1215.
[1913] 2022 Conn. Acts 22-101, H.B. No. 5301.
[1914] 2022 Ga. Laws Act 728, SB 379.
[1915] 2022 La. Acts No. 308, SB No. 261.
[1916] 2022 Me. Acts Ch. 722, H.P. 1349, L.D. 1816.
[1917] 2022 Me. Acts Ch. 174, S.P. 267, L.D. 680.
[1918] 2022 Md. Laws Ch. 623, HB 1446.
[1919] 2022 N.J. Laws P. L. c 81, A. 4224; 2002 N.J. Laws, 2022 P.L. c. 82, A. 4225.
[1920] 2022 Okla. Sess. Laws HB 2926.

adopted a dual admissions policy for a person who satisfies the admission requirements of a two-year institution and a public university while pursuing a degree program within a transfer pathway program of study.[1921] Utah transferred the data resource center from the department of workforce services to the system of higher education and expanded the duties of the center by requiring the center to collect and promote access to data from institutions of higher education.[1922] Virginia required the state council of higher education to maintain on its website a comparison of each baccalaureate public institution of higher education to each other baccalaureate public institution of higher education on nine measures, including admission test scores, tuition costs, debt accumulation, graduation rates, and wages at five- and twenty-year marks.[1923] Washington required the apprenticeship council to establish an economic or industry sector-based platform for existing registered apprenticeship programs or when a new program gains approval.[1924]

Eleven states enacted fourteen bills to provide direction for teacher education programs at the university level. Arizona added a requirement for teacher certification programs to instruct in best practices for social media and cellphone use between students and school personnel.[1925] Hawaii required the University of Hawaii to establish K-12 expanded teaching cohort programs in each county for students who are pursuing undergraduate degrees in education.[1926] Indiana allowed teacher preparation programs to report admission practices to an additional accrediting entity that had not been previously recognized by statute.[1927] Iowa changed the hour participation requirements for students in teacher preparation programs.[1928] Louisiana required dyslexia education as a component of teacher education programs.[1929] Louisiana required the state department of education to review laws pertaining to teacher training and submit a report to legislative bodies on that subject.[1930]

Missouri directed the state board of education to align literacy and reading instruction coursework for teacher education programs across all content areas touching on reading and special education

---

[1921] 2022 Tenn. Pub. Acts Ch. No. 794, S.B. No. 2531, Sub. H.B. No. 2115.
[1922] 2022 Utah Laws S.B. 226.
[1923] 2022 Va. Acts Ch. 344, S. 738; 2022 Va. Acts Ch. 365, H. 355.
[1924] 2022 Wash. Laws Ch. 156, S.B. 5600.
[1925] 2022 Ariz. Sess. Laws Ch. 367, H.B. 2017.
[1926] 2022 Haw. Sess. Laws Act 141, SB 2359.
[1927] 2022 Ind. Acts Pub. Law 41, SB 91.
[1928] 2022 Iowa Acts HF 2081.
[1929] 2022 La. Acts No. 607, HB No. 136.
[1930] 2022 La. Acts No. 338, HB No. 509.

certification. The act included detailed content which must be taught by the teacher education programs.[1931] New Jersey directed educator preparation programs to require candidates to complete a performance-based assessment within the educator preparation program.[1932] Pennsylvania adopted a talent recruitment grant program within the department of education as a competitive grant program for institutions of higher education to increase participation in the education workforce.[1933] South Carolina required the state board of education to develop and publish a teacher preparation report card as a method of evaluation of teacher education programs.[1934]

Tennessee required teacher training programs to provide instruction on strategies for virtual instruction.[1935] Tennessee required educator preparation providers approved by the state board of education to include on the annual report card required pursuant to Tenn. Code § 49-5-108, the state department's review of the provider's implementation of instruction aligned with foundational literacy skills.[1936] Tennessee also required the state department of education to produce an annual report concerning the efficacy of training on reading instruction provided by educator preparation providers and authorized the state board of education to place low-scoring preparation providers on probation.[1937] Virginia required public and private institutions of higher education providing training for teacher certification to require students to demonstrate mastery in science-based reading research and evidence-based literacy instruction.[1938]

Two states adopted acts regarding school administrator certification and training programs. North Carolina removed references to the Transforming Principal Preparation Program and retained references to the Principal Fellows Program in provisions regarding principal licensure.[1939] Pennsylvania directed that school safety and mental health services must be included in the training programs for school administrators.[1940]

States continued to enact measures regarding college-level athletics, beginning with additional name, image, and likeness (NIL)

[1931] 2022 Mo. Laws SB 681 & 662; § 161.097.
[1932] 2022 N.J. Laws P.L. c. 129, S. 896.
[1933] 2022 Pa. Laws Act No. 55, HB 1642, Section 29.
[1934] 2022 S.C. Acts 185, H. 3591.
[1935] 2022 Tenn. Pub. Acts Ch. No. 936, H.B. No. 1964, Sub. S.B. No. 2369.
[1936] 2022 Tenn. Pub. Acts Ch. No. 974, S.B. No. 2163, Sub. H.B. No. 2343.
[1937] 2022 Tenn. Pub. Acts Ch. No. 975, S.B. No. 2181, Sub. H.B. No. 2057.
[1938] 2022 Va. Acts Ch. 757, H. 419.
[1939] 2022 N.C. Sess. Laws Ch. 71, H.B. 159.
[1940] 2022 Pa. Laws Act No. 55, HB 1642, section 19.

policies. Connecticut amended its NIL policy for student-athletes in institutions of higher education to prohibit a requirement by an institution to allow a student athlete to use or consent to the use of any institutional marks.[1941] Illinois permitted student athletes to retain an agent for any matter or activity relating to compensation for the use of the name, image, likeness, or voice of the student athlete.[1942] Louisiana amended its NIL statute to strike a provision prohibiting postsecondary institutions or their officers or employees to steer compensation to current or prospective athletes.[1943] Maine adopted an NIL act for college or university student athletes allowing monetization of NIL, as well as for autographs.[1944] Mississippi amended a provision regarding NIL rights of student athletes to stipulate that payment of wages and benefits to a student-athlete for work actually performed for services unrelated to a student-athlete's publicity rights or other intellectual or intangible property rights of a student-athlete under federal or state law is not considered "compensation" under the NIL act.[1945]

Kentucky provided protections for student athletes seeking compensation for their NIL.[1946] New York allowed student-athletes to receive compensation including for the use of a student's NIL and for student-athletes to seek professional representation.[1947] Tennessee amended a provision permitting intercollegiate athletes to earn compensation for use of the athlete's NIL to specify that compensation must not be provided in exchange for athletic performance or attendance at an institution.[1948] Virginia prohibited public or private institutions of higher education from preventing a student-athlete from earning compensation for the use of his NIL but placed guardrails in compensation in connection with alcohol, adult entertainment, cannabis, controlled substances, performance-enhancing drugs, drug paraphernalia, tobacco, weapons, and casinos or gambling.[1949]

One state, Ohio, added an act regarding the wearing of religious apparel with athletic uniforms. Ohio prohibited any public or nonpublic school, school district, interscholastic conference, or organization that regulates interscholastic athletics to adopt a rule, bylaw, or other regulation that prohibits or creates any obstruction

---

[1941] 2022 Conn. Acts 22-11, S.B. No. 20.
[1942] 2022 Ill. Laws Pub. Act 102-0892, HB 1175.
[1943] 2022 La. Acts No. 307, SB No. 250.
[1944] 2022 Me. Acts Ch. 544, S.P. 663, L.D. 1893.
[1945] 2022 Miss. Laws S.B. No. 2690.
[1946] 2022 Ky. Acts Ch. 12, SB 6.
[1947] 2022 N.Y. Laws Ch. 622, S. 5891.
[1948] 2022 Tenn. Pub. Acts Ch. No. 845, H.B. No. 2249, Sub. S.B. No. 2392.
[1949] 2022 Va. Acts Ch. 510, H. 507; 2022 Va. Acts Ch. 638, S. 223.

to wearing religious apparel when competing or participating in interscholastic athletics or extracurricular activities. The act provides an exception if a legitimate danger to participants is identified due to wearing the religious apparel. The act defines "wearing religious apparel" as wearing of headwear, clothing, jewelry, or other coverings while observing a sincerely held religious belief.[1950]

Two states adopted prohibitions against male athletes competing on women teams. South Dakota required teams and sports at the college and scholastic levels, as well as associations governing teams and sports, to designate the activities based upon the biological sex at birth of participating students. Only female students may participate in any team, sport, or athletic event designated as being for females, women, or girls. Failure to comply with this provision is a limited waiver of sovereign immunity for relief authorized in an added section, which provides students a private cause of action for relief against the school, college, or association.[1951]

Tennessee prohibited males from participating in public higher education sports that are designated for females.[1952]

One state, Michigan, constructed two categories of students who may not participate in college athletics. Michigan prohibited students from participating in intercollegiate sports if they are in a five-year high school program and taking college-level courses,[1953] or in dual enrollment career and technical programs.[1954]

Two states enrolled three acts about employment law in the college setting. For a community college that has adopted a merit system for its employees, California required a permanent employee who accepts a promotion and fails to complete the probationary period for that promotional position to be employed in the classification from which the employee was promoted.[1955] California also prohibited the suspension without pay, suspension, or demotion with a reduction in pay, or dismissal of a permanent employee of a school district or community college district who timely requests a hearing on charges against the employee, unless the employer demonstrated by a preponderance of the evidence that the employee engaged in criminal misconduct, misconduct that presents a risk of harm to pupils or students, staff or property, or committed habitual

---

[1950] 2022 Ohio Laws S.B. No. 181.
[1951] 2022 S.D. Laws S.B. 46.
[1952] 2022 Tenn. Pub. Acts Ch. No. 1005, S.B. No. 2153, Sub. H.B. No. 2316.
[1953] 2022 Mich. Pub. Acts 230, HB 6040.
[1954] 2022 Mich. Pub. Acts 229, HB 6039.
[1955] 2022 Cal. Stat. Ch. 150, S.B. No. 874.

violations of the district's policies or regulations.[1956] Tennessee required boards of regents and trustees governing public higher education institutions to publish the grievance procedure for support staff employees on their websites.[1957]

Campus safety issues brought legislation to deal with such issues as sexual assault, discipline policy, substance abuse, medications on campus, bullying and hazing, and other challenges to student wellbeing. Four states passed six acts regarding sexual assault, sexual violence, or sexual harassment on campuses. California required the university systems and the community college system to post educational and preventive information on sexual violence and sexual harassment on their internet websites.[1958] California also required public postsecondary institutions of higher education to extend services for victims of sexual assault and domestic violence, independent of campus Title IX offices.[1959] Finally, California required the trustees of the state university system, and requested the regents of the university system, to develop content and presentation standards and a model internet website template regarding the steps a campus community member who is a survivor of sexual assault may take immediately following the assault.[1960]

Louisiana required the board of regents of public postsecondary institutions of higher education to consult with the power-based violence review panel and with select committees on women and children in providing a report to the governor and legislative-branch leadership on power-based violence, which includes intimidation and sexual assault behaviors.[1961] Maine required all institutions of higher education, including public, private, nonprofit, or for-profit postsecondary institutions, to have policy and procedures regarding sexual violence, intimate partner violence, and stalking.[1962] Pennsylvania added the concepts of dating violence, domestic violence, and stalking prevention to provisions related to sexual violence prevention in colleges and universities.[1963]

Three states enrolled acts regarding college-level disciplinary conduct codes. Kentucky required governing boards of public postsecondary institutions to adopt a student code of conduct for nonacademic violations which might be punishable by suspension or

---

[1956] 2022 Cal. Stat. Ch. 913, A.B. No. 2413.
[1957] 2022 Tenn. Pub. Acts Ch. No. 891, S.B. No. 2666, Sub. H.B. No. 2568.
[1958] 2022 Cal. Stat. Ch. 798, A.B. No. 2683.
[1959] 2022 Cal. Stat. Ch. 556, A.B. No. 1467.
[1960] 2022 Cal. Stat. Ch. 115, A.B. No. 1968.
[1961] 2022 La. Acts No. 689, SB No. 297.
[1962] 2022 Me. Acts Ch. 733, S.P. 572, L.D. 1727.
[1963] 2022 Pa. Laws Act No. 55, HB 1642, Section 45.

expulsion and outlined procedures for determining wrongdoing and consequences.[1964] Louisiana required public postsecondary institutions to adopt a policy regarding disciplinary proceedings for students, including procedural aspects of discipline.[1965] Tennessee extended agency rules scheduled to expire under the state's administrative procedures act, specifically related to the student code of conduct at the University of Tennessee and rules regarding Title IX compliance at Austin Peay State University.[1966]

California passed three acts regarding campus surveys of student safety. California required the chancellors for the state university system and the community colleges, and requested that the chancellor for the university system, to participate in creating questions for an online survey regarding campus safety.[1967] California also required each community college district with an instructional service agreement with a public safety agency to annually submit a copy of the agreement to the community colleges chancellor's office.[1968] In a third act, California required the chancellor of the state university system to convene a workgroup to evaluate and report on alternative options to current emergency response programs on campuses of the system, as well as alternative dispute resolution options to resolve employee conflicts.[1969]

Two states addressed hazing. Virginia required public and private institutions of higher education to provide training for members of student organizations about the dangers of hazing.[1970] Washington added provisions to its anti-hazing legislation in institutions of higher education, to expand the definition of hazing, require the provision for students of educational programming on hazing, and the creation of hazing-prevention committees at each public institution of higher education.[1971]

Two states addressed mental health and suicide. California required community colleges and universities to establish a mental health hotline for students and to print information about the hotline on student identification cards.[1972] Ohio required the chancellor to annually issue a report about the mental health and

---

[1964] 2022 Ky. Acts Ch. 159, HB 290.
[1965] 2022 La. Acts No. 464, HB No. 364.
[1966] 2022 Tenn. Pub. Acts Ch. No. 1024, S.B. No. 1748, Sub. H.B. No. 1827.
[1967] 2022 Cal. Stat. Ch. 928, A.B. No. 1712.
[1968] 2022 Cal Stat. Ch. 930, A.B. No. 1942.
[1969] 2022 Cal. Stat. Ch. 931, A.B. No. 1997.
[1970] 2022 Va. Acts Ch. 693, H. 525; 2022 Va. Acts Ch. 694, S. 439.
[1971] 2022 Wash. Laws Ch. 209, H.B. 1751.
[1972] 2022 Cal. Stat. Ch. 183, A.B. No. 2122.

wellness services and initiatives of state institutions of higher education.[1973]

Two states addressed opioid abuse. California required the governing boards over community colleges and the state university system to provide educational and preventive information about opioid overdose, the use and location of opioid overdose reversal medication, and the medication through campus health centers.[1974] New York required training of resident assistants in college housing in the administration of opioid antagonists.[1975]

Two states permitted alcohol on campus, with restrictions. Maryland authorized a licensing board to issue a beer, wine, and liquor license to a university or college that offers a hospitality and tourism management degree program.[1976] Michigan permitted alcohol to be served at a building at Lake Superior State University.[1977]

Two other safety-related provisions were adopted. Tennessee added requirements for institutions of higher education to report criminal activity.[1978] California extended authority to charge persons for trespass of a school campus or facility to private universities.[1979]

Two states adopted acts regarding student housing. California required the chancellors of the state university system and the community colleges, and requested the chancellor of the university system, to collect and post on their websites data on campus-owned, campus-operated, or campus-affiliated student housing.[1980] Maryland required higher education institutions to provide information to students who are applying to be a resident of student housing regarding the implications for students living in a corporation student housing project.[1981]

Other higher education-related acts approved in 2022 are detailed below. California required each community college campus to allow current students, staff, or faculty to declare an affirmed name, gender, or both name and gender identification.[1982] California also required institutions of higher education to include in the institution's requirements for recognition of a sorority and fraternity a requirement that the sorority or fraternity submit information

---

[1973] 2022 Ohio Laws Sub. S.B. No. 135.
[1974] 2022 Cal. Stat. Ch. 218, S.B. No. 367.
[1975] 2022 N.Y. Laws Ch. 580, S. 3448.
[1976] 2022 Md. Laws Ch. 760, HB 856.
[1977] 2022 Mich. Pub. Acts 216, HB 5623.
[1978] 2022 Tenn. Pub. Acts Ch. No. 958, H.B. No. 2730, Sub. S.B. No. 2830.
[1979] 2022 Cal. Stat. Ch. 134, S.B. No. 748.
[1980] 2022 Cal. Stat. Ch. 593, A.B. No. 2459.
[1981] 2022 Md. Laws Ch. 183, HB 385; 2022 Md. Laws Ch. 184, SB 560.
[1982] 2022 Cal. Stat. Ch. 932, A.B. No. 2315.

annually regarding activities, conduct, and discipline.[1983] Colorado created the position of foster care coordinator within the department of higher education to support college-age foster care students.[1984]

Colorado directed postsecondary institutions to permit veterans to audit higher education courses.[1985] Colorado also allowed a student enrolled in an institution of higher education outside of Colorado to postpone jury duty.[1986] Kansas transferred authority for postsecondary driver's education programs and driver training schools to the department of revenue.[1987] Kentucky created a center for cannabis research at the University of Kentucky.[1988] Maine permitted Eastern Maine Community College to provide credentialing for an education technician III, but specified that persons with this certification are not eligible for an emergency teacher certificate.[1989] Maryland allowed an employee of the University of Maryland, Baltimore Campus to solicit gifts or proposals for grants for the benefit of the university medical system corporation.[1990] New York directed institutions of higher education to cooperate with the department of agriculture and markets in developing and producing guidance and educational materials for farmers on the use of "agrivoltaics" in farming.[1991]

North Carolina required internship programs, whether time-based, competency-based, or hybrid approach, to conform to the requirements of federal law at 29 C.F.R. § 29.5.[1992] Tennessee required a state governmental entity or an institution of higher education receiving a complaint alleging that antisemitism has occurred on the premises of an institution of higher education, or through electronic outreach from an institution of higher education, to take into consideration the working definition of antisemitism adopted by the International Holocaust Remembrance Alliance (IHRA) in determining whether the alleged act was motivated by antisemitic intent.[1993] Virginia required every offeror awarded a contract by a public institution of higher education for a construction project with a total cost of $5 million or more to disclose any contributions the offeror has made within the previous five-year period totaling $25,000 or more, with failure to report bringing a

---

[1983] 2022 Cal. Stat. Ch. 268, A.B. No. 524.
[1984] 2022 Colo. Sess. Laws SB 8.
[1985] 2022 Colo. Sess. Laws HB 1407.
[1986] 2022 Colo. Sess. Laws HB 1032.
[1987] 2022 Kan. Sess. Laws SB 215.
[1988] 2022 Ky. Acts Ch. 239, HB 604.
[1989] 2022 Me. Acts Ch. 156, S.P. 393, L.D. 1207.
[1990] 2022 Md. Laws Ch. 621, HB 907; 2022 Md. Laws Ch. 622, SB 589.
[1991] 2022 N.Y. Laws Approval Memo 27, S. 7861.
[1992] 2022 N.C. Sess. Laws Ch. 71, H.B. 159.
[1993] 2022 Tenn. Pub. Acts Ch. No. 1075, H.B. No. 2673, Sub. S.B. No. 2864, § 2.

$500 civil penalty.[1994] Washington amended provisions related to ethics of postsecondary faculty in performing their duties, especially with respect to grants and contracts. Each governing board is required to address ethical duties in policy and provide a copy of the policy to the executive ethics board upon approval.[1995]

Conclusion

This chapter describes and sorts legislative acts adopted by the United States Congress and each of the fifty state legislatures and general assemblies during the 2022 calendar year. The secondary author began researching and reporting for this chapter with the 1998 legislative year, when only five education-related acts were reported at the federal level and 248 education-related acts were enacted by state legislative bodies collectively. This chapter reported 1,480 education-related legislative acts for the 2021 legislative year, and now reports 1,319 acts in 2022. The following chart represents the continuing trend of accelerating numbers of education-related acts since 1998, with peaks in 2011, 2019, and 2021.

Years	Number of Acts Reported
1998	253 acts
1999-2001	430 acts on average annually
2002-2006	630 acts on average annually
2007-2009	890 acts on average annually
2010	1,050 acts
2011	1,225 acts
2012	830 acts
2013	922 acts

[1994] 2022 Va. Acts Ch. 96, S. 210; 2022 Va. Acts Ch. 97, H. 19.
[1995] 2022 Wash. Laws Ch. 173, S.B. 5854.

2014	819 acts
2015	864 acts
2016	671 acts
2017	960 acts
2018	919 acts
2019	1,233 acts
2020	799 acts
2021	1,480 acts
2022	1,319 acts

The data above demonstrate that legislative bodies produced more education-related legislation in 2021 than had been recorded in earlier years, going back to 1998. The amount of legislation passed in 2022 totaled between the two peaks in 2019 and 2021. The following chart describes the number of acts reported in each category of education-related legislation passed in 2022.

Categories	Number of Acts Reported
Federal Legislation	10
State Legislation:	
Accountability and School Reform	34
Athletics	17
Attendance, Promotion, and Graduation	61
Buildings and Grounds	31
Curricular Requirements	69
Employment	167

Finance and School Business	60
Governance and School Leadership	260
Parental and Student Rights	74
Program Development	72
School Choice	19
School Safety	118
Students with Disabilities	39
Technology	8
Transportation	23
Higher Education	249

In recent years, higher education-related legislation has repeatedly been the category with the most legislative acts. However, in 2022, the category with the most numerous legislative acts was governance and school leadership, with 260 acts. The number of acts passed by the Georgia Assembly were just over half of the total acts, with 129 acts "reconstituting" named school districts, five acts changing the membership of named school districts, and one act changing the election for one school district. For scope, Georgia has 181 school districts, including 159 county school districts, 21 city school districts, and one school district for the juvenile justice system. Also, South Carolina passed 44 acts in 2022 directing consolidation or reapportionment of local school districts. These high numbers of intervention at the school board level support the theory that Southern states, with constitutions adopted after Reconstruction and designed to limit local control, continue to intercede in local governance affairs more frequently than states outside the South.

Higher education-related legislation in 2022 represented the second-greatest number of legislative acts among the subject headings for this chapter, with 249 acts. In 1998, thirteen states enrolled eighteen acts about higher education. In 1999, sixteen states added thirty-five more acts about higher education. From 2000 to 2005, on average, twenty-nine states annually added fifty-four acts related to higher education. Then, the amount of higher education-related legislation accelerated dramatically each year until 2011, with 94 acts in 2006; 170 acts in 2007; 151 acts in 2008; 141 acts in 2009; 218 acts in 2010; and 257 acts in 2011. The first decade of the new century marked a change in how legislatures treated higher education because it was the time in which legislatures began interacting with higher education institutions differently, more like K-12 schools, with more direct involvement about decisions within the institutions. In subsequent years, the number of higher education-related acts remained relatively high, as follows: 150 acts in 2012; 147 acts in 2013; 151 acts in 2014; 173 acts in 2015; 102 acts in 2016; 147 acts in 2017; 167 acts in 2018; 263 acts in 2019; 152 acts in 2020; 314 acts in 2021; and 249 acts in 2022. In the current decade, higher education-related legislation was the most numerous legislative category every year, except in 2016, when school safety legislation was most numerous, and in 2022, when governance and school leadership acts were more numerous.

In 2022, legislation about higher education continued to emphasize the recognition and planning for student "pathways," a term which first appeared in legislation in 2019. At first, the term seemed to relate to legislative decisions to put more resources in career-technology courses and programs, beginning in middle school and projecting into community colleges and other postsecondary institutions. By 2021, "pathways" connoted a requirement that secondary students and students in technical centers, community colleges, and universities be made more aware of careers that do not require a college education, and that educational institutions must provide data for students to know the costs and benefits of training for different careers. By 2021, the meaning of "pathways" expanded to incorporate internships, paid apprenticeships, and industry certification. In 2022, the term "pathways" matured to include more infrastructure for career paths through career-technology programs and to recognize that the word "pathways" still stresses the career-technology side of schooling. However, in 2022 acts, the word "pathways" also refers to the more traditional path for a student, from elementary school, to middle school and high school, to postsecondary school, and possibly graduate and professional school—and the places where the paths cross, offer dual credit, and provide the option for students to switch paths more than once.

Last year saw adoption of acts that will likely bring First Amendment litigation against public institutions of higher education. In one group of acts, states had competing views apparently derived from public forum doctrine about what kind of forum they intended to create on university campuses. Two states had a broad view of a limited public forum, essentially leaving most university grounds as a place for speech, with few manner, place, or time restrictions. Two other states asked work groups to fashion a policy about the public's right to speak on university property. Another set of acts prohibited the discussion of "divisive concepts" on university property. Similar acts appeared in other states in recent years, perhaps as evidence of culture wars based upon alternative views about the nature of public institutions of higher education and their role in society.

The authors reported that the 2000 legislative year was the first year in which legislators interceded directly in an academic program in public institutions of higher education. When they did, it was usually in teacher education programs. In 2021, twelve acts were adopted in which legislative bodies provided direction to teacher education programs, including what was to be taught, what was a preferred model of instruction, and how it was to be evaluated. In 2022, eleven states added fourteen more acts placing requirements on teacher education programs. Only two of those prescriptions appear to be calculated to address teacher shortages. Many of the acts added requirements, thereby lengthening programs and delaying getting more teachers into the classroom.

The number of scholarships for those connected to the military and other individuals were less in 2022 compared to previous years, but new scholarships continued to be added, along with resident tuition status and fee waivers. States continued to erect structures to provide better oversight over the functions of private proprietary schools, which are also legislative measures calculated to support affordability.

States directed public postsecondary institutions to continue to address campus safety, particularly with respect to sexual violence. Besides policies on sexual violence, states required policies on student conduct codes, asked for safety surveys, and spoke to a smattering of other safety topics like suicide prevention, mental health counseling, and opioid addiction.

Legislation on three issues related to athletics in higher education appeared in 2022. More states authorized college student-athletes to negotiate name, image, and likeness (NIL) agreements. Eight states prohibited male student-athletes to participate in women's sports, and one state added an act permitting the wearing of athletic uniforms accessorized with religious symbols.

Legislation related to school employment was the third most-common category of legislation in 2022, with 167 acts recorded. The number of employment-related acts averaged 65 acts annually from 2000-2005; 85 acts in 2006; 157 acts in 2007; 107 acts in 2008; 113 acts in 2009; 151 acts in 2010; 183 acts in 2011; 127 acts in 2012; 95 acts in 2013; 94 acts in 2014; 102 acts in 2015; 57 acts in 2016; 124 acts in 2017; 155 acts in 2018; 148 acts in 2019; 98 acts in 2020; 156 acts in 2021; and, 167 acts in 2022. In recent years, school employment-related legislation has competed with school safety-legislation for second place for most numerous.

The dominant concern in legislative activity related to employment was the continuing and deepening shortage of classroom teachers and other school personnel. Of the 167 total employment-related acts enrolled in 2022, 96 of the acts were about addressing teacher shortages. Seventeen states approved thirty-two acts attempting to speed new teachers into placement by decreasing certification requirements and normalizing alternative certificates. Barriers such as tests, degrees, and evaluation were put in place earlier to improve quality, but were worked around last year. Alternative certificates were upgraded to full certificates; a live person in the classroom available to teach while still in a training program is considered equal to a person who has completed training. As noted above, in higher education-related legislation, state legislatures were stepping in to dictate higher standards for what is taught in teacher education programs, thereby increasing certificate prerequisites and delaying the speed of getting teachers into the classroom. However, in the area of employment-related legislation, legislatures are clearly at cross-purposes. While one policy direction wants better quality teachers, perhaps legislatures are willing to sacrifice quality to assure that someone is in the classroom.

There is evidence that legislative bodies understood the tradeoffs they were making on quality, and they took additional measures to mitigate the damage to instructional quality. Many states adopted incentive programs to address teacher and other educator shortages, including scholarships, loan forgiveness, and housing. Several states permitted retired teachers to return to the classroom without sacrificing their retirement income. Ten states adopted eleven acts regarding professional development, which may in part be a policy option to improve teacher quality while they are serving in the classroom.

State legislative bodies adopted 118 school safety-related acts in 2022, making it the fourth-most numerous category of legislation. For comparison, there were 107 school safety-related acts enrolled in 1999, the year of violence at Columbine High School, and 100 more acts were adopted each of the next two years. From 2002 to 2004, approximately fifty school safety acts were passed each year. The following number of acts were signed into law in subsequent years: 81 acts in 2005; 70 acts in 2006; 122 acts in 2007; 81 acts in 2008; 97 acts in 2009, 54 acts in 2010; 87 acts in 2011; 55 acts in 2012; 88 acts in 2013; 88 acts in 2014; 110 acts in 2015; 115 acts in 2016; 120 acts in 2017; 155 acts in 2018; 190 acts in 2019; 100 acts in 2020; 135 acts in 2021; and 118 acts in 2022. School safety was the most-numerous category of legislation only once during this decade, in 2016. In the other years, it exchanged second and third place with employment. In 2022, school safety-related legislation dropped to fourth place, due to the flood of school board-related local governance acts in Georgia and South Carolina.

School safety-related acts in the last calendar year spotlighted safety planning that is more comprehensive in nature with more actors, especially law enforcement, involved in the plan's creation. A few of these acts indicate the rationale for law enforcement involvement is linked to requirements of critical incident mapping and threat assessment. Several states have had the foresight to make school safety plans, or portions of school safety plans, not disclosable under state freedom of information acts. The desired school safety plans understand that threats to schools and schoolchildren are much broader than traditionally thought, including fire, flooding, weather and climatic incidents, violence, biologic and medical emergencies, civil unrest, cyber-attack, and hazardous materials. Safety training stresses interaction opportunities to practice coordination of responsibilities to make certain that in the absence of leaders, others are capable to step in. Another element of safety planning is in the area of discipline policy. Several states called for student discipline that is inclusive, with rational consequences, based upon best practices for guiding student behavior. Of the few remaining states that had not yet banned corporal punishment, one state elected to ban it throughout the state. Another state, while previously banning corporal punishment in school districts, added a ban for corporally punishing students who are educated in state agency schools.

Several states added measures to improve student mental health including the addition of trained personnel with job titles denoting primary responsibility for assisting students and staff in dealing with mental health issues. Many states required the addition of professional development and training in dealing with mental health challenges. An area of concern, closely related to mental health, is the need for suicide prevention. Several states required the identification of personnel to serve in a training and leadership role in suicide prevention, and many states also required professional development in suicide prevention for all staff.

Milton Keynes UK
Ingram Content Group UK Ltd.
UKHW020634101024
2102UKWH00059B/587